Hands-On Ethical Hacking and Network Defense

By
Michael T. Simpson

THOMSON

COURSE TECHNOLOGY

Australia • Canada • Mexico • Singapore • Spain • United Kingdom • United States

Hands-On Ethical Hacking and Network Defense

is published by Thomson Course Technology

Managing Editor:
William Pitkin III

Production Editor:
Pamela Elizian

Technical Editor and Contributing Author:
Randy Weaver

Editorial Assistant:
Allison Murphy

Compositor:
GEX Publishing Services

Product Manager:
Amy M. Lyon

Senior Manufacturing Coordinator:
George Morrison

Quality Assurance Coordinator:
Christian Kunciw

Cover Design:
Steve Deschene

Text Designer:
GEX Publishing Services

Developmental Editor:
Lisa M. Lord

Product Marketing Manager
Gayathri Baskaran

Associate Product Manager:
Sarah Santoro

TABLE OF
Contents

CHAPTER FOUR
Footprinting and Social Engineering   **61**

CHAPTER FIVE
Port Scanning   **89**

CHAPTER SIX
Enumeration   **109**

Preface

I started the Institute for Security and Open Methodologies (ISECOM) in January 2001, because I didn't want to be part of the problem any more. Since that time, hundreds of other professionals have joined with ISECOM because they felt the same way. Thousands have contacted ISECOM to be part of the community, and millions have downloaded our standards and documents. We continue to work as an open-source community and provide politically free and commercially free security research, such as the Open Source Security Testing Methodology Manual (OSSTMM) and Hacker Highschool. Our efforts are supported and funded by the security community through certification programs, such as the OSSTMM Professional Security Tester (OPST) and OSSTMM Professional Security Analyst (OPSA). These programs are growing, open accreditation projects for creating walk-the-walk security professionals who have learned critical thinking and prove they can do what they're certified to do. (What good is just knowing arbitrary security facts and definitions?) Many countries already require OPST or OPSA for security personnel and managers. And as the need for critical minds with the ability for security analysis grows, ISECOM will continue to keep me from being part of the problem as a security researcher, manager of projects, and leader of volunteers. And you?

Your continued self-education and your applied knowledge require consistent attention if you expect to be not only a security professional, but also a security/safety-minded citizen. Consider your place today if you were to serve on a jury in a computer-trespassing crime. Are you qualified to make a decision about someone's life based on the evidence? Can you consider yourself a peer of the defendant? Today, security failures already destroy lives through identity theft, ruined businesses, false imprisonment, overhyped prison sentences, and improperly secured, high-frequency microprocessors affecting medicine dispensers and guidance systems. If you think of yourself as just someone who makes Web sites safe, you couldn't be more wrong. Web sites are responsible for information that affects people. Being involved in security decisions is to be responsible for human lives. And every year, your direct effect on protecting those lives, their liberties, and their privilege to pursue happiness becomes even greater. There's no room for laziness.

Do you think about how the tools you run to test security are generally limited by the anticipated outcomes the tool designer knows or that the tool designer might not know enough about the subject? (Many open-source tools are written to help the developer understand a concept.) And even the second tool you used to verify the first could impose the exact same limitations. (Yes, developers borrow from each other and not always to improve accuracy.)

You research, review, verify, question, correlate, and analyze. You make decisions based on what you have determined to be true and not what everyone else is saying. You find facts and don't shy away from the results just because they might be contrary to popular opinion. Again, consider your education and how you have spent your life being taught. You're not reading this book to be taught, however. You're reading it to learn.

I don't know where you'll be in five or ten years, but even if you're not a security professional, I'm sure you'll be able to affect security in my life through commentary, decision, vote, or inaction. If you wake up now and make the difference in yourself, I win. If you open up someone else's eyes as well, we've both won.

Pete Herzog

Managing Director, ISECOM

Pete Herzog is an American in Barcelona who founded the nonprofit ISECOM to uphold the OSSTMM ideals of doing security the right way through verification and fact. Besides being the full-time Managing Director of open-source projects at ISECOM, Pete is a professor of business information security and IT security at two Barcelona-based universities and a part-time consultant. He trains ISECOM security trainers twice a year and coordinates with other security organizations to offer a pragmatic, full-spectrum yearly security class called ISESTORM.

Introduction

The need for security professionals who understand how attackers compromise networks is growing each day. You can't pick up a newspaper without seeing an article on identification theft or credit card numbers stolen from unprotected databases. Companies rely on skilled professionals to conduct attacks on their networks as a way to discover vulnerabilities before attackers do. "Ethical hacker" is one term used to describe these professionals; others are "security tester" or "penetration tester."

This book is not intended to provide comprehensive training in security testing or penetration testing. It does, however, introduce security testing to those who are new to the field. This book is intended for novices who have a thorough grounding in computer and networking basics but want to learn how to protect networks by using an attacker's knowledge to compromise network security. By understanding what tools or methodologies a hacker uses to break into a network, security testers can protect a system from these attacks.

The purpose of this book is to guide you toward becoming a skilled security tester. This profession requires creativity and critical thinking, which are sometimes difficult skills to learn in an academic environment. However, with an open mind and a willingness to learn, you can think outside the box and learn to ask more questions than this book or your instructor poses. Being able to dig past the surface to solve a problem takes patience and the willingness to admit that sometimes there's no simple answer.

There's more to conducting a security test than running exploits against a system and informing your client of existing vulnerabilities. Isn't it possible that you neglected to test for some areas that might be vulnerable to attacks? Haphazard approaches undermine the security profession and expose companies to theft. The purpose of this book is to offer a more structured approach to conducting a security test and to introduce the novice to professional certifications available in this growing field.

Intended Audience

Although this book can be used by people with a wide range of backgrounds, it's intended for those with a Security+ and Network+ certification or equivalent. A networking background is necessary so that you understand how PCs operate in a networked environment and can work with a network administrator when needed. In addition, readers must have knowledge of how to use a computer from the command line and how to use popular operating systems, such as Windows 9x, 2000, and XP and Linux.

This book can be used at any educational level, from technical high schools and community colleges to graduate students. Current professionals in the public and private sectors can also use this book.

Chapter Descriptions

Here is a summary of the topics covered in each chapter of this book:

Chapter 1, "Ethical Hacking Overview," defines what an ethical hacker can and cannot do legally. The roles of security and penetration testers are described, and certifications that are current at the time of publication are reviewed.

Chapter 2, "TCP/IP Concepts Review," describes the layers of the TCP model and reviews IP addressing along with binary, octal, and hexadecimal numbering systems.

Chapter 3, "Network and Computer Attacks," defines malicious software and how to protect against malware attacks. Intruder attacks and physical security are also addressed.

Chapter 4, "Footprinting and Social Engineering," explores the use of Web tools as well as personal interchanges used to gather information.

Chapter 5, "Port Scanning," demonstrates the types and uses of port-scanning tools, explains how to conduct ping sweeps, and gives you an overview of shell scripting.

Chapter 6, "Enumeration," defines the tools for enumerating operating systems, such as NetWare, Microsoft, and UNIX/Linux.

Chapter 7, "Programming for Security Professionals," introduces and reviews computer programming concepts as they relate to network and computer security.

Chapter 8, "Microsoft Operating System Vulnerabilities," discusses the tools for identifying vulnerabilities in Microsoft systems and services. Best practices for hardening the system are also covered.

Chapter 9, "Linux Operating System Vulnerabilities," discusses tools and countermeasures for protecting Linux systems.

Chapter 10, "Hacking Web Servers," explains Web appliances, applications, and vulnerabilities and the tools used by Web attackers as well as security testers.

Chapter 11, "Hacking Wireless Networks," details the history of IEEE wireless standards. Wardriving and wireless hacking tools and countermeasures are covered.

Chapter 12, "Cryptography," explains the history and uses of cryptography and offers examples of some cryptography attacks.

Chapter 13, "Protecting Networks with Security Devices," provides an overview of the hardware and software security devices used to protect networks.

Appendix A, "Legal Resources," examines state laws affecting network security.

Appendix B, "Resources," includes a sample contract for an IT professional consultant, lists additional reference books, and lists the URLs referenced throughout the book.

Appendix C, "Documentation Forms for Penetration Tests," contains a sample executive summary report and technical report a security tester could submit after conducting a security test.

Features

To help you fully understand computer and network security, this book includes many features designed to enhance your learning experience:

- **Chapter Objectives.** Each chapter begins with a detailed list of the concepts to be mastered in that chapter. This list gives you a quick reference to the chapter's contents and serves as a useful study aid.

- **Figures and Tables.** Screenshots are used as illustrations and guidelines to assist the reader in using security tools and creating computer programs. For tools not included with the book or that aren't offered in free demo versions, figures have been added to show the tool's interface. Tables are used throughout the book to present information in an organized, easy-to-grasp manner.

- **Security Bytes.** Each chapter includes several topical snippets and real-world experiences pertaining to the security aspects of that chapter's material.

- **Chapter Summaries.** Each chapter's material is followed by a summary of the concepts introduced in that chapter. These summaries are a helpful way to review the ideas covered in each chapter.

- **Key Terms.** Following the Chapter Summary, a list of all new terms introduced in the chapter with boldfaced text are gathered together in the Key Terms list, with full definitions for each term. This list encourages a more thorough understanding of the chapter's key concepts and is a useful reference.

- **Review Questions**.   The end-of-chapter assessment begins with a set of review questions that reinforces the main concepts in each chapter. These questions help you evaluate and apply the material you have learned.

- **Hands-on Activities**.   One of the best ways to reinforce learning about network security and security testing is to practice using the many tools security testers use. Each chapter in this book contains many Hands-on Activities that give you experience applying what you have learned.

- **Case Projects**.   At the end of each chapter are Case Projects covering concepts you have learned in the chapter. To complete these projects, you must draw on real-world common sense as well as your knowledge of the technical topics covered to that point in the book. Your goal for each project is to come up with answers to problems similar to those you'll face as a working security tester.

- **CD-ROM**.   The book includes a bootable CD that allows students to used a *NIX-based operating system on a classroom or home computer running a Windows OS. Many security-testing tools are included on the CD as well as a copy of the OSSTMM, so students have quick access to the methods used to conduct a security test.

Text and Graphic Conventions

Where appropriate, additional information and exercises have been added to this book to help you better understand the topic at hand. Icons throughout the text alert you to additional materials. The following icons are used in this book:

 The Note icon draws your attention to additional helpful material related to the subject being covered.

 Tips based on the authors' experience offer extra information about how to attack a problem or what to do in real-world situations.

 The Caution icons warn you about potential mistakes or problems and explain how to avoid them.

 Each hands-on activity in this book is preceded by the Hands-On icon and a description of the exercise that follows.

 These icons mark Case Projects, which are scenario-based assignments. In these extensive case examples, you are asked to apply independently what you have learned.

INSTRUCTOR'S MATERIALS

The following additional materials are available when this book is used in a classroom setting. All the supplements available with this book are provided to instructors on a single CD. You can also retrieve these supplemental materials from the Course Technology Web site, *www.course.com*, by going to the page for this book, under "Download Instructor Files & Teaching Tools."

Electronic Instructor's Manual. The Instructor's Manual that accompanies this book includes the following items: additional instructional material to assist in class preparation, including suggestions for lecture topics; recommended lab activities; tips on setting up a lab for Hands-On Projects; and solutions to all end-of-chapter materials.

ExamView Test Bank. This cutting-edge Windows-based testing software helps instructors design and administer tests and pretests. In addition to generating tests that can be printed and administered, this full-featured program has an online testing component that allows students to take tests at the computer and have their exams automatically graded.

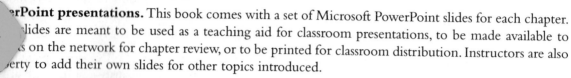

PrPoint presentations. This book comes with a set of Microsoft PowerPoint slides for each chapter. slides are meant to be used as a teaching aid for classroom presentations, to be made available to s on the network for chapter review, or to be printed for classroom distribution. Instructors are also erty to add their own slides for other topics introduced.

Figure files. All the figures in the book are reproduced on the Instructor's Resources CD. Similar to the PowerPoint presentations, they are included as a teaching aid for classroom presentation, to make available to students for review, or to be printed for classroom distribution.

Lab Requirements

The Hands-on Activities in this book help you apply what you have learned about conducting a security or penetration test. The following section lists the minimum hardware requirements for completing all the Hands-on Activities in this book. In addition to the items listed, students must be able to download and install demo versions of software.

Minimum Lab Requirements

- Lab computers that boot to Windows XP SP2. The Windows XP firewall as well as any third-party firewall software should be turned off.

- Access to the Internet, with each computer configured to receive IP configuration information from a router running DHCP.

- Lab computers must have a CD-ROM drive that allows for bootable CDs.

The steps and projects in this book are designed with the following hardware and software requirements in mind.

OPERATING SYSTEMS AND HARDWARE

Windows XP SP2

Use a standard installation of XP Professional. The computer running Windows XP should meet the following minimum requirements:

- CD-ROM drive
- VGA or higher monitor
- Hard disk partition of 4 GB or more
- Mouse or other pointing device
- Keyboard
- 128 MB RAM

Security Testing Tools

This book includes hands-on activities that involve using many security tools that are on the CD or can be downloaded from the Internet as freeware, shareware, or free demo versions. Because Web site addresses change frequently, use a search engine to find software if the address noted in an activity is no longer valid.

In addition, you use Microsoft Office Word (or other word processing software) and need to have e-mail software, such as Microsoft Outlook Express, installed on your computer.

Even though you aren't required to use a remote attack network to do the hands-on activities, *www.hackerhighschool.org* offers schools using this book a one-year license at a nominal fee to access such a network. Students can perform attacks on a remote network without the risk of breaking the law and can also purchase the license for home use if they like.

ACKNOWLEDGMENTS

I would like to express my appreciation to Managing Editor Will Pitkin, who asked me to do this project long before others saw the need for such an endeavor. I would like to thank the entire editorial and production staff for their dedication and fortitude during this project, including Amy Lyon, the Product Manager, and Pam Elizian, the Production Editor. Special thanks to Lisa Lord, the Developmental Editor and my savior when deadlines required a helping hand. I would also like to thank the testers in the Manuscript Quality Assurance Department: Christian Kunciw, Serge Palladino, and Danielle Shaw. I also appreciate the careful reading and thoughtful suggestions of Technical Editor Randy Weaver, and would like to thank FBI Special Agent Arnold Laanui, Jr., Cybercrime Squad, for his input and patience. In addition, I would like to thank the team of peer reviewers who evaluated each chapter and offered helpful suggestions and contributions:

Larry Anderson	Metropolitan Community College
Bob Bruen	Springfield Technical Community College
Don Husmann	Heald College
David Pope	Ozarks Technical Community College
Erich Spengler	Moraine Valley Community College

I would also like to express appreciation to security testers and IT colleagues who kept me on track and offered assistance: Pete Herzog; Jeff Williams, CEO Aspect Security, Inc.; Nmap creator Fyodor (*http://insecure.org*); Wilson Steiger; Curt Cavanaugh; Dominic Monteleone; Mountain Lion Consulting; my undergraduate and graduate students at the University of Phoenix, who keep me current; and last, but not least, Gloria Goldstein, who spent countless hours reading through hundreds of pages of text and never stopped giving me encouraging words.

DEDICATION

This book is dedicated to my best friend and wife, Claudia, who sacrificed many candlelight dinners, walks on the beach, tennis matches with Jeff and Shelley, and weekends together so that I could sit in front of a computer monitor and write.

1

ETHICAL HACKING OVERVIEW

After reading this chapter and completing the exercises, you will be able to:

♦ Describe the role of an ethical hacker

♦ Describe what you can do legally as an ethical hacker

♦ Describe what you cannot do as an ethical hacker

The term "ethical hacker" might seem like an oxymoron—sort of like an ethical pickpocket or ethical embezzler. In this chapter, you learn that ethical hackers are employed or contracted by a company to do what illegal hackers do: break in. Why? Companies need to know what, if any, parts of their security infrastructure are vulnerable to attack. To protect a company's network, many security professionals recognize that knowing what tools the bad guys use and how they think enables them to better protect (harden) a network's security.

Remember the old adage: You're only as secure as your weakest link. The bad guys spend lots of time and energy trying to find that weak link. This book provides the tools you need to protect a network and shares some approaches an ethical hacker—or a "penetration tester"—might use to discover vulnerabilities in a network. It is by no means a definitive book on ethical hacking. Rather, it gives you a good overview of a penetration tester's role and activities to assist you in developing the skills you need to protect a network from attack. This book helps you understand how to protect a network when you discover the methods the bad guys (hackers) or the good guys (ethical hackers) use to break into a network. It also helps you select the most appropriate tools to make your job a lot easier.

Understanding what laws might affect you when performing your network security job is important, especially if you use the penetration testing methods outlined in this book. Also, understanding the importance of having a contractual agreement with a client before performing any aspects of a penetration test might help you avoid breaking the law.

Introduction to Ethical Hacking

Ethical hackers are sometimes employed by companies to perform penetration tests. In a **penetration test**, an ethical hacker attempts to break into a company's network to find the weakest link in that network or one of its systems. In a **security test**, the tester does more than attempt to break in; he or she also analyzes the company's security policy and procedures and reports any vulnerabilities to management.

Security testing takes penetration testing to a higher level. As Peter Herzog states in the *Open Source Security Testing Methodology Manual*, "[Security testing] relies on a combination of creativeness, expansion of knowledge bases of best practices, legal issues, and client industry regulations as well as known threats and the breadth of the target organization's security presence (or point of risk)." These issues are just some of the factors security testers must examine. In doing so, they alert companies to the areas that need to be monitored or secured. As a security tester, you can't make a network impenetrable. The only way to do that is to unplug the network cable from the wall. When you discover vulnerabilities or holes in a network, you can spend time correcting them. This might entail anything from installing the latest security patch or hotfix to upgrading the operating system (OS).

If your job is merely a penetration tester, you simply need to give your findings to the company. Then it's up to the company to make the final decision on how to use the information you have supplied. However, as a security tester, your position might require you to also offer solutions to secure or protect the network. This book assumes your position is that of a network security professional in charge of protecting a corporate network, so the emphasis is on using a security tester's skills to secure or protect a network.

This book addresses how to find vulnerabilities in a network and correct them. Your job is to document all the vulnerabilities you find and alert management and IT staff of areas that need special attention.

The Role of Security and Penetration Testers

A **hacker** accesses a computer system or network without the authorization of the system's owner. By doing so, a hacker is breaking the law and can go to prison. Those who break into systems to steal or destroy data are often referred to as **crackers**; hackers might simply want to prove how vulnerable a system is by accessing the computer or network without destroying any data. For the purpose of this book, no distinction is made between the terms "hackers" and "crackers." The U.S. Department of Justice labels all illegal access to computer or network systems as "hacking," and this book follows that usage.

An ethical hacker is a person who performs most of the same activities a hacker does, but with the owner or company's permission. This is a big distinction and can mean the difference between going to jail or not going to jail. Ethical hackers are usually contracted to perform penetration tests or security tests. Companies realize that intruders might attempt to access their network resources and are willing to pay for someone to discover these vulnerabilities first. Companies would rather pay a "good hacker" to discover problems in their current network configuration than have a "bad hacker" discover those vulnerabilities. Bad hackers spend many hours scanning systems over the Internet looking for openings or vulnerable systems.

Some hackers are skillful computer operators, but others are younger inexperienced people who experienced hackers refer to as **script kiddies** or **packet monkeys**. These derogatory terms depict hackers as people who copy code from knowledgeable programmers instead of creating the code themselves. Many experienced penetration testers can write computer programs or scripts by using Practical Extraction and Report Language (Perl) or the C programming language to carry out network attacks. A **script** is a set of instructions that runs in sequence to perform tasks on a computer system.

An Internet search on IT job recruiter sites for "penetration tester" produces hundreds of job announcements, many from Fortune 500 companies looking for experienced applicants. A typical ad might include the following requirements:

- Perform vulnerability, attack, and penetration assessments in Internet, intranet, and wireless environments

- Perform discovery and scanning for open ports and services

- Apply appropriate exploits to gain access and expand access as necessary
- Participate in activities involving application penetration testing and application source code review
- Interact with the client as required throughout the engagement
- Produce reports documenting discoveries during the engagement
- Debrief with the client at the conclusion of each engagement
- Participate in research and provide recommendations for continuous improvement
- Participate in knowledge sharing

Penetration testers and security testers usually have a laptop computer configured with multiple OSs and hacking tools. The CD accompanying this book contains the Linux OS and many tools needed to conduct actual network attacks. This collection of tools for conducting vulnerability assessments and attacks is sometimes referred to as a "tiger box." You can order tiger boxes on the Internet, but if you want to gain more experience, you can install multiple OSs and security tools on your own system. Learning how to install an OS is not covered in this book, but you can easily find books on this topic. The procedure for installing security tools varies, depending on the OS in use. Later in this book, you have a chance to install a Linux-based tool.

Activity 1-1: Determining the Corporate Need for Penetration Testers

Time Required: 10 minutes

Objective: Discover the many corporations looking to employ penetration testers.

Description: Many companies are eager to employ or contract penetration testers for their corporate networks. In this activity, you search the Internet for job postings using the keywords "penetration tester" and read some job descriptions to determine the IT skills (as well as any non–IT skills) most companies want an applicant to possess.

1. Start your Web browser, enter the URL **www.monster.com**, and then press **Enter**.
2. Click the **Search Jobs** icon on the home page. If you're prompted to create a Monster account, click **Not today, thanks**, and then click **Next**.
3. In the Enter Key Words dialog box, type **penetration tester** and then click the **Get Results** icon.
4. Note the number of positions found by scrolling to the bottom of the first page. Select three to five positions and read the job description information.
5. When you're finished, close your Web browser.

Penetration-Testing Methodologies

Ethical hackers who perform penetration tests use one of these models:

- White box model
- Black box model
- Gray box model

In the **white box model**, the tester is told what network topology and technology the company is using and is given permission to interview IT personnel and company employees. For example, the company might print a network diagram showing all the company's routers, switches, firewalls, and intrusion-detection systems (IDSs) as well as the OSs running on client computers and the company's servers (see Figure 1-1).

This makes the penetration tester's job a little easier than using the black box model. In the **black box model**, management does not divulge to staff that penetration testing is being conducted, nor does it give the tester any diagrams or describe what technologies the company is using. This model puts the burden on the tester to find this information by using techniques you learn throughout this book. This model also helps

NetWare servers

Figure 1-1   A sample network diagram

management see whether the company's security personnel are able to detect an attack. The **gray box model** is a hybrid of the white and black box models. In this model, the company gives a tester only partial information. For example, the tester might get information about which OSs are used, but not get any network diagrams.

Security Bytes

Hospitals often check the intake procedures medical staff perform by using interns and nurses as "potential patients." In one psychiatric hospital, intake staff were told in advance that some potential patients would be doctors or nurses. It was surprising that the number of patients admitted that month was unusually low, even though none of the patients were interns or nurses. In the same vein, if a company knows that it's being monitored to assess the security of its systems, employees might behave more vigilantly and adhere to existing procedures. Many companies don't want this false sense of security; they want to see how personnel operate without forewarning that someone might attempt to attack their network.

Certification Programs for Network Security Personnel

As most IT professionals are aware, professional certification is available in just about every area of network security. Whether you are a security professional, computer programmer, database administrator, or wide area network (WAN) specialist, professional organizations offer enough certifications and exams to keep you busy for the rest of your career. The following sections cover the most popular IT security certifications and briefly describe some exam requirements. To prepare for these certifications, CompTIA Security+ and Network+ certifications (or equivalent knowledge) are helpful. For more details, visit the CompTIA Web site at *www.comptia.org*.

Certified Ethical Hacker (CEH)

The International Council of Electronic Commerce Consultants (EC-Council) has developed a certification designation called **Certified Ethical Hacker (CEH)**. Currently, the CEH exam is based on 21 domains (subject areas) with which the tester must be familiar. Knowledge requirements change periodically, so if you're interested in taking this exam, you should visit EC-Council's Web site (*www.eccouncil.org*) for the most up-to-date information. These are the 21 domains tested for the CEH exam:

- Ethics and legal issues
- Footprinting
- Scanning
- Enumeration

- System hacking

- Trojan programs and backdoors

- Sniffers

- Denial of service

- Social engineering

- Session hijacking

- Hacking Web servers

- Web application vulnerabilities

- Web-based password-cracking techniques

- SQL injection

- Hacking wireless networks

- Viruses and worms

- Hacking Novell

- Hacking Linux

- Intrusion detection systems (IDSs), firewalls, and honeypots

- Buffer overflows

- Cryptography

As you can see, you must be familiar with a vast amount of information to pass this multiple-choice exam. Although you do need a general knowledge of these 21 domains for the exam, in the workplace, you will most likely be placed on a team that conducts penetration tests. This team, called a **red team** in the industry, is composed of people with varied skills who perform the tests. For example, a red team might include a computer programming expert who can perform SQL injection or other programming vulnerability testing. (You learn more about SQL injection in Chapter 10 and programming fundamentals in Chapter 7.) The team might also include a network expert who's familiar with port vulnerabilities and IDS, router, or firewall vulnerabilities. It's unlikely that one person will perform all the tests. However, passing the exam requires general knowledge of all the domains listed. Reading this book and working through the activities and case projects will help you gain this knowledge.

Open Source Security Testing Methodology Manual (OSSTMM) Professional Security Tester

The **OSSTMM Professional Security Tester (OPST)** certification is designated by the **Institute for Security and Open Methodologies (ISECOM)**, a nonprofit organization that provides security training and certification programs for security professionals. The OPST certification uses the **Open Source Security Testing Methodology Manual (OSSTMM)**, written by Peter Herzog, as its standardized methodology. This manual is one of the most widely used security testing methodologies to date and is available on the CD accompanying this book. You'll use many of its methodologies throughout this book. Because the manual is updated periodically, you should check the ISECOM site (*www.isecom.org*) regularly to download the most current version.

The exam covers some of the following topics:

- *Professional*—Rules of engagement (defining your conduct as a security tester)

- *Enumeration*—Internet packet types, denial-of-service testing

- *Assessments*—Network surveying, controls, competitive intelligence scouting

- *Application*—Password cracking, containment measures

- *Verification*—Problem solving, security testing

The exam requires testers to not only answer multiple-choice questions, but also successfully conduct security testing on an attack network. This practical-application portion of the exam ensures that testers can apply their knowledge to a real-world setting. For more information about this certification, visit *www.isecom.org*.

Certified Information Systems Security Professional (CISSP)

The **Certified Information Systems Security Professional (CISSP)** certification for security professionals is issued by the International Information Systems Security Certifications Consortium (ISC^2). Even though the CISSP certification is not geared toward the technical IT professional, it has become one of the standards for many security professionals. The exam doesn't require testers to have technical knowledge in IT; it tests security-related managerial skills. CISSPs are usually more concerned with policies and procedures than the actual tools for conducting security tests or penetration tests, so they don't need the skill set of a technical security professional. The exam covers questions from the following 10 domains:

- Access control systems and methodology
- Telecommunications and network security
- Security management practices
- Application and systems development security
- Cryptography
- Security architecture and models
- Operations security
- Business continuity planning and disaster recovery planning
- Laws, investigations, and ethics
- Physical security

For more information about this certification, visit *www.isc2.org*.

SANS Institute

The **SysAdmin, Audit, Network, Security (SANS) Institute** offers training and IT security certifications through **Global Information Assurance Certification (GIAC)**. It also disseminates research documents on computer and network security worldwide at no cost. One of the most popular SANS Institute documents is the Top 20 list, which details the most common network exploits and suggests ways of correcting vulnerabilities. This list offers a wealth of information for penetration testers or security professionals, and you take a closer look at it in Activity 1-2. For more information on security certification exams, visit *www.sans.org* or *www.giac.org*.

Which Certification Is Best?

Deciding which certification exam or path to take can be difficult. Penetration testers need to have the technical skills to perform their duties effectively. They must also have a good understanding of networks and the role of management in an organization, have skills in writing and verbal communication, and have a desire to continue learning. Any certification, if it encourages you to read and study more, is worth its weight in gold. The argument that certification is just a piece of paper can be countered by saying "So is a hundred dollar bill, but it's nice to have in your wallet!" The danger of certification exams is that some participants simply memorize terminology and don't have a good grasp of the subject matter or complex concepts, much like students who have managed to pass a final exam by cramming and then forgetting most of the information after taking the test. Use the time you spend studying for a certification exam wisely, discovering areas in which you might need improvement instead of memorizing answers to questions.

This book assists you in acquiring the skills you need to become a competent IT security professional and pass any exam that covers ethical hacking, penetration testing methodologies, and network topologies and technologies. But regardless of the exam you take, the most critical concept to keep in mind is that there are laws governing what you can or cannot do as an ethical hacker, security tester, or penetration tester. Following the laws and behaving ethically are more important than passing an exam.

Again, visit Web sites for the organizations conducting certification testing because exam requirements change as rapidly as technology does. For example, several years ago the CISSP exam had no questions on wireless networking because the technology was not widely available, but now the exam covers wireless technology.

Activity 1-2: Examining the Top 20 List

ACTIVITY

Time Required: 15 minutes

Objective: Examine the SANS list of the most common network exploits.

Description: As fast as IT security professionals attempt to correct network vulnerabilities, someone creates new exploits. Network security professionals must keep up to date on those exploits. In this activity, you examine some of the current exploits used to attack networks. Don't worry—you won't have to memorize your findings. This activity simply gives you an introduction to the world of network security.

1. Start your Web browser, enter the URL **www.sans.org**, and then press **Enter**.

2. Click the **Top 20 List** icon on the home page. (Because home pages from Web sites change as rapidly as the price of gas, you might have to search to locate the icon.)

3. Read the content of the SANS Top 20 list. Because this document changes to reflect the many new exploits created daily, choose any Windows exploit by scrolling below the introduction and then clinking a link. Microsoft SQL Server (MSSQL) has been listed as having vulnerabilities, for example, and you might still see it in the list.

4. Note the heading "How to Determine if you are Vulnerable," and read this section.

5. Scroll down the document, and read the section "How to Protect Against It," noting possible remedies you might try to correct the vulnerability. Does the remedy use a third-party tool or one that can be downloaded from Microsoft?

6. Scroll down to the section on UNIX. Choose one of the vulnerabilities for the UNIX system by clicking the link under the "Top Vulnerabilities to UNIX Systems" heading.

7. Note the operating systems affected by the vulnerability in the "Operating Systems Affected" section.

8. Read the section "How to Determine if you are Vulnerable."

9. Scroll down the document, and read the section "How to Protect Against It," noting possible remedies for correcting the vulnerability. Are there software patches offered by vendors? Does the vendor offer any step-by-step directions for IT professionals?

10. When you're finished, close your Web browser.

WHAT YOU CAN DO LEGALLY

Because laws involving computer technology change as rapidly as technology itself, you must continuously keep abreast of what's happening in your area of the world. What is legal in Des Moines might not be legal in Indianapolis. Finding out what's legal in your state or country can be just as difficult as performing penetration tests, however. Many state officials aren't aware of the legalities surrounding computer technology. This confusion also makes it difficult to prosecute wrongdoers in computer crimes. The average citizen on a jury doesn't want to send a person to jail for doing something the state prosecutor hasn't clearly defined as illegal.

As a security tester, you must be aware of what you're allowed to do and what you should not or cannot do. For example, some security testers know how to pick a deadbolt lock, so a locked door wouldn't deter them from getting physical access to a server. However, testers must be knowledgeable about the laws for possessing lockpicks before venturing out to a corporate site with tools in hand. In fact, laws vary from state to state and country to country. In some states, the mere possession of lockpicking tools constitutes a crime, whereas other states allow possession as long as a crime has not been committed. In one state, you might be charged with a misdemeanor for possessing burglary tools; in another state, you might be charged with a felony.

Laws of the Land

As with lockpicking tools, some hacking tools on your computer might be illegal to possess. You should contact local law enforcement agencies and ask about the laws for your state or country before installing hacking software on your laptop. You can see how complex this issue gets as you travel from state to state or from country to country. New York City might have one law, and a quick drive over the George Washington Bridge brings you to the laws of New Jersey. Table A-1, in Appendix A, compares Vermont's computer crime statutes to New York's to demonstrate the variety of verbiage the legal community uses.

Laws are written to protect society, but often the written words are open to interpretation. That's why we have courts and judges. In Hawaii, the state must prove that the person charged with committing a crime on a computer had the "intent to commit a crime." So scanning a network in itself is not a crime in Hawaii. Also, the state has the even more difficult task of having to prove that the computer used in committing a crime has been used by only one person—the one alleged to have committed the crime. If the person charged with the crime claims that more than one person in his office or home has access to the computer that was used to gather evidence of wrongdoing, the state can't use that computer as evidence.

What do these laws have to do with a network security professional using penetration-testing tools? Hacking tools that allow you view a company's network infrastructure are not as clearly defined as possession of burglary tools because laws for computer hacking tools haven't been able to keep up with the speed of technological advances. Is it legal to take pictures with your 35-mm camera of the exterior and interior of a bank? Security personnel at a bank in Hawaii say you would be asked to stop taking pictures and leave the premises. Arnold Laanui, Jr., an FBI spokesperson, put it in simple terms: You can be asked to stop taking photographs if you're on private property. Taking pictures across the street from the bank with a zoom lens is legal, but if you used the photographs to commit a crime in the future, an attorney would tell you the charges against you might be more serious. Because of the fear of terrorism, in certain parts of the United States and many parts of Europe, taking pictures of bridges, train stations, and other public areas is illegal. Yet running a computer program that gives an attacker an overview and detailed description of a company's network infrastructure is not seen as a threat by most.

The point of mentioning all these laws and regulations is to make sure you're aware of the dangers of being a security tester or a student learning hacking techniques. Table 1-1 lists just a fraction of the cases prosecuted in 2004; in these cases, many people have been sentenced to a substantial prison term for "hacking," the term used by the Department of Justice. Most attacks involved more than just scanning a business, but this information shows how the government is getting more serious about punishment for cybercrimes. Some of the most infamous cases are hacks carried out by college students, such as the eBay hack of 1999. As you read the cases in Table 1-1, note that some hackers used software to crack passwords of logon accounts. This act, performed by many security professionals when given permission to do so by a network's owner, is a federal offense when done without permission and can add substantial prison time to a hacker's sentence.

Table 1-1   An overview of recent hacking cases

State/Year	Description
North Carolina 2004	Brian A. Salcedo was sentenced to 108 months for hacking Lowe's store system to steal credit card numbers from customers. The longest prison sentence for a hacking-related crime before this case was for Kevin Mitnick, who was sentenced to 68 months.
New York 2004	Neal Cotton, a disgruntled network administrator who was fired by Cyber City, a computer consulting company, decided to attack his former employer's network and wipe out files and company data. He faces up to 10 years of prison time and a $250,000 fine.

Table 1-1   An overview of recent hacking cases (continued)

State/Year	Description
Massachusetts 2004	Patrick Angle, a former employee of a high-technology firm in Boston, was charged with hacking into his former employer's network and deleting source code for a program he and others developed. If found guilty, Angle faces up to 10 years in prison, a $250,000 fine, and restitution. He's alleged to have deleted log files to cover his tracks and to have changed the root password to the server so that other employees couldn't correct the problems he created.
California 2004	Even though this indictment happened in Los Angeles, the case involves several states and other countries. Calin Mateias, a 24-year-old Romanian hacker, was charged with conspiring to steal more than $10 million in computer equipment from Ingram Micro, a computer distribution company. Mateias is alleged to have hacked into Ingram Micro's online ordering system, placed fraudulent orders for computers, and had the equipment mailed to members of his team located throughout the United States. The indictment includes five others in Florida, Georgia, Virginia, and Alaska. If found guilty, Mateias faces up to 90 years in prison. The five U.S citizens face from 25 to 35 years in prison. Most were in their early to mid-20s.
Washington 2004	Laurent Chavet, a former Alta Vista employee, was charged with hacking into a protected computer to steal source code and causing $5000 of damage to the computer. If found guilty, the two-count indictment carries a 10-year sentence, a $500,000 fine, and possible restitution.
New York 2004	Peter Borghard, a former network administrator for a Manhattan-based ISP, was sentenced to five months in prison and five months of home confinement for hacking into his former employer's system. He was also ordered to pay restitution of $118,030. In two separate attacks in January 2003, Borghard destroyed data and wiped out configuration settings using a slave computer located in a cubicle at a company Borghard had worked at before joining the ISP. His attacks temporarily crippled systems and deprived the ISP's customers of services. Despite attempts to erase evidence of the attack, Borghard was apprehended by the FBI's computer forensics analysis.
Louisiana 2004	David Jeanesonne, 43, was arrested for allegedly transmitting a worm that caused WebTV users who opened an e-mail attachment to dial 911 instead of the ISP's telephone number. He faces up to 10 years in prison and a $250,000 fine.
Texas 2004	A former CEO of a Dallas-based car parts distribution company as well as his CTO and a computer consultant were indicted by the U.S. Attorney's office for intruding into a competitor's database to gain competitive advantage. If found guilty, they face up to 10 years in prison and a $250,000 fine. They were also charged with five counts of computer password trafficking; each count carries a one-year sentence and a $100,000 fine. To access the car parts database, they needed access to legitimate user names and passwords to the system. Obtaining logon names and passwords illegally can be dangerous and expensive.
California 2004	Jerome T. Heckenkamp, a 24-year-old computer science graduate student, pled guilty to unauthorized access to eBay and Qualcomm Computer systems in 1999. Heckenkamp was known as MagicFX. A 16-count indictment was consolidated in 2003, and Heckenkamp's sentence, after plea agreements, could be eight months to three years in prison.
New York 2004	Adrian Lamo, 23, known as the "Homeless Hacker," pled guilty to hacking the *New York Times* computer network. He was sentenced to six months of house arrest and a $65,000 fine. One can only imagine how a homeless 23-year-old could be under house arrest, but the prosecutor said that Lamo will have a felony conviction on his record for the rest of his life.

Is Port Scanning Legal?

Some states look at port scanning (a method used to find open ports on a system, covered in Chapter 5) as noninvasive or nondestructive in nature and deem it legal. This is not always the case, however, so you must still be prudent before you start using penetration-testing tools. In some cases, a company has filed criminal charges against a hacker for scanning its system. In one case, however, a Georgia judge ruled that no damage was done to the network, so the charges were dismissed. It's just a matter of time before a business will claim that its network is also private property, and it should have the right to say that scanning is not allowed. Because the federal government currently doesn't see such infringements as a violation of the U.S. Constitution, it allows each state to address these issues separately. However, a company could bring similar charges against you if you decide to practice using the tools you learn about in this book. Even if you were found innocent in your state, the legal costs could be damaging to your business or personal finances. Therefore, finding out what your state laws are before using what you learn in this book is essential, even if you're using the tools for the benefit of others, not criminal activity.

You might also want to read your ISP contract, specifically the section usually called "Acceptable Use Policy." Most people quickly glance over and accept the terms of their contract. Figure 1-2 is an excerpt from an actual ISP contract. Notice that section (c) might create some problems if you run scanning software that subsequently slows down network access or prevents users from accessing network components.

Acceptable Use Policy

(a) PacInfo Net makes no restriction on usage provided that such usage is legal under the laws and regulations of the State of Hawaii and the United States of America and does not adversely affect PacInfo Net customers. Customer is responsible for obtaining and adhering to the Acceptable Use Policies of any network accessed through PacInfo Net services.

(b) PacInfo Net reserves the right without notice to disconnect an account that is the source of spamming, abusive, or malicious activities. There will be no refund when an account is terminated for these causes. Moreover, there will be a billing rate of $125 per hour charged to such accounts to cover staff time spent repairing subsequent damage.

(c) Customers are forbidden from using techniques designed to cause damage to or deny access by legitimate users of computers or network components connected to the Internet. PacInfo Net reserves the right to disconnect a customer site that is the source of such activities without notice.

Figure 1-2   An example of an acceptable use policy

Another ISP responded to an e-mail about the use of scanning software with the following message:

> *Any use of the Service that disturbs the normal use of the system by HOL or by other HOL customers or consumes excessive amounts of memory or CPU cycles for long periods of time may result in termination pursuant to Section 1 of this Agreement. Users are strictly prohibited from any activity that compromises the security of HOL's facilities. Users may not run IRC "bots" or any other scripts or programs not provided by HOL.*

> *Regards,*

> *Customer Support*
> *Hawaii Online*

The statement that prohibits the use of Internet Relay Chat (IRC) bots or any other scripts or programs not provided by the ISP might be the most important for penetration testers. An IRC "bot" is a program that sends automatic responses to users, giving the appearance of a person being present on the other side of the connection. For example, a bot can be created that welcomes new users joining a chat session, even though a person isn't actually present to welcome them. Even if you have no intentions of creating a bot, the "any other scripts or programs" clause should still raise an eyebrow.

Table A-2 in Appendix A shows which legal statutes to look at before you begin your journey. The statutes listed in the table might have changed since the writing of this book, so keeping up with your state laws before trying out penetration-testing tools is important. In Activity 1-3, you research the laws of the state in which you reside, using Table A-2 as a guide.

Activity 1-3: Identifying Computer Statutes in Your State or Country

Time Required: 30 minutes

Objective: Learn what laws might prohibit you from hacking a network or computer system in your state or country.

Description: For this activity, use Internet search engines to gather information on computer crime in your state (or a state selected by your instructor). You have been hired by ExecuTech, a security consulting company, to gather information on any new statutes or laws that might have an impact on the security testers the company employs. Write a one-page memo to Bob Lynch, director of security and operations, listing any applicable statutes or laws and offering recommendations to management. For example, you might note in your memo that conducting a denial-of-service attack on a company's network is illegal because the state's penal code prohibits such an attack unless authorized by the owner.

Federal Laws

You should also be aware of applicable federal laws when conducting your first security test (see Table 1-2). Federal computer crime laws are getting more specific about cybercrimes and intellectual property issues. In fact, the government now has a new branch of computer crime called computer hacking and intellectual property (CHIP).

Table 1-2 Federal computer crime laws

Federal Law	Description
The Computer Fraud and Abuse Act. Title 18, Crimes and Criminal Procedure. Part I: Crimes, Chapter 47, Fraud and False Statements, Sec. 1030: Fraud and related activity in connection with computers	This law makes it a federal crime to access classified information or financial information without authorization.
Electronic Communication Privacy Act. Title 18, Crimes and Criminal Procedure. Part I: Crimes, Chapter 119, Wire and Electronic Communications Interception and Interception of Oral Communications, Sec. 2510: Definitions and Sec. 2511: Interception and disclosure of wire, oral, or electronic communications prohibited	This laws prevents you from intercepting any communication, regardless of how it was transmitted.
U.S. Patriot Act Sec. 217. Interception of Computer Trespasser Communications	This law amends Chapter 119 of Title 18, U.S. Code.
Stored Wire and Electronic Communications and Transactional Records Act. Title 18, Crimes and Criminal Procedure. Part I: Crimes, Chapter 121, Stored Wire and Electronic Communications and Transactional Records Act, Sec. 2701: Unlawful access to stored communications (a) Offense. Except as provided in subsection of this section whoever (1) intentionally accesses without authorization a facility through which an electronic communication service is provided; or (2) intentionally exceeds an authorization to access that facility; Sec. 2702: Disclosure of contents	This law defines unauthorized access to computers that store classified information.

Security Bytes

NOTE Even though you might think you're following the requirements set forth by the client who hired you to perform a security test, don't assume that management will be happy with your results. One tester was reprimanded by a manager who was upset that the security testing revealed all the logon names and passwords to the tester. The manager believed that the tester shouldn't know this information and considered stopping the security testing.

Activity 1-4: Examining Federal Computer Crime Laws

Time Required: 15 minutes

Objective: Increase your understanding of U.S. federal laws related to computer crime.

Description: For this activity, use Internet search engines to gather information on U.S. Code, Title 18, Sec. 1030, which covers fraud and related activity in connection with computers. Write a summary explaining how this law can affect ethical hackers and security testers.

WHAT YOU CANNOT DO LEGALLY

After reading through the state and federal laws on computer crime, you can see that accessing a computer without permission, destroying data, or copying information without the owner's permission is illegal. It doesn't take a law degree to understand that certain actions are illegal, such as installing worms or viruses on a computer network that deny users access to network resources. As a security tester, you must be careful that your actions don't prevent customers from doing their jobs. If you run a program that uses network resources to the extent that a user is denied access to a network resource, you have violated federal law. For example, denial-of-service (DoS) attacks, covered in Chapter 3, should not be initiated on your customer's networks.

Get It in Writing

As discussed earlier, you can inadvertently cause a DoS attack by running certain hacking programs on a customer's network. This is what makes your job difficult, especially if you're conducting security tests as an independent contractor hired by a company, versus being an employee of a large security company that has a legal team to draw up a contract with the client. Employees of a security company are protected under the company's contract with the client.

For the purposes of this book, assume you're an independent contractor who needs a little guidance in creating a written contract. Some contractors don't believe in written contracts, thinking they undermine their relationships with clients. The old handshake and verbal agreement work for many computer consultants, but of course you have to be the final judge on whether this approach is right for you. Some think it's a matter of trust. Others argue that trust has nothing to do with it; a written contract is just good business. Consultants who have worked on a project and not received payment from the client usually vote yes on the contract question. Users often aren't convinced about the importance of backing up important documents until their computers crash. Don't be like them and wait until you're in court to wish you had something in writing.

As an independent contractor in computer consulting, you would probably have some experience with contracts. If you want additional information, you can consult books on working as an independent contractor, such as *The Computer Consultant's Guide* by Janet Ruhl (ISBN: 0471176494, 1997) and *Getting Started in Computer Consulting* by Peter Meyer (ISBN: 0471348139, 1999). The Internet can also be a helpful resource for finding free contract templates that can be modified to fit your business situation. However, having an attorney read over your contract before it's signed is a good investment of your time and money. The modifications you make might create more problems than no contract at all.

Are you concerned? Good. Most textbooks or courses on ethical hacking gloss over this topic, yet it's the most important part of the profession. If your client gives you a contract drawn up by its legal team, consulting a lawyer can save you time and money. Attempting to understand a contract written by a team of attorneys representing the company's best interests warrants an attorney on your side looking out for your best interests. The complexity of law is too much for most laypeople to understand. It's difficult enough to keep up with computer technology. Both fields are changing constantly, but law is even more complex, as it changes from state to state.

Figure B-1 in Appendix B shows an example of a contract you might want to use, with modifications, after joining the Independent Computer Consultants Association (ICCA). Read through the legal language in this figure, and then do Activity 1-5.

Activity 1-5: Understanding a Consulting Contract

Time Required: 30 minutes

Objective: Increase your understanding of a consulting contract.

Description: For this activity, review the sample contract shown in Appendix B. This contract can't be used unless you're a member of the ICCA, but it's an excellent example of how a contract might be worded. After reading the contract, write a one-page summary discussing the areas you would modify or add to. Include what important areas are missing for a penetration tester, if any.

Security Bytes

Because the job of an ethical hacker is relatively new, the laws are constantly changing. Even though a company has hired you to test its network for vulnerabilities, be careful that you aren't breaking any laws for your state or country. If you're worried that one of your tests might slow down the network because of excessive bandwidth use, that concern should signal a red flag. The company might consider suing you for lost time or monies caused by this delay.

Ethical Hacking in a Nutshell

After reading all the dos and don'ts, you might have decided to go into a different profession. Before switching careers, however, take a look at the different skills a security tester needs to help determine whether you have what it takes to do this job:

- *Knowledge of network and computer technology*—As a security tester, you must have a good understanding of networking concepts. You should spend time learning and reviewing TCP/IP and routing concepts and be able to read network diagrams. If you don't have experience working with networks, it's important that you start now. Being a security tester is impossible without a high level of expertise in this area. You should also have a good understanding of computer technology and OSs. Read as much as you can on the OSs in use today, paying particular attention to *nix (UNIX and Linux) systems and Microsoft OSs because most of your security testing will be done on these popular systems.

- *Ability to communicate with management and IT personnel*—Security testers need to be good listeners and must be able to communicate verbally and in writing with members of management and IT personnel. Explaining your findings to CEOs might be difficult, especially if they don't have a technical background. Your reports should be clear and succinct and offer constructive feedback and recommendations.

- *An understanding of the laws that apply to your location*—As a security tester, you must be aware of what you can or can't do legally. This can be difficult when working with global companies, as laws can vary widely in other countries.

- *Ability to apply the necessary tools to perform your tasks*—Security testers must have a good understanding of the tools available for conducting security tests. More important, you must be able to think outside the box by discovering, creating, or modifying tools when current tools don't meet your needs.

Security Bytes

If being liked by others is important to you, you might want to consider a different profession than penetration testing. If you're good at your job, many IT employees resent you discovering vulnerabilities in their systems. In fact, it's the only profession in which the better you do your job, the more enemies you make!

CHAPTER SUMMARY

- ❏ Many companies hire ethical hackers to perform penetration tests. The purpose of a penetration test is to discover vulnerabilities in a network. A security test is performed by a team of people with varied skill sets, sometimes referred to as a red team.

- ❏ Penetration tests are usually conducted by using three different models: white box model, black box model, and gray box model. The model the tester uses is based on the amount of information the customer is willing to supply. In some tests, the customer doesn't want the tester to have access to any of the company's information. In other words, the customer is saying "Find out what you can about my company without my help."

❑ Security testers can earn certifications from multiple sources. The most popular certifications are CEH, CISSP, and OPST. Each certification requires taking an exam and covers different areas the tester must master. Because test requirements change periodically, visiting the certification company's Web site to verify exam requirements is important.

❑ As a penetration tester, you must be aware of what you're legally allowed or not allowed to do. Contacting your local law enforcement agency is a good place to start before beginning any security testing.

❑ Your ISP might have an acceptable use policy in the contract you signed. It could limit your ability to use many of the tools available to security testers. Running scripts or programs not authorized by the ISP can result in termination of services.

❑ State and federal laws pertaining to computer crime should be understood before conducting a security test. Federal laws are applicable for all states, whereas state laws can vary. Being aware of the laws that apply is imperative.

❑ Get it in writing. As an independent contractor, having the client sign a written contract allowing you to conduct the penetration test before you begin is critical. You should also have an attorney read the contract, especially if you or the company representative made any modifications.

KEY TERMS

black box model — Management does not divulge to IT security personnel that penetration testing will be conducted, nor does it give the testing team a description of the network topology. In other words, penetration testers are on their own.

Certified Ethical Hacker (CEH) — A certification for security testers designated by the EC-Council.

Certified Information Systems Security Professional (CISSP) — Non-vendor-specific certification issued by the International Information Systems Security Certifications Consortium, Inc. (ISC^2). Visit *www.isc2.org* for more information.

crackers — Hackers who break into systems with the intent of doing harm or destroying data.

ethical hackers — Users who access a computer system or network with the owner's permission.

Global Information Assurance Certification (GIAC) — An organization founded by the SANS Institute in 1999 to validate the skills of security professionals. GIAC certifications encompass many areas of expertise in the security field. Visit *www.giac.org* for more information.

gray box model — A hybrid of the black box model and the white box model. For example, the company might give a tester some information about which OSs are running, but not provide any network topology information (diagrams of routers, switches, intrusion-detection systems, firewalls, and so forth).

hacker — A user who accesses a computer system or network without authorization from the owner.

Institute for Security and Open Methodologies (ISECOM) — ISECOM is a nonprofit organization that provides security training and certification programs for security professionals. Visit *www.isecom.org* for more information.

Open Source Security Testing Methodology Manual (OSSTMM) — This security manual developed by Peter Herzog has become one of the most widely used security testing methodologies to date. Visit *www.osstmm.org* for more information.

OSSTMM Professional Security Tester (OPST) — An ISECOM-designated certification for penetration testers.

packet monkeys — A derogatory term for unskilled crackers or hackers who steal program code to hack into network systems instead of creating the programs themselves.

penetration test — In this test, a security professional performs an attack on a computer network with permission from the network's owner.

red team — A group of penetration testers who work together to attack a network.

script — Lines of code that run in sequence to perform tasks on a computer. Many experienced penetration testers write or modify scripts using the Perl or C programming language.

script kiddies — Similar to packet monkeys, a term for unskilled hackers or crackers who use scripts or computer programs written by others to penetrate networks.

security test — In this test, a security professional performs an attack on a network; in addition, the tester analyzes the organization's security policy and procedures and reports any vulnerabilities to management.

SysAdmin, Audit, Network, Security (SANS) Institute — Founded in 1989, this organization conducts training worldwide and offers multiple certifications through GIAC in many aspects of computer security and forensics.

white box model — In this model, testers can speak with company staff and are given a full description of the network topology and technology.

REVIEW QUESTIONS

1. The U.S. Department of Justice defines a hacker as which of the following?

   a. a person who accesses a computer or network without the owner's permission

   b. a penetration tester

   c. a person who uses telephone services without payment

   d. a person who accesses a computer or network system with the owner's permission

2. A penetration tester is _____ .

   a. a person who accesses a computer or network without permission from the owner

   b. a person who uses telephone services without payment

   c. a security professional who's hired to hack into a network to discover vulnerabilities

   d. a hacker who accesses a system without permission, but does not delete or destroy files

3. Some experienced hackers refer to inexperienced hackers who copy or use prewritten scripts or computer programs as which of the following? (Choose all that apply.)

   a. script monkeys

   b. packet kiddies

   c. packet monkeys

   d. script kiddies

4. What three models do penetration testers use to perform penetration tests?

5. A team composed of people with varied skills used to penetrate a network is referred to as which of the following?

   a. green team

   b. blue team

   c. black team

   d. red team

6. How can you find out which computer crime laws are applicable in your state?

   a. Contact your local law enforcement agencies.

   b. Contact your ISP provider.

   c. Contact your local computer store vendor.

   d. Call 911.

7. What portion of your ISP contract might affect your ability to conduct a penetration test over the Internet?

   a. scanning policy

   b. port access policy

   c. acceptable use policy

   d. warranty policy

8. If you run a program in New York City that uses network resources to the extent that a user is denied access to a network resource, what type of law have you violated?

   a. city

   b. state

   c. local

   d. federal

9. Which federal law prohibits unauthorized access of classified information?

   a. Computer Fraud and Abuse Act, Title 18

   b. Electronic Communication Privacy Act

   c. Stored Wire and Electronic Communications and Transactional Records Act

   d. Fifth Amendment

10. Which federal law prohibits intercepting any communication, regardless of how it was transmitted?

    a. Computer Fraud and Abuse Act, Title 18

    b. Electronic Communication Privacy Act

    c. Stored Wire and Electronic Communications and Transactional Records Act

    d. Fourth Amendment

11. Which federal law amended Chapter 119 of Title 18, U.S. Code?

    a. Computer Fraud and Abuse Act, Title 18

    b. Electronic Communication Privacy Act

    c. Stored Wire and Electronic Communications and Transactional Records Act

    d. U.S. Patriot Act, Sec. 217: Interception of Computer Trespasser Communications

12. To determine whether scanning is illegal in your area, you should do which of the following?

    a. Refer to U.S. Code.

    b. Refer to the U.S. Patriot Act.

    c. Refer to state laws.

    d. Contact your ISP.

13. What organization offers the Certified Ethical Hacker (CEH) certification exam?

    a. International Information Systems Security Certifications Consortium (ISC^2)

    b. EC-Council

    c. SANS Institute

    d. GIAC

14. What organization designates an individual as a CISSP?

    a. International Information Systems Security Certifications Consortium (ISC^2)

    b. EC-Council

    c. SANS Institute

    d. GIAC

15. What organization designates an individual as an OPST?

    a. International Information Systems Security Certifications Consortium (ISC^2)

    b. EC-Council

    c. SANS Institute

    d. ISECOM

16. As a security tester, what should you do before installing hacking software on your computer?

    a. Check with your local law enforcement agencies.

    b. Contact your hardware vendor.

    c. Contact the software vendor.

    d. Contact your ISP.

17. Before using hacking software over the Internet, you should contact which of the following? (Choose all that apply.)

    a. your ISP

    b. your vendor

    c. local law enforcement authorities to check for compliance

    d. the FBI

18. What organization issues the Top 20 list of current network exploits?

    a. SANS Institute

    b. ISECOM

    c. EC-Council

    d. OPST

19. A written contract is not necessary when a friend recommends a client. True or False?

20. A security tester should possess which of the following attributes? (Choose all that apply.)

    a. good listening skills

    b. knowledge of networking and computer technology

    c. good verbal and written communications skills

    d. an interest in securing networks and computer systems

CASE PROJECTS

CASE PROJECTS

Case 1-1: Determining Legal Requirements for Penetration Testing

K. J. Williams Corporation, a large real estate management company in Maui, Hawaii, has contracted your computer consulting company to perform a penetration test on its computer network. The company owns property that houses a five-star hotel, golf courses, tennis courts, and restaurants. Claudia Mae, the vice president, is your only contact for the company. You won't be introduced to any IT staff or employees to avoid undermining the tests you're conducting. Claudia wants to determine what you can find out about the company's network infrastructure, network topology, and any discovered vulnerabilities, without any assistance from her or company personnel.

Based on the preceding information, write a report for your instructor outlining the steps you should take before beginning penetration tests of the K. J. Williams Corporation. Research the laws that apply to the state where the company is located, and be sure to reference any federal laws that might apply to what you have been asked to do.

CASE PROJECTS

Case 1-2: Understanding the Rules of Engagement for Security Testers

You are a new security tester just hired by Security Consulting Company (SCC). Your supervisor wants to be sure you don't violate any of the company's policies before sending you out on your first assignment. Shelley Canon, the vice president of SCC, wants you to read the rules of engagement section of the OSSTMM.

Write a memo to Shelley Canon summarizing the rules of engagement section of the OSSTMM (located on this book's CD). The memo should describe the purpose of the rules of engagement and include answers to the following questions:

1. When is it permissible to release the names of past clients?

2. If you are not able to penetrate a customer's network, is it permissible to offer your services free of charge?

3. When is it permissible to conduct denial-of-service attacks on a customer's network?

2

TCP/IP CONCEPTS REVIEW

> **After reading this chapter and completing the exercises, you will be able to:**
>
> ◆ Describe the TCP/IP protocol stack
> ◆ Explain the basic concepts of IP addressing
> ◆ Explain the binary, octal, and hexadecimal numbering systems

Almost everything you do as a network security analyst or security tester depends on your understanding of networking concepts and knowledge of Transmission Control Protocol/Internet Protocol (TCP/IP). This book assumes you already have a thorough knowledge of networking concepts and TCP/IP. This chapter serves as a quick review of how both topics relate to IT security and security testers. In the activities and case projects, you apply your knowledge of TCP/IP and networking concepts to security-testing techniques.

Most of the tools both hackers and security testers use run over IP, which is the de facto standard of network protocols. However, it was developed without security functions in mind, so there's a need for professionals who have the knowledge and skills to tighten up many of the security holes resulting from the use of IP.

In this chapter, you examine the TCP/IP protocol stack and IP addressing and review the binary, octal, and hexadecimal numbering systems and the ports associated with services that run over TCP/IP.

OVERVIEW OF TCP/IP

For computers to communicate with one another over the Internet or across an office, they must speak the same language. This language is referred to as a **protocol**, and the most widely used is **Transmission Control Protocol/Internet Protocol (TCP/IP)**. No matter what medium connects computers on a network—copper wires, fiber-optic cables, or a wireless setup—the same protocol must be running on all computers if communication is going to function correctly. Sticking your chopsticks in the communal rice bowl after eating in a Japanese restaurant is considered a major error in protocol. Similarly, attempting to have a computer running Novell's Internetwork Packet Exchange/Sequenced Packet Exchange (IPX/SPX) protocol connect to a Windows Server 2003 server running TCP/IP would produce a protocol error that prevents network communication. Dissatisfied users who can't connect to the server would have negative reactions, in the same way that Japanese citizens would be upset at your lack of manners.

Security Bytes

NOTE

Even though IPX/SPX is not widely used today, many corporations have legacy systems that rely on it. In fact, some users separate their internal networks from the outside world by running IPX/SPX internally. An intruder attempting to attack a network over the Internet would be blocked when the protocol changes from TCP/IP to IPX/SPX. This tactic is referred to as "the poor man's firewall." Of course, it's not a recommended solution for protecting a network, but as a network security professional, you might see it used.

Although you have already studied TCP/IP, a little review is helpful to make sure you have a thorough understanding. TCP/IP is more than simply two protocols (TCP and IP). It's usually referred to as the TCP/IP stack, which contains four distinct layers (see Figure 2-1). The network layer is concerned with physically moving electrons across a media or wire, and the Internet layer is responsible for routing packets by using IP addresses. The transport layer is concerned with controlling the flow of data, sequencing packets for reassembly, and encapsulating the segment with a TCP or User Datagram Protocol (UDP) header. The application layer is where applications and protocols, such as HTTP and Telnet, operate.

| **Application layer** |
| This layer includes network services and client software. |
| **Transport layer**
TCP/UDP services

This layer is responsible for getting data packets to and from the application layer by using port numbers. TCP also verifies packet delivery by using acknowledgments. |
| **Internet layer**

This layer uses IP addresses to route packets to their appropriate destination network. |
| **Network layer**

This layer represents the physical network pathway and the network interface card. |

Figure 2-1   The TCP/IP protocol stack

This chapter discusses only the application, transport, and Internet layers, covered in the following sections.

The Application Layer

The application layer protocols are the front ends to the lower-layer protocols in the TCP/IP stack. In other words, this layer is what you can see and touch. Table 2-1 lists some of the main applications and protocols that run at this layer. These applications and protocols are mentioned again later in the "TCP Ports" section.

Table 2-1 Application layer programs

Application	Description
Hypertext Transfer Protocol (HTTP)	The primary protocol used to communicate over the World Wide Web (see RFC-2616 at *www.ietf.org* for details)
File Transfer Protocol (FTP)	Allows different operating systems to transfer files between one another
Simple Mail Transfer Protocol (SMTP)	The main protocol for transmitting e-mail messages across the Internet
Simple Network Management Protocol (SNMP)	Primarily used to monitor devices on a network, such as remotely monitoring a router's state
Secure Shell (SSH)	Enables a remote user to log on to a server and issue commands
Internet Relay Chat (IRC)	Enables multiple users to communicate over the Internet in discussion forums
Telnet	Enables users to remotely log on to a server

The Transport Layer

The transport layer is where data is encapsulated into segments. A segment can use TCP or UDP as its method for connecting to and forwarding data to a destination host (or node). TCP is a **connection-oriented** protocol, which means the sender doesn't send any data to the destination node until the destination node acknowledges that it's listening to the sender. In other words, a connection is established before data is sent. For example, if Computer A wants to send data to Computer B, it sends Computer B a **SYN** packet first. A SYN packet is a query to the receiver, much like asking "Hello, Computer B. Are you there?" Computer B sends back an acknowledgment called a **SYN-ACK** packet, which is like replying "Yes, I'm here. Go ahead and send." Finally, Computer A sends an **ACK** packet to Computer B in response to the SYN-ACK. This process, called a **three-way handshake**, involves the following steps:

1. Host A sends a TCP packet with the SYN flag set (that is, a SYN packet) to Host B.

2. After receiving the packet, Host B sends Host A its own SYN packet with an ACK flag (a SYN-ACK packet) set.

3. In response to the SYN-ACK packet from Host B, Host A sends Host B a TCP packet with the ACK flag set (an ACK packet).

TCP Segment Headers

As a security professional, you should know the critical components of a TCP header: TCP flags, the initial sequence number (covered later in "Initial Sequence Number (ISN)"), and source and destination port numbers (covered later in "TCP Ports"). Hackers abuse many of these TCP header components; for example, when port scanning, many hackers use the method of sending a packet with a SYN-ACK flag set even though a SYN packet was not sent first. Security testers also use this method, but for legitimate purposes. You need to understand these components before learning how they can be abused. Then, and only then, can you check whether your network has vulnerabilities in these areas. Remember, to protect a network, you need to know the basic methods of hacking into networks. You examine more details on TCP headers in Activity 2-1.

TCP Flags

Each **TCP flag** occupies one bit of the TCP segment and can be set to 0 (off) or 1 (on). These are the six flags of a TCP segment:

- *SYN flag*—The synthesis flag signifies the beginning of a session.
- *ACK flag*—The acknowledgment flag acknowledges a connection and is sent by a host after receiving a SYN-ACK packet.
- *PSH flag*—The push flag is used to deliver data directly to an application. Data is not buffered, but is sent immediately.
- *URG flag*—This flag is used to signify urgent data.
- *RST flag*—The reset flag resets or drops a connection.
- *FIN flag*—The finish flag signifies that the connection is finished.

Initial Sequence Number (ISN)

The **initial sequence number (ISN)** is a 32-bit number that tracks the packets received by the node and enables the reassembly of large packets that have been broken up into smaller packets. In Steps 1 and 2 of the three-way handshake, an ISN is sent. That is, the ISN from the sending node is sent with the SYN packet, and the ISN from the receiving node is sent back to the sending node with the SYN-ACK packet. This ISN can be quite a large number because 2^{32} allows a range of numbers from zero to more than four billion.

Security Bytes

A TCP header's ISN might not seem important to network security professionals who aren't familiar with penetration testing or hacking techniques. However, numerous network attacks have used **session hijacking**, which is an attack that relies on guessing the ISNs of TCP packets. One of the most famous is Kevin Mitnick's attack on the Japanese corporation Tsutomu Shimomura, called an IP sequence attack. Understanding TCP flags and the basic elements of a TCP packet can go a long way toward understanding how a hacker thinks—and how you should think. To become a better security professional, try to discover vulnerabilities or weaknesses as you study the basics. Too many network security professionals wait for hackers to discover vulnerabilities in a network instead of beating them at their own game.

Activity 2-1: Viewing RFC-793

Time Required: 30 minutes

Objective: Examine the details of the components of a TCP segment and understand how to make use of Request for Comments (RFC) documents.

Description: As an IT security professional, the amount of available information can be overwhelming. To protect corporate resources (or "assets," as they're commonly called), you're expected to be skillful in many areas. To gain the necessary skills in your profession, you should know where to look for technical information that helps you better understand a particular technology. Want to know how the Domain Name Service (DNS) works? Want a better understanding of Dynamic Host Configuration Protocol (DHCP)? Reading the RFCs on these topics can answer any questions you might have. In this activity, you examine the details of a TCP segment and get an overview of some TCP header components. You won't have to memorize your findings. This is merely an introduction to the wonderful world of RFCs.

1. Start your Web browser, type **http://www.ietf.org** in the Address text box, and then press **Enter**.

2. On the Internet Engineering Task Force home page, click the **RFC Pages** icon from the menu. (If time permits, you might want to navigate to the many other available selections for information on useful topics.)

3. Read the instructions on the Request for Comments page, type **793** in the RFC number text box, and then click **go**. Note the title page of this RFC.

4. Scroll down the document and read the table of contents to get an overview of this document's information. Read through Sections 2.6, 2.7, and 2.8 to get a better idea of how TCP works. (Note that Section 2.6 discusses reliable communication.)

5. Scroll down to Section 3.1, "Header Format." The diagram might not be what you're used to seeing in computer documentation, but it's typical of what you see in an RFC. The numbers at the top make it easier for you to see the position of each bit. For example, the upper 0, 1, 2, and 3 show you that there are a total of 32 bits (0 to 31) across this segment. Note that the source port and destination port fields are 16 bits long, and that both the ISN and the acknowledgment number are 32 bits long.

6. Read through the section and note the use of the binary numbering system (covered in more detail later in this chapter).

7. Scroll down to Section 3.4, "Establishing a connection," and skim the description of a three-way handshake. The author does a nice job of simplifying this process and adds a little humor about why an ACK doesn't occupy sequence number space. Many RFC authors have a knack for explaining complex material in an easy-to-understand manner.

8. Scroll through the rest of the document to get an overview of what's covered. You can read the entire document later, if you like.

9. Close your Web browser.

TCP Ports

A TCP packet has two 16-bit fields containing the source and destination port numbers. A **port** is the logical, not physical, component of a TCP connection. A port identifies the service that's running. For example, the HTTP service uses port 80. Understanding ports is important so that you know how to stop or disable services that aren't being used on your network. The more services you have running on a server, the more ports are open for a potential attack. In other words, securing a house with 1000 open doorways is more difficult than securing a house with only 10 open doorways.

NOTE

Security Bytes
The most difficult part of a network security professional's job is balancing system security with ease of use and availability for users. Closing all ports and stopping all services would certainly make your network more secure, but your users couldn't connect to the Internet, send or receive e-mail, or access any network resources. So your job is to allow users to work in a secure network environment without preventing them from using services such as e-mail, Web browsing, and the like. This is not an easy task, as you'll see throughout this book.

A possible 65,535 TCP and UDP port numbers are available, but the good news is that only 1023 are considered well-known ports. To see the list of well-known ports, visit the **Internet Assigned Numbers Authority (IANA)** at *www.iana.org*. Select the Protocol Number Assignment Services option on the home page and then click the letter "P". Select System under the Port Numbers heading, and peruse the document. Because Web pages can change, you might find these port numbers in a different location. (See the following Note.) There's probably more information than you need, but navigating to these Web sites gives you practice searching for information. A good security professional knows how to find answers by using a structured methodology.

NOTE
You can access the well-known port page by entering *www.iana.org/ assignments/port-numbers* as the URL, but you bypass the IANA home page, which has more information and access to the IANA Whois service. This service is covered later in Chapter 4, but you can review it while browsing the IANA page.

Don't worry about memorizing those 1023 ports. Luckily, that isn't necessary. However, you should memorize the following TCP ports and the services they represent. Much of what you do as a security professional and penetration tester relies heavily on understanding this information.

- *Ports 20 and 21 (File Transfer Protocol)*—FTP has been around as long as the Internet. It was the de facto standard for moving or copying large files and is still used today, although to a lesser extent because of the popularity of HTTP. FTP uses port 20 for data transfer and port 21 for overhead. FTP requires entering a logon name and password and is more secure than Trivial File Transfer Protocol (TFTP, covered later in this list). Figure 2-2 shows the logon screen displayed when attempting to connect to a Cisco FTP site.

Figure 2-2   Connecting to an FTP site

- *Port 25 (Simple Mail Transfer Protocol)*—E-mail servers listen on this port. If you attempt to send e-mail to a remote user, your computer connects to port 25 on a mail server.

- *Port 53 (Domain Name Service)*—If a server on your network uses DNS, it's using port 53. Most networks require a DNS server so that users can connect to Web sites with URLs instead of IP addresses. When a user enters a URL, such as *www.yahoo.com*, the DNS server resolves the name to an IP address. The DNS server might be internal to the company, or each computer might be configured to point to the IP address of a DNS server that's serviced by the company's ISP.

- *Port 69 (Trivial File Transfer Protocol)*—Many network engineers use the TFTP service to transfer router and backup router configurations.

- *Port 80 (Hypertext Transfer Protocol)*—Most certification exams have a question about port 80 being used for HTTP. Port 80 is used when you connect to a Web server. If security personnel decided to filter out HTTP traffic, almost every user would notice a problem on the network.

Security Bytes

NOTE
Often technical personnel who aren't familiar with security techniques think that restricting access to ports on a router or firewall can protect a network from attack. This is easier said than done. After all, if a firewall prevents any traffic from entering or exiting a network on port 80, you have indeed closed a vulnerable port to access from hackers. However, you have also closed the door to Internet access for your users, which probably isn't acceptable to your company. The tricky (and almost impossible) part for security personnel is attempting to keep out the bad guys while allowing the good guys to work and use the Internet. As you progress through this book, you'll see that as long as users can connect to the Internet through an open port, attackers can get in. It's that simple. If a user can get out, an attacker can get in!

2

- *Port 110 (Post Office Protocol 3)*—To retrieve e-mail from a mail server, you most likely access port 110. An enhanced e-mail retrieving protocol, IMAP4, is also available and is covered later in this list. POP3 is still around, however, and is one of the most common e-mail retrieval systems.

- *Port 119 (Network News Transport Protocol)*—This port is used to connect to a news server for use with newsgroups.

- *Port 135 (Remote Procedure Call)*—This port, used by Microsoft RPC, is critical for the operation of Microsoft Exchange Server as well as Active Directory, available in Windows 2000 Server and Windows Server 2003 operating systems.

- *Port 139 (NetBIOS)*—This port is used by Microsoft's NetBIOS Session Service to share resources. NetBIOS is covered in Chapter 8.

- *Port 143 (Internet Message Access Protocol 4)*—IMAP4 uses this port to retrieve e-mail.

Activity 2-2: Connecting to Port 25 (SMTP)

ACTIVITY

Time Required: 30 minutes

Objective: Use the Telnet command to access port 25 on your mail server, log on, and send an e-mail message to a recipient.

Description: As an IT security professional, you should be aware of the ports used over a network infrastructure. A good way to test whether a service is running on a server is to telnet to the port using that service. For example, the SMTP service uses port 25. In this activity, you telnet into your classroom's mail server from your computer running Windows XP Professional. If your classroom doesn't have a mail server configured, connect to your ISP's mail server and send an e-mail to a recipient from your e-mail account.

If you can't connect to a mail server using the commands in Activities 2-2 and 2-3, you should still read through the steps and examine the figures to give you an idea of what a successful Telnet connection looks like.

NOTE

1. To open a command prompt window, click **Start**, **Run**, type **cmd** in the Open text box, and then press **Enter**.

2. Type the command **telnet** *RemoteMailServer* **25** (substitute your own server name for *Remote-MailServer*), and press **Enter**. Note that you must enter the port number of the service you're attempting to connect to. In this case, you use port 25 for SMTP.

3. After receiving the prompt shown in Figure 2-3, type **helo** *LocalDomainName*. The mail server accepts almost anything you enter after the Helo command as valid, but you should use your actual domain name.

```
220 leka04.aloha.net ESMTP Postfix
helo leka04.aloha.net
250 leka04.aloha.net
mail from: mike@ntsconsulting.net
250 Ok
rcpt to: ntscon@aloha.net
250 Ok
data
354 End data with <CR><LF>.<CR><LF>
I prefer doing email from Paris!
.
250 Ok: queued as 1289EA0F5
quit
221 Bye

Connection to host lost.

C:\Documents and Settings>
```

Figure 2-3   Using Telnet to send e-mail

4. You can now enter your e-mail address, which is displayed in the recipient's From field. You can enter a bogus address, as shown in Figure 2-3, which is how someone can spoof an e-mail, but you should enter your correct e-mail address for this activity. Type **mail from:** *YourMailAccount*, and press **Enter**.

5. You should receive a "250 OK" message. You can now enter the recipient's e-mail address. (You can also send a message to yourself.) Type **rcpt to:** *RecipientMailAccount*, and press **Enter**.

6. After receiving a "Recipient OK" message, you're ready to start creating your message. Type **data** and press **Enter**. Type your message, press **Enter**, and then type a single period to end your message. You should receive a message saying that your e-mail was queued.

TIP

If you make a typo, you have to re-enter your commands. Pressing Backspace or using the arrow keys doesn't work.

7. To end your Telnet session, type **quit** and press **Enter**. The "Bye" message from the mail server is displayed, and then you see the "Connection to host lost" message shown in Figure 2-3.

8. Exit the command prompt window, and close any open windows.

ACTIVITY

Activity 2-3: Connecting to Port 110 (POP3)

Time Required: 30 minutes

Objective: Use the Telnet command to access port 110 on your mail server, log on, and retrieve an e-mail message that has been sent to your e-mail account.

Description: The POP3 service uses port 110. In this activity, you telnet into your classroom's mail server from your computer running Windows XP Professional. If your classroom doesn't have a mail server configured, connect to your ISP's mail server and retrieve an e-mail message that has been sent to your mailbox.

1. Open a command prompt window. (Refer to Step 1 in Activity 2-2, if necessary.)

2. Type **telnet** *RemoteMailServer* **110** (substitute your own server name for *RemoteMailServer*), and press **Enter**.

3. After receiving the +OK message (see Figure 2-4), you must enter the user command that allows you to log on to your account. Type **user** *YourMailAccount*, and press **Enter**.

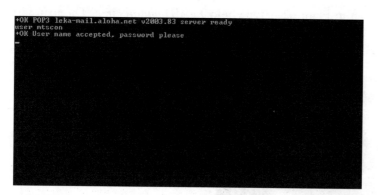

Figure 2-4 Logging on to an e-mail server

4. Next, you're prompted to enter your password. Type *YourPassword*, and press **Enter**.

5. After being authenticated by the mail server, you receive a message similar to Figure 2-5 showing the number of messages in your mailbox. To list all the messages, type **list** and press **Enter**.

Figure 2-5   Viewing e-mail messages in a mailbox

6. To retrieve a specific message, you use the Retr command followed by the message number. For example, to retrieve message number 1, enter **retr 1** and press **Enter** (see Figure 2-6).

```
retr 1
+OK 1648 octets
Return-Path: <mike@mtsconsulting.net>
X-Original-To: mtscon@aloha.net
Delivered-To: mtscon@aloha.net
Received: from localhost (localhost [127.0.0.1])
        by localhost.aloha.net (Postfix) with ESMTP id D1EBAA3706
        for <mtscon@aloha.net>; Thu, 14 Oct 2004 16:46:55 -1000 (HST)
Received: from kou.aloha.net ([127.0.0.1])
    by localhost (kou.aloha.net [127.0.0.1]) (amavisd-new, port 10024) with LMTP
    id 76343-01-99 for <mtscon@aloha.net>; Thu, 14 Oct 2004 16:46:55 -1000 (HST)
Received: from smtpout01-03.mesa1.secureserver.net (smtpout01-03.mesa1.secureser
ver.net [64.202.165.78])
        by kou.aloha.net (Postfix) with SMTP id E99F1A3526
        for <mtscon@aloha.net>; Thu, 14 Oct 2004 16:46:54 -1000 (HST)
Received: (qmail 24943 invoked from network); 15 Oct 2004 02:46:54 -0000
Received: from unknown (HELO webmail01.mesa1.secureserver.net) (64.202.166.114)
    by smtpout01-03.mesa1.secureserver.net with SMTP; 15 Oct 2004 02:46:54 -0000
Received: (qmail 3414 invoked by uid 99); 15 Oct 2004 02:46:54 -0000
Message-ID: <20041015024654.3413.qmail@webmail01.mesa1.secureserver.net>
Date: Thu, 14 Oct 2004 19:46:54 -0700
From: mike@mtsconsulting.net
Subject: Using POP3
To: mtscon@aloha.net
MIME-Version: 1.0
Content-Type: TEXT/html; CHARSET=US-ASCII
X-Virus-Scanned: by amavisd-new at aloha.net
X-Spam-Status: No, hits=2.9 tagged_above=0.0 required=6.0 tests=HTML_30_40,
  HTML_MESSAGE, HTML_MIME_NO_HTML_TAG, MIME_HTML_ONLY, NO_REAL_NAME
X-Spam-Level: **
Status: RO

<div>Hi Mike. Did you know you could read this message using the telnet
command?</div>
<div> </div>
<div>Thanks,</div>
<div> </div>
<div>Claudia</div>
```

Figure 2-6   Retrieving an e-mail message

7. To view the open ports on your Windows XP system, you can use the Netstat command. Figure 2-7 shows the result of running Netstat while several ports are open. Open another command prompt window, type **netstat**, and press **Enter**.

```
C:\Documents and Settings>netstat

Active Connections

  Proto  Local Address          Foreign Address        State
  TCP    msimpson:1135          email20.uophx.edu:993  ESTABLISHED
  TCP    msimpson:1161          mail.aloha.net:pop3     ESTABLISHED
  TCP    msimpson:1162          mail.aloha.net:smtp     ESTABLISHED
  TCP    msimpson:1165          167.68.24.98:http       ESTABLISHED
  TCP    msimpson:1166          167.68.24.98:http       ESTABLISHED

C:\Documents and Settings>
```

Figure 2-7   Using the Netstat command to view open ports

8. If the results show no active ports open, minimize the command prompt window, and start your Web browser.

9. Connect to any Web site. Maximize the command prompt window, type **netstat** again, and press **Enter**. Note the new entry indicating that port 80 (HTTP) is now being used.

10. To exit your Telnet session, type **quit** and press **Enter**.

11. Close the command prompt window and any other open windows.

User Datagram Protocol (UDP)

User Datagram Protocol (UDP) is a fast but unreliable delivery protocol that also operates on the transport layer. Imagine trying to compete in the mail courier business and touting that your service was fast but unreliable. It would probably be difficult to sell. However, UDP is a widely used protocol on the Internet because of its speed. UDP doesn't need to verify whether the receiver is listening or ready to accept the packets. The sender doesn't care—it just sends, even if the receiver isn't ready to accept the packet. See why it's faster? Some applications that use UDP, such as e-mail programs, have built-in utilities to warn recipients of undeliverable messages, but UDP doesn't. In other words, it depends on the higher layers of the TCP/IP stack to handle these problems. Think of UDP as someone announcing over a loudspeaker that school will be closed that afternoon. Some lucky students will hear the message, and some won't. This type of delivery protocol is referred to as **connectionless**.

The Internet Layer

The Internet layer of the TCP/IP stack is responsible for routing a packet to a destination address. This is done by using a logical address, called an IP address. Like UDP, IP addressing packet delivery is connectionless. IP addressing is covered in more detail in the "IP Addressing" section, but first take a look at another protocol that operates at the Internet layer.

Internet Control Message Protocol

Internet Control Message Protocol (ICMP) is used to send messages that relate to network operations. For example, if a packet cannot reach its destination, you might see the "Destination Unreachable" error.

ICMP makes it possible for network professionals to troubleshoot network connectivity problems (with the Ping command) and to track the route a packet traverses from a source IP address to a destination IP address (with the Traceroute command). Security professionals can use ICMP type codes (see Table 2-2) to block ICMP packets from entering or leaving a network. For example, a router can be configured to not allow an ICMP packet with the type code 8 to enter a network. Try pinging *www.microsoft.com* and see what happens. Microsoft does not allow its IP address to be pinged, which is the type code 8 (Echo).

NOTE

For a more detailed description of ICMP, see RFC-792.

Table 2-2 ICMP type codes

ICMP Type Code	Description
0	Echo Reply
3	Destination Unreachable
4	Source Quench
5	Redirect
6	Alternate Host Address
8	Echo
9	Router Advertisement
10	Router Solicitation

Table 2-2   ICMP type codes (continued)

ICMP Type Code	Description
11	Time Exceeded
12	Parameter Problem
13	Timestamp
14	Timestamp Reply
15	Information Request
16	Information Reply
17	Address Mask Request
18	Address Mask Reply
19	Reserved (for Security)
20–29	Reserved (for Robustness Experiment)
30	Traceroute
31	Datagram Conversion Error
32	Mobile Host Redirect
33	IPv6 Where-Are-You
34	IPv6 I-Am-Here
35	Mobile Registration Request
36	Mobile Registration Reply
37	Domain Name Request
38	Domain Name Reply
39	Skip
40	Photuris
41–255	Reserved

IP ADDRESSING

An IP address consists of four bytes divided into two components: a network address and a host address. Based on the starting decimal number of the first byte, you can classify IP addresses as Class A, Class B, or Class C, as shown in Table 2-3.

Table 2-3   TCP/IP address classes

Address Class	Range	Address Bytes	Number of Networks	Host Bytes	Number of Hosts
Class A	1–127	1	127	3	16,777,214
Class B	128–191	2	16,128	2	65,534
Class C	192–223	3	2,097,152	1	254

NOTE

Class D and Class E addresses are reserved for multicast and experimental addressing, respectively, and are not covered in this chapter.

From Table 2-3, you can determine, for example, that a user with the IP address 193.1.2.3 has a Class C address, and a user with the IP address 9.1.2.3 has a Class A address. An IP address is composed of four bytes (an octet). An octet is equal to eight bits, which equals one byte, so you sometimes see an IP address defined as four octets instead of four bytes. The following list describes each address class:

- *Class A*—The first byte of a Class A address is reserved for the network address, making the last three bytes available to assign to host computers. Because a Class A address has a three-octet host address, Class A networks can support more than 16 million host computers. (For more information on determining how many hosts a network can support, see the next section, "Reviewing the Binary Numbering System.") The number of Class A Internet addresses is limited, so these addresses are reserved for large corporations and governments. Class A addresses have the format *network.node.node.node*.

- *Class B*—These address are evenly divided between a two-octet network and a two-octet host address, allowing more than 65,000 host computers per Class B network address. Large organizations and Internet service providers are often assigned Class B Internet addresses. Class B addresses have the format *network.network.node.node*.

- *Class C*—These addresses have a three-octet network address and a one-octet host address, resulting in more than 2 million Class C Internet addresses. Each address supports up to 254 host computers. These addresses are usually available for small businesses and home use. They have the format *network.network.network.node*.

In addition to a unique network address, each network must be assigned a subnet mask, which helps identify the network address bits from the host address bits. As a network security professional, you should understand subnetting, which is covered in the Network+ curriculum. Many utilities return information based on IP address and subnet information, so a thorough understanding of these concepts is important. In addition, when conducting a penetration test, you might be required to determine which hosts are on a specific network segment, so be sure to review this topic if you're not familiar with subnetting networks or recognizing when a network is subnetted.

Planning IP Address Assignments

When IP addresses are assigned, companies need to assign a unique network address to each network segment that's separated by a router. For example, suppose a company has been issued two IP addresses: 193.145.85.0 and 193.145.86.0. Looking at the first byte of each address, the company determines that both are Class C addresses. With a default subnet mask of 255.255.255.0, 254 host addresses can be assigned to each segment. You use the formula $2^x - 2$ for this calculation. For this example, x equals 8 because there are eight bits in the fourth octet:

$$2^8 - 2 = 254$$

You must subtract 2 in the formula because the network portion and host portion of an IP address can't contain all 1s or all 0s. Remember, you can't assign a network user the IP address 192.168.8.0.

Also, you can't give a user an address of 192.168.8.255 because it would produce all 1s in the host portion of an IP address; this address is reserved as a broadcast address to all nodes on the segment 192.168.8.0.

To access entities and services on other networks, each computer must also have the IP address of its gateway. Before sending a packet to another computer, the TCP/IP Internet layer uses your computer's subnet mask to determine the destination computer's network address. If this address is different from the sending computer's network address, the sending computer relays the packet to the IP address specified in the gateway parameter. The gateway computer then forwards the packet to its next destination. In this way, the packet eventually reaches the destination computer.

For example, if a Linux server has the IP address 192.168.8.2 and the subnet mask 255.255.255.0, and a user has a computer with the IP address 192.168.9.200 and the subnet mask 255.255.255.0, the company must configure a default gateway address. The default gateway sends the user to a router, which routes the user to the different network segment. If the default gateway isn't configured on the user's computer, and this user attempts to use the Ping command to contact the server, he or she gets the "Destination Unreachable" message (see Table 2-2). The user's computer can't connect to the other host—a Linux server located on a different network segment—because there's no router to help it. The router's job is to take those packets, which are not on the same network segment, and send them on their way.

As a network security professional, you must understand these basic network concepts before attempting to conduct a penetration test on a network, especially one that's been subnetted. In a subnetted network it might be easy to mistake a broadcast address as a valid host address, a major blunder that could cause a denial-of-service attack after thousands of packets are sent to all hosts on a network instead of to the one host you were trying to reach.

Overview of Numbering Systems

As a security professional, your knowledge of numbering systems will also come into play. The following sections offer a quick review of the binary, octal, and hexadecimal numbering systems.

Reviewing the Binary Numbering System

You learned base 10 math in elementary school, although you might not have realized it at the time. When you see the number 3742, for example, you quickly recognize it as three thousand seven hundred and forty-two. By placing each number in a column, as shown in the following lines, you can see that each number has a different value and magnitude. This numbering system uses 10 as its base and goes from right to left, multiplying the base number in each column by an exponent starting from zero. Valid numbers in base 10 are 0 through 9. That is, each column can contain any number from 0 to 9.

```
1000    100    10    1
10³     10²    10¹   10⁰
3       7      4     2
```

As you can see, 3742 is obtained by multiplying 3 by 1000, 7 by 100, 4 by 10, and 2 by 1, and then adding the values.

The binary system, on the other hand, uses the number 2 as its base. Each binary digit, or bit, is represented by a 1 or 0. Bits are usually grouped by eight because a byte contains eight bits. Computer engineers chose this numbering system because logic chips make binary decisions based on true or false, on or off, and so forth. With eight bits, a computer programmer can represent 256 different colors for a video card, for example. (Two to the power of eight, or 2^8, equals 256.) Therefore, black can be represented by 00000000, white by 11111111, and so on.

Another example of using binary numbering can be seen in file permissions for users: r (read), w (write), or x (execute). A 1 represents having the permission and a 0 means removing the permission. Therefore, 111 (rwx) would mean all permissions apply, and 101 (r-x) would mean the user could read and execute the file but not write to it. (The - symbol indicates that the permission isn't granted.) Those familiar with UNIX will recognize this numbering system. To make it a little easier, UNIX allows using the decimal equivalent of binary numbers. So for the binary 111, you would enter the decimal number 7. For the binary 101, you would enter the decimal number 5. Confused? You'll be a binary expert in a few minutes, so hang in there.

To simplify the concept of binary numbers, think of a room with two light switches, and consider how many different combinations of positions you could use for the switches. For example, both switches could be off, Switch 1 could be off and Switch 2 could be on, and so forth. Here's a binary representation of these switch positions:

```
0  0  (off, off)
0  1  (off, on)
1  0  (on, off)
1  1  (on, on)
```

The two switches have four possible occurrences, or 2^x power; x represents the number of switches (bits) available. For the light switches, x equals 2.

Examples of Determining Binary Values

Now that you've been introduced to the basic concepts, you can see how bits are used to notate binary numbers. First, however, you must learn and memorize the columns for binary numbers, just as you did for base 10:

```
128    64    32    16    8    4    2    1
```

From right to left, these numbers represent increasing powers of two. Using the preceding columns, try to determine the value of a sample binary number:

128	64	32	16	8	4	2	1
2^7	2^6	2^5	2^4	2^3	2^2	2^1	2^0
0	1	0	0	0	0	0	1

The byte in the preceding example represents the decimal number 65. You calculate this value by adding each column containing a 1 (64 + 1). Now try another example:

128	64	32	16	8	4	2	1
2^7	2^6	2^5	2^4	2^3	2^2	2^1	2^0
0	1	0	0	0	0	0	1

To convert the binary number to decimal (base 10), add the columns that contain 1s:

128 + 64 + 1 = 193

Adding the values in these columns can be tedious, but in the following section, you learn some tricks of the trade to help you translate binary to decimal quickly. However, make sure to memorize each binary column before working through the remaining examples in this chapter.

Understanding Nibbles

Psychologists have found that people have difficulty memorizing numbers of seven digits or more. This is why telephone numbers have only seven digits and why a dash follows the first three numbers; the dash gives your brain a chance to pause before moving on to the next four numbers.

Likewise, binary numbers are easier to read when there is a separation between them. For example, 1111 1010 is easier to read than 11111010. If you need to convert a binary number written as 11111010, you should visualize it as 1111 1010. In other words, you break the byte into two nibbles (sometimes spelled "nybbles"). A nibble is half a byte, or four bits. The four bits on the left side are called the high-order nibble, and the four bits on the right are the low-order nibble.

The following examples show how to convert a low-order nibble to a decimal number. Note the pattern at work among the binary numbers as you proceed through the examples:

```
0000 = 0
0001 = 1
0010 = 2
0011 = 3
0100 = 4
0101 = 5
0110 = 6
0111 = 7
1000 = 8
1001 = 9
1010 = 10
1011 = 11
1100 = 12
1101 = 13
1110 = 14
1111 = 15
```

The largest decimal number you can represent with four low-order bits is 15. You should memorize these numbers if you can, especially the ones that have convenient memory aids. For example, 1010 is equal to the decimal number 10. Just remember the phrase "It's 10, silly, 10!" 1011 is just as easy: "Not 10, but 11." You can make up your own tricks, but you can always simply add the columns if you forget.

You can also practice converting decimal numbers into binary numbers by using license plate numbers as you drive to work. For example, if a license plate number ends with 742, you should visualize 0111, 0100, 0010. (You can eliminate the leading zeros after a few days of practice.) When you get comfortable with the low-order nibble and can quickly identify a sequence of four bits, you can move to the high-order side.

For example, what does the binary number 1010 1010 equal in decimal? On the low-order side, you can quickly convert 1010 to the decimal number 10. The high-order side is also 10, but it's 10 times 16, or 160. You can always add the columns if you're confused:

```
128 + 32 = 160
```

Any value in the high-order nibble is multiplied by the number 16. For example, the binary number 0010 0000 is equal to 32. You can multiply the nibble value of 2 by 16, but in this case it's easier to immediately recognize the 1 in the 32 column, which makes the answer 32.

You should memorize the following high-order nibble values, which will help you with subnetting. As you should recall from subnetting basics, 128, 192, 224, and so on are used as subnet masks.

```
1000 = 128
1100 = 192
1110 = 224
1111 = 240
```

If you recognize 1111 0000 as 240, the binary number 1111 1000 should be easy to calculate as 248. By the same token, the binary number 1111 1111 is equal to the decimal 255, or 240 + 15, the largest number you can represent with eight bits.

TIP To help you convert numbers correctly, note that all odd numbers have the low-order bit turned on. For example, 1001 cannot be an even number, such as 10 or 8, because the low-order bit is turned on. You can also guess that the number is larger than 8 because the 8 column bit is turned on. Similarly, you can identify 0101 as converting to a decimal number lower than 8 because the 8 column is not turned on, and identify it as an odd number because the low-order bit is on.

TIP There are other easy ways to memorize and break down binary numbers. For example, note that 1010 is 10, and 0101 converts to half of 10: 5. The two numbers are mirror images of each other in binary, and one number is half of the other in decimal. In the same way, 1110 equals 14 and 0111 is 7. In the high-order nibble, 1110 equals 224, and 0111 in the high-order nibble equals 112 (half of 224). This trick helps you convert binary numbers quickly. For example, the binary number 0101 1010 equals 90. In this number, the high-order nibble converts to 80 because 1010 would equal 160. The low-order nibble converts to 10, and quick addition gives you the final answer of 90.

Reviewing the Octal Numbering System

An octal number is written as a digit from 0 to 7. An octal number is a base 8 number, which uses eight symbols: 0, 1, 2, 3, 4, 5, 6, and 7. Because you're a binary expert now, it's easy to see how binary converts to octal. An octal digit can be represented with only three bits because the largest digit in octal is 7. The number 7 is written as 00000111, or 111 if you drop those leading zeros. The binary equivalent of the octal number 5 is then 101.

To see how this concept relates to network security, take a look at UNIX permissions. Octal numbering is used to express the following permissions on a directory or a file: Owner permissions, Group permissions, and Other permissions. For a directory, (rwxrwxrwx) means that the owner of the directory, members of a group, and everyone else (Other) have read, write, and execute permissions for that directory.

Because each category has three unique permissions, and each permission can be expressed as true or false (on or off), three bits are used. You don't need all eight bits because three bits (rwx) are enough. Recall from binary numbering that 0 is counted as a number, so with three bits, there are eight possible occurrences: 000, 001, 010, 011, 100, 101, 110, and 111. Using octal numbering, 001 indicates that the execute (x) permission is granted, 010 indicates that the write (w) permission is granted, but not read and execute, and so on. The octal number 7 indicates all 1s (111), or 1 + 2 + 4. So in *NIX systems, 777 (in binary, 111 111 111) indicates that the Owner, Group, and Other have all permissions (rwx) to a file or folder.

Reviewing the Hexadecimal Numbering System

A hex number is written with two characters, each representing a nibble. Hexadecimal is a base-16 numbering system, so its valid numbers range from 0 to 15. Like base 2 (binary), hex uses exponents that begin with 0 and increase from right to left:

```
4096    256     16      1
16³     16²     16¹     16⁰
A       0       C       1
```

Fortunately, in hex you have to memorize only the final two columns: 1 and 16. As you can see from the preceding example, the value contains alphabetic characters—valid hex numbers range from 0 to 15, and hex solves the problem of expressing two-digit numbers in a single slot by using letters. For example, A represents the number 10, B stands for 11, C is 12, D is 13, E is 14, and F is 15.

Hex numbers are sometimes expressed with a "0x" in front of them. For example, 0x10 equals decimal number 16. As with decimal and binary numbers, you multiply the value in each column by the value of the column to determine hex numbers. In the previous example, you simply multiply 1 by 16 to get 16. To convert a hex number to binary, you write each nibble from left to right. For example, 0x10 is 0001 0000 in binary and 0x24 is 0010 0100.

Activity 2-4: Working with Binary and Octal Numbering

Time Required: 30 minutes

Objective: Apply your skills in binary and octal numbering to configuring *NIX directory and file permissions.

Description: As a network security professional, you need to understand different numbering systems. For example, if you work with routers, you might have to create access control lists (ACLs) that filter inbound and outbound network traffic. Most of these ACLs require understanding binary numbering; similarly, if you're hardening a Linux system, your understanding of binary helps you create the correct umask and permissions. UNIX uses base 8 (octal) numbering for creating directory and file permissions. You don't need to do this activity on a computer; you can simply use a pencil and paper.

1. Write the octal equivalents for the following binary numbers: 100, 111, 101, 011, and 010.

2. Write how to express *NIX Owner permissions of r-x in binary. (The - symbol indicates that the permission isn't granted.) What is the octal representation of the binary number you calculated? (The range of numbers expressed in octal is 0 to 7. Because *NIX has three sets of permissions, three sets of three binary bits logically represent all possible permissions.)

3. In binary and octal numbering, how do you express granting read, write, and execute permission to the Owner of a file and no permissions to anyone else?

4. In binary and octal numbering, how do you express granting read, write, and execute permission to the Owner of a file, read and write permission to Group, and read permission to Other?

5. In UNIX, a file can be created by using a umask, which enables you to modify the default permissions for a file or directory. For example, a directory has the default permission of octal 777. If a UNIX administrator creates a directory with a umask of octal 020, what effect does this have on the directory? (*Hint:* To calculate the solution, you can subtract the octal umask value from the octal base permission.)

6. The default permissions for a file on your UNIX system is octal 666. If a file is created with a umask of octal 022, what are the effective permissions? Calculate your results.

CHAPTER SUMMARY

❑ TCP/IP is the most widely used protocol for communication over the Internet. The TCP/IP stack consists of four layers that perform different functions: network access, application, transport, and Internet.

❑ The application layer protocols are the front end of the lower-layer protocols. Examples of protocols that operate at this layer are HTTP, SMTP, Telnet, and SNMP.

❑ The transport layer is responsible for encapsulating data into segments and uses UDP or TCP headers for connections and for forwarding data. TCP is a connection-oriented protocol. UDP is a connectionless protocol.

❑ The critical components of TCP segment headers are TCP flags, the initial sequence number (ISN), and source and destination port numbers.

❑ TCP ports identify the services running on a system. Port numbers from 1 to 1023 are considered well-known ports. A total of 65,535 port numbers are available.

❑ The Internet layer is responsible for routing a packet to a destination address. IP addresses as well as ICMP messages are used in this layer. IP, like UDP, is a connectionless protocol. ICMP is used to send messages related to network operations. A type code identifies the ICMP message type and can be used to filter out network traffic.

❑ IP addressing consists of four bytes, also called octets, which are divided into two components: a network address and a host address. Three classes of addresses are used on the Internet: Class A, B, and C.

❑ The binary numbering system is used primarily because logic chips make binary decisions based on true or false, on or off. Binary numbers are represented by 0 or 1.

❑ The octal numbering system (base 8) uses numbers from 0 to 7. Only three bits of the binary numbering system are used because the highest number in base 8 is the number 7, which can be written with three binary bits: 111.

❑ Hexadecimal is a base-16 numbering system that uses numbers from 0 to 15. After 9, the numbers 10, 11, 12, 13, 14, and 15 are represented as A, B, C, D, E, and F, respectively.

KEY TERMS

ACK — A TCP flag that acknowledges a TCP packet with SYN-ACK flags set.

connection-oriented — A method of transferring data over a network that requires a session connection before data is sent. With TCP/IP, this step is accomplished by sending a SYN packet.

connectionless — With a connectionless protocol, no session connection is required before data is transmitted. UDP and IP are examples of connectionless protocols.

initial sequence number (ISN) — A number that keeps track of what packets a node has received.

Internet Assigned Numbers Authority (IANA) — The organization responsible for assigning IP addresses.

Internet Control Message Protocol (ICMP) — The protocol used to send informational messages and test network connectivity.

port — The logical component of a connection that identifies the service running on a network device. For example, port 110 is the POP3 mail service.

protocol — A language used to transmit data across a network infrastructure.

session hijacking — An attack on a network that requires guessing ISNs. *See also* initial sequence number (ISN).

SYN — A TCP flag that signifies the beginning of a session.

SYN-ACK — A reply to a SYN packet sent by a host.

TCP flag — The six flags in a TCP header are switches that can be set to on or off to indicate the status of a port or service.

three-way handshake — The method the transport layer uses to create a connection-oriented session.

Transmission Control Protocol/Internet Protocol (TCP/IP) — The main protocol used to connect computers over the Internet.

User Datagram Protocol (UDP) — A fast, unreliable transport layer protocol that is connectionless.

REVIEW QUESTIONS

1. The Netstat command indicates that POP3 is in use on a remote server. Which port is the remote server most likely using?

   a. port 25

   b. port 110

   c. port 143

   d. port 80

2. At a Windows XP computer, what command can you enter to show all open ports being used?

   a. Netstat

   b. Ipconfig

   c. Ifconfig

   d. Nbtstat

3. Which protocol uses UDP?

   a. FTP

   b. Netstat

   c. Telnet

   d. TFTP

4. Which protocol offers guaranteed delivery and is connection-oriented?

   a. UDP

   b. IP

   c. TCP

   d. TFTP

5. TCP communication could be likened to which of the following?

   a. announcement over a loudspeaker

   b. bullhorn at a sporting event

   c. Internet traffic

   d. telephone conversation

6. Which of the following protocols is connectionless? (Choose all that apply.)

   a. UDP

   b. IP

   c. TCP

   d. SPX

7. Which command verifies the existence of a node on a network?

   a. Ping

   b. Ipconfig

   c. Netstat

   d. Nbtstat

8. FTP offers more security than TFTP. True or False?

9. List the three components of the TCP/IP three-way handshake.

10. What protocol is used for reporting or informational purposes?

    a. IGMP

    b. TCP

    c. ICMP

    d. IP

11. List the six flags of a TCP packet.

12. A UDP packet is usually smaller than a TCP packet. True or False?

13. What port, other than port 110, is used to retrieve e-mail?

    a. port 25

    b. port 143

    c. port 80

    d. port 135

14. What port does DNS use?

    a. port 80

    b. port 69

    c. port 25

    d. port 53

15. What command is used to log on to a remote server, computer, or router?

    a. Ping

    b. Traceroute

    c. Telnet

    d. Netstat

16. Which of the following is *not* a valid octal number?

    a. 5555

    b. 4567

    c. 3482

    d. 7770

17. The initial sequence number (ISN) is set at what step of the TCP three-way handshake?

    a. 1, 2, 3

    b. 1, 3

    c. 1

    d. 1 and 2

18. A Ping command initially uses which ICMP type code?

    a. type 0

    b. type 8

    c. type 14

    d. type 13

19. "Destination Unreachable" is designated by which ICMP type code?

   a. type 0

   b. type 14

   c. type 3

   d. type 8

20. What is the hexadecimal equivalent of the binary number 1111 1111?

   a. FF

   b. 255

   c. EE

   d. DD

CASE PROJECTS

Case 2-1: Determining the Services Running on a Network

K. J. Williams Corporation has multiple operating systems running in its many branch offices. Before conducting a penetration test to determine the vulnerabilities you need to correct, you must analyze the services currently running on the corporation's network. Steven Schoen, a member of your security team who is experienced in computer programming and database design but weak in networking concepts, wants to be briefed on the network topology issues for the K. J. Williams Corporation.

Write a memo to Steven summarizing the possible port numbers and services that run on most networks. The memo should discuss the concepts of well-known ports and give a brief description of the most popular ports: 20, 21, 23, 25, 53, and 110.

Case 2-2: Investigating Possible E-mail Fraud

The vice president of K. J. Williams Corporation says he received a hostile e-mail message from an employee in the Maui office. Human Resources has informed him that the contents of the message are grounds for termination, but the vice president wonders whether the employee did indeed send the message. When confronted, the employee claims he never sent the message and doesn't understand why the message shows his return address.

Write a memo to the vice president outlining the steps an employee might have taken to create the hostile e-mail message and to make it appear to come from the innocent employee's account. Be sure to include some of the SMTP commands the culprit might have used.

# CHAPTER 3

NETWORK AND COMPUTER ATTACKS

**After reading this chapter and completing the exercises,
you will be able to:**

♦ Describe the different types of malicious software

♦ Describe methods of protecting against malware attacks

♦ Describe the types of network attacks

♦ Identify physical security attacks and vulnerabilities

As a network security professional, you need to be aware of attacks an intruder can make on your network. Attacks are any attempts by unauthorized users to access network resources or systems. To do this, you must have a good understanding of network security and computer security. Network security involves protecting the network infrastructure. However, network security professionals must also be concerned with protecting standalone systems. Therefore, computer security is necessary to protect computers and laptops that aren't part of a network infrastructure but that still contain information the company believes is important or confidential. In many cases, protective measures involve examining physical security issues, right down to checking door locks, and assessing the risks associated with a lack of physical security.

This chapter gives you a strong foundation on what attackers are doing. Just as law enforcement personnel must be aware of the methods criminals use, you must have an understanding of what computer attackers are up to. How can a denial-of-service attack be used to shut down a company? How can worms and viruses be introduced into a company's corporate database? Can a laptop or desktop computer be removed from your office with little risk of the intruder being caught or stopped? In this chapter, you get an overview of attack methods and protective measures. To understand the importance of physical security, you also learn that an unscrupulous in-house employee can pick a lock in seconds.

MALICIOUS SOFTWARE (MALWARE)

Many network attacks are malicious attacks that are initiated to prevent a business from operating. **Malware** is malicious software, such as a virus, worm, or Trojan program, introduced to a network for just that reason. The goal is to destroy or corrupt data or to shut down a network or computer system. The following sections cover the different types of malware that attackers use.

Viruses

A **virus** is a computer program that attaches itself to an executable file or application. It can replicate itself, usually through an executable program attached to an e-mail. The key word is "attaches." A virus does not stand on its own. It can't replicate itself or operate without the presence of a host program. A virus attaches itself to a host program, just as the flu attaches itself to a host organism. No matter how skilled you are as a security professional, if you don't prevent viruses from being installed on computers in your organization, you have a problem. After the virus attaches itself to a program, such as Microsoft Word, it performs whatever the creator designed it to do. For example, Figure 3-1 shows a virus attached to a .zip file. The virus sender uses a common ploy: purported naked pictures of his wife. This ploy lures a naive computer user into clicking and therefore running the attached infected file.

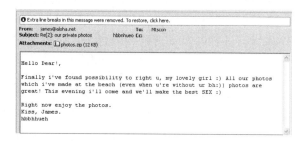

Figure 3-1   A virus attached to an e-mail message

The bad news about viruses is that there's no foolproof method of preventing them from attaching themselves to your computer. Many antivirus software packages are available, but none can guarantee protection because a new virus—for example, one created five minutes ago—wouldn't show up in the software's virus signature files. Antivirus software compares **virus signature files** against the programming code of known viruses; if there's a match, the program warns you that the program you're installing is infected. If the virus is not known, however, the antivirus software doesn't see a match. Therefore, regularly updating virus signature files is crucial. Many antivirus software packages offer automatic updates. For example, with Norton AntiVirus Enterprise Edition, administrators can configure a server that's responsible for pushing new antivirus updates to client computers in an organization.

Table 3-1 shows some common viruses that have plagued computer systems. As of this writing, thousands more viruses are being created. Listing all known viruses would take up this entire book.

Table 3-1   Computer viruses

Virus	Description
W32/Bagle.AV	Detected in 2004, this virus is usually sent to users as an attachment to an e-mail message. The attachment is often a file named Price.cpl or Joke. The virus allows the remote attacker to open a backdoor to your system. Many ISPs recognize this virus and warn e-mail recipients of the potential attack.
W32/MyDoom	This virus spreads through e-mail by using its own SMTP engine. It also creates a backdoor to the attacked system.

Table 3-1 Computer viruses (continued)

Virus	Description
W32/Novarg.A	This virus affects any system running Microsoft Windows (all versions from Windows 95 and up). The virus modifies the Registry and opens TCP ports 3127 to 3198, enabling it to access the remote computer later.
W32/Mimail	This mass-mailer virus attacks a computer with an infected attachment called Message.html contained in a .zip file.

It seems that many people have nothing but time on their hands when it comes to creating these destructive programs. The following warning was sent to a user with a file called Price.cpl attached to the e-mail. The e-mail provider rejected sending the e-mail because the attachment was recognized as a potential virus.

```
This message was created automatically by mail delivery software.
A message that you sent could not be delivered to one or more of
its recipients. This is a permanent error. The following
address(es) failed:
CustomerService@MSIGroupInc.com
    This message has been rejected because it has
    a potentially executable attachment "Price.cpl"
    This form of attachment has been used by
    recent viruses or other malware.
    If you meant to send this file then please
    package it up as a zip file and resend it.
[Message header deleted for brevity]
        boundary="--------sghsfzfldbjbzqmztbdx"
----------sghsfzfldbjbzqmztbdx
Content-Type: text/html; charset="us-ascii"
Content-Transfer-Encoding: 7bit
<html><body>
:))

<br>
</body></html>
----------sghsfzfldbjbzqmztbdx
Content-Type: application/octet-stream; name="Price.cpl"
Content-Transfer-Encoding: base64
Content-Disposition: attachment; filename="Price.cpl"
```

TVqQAAMAAAAEAAAA//8AALgAAAAAAAAQAAAAAAAAAAAAAAAAAAAAAAAAAAAAAAAA
AAAAAAAAAAAAAgAAAA4fug4AtAnNIbgBTM0hVGhpcyBwcm9ncmFtIGNhbm5vdCBi
ZSBydW4gaW4gRE9TIG1vZGUuDQ0KJAAAAAAAAABQRQAATAEDAA+kgUEAAAAAAAAAO
AADiELAQUMAAwAAAACAAAAAAAAAQBUAAAAQAAAIAAAAAAEAAQAAAAgAABAAAAAAAA
AAA
```
[Several pages of code cut for brevity]
GWxWigppFLPigOA6Iqb3ZYDSw1XilsV7d6oVtwKiyKmr4PDWUmgExWU6UOIHF6MK1Q
pBexfKQoD6cNpr9elby7KaodMn9OajUYhI89GZ0TN1mpSHgZTXY+Ahx+NCkmcrKuwk
rAHpUVFB13SzE3uIwvTQoZEU9kN6Jqsm2aMnsyrFibrBp4voRwv6diDqGfRRpprwZK
AK81F1dMNaqmBlOzbkAzqZeKAnWDoGm7rx4WJEJhMA9PhmgRULBlwHJRNbDESZCWNB
UuWgAVvQ8Mh6RWTpNRT7tllLaWqwF8XoKZZ4BJtxGGnYWZS3Qvoj4DEJVZJY4Vqlpz
FVjGZFe7gINFdmEHhFKduVyiMbZqwZozp0oUqm44BwNnDx+YEZYpVZIGd5ytoniznc
RDYI6aY14sJlkIhC8uQT6yVW9EFBhFrTszSoYRJY5DJzdgtKiJfTULswC+f10GAJoT
iQZvFliarpRse0S+nQVQjF2SjKFNHjekwmQ3fbhSL4K+DxCtZDpLBWyncpWdFChbAb
QzNSOxODuPwqoJCotamiRfBAUTFnCeGgaFs4MZo3OGKKBUJkCEFGV5vWeVRCxHKzwY
Im2SRFN4XlEgeAEaPg5iBXhMFxqQGi4GOXYhxmW2jGiqvmGWxZQFXJcSwYMUoo8CDW
Gbbw==

This cryptic code looks odd because it has been encoded in base 64. As you'll recall from Chapter 2, base 2 (binary), base 8 (octal), and base 16 (hexadecimal) are common numbering systems that computers use. Base
```

64 is another one you should know. Typically, it's used to reduce the size of e-mail attachments. Valid characters for base 64 are shown in the following chart:

Character or Symbol	Representation in Base 64
Uppercase A to Z	0–25
Lowercase a to z	26–51
Numerals 1 to 9	52–61
+ and / symbols	62, 63

To represent 0 to 63 characters, you need only six bits, or 2^6. So the binary representation of the letter A is 000000, B is 000001, C is 000010, and so on. Z is represented as 011001. Just remember that the high-order bit is the 32 column, not the 128 column, as with eight bits. The lowest number you can represent with six bits is 000000 (0), and the highest number is 111111 (63). To convert a base 64 number to its decimal equivalent, simply break the sequence into groups of four characters, and represent each character by using six bits (24 bits = 6 × 4).

To see how this works, take a look at a simple example. To convert the base 64 string SGFwcHkgQmlydGhkYXk= into its decimal equivalent, you use the following steps. In this example, the first four characters—S, G, F, and w—are written as three eight-bit numbers (24 bits = 3 × 8).

1. Convert the decimal value of each letter to binary:

    S = 18 decimal, binary 010010

    G = 6 decimal, binary 000110

    F = 5 decimal, binary 000101

    w = 48 decimal, binary 110000

2. Rewrite the four binary groups into three groups of eight bits. For example, starting with the lower-order bit of the binary equivalent of w, writing from right to left produces [01]110000. The bracketed binary numbers represent the first two lower-order bits from the F binary equivalent, 1 and 0:

    01001000 01100001 01110000

3. Convert the binary into its decimal equivalent:

    01001000 = 72 ASCII   H

    01100001 = 97 ASCII   a

    01110000 = 112 ASCII   p

Repeat Steps 1 to 3 for the next four base 64 numbers, cHkg, until each letter's base 64 number is converted. (One or two equal signs are used when three bytes [24 bits] aren't needed to represent the integer.) What does the base 64 string convert to? Your answer should be "Happy Birthday."

Base 64 decoders are available for purchase at retail outlets and online. As a security professional, you don't need to know how to manually convert base 64 code, but it's important to see how numbering systems are used in practical applications, not just academic exercises. Running a base 64 decoder on the Price.cpl code reveals the following suspicious programming code:

```
This program cannot be run in DOS mode.
user32.dll CloseHandle() CreateFileAb GetWindowsDirectory
WriteFile
strcat kernel32.dll Shell Execute shell32 KERNEL32.DLL USER32.DLL
GetProcAddress LoadLibrary ExitProcess Virtual FreeMessageBox
```

This code shows something suspicious happening that's contained in an attachment. The first line, "This program cannot be run in DOS mode," identifies the text that follows as a program. This alerts you that the e-mail attachment contains a hidden computer program. Also, a shell being executed adds to the suspicious nature of the Price.cpl attachment. A **shell** is an executable piece of programming code that should not appear in an e-mail attachment. References to User32.dll and especially Kernel32.dll should raise a red flag. You can see that the e-mail provider's rejection of this e-mail was valid.

Activity 3-1: Identifying New Computer Viruses

Time Required: 30 minutes

Objective: Examine some current computer virus threats.

Description: As a network security professional, you must keep abreast of the many new viruses that might attack your network infrastructure. If one computer is compromised, all the computers in your network could be compromised. Many firewalls don't detect a virus attached to an executable program or a macro virus (covered later in this section), so security professionals need to train users on the dangers of installing software, including games and screen savers, on a computer. Remember, a firewall doesn't look at packets internal to the network, so a virus can spread internally within an organization regardless of how effective your firewall is. A good place to gain knowledge of new viruses is the Internet.

1. Start your Web browser, type **http://www.cert.org/advisories** in the Address text box, and then press **Enter**.

2. On the Advisories page, select an entry from the list. What operating systems are affected by the virus or worm you selected?

3. Give a brief description of the virus or worm you selected and ways to remove or prevent infection from the virus or worm.

4. In your Web browser, enter **www.symantec.com** and press **Enter**.

5. On the Symantec home page, click the **Latest Threats** link.

6. List the five most recent viruses or worms displayed on this page.

7. Select one of the viruses or worms you listed in Step 6, and briefly describe its technical details. Are any solutions for removing the virus or worm available? If so, what are they?

8. Close your Web browser.

Security Bytes

Security professionals have many resources for finding information on current vulnerabilities or possible network attacks. There are excellent Web sites you can visit to learn about OS and application vulnerabilities. One site that should be bookmarked in any security professional's Web browser is the Mitre Corporation's Common Vulnerabilities and Exposures site at *www.cve.mitre.org*. Other helpful sites are *www.osvdb.org/*, *www.packetstormsecurity.com/*, *http://archives.neohapsis.com/*, *www.neworder.box.sk/*, *www.securityfocus.com/search*, Microsoft Security Bulletins at *www.microsoft.com/security/bulletins/default.mspx*, *www.kb.cert.org/vuls*, and, of course, *www.google.com*.

By identifying all the vulnerabilities associated with a customer's OSs and applications, you can determine which type of attack to use on a network when conducting a security test. You might also discover a vulnerability associated with a different OS that could be used to compromise your client's OS. Remember to think outside the box. Security testing is more than memorizing tools and rules; it relies heavily on creativity and imagination.

No standard definitions of terms are currently available in the computer security field. Hence, security professionals sometimes use the terms "vulnerability" and "exposure" interchangeably. In this book, for the sake of simplicity, the terms are used in the broad sense to mean a flaw in a protection process that an unauthorized person might take advantage of. One difficulty in writing a book on network security is the varying terminology that professionals use. The OSSTMM attempts to solve this problem, but until all professional organizations adopt one standard, ambiguity will prevail.

Macro Viruses

A **macro virus** is a computer virus encoded as a macro in programs that support a macro language, such as Visual Basic Application (VBA). For example, you can write a macro, which is basically a list of commands, in Microsoft Word that highlights the contents of a document (Ctrl+A), copies the selected data (Ctrl+C), and then pastes the information into a different part of the document (Ctrl+V). Macro language commands that open and close files, however, can be used in destructive ways. These commands can be set to run automatically as soon as a data file is opened or clicked on, as in an e-mail attachment. The most infamous macro virus is Melissa, which appeared in 1999. The virus was initiated after a user opened an infected document; the virus then sent an e-mail message to the first 50 entries it located in the infected computer's address book.

In the past, viruses were created by computer programmers who found the challenge of creating a destructive program rewarding. Today, even nonprogrammers can easily create macro viruses. In fact, anyone with Internet access can go to many Web sites to learn how to create a macro virus step by step. This adds to the problems you must deal with as a security professional. It's helpful to put yourself in the computer criminal's frame of mind. You have to begin thinking like the bad guys and, like an FBI profiler, understand the perverse mind of a computer criminal. A good place to start is visiting Web sites of virus creators and seeing what they have to say. For example, a search for "Macro Virus Tutorial" at *www.google.com* directs you to many different Web sites. The following excerpt was taken from the site *http://web.textfiles.com/virus/mactut.txt*:

 Connecting to Web sites such as this one can be dangerous. There's a risk in connecting to sites that offer hacking tools or information on creating viruses. Many of these sites contain Trojan programs and viruses that might compromise your computer.

LEGALESE

I SHALL NOT BE HELD RESPONSIBLE FOR ANY DAMAGE CREATED BE IT DIRECT OR INDIRECT USE OF THE PUBLICISED MATERIAL. THIS DOCUMENT IS COPYRIGHT 1996 TO ME, DARK NIGHT OF VBB. HEREWITH I GRANT ANYBODY LICENSE TO REDISTRIBUTE THIS DOCUMENT AS LONG AS IT IS KEPT IN WHOLE AND MY COPYRIGHT NOTICE IS NOT REMOVED. SO IF I FIND ANY LAMERS WHO JUST TAKE THE CODE PUBLISHED HERE AND SAY IT IS THEIR OWN I WILL SEE THAT THEY'LL BE PUNISHED.(BELIEVE IT OR NOT :-))!!!

INTRODUCTION

MANY OF YOU MAY BE WONDERING RIGHT NOW WHO I AM AND WHO VBB IS. COME ON LAMERS! GET ALIVE. VBB IS ONE OF THE COOLEST VIRUS GROUPS AROUND. YOU CAN'T TELL ME YOU'VE NEVER HEARD OF US. WELL, OK I'LL ADMIT IT. WE'RE NOT THAT POPULAR YET, BUT THAT'LL COME. SO FOR NOW HERE'S MY CONTRIBUTION TO THE GROUP AS THE LEADER. WELCOME TO THE MACRO VIRUS WRITING TUTORIAL PART 1! ENJOY!!

THE TOOLS

FIRST OF ALL YOU'LL NEED MS WORD 6.0 OR UP (DUH), THEN YOU MAY WANT TO GET VBB'S MACRO DISASSEMBLER BY AURODREPH SO THAT YOU CAN STUDY ENCRYPTED MACROS. ALSO YOU SHOULD MAKE BACK-UPS OF

3

YOUR NORMAL.DOT TEMPLATE IN YOUR WINWORD6\TEMPLATE\ DIRECTORY, AS THIS IS THE DOCUMENT COMMONLY INFECTED BY MACRO VIRII. SO WATCH OUT. ALSO I RECOMMEND TO HAVE AT LEAST A SMALL KNOWLEDGE OF WORD BASIC, SO THAT YOU KIND A KNOW WHAT'S GOING ON. WELL, THAT'S IT. YOU'VE MADE IT THIS FAR. IT'S NOW TIME TO GET INTO THE MACRO VIRUS GENERALS . . . .

The rest of the document was deleted because of space constraints. However, you can see that finding information on creating a macro virus is all too easy.

Activity 3-2: Identifying Macro Viruses

Time Required: 30 minutes

Objective: Examine macro viruses that are current threats to computer users.

Description: Many antivirus programs detect macro viruses, so you need to know how to turn off the feature that enables macros to run automatically without prompting the user first. You should also be aware of new macro viruses. Again, the Internet is an excellent resource.

1. Start your Web browser, type **http://www.google.com** in the Address text box, and then press **Enter**.

2. On the search page, enter **macro virus** in the Search box.

3. List some of the current macro virus threats your search returned.

4. Select one of the macro viruses you listed in Step 3. Use the name of the macro to search for more information about the virus. Are any fixes available?

5. Begin a new Google query by entering **macro virus tutorial** in the Search box and clicking **Search**. Did you locate any sites with instructions on creating a macro virus? If not, attempt the search again with a different search engine.

6. Read the tutorial information on a site you discovered in Step 5. Does creating a macro virus seem difficult or easy?

7. Close your Web browser.

Worms

A **worm** is a computer program that replicates and propagates itself without having to attach itself to a host (unlike a virus, which needs to attach itself to a computer program or host). The most infamous worms are Code Red (covered in Activity 3-3) and Nimda. Theoretically, a worm that replicates itself multiple times to every user it infects can infect every computer in the world over a short period. This result is unlikely, but as with many pyramid schemes, it's easy to see how a worm can propagate throughout an entire network and even across the Internet.

Table 3-2 describes some of the most infamous worms that have cost businesses millions of dollars in damage as a result of the lost productivity caused by computer downtime and the time spent recovering lost data, reinstalling programs and operating systems, and hiring or contracting IT personnel. Security professionals are also working to protect automated teller machines (ATMs) from worm attacks, such as the Slammer and Nachi worms. Cyberattacks against ATMs are a serious concern for the banking industry and law enforcement agencies worldwide.

Table 3-2   Common computer worms

Worm	Description
W32.Mydoom.aK@mm	Detected in 2004, this worm exploits Internet Explorer's remote buffer overflow vulnerability and spreads itself by using e-mail addresses it discovers on the attacked computer. The worm can also allow unauthorized access to the attacked computer. It affects Windows 95 and later.
W32/Sasser	Detected in 2004, the worm exploits a buffer overflow vulnerability in Windows Local Security Authority Service Server (LSASS) and allows a remote attacker to run code with system privileges. For more information, see Microsoft Security Bulletin MS04-011 (*www.microsoft.com/security/bulletins/default.mspx*).
W32/Sobig.F Worm	Detected in 2003, this worm requires a user to run an attachment or runs if the e-mail program automatically opens an attachment. The worm modifies entries in the attacked computer's Registry, attempts to contact remote IP addresses, and scans the computer for valid e-mail addresses.
MS-SQL Server Worm	Detected in 2003, this worm affects Microsoft SQL Server 2000 and Microsoft Desktop Engine (MSDE) 2000. After attacking a computer, the worm creates packets and sends them to randomly chosen IP addresses on UDP port 1434. If the packet is sent to a computer that's also vulnerable to the exploit, it propagates and infects other computers.
Apache/mod_ssl Worm	Detected in 2002, this worm affects Linux systems running Apache OpenSSL. The worm scans for vulnerable systems on TCP port 80 and then attempts to deliver the exploit code through TCP port 443. If the system does get infected with the worm, it begins spreading the worm to other systems on the network. See VU#102795 and CA-2002-23 at *www.kb.cert.org/vuls* for more information. This site cross-references the vulnerabilities listed at *www.cve.mitre.org*.
Slammer	Detected in 2003, this worm was purported to have shut down more than 13,000 ATMs of one of the largest banks in America by infecting database servers located on the same network.
Nachi	Detected in 2003, this worm also affected ATMs in several banks by compromising the RPC DCOM vulnerability of Windows XP.

ACTIVITY

Activity 3-3: Identifying the Code Red Worm

Time Required: 15 minutes

Objective: Examine the Code Red worm.

Description: The Code Red worm wreaked havoc on networks. As a network security professional, you should be aware of past attacks because history often repeats itself.

1. Start your Web browser, type **http://www.google.com** in the Address text box, and then press **Enter**.

2. On the search page, enter **Code Red** in the Search box.

3. If the search does not display CERT Advisory as the first site, change your search to look specifically for **CA-2001-19**. You had a chance to visit the CERT Web site in Activity 3-1. If time permits, visit *www.cert.org* again for information about this federally funded research center specializing in Internet security. This site is an excellent place to research current vulnerabilities and security alerts.

4. What vulnerability did the worm use to propagate itself?

5. What port did Code Red use to connect to the attacked server?

6. Did the worm deface or destroy any Web pages?

7. What solutions were offered for infected computers?

8. Close your Web browser.

Trojan Programs

One of the most insidious attacks against networks and home computers worldwide is **Trojan programs**, which disguise themselves as useful computer programs or applications and can install a **backdoor** or **rootkit** on a computer. Backdoors or rootkits are computer programs that give attackers a means of regaining access to the attacked computer later. A rootkit is created after an attack and usually hides itself within the OS tools, so it's almost impossible to detect. Back Orifice is still one of the most common Trojan programs used today. It allows attackers to take full control of the attacked computer, similar to the way Microsoft Windows XP Remote Desktop functions, except that Back Orifice works without the user's knowledge. The program has been around since 1999, but it's now marketed as an administrative tool rather than a hacking tool. Table 3-3 lists some of the ports Trojan programs use.

Table 3-3   Trojan programs and ports

Trojan Program	TCP Ports Used
W32.Korgo.A	13, 2041, and 3067
Backdoor.Rtkit.B	445
Backdoor.Systsec, Backdoor.Zincite.A	1034
W32.Beagle.Y@mm	1234
Trojan.Tilser	6187
Backdoor.Hacarmy.C, Backdoor.Kaitex, Backdoor.Clt, Backdoor.IRC.Flood.E, Backdoor.Spigot.C, Backdoor.IrcContact, Backdoor.DarkFtp, Backdoor.Slackbot.B	6667
Backdoor.Danton	6969
Backdoor.Nemog.C	4661, 4242, 8080, 4646, 6565, and 3306

The programmer who wrote Backdoor.Slackbot.B can control a computer by using Internet Relay Chat (IRC), which is on port 6667. A good software or hardware firewall would most likely identify traffic that's using unfamiliar ports, but Trojan programs that use common ports, such as TCP port 80 (HTTP) or UDP port 53 (DNS), are more difficult to detect. Also, many home users or small businesses don't use software or hardware firewalls.

Security Bytes

Many software firewall products are available, such as Zone Alarm, BlackIce, and McAfee Desktop Firewall. They do a good job of recognizing port-scanning programs or information from a computer attempting to leave a questionable port. However, many of these programs prompt the user to allow or disallow such traffic. The problem is that many users who are not aware of these Trojan programs simply click the Allow check box when warned about suspicious activity on a port. Also, many Trojan programs use standard ports to conduct their exploits, which makes it difficult for average users to distinguish between suspicious activity and normal Internet traffic. You should educate your network users about these basic concepts if there's no corporate firewall or a corporate policy establishing rules or restrictions.

Spyware

If you do a search on the keyword "spyware," you'll be bombarded with hundreds of links. Some simply tout spyware removal, but some install spyware on a computer when the user clicks the Yes button in a dialog box asking whether the computer should be checked for spyware (see Figure 3-2). When you click the Yes button, the spyware installation begins.

Figure 3-2   A spyware initiation program

A **spyware** program sends information from the infected computer to the person who initiated the spyware program on your computer. This information could be confidential financial data, passwords, PINs—just about any data stored on your computer. You need to make sure your users understand that this information collection is possible and that spyware programs can register each keystroke entered. It's that simple. This type of technology not only exists, but is prevalent. It can be used to record and send everything a user enters to an unknown person located halfway around the world. Tell your users they shouldn't assume that just because they're sitting in an office with the doors and windows locked, they're safe from an intruder.

Activity 3-4: Identifying Spyware

Time Required: 30 minutes

Objective: Examine prevalent spyware programs.

Description: Network security professionals know that spyware is one of the worst types of malicious attacks on corporate networks. Spyware can be installed on any computer through various means; the most common approach is installing spyware automatically after a user clicks a hyperlink or runs a program without verifying its authenticity. You should be aware of any new spyware programs as well as software that can remove spyware from a computer.

1. Start your Web browser, type **http://www.google.com** in the Address text box, and then press **Enter**.

2. Type **spyware** in the Search box and press **Enter**.

3. List some of your search results.

4. Write a description of spyware based on one of the sites you listed in Step 3.

5. In your Web browser, enter **www.spywareguide.com/**, and press **Enter**.

6. On the home page, click the **List of Products** link.

7. Click one of the links you found in Step 6, and write a brief description of the spyware. (*Note:* The list is in alphabetical order; you can scroll it with the arrow keys.)

8. Close your Web browser.

Adware

The difference between spyware and **adware** is a fine line. Both programs can be installed without the user being aware of their presence. Adware, however, sometimes displays a banner that notifies the user of its presence. Adware's main purpose is to determine a user's purchasing habits so that Web browsers can display advertisements tailored to that user. The biggest problem with adware is that it slows down the computer it's running on.

Security Bytes

Network security begins with each user understanding how vulnerable a computer is to attack. However, being aware of malware's presence, just as you're aware of unscrupulous telemarketers who call you during dinnertime, can better equip you to make valid decisions. If someone offers to sell you property in Tahiti for $99.95 over the telephone and asks for your credit card number, you'd refuse. Computer users should be just as skeptical when prompted to click an OK button or install a free computer game.

PROTECTING AGAINST MALWARE ATTACKS

Protecting an organization from malware attacks is difficult because new viruses, worms, and Trojan programs appear daily. Fortunately, many malware programs are detected by antivirus programs. Figures 3-3 and 3-4 show Symantec antivirus software detecting a remote program attempting to install a virus and a Trojan program. It's important to educate users about these types of attacks as well as other attacks, covered later in this section.

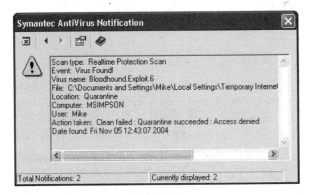

Figure 3-3 Detecting a virus

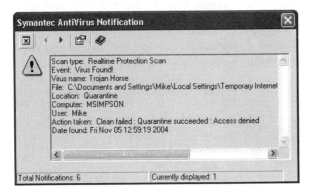

Figure 3-4 Detecting a Trojan program

Educating Your Users

No matter how hard you try to protect a network from malware being introduced, the most effective approach is conducting structured training of all employees and management. In fact, many U.S. government organizations make security awareness programs mandatory, and many private-sector companies are following their example. A simple but effective method of educating users is e-mailing monthly security updates to all employees to inform them of the most recent viruses, spyware, and adware detected on the Internet.

To help prevent viruses from being introduced into corporate networks, the most important recommendation you should make to a client is to update virus signature files as soon as they're available from the vendor. Most antivirus software does this automatically or prompts the user with an icon displayed on the taskbar. An organization can't depend on employee vigilance to protect its systems, so centralizing all antivirus software updates from a corporate server is prudent.

To counter the introduction of spyware and adware into a corporate network, you might need to download additional software from the Internet. Many antivirus software packages don't fully address the problem of spyware and adware. As of this writing, the two most popular spyware and adware removal programs are SpyBot and Ad-Aware. Both are free and easy to install and can be downloaded from *www.pcworld.com/ downloads*. Many other Web sites offer these programs, but remember to use caution when downloading any programs from unknown Web sites.

You can also help protect a network by implementing a firewall (covered in more detail in Chapter 13). Many of the top antivirus software companies also offer software firewalls for home users or small businesses that do not have a hardware firewall or an intrusion detection system (IDS) installed. Companies that have firewalls can follow the configuration instructions at many of the antivirus sites. For example, the W32/Sobig.F worm uses UDP port 8998 to contact the attacker's server. By blocking all outbound traffic on this port, you can prevent this attack from occurring. Also, many services are started by default on a computer system, and they don't need to be. For example, the average home user or small-business owner doesn't typically use Telnet. This service should not be active on most computers because Telnet is vulnerable to many outside attacks.

Avoiding Fear Tactics

You'd be surprised how many users don't know that clicking an icon in an e-mail message can activate a virus or Trojan program or that another person can access their computers from a remote location. Consequently, some security professionals use fear tactics to scare users into complying with security measures. Their approach is to tell users that if they don't take a particular action, their computer systems will be attacked by every malcontent who has access to the Internet. This method is sometimes used to generate business for security testers and is not only unethical, but also against the OSSTMM's Rules of Engagement. The rule states: "The use of fear, uncertainty, and doubt may not be used in the sales or marketing presentations, websites, supporting materials, reports, or discussion of security testing for the purpose of selling or providing security tests. This includes but is not limited to crime, facts, criminal or hacker profiling, and statistics."

Your approach to users or potential customers should be promoting awareness rather than instilling fear. You should point out to users how important it is not to install computer programs—especially those not approved by the company—on their desktops because of the possibility of introducing malware. Users should be aware of potential threats, not terrified by them.

In addition, when training users, be sure to build on the knowledge they already have. For example, some users are familiar with Windows XP Remote Assistance or other remote control programs, such as PC AnyWhere. Users' experience with these programs makes the job of explaining how an intruder can take control of their computers easier because they already know the technology is available.

INTRUDER ATTACKS ON NETWORKS AND COMPUTERS

An **attack** is defined as any attempt by an unauthorized person to access or use network resources or computer systems. **Network security** is concerned with the security of computers or devices that are part of a network infrastructure. **Computer security** is defined as securing a standalone computer that's not part of a network infrastructure. The FBI, CIA, and Interpol warn that computer crime is the fastest growing type of crime worldwide. After all, attacking a corporate network from the comfort of home is much easier than breaking into a business at 3:00 a.m. Speaking on the subject of the difficulty of prosecuting computer criminals, FBI agent Arnold Aanui, Jr., from the Honolulu FBI Cybercrime Division stated: "Even if the FBI tracks down the computer used in a crime, if more than one person has access to that computer, the FBI can't arrest the alleged perpetrator because any one of the users might have committed the crime." Until the laws change so that the punishment for committing these crimes becomes more of a deterrent, security professionals will be busy for many years.

Security Bytes

Not too long ago, in an affluent neighborhood in Hawaii, the FBI stormed into a quiet residential home with warrants in hand, prepared to arrest the occupant and confiscate his desktop computer, which was alleged to contain records of drug transactions and other incriminating evidence. While FBI personnel were cautiously entering the front of the house, they heard a gunshot from a rear bedroom. When they entered the room, they saw a man seated on the bed and a 12-gauge shotgun leaned against a closed door. He had just emptied a round into the computer, destroying the hard drives so thoroughly that the data couldn't be recovered. The FBI agents could have tried sending the disks to a lab that specialized in data recovery from hard disks, but decided not to because they believed they had enough evidence from other sources. Criminals of all sorts use computers to commit computer crimes but also as tools to run their "businesses" more efficiently. The FBI would probably have gotten better results by hiring a security tester to access the computer.

Denial-of-Service Attacks

As the name implies, a **denial-of-service (DoS) attack** prevents legitimate users from accessing network resources. Some forms of DoS attacks don't even involve computers. For example, intentionally looping a document on a fax machine by taping two pages together can use up reams of paper on the destination fax machine, thus preventing others from using it. In a DoS attack that does involve computers, attackers aren't attempting to access information from your servers. However, they might be using the attack to cripple the network until it's vulnerable to a different type of attack.

As a network security tester, you don't usually install a virus or worm on a customer's computer. Seldom does a penetration tester or an ethical hacker perform this type of testing. Similarly, you should know how a DoS attack can take place and attempt to protect the business from it, but conducting the attack yourself isn't wise. Doing so would be like a safety consultant blowing up a refinery after being hired to look for safety hazards or vulnerabilities. You simply need to prove the attack could be carried out.

Distributed Denial-of-Service Attacks

A **distributed denial-of-service (DDoS) attack** is an attack on a host from multiple servers or workstations. In a DDoS attack, a network could be flooded with literally billions of packets; typically, each participant in the attack contributes only a small number of the total packets. For example, if one server bombards an attacked server with hundreds or even thousands of packets, network bandwidth could be used to the point that legitimate users notice a performance degradation or loss of speed. Now multiply that one server bombarding the attacked server by 1000 servers or even 10,000 servers, with each server sending several thousand IP packets to the attacked server. There you have it: a DDoS attack. Keep in mind that participants in the attack often aren't aware their computers are taking part in the attack. They, too, have been attacked by the culprit. In fact, in one DDoS attack, a company was flooded with IP packets from thousands of Internet core routers and Web servers belonging to Yahoo.com.

Buffer Overflow Attacks

A number of buffer overflow attacks have taken place on many different OSs over the years. In a **buffer overflow attack**, a programmer finds a vulnerability in poorly written code that doesn't check for a defined amount of space utilization. For example, if a program defines a buffer size of 100 MB (the total amount of memory the program is supposed to use), and the program writes data over the 100 MB mark without triggering an error or preventing this occurrence, you have a buffer overflow. Basically, the attacker writes code that overflows the buffer; this is possible because the buffer capacity hasn't been defined correctly in the program. The trick is to not fill the overflow buffer with meaningless data, but to fill it with executable program code. That way, the OS runs the code and the attacker's program does something harmful. Usually, the code elevates the attacker's permissions to that of an administrator or gives the attacker the same privileges as the owner or creator of the poorly written program. Table 3-4 describes some current buffer overflow vulnerabilities.

Table 3-4   Buffer overflow vulnerabilities

Buffer Overflow	Description
Solaris X Window Font Service	This buffer overflow affects the Sun Microsystems Solaris 2.5.1, 2.6, 7, 8, and 9 and the Solaris X Window Font Service systems. It allows an attacker to run arbitrary code in memory. See VU#312313 (*www.kb.cert.org/vuls*) for more information.
Windows Workstation	Microsoft Security Bulletin MS03-049 (*www.microsoft. com/security/bulletins/default.mspx*) discusses this buffer overflow vulnerability, which makes it possible for the attacker to run arbitrary code placed in memory.
Remote Sendmail	This buffer overflow vulnerability affects all versions of Sendmail Pro and some versions of Sendmail Switch. The vulnerability allows the attacker to gain root privileges on the attacked system. See VU#398025 for more details.
Microsoft Windows Messenger Service	The Windows Messenger Service has a buffer overflow vulnerability that enables the attacker to run arbitrary code and gain privileges to the attacked system.
Microsoft Windows Help and Support Center	Contains buffer overflow in code used to handle Human Communications Protocol (HCP). A buffer overflow security vulnerability in the Help and Support Center function affects Windows XP and Windows Server 2003. The vulnerability allows the attacker to create a URL that could run arbitrary code at the local computer security level when the user enters that URL.
Sendmail	All systems running Sendmail versions before 8.12.10, including UNIX and Linux systems, are vulnerable to a buffer overflow attack that enables the attacker to possibly elevate privileges to that of the root user.
Microsoft RPCSS Service	There are two buffer overflow vulnerabilities in the RPCSS Service, which handles DCOM messages. This service is enabled by default on many versions of Microsoft Windows, but the vulnerability affects only Microsoft Windows 2000 systems. For more information, see VU#483492 and VU#254236.
Microsoft Internet Explorer	A total of five vulnerabilities affect Microsoft systems running Internet Explorer 5.01, 5.50, and 6.01. For more information, see Microsoft Security Bulletin MS03-032.

In defense of computer programmers, many are not trained to write programs with computer security in mind. In the past, programs were written for ease of use and to create efficient executable code that ran quickly and used as few computer resources as possible. Today, the trend is to make sure programmers are aware of how their code might be vulnerable to attack, but it's going to take a while before checking for security vulnerabilities becomes standard practice. Most universities do not offer courses on writing computer programs with security in mind. At Microsoft, computer programmers are now rewarded for writing code that doesn't show up later as a vulnerability in the system. In Activity 3-5, you take a look at some Microsoft programs that overlooked the security factor in their program design.

Activity 3-5: Identifying Microsoft Buffer Overflow Vulnerabilities

Time Required: 30 minutes

Objective: Examine Microsoft buffer overflow vulnerabilities.

Description: As a network security professional conducting a security test on a customer's network, you need to investigate any vulnerabilities that might be used. After discovering vulnerabilities that might affect a client's network, you must create documentation of your findings and make recommendations to correct the problem. In this activity, you examine buffer overflow vulnerabilities of Microsoft programs and learn what solutions or recommendations you might give to customers.

1. Start your Web browser, type **www.microsoft.com** in the Address text box, and then press **Enter**.

2. In the Search Microsoft.com for text box, type **MS03-041** and press **Enter**.

3. Click the **Microsoft Security Bulletin MS03-041** link.

4. Scroll down the document and click to expand the **Technical Details** option.

5. If the user who activated the ActiveX control from the attacked workstation was logged on as Administrator, what rights would you, the attacker, have?

6. What recommendations would you give a customer running Microsoft Windows 2000, Service Pack 2?

7. On the Microsoft Security Bulletin page, type **MS03-042** in the Search text box and press **Enter**.

8. On the search page, click the **Microsoft Security Bulletin MS03-042** link.

9. Scroll down the document and click to expand the **Technical Details** option.

10. Which ActiveX control has a buffer overflow vulnerability?

11. If the customer is running Microsoft Windows XP, what recommendation would you give?

12. Close your Web browser.

The previous activity gives you insight into how buffer overflows are used to exploit an OS. Usually, a buffer overflow's main purpose is to insert code into the overwritten area of memory that elevates the attacker's permissions to that of the user.

Ping of Death Attacks

The **Ping of Death attack**, a type of DoS attack, is not as common as it was during the late 1990s. The attacker simply creates an ICMP packet (discussed in Chapter 2) that's larger than the maximum allowed 65,535 bytes. The large packet is fragmented into smaller packets and reassembled at its destination. The user's system at the destination point can't handle the reassembled oversized packet, thereby causing the system to crash or freeze.

Session Hijacking

Session hijacking enables an attacker to join a TCP session and make both parties think he or she is the other party. This attack, discussed briefly in Chapter 2 in relation to ISNs, is a complex attack that's beyond the scope of this book.

Addressing Physical Security

Protecting a network from attacks is not always a software issue. You should have some basic skills in protecting a network from physical attacks as well. No matter how effective your firewall is, you must secure your servers and computers from an attack from within your organization. In fact, there's a higher chance that a hacker who breaks into the network is from inside your company rather than outside.

Security Bytes

Recently, on a military base in Hawaii, a pickup truck parked in front of an office building, and the driver entered the building and walked into an empty office. He disconnected one of the computers from the network, carried it out of the office, placed it in the truck's flatbed, and drove off, never to be seen again. When upper management questioned the staff, employees said they remembered seeing someone walking out of the building with the computer, but they assumed he was a help desk employee. Physical security is only as strong as the weakest link. All employees need to be aware of what's happening in their work environment. For example, if they notice a stranger is sitting in front of a computer downloading files, they should contact security and then confront the person. Employees should be vigilant and not depend on security personnel alone to pay attention.

Keyloggers

Keyloggers are devices or computer programs that can be used to capture keystrokes on a computer. Software keyloggers behave like Trojan programs and are loaded on a computer. A hardware keylogger is a small device, often smaller than an inch long. It can usually be installed on a computer in less than 30 seconds. It's a simple matter of unplugging a keyboard from a computer, plugging the small attachment into the keyboard input jack, and then plugging the keylogger jack into the computer's keyboard port. After installing the hardware, most vendors require you to run a word processing program, such as WordPad, and then enter the vendor-supplied password in the blank document. After entering the password, a menu is displayed. Some common hardware keyloggers are KeyKatcher and KeyGhost. In Figure 3-5, the KeyKatcher keylogger program captured a private message sent in an e-mail; the sender is informing Bob that he's going to quit his job. If you're conducting a security test on a system and need to obtain passwords, keyloggers can be a helpful tool.

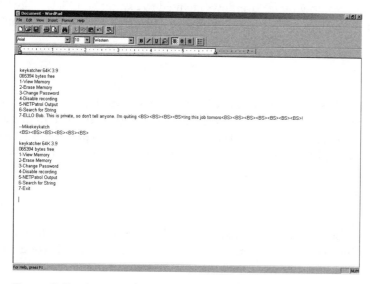

Figure 3-5 An e-mail message captured by KeyKatcher

Most keylogger products display similar menus that allow the system to begin capturing keystrokes the user enters. Figure 3-6 shows the menu in a different keylogger product from KeyGhost. This product has more storage area for capturing data. Both products can be quite useful when conducting a security test or penetration test for a company and can be installed and configured in a few minutes. The products were created for companies or even parents who want to monitor computers. Both include a plastic, tubelike covering that can be melted with a lighted match onto the connection so that the user can't unplug the unit before conducting questionable activity on the computer.

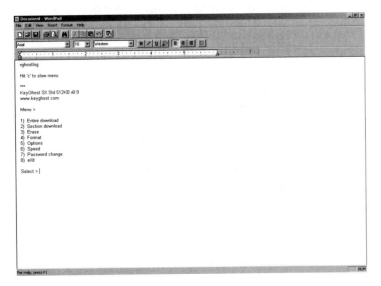

Figure 3-6   The KeyGhost menu

Unfortunately, attackers can also use keylogger devices. An unscrupulous employee can connect the device to a manager's computer and retrieve confidential information later. Installing this device does require actually physically sitting in front of the computer, which might pose a problem if the manager's office is locked. However, as mentioned previously, keyloggers are also available as software (spyware) that's loaded on a computer, and retrieved information can be e-mailed or transferred to a remote location.

When doing random visual tests of computers in your organization, keep an eye out for any suspicious hardware attached to the keyboard cable that wasn't installed by security personnel. This is a simple way to monitor for keyloggers. Conducting weekly random searches of computers might turn up some hardware, such as keyloggers or even computer systems, that the company didn't install.

Behind Locked Doors

As a security professional, you should be aware of the types of locks used to secure a company's assets. If an intruder gets physical access to a server, whether it's running Linux, Microsoft, or another OS, it doesn't matter how good your firewall or IDS is. Encryption or Public Key Infrastructure (PKI) enforcements don't help in this situation, either. If an intruder can sit in front of your server, he or she can hack it. Simply put, *lock up your server.*

In the same way that terrorists can learn how to create a bomb by doing research on the Internet, attackers can find countless articles about lock picking. One such paper, "MIT Guide to Lock Picking" by an author calling himself Ted the Tool, discusses the vulnerabilities of tumbler locks. The details of lock picking are beyond the scope of this book, but after a week or two of practice, the average person can learn how to pick a deadbolt lock in less than five minutes. Those who have more time on their hands, such as hackers, can learn to pick a deadbolt lock in under 30 seconds. If you're responsible for protecting a network infrastructure that has night-shift workers, don't assume that locked doors or cabinets can keep out unscrupulous employees with time on their hands. Typically, fewer employees are around during nonstandard business hours, which makes it easier for an employee to get into areas to which he or she might not normally have access. Your server room should have the best lock your company can afford. Take the time to look into locks that organizations such as the Department of Defense use, where protecting resources might be a life-or-death situation. It's not unheard of for such an organization to spend $5000 to $10,000 on a lock.

Rotary locks that require pushing in a sequence of numbered bars are more difficult to crack than deadbolt locks. However, neither lock type keeps a record of who has entered the locked room, so some businesses require using card access for better security. With this method, a card is scanned and access is given to the card holder while documenting the time of entry. This method also makes it possible for one card to offer access to several doors in a company without having to issue multiple keys or having users memorize different combinations.

Security Bytes

Some legitimate sites offer tools and manuals on lock picking for police or security professionals. You might have to fill out some forms, but it could be worth your while if you plan to become a security professional. For example, if you're conducting a security test on an organization that has a locked server room and you want to gain access, knowing how to pick a lock could be beneficial. Remember, however, that you must get written permission from management before conducting this level of testing.

Most police officers take a class to learn the basics of lock picking. When ordering lock-picking tools, be aware that many states or countries consider the mere possession of these tools a crime. Possession of burglary tools in New York City is a misdemeanor, and in Arizona, it's a felony. Hawaii, on the other hand, allows possessing the tools as long as they aren't used to commit a crime. Remember, possession of certain hacking tools is also illegal.

CHAPTER SUMMARY

- ❏ Network security professionals must be aware of attacks that can take place both on network infrastructures and on standalone computers.

- ❏ Intruder network and computer attacks can be perpetrated by insiders as well as remote users.

- ❏ Malicious software (malware), such as viruses, worms, and Trojan programs, are attacks that can be made on a network or computer. A virus is a computer program that attaches itself to a program or host. A worm is a computer program that's able to replicate and propagate itself without attaching itself to a program or host. A Trojan program disguises itself as a useful computer program or application and can install a backdoor or rootkit on a computer.

- ❏ Users can inadvertently install spyware programs, thinking they are installing software to protect their computers. Spyware can record information from a user's computer and send it to the attacker.

- ❏ Adware programs can also be installed without users' knowledge. They are used to discern users' buying patterns for the purpose of sending Web advertisements tailored to their buying habits, but can slow down a computer system.

- ❏ A denial-of-service (DoS) attack denies authorized users access to network resources. The attack is usually accomplished through excessive use of bandwidth.

- ❏ A distributed denial-of-service (DDoS) is an attack on a host from multiple servers or computers.

- ❏ The main purpose of buffer overflows is to insert executable code into an area of memory that elevates the attacker's permissions to that of the user.

- ❏ In a Ping of Death attack, the attacker crafts an ICMP packet to be larger than the maximum 65,535 bytes. This causes the recipient system to crash or freeze. Most systems today are not affected by this exploit.

- ❏ In session hijacking, the attacker joins a TCP session and makes both parties think he or she is the other party.

□ Physical security is everyone's responsibility. All desktop systems and servers must be secured.

□ Keyloggers make it possible to monitor what's being entered on a computer system. They can easily be installed on a keyboard connector and use a word processor to store information. Security personnel should conduct random checks of computer hardware to detect these devices.

3

Key Terms

adware — Software that can be installed without user knowledge; its main purpose is to determine users' purchasing habits.

attack — Any attempt of an unauthorized person to access or use resources of a network or computer system.

backdoor — A program that can be used to gain access to a computer system at a later date.

buffer overflow attack — An exploit written by a programmer that finds a vulnerability in poorly written code that doesn't check for a predefined amount of space usage and writes executable code in this overflow area.

computer security — The security of standalone computers that are not part of a network infrastructure.

denial-of-service (DoS) attack — An attack made to deny legitimate users from accessing network resources.

distributed denial-of-service (DDoS) attack — An attack made on a host from multiple servers or workstations to deny legitimate users from accessing network resources.

keyloggers — Hardware devices or software (spyware) that record keystrokes made on a computer and store the information for later retrieval.

macro virus — A computer program written in a macro programming language, such as Visual Basic Application.

malware — Malicious software, such as a virus, worm, or Trojan program, that is used to shut down a network and prevent a business from operating.

network security — The security of computers or devices that are part of a network infrastructure.

Ping of Death attack — A crafted ICMP packet larger than the maximum 65,535 bytes. It causes the recipient system to crash or freeze.

rootkit — A set of tools created after an attack for later use by the attacker.

shell — An interface to an operating system that enables system commands to be executed.

spyware — Software installed on users' computers without their knowledge that records personal information from the source computer and sends it to a destination computer.

Trojan program — A computer program that disguises itself as a legitimate program or application but has a hidden payload that might send information from the attacked computer to the creator or to a recipient located anywhere in the world.

virus — A computer program that attaches itself to an application or a program.

virus signature files — Antivirus software compares these files against the programming code of known viruses to determine whether a program you're installing is infected.

worm — A computer program that replicates and propagates without needing a host or program.

Review Questions

1. What is the main purpose of malware?

   a. to do harm to a computer system

   b. to learn passwords

   c. to discover open ports

   d. to identify an operating system

2. A computer _____ relies on a host system to propagate throughout a network.

   a. worm

   b. virus

   c. program

   d. sniffer

3. A computer exploit that attacks computer systems by substituting executable code in areas of memory not protected because of poorly written code is called a _____ .

   a. buffer overflow

   b. Trojan program

   c. virus

   d. worm

4. Which of the following exploits might hide its destructive payload in a legitimate software application or game?

   a. Trojan program

   b. macro virus

   c. worm

   d. buffer overflow

5. Antivirus software should be updated annually. True or False?

6. Which of the following does not attach itself to a program but can replicate itself?

   a. worm

   b. virus

   c. Trojan

   d. buffer overflow

7. Which of the following is an example of a macro programming language?

   a. C++

   b. Windows XP

   c. Visual Basic

   d. Visual Basic Application (VBA)

8. One purpose of adware is to determine users' purchasing habits. True or False?

9. List three types of malware.

10. The software or hardware component that records each keystroke a user enters into a word processing document is called a _____ .

    a. sniffer

    b. keylogger

    c. Trojan program

    d. buffer overflow

11. List three worms or viruses that use e-mail as a form of attack.

12. The Ping of Death is an exploit that sends multiple ICMP packets to a host faster than the host can handle. True or False?

13. What type of network attack relies on multiple servers participating in an attack on one host system?

   a. Trojan attack

   b. buffer overflow

   c. denial-of-service attack

   d. distributed denial-of-service attack

14. What exploit is used to elevate the permissions of a network attacker by writing executable code in the computer's memory?

   a. Trojan program

   b. buffer overflow

   c. Ping of Death

   d. buffer variance

15. What component can be used to reduce the risk of a Trojan program or rootkit sending information from an attacked computer to a remote host?

   a. base 64 decoder

   b. keylogger

   c. Telnet

   d. firewall

16. To reduce the risk of a virus attack on a network, you should do which of the following?

   a. Use antivirus software.

   b. Educate users about opening attachments from suspicious e-mail.

   c. Keep virus signature files current.

   d. All of the above.

17. The base-64 numbering system uses _____ bits to represent a character.

   a. 4

   b. 6

   c. 7

   d. 8

18. An exploit that leaves an attacker with another way to compromise a network later is called a _____ .

   a. root tool

   b. worm

   c. backroot

   d. backdoor

19. A good place to begin your search for vulnerabilities of Microsoft products is to review _____ .

   a. hacking Web sites

   b. Microsoft Security Bulletins

   c. newsgroup references to vulnerabilities

   d. user manuals

20. An exploit discovered for one operating system might also be effective on another operating system. True or False?

CASE PROJECTS

Case 3-1: Determine Vulnerabilities for a Database Server

You have interviewed Wilson Steiger after conducting your initial security testing of the K. J. Williams Corporation. Mr. Steiger is an IT staff member at K. J. Williams. He informs you that the company is running Oracle8*i* for its personnel database. You decide to do some research on whether Oracle8*i* has any known vulnerabilities that you can include in your report to Mr. Steiger. You don't know whether Mr. Steiger has installed any patches or software fixes; you simply want to create a report with general information.

Based on the preceding information, write a memo to Mr. Steiger addressing any CVEs (common vulnerabilities and exposures) or CAN (candidate) documents you found related to Oracle8*i*. If you do find vulnerabilities, your memo should include recommendations and be written in a way that doesn't generate fear or uncertainty, but encourages prudent decision making.

Case 3-2: Investigate Possible Vulnerabilities of Microsoft IIS 5.0

Carrell Jackson, the Web developer for K. J. Williams, has informed you that Microsoft IIS 5.0 is being used for the company's Web site. He is proud of the direction the Web site is taking and says that the company currently has more than 1000 hits per week. Customers can now reserve hotel rooms, reserve tee times for several golf courses, and make reservations at any of the facility's many restaurants. Customers can enter their credit card information and receive their confirmations via e-mail.

Based on the preceding information, write a memo to Mr. Jackson listing any CVE or CAN documents related to known vulnerabilities of IIS 5.0, if any. If you do find vulnerabilities, your memo should include recommendations and be written in a way that doesn't generate fear or uncertainty, but encourages prudent decision making.

4

FOOTPRINTING AND SOCIAL ENGINEERING

After reading this chapter and completing the exercises, you will be able to:

♦ Use Web tools for footprinting

♦ Conduct competitive intelligence

♦ Describe DNS zone transfers

♦ Identify the types of social engineering

In this chapter, you learn how to use tools readily available on the Internet to find out how a company's network is designed. You also learn the skills needed to conduct competitive intelligence and how to use those skills for information gathering. Before you conduct a security test on a network, you need to perform most, if not all, of the footprinting tasks covered in this chapter.

This chapter also explains the tactics of attackers who use social engineering to get information from a company's key employees. In addition, you examine some of the less glamorous methods attackers use—such as looking through garbage cans, wastepaper baskets, and dumpsters for old computer manuals, discarded disks, and other materials—to obtain information that can enable them to break into a network.

USING WEB TOOLS FOR FOOTPRINTING

In movies, before a thief robs a bank or steals jewelry, he "cases the joint" by taking pictures and getting floor plans. Movie thieves are usually lucky enough to get schematics of alarm systems and air-conditioning ventilation systems, too. At least, that's how Hollywood portrays thieves. Any FBI agent would tell you that most real-life thieves aren't that lucky. However, the smart ones who don't get caught are meticulous and cautious. Many attackers do case the joint to look over the location, find weaknesses in the security system, and determine what types of locks and alarm systems are being used. They try to gather as much information as possible before committing a crime.

As a security tester, you, too, must find out as much as you can about the organization that hired you to test its network security. That way, you can advise management of any problem areas. In computer jargon, the process of finding information on a company's network is called **footprinting**. The security tester (or attacker) tries to discover as much as possible about the organization and its network. Table 4-1 lists some of the many tools available for footprinting.

Table 4-1 Summary of Web tools

Tool	Function
Google groups (*http://groups.google.com*)	Search for e-mail addresses in postings in technical or nontechnical newsgroups
Whois (*www.arin.net* or *www.whois.net*)	Gather IP and domain information
SamSpade (*www.samspade.org*)	Gather IP and domain information; versions available for UNIX and Windows OSs
Google search engine (*www.google.com*)	Search for Web sites and company data
Namedroppers (*www.namedroppers.com*)	Run a domain name search; more than 30 million domain names updated daily
White Pages (*www.whitepages.com*)	Conduct reverse phone number lookups and retrieve address information
Metis (*www.severus.org/sacha/metis*)	Gather competitive intelligence from Web sites
Dig (command available on all *NIX-based systems; can be downloaded from *http://pigtail.net/LRP/dig/* for Microsoft platforms)	Perform DNS zone transfers; replaces the Nslookup command
Host (command available on all *NIX-based systems; Hostname can be downloaded from *http://sysinternals.com/ntw2k/source/misc.shtml* for Windows platforms)	Obtain host IP and domain information; can also be used to initiate DNS zone transfers
Netcat (command available on all *NIX-based systems; can be downloaded from *http://atstake.com/research/tools* for Windows platforms)	Read and write data to ports over a network
Wget (command available on all *NIX-based systems; can be downloaded from *http://gnu.org/software/wget/wget.html* for Microsoft platforms)	Retrieve HTTP, HTTPS, and FTP files over the Internet
Paros (*www.parosproxy.org*)	Capture Web server information and possible vulnerabilities in a Web site's pages that could allow exploits such as SQL injection and buffer overflows

NOTE Many command-line utilities included by default for *NIX systems aren't part of a Windows environment. For example, the Dig, Host, Netcat, and Wget commands don't work at the command prompt of a Windows XP computer. You can download Windows versions from the Web sites listed in Table 4-1. Security testers should spend time learning to use these command-line tools on a Linux or *NIX-based system.

In this chapter, you use the Whois utility to get information about a company's Web presence and use tools such as the Dig command, SamSpade, and DNS zone transfers to determine computers' IP address ranges and host names.

Security Bytes

Each year, Department of Defense (DoD) employees are required to complete security awareness training that emphasizes the dangers of terrorists or spies being able to collect nonclassified information. This information, available to most Americans, can be found by reading newspapers and listening to the news. By putting small pieces of information together, terrorists can get a full picture of the DoD's activities. The DoD wants its employees to realize that discussing seemingly inconsequential information might be more dangerous than imagined. This information, when combined with additional information, can be damaging to national security.

For example, a sailor meets a friend in a restaurant and mentions that he'll be gone for six months. That same day, a civilian working for the DoD mentions over lunch at a restaurant that she has to work a lot of overtime ordering increased supplies. As you can see, terrorists could easily pick up both pieces of information by listening in on conversations. This might sound farfetched, but it's one of the major methods of gathering intelligence. The point is that you, too, need to pay attention to all the information that's available, whether it's information on a Web site, in e-mail headers, or in an employee's statement in an interview. Unfortunately, attackers are checking Web pages and newsgroups, examining IP addresses of companies, and looking for postings from IT personnel asking specific questions about operating systems or firewall configurations. Remember, too, that after gathering a piece of information, you shouldn't stop there. Continue to dig to see what else potential attackers could discover.

Conducting Competitive Intelligence

If you want to open a piano studio to compete against another studio that has been in your neighborhood for many years, getting as much information as possible about your competitor is wise. How could you know the studio was successful without being privy to its bank statements? First, many businesses fail after the first year, so the studio being around for years is a testament to the owner doing something right. Second, you can simply park your car across the street from the studio and count the students to get a good idea of the number of clients. You can easily find out the cost of lessons by calling the studio or looking for ads in newspapers, flyers, telephone books, billboards, and so on. Numerous resources are available to help you discover as much as is legally possible about your competition. Business people have been doing this for years. Now this information gathering, called **competitive intelligence**, is done on an even higher level through technology. As a security professional, you should be able to explain to the company that hired you all the methods competitors use to gather information. To limit the amount of information a company makes public, you should have a good understanding of what a competitor would do to discover confidential information.

Security Bytes

Just because you're able to find out information about a company and its employees doesn't mean you should divulge that information. For example, say you find that an employee is visiting a dating service Web site or questionable newsgroups. This activity doesn't jeopardize the company in any way, however, so as a security professional conducting a security test, you're not obligated to inform the company. Depending on the laws of your country or state, privacy issues might affect your decision on how to handle this situation. A security professional and company officials can be sued for releasing confidential information of this nature.

Analyzing a Company's Web Site

Network attacks often begin by gathering information from a company's Web site. Web pages are an easy way for attackers to discover critical information about an organization. Many tools are available for this type of information gathering. For example, Paros is a powerful tool for UNIX and Windows OSs that can be downloaded free (*www.parosproxy.org*). Paros requires having Java J2SE installed, which can be downloaded from *www.sun.com*. After you install Paros on a Windows server, a desktop icon is displayed for running the program. Figure 4-1 shows the main window of Paros.

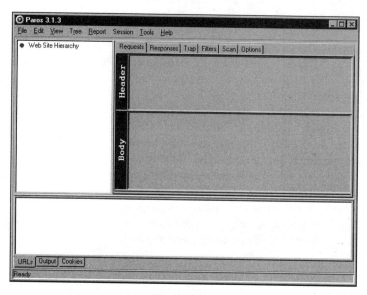

Figure 4-1   The main window of Paros

To search for a Web site using Paros, click Tools, Spider from the menu. Enter the Web site's URL, as shown in Figure 4-2.

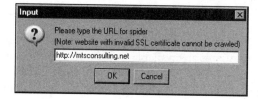

Figure 4-2   Entering a URL in the Input dialog box

In a matter of seconds, the file names of every Web page the site contains are displayed (see Figure 4-3).

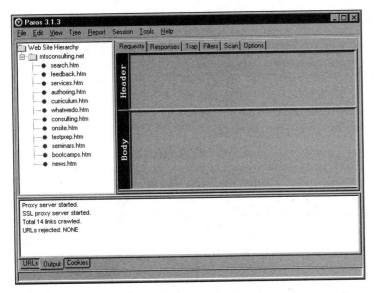

Figure 4-3   Displaying file names of all Web pages on a site

Next, click Tree, Scan All from the menu, After a minute or so, depending on the Web site's size, you get a report similar to the one in Figure 4-4. This report can show an attacker how a Web site is structured and lists Web pages that can be investigated for further information.

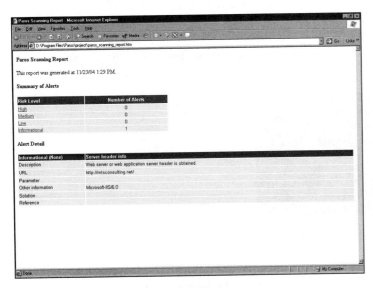

Figure 4-4   The Paros scanning report

As you can see, the scan feature enables you to test areas of the site that might have problems. Any vulnerabilities in the Web site are indicated in the Risk Level column as High. In this example, the risk level is flagged as Informational. However, the scan indicates what version of IIS is used for this Web site, which can be useful information for conducting further investigations or testing. Gathering competitive intelligence through scans of this type is time consuming, and the more you find out, the deeper you want to dig. Setting a reasonable time frame for this phase of your investigation is important, or you might spend too much time on this activity. On the other hand, you don't want to rush your information gathering because much of what you learn can be used for further testing and investigation. The following section covers additional tools you can use for gathering information.

Using Other Footprinting Tools

The Whois utility is a commonly used tool for gathering IP address and domain information. With just a company's Web address, you can discover a tremendous amount of information. Unfortunately, attackers can also make use of this information. Often companies don't realize that they're publishing information on the Web that computer criminals can use. The Whois utility gives you information on a company's IP addresses and any other domains the company might be part of. In Activity 4-1, you practice using Whois with other tools, such as the Host command, for footprinting purposes.

Activity 4-1: Using Footprinting Tools

Time Required: 30 minutes

Objective: Learn how to use footprinting tools, such as the Whois utility and the Host command.

Description: IT security professionals need to know which tools can be used to gather information about networks. With the Whois utility, you can discover which network configuration factors might be used in attacking a network. You also examine other commands for gathering additional details.

1. Start your Windows XP Professional system with the classroom Linux CD. Select a shell of your choosing, type the command **host mit.edu**, and press **Enter**. (To select a shell, right-click your desktop and click **Terminal**.)

> The Host command entered in Step 1 performs a reverse DNS lookup and returns an IP address. This IP address is then used in the whois.arin.net command later in this activity.

2. To see the options you can use with the Host command, type **host –h** in the Linux shell and press **Enter** (see Figure 4-5).

```
root@1[root]# host -h
Usage:      host [-v] [-a] [-t querytype] [options] name [server]
Listing:    host [-v] [-a] [-t querytype] [options] -l zone [server]
Hostcount:  host [-v] [options] -H [-D] [-E] [-G] zone
Check soa:  host [-v] [options] -C zone
Addrcheck:  host [-v] [options] -A host
Listing options: [-L level] [-S] [-A] [-p] [-P prefserver] [-N skipzone]
Common options: [-d] [-f|-F file] [-I chars] [-i|-n] [-q] [-Q] [-T] [-Z]
Other options:  [-c class] [-e] [-m] [-o] [-r] [-R] [-s secs] [-u] [-w]
Special options: [-O srcaddr] [-j minport] [-J maxport]
Extended usage: [-x [name ...]] [-X server [name ...]]
root@1[root]#
```

Figure 4-5   Options to use with the Host command

3. To understand what each option does, type **man host** in the shell (see Figure 4-6). On *NIX systems, the Man command is used to display topics from the help manual.

4. After you scroll through the man page to get a good overview of the Host command, press **Q** to exit.

5. To recall the IP address you obtained in Step 1, press the **up arrow** key until you see your original Host command. When you find it, press **Enter** to run it again.

6. Next, type **nc whois.arin.net** (to run the Netcat command) and press **Enter**. The Netcat command enables you to read and write data across a network to almost every port. This command returns a "no port(s) to connect to" error because you didn't assign a port for the *whois.arin.net* URL, which is port 43.

7. Press the **up arrow** key to return to the previous command, type **43** at the end of the command, and then press **Enter**.

```
host(1)                                                      host(1)

NAME
      host - query nameserver about domain names and zones

SYNOPSIS
      host [-v] [-a] [-t querytype] [options]  name [server]
      host [-v] [-a] [-t querytype] [options] -l zone [server]
      host [-v] [options] -H [-D] [-E] [-G] zone
      host [-v] [options] -C zone
      host [-v] [options] -A host

      host [options] -x [name ...]
      host [options] -X server [name ...]

OPTION SYNTAX
      Besides the traditional short options (one letter with single dash, and
      an optional value as separate argument), there are now also long
      options in the format --keyword[=value]. Many (but not all) short
      options have a long equivalent. There are several long options without
      a short equivalent. The long options are not yet documented in this
      manual page, but a summary of the existing long options, and the map-
      ping to their short alternative, is available via the command
      host --help.

DESCRIPTION
      host looks for information about Internet hosts and domain names. It
      gets this information from a set of interconnected servers that are
      spread across the world. The information is stored in the form of
      "resource records" belonging to hierarchically organized "zones".

      By default, the program simply converts between host names and Internet
      addresses. However, with the -t, -a and -v options, it can be used to
      find all of the information about domain names that is maintained by
      the domain nameserver system. The information printed consists of var-
      ious fields of the associated resource records that were retrieved.

      The arguments can be either host names (domain names) or numeric Inter-
      net addresses.

      A numeric Internet address consists of four numbers separated by dots,
      eg. 192.16.199.1, representing the four bytes of the 32-bit address.
      The numbers are interpreted in hexadecimal if they begin with "0x", in
      octal if they begin with "0" and in decimal otherwise.
      The default action is to look up the associated host name.

      A host name or domain name consists of component names (labels) sepa-
      rated by dots, e.g. nikhefh.nikhef.nl
      The default action is to look up all of its Internet addresses.

Manual page host(1) line 1
```

Figure 4-6   The man page for the Host command

8. Next, you need to supply one more piece of information: the IP address of mit.edu. Type the IP address you found from using the Host command in Step 1, and press **Enter**. You should see a screen similar to the one in Figure 4-7. What information returned in this screen could be used by attackers if a private company instead of an academic domain were being examined? What problems, if any, do you think might occur when using a person's name and telephone number instead of a title or job position?

9. Close your shell.

For those who find using a GUI tool easier than typing commands at a shell, SamSpade at *www.samspade.org* might be the tool for you (see Figure 4-8). This tool, available for UNIX and Windows OSs, is as easy to use as a Web search engine.

Figure 4-9 shows another GUI product called Greenwich (*http://directory.fsf.org/All_Packages_in_Directory/Greenwich.html*) that conducts Whois queries on .edu sites only.

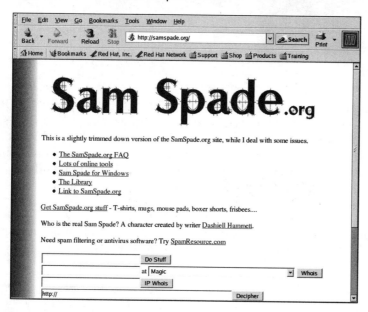

```
root@3[root]# host mit.edu
mit.edu                   A         18.7.22.69
root@3[root]# nc whois.arin.net 43
18.7.22.69

OrgName:     Massachusetts Institute of Technology
OrgID:       MIT-2
Address:     Room W92-190
Address:     77 Massachusetts Avenue
City:        Cambridge
StateProv:   MA
PostalCode:  02139-4307
Country:     US

NetRange:    18.0.0.0 - 18.255.255.255
CIDR:        18.0.0.0/8
NetName:     MIT
NetHandle:   NET-18-0-0-0-1
Parent:
NetType:     Direct Assignment
NameServer:  STRAWB.MIT.EDU
NameServer:  W20NS.MIT.EDU
NameServer:  BITSY.MIT.EDU
Comment:
RegDate:
Updated:     1998-09-26

TechHandle:  JIS-ARIN
TechName:    Schiller, Jeffrey
TechPhone:   +1-617-253-8400
TechEmail:   jis@mit.edu

OrgTechHandle: JIS-ARIN
OrgTechName:   Schiller, Jeffrey
OrgTechPhone:  +1-617-253-8400
OrgTechEmail:  jis@mit.edu

# ARIN WHOIS database, last updated 2004-11-21 19:10
# Enter ? for additional hints on searching ARIN's WHOIS database.
root@3[root]#
```

Figure 4-7   The Whois output screen

Figure 4-8   The SamSpade Web site

Using E-mail Addresses

After seeing the information you can obtain with the Host command, you might wonder what else you can do. Knowing a user's e-mail address can help you dig even further. Based on an e-mail account listed in DNS output, you might discover that the company's e-mail address format is first name initial, followed by last name and the @*companyname.com* sequence. You can guess other employees' e-mail accounts by getting a company phone directory or searching the Internet for any @*companyname.com* references. *Groups.google.com* is the perfect tool for this job. In Activity 4-2, you use it to find corporate e-mail addresses.

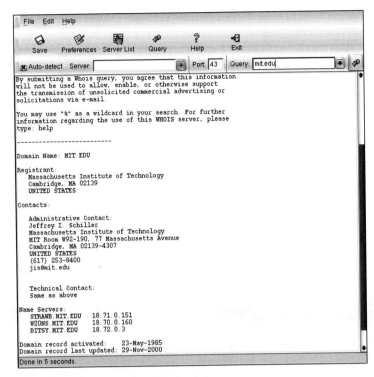

Figure 4-9 The Greenwich interface

Activity 4-2: Identifying Corporate E-mail Accounts

Time Required: 30 minutes

Objective: Determine e-mail addresses for corporate employees.

Description: Knowing the e-mail addresses of corporate employees can help you discover security vulnerabilities and gain competitive intelligence data. For example, you might discover that an employee has joined a newsgroup using his or her corporate e-mail account and shared proprietary information about the company. IT employees, when posting technical questions to a newsgroup, might reveal detailed information about the company's firewall or IDS, or a marketing director might mention a new ad campaign strategy the company is considering.

1. Start your Web browser, enter **http://groups.google.com**, and then press **Enter**.

2. On the search page, enter **@microsoft.com**, and press **Enter**. This is a fast and easy way to find e-mail accounts of people posting questions to the Microsoft domain.

3. Scroll down the list of items and try to find postings from employees who work at different companies. (*Hint*: Choose entries containing Re: in the listing. They are usually responses to questions sent by employees.) The list will vary, but it should give you an idea of the danger in using a company's e-mail address when posting questions to forums or newsgroups.

Remember, messages posted to newsgroups aren't private. People can look up newsgroup messages for many years. As a security tester, you should recommend that employees use a Web-based e-mail account (such as Hotmail), rather than their corporate e-mail accounts, for posting messages to newsgroups.

4. From a new query in groups.google.com, enter **@checkpoint.com.** Now you can find out who is posting questions to the firewall company Checkpoint. Most likely, the postings are from users of this firewall product. Can you see how an attacker could use this information?

5. Scroll through the list and look for questions from employees of the firewall company and customers wanting advice. Could attackers use this information for negative purposes?

6. When you're done, close your Web browser.

NOTE

To avoid revealing personal information, specific e-mail addresses weren't used in Activity 4-2. However, if you know a user's e-mail address, you can enter it directly in the *groups.google.com* search page. In Case Project 4-1, you get a chance to search on a specific e-mail address. If you were conducting a security test in the real world, you would search for e-mail accounts of IT staff and other key personnel.

Using HTTP Basics

As you learned in Chapter 3, HTTP operates on port 80. A security tester can pull information from a Web server by using the HTTP language set (commands). Don't worry; you won't have to learn too many codes to get data from a Web server. You've probably seen HTTP client error codes before, such as 400 Bad Request. A basic understanding of HTTP can be beneficial to security testers. If you know the return codes a Web server generates, you can determine what OS is being used on the computer where you're conducting a security test. Table 4-2 lists common HTTP client errors, and Table 4-3 lists HTTP server errors that might occur.

Table 4-2   HTTP client errors

Error	Description
400 Bad Request	Request not understood by server
401 Unauthorized	Request requires authentication
402 Payment Required	Reserved for future use
403 Forbidden	Server understands request but refuses to comply
404 Not Found	Unable to match request
405 Method Not Allowed (methods are covered later in this section)	Request not allowed for the resource
406 Not Acceptable	Resource does not accept your request
407 Proxy Authentication Required	Client must authenticate with proxy
408 Request Timeout	Request not made by client in allotted time
409 Conflict	Request could not be completed due to an inconsistency
410 Gone	Resource is no longer available
411 Length Required	Content length not defined
412 Precondition Failed	Request header fields evaluated as false
413 Request Entity Too Large	Request larger than server is able to process
414 Request-URI (Uniform Resource Identifier) Too Long	Request-URI is longer than the server is willing to accept

Table 4-3   HTTP server errors

Error	Description
500 Internal Server Error	Request could not be fulfilled by server
501 Not Implemented	Server does not support request
502 Bad Gateway	Server received invalid response from upstream server
503 Service Unavailable	Server is unavailable due to maintenance or overload
504 Gateway Timeout	Server did not receive a timely response
505 HTTP Version Not Supported	HTTP version not supported by server

In addition, you need to understand some of the available HTTP methods, shown in Table 4-4. You don't have to be fluent in using HTTP methods, but you need to be well versed enough to use the most basic HTTP method: GET / HTTP/1.1.

TIP

For a more detailed definition of HTTP methods, see RFC-2616.

Table 4-4 HTTP methods

Method	Description
GET	Retrieves data by URI (Uniform Resource Identifier)
HEAD	Same as the GET method, but retrieves only the header information of an HTML document, not the document body
OPTIONS	Requests information on available options
TRACE	Starts a remote application-layer loopback of the request message
CONNECT	Used with a proxy that can dynamically switch to a tunnel connection, such as Secure Socket Layer (SSL)
DELETE	Requests that the origin server delete the identified resource
PUT	Requests that the entity be stored under the Request-URI
POST	Allows data to be posted (that is, sent to a Web server)

If you know HTTP methods, you can send a request to a Web server and, from the generated output, determine what OS the Web server is using. You can also find other information that could be used in an attack. Remember from Chapter 3 how easy it is to find vulnerabilities or exploits that can be used on a Web browser or Web server. After you determine which OS version a company is running, you can search for any exploits that might be used against that network's systems.

Activity 4-3: Using HTTP to View Web Banners

Time Required: 30 minutes

Objective: Determine Web server information by using HTTP methods.

Description: Armed with the information gathered from a company Web server by using basic HTTP methods, a security tester can then discover system vulnerabilities and use this information for further testing. For example, querying a Web server might reveal that the server is running the Linux OS and using Apache software. In this activity, you use the Netcat command to connect to port 80 and then use the HTTP language.

If you can't get results in this activity by using mit.edu, perhaps the Web site has changed its security and won't allow the HEAD or OPTIONS methods to be used. If this is the case, try using isecom.org instead of mit.edu.

1. Start your Windows XP system from the Linux CD and open a shell of your choice. At the prompt, type **nc mit.edu 80** and press **Enter**. (Port 80 is the HTTP port.)

2. On the next line, type **OPTIONS / HTTP/1.1** and press **Enter**. (Note the spaces around the slash character between the words OPTIONS and HTTP.)

3. On the next line, type **127.0.0.1** and then press **Enter** twice. After several seconds, you see the screen shown in Figure 4-10.

```
root@3[root]# nc mit.edu 80
OPTIONS / HTTP/1.1
HOST: 127.0.0.1

HTTP/1.1 200 OK
Date: Mon, 22 Nov 2004 21:43:56 GMT
Server: MIT Web Server Apache/1.3.26 Mark/1.4 (Unix) mod_ssl/2.8.9 OpenSSL/0.9.6g
Content-Length: 0
Allow: GET, HEAD, OPTIONS, TRACE

root@3[root]#
```

Figure 4-10 Using the OPTIONS HTTP method

4. What information generated from the Netcat command might be useful to a security tester? What other options are available when accessing this Web server? [*Note:* Use Figure 4-10 to answer the question if the command doesn't work at this time.]

5. From your Linux shell, type **nc mit.edu 80** and press **Enter**.

6. On the next line, type **HEAD / HTTP/1.0** and press **Enter** twice to retrieve header information. Your screen should look similar to Figure 4-11. Note the additional information the HEAD method produced, such as indicating that the connection has been closed and specifying the content length (16554 bytes).

```
root@3[root]# nc mit.edu 80
HEAD / HTTP/1.0

HTTP/1.1 200 OK
Date: Mon, 22 Nov 2004 22:11:02 GMT
Server: MIT Web Server Apache/1.3.26 Mark/1.4 (Unix) mod_ssl/2.8.9 OpenSSL/0.9.
Last-Modified: Mon, 22 Nov 2004 04:59:22 GMT
ETag: "71d07c0-40aa-41a1722a"
Accept-Ranges: bytes
Content-Length: 16554
Connection: close
Content-Type: text/html

root@3[root]#
```

Figure 4-11   Using the HEAD HTTP method

7. Close your Linux shell.

TIP

To see additional parameters that can be used with the Netcat command, you can type nc -h at the shell prompt (see Figure 4-12).

```
root@3[root]# nc -h
[v1.10]
connect to somewhere:   nc [-options] hostname port[s] [ports] ...
listen for inbound:     nc -l -p port [-options] [hostname] [port]
options:
        -e prog             program to exec after connect [dangerous!!]
        -b                  allow broadcasts
        -g gateway          source-routing hop point[s], up to 8
        -G num              source-routing pointer: 4, 8, 12, ...
        -h                  this cruft
        -i secs             delay interval for lines sent, ports scanned
        -l                  listen mode, for inbound connects
        -n                  numeric-only IP addresses, no DNS
        -o file             hex dump of traffic
        -p port             local port number
        -r                  randomize local and remote ports
        -q secs             quit after EOF on stdin and delay of secs
        -s addr             local source address
        -t                  answer TELNET negotiation
        -u                  UDP mode
        -v                  verbose [use twice to be more verbose]
        -w secs             timeout for connects and final net reads
        -z                  zero-I/O mode [used for scanning]
port numbers can be individual or ranges: lo-hi [inclusive]
root@3[root]#
```

Figure 4-12   Netcat parameters

Other Methods of Gathering Information

So far, you have learned several methods for gathering information from company Web sites and e-mail addresses. With just a URL, you can determine which Web server and OS a company is using and learn the names of IT personnel, for example. You need to be aware of other methods used to gather information about a company. Some of these methods, such as using cookies and Web bugs, are unscrupulous.

Detecting Cookies and Web Bugs

A **cookie** is a text file generated by a Web server and stored on a user's browser. The information in this file is sent back to the Web server when the user returns to the Web site. For example, a returning customer can be shown a customized Web page when he or she revisits an online store's Web site. Some cookies can cause security issues because unscrupulous people might store personal information in cookies that can be used to attack a computer or server.

A **Web bug** is a 1-pixel × 1-pixel image file referenced in an <IMG> tag, and it usually works with a cookie. Its purpose is similar to that of spyware and adware: to get information about the person visiting the Web site. Web bugs are not from the same Web site as the Web page creator. They come from third-party companies specializing in data collection. Security professionals need to be aware of cookies and Web bugs to keep these information-gathering tools off company computers.

Activity 4-4: Discovering Cookies on Web Browsers

Time Required: 30 minutes

Objective: Determine whether cookies are present in Web pages.

Description: Many companies include cookies in their Web pages to gather information about visitors to their Web sites. This information might be used for competitive intelligence or, for example, to determine visitors' buying habits. Security professionals should know how to verify whether a Web page contains cookies.

1. Start your Windows XP system from the Linux CD, and open the Mozilla Firefox Web browser. If you have been using this browser and didn't need to boot from the CD, cookies are probably loaded on your computer already, so you need to clear the cookies and then visit a new site.

2. First, to clear any cookies from your computer, click **Tools**, **Options** from the browser menu. In the Options dialog box, click the **Privacy** icon at the left (see Figure 4-13). Click to expand the **Cookies** selection, and then click the **Stored Cookies** button.

Figure 4-13 The Privacy dialog box in Mozilla Firefox

3. In the Cookie Manager dialog box, click the **Remove All Cookies** button. Your screen should look like Figure 4-14.

4. Click **OK**, and then click **OK** again to close the Privacy dialog box.

5. Type **www.amazon.com** in your browser's Address text box and press **Enter**. Return to the Privacy dialog box and click **Stored Cookies** again. If any cookies are listed, simply click one to view information about it. Do any of the cookies have personal information stored?

6. If time permits, visit some sites that require signing in with an account logon and password. See whether these sites create any cookies with personal information.

7. Click the **Cancel** button twice to return to the Amazon Web page.

8. Close your Web browser.

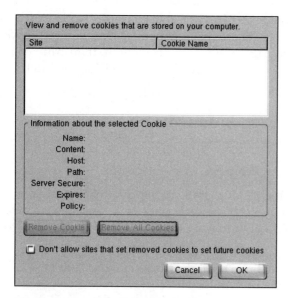

Figure 4-14   Removing cookies

Activity 4-5: Installing Web Bug Detector Software

Time Required: 30 minutes

Objective: Install Web bug detector software on your Windows XP computer and examine a Web bug.

Description: Web bugs are from third-party companies and are considered more invasive than cookies. As a security professional, you should know how to verify whether a Web page contains Web bugs.

1. Restart your system if it's not booted in Windows XP. Start your Internet Explorer Web browser, type **www.bugnosis.org/download.html** in the Address text box, and press **Enter**.

2. Click **Bugnosis** in the Then fetch and install column, and then click **Run** in the File Download - Security Warning dialog box.

3. If you receive a Security Warning dialog box again, click **Run**. Follow the prompts to install the product, accepting all the defaults. When the installation is finished, close all browser windows, and then restart your browser. (*Note*: If you see a message box asking whether you want to download the latest settings for Bugnosis, click **Yes**.) When your browser opens, you see the Bugnosis toolbar added (see Figure 4-15).

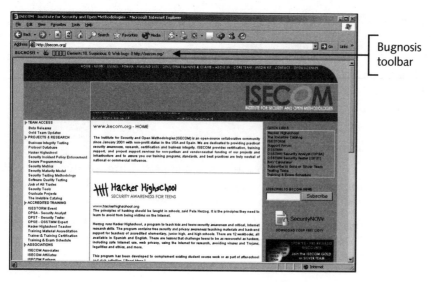

Figure 4-15   The Bugnosis toolbar

4. Next, you visit a Web site that has many known Web bugs. Type **www.wired.com** as the URL, and press **Enter**. Note the status bar information and diagnosis of the software. (*Note*: If you have a firewall on your network, you might see a popup message stating that the site isn't accessible. If so, you need to configure the firewall to allow you to visit that Web site.)

5. Did Bugnosis detect any Web bugs? If yes, what criteria were used?

6. If time permits, visit some other sites and note the results. This type of research can be time consuming but interesting.

7. Close your Web browser.

4

Using Domain Name Service (DNS) Zone Transfers

Another way to gather information when footprinting a network is through DNS. As you know from learning basic networking concepts, DNS is the network component responsible for resolving host names to IP addresses. People don't like memorizing numbers. They would much rather memorize a URL, such as *www.oracle.com*, than an IP address. Unfortunately, using URLs comes at a high price. DNS is one of the major areas of potential vulnerability for network attacks.

Without going into too much detail, DNS uses name servers to do just that: resolve names. After you determine what name server a company is using, you can attempt to transfer all the records for which the DNS server is responsible. A zone transfer can be done by using the Dig and Host commands. (For those familiar with the Nslookup command, Dig is now the recommended command.) To determine a company's primary DNS server, you can look for a DNS server containing a Start of Authority (SOA) record. The SOA shows for which zones or IP addresses the DNS server is responsible. After you determine which server has that record, you can perform a zone transfer. **Zone transfers** enable you to see all the host computers on a network. In other words, they give you an organization's network diagram. You can see all the hosts on a network and use this information to attack other servers or computers that are part of the network infrastructure.

Activity 4-6: Identifying IP Addresses by Using Zone Transfers

Time Required: 30 minutes

Objective: Perform a zone transfer on a DNS server.

Description: When footprinting a network, it is important to obtain the IP addresses and host names of all servers, computers, and other nodes connected to the network. With commands such as Dig or Host, you can perform zone transfers of all DNS records. You can then use this information to create network diagrams and establish a good visual picture of how the network is organized. For example, you can see how many hosts are on the network and how many subnets have been created.

In this example, mit.edu is used to demonstrate conducting a zone transfer. At the time of the writing of this book, it worked. However, many universities are tightening security and no longer allow zone transfers, but you should still know the steps to perform a zone transfer.

1. Boot your computer to Linux and start a shell of your choice. From the shell, type **dig soa mit.edu**, and press **Enter**. You should see a screen similar to Figure 4-16. Three name servers, indicated by "NS," are listed: STRAWB.mit.edu, BITSY.mit.edu, and W2ONS.mit.edu. (This information might change by the time you read this book. If so, ask your instructor for guidelines.)

2. To perform a zone transfer on the BITSY.mit.edu DNS server, type **dig @BITSY.mit.edu mit.edu axfr** and press **Enter**. BITSY.mit.edu is the server on which you're attempting the zone transfer, and the second mit.edu statement is the domain where the server is located.

3. After a short wait, your screen should fill with thousands of records. Press **Ctrl+C** to stop the transfer.

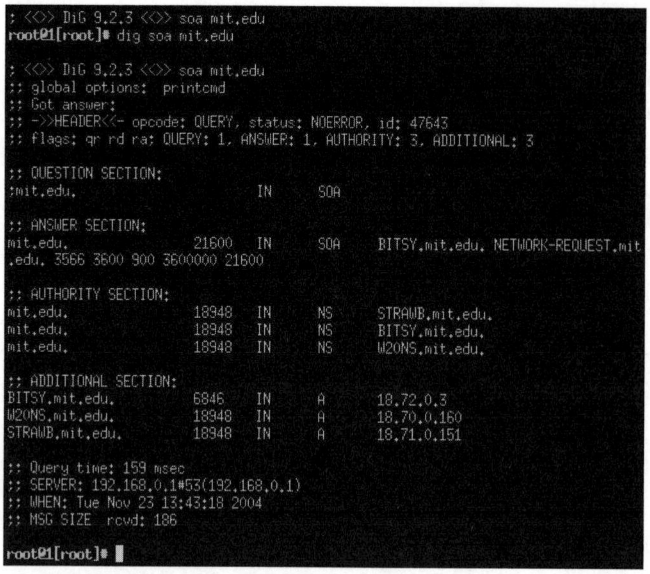

```
; <<>> DiG 9.2.3 <<>> soa mit.edu
root@1[root]# dig soa mit.edu

; <<>> DiG 9.2.3 <<>> soa mit.edu
;; global options:  printcmd
;; Got answer:
;; ->>HEADER<<- opcode: QUERY, status: NOERROR, id: 47643
;; flags: qr rd ra; QUERY: 1, ANSWER: 1, AUTHORITY: 3, ADDITIONAL: 3

;; QUESTION SECTION:
;mit.edu.                   IN     SOA

;; ANSWER SECTION:
mit.edu.           21600   IN     SOA    BITSY.mit.edu. NETWORK-REQUEST.mit
.edu. 3566 3600 900 3600000 21600

;; AUTHORITY SECTION:
mit.edu.           18948   IN     NS     STRAWB.mit.edu.
mit.edu.           18948   IN     NS     BITSY.mit.edu.
mit.edu.           18948   IN     NS     W20NS.mit.edu.

;; ADDITIONAL SECTION:
BITSY.mit.edu.      6846   IN     A      18.72.0.3
W20NS.mit.edu.     18948   IN     A      18.70.0.160
STRAWB.mit.edu.    18948   IN     A      18.71.0.151

;; Query time: 159 msec
;; SERVER: 192.168.0.1#53(192.168.0.1)
;; WHEN: Tue Nov 23 13:43:18 2004
;; MSG SIZE  rcvd: 186

root@1[root]#
```

Figure 4-16   Using the Dig command

4. Do the transfer again, but this time use the |less parameter by typing **dig @BITSY.mit.edu mit.edu axfr |less** and pressing **Enter**.

5. Press **Enter** or the **spacebar** to view additional records, and then press **q** to quit.

6. To do the same zone transfer with the Host command, type **host –l –v –t any mit.edu** and press **Enter**.

7. How many records is the DNS server responsible for? (*Hint:* You can run the command without the |less parameter and wait until the summary page is displayed.)

8. When you're finished viewing the records, close the shell and shut down your Linux system.

The tools you've just learned about aren't the only way to get information. Sometimes information about a company is gathered by using nontechnical skills. In fact, the best hackers aren't necessarily the most technically adept people. Instead, they possess a more insidious—and often underestimated—skill called social engineering, discussed in the following section.

INTRODUCTION TO SOCIAL ENGINEERING

The art of social engineering has been around much longer than computers. **Social engineering** means using a knowledge of human nature to get information from people. In computer attacks, the information is usually a password to a network or other information an attacker could use to compromise a network. A salesperson can get personal information about customers, such as income, hobbies, social life, drinking habits, music preferences, and the like, just by asking the customer the right questions. A salesperson uses charm and sometimes guile to relax customers. In a sense, a salesperson attempts to bond with customers by pretending to be empathetic with them. After leaving the store, customers might regret some of the information they freely gave, but if the salesperson was personable, they might not think twice about the personal information the salesperson elicited. Social engineers might also use persuasion tactics, intimidation, coercion, extortion, and even blackmail to gather the information they need. They are probably the biggest security threat to networks and the most difficult to protect against.

You have probably heard the saying "Why try to crack a password when you can simply ask for it?" Many attackers do just that: They ask for it. Unfortunately, many users give attackers everything they need to break into a network. Anyone who has worked at a help desk or in network support knows this to be true. Even if a company policy states that passwords must not be given to anyone, users often think this policy doesn't apply to IT personnel. How many times have users said their passwords out loud when an IT technician is seated in front of their computers? IT personnel don't want to know a user's password. They especially don't want a user to say it aloud or on the telephone or to type it in e-mails. Yet users often don't consider their company passwords private, so they don't guard passwords as they might PINs for their ATM cards. They might not think that what they have on their company's computers is important or would be of interest to an attacker. Social engineers know how to put these types of users at ease. The following is an example of a typical social-engineering tactic:

First, the social engineer poses as "Mike," a name he found after performing a zone transfer and examining the company's DNS server. Mike might not be the current IT point of contact (POC), but it doesn't matter. Depending on the company's size, most users often don't know everyone on the IT staff. The social engineer then places a call for Sue, an employee name he found from the zone transfer information and several company Web pages that showed the format of e-mail addresses. To get the phone number, he simply calls the company's main switchboard and asks for Sue. Then he says he wants to leave a message for Sue and asks to be directed to her voicemail. "Sue's in the office now," replies the friendly receptionist. "Would you like me to connect you to her?" The social engineer says "Darn, my other line is ringing. I misplaced her extension. Can you please give me her extension number and I'll call her back in a few minutes? I really have to get that call."

In this exchange, his tactic is to create a sense of urgency yet remain cordial. It usually works because most receptionists don't see a problem with connecting a caller to an employee or giving an employee's direct number or extension. After all, the caller knows Sue's name and seems to know her. "Extension 4100," the receptionist says. "Thanks! Gotta go," the social engineer replies.

After 30 minutes or so, the social engineer calls the company again. "Hello. Extension 4101, please," he asks. The receptionist connects him, and a man answers "Bob Smith, Accounting." "Sorry, Bob. Mike here. I was calling Sue, but I guess I got your extension by mistake. Sue was having a problem connecting to the Internet, so we're checking IP address information. We just fixed her system. Are you also having a problem?" Bob says "It looks like only the accounting department is having a problem with the VLAN config." Mike then asks, "Still running Windows XP?" Bob answers no, but tells Mike which operating system he's using. Bob probably feels as though he knows Mike, even though he doesn't.

Another way to find out how the IT staff operates is for Mike to pose as Bob and call in with a question or problem he's having. Mike would then learn how the help desk person handles the call. Does the help desk issue a help ticket? Does Bob have to give any information to the caller other than his name and phone number? Many help desk offices require assigning a unique number to the help call until the problem is solved.

The social engineer used Sue's name to give his call more credibility. Also, because he had gathered information about the operating system through other means, he took advantage of that knowledge, as shown by his Windows XP question. Mike might try to go for the kill now, or he might decide to attempt the final attack with Sue. If he calls her, he can talk about Bob as though they're old friends. What he wants is Bob or Sue's password. He might try the following ploy: "Bob, there's a good chance we'll have to shut down accounting's network connectivity for an hour or so. I could reduce this time for your system to five minutes if I could work on the problem from here. Only problem is I need your password. I already have your logon account as bsmith@kjwilliams.com. Is that correct?" Chances are good that Bob will give his password to Mike over the telephone.

Not all social engineering takes place on the telephone, but it's probably the most common method because it's anonymous and allows the social engineer to carry out multiple attacks in the same organization. This can be more difficult if one or two employees hear different stories from the same person. However, a well-dressed person carrying a clipboard can also be successful in gathering information from employees. This approach requires more courage because the social engineer has to face the people from whom he's attempting to gather information.

Social engineers study human behavior. They can recognize personality traits, such as shyness or insecurity, and understand how to read body language: slouched shoulders, avoidance of eye contact, nervous fidgeting, and so on. If the ploy is conducted over the telephone, the person's tone of voice can give the social engineer clues. Many profess to practice on people they date or try to get useless information from unsuspecting victims just to hone their skills. Like a tiger seeking out the weakest gazelle in the herd, social engineers can identify the most vulnerable person in an organization. They know who to approach and who to avoid.

Security Bytes

The most difficult job of a security professional is preventing social engineers from getting crucial information from company employees. No matter how thorough a security policy is or how much money is spent on firewalls and intrusion detection systems (IDSs), employees are still the weakest link in an organization. Attackers know this fact and use it. Employees must be trained and tested periodically on security practices. Just as fire drills help prepare people to evacuate during a fire, random security drills can improve a company's security practices. For example, randomly selecting and testing employees each month to see whether they would give their passwords to someone within or outside the organization is a good way to see if your security memos are being read and followed.

Social engineers use many different techniques in their attempts to gain information from unsuspecting people:

- *Urgency*—"I need the information now or the world will come to an end!" For example, a social engineer might tell a user that he needs the information quickly or the network will be down for a long time, thus creating a false sense of urgency.

- *Quid pro quo*—"I can make your life better if you give me the information I need." The social engineer might promise the user faster Internet access, for example, if he or she helps the social engineer.

- *Status quo*—"Everyone else is doing it, so you should, too." By using the names of other employees, a social engineer can easily convince others to reveal their passwords.

- *Kindness*—This tactic is probably the most dangerous weapon social engineers wield. People want to help those who are kind to them. The saying "It's easier to catch flies with honey than with vinegar" also applies to social engineering.

- *Position*—Convincing an employee that you're in a position of authority in the company can be a powerful means of gaining information. This is especially true in the military, where rank has its privileges. Social engineers can claim that a high-ranking officer is asking for the information, so it's imperative that it be given as quickly as possible.

Security Bytes

As a security tester, you should never use social-engineering tactics unless the person who hired you gives you permission in writing. You should also confirm on which employees you're allowed to perform social-engineering tests, and document the tests you conduct. Your documentation should include the responses you received, and all test results should, of course, be confidential. Figures 4-17 and 4-18 show social-engineering templates included in the OSSTMM. You can print them from your copy of the OSSTMM on the book's CD.

It is important to train users not to give outsiders any information about operating systems. Employees should also be taught to confirm that the person asking questions is indeed the person he or she claims to be. Employees shouldn't be embarrassed to ask the person for a company telephone number to call back instead of trusting the person on the other end of the phone line. Simply making employees aware that most hacking is done through social engineering, not computer programming skills, can make them more aware of how attackers operate.

OSSTMM Social Engineering Template

Company	
Company Name	
Company Address	
Company Telephone	
Company Fax	
Company Web Page	
Products and Services	
Primary Contacts	
Departments and Responsibilities	
Company Facilities Location	
Company History	
Partners	
Resellers	
Company Regulations	
Company Info Security Policy	
Company Traditions	
Company Job Postings	
Temporary Employment Availability	
Typical IT Threats	
People	
Employee Information	
Employee Names and Positions	
Employee Place in Hierarchy	
Employee Personal Pages	
Employee Best Contact Methods	
Employee Hobbies	
Employee Internet Traces (SENET, Forums)	
Employee Opinions Expressed	
Employee Friends and Relatives	
Employee History (Including Work History)	
Employee Character Traits	
Employee Values and Priorities	
Employee Social Habits	
Employee Speech and Speaking Patterns	
Employee Gestures and Manners	

Figure 4-17   Social Engineering Template

OSSTMM Social Engineering Telephone Attack Template

Attack Scenario	
Telephone #	
Person	
Description	
Results	

Figure 4-18   Social Engineering Telephone Attack Template

The Art of Shoulder Surfing

Another method social engineers use to gain access to information is **shoulder surfing**. A shoulder surfer is a person skilled at reading what users enter on their keyboards, especially logon names and passwords. This skill certainly takes practice, but with enough time, it can be mastered easily. Shoulder surfers also use this skill to read PINs entered at ATMs or to detect long-distance authorization codes that callers dial. ATM theft is much easier than computer shoulder surfing because a keypad has fewer characters to memorize than a computer keyboard. If the person throws away the receipt in a trash can near the ATM, the shoulder surfer can match the PIN with an account number and then create a fake ATM card. Often shoulder surfers use binoculars or high-powered telescopes to observe PINS being entered, making it difficult to protect against this attack.

Security Bytes

A common tactic of shoulder surfers is using camera cell phones to take photos of unaware shoppers' credit cards in supermarkets and stores. With this technique, they can get the credit card number and expiration date. Combining this technique with observing the shopper entering his or her PIN increases the risk of identity theft.

Many keyboard users don't follow the traditional fingering technique taught in typing classes. Instead, they hunt and peck using two or three fingers. However, shoulder surfers train themselves to memorize key positions on a standard keyboard. Armed with this knowledge, they can determine which keys are being pressed by noticing the location on the keyboard, not which finger the typist is using.

Shoulder surfers also know the popular letter substitutions most people use when creating passwords: s equals $, a equals @, i equals 1, o equals 0, and so forth. Many users think p@$$w0rd is difficult to guess, but it's not for a skilled shoulder surfer. In addition, many users are required to use passwords containing special characters, and often they type these passwords more slowly to make sure they enter the correct characters. Slower typing makes a shoulder surfer's job easier.

Security Bytes

With so many people taking their laptops to the airport, commercial airlines warn customers to be aware of shoulder surfers. In the tight confines of an airplane, someone could easily observe the keys pressed and read the data on a laptop monitor. Products that prevent off-axis viewing of screens, such as screen overlays or a security lens, are recommended for travelers. Many employees conduct business on airplanes, and shoulder surfers can use the information gathered there to compromise computer systems at the company.

To help prevent shoulder-surfing attacks, you must educate your users not to type logon names and passwords when someone is standing directly behind them—or even standing nearby. You should also caution users about typing passwords when someone nearby is talking on a cell phone because of the wide availability of camera phones. To further reduce the risk of shoulder surfing, make sure all computer monitors face away from the door or the cubicle entryway. Warn your users to change their passwords immediately if they suspect someone might have observed them entering their passwords.

4

NOTE

Security Bytes

When you're entering your long-distance access code at a pay phone, a shoulder surfer holding a calculator while "talking" on the next phone can simply enter each number you have dialed into his calculator. With this method, he doesn't have to memorize a long sequence of numbers. The calculator entry contains the access code he needs to place a long-distance call charged to your phone card.

The Art of Dumpster Diving

Another method social engineers use to gain access to information is **dumpster diving**. Although it's certainly not a glamorous form of gathering information, you'd be surprised at what you can find by examining someone's trash. For example, discarded computer manuals can indicate what OS is being used. If the discarded manual is for Windows NT 4.0, there's a good chance the newer system is a Microsoft OS, such as Windows Server 2003. Sometimes network administrators write notes in manuals or even jot down passwords, and social engineers can make use of this information.

Company telephone directories are another source of information. A dumpster diver who finds a directory listing company employees can use this information to pose as an employee for the purpose of gathering information. Company calendars with meeting schedules, employee vacation schedules, and so on can be used to gain access to offices that won't be occupied for a specified time period. Trash can be worth its weight in gold for the dumpster diver who knows what to do with it. Here are some other items that can be useful to dumpster divers:

- Financial reports
- Interoffice memos
- Discarded computer programs
- Company organizational charts showing managers' names
- Resumes of employees
- Company policy or systems and procedures manuals
- Professional journals or magazines
- Utility bills
- Solicitation notices from outside vendors
- Regional manager reports
- Quality assurance reports
- Risk management reports
- Minutes of meetings
- Federal, state, or city reports

Dumpster diving can produce a tremendous amount of information, so it is important to educate your users on the importance of proper trash disposal. Disks or hard drives containing company information should be formatted with software that writes binary zeros to all portions of the disks. This should be done at least seven times to ensure that all previous data is unreadable. Old computer manuals should be discarded offsite so that dumpster divers can't associate the manuals with the company. Before disposal, all these items should be placed in a locked room with adequate physical, administrative, and technical safeguards. All documents should be shredded, even if the information seems innocuous. Social engineers know how to pull together information from many different sources. Putting a puzzle together from many small pieces makes it possible for attackers to break into a network.

The Art of Piggybacking

Sometimes security testers need to enter part of a building that's restricted to authorized personnel. In this case, a tester or an attacker uses a technique called **piggybacking**. Piggybacking is trailing closely behind an employee who has access to an area without the person realizing that you didn't use a PIN or a security badge to enter the area. Those skilled in piggybacking watch authorized personnel enter secure areas and wait for the opportune time to quickly join them at the security entrance. They count on human nature and the desire of others to be polite to hold open a secured door. This ploy usually works, especially if the piggybacker has both hands full and seems to be struggling to remove an access card from a purse or pants pocket. Some piggybackers wear a fake badge around their necks or pretend to scan a security card across a card reader. If they are detected, they might say their card has been giving them problems and use their social-engineering skills to convince the security guard to let them through.

NOTE

Security Bytes

A well-dressed security tester walked into a hospital with a wireless laptop and sat down in the waiting area adjacent to the nurses' station. He was able to access passwords and logon information on his laptop and collected data for more than a week without being questioned by security or hospital personnel. In fact, the security tester felt as though he was invisible. Doctors, nurses, administrators, and other hospital personnel never questioned the presence of the stranger in their midst, even though he had covered most of the waiting room table with legal pads and his laptop. After the security test was completed, it was determined that everyone thought the stranger was working for someone else in the area. No one felt responsible for finding out who the stranger was and why he was there.

ACTIVITY

Activity 4-7: Learning Piggybacking Skills

Time Required: 30 minutes

Objective: Learn how piggybacking can be used to gain access to restricted areas.

Description: In this activity, you learn the piggybacking skills used to gain access to areas restricted to authorized personnel. Assume you're conducting a security test and need access to a company's server room. To enter the room, you must scan an access card over a card reader, and then push open a door within several seconds, during which time a bell rings softly. If the door isn't opened in the allotted time, the card must be swiped again. Form teams of two and demonstrate to the class how you would use piggybacking to get into the classroom if it was secured. One student should pretend to be an authorized user while the other student uses piggybacking techniques to gain entry.

A good preventive measure against piggybacking is the use of turnstiles at areas where piggybacking can occur. However, the best preventive measure is to train personnel to notify security when they notice a stranger in a restricted area. Employees must feel a vested interest in area security and should not rely on security personnel. Employees should be taught not to hold secured doors open for anyone, even people they know. Educate your users to get in the habit of making sure all employees use their access cards to gain entry into a restricted area and to report any suspicious or unknown people to security.

CHAPTER SUMMARY

- ❑ Footprinting is the process of gathering network information with Web tools and utilities. Some of the Web tools used to gather information about a network infrastructure include Whois.arin.net, Namedroppers, Google, and the Host and Dig commands.

- ❑ Corporate information can be obtained by using competitive intelligence gathered through observation and Web tools.

- ❑ IP addresses and domain names can be obtained by using tools such as SamSpade and the Dig and Host commands.

- ❑ Security testers must be aware of how cookies and Web bugs can be used to retrieve information and access data without a user's knowledge.

- ❑ Zone transfers can be used to obtain a network's topology and to view all the network's host computers and domains.

- ❑ Social engineering is the ability to use an understanding of human nature to get information from unsuspecting people.

- ❑ Social engineers use many methods to convince users to give them information, such as creating a false sense of urgency, pretending to have a position of authority, being kind and friendly, offering something in return for complying with the request, or giving the impression that everyone else has complied with the request.

- ❑ Educating company personnel about social-engineering attacks is important, but random testing can also be done to ensure that employees are following company policies.

- ❑ Attackers use techniques such as shoulder surfing, dumpster diving, and piggybacking to obtain confidential information.

KEY TERMS

competitive intelligence — A means of gathering information about a business or an industry by using observation, accessing public computer information, speaking with employees, and so on.

cookie — A text file containing a message sent from a Web server to a user's Web browser to be used later when the user revisits the Web site.

dumpster diving — Gathering information by examining the physical trash that people thoughtlessly discard.

footprinting — Gathering information about a company before performing a security test or an attack.

piggybacking — A method attackers use to gain access to restricted areas in a company. The attacker closely follows an employee and enters the area with that employee.

shoulder surfing — The ability of an attacker to observe the keys a user types when entering a password by simply looking over the unaware user's shoulder.

social engineering —Using an understanding of human nature to obtain information from people.

Web bug — A small graphic image referenced in an <IMG> tag. This image is created by a third-party company specializing in data collection.

zone transfer — A method of transferring records from a DNS server to use in analysis of a network.

REVIEW QUESTIONS

1. Which of the following is a fast and easy way to gather information about a company? (Choose all that apply.)

   a. Conduct port scanning.

   b. Perform a zone transfer of the company's DNS server.

   c. View the company's Web site.

   d. Look for company ads in phone directories.

2. To find information about the key IT personnel responsible for a company's domain, you might use which of the following tools? (Choose all that apply.)

   a. Whois

   b. Whatis

   c. SamSpade

   d. Nbtstat

3. _____ is one of the components most vulnerable to network attacks.

   a. TCP/IP

   b. WINS

   c. DHCP

   d. DNS

4. Which of the following contains host records for a domain?

   a. DNS

   b. WINS

   c. Linux server

   d. UNIX Web clients

5. Which of the following is a good Web site for gathering information on a domain?

   a. *www.google.com*

   b. *www.namedroppers.com*

   c. *www.samspade.org*

   d. *www.arin.net*

   e. all of the above

6. A cookie can store information about a Web site's visitors. True or False?

7. List three tools you can use to find IP address information.

8. What is one way to gather information about a domain?

   a. View the header of an e-mail you send to an e-mail account that doesn't exist.

   b. Run the Ipconfig command.

   c. Run the Ifconfig command.

   d. Connect via Telnet to TCP port 53.

9. Which of the following is one method of gathering information about the operating systems a company is using?

   a. Search the Web for e-mail addresses of IT employees.

   b. Connect via Telnet to the company's Web server.

   c. Ping the URL and analyze ICMP messages.

   d. Use the Ipconfig /os command.

10. Which of the following commands displays information about the primary DNS server for the mit. edu domain?

    a. host –t mit.edu

    b. host –t soa mit.edu

    c. host –t prim mit.edu

    d. host –t all mit.edu

11. When conducting competitive intelligence, which of the following is a good way to determine the size of a company's IT support staff?

    a. Review job postings on Web sites such as *www.monster.com* or *www.dice.com.*

    b. Use the Nslookup command.

    c. Perform a zone transfer of the company's DNS server.

    d. Use the host –t command.

12. If you're trying to find newsgroup postings by IT employees of a certain company, which of the following Web sites should you visit?

    a. *groups.google.com*

    b. *www.google.com*

    c. *www.samspade.com*

    d. *www.arin.org*

13. Which of the following tools can assist you in finding information about an organization and its employees? (Choose all that apply.)

    a. *www.google.com*

    b. *groups.google.com*

    c. Netcat

    d. Nmap

14. What is the first method a security tester should attempt to obtain a password for a computer on the network?

    a. Use a scanning tool.

    b. Install a sniffer on the network.

    c. Ask the user.

    d. Install a password-cracking program.

15. Most social engineers use _____ to gather the information they need.

    a. the Internet

    b. the telephone

    c. a company intranet

    d. e-mail

16. Obtaining a user's password by observing the keys he or she presses is called which of the following?

    a. password hashing

    b. password crunching

    c. piggybacking

    d. shoulder surfing

17. Shoulder surfers can use their skills to find which of the following pieces of information? (Choose all that apply.)

    a. passwords

    b. ATM PINs

    c. long-distance access codes

    d. open port numbers

18. Entering a restricted area of a company by following closely behind an authorized person is referred to as _____ .

    a. shoulder surfing

    b. piggybacking

    c. false entering

    d. social engineering

19. What social-engineering technique involves telling an employee that you're calling from the CEO's office and need certain information ASAP? (Choose all that apply.)

    a. urgency

    b. status quo

    c. position of authority

    d. quid pro quo

20. Before conducting a security test using social-engineering tactics, what should you do?

    a. Set up an appointment.

    b. Document all findings.

    c. Get written permission from the person who hired you to conduct the security test.

    d. Get written permission from the department head.

CASE PROJECTS

CASE PROJECTS

Case 4-1: Using an E-mail Address to Determine the Operating System

K. J. Williams Corporation has multiple operating systems running in its many offices. Before conducting a security test to determine the vulnerabilities you need to correct, you want to determine whether any operating systems are running that you're not aware of. Network Administrator/Security Officer Mike Constantine is resistant to giving you information after he learns you're there to discover network security vulnerabilities. He sees you as a threat to his position. After several hours of interviews, you can ascertain only that Mike's personal e-mail address is mtscon@aloha.net and that Oracle8*i* is running on one of the company's systems.

Based on the preceding information, answer the following questions:

1. What tools might you use after learning Mr. Constantine's e-mail address?

2. What did you determine after entering Mr. Constantine's e-mail address in the *groups.google.com* Web site?

3. Could the information you learned from *groups.google.com* be used to conduct vulnerability testing or exploits?

Write a memo to the IT chief informing her of the possibility of a NetWare server being part of the company's network infrastructure. Make sure your memo explains how this information was obtained and ensure that it offers constructive feedback. Your memo should not point a finger at any company employees; rather, it should discuss the problems on a general level.

Case 4-2: Using Dumpster-diving Skills

You have observed that K. J. Williams Corporation uses Alika's Cleaning Company for its janitorial services. The company's floors are vacuumed and mopped each night, and the trash is collected in large bins that are placed outside for pickup on Tuesdays and Fridays. You decide to visit the dumpster Thursday evening after the cleaning crew leaves the facility. Wearing surgical gloves and carrying a large plastic sheet, you place as much of the trash onto the sheet as possible. Sorting through the material, you find the following items: a company telephone directory; a Windows NT complete training kit; 23 outdated Oracle magazines; notes that appear to be computer programs written in HTML, containing links to a SQL Server database; 15 company memos from key employees; food wrappers; an empty bottle of expensive vodka; torn copies of several resumes; an unopened box of new business cards; and an old pair of women's running shoes.

Based on the preceding information, write a two-page report explaining the relevance these items have. What recommendations, if any, might you give to K. J. Williams management?

5

PORT SCANNING

After reading this chapter and completing the exercises, you will be able to:

♦ Describe port scanning

♦ Describe different types of port scans

♦ Describe various port-scanning tools

♦ Explain what ping sweeps are used for

♦ Explain how shell scripting is used to automate security tasks

Port scanning, also referred to as service scanning, is the process of scanning a range of IP addresses to determine what services are running on a network. As you learned in Chapter 2, the open ports on a computer identify the services running on that computer. For example, HTTP uses port 80 to connect to a Web service. Instead of pinging each IP address in an IP address range and waiting for an ICMP Echo Reply (type 0) to see whether a computer can be reached, you can use scanning tools to simplify this procedure. After all, manually pinging several thousand IP addresses is time consuming.

Port-scanning tools can be complex, so you need to devote time to learning their strengths and weaknesses and understanding how and when you should use these tools. In this chapter, you look at port-scanning tools that enable you to identify services running on a network and use this knowledge to conduct a security test.

INTRODUCTION TO PORT SCANNING

In Chapter 4, you performed a zone transfer using the Dig command to determine the IP addresses of a network. Suppose the zone transfer indicated that a company is using a subnetted Class C address with 126 available host IP addresses. How do you verify whether all those addresses are being used by computers that are up and running? You use a port scanner to ping the range of IP addresses you discovered.

A more important question a security tester should ask is, "What services are running on the computers that were successfully pinged?" **Port scanning** is a method of finding out which services a host computer offers. For example, if a server is hosting a Web site, is it likely that the server has port 80 open? Are any of the services vulnerable to attacks or exploits? Are any services not being filtered by a firewall, thus making it possible to load a Trojan program that can send information from the attacked computer? Which computer is most vulnerable to an attack? You already know how to search for known vulnerabilities by using the Common Vulnerabilities and Exposures Web site (*www.cve.mitre.org*). There are also port-scanning tools that identify vulnerabilities. For example, AW Security Port Scanner (*www.atelierweb.com*), a reasonably priced commercial scanner with a GUI interface (see Figure 5-1), shows the type of Trojan known to operate on a particular port. Using this tool, an attacker can quickly identify a vulnerable port and then launch an exploit to attack the system.

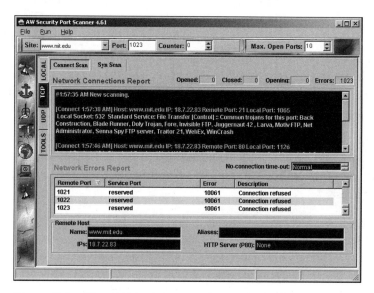

Figure 5-1   The AW Security Port Scanner interface

As a security tester, you need to know which ports attackers are going after so those ports can be closed or protected. Security professionals must scan all ports when doing a test, not just the well-known ports (ports 1 to 1023, the most common, are covered in Chapter 2). Many computer programs use port numbers outside the range of well-known ports. For example, pcAnywhere operates on ports 65301, 22, 5631, and 5632. A hacker who discovers that port 65301 is open might want to check the information at the Common Vulnerabilities and Exposures Web site for a possible vulnerability in pcAnywhere. After a hacker discovers an open service, finding a vulnerability or exploit isn't too difficult.

Security Bytes

NOTE

Most security testers and hackers argue that port scanning is legal simply because it doesn't invade others' privacy; it merely discovers whether the party being scanned is available. The typical analogy is a person walking down the street and turning the doorknob of every house along the way. If the door opens, the person notes that the door is open and proceeds to the next house. Of course, entering the house would be a crime in most parts of the world, just as entering a computer system or network without the owner's permission is a crime.

Port scanning helps you answer questions about open ports and services by enabling you to quickly scan thousands or even tens of thousands of IP addresses. Many port-scanning tools produce reports of their findings, and some give you best-guess assessments of which OS is running on a system. Most, if not all, scanning programs report **open ports**, **closed ports**, and **filtered ports** in a matter of seconds. When a Web server needs to communicate with applications or other computers, for example, port 80 is opened. An open port allows access to applications and can be vulnerable to an attack. A closed port does not allow entry or access to a service. For instance, if port 80 is closed on a Web server, users wouldn't be able to access Web sites. A scanner that reports a port as filtered might indicate that a firewall is being used to allow specified traffic in or out of the network.

5

TYPES OF PORT SCANS

Before delving into using port-scanning tools, take a look at the types of scans that can be used for port scanning:

- *SYN scan*—In a normal TCP session, a packet is sent to another computer with the SYN flag set. The receiving computer sends back a packet with the SYN/ACK flag set, indicating an acknowledgment. The sending computer then sends a packet with the ACK flag set. If the port to which the SYN packet is sent is closed, the computer responds to the SYN packet with an RST/ACK packet. If a SYN/ACK packet is received by an attacker's computer, it quickly responds with an RST/ACK packet, closing the session. This is done so that a full TCP connection is never made and logged as a transaction. In this sense, it is "stealthy." After all, you don't want a transaction to be logged showing the IP address that connected to the attacked computer.

- *Connect scan*—This type of scan relies on the OS of the attacked computer, so it's a little more risky to use. A connect scan is similar to the SYN scan, except that it does complete the three-way handshake. This means the attacked computer most likely logs the transaction or connection, indicating that a session took place. Therefore, unlike a SYN scan, a connect scan is not stealthy and is easily detected.

- *NULL scan*—In a NULL scan, all the packet flags are turned off. A closed port responds to a NULL scan with an RST packet, so if no packet is received, the best guess is that the port is open.

- *XMAS scan*—In this type of scan, the FIN, PSH, and URG flags are set. (Refer to Chapter 2 for a review of the different flags.) Closed ports respond to this type of packet with an RST packet. This scan can be used to determine which ports are open. An attacker could send this packet to port 53 on a system and see whether an RST packet is returned. If not, the DNS port might be open.

- *ACK scan*—Attackers typically use ACK scans to get past a firewall (or other filtering device). A filtering device looks for the SYN packet, the first packet in the three-way handshake, that the ACK packet was part of. Remember this packet order: SYN, SYN/ACK, and ACK. If the attacked port returns an RST packet, the packet filter was fooled, or there's no packet-filtering device. In either case, the attacked port is considered to be "unfiltered."

- *FIN scan*—In this type of scan, a FIN packet is sent to the target computer. If the port is closed, it sends back an RST packet. When a three-way handshake ends, both parties send a FIN packet to end the connection.

- *UDP scan*—In this type of scan, a UDP packet is sent to the target computer. If the port sends back an ICMP "Port Unreachable" message, the port is closed. Again, not getting that message might imply the port is open, but this isn't always true. A firewall or packet-filtering device could undermine your assumptions.

A computer that receives a SYN packet from a remote computer responds to the packet with a SYN/ACK packet if its port is open. Recall that in a three-way handshake, the SYN packet is sent from one computer, a SYN/ACK is sent from the receiving computer back to the sender, and finally, the sender sends an ACK packet to the receiving computer. If a port is closed and it receives a SYN packet, it sends back an RST/ACK packet. Determining whether a port is filtered is more complex. Many scanning tools, such as Nmap, use a best-guess approach. That is, if a UDP packet doesn't receive a response from the receiving port, many scanning tools report that the port is open.

Security Bytes

NOTE

In one case in Canada, a man was charged and found guilty of scanning a company's computers. The company actually prosecuted him for using micro-watts of its power for him to perform the scan. Using the company's electric power without the company's permission was considered a crime—petty, yes, but effective. To play it safe, it's wise to get permission from a company if you're going to perform an intensive scan on its network infrastructure. If your scan slows down a network's traffic, the company might argue that a low-level DoS attack was performed. As you know, this type of attack is illegal.

USING PORT-SCANNING TOOLS

Hundreds of port-scanning tools are available for both hackers and security testers. Some are commercial, and some are freeware or open source. How do you decide which tool to use? Not all are accurate, so using more than one port-scanning tool is recommended. In addition, becoming familiar with a variety of tools is wise. Although you should practice often with a tool to gain proficiency in using it, don't fall into the trap of using one tool exclusively.

Nmap

Originally written for *Phrack* magazine in 1997 by Fyodor, **Nmap** has become one of the most popular port scanners available and constantly adds features, such as OS detection and fast multiple-probe ping scanning. Nmap also has a GUI version called Xnmap that makes it easier to work with some of the complex options. Nmap has been modified and enhanced over the years because, like many other security tools, it's open source. If bugs are found, users can offer suggestions for correcting them.

Nmap is referred to many times in this book because it's currently the standard tool for security professionals. Regardless of the other port-scanning tools available, any security tester with a modicum of experience has worked with Nmap. As a beginning student, you can use it for every part of a security or penetration test, but remember to build proficiency in all the tools discussed in this book.

Security Bytes

NOTE

As most security professionals will tell you, Hollywood seldom depicts attackers actually hacking into a system. They are usually using a GUI program, frantically clicking the mouse or typing a decryption algorithm. One exception is *The Matrix Reloaded*. The female protagonist, Trinity, sits in front of a computer terminal and runs Nmap. She discovers that port 22 (SSH) is opened, runs an SSHv1 CRC32 exploit (an actual bug in SSH) that allows her to change the root password to "Z1ON0101," and then proceeds to shut down the grid. Moral of the story? Know your tools and exploits, and you might save the world.

You won't have to memorize how each flag is set when performing a port scan with Nmap. In fact, just typing the command nmap 193.145.85.201 scans every port on the computer with that IP address. However, port scanning can be an involved process. Some attackers want to be hidden from network devices or IDSs that recognize an inordinate amount of pings or packets being sent to their networks, so they use stealth attacks that are more difficult to detect. In the following activities, you become familiar with the basic Nmap command and then learn some of the more complex options.

Activity 5-1: Getting to Know Nmap

ACTIVITY

Time Required: 30 minutes

Objective: Learn the basic commands and syntax of Nmap.

Description: In this activity, you're introduced to using Nmap, a popular port scanner, to see how it's used to do quick scans of a network. You send a SYN packet to a host on the attack network your instructor has supplied. In this example, the attack network IP addresses are 193.145.85.201 to 193.145.85.211, but your attack range might be different. Please follow all the rules of engagement, and do not perform port scanning on any systems not included in the IP range your instructor has given you.

1. Start your Windows XP Professional system with the Linux CD. Open a shell of your choice, and enter the command **nmap –h**. Your screen should look like Figure 5-2.

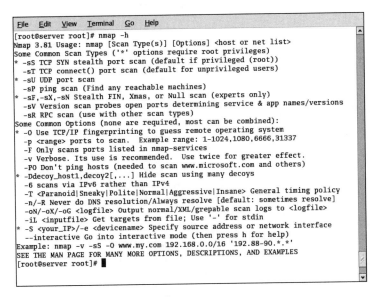

```
File  Edit  View  Terminal  Go  Help
[root@server root]# nmap -h
Nmap 3.81 Usage: nmap [Scan Type(s)] [Options] <host or net list>
Some Common Scan Types ('*' options require root privileges)
* -sS TCP SYN stealth port scan (default if privileged (root))
  -sT TCP connect() port scan (default for unprivileged users)
* -sU UDP port scan
  -sP ping scan (Find any reachable machines)
* -sF,-sX,-sN Stealth FIN, Xmas, or Null scan (experts only)
  -sV Version scan probes open ports determining service & app names/versions
  -sR RPC scan (use with other scan types)
Some Common Options (none are required, most can be combined):
* -O Use TCP/IP fingerprinting to guess remote operating system
  -p <range> ports to scan.  Example range: 1-1024,1080,6666,31337
  -F Only scans ports listed in nmap-services
  -v Verbose. Its use is recommended.  Use twice for greater effect.
  -P0 Don't ping hosts (needed to scan www.microsoft.com and others)
* -Ddecoy_host1,decoy2[,...] Hide scan using many decoys
  -6 scans via IPv6 rather than IPv4
  -T <Paranoid|Sneaky|Polite|Normal|Aggressive|Insane> General timing policy
  -n/-R Never do DNS resolution/Always resolve [default: sometimes resolve]
  -oN/-oX/-oG <logfile> Output normal/XML/grepable scan logs to <logfile>
  -iL <inputfile> Get targets from file; Use '-' for stdin
* -S <your_IP>/-e <devicename> Specify source address or network interface
  --interactive Go into interactive mode (then press h for help)
Example: nmap -v -sS -O www.my.com 192.168.0.0/16 '192.88-90.*.*'
SEE THE MAN PAGE FOR MANY MORE OPTIONS, DESCRIPTIONS, AND EXAMPLES
[root@server root]# 
```

Figure 5-2   The Nmap Help screen

2. The Nmap Help screen lists the available commands. After reviewing the parameters, write down three options that can be used with the Nmap command.

3. To send a SYN packet to one of the IP addresses in your assigned IP range, type **nmap –sS –v 193.145.85.201** and press **Enter**. What were the results of your SYN scan?

4. Next, try sending a new SYN packet to a different IP address in your attack range. What are the results of this new scan? Did you see any differences? If so, list them.

5. Nmap can scan through a range of IP addresses, so manually entering one IP address at a time isn't necessary. To send a SYN packet to each IP address in your attack range, type **nmap –sS –v 193.145.85.201–211** and press **Enter**. To see the output in a format you can scroll, press the **up arrow** key and add the **|less** option to the end of your Nmap command. The command should look like this: nmap –sS –v 193.145.85.201–211 |less.

6. Next, add one more parameter to your Nmap command to determine which computers in your IP address range have the SMTP service or HTTP service running. Using what you've learned so far in this activity, enter the command and note the output. (*Hint:* What ports do SMTP and HTTP use?) The command's output might vary, but what's important is to learn how to build on the Nmap command. You can select specific ports in your Nmap command, so not all 65,000 ports have to be scanned.

7. Leave the Linux shell open for the next activity.

5

Security Bytes

A security professional came to work one evening and noticed that the company's firewall had crashed because someone ran a port-scanning program on the network using ACK packets. Many attackers use ACK scans to bypass packet-filtering devices (such as firewalls, discussed in Chapter 13). In this case, the company's firewall was disabled when flooded with tens of thousands of ACK packets bombarding its stateful routing tables. This ACK scan was a DoS attack on the network. Remember that DoS attacks are illegal, so don't get complacent when running port scans on networks. Always have the network owner's written permission before doing a port scan.

Activity 5-2: Using Additional Nmap Commands

Time Required: 30 minutes

Objective: Perform more complex port-scanning attacks with Nmap.

Description: In this activity, you continue to use Nmap to do port scanning on your attack network. You add to the parameters used in Activity 5-1 and send FIN, XMAS, and ACK packets to selected ports. You should practice these commands until they are second nature, but Fyodor developed a well-written help page (called a "man page" in UNIX circles) that you can use as a helpful resource. You begin this activity by looking at this help page.

1. If you're not already in a Linux shell, start your Windows XP Professional system with your Linux CD. Start any shell of your choosing, and at the command prompt, type **man nmap**. You can see that this command produces more information than the Nmap –h command. Don't be overwhelmed. You don't have to memorize the manual; just know it's there when you need it.

2. Open another shell so that you can run Tcpdump, which allows you to see the traffic generated from the packets you're creating. Like Ethereal, Tcpdump is a protocol packet analyzer and is included on the book's CD. You might want to get into the habit of having Tcpdump running in the background in a different shell. Type **tcpdump –h** in the new window, and press **Enter** to view the parameters you can use with this command.

3. You can type man tcpdump to examine this tool's help manual, but that isn't necessary now. Just type **tcpdump** and press **Enter**. Your network adapter card is now listening for traffic over the network.

4. Referring to the Nmap help pages for guidance, enter the command for sending a FIN packet to five of the computers in your IP attack range. Look at the traffic generated from your FIN scan. What responses did your computer receive, if any?

5. Next, enter the command to send an XMAS packet to the same five computers selected in the FIN scan. What are the results?

6. Finally, enter the Nmap command for sending an ACK packet to the same five computers. What responses did your computer receive, if any?

7. Close all shells.

Unicornscan

A new kid on the block, Unicornscan was developed in 2004 to assist security testers in conducting tests on large networks and to consolidate many of the tools needed for large-scale endeavors. The developers thought that many current products were too slow to scan thousands of IP addresses. Also, maintaining several security tools can be daunting, so the Unicornscan developers created a product to meet all the needs of security testers.

Unicornscan running on a typical Pentium computer can scan one port on each IP address of a Class B network. That equates to scanning 65,535 computers in three to seven seconds, which brings UDP scanning to a new level. Most scanners using UDP scans make only best guesses when trying to determine whether a port is closed, open, or filtered. As mentioned earlier, UDP scanning has been considered an unreliable method of discovering live systems on a network. Although Unicornscan can handle port scanning using TCP, ICMP, and IP, it optimizes UDP scanning beyond the capabilities of any other port scanner. You can download this software free from *www.unicornscan.org*.

NetScanTools Pro 2004

An entire chapter could be devoted to this robust and easy-to-use commercial port-scanning product, which includes many tools. NetScanTools Pro 2004 should be part of your security toolkit because it offers tools for *NIX systems as well as Windows systems. For more information on this product, visit *www.netscantools.com/ nstpro_nslookup.html*. Many of the features in a command-line utility, such as Nmap, Unicornscan, and the like, are here, but in an easy-to-use GUI interface, shown in Figure 5-3.

The scanning feature is only a small part of this product. Using NetScanTools, you can do security testing in some of the following areas:

- View possible database vulnerabilities.
- View e-mail account vulnerabilities.
- Perform DHCP server discovery.
- View IP packets.
- Look up name servers.
- Conduct OS fingerprinting.

With just a right-click on an IP address returned in the scan, you get a long list of options, shown in Figure 5-4.

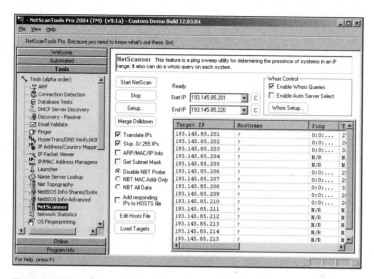

Figure 5-3   The NetScanTools Pro 2004 interface

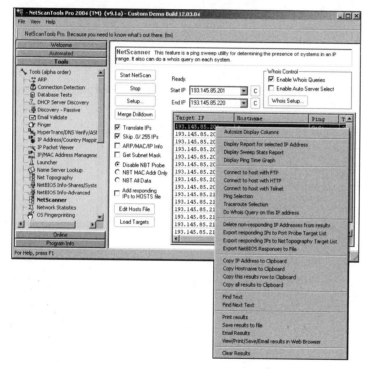

Figure 5-4   Menu of available NetScanTools options

Nessus

Security testers should also investigate **Nessus**, a tool first released in 1998. Like Nmap, Nessus is open source, so you can download it free from *www.nessus.org*. Nessus uses a client/server technology that enables security testers to conduct testing from different locations (servers) within a network and to use different client OSs. The server portion of the product runs on any *NIX platform, but the Nessus client can be UNIX or Windows. Nessus functions much like a database server, performing complex queries while the client interfaces with the server to simplify reporting or configuration.

What makes the product unique is the ability to update security check plug-ins when they become available. (To do this, enter the nessus-update-plugins command at the console.) A Nessus plug-in is a security test program (script) that can be selected from the client interface (see Figure 5-5). The person who writes the plug-in decides whether to designate a plug-in as dangerous, and the plug-in author's judgment on what's considered dangerous might differ from yours. Therefore, clicking the button labeled "Enable all but dangerous plugins" is a wise selection before you start a scan.

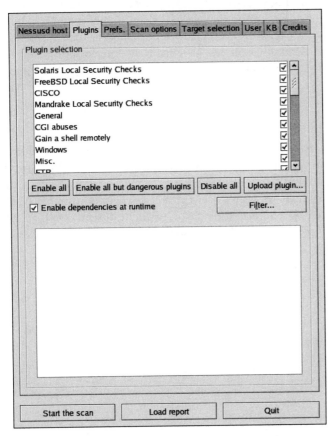

Figure 5-5   Nessus plug-ins

A Nessus scan isn't limited to determining which services are running on a port. Nessus plug-ins can also determine what vulnerabilities are associated with those services, as shown in Figure 5-6. (You use Nessus again in subsequent chapters of this book.)

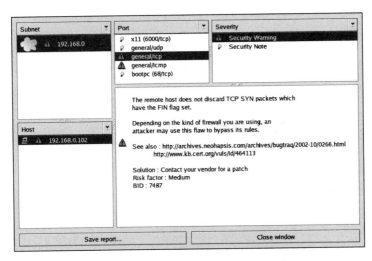

Figure 5-6   Nessus discovers a vulnerability

CONDUCTING PING SWEEPS

Port scanners can also be used to conduct a **ping sweep** of a large network to identify which IP addresses belong to active hosts. In other words, to find out which hosts are "alive," ping sweeps simply ping a range of IP addresses and see what type of response is returned. The problem with relying on ping sweeps to identify live hosts is that a computer might be shut down at the time of the sweep, indicating that the IP address does not belong to a live host. Another problem with ping sweeps is that many network administrators configure nodes to not respond to an ICMP Echo Request (type 8) with an ICMP Echo Reply (type 0). This doesn't mean the computer isn't alive; it just means it isn't replying to the attack computer at that moment. Add to that the possibility of a firewall filtering out ICMP traffic, and you have many reasons for using caution when running ping sweeps. Many tools can be used to conduct a ping sweep of a network, and you learn about some in the following sections.

Fping

With the **Fping** tool, you can ping multiple IP addresses simultaneously. The program can be downloaded free at *www.fping.com/download*. It can accept a range of IP addresses manually entered at a shell, or a file can be created containing multiple IP addresses and used as input to the Fping command. For example, the fping -f ip_address.txt command uses ip_address.txt, which contains a list of IP addresses, as its input file. Most likely, the file is created with a shell-scripting language, so you don't need to type the thousands of IP addresses for a ping sweep on a Class B network, for example. Figure 5-7 shows some parameters you can use with the Fping command.

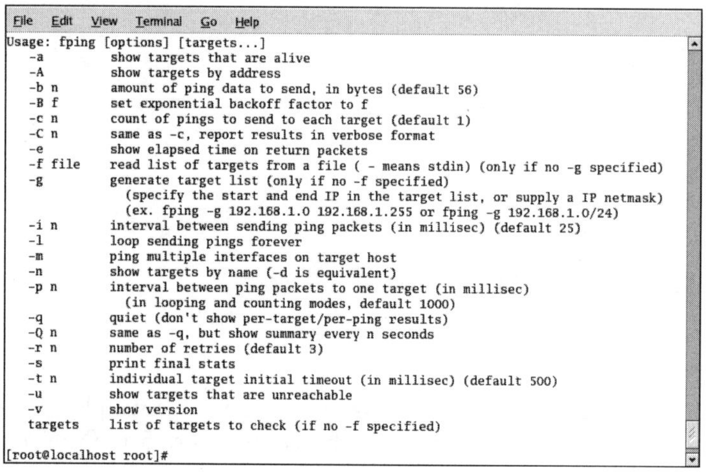

```
File  Edit  View  Terminal  Go  Help
Usage: fping [options] [targets...]
   -a          show targets that are alive
   -A          show targets by address
   -b n        amount of ping data to send, in bytes (default 56)
   -B f        set exponential backoff factor to f
   -c n        count of pings to send to each target (default 1)
   -C n        same as -c, report results in verbose format
   -e          show elapsed time on return packets
   -f file     read list of targets from a file ( - means stdin) (only if no -g specified)
   -g          generate target list (only if no -f specified)
               (specify the start and end IP in the target list, or supply a IP netmask)
               (ex. fping -g 192.168.1.0 192.168.1.255 or fping -g 192.168.1.0/24)
   -i n        interval between sending ping packets (in millisec) (default 25)
   -l          loop sending pings forever
   -m          ping multiple interfaces on target host
   -n          show targets by name (-d is equivalent)
   -p n        interval between ping packets to one target (in millisec)
               (in looping and counting modes, default 1000)
   -q          quiet (don't show per-target/per-ping results)
   -Q n        same as -q, but show summary every n seconds
   -r n        number of retries (default 3)
   -s          print final stats
   -t n        individual target initial timeout (in millisec) (default 500)
   -u          show targets that are unreachable
   -v          show version
   targets     list of targets to check (if no -f specified)

[root@localhost root]#
```

Figure 5-7   Fping parameters

To ping sweep a range of IP addresses without using an input file, you use the command fping -g *BeginningIPaddress Ending IPaddress*. The -g parameter is used when no input file is available. For example, the fping -g 193.145.85.201 193.145.85.220 command returns the results shown in Figure 5-8.

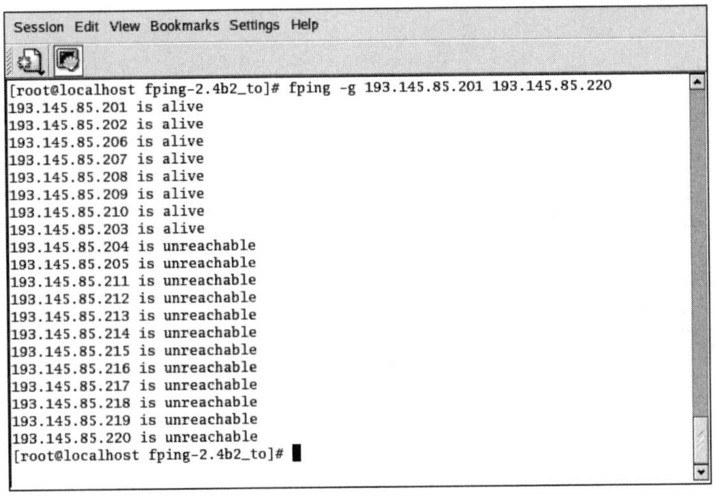

Figure 5-8 Results of an Fping command

Hping

You can also use the **Hping** tool (*www.hping.org/download*) to perform ping sweeps. However, many security testers use it to bypass filtering devices by allowing users to fragment and manipulate IP packets. This tool offers a wealth of features, and security testers should spend as much time as possible learning the intricacies of this advanced port-scanning tool. For a quick overview, type the hping –help | less command at any shell, and browse through some of the parameters you can use (see Figures 5-9, 5-10, and 5-11). As you can see, many parameters can be added to the Hping command, enabling you to craft an IP packet to your liking. In Activity 5-3, you craft an IP packet, and you can refer to these figures when using the Hping tool.

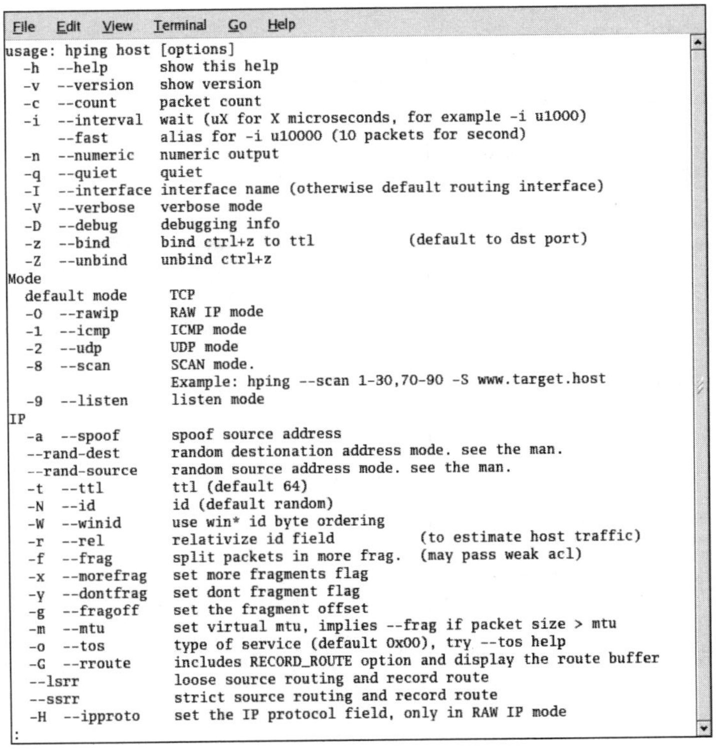

Figure 5-9 Hping help, page 1

```
File   Edit   View   Terminal   Go   Help
ICMP
  -C  --icmptype    icmp type (default echo request)
  -K  --icmpcode    icmp code (default 0)
      --force-icmp  send all icmp types (default send only supported types)
      --icmp-gw     set gateway address for ICMP redirect (default 0.0.0.0)
      --icmp-ts     Alias for --icmp --icmptype 13 (ICMP timestamp)
      --icmp-addr   Alias for --icmp --icmptype 17 (ICMP address subnet mask)
      --icmp-help   display help for others icmp options
UDP/TCP
  -s  --baseport    base source port              (default random)
  -p  --destport    [+][+]<port> destination port(default 0) ctrl+z inc/dec
  -k  --keep        keep still source port
  -w  --win         winsize (default 64)
  -O  --tcpoff      set fake tcp data offset       (instead of tcphdrlen / 4)
  -Q  --seqnum      shows only tcp sequence number
  -b  --badcksum    (try to) send packets with a bad IP checksum
                    many systems will fix the IP checksum sending the packet
                    so you'll get bad UDP/TCP checksum instead.
  -M  --setseq      set TCP sequence number
  -L  --setack      set TCP ack
  -F  --fin         set FIN flag
  -S  --syn         set SYN flag
  -R  --rst         set RST flag
  -P  --push        set PUSH flag
  -A  --ack         set ACK flag
  -U  --urg         set URG flag
  -X  --xmas        set X unused flag (0x40)
  -Y  --ymas        set Y unused flag (0x80)
      --tcpexitcode use last tcp->th_flags as exit code
      --tcp-timestamp enable the TCP timestamp option to guess the HZ/uptime
Common
  -d  --data        data size              (default is 0)
  -E  --file        data from file
  -e  --sign        add 'signature'
  -j  --dump        dump packets in hex
  -J  --print       dump printable characters
  -B  --safe        enable 'safe' protocol
  -u  --end         tell you when --file reached EOF and prevent rewind
  -T  --traceroute  traceroute mode        (implies --bind and --ttl 1)
:
```

Figure 5-10   Hping help, page 2

```
File   Edit   View   Terminal   Go   Help
      --icmp-ts     Alias for --icmp --icmptype 13 (ICMP timestamp)
      --icmp-addr   Alias for --icmp --icmptype 17 (ICMP address subnet mask)
      --icmp-help   display help for others icmp options
UDP/TCP
  -s  --baseport    base source port              (default random)
  -p  --destport    [+][+]<port> destination port(default 0) ctrl+z inc/dec
  -k  --keep        keep still source port
  -w  --win         winsize (default 64)
  -O  --tcpoff      set fake tcp data offset       (instead of tcphdrlen / 4)
  -Q  --seqnum      shows only tcp sequence number
  -b  --badcksum    (try to) send packets with a bad IP checksum
                    many systems will fix the IP checksum sending the packet
                    so you'll get bad UDP/TCP checksum instead.
  -M  --setseq      set TCP sequence number
  -L  --setack      set TCP ack
  -F  --fin         set FIN flag
  -S  --syn         set SYN flag
  -R  --rst         set RST flag
  -P  --push        set PUSH flag
  -A  --ack         set ACK flag
  -U  --urg         set URG flag
  -X  --xmas        set X unused flag (0x40)
  -Y  --ymas        set Y unused flag (0x80)
      --tcpexitcode use last tcp->th_flags as exit code
      --tcp-timestamp enable the TCP timestamp option to guess the HZ/uptime
Common
  -d  --data        data size              (default is 0)
  -E  --file        data from file
  -e  --sign        add 'signature'
  -j  --dump        dump packets in hex
  -J  --print       dump printable characters
  -B  --safe        enable 'safe' protocol
  -u  --end         tell you when --file reached EOF and prevent rewind
  -T  --traceroute  traceroute mode        (implies --bind and --ttl 1)
      --tr-stop     Exit when receive the first not ICMP in traceroute mode
      --tr-keep-ttl Keep the source TTL fixed, useful to monitor just one hop
      --tr-no-rtt   Don't calculate/show RTT information in traceroute mode
ARS packet description (new, unstable)
      --apd-send    Send the packet described with APD (see docs/APD.txt)
(END)
```

Figure 5-11   Hping help, page 3

If you decide to use ping sweeps, be careful not to include the broadcast address in your range of addresses. You can do this by mistake if subnetting is used in an organization. For example, if the IP address 193.145.85.0 is subnetted with a 255.255.255.192 subnet mask, four subnets are created: 193.145.85.0, 193.145.85.64, 193.145.85.128, and 193.145.85.192. The broadcast addresses for each subnet are 193.145.85.63, 193.145.85.127, 193.145.85.191, and 193.145.85.255, respectively. If a ping sweep was inadvertently activated on the range of hosts 193.145.85.65 to 193.145.85.127, an inordinate amount of traffic could flood through the network because the broadcast address of 193.145.85.127 was included. This would be more of a problem on a Class B address, but if you perform ping sweeps, having your client sign a written agreement authorizing such testing is crucial.

5

Crafting IP Packets

Packets contain source IP addresses as well as destination IP addresses. A packet also contains information about the flags you learned earlier: SYN, ACK, FIN, Connect, and so on. You can create a packet with a particular flag set. For example, if you aren't satisfied with the response received from the host computer after sending a SYN packet, you can create another packet with the FIN flag set. The SYN flag might have returned a "closed port" message, but a FIN packet sent to the same computer might return a "filtered port" message. You can craft any type of packet you like. Hping and Fping are helpful tools for crafting IP packets, and you work with both tools in Activity 5-3.

Activity 5-3: Crafting IP Packets with Fping and Hping

Time Required: 30 minutes

Objective: Learn to create IP packets with Fping and Hping.

Description: In this activity, you see how IP packets are crafted to enable security testers to find out what services are running on a network. The more ways you know how to send a packet to an unsuspecting port on a computer and get a response, the better. If a computer doesn't respond to an ICMP packet sent to a particular port, it doesn't mean that any packet sent to that same port will get the same response. You might need to send different packets to an attacked computer to get the results you need to do a thorough security test.

1. If necessary, start your Windows XP Professional system with the Linux CD. Open a shell of your choice, type the command **fping –h** and press **Enter**.

2. To see the computers that are alive in the range of IP addresses your instructor gave you, type **fping –g** *BeginningIPaddress EndingIPaddress* and press **Enter**. Note the results. (Be sure to use the beginning and ending IP addresses in your assigned IP range.)

3. Next, type **hping –S** *IPAddressAttackComputer* (substituting an address from the IP attack network your instructor gave you) and press **Enter**. By using the –S parameter, you have just crafted a TCP SYN packet.

4. Open another shell, type **tcpdump**, and press **Enter**.

5. Arrange both shell windows next to each other so that you can observe what happens after entering the Hping command. From the shell that's not running Tcpdump, press **Ctrl+C** to return to the command prompt, type **hping –S** *IPaddressAttackComputer*, and press **Enter**. Watch the Tcpdump window fill with the traffic that's generated. To stop Tcpdump from capturing packets, press **Ctrl+C**.

6. If time permits, consult the Hping help pages (refer to Figures 5-9, 5-10, and 5-11, if needed) and experiment with creating different types of packets. Note the difference in the network traffic that's generated in the Tcpdump output. Security testers need to understand how slight differences in packets sent to an attacked computer can produce varied results. For example, if a computer doesn't respond to a SYN packet, try sending an ACK packet. What happens when a FIN packet is sent? If you aren't having any success, try sending the same packets to different ports. Does this change the response from the attacked computer?

7. When you're done, close both shells.

UNDERSTANDING SHELL SCRIPTING

Some tools might need to be modified to better suit your needs as a security tester. Creating a customized script—a computer program that automates a task that takes too much time to perform manually—can be a time-saving solution. As mentioned earlier, Fping can use an input file to perform ping sweeps. Manually creating an input file with thousands of IP addresses isn't worth the time. Instead, most security testers rely on their basic programming skills to write a script for creating an input file.

Scripting Basics

If you have worked with DOS batch programming, shell script programming will be familiar. If you're from a networking background and new to programming, however, this topic might seem a little overwhelming. Don't panic. Chapter 7 focuses on getting nonprogrammers up to speed. A script or batch file is a text file containing multiple commands that are normally entered manually at the command prompt. If you see that you're using a set of commands repeatedly to perform the same task, that task might be a good candidate for a shell script. You can then run the file or program by using just one command. The best way to learn how to create a shell script is by doing it, so you get an opportunity to practice writing one in Activity 5-4.

ACTIVITY

Activity 5-4: Creating an Executable Shell Script

Time Required: 45 minutes

Objective: Learn to create, save, and run a shell script.

Description: Many hacking tools are written in script languages, such as VBScript or JavaScript. In this activity, you create a script that populates a file with a range of IP addresses. This type of file could be used as an input file for Nmap or Fping.

1. If necessary, start your Windows XP Professional system with the Linux CD. Open a shell of your choice, type **vi Myshell**, and then press **Enter**.

2. To activate the screen, press **Esc** and then type the letter "i." Make sure Caps Lock is not activated because the vi program is case sensitive, and you can get strange results if you don't pay careful attention to letter case. The bottom of the screen should indicate that you're in Insert mode. Insert mode enables you to enter text in this vi shell screen. If this is your first time using the vi editor, you might need to use Table 5-1 for a quick reference. For a more detailed description of this versatile editor, type **man vi** and press **Enter**.

Table 5-1   Summary of vi commands

vi Commands	Description
j	Moves the insertion point down one line
k	Moves the insertion point up one line
h	Moves the insertion point back one character
l (lowercase L)	Moves the insertion point forward one character
Enter key	Moves the insertion point to the beginning of the next line
a	After pressing the Esc key, appends text after the insertion point
i	After pressing the Esc key, inserts text before the insertion point
Delete key	Overwrites the last character when in Insert mode
x	Deletes current character
dd	Deletes current line
dw	Deletes the current word
p	Replaces the text previously deleted
ZZ	Exits vi and saves all changes
wq	Writes changes and quits the edit session

3. First, type **#!/bin/sh** and press **Enter**. This line is important because it identifies the file you're writing as a shell script. You should enter a few lines of documentation in any scripts or programs you write because they help with program modifications and maintenance done later. When a line is used for documentation purposes, it is preceded with a # character.

CAUTION   Make sure the slashes point in the correct direction (/). Microsoft users often make this mistake because they're used to typing backward slashes (\).

5

4. The second line is the name of the script you are creating. Type **# Myshell** and press **Enter**. If this script were being used in a production setting, you would also enter the date and your name.

5. Read the paragraph about the purpose of the script, but don't type it in your script. Your script should have only #!/bin/sh and # Myshell statements so far.

6. Next, type **network_id="193.145.85."** and press **Enter**. Be sure to include the quotation marks and the last period after the number 85. Because you aren't actually using these IP addresses, it doesn't matter what address you use.

7. Type **count=0** and press **Enter**. You're initializing the count variable to zero, which is always wise because a variable shouldn't be used in a program without having a value set. You learn more about setting values for variables in Chapter 7.

8. You can skip the documentation (shown in Figure 5-12) and start to enter the crucial program code. You need your program to add the number 1 to the 193.145.85. network ID, and to continue adding and incrementing numbers to the network ID until a range of IP addresses from 193.145.85.1 through 193.145.85.254 is written to a file named ip_address.txt. In programming lingo, this process is called looping. To avoid creating an endless loop, you need to add a condition to the while statement. Type **while ["$count" –le 253]** and press **Enter**. Note the spaces within the square brackets and pay close attention to the use of quotation marks and dollar signs.

9. Next, type **do** and press **Enter**. This is where you want the program to perform its main task. The action takes place between the do statement and the done statement. First, to increment the count variable by 1, type **count=$(($count+1))**, paying careful attention to the parentheses, and then press **Enter**.

10. The next line is covered in more detail in Chapter 7. For now, just understand that you can use the printf function to write data to a file. Type **printf "%s%s\n" $network_id $count >> ip_address.txt** and press **Enter**. The >> characters are used to add each IP address to the end of the ip_address.txt file.

11. Type **exit 0**. Figure 5-12 shows the entire script. Save your hard work by pressing **Esc** and typing **:** (the colon character). At the : prompt, type **wq**, and press **Enter**.

12. Now that you have saved your script, you need to make it executable so that you can run it. From the command line, type **chmod +x Myshell** and press **Enter**.

13. To run your script, type **./Myshell** and press **Enter**. Because your script doesn't create any output to the screen, you need to examine the contents of the ip_address.txt file to see whether it worked.

14. Type **cat ip_address.txt**. How many IP addresses were created in the ip_address.txt file?

15. Close the shell, and shut down your system.

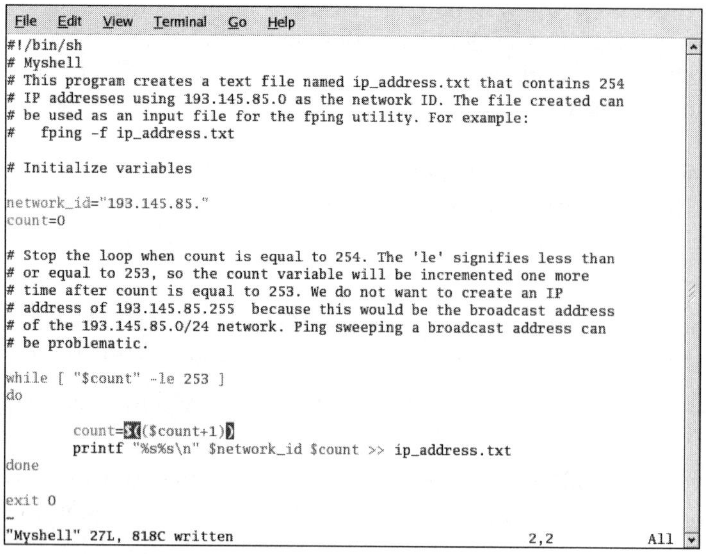

```
File  Edit  View  Terminal  Go  Help
#!/bin/sh
# Myshell
# This program creates a text file named ip_address.txt that contains 254
# IP addresses using 193.145.85.0 as the network ID. The file created can
# be used as an input file for the fping utility. For example:
#   fping -f ip_address.txt

# Initialize variables

network_id="193.145.85."
count=0

# Stop the loop when count is equal to 254. The 'le' signifies less than
# or equal to 253, so the count variable will be incremented one more
# time after count is equal to 253. We do not want to create an IP
# address of 193.145.85.255  because this would be the broadcast address
# of the 193.145.85.0/24 network. Ping sweeping a broadcast address can
# be problematic.

while [ "$count" -le 253 ]
do

        count=$(($count+1))
        printf "%s%s\n" $network_id $count >> ip_address.txt
done

exit 0
~
"Myshell" 27L, 818C written                    2,2          All
```

Figure 5-12   A shell script

CHAPTER SUMMARY

❑ Port scanning, also referred to as service scanning, is the process of scanning a range of IP addresses to determine what services are running on a system or network.

❑ Different port scans might elicit different information, so security testers need to be aware of the port scan types, such as SYN, ACK, FIN, and so on.

❑ A multitude of port-scanning tools are available to security testers. The most popular are Nmap, Nessus, and Unicornscan.

❑ Ping sweeps are used to determine which computers on a network are "alive" (computers the attack computer can reach).

❑ Using shell scripting can help security professionals by automating many time-consuming tasks.

KEY TERMS

closed ports — Ports are designated as closed when they're not listening or responding to a packet.
filtered ports — Ports designated as not open or closed, but possibly filtered by a network-filtering device, such as a firewall.
Fping — An enhanced Ping utility for pinging multiple targets simultaneously.
Hping — An enhanced Ping utility for creating TCP and UDP packets to be used in port-scanning activities.
open ports — Ports are designated as open when they respond to packets.
Nessus — A security tool installed on a *NIX operating system (server) that conducts port scanning, OS identification, and vulnerability assessments. A client computer (*NIX or Microsoft OS) must connect to the server to perform the tests.
Nmap — A security tool used to identify open ports and detect services and OSs running on network systems.
ping sweep — Pinging a range of IP addresses to identify live systems on a network.
port scanning — A method of finding out which services a host computer offers.

REVIEW QUESTIONS

1. Security testers and hackers use which of the following to determine the services running on a host and the vulnerabilities associated with those services?

   a. zone transfers

   b. zone scanning

   c. encryption algorithms

   d. port scanning

2. What is the most popular port-scanning tool used today?

   a. Netcat

   b. Netstat

   c. Nmap

   d. Nslookup

3. To receive extensive Nmap information and examples of the correct syntax to use in a Linux shell, which of the following commands should you type?

   a. nmap –h

   b. nmap –help

   c. nmap ?

   d. man nmap

4. To receive a brief summary of Nmap commands in a Linux shell, which of the following should you do?

   a. Type nmap –h.

   b. Type nmap –help.

   c. Type help nmap.

   d. Press the F1 key.

5. Which of the following Nmap commands sends a SYN packet to a computer with an IP address of 193.145.85.210? (Choose all that apply.)

   a. nmap –sS 193.145.85.210

   b. nmap –v 193.145.85.210

   c. nmap –sA 193.145.85.210

   d. nmap –sF 193.145.85.210

6. Which flags are set on a packet sent with the nmap –sX 193.145.85.202 command? (Choose all that apply.)

   a. FIN

   b. PSH

   c. SYN

   d. URG

7. Which Nmap command verifies whether the SSH port is open on any computers on the 192.168.1.0 network? (Choose all that apply.)

   a. nmap –v 192.168.1.0-254 –p 22

   b. nmap –v 192.168.1.0-254 –p 23

   c. nmap –v 192.168.1.0-254 –s 22

   d. nmap –v 192.168.1.0/24 –p 22

8. A closed port responds to a SYN packet with a(n) _____ packet.

   a. FIN

   b. SYN-ACK

   c. SYN

   d. RST

9. Which type of scan is usually used to bypass a firewall or packet-filtering device?

   a. an ACK scan

   b. a SYN scan

   c. an XMAS scan

   d. a FIN scan

10. Security testers can use Hping to bypass filtering devices. True or False?

11. A FIN packet sent to a closed port responds with a(n) _____ packet.

    a. FIN

    b. SYN-ACK

    c. RST

    d. SYN

12. A(n) _____ scan sends a packet with all flags set to NULL.

    a. NULL

    b. VOID

    c. SYN

    d. XMAS

13. What is a potential danger of performing a ping sweep on a network?

    a. including a broadcast address in the ping sweep range

    b. including a subnet IP address in the ping sweep range

    c. including the subnet mask in the ping sweep range

    d. including the intrusion detection system's IP address number in the ping sweep range

14. Port scanning provides the state for all but which of the following ports?

    a. closed

    b. open

    c. filtered

    d. buffered

15. A NULL scan requires setting the FIN, ACK, and URG flags. True or False?

16. Why does the fping -f 193.145.85.201 193.145.85.220 command cause an error?

    a. An incorrect switch is used.

    b. The IP range should be indicated as 193.145.85.201–220.

    c. There is no such command.

    d. IP ranges are not allowed with this command.

17. In basic network scanning, ICMP Echo Requests (type 8) are sent to host computers from the attacker, who waits for which type of packet to confirm that the host computer is alive?

    a. ICMP SYN-ACK packet

    b. ICMP SYN packet

    c. ICMP Echo Reply (type 8)

    d. ICMP Echo Reply (type 0)

18. To bypass some ICMP-filtering devices on a network, an attacker might send which type of packets to scan the network for vulnerable services? (Choose all that apply.)

   a. PING packets

   b. SYN packets

   c. ACK packets

   d. ECHO request packets

19. Which of the following is a tool for creating a custom TCP/IP packet and sending it to a host computer?

   a. Tracert

   b. Traceroute

   c. Hping

   d. Nmaping

20. Fping does not allow users to ping multiple IP addresses simultaneously. True or False?

CASE PROJECTS

Case 5-1: Obtaining Information on a Network's Active Services

After conducting a zone transfer and running various security tools on the K. J. Williams network, you're asked to write a memo to the IT manager, Bob Jones, detailing which tools you used to determine the services running on his network. Mr. Jones is curious about how you obtained this information. You decide to consult the OSSTMM and read Section C on port scanning and the "Internet Technology Security" section, particularly the material on identifying services, so that you can better address his concerns.

Based on the preceding information, write a one-page memo to Mr. Jones explaining the steps you took to find this information. Your memo should mention any information you found in the OSSTMM that relates to this stage of your testing.

Case 5-2: Finding Port-Scanning Tools

The company that has employed you as a security tester has asked you to research any new tools that might help you perform your duties. It has been noted that some of the tools your company is currently using have flaws or do not meet the company's expectations. Your manager, Gloria Petrelli, has asked that you research any new or improved products currently on the market.

Based on the preceding information, write a one-page report for Ms. Petrelli describing some port-scanning tools that might be useful to your company. The report should include available commercial tools and their cost.

6

ENUMERATION

After reading this chapter and completing the exercises, you will be able to:
♦ Describe the enumeration step of security testing
♦ Enumerate Microsoft OS targets
♦ Enumerate NetWare OS targets
♦ Enumerate *NIX OS targets

Enumeration takes port scanning to the next level. Now that you know how to discover live systems on a network, the next steps are finding what resources are shared on the systems, discovering logon accounts and passwords, and gaining access to network resources. Enumeration involves connecting to a system, not just identifying that a system is present on a network. Hackers aren't satisfied with knowing that computer systems are running on a network. Their goals are to find live systems and gain access to them. For security testers, enumeration is a more intrusive part of testing, and not having permission from the network's owner for this step could result in being charged with a criminal offense. Enumeration is the step in which you attempt to retrieve information and gain access to servers by using company employees' logon accounts. Knowledge of operating systems and how they store information can be helpful in enumeration. Not knowing how shares are handled in Microsoft OSs or how Novell manages files and folders, for example, can make it more difficult to access information or see possible vulnerabilities in these systems. In this chapter, you learn some basics of various OSs and the tools for enumerating them. Some of these tools have been covered previously and some are new, but they all make enumeration as easy as entering a single command or clicking a mouse button.

INTRODUCTION TO ENUMERATION

In previous chapters, you have seen how to perform a zone transfer, use the Dig command, and discover what computers are alive on a network. What's the next step in security testing? **Enumeration** is the process of extracting the following information from a network:

- Resources or shares on the network
- User names or groups assigned on the network
- The last time a user logged on as well as his or her password

To determine what resources or shares are on a network, security testers must first determine what OS is being used via port scanning and footprinting. If a network is running a Microsoft OS, for example, testers can use specific tools to view those shares and possibly access resources. Enumeration is more intrusive because you're not just identifying a resource; you're attempting to access it. It goes beyond passive scanning of a network to find open ports. Sometimes this process entails guessing passwords after determining a user name.

Before you jump into using enumeration tools, however, you learn how to install a Linux tool in Activity 6-1. Microsoft users have become accustomed to the simplicity of installation programs, which typically require simply clicking a series of Next buttons. Downloading and installing Linux OS products is a little more complex, but after some practice, you'll be comfortable installing these products, too. In Activity 6-1, you install NBTscan (NBT is an abbreviation for NetBIOS over TCP/IP), a tool for enumerating Microsoft OSs. You use this tool later in the chapter for subsequent activities.

Activity 6-1: Installing NBTscan on a Linux OS

Time Required: 30 minutes

Objective: Learn how to download, unzip, and create an executable program on a Linux operating system.

Description: In this activity, you download a Linux-based tool and prepare it to run as an executable program in a Linux OS. This tool, called NBTscan, is used to find systems running NetBIOS.

1. Start your Windows XP Professional system with the Linux CD. Open a shell of your choice and start a Web browser. Type the URL **www.inetcat.org/software/nbtscan.html** and press **Enter**. (A WIN32 version is also available, but in this activity, you're practicing installing Linux programs.) Click the **Download NBTscan sources** link. Next, you're prompted to open the file or save it to disk. Click the **Save to Disk** option.

2. Next, you're prompted for a directory to save the program. Create a directory called **NBTscan** and save the file in this directory. You can open a shell and type the command **mkdir NBTscan** or click the icon labeled "Create new directory" shown in Figure 6-1. Where you save the file doesn't matter because the Linux CD uses RAM for the programs and files with which you're working, so the file disappears the next time your computer is restarted.

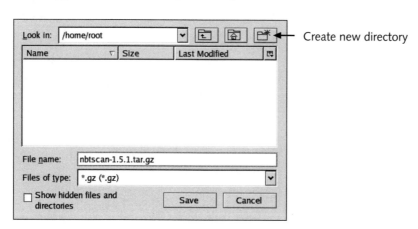

Figure 6-1   Creating a new directory

The program you have downloaded is nbtscan-1.5.1.tar.gz. The "tar" extension stands for *tape archive*. The **Tar command** combines multiple files and folders into one big file, but it doesn't compress the files and folders.

Windows users are used to seeing the .zip extension on compressed files. UNIX users, however, are familiar with the .gz extension, which means the Gzip utility was used to compress the file. For example, to compress the BigFile.tar file, you use the command gzip BigFile.tar. This command produces a file named BigFile.tar.gz. To unzip (uncompress) this file, you use the command gzip -d BigFile.tar.gz.

Files with a .tgz extension can also be uncompressed with the gzip -d command.

3. Open any shell, and change to the **NBTscan** directory. To uncompress the nbtscan-1.5.1.tar.gz file, type **gzip –d nbtscan-1.5.1.tar.gz** and press **Enter**. To see what this command does, type **ls** and press **Enter** (see Figure 6-2).

You can also enter the command tar -zxvf nbtscan-1.5.1.tar.gz to unzip and untar the downloaded file in one step. In addition, to reduce possible typos and save time, you can press Tab after entering one or two characters of the file name. The file name is then filled in automatically.

```
File   Edit   View   Terminal   Go   Help
[root@localhost NBTscan]# ls
nbtscan-1.5.1.tar.gz
[root@localhost NBTscan]# gzip -d nbtscan-1.5.1.tar.gz
[root@localhost NBTscan]# ls
nbtscan-1.5.1.tar
[root@localhost NBTscan]#
```

Figure 6-2   Using the Gzip command

4. Note that you now have a tar file in the directory. To unpack the files or directories in this file, you need to use the Tar command. Type **tar –xvf nbtscan-1.5.1.tar** and press **Enter**. Figure 6-3 shows the files contained in the tar file.

```
File   Edit   View   Terminal   Go   Help
[root@localhost NBTscan]# tar -xvf nbtscan-1.5.1.tar
nbtscan-1.5.1a/
nbtscan-1.5.1a/ChangeLog
nbtscan-1.5.1a/config.guess
nbtscan-1.5.1a/config.sub
nbtscan-1.5.1a/configure
nbtscan-1.5.1a/configure.in
nbtscan-1.5.1a/COPYING
nbtscan-1.5.1a/errors.h
nbtscan-1.5.1a/install-sh
nbtscan-1.5.1a/list.c
nbtscan-1.5.1a/list.h
nbtscan-1.5.1a/Makefile.in
nbtscan-1.5.1a/nbtscan.c
nbtscan-1.5.1a/range.c
nbtscan-1.5.1a/range.h
nbtscan-1.5.1a/README
nbtscan-1.5.1a/statusq.c
nbtscan-1.5.1a/statusq.h
nbtscan-1.5.1a/time.h
nbtscan-1.5.1a/config.log
nbtscan-1.5.1a/config.status
nbtscan-1.5.1a/configure.in.old
[root@localhost NBTscan]#
```

Figure 6-3   List of files in the tar file

TIP

For more information on using the Tar command, type **man tar** and press Enter.

5. Type **ls -l** and press **Enter** to see your directory's contents. Note that the nbtscan-1.5.1a directory was created. To change to that directory, type **cd nbtscan-1.5.1a** and press **Enter**. Next, type **ls** and press **Enter** to see the directory's contents, shown in Figure 6-4.

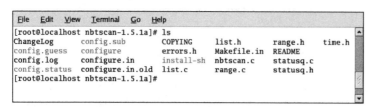

```
File  Edit  View  Terminal  Go  Help
[root@localhost nbtscan-1.5.1a]# ls
ChangeLog      config.sub      COPYING      list.h       range.h     time.h
config.guess   configure       errors.h     Makefile.in  README
config.log     configure.in    install-sh   nbtscan.c    statusq.c
config.status  configure.in.old list.c      range.c      statusq.h
[root@localhost nbtscan-1.5.1a]#
```

Figure 6-4   Contents of the nbtscan-1.5.1a directory

6. Before installing a new program on your computer, you should always review the README file. To do this, type **cat README | less** and press **Enter**. Scan through the document, which gives you a preview of the following steps. When you're done, press **q** to quit the README file.

7. Next, type **./configure** and press **Enter**. Your screen should fill with many lines of code. This command is a script that checks to make sure everything is configured correctly. It sends results and builds a file called Makefile, which contains all the programs included in the downloaded package.

8. When the scrolling stops, type **make** and press **Enter** to run the make program, which automates the compilation of programs in the Makefile. Otherwise, you would have to compile all the programs manually.

9. Next, type **make install** and press **Enter**. This command runs the make program again, but this time it uses the Install program included in the Makefile, which contains installation instructions. NBTscan is now loaded on your computer. To view information about the program, type **nbtscan -h | less** and press **Enter**. Figure 6-5 shows the output of the command to scan a range of IP addresses. Note that a computer named SALESMGR is located on the 192.168.0.0 network with an IP address of 192.168.0.100. The command also reveals the computer's MAC address.

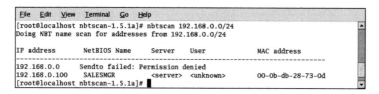

```
File  Edit  View  Terminal  Go  Help
[root@localhost nbtscan-1.5.1a]# nbtscan 192.168.0.0/24
Doing NBT name scan for addresses from 192.168.0.0/24

IP address      NetBIOS Name    Server    User        MAC address
------------------------------------------------------------------------
192.168.0.0     Sendto failed: Permission denied
192.168.0.100   SALESMGR        <server>  <unknown>   00-0b-db-28-73-0d
[root@localhost nbtscan-1.5.1a]#
```

Figure 6-5   NBTscan finds a computer named SALESMGR

10. If time permits and any computers on your classroom network are running Windows XP, try using the Nbtscan command on the network to see whether any computers are identified. If all the computers in your classroom are running Linux, however, Nbtscan doesn't return any results because Linux doesn't use NetBIOS.

11. Close the Linux shell, and leave your system running for the next activity.

Security Bytes

This book is by no means a how-to manual on using Linux, but security testers should know how to install tools on a Linux OS. Even though the activities in this book use a bootable Linux CD, you might consider downloading or purchasing Linux and installing it on your computer. Practicing installing and using new tools is one of the quickest ways to learn security-testing skills. A laptop computer that can be devoted to security testing is helpful, too. You can partition the hard drive and install Windows XP on one partition and Linux on the other. You can then create a Tools directory on both partitions and download security tools from the Internet. Most security professionals have a large arsenal of tools installed and ready to use on their laptop computers.

Although installing a tool in a Linux environment is often more challenging than installing software in a Windows environment, that's not true for all Linux tools. Installing Nessus, one of the most powerful security tools, is much easier than the process in Activity 6-1. The Nessus developer created a shell script that does everything for you, so there's no need to issue commands for uncompressing a tar file and creating an executable file.

ENUMERATING MICROSOFT OPERATING SYSTEMS

To understand how an attacker might gain access to resources or shares on a Microsoft network, in this section you take a brief look at Microsoft OSs. Chapter 8 delves into more detail on Microsoft attacks; this chapter merely highlights the Microsoft OS as it relates to enumeration. Table 6-1 describes Microsoft OSs beginning with Windows 95 and ending with Windows Server 2003.

Many of the enumeration techniques that work with older Windows OSs still work with the newer versions.

Table 6-1   Microsoft OS descriptions

Microsoft Operating System	Description
Windows 95	Windows 95 is the first Microsoft GUI product that did not rely on DOS. It was the beginning of plug and play and the ActiveX standard used today in all Windows versions. Probably the biggest enhancement was the Registry, a database that stores information about the system's hardware and software. Previously, this information was stored in files. Windows 95 ran on standalone computers and on computers that shared information across a network. It used the FAT16 file system.
Windows 98 and Me	More stable than its predecessor, with an improved file system (FAT32), new hardware support, and better backup and recovery tools. The enumeration process for Windows Me is the same as for Windows 98.

Table 6-1 Microsoft OS descriptions (continued)

Microsoft Operating System	Description
Windows NT 3.51 Server/Workstation	Microsoft created this OS with security in mind and to enhance the network functionality of its desktop OSs. Domains were emphasized instead of workgroups. Instead of peer-to-peer networks, a client-server model was created in which a server was responsible for authenticating users and giving them access to resources on a network. This concept made it possible to have many computers in a domain versus a limited number of computers in a workgroup. Also, NTFS and FAT partitions can't see, read, or write to one another. They cannot interact. NTFS was implemented to replace FAT16 and FAT32 because of the difficulty in implementing security in these file systems. NTFS enabled file level security features not possible in or supported by FAT.
Windows NT 4.0 Server/Workstation	These upgrades of the Windows NT 3.51 products had improved GUIs and performance.
Windows 2000 Server/Professional	In these upgrades of the NT series, Microsoft replaced the Registry with Active Directory for object storage. Millions of objects (such as users, printers, and other network resources) could be stored by using the X.500 directory service standard. Active Directory was more scalable and used Lightweight Directory Access Protocol (LDAP) rather than the high-overhead protocols X.500 used, so larger network infrastructures could be supported. Enumeration of these OSs includes enumerating Active Directory.
Windows XP Professional	XP Professional takes some of the most useful features of Windows 2000, such as standards-based security and improved manageability using the Microsoft Management Console (MMC), and blends it with an improved user interface and better Plug and Play support. Microsoft made significant security improvements to XP in the kernel data structures, making them read-only to prevent rogue applications from affecting the core of the operating system, and implemented Windows File Protection to prevent core system files from being overwritten. Despite these improvements, the enumeration processes used for earlier versions of Windows still work much the same in Windows XP Professional.
Windows Server 2003	The newest Microsoft OS has improvements in some security areas, such as Internet Information Services (IIS). Windows Server 2003 encompasses four versions; each is targeted to different markets with different features. Generally, all 2003 versions include Remote Desktop, load balancing, and VPN support. EFS, management services such as Windows Management Instrumentation (WMI), and .NET application services are also common to the four versions. The higher-end versions offer better support for PKI, certificate services, and Active Directory as well as other enhancements to reliability, scalability, manageability, and security. Again, even with Microsoft's improvements to security and stability of these systems, enumeration techniques described for other Microsoft versions are effective with the Windows Server 2003 family.

NetBIOS Basics

Before learning how to enumerate Microsoft products, you need to review the basics of how **Network Basic Input Output System (NetBIOS)** works. NetBIOS is a Microsoft programming interface that allows computers to communicate across a local area network (LAN). Most Windows OSs use NetBIOS to share files and printers.

In addition, the computer names you assign to Windows systems are called NetBIOS names. NetBIOS names have a limit of 16 characters; the last character is reserved for a special hexadecimal number (00 to FF) that identifies the type of service running on the computer. So you can use only 15 characters for a computer name, and NetBIOS automatically adds the last character, which identifies the service that has registered with the OS. For example, if a computer named SALESREP is running the Server service, the OS stores this information in a NetBIOS table.

A NetBIOS name must be unique on a network, so you can't have two computers with the same NetBIOS name. Table 6-2 lists the NetBIOS suffixes that correspond to the services, or resource types, running on a computer. You don't need to memorize all these suffixes, but several are critical because they identify the computer or server being enumerated as a standalone computer or a domain controller. Hackers often spend more time attacking computers identified as domain controllers because they can offer more information, including logon names for user accounts and network resources.

Table 6-2   NetBIOS names and suffixes

NetBIOS Name	Suffix	Description
<computer name>	00	The Workstation service registered the computer name (also referred to as the NetBIOS name).
<_MSBROWSE_>	01	Signifies that the computer is the master browser on the network. The master browser is responsible for notifying all computers on the network of any NetBIOS name changes or additions.
<computer name>	03	The computer is registered by the Messenger service, which the client uses when sending and receiving messages.
<computer name>	06	Registered by Routing and Remote Access Service (RRAS).
<computer name>	1F	Network Dynamic Data Exchange (NetDDE) services have been started on the computer. NetDDE is a system process that runs on Microsoft OSs to facilitate the exchange of network data.
<computer name>	20	Registered by the Server service. A computer must have this service running to share printers or files.
<computer name>	21	Registered by Remote Access Service (RAS).
<computer name>	22	Registered by the Microsoft Exchange Interchange service.
<computer name>	23	Registered by the Microsoft Exchange Store service. The store is where mailboxes and public folders are stored.
<computer name>	24	Registered by the MS Exchange Directory service.
<computer name>	30	Registered by the Modem Sharing Server Service.
<computer name>	31	Registered by the Modem Sharing Client Service.
<computer name>	43	Registered by the Systems Management Server (SMS) remote control client. SMS enables administrators to take control of a client computer for troubleshooting and administration.
<computer name>	44	Indicates that the SMS remote control tool is running on this computer.
<computer name>	45	Signifies that SMS remote chat is enabled on this computer.

Table 6-2 NetBIOS names and suffixes (continued)

NetBIOS Name	Suffix	Description
<computer name>	46	Signifies that SMS remote transfer is enabled on this computer.
<computer name>	4C	Indicates that DEC Pathworks TCP/IP is configured on the computer.
<computer name>	52	Also indicates that DEC Pathworks is configured on the computer.
<computer name>	87	Signifies that MS Exchange Message Transfer Agent (MTA) is running on this computer.
<computer name>	6A	Indicates that Microsoft Exchange Internet Mail Connector (IMC) is running.
<computer name>	BE	Signifies that Netmon Agent (a Microsoft network-monitoring tool) is running.
<computer name>	BF	Indicates that the Netmon application is running.
<username>	03	Indicates that the Messenger service is running.
<domain name>	00	Indicates that the Domain Name Service (DNS) is running.
<domain name>	1B	Identifies the computer as a domain master browser.
<domain name>	1C	Identifies the computer as a domain controller.
<domain name>	1D	Identifies the computer as a master browser.
<domain name>	1E	Signifies that Browser Services Election is running.
<iNet~Services>	1C	Indicates that Internet Information Services (IIS) is running.
<IS-computername>	00	Also indicates that IIS is running.

NetBIOS Null Sessions

One of the biggest vulnerabilities of NetBIOS systems is a **null session**, which is an unauthenticated connection to a Windows computer using no logon and password values. Many of the enumeration tools covered in this chapter establish a null session to gather information such as logon accounts, group membership, and file shares from an attacked computer. This vulnerability has been around for more than a decade and is still present in recent Windows OSs, including Windows XP.

NetBIOS Enumeration Tools

The Nbtstat command is a powerful enumeration tool included with the Microsoft OS. To display the NetBIOS table, you issue the Nbtstat -a *IPaddress* command. Figure 6-6 shows the entry SALESREP <20>. The "20" represents the Server service running on the SALESREP computer. The NetBIOS table also shows that ZIONBANK is a domain controller, as indicated by the 1C suffix, and even reveals the logged-on user's name: Administrator.

Another built-in Microsoft tool is the Net view command, which gives you a quick way to see whether there are any shared resources on a computer or server. To see the syntax for this command, type net view ? at the command prompt, as shown in Figure 6-7.

You can also use the IP address of the computer you discovered when using port-scanning tools. For example, Figure 6-8 shows the command being used on a remote Windows 98 computer. A share name called EMPPASSWORDS is retrieved with the command. The next command an attacker could use against this computer is \\192.168.0.106\emppasswords to retrieve user passwords.

Although you can download or buy enumeration tools, you should learn how to take advantage of the tools already available in the Microsoft OS. A simple command-line utility can give you the name of a logged-on user, and a guess of that user's password can give you access to the system quickly. Many password-guessing programs are available that can determine a password in a matter of seconds. One such program the Department of Defense uses is L0phtcrack. (This tool used to be free, but now you can order it for a small fee

```
C:\Documents and Settings>nbtstat -a salesrep

Local Area Connection:
Node IpAddress: [192.168.0.100] Scope Id: []

            NetBIOS Remote Machine Name Table

    Name               Type         Status
    ---------------------------------------------
    SALESREP     <00>  UNIQUE     Registered
    SALESREP     <20>  UNIQUE     Registered
    ZIONBANK     <00>  GROUP      Registered
    ZIONBANK     <1C>  GROUP      Registered
    ZIONBANK     <1B>  UNIQUE     Registered
    SALESREP     <03>  UNIQUE     Registered
    ZIONBANK     <1E>  GROUP      Registered
    INet~Services<1C>  GROUP      Registered
    ZIONBANK     <1D>  UNIQUE     Registered
    IS~SALESREP...<00> UNIQUE     Registered
    ..__MSBROWSE__.<01>GROUP      Registered
    ADMINISTRATOR<03>  UNIQUE     Registered

    MAC Address = 00-50-DA-63-EB-BE

C:\Documents and Settings>
```

Figure 6-6   Using the Nbtstat command

```
C:\Documents and Settings>net view
Server Name         Remark

---------------------------------------------------------------
\\SAMBA              Manager
\\SECURITYTESTER
\\SERVER              server
The command completed successfully.


C:\Documents and Settings>net view ?
The syntax of this command is:


NET VIEW
[\\computername [/CACHE] | /DOMAIN[:domainname]]
NET VIEW /NETWORK:NW [\\computername]


C:\Documents and Settings>
```

Figure 6-7   Viewing help for the Net view command

```
C:\Documents and Settings>net view \\192.168.0.106
Shared resources at \\192.168.0.106

MTS CONSULTING

Share name    Type  Used as  Comment

----------------------------------------------------------
CDDRV         Disk
EMPPASSWORDS  Disk
WIN98-SYSTEM  Disk
The command completed successfully.


C:\Documents and Settings>
```

Figure 6-8   Using the Net view command with an IP address

from *www.atstake.com/downloads*). However, security testers can often guess passwords without needing a special program because some users are lazy about creating passwords. For example, many users, despite guidelines in company security policies, use simple passwords, such as "password" or "p@$$w0rd."

Activity 6-2: Using Built-in Microsoft NetBIOS Tools

Time Required: 30 minutes

Objective: Learn to use the Microsoft Nbtstat, Net view, and Net use commands.

Description: In this activity, you look at the tools available for viewing NetBIOS services and shares. After using the Nbtstat command to discover a computer or server on a network that's sharing a resource, you can use the Net view and Net use commands to see whether any computers are sharing resources and possibly access those resources from your XP computer.

1. If your computer is running Linux, remove the Linux CD and restart your computer. You can also type **init 0** at a shell and press **Enter** to shut down your Linux system. Then start your computer in Windows XP Professional.

2. Right-click **Start** and click **Explore**. In the Start Menu window, click **Local Disk (C:)** and then click **File** on the menu bar, point to **New**, and click **Folder**. Name the new folder *YourFirstName*, and then click **Enter.**

3. Right-click the folder you just created and click **Sharing and Security**. In the Properties dialog box, click to enable the **Share this folder on the network** check box, and accept the share name by clicking **OK**.

4. Click **Start**, point to **All Programs**, point to **Accessories**, and click **Command Prompt**. In the command prompt window, type **ipconfig** and press **Enter**. Write down your IP address and tell it to your partner.

5. Next, type **net view ***PartnersIPaddress* and press **Enter**. What does the command produce as output?

6. You use the Net use command to connect to a computer containing the shared folders or files. To see the information this command returns, type **net use ?** and press **Enter**. Your screen should look like Figure 6-9.

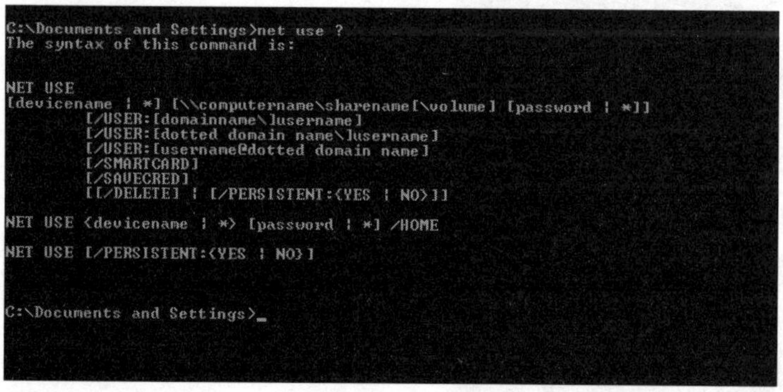

```
C:\Documents and Settings>net use ?
The syntax of this command is:

NET USE
[devicename | *] [\\computername\sharename[\volume] [password | *]]
        [/USER:[domainname\]username]
        [/USER:[dotted domain name\]username]
        [/USER:[username@dotted domain name]
        [/SMARTCARD]
        [/SAVECRED]
        [[/DELETE] | [/PERSISTENT:{YES | NO}]]

NET USE {devicename | *} [password | *] /HOME

NET USE [/PERSISTENT:{YES | NO}]


C:\Documents and Settings>_
```

Figure 6-9   Viewing help for the Net use command

7. After reading the help screen, type **net use ***PartnersIPaddress******PartnersSharedFolder*. What are the results of this command?

8. At the command prompt, type **nbtstat -A** *PartnersIPaddress*. What are the results of this command?

9. At the command prompt, type **exit** and press **Enter**. Leave Windows XP running for the next activity.

Additional Enumeration Tools

As you have seen, Microsoft has several built-in tools that can assist you in enumerating NetBIOS systems. In the following sections, you examine some additional tools for enumerating NetBIOS systems.

NetScanTools Pro

NetScanTools Pro (introduced in Chapter 5) produces a graphical view of NetBIOS running on a network. As shown in Figure 6-10, a comment in the analysis section on the right identifies a NetBIOS Session service found on port 139 and states that it's a "probable unprotected Windows computer." Ports 135 to 139 are the most vulnerable to NetBIOS attacks.

NetScanTools also enumerates any shares running on the computer. For example, Figure 6-11 lists \\SALESMGR\Printer2 as a shared printer.

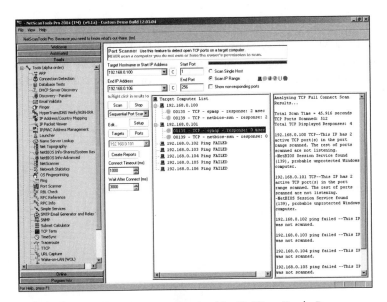

Figure 6-10 The enumeration tool in NetScanTools Pro

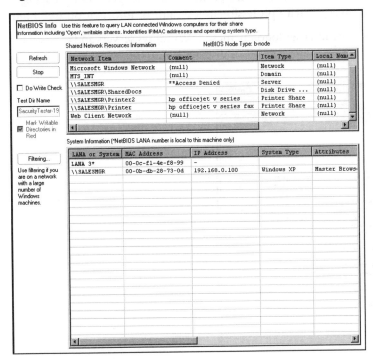

Figure 6-11 Enumerating shares in NetScanTools Pro

In Figure 6-11, the \\SALESMGR entry displays "**Access Denied" in the Comment column, but the \\SALESMGR\SharedDocs Comment entry is blank in this column. To see whether access is available for this shared resource, an attacker simply enters the Universal Naming Convention (UNC) name—\\SALESMGR\SharedDocs—in the Run dialog box in Windows.

DumpSec

DumpSec, a popular enumeration tool for Microsoft systems, is produced by Foundstone, Inc., and can be downloaded from *www.systemtools.com*. The information you can gather with this software is astonishing. For example, after connecting to a Windows server, you can download—or, as it's called in DumpSec, "dump"—the following information:

- Permissions for shares
- Permissions for printers
- Permissions for the Registry
- Users in column or table format
- Policies (such as local, domain, or group policies)
- Rights
- Services

Hyena

Hyena, available at *www.systemtools.com*, is an excellent GUI product for managing and securing Microsoft OSs. The interface is easy to use and gives security professionals a wealth of information (see Figure 6-12).

With just a click, you can look at the shares and user logon names for Windows servers and domain controllers. If any domains or workgroups are on the network, this tool displays them, too.

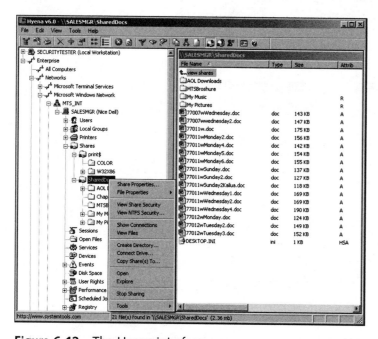

Figure 6-12   The Hyena interface

Hyena can also display a graphical representation of the following areas:

- Microsoft Terminal Services
- Microsoft Windows Network
- Web Client Network
- Find User/Group

NessusWX

Chapter 5 introduced the Nessus tool, which operates with a client/server methodology. First the Nessus server is configured and connects to the network; then a Nessus client is configured to connect to the Nessus server. Nessus runs on any *NIX system, but Nessus client software (NessusWX, available for download at *www.nessus.org* or at *http://nessuswx.nessus.org* for the Windows version) can run on both *NIX and Windows OSs. NessusWX is easy to install and takes just minutes to configure. This tool can come in handy when you need to enumerate different OSs on a large network and have multiple servers dispersed throughout an organization. You can use a laptop running Windows XP and NessusWX to connect to any Nessus server.

Double-click the NessusWX desktop icon to display a session window similar to the one in Figure 6-13. The window is blank if you haven't established any sessions to computers on a network. When you create a session, you can name it so that it's easier to return later and continue your enumeration. The names can be descriptive or just the default Session1, Session2, and so on that Nessus supplies. Remember that the XP client is not the computer that's attacking or scanning the target. That's the job of the Nessus server, so the Nessus server must be up and running before you attempt to connect to it.

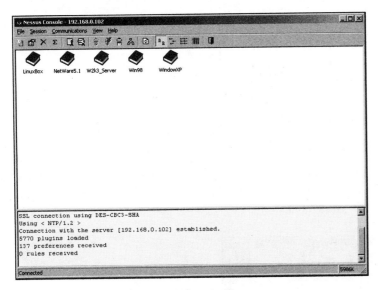

Figure 6-13   The session window in Nessus

To connect your Nessus client to the Nessus server, click Communications, Connect from the menu in the session window. The Connect dialog box opens, as shown in Figure 6-14. The Name drop-down list in the Server section of the Connect dialog box lets you choose to which Nessus server you want to connect. It's possible to have more than one Nessus server on a network, but in this example, the security tester has selected the 192.168.0.102 server.

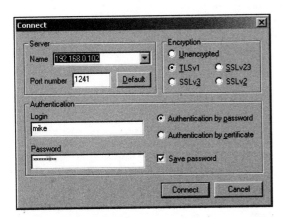

Figure 6-14   The Connect dialog box

A Nessus user account called Mike was created and a password was assigned. on the Nessus server. A client must log on to the server with these credentials to be authenticated. The XP computer can then choose a computer to test in the session window shown previously in Figure 6-13.

Figures 6-15 through 6-20 show Nessus in action. In Figure 6-15, the host system, identified as 192.168.0.106, displays eight NetBIOS names that Nessus has gathered. Nessus identifies the computer as LAPTOP and determines that the currently logged-on user is Administrator. This information could be used to launch an attack.

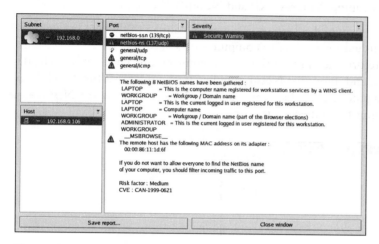

Figure 6-15   Nessus enumerates a NetBIOS system

The Windows 98 computer that Nessus is enumerating indicates a high severity error (see Figure 6-16). Nessus displays four shares the tester can access: IPC$, EMPPASSWORDS, WIN98-SYSTEM, and CDDRV. A hacker would probably be drawn to the EMPPASSWORDS share to discover employee passwords. Note that Nessus also offers a solution to this vulnerability.

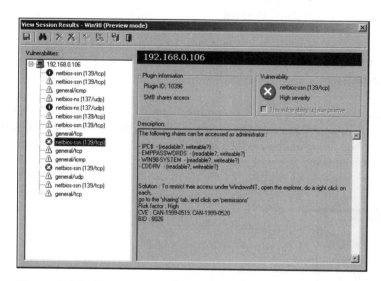

Figure 6-16   Enumerating shares in Nessus

Figure 6-17 shows Nessus identifying another high-severity error—in this case, a password vulnerability.

Nessus is also helpful in identifying the OS and service pack running on a computer. Figure 6-18 shows that the system with the IP address 192.168.0.101 is running Windows XP with Service Pack 2 (SP2) installed.

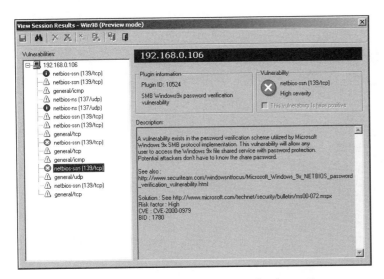

Figure 6-17   Nessus enumerates password information

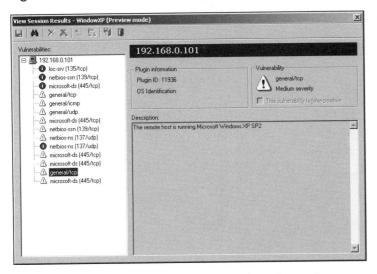

Figure 6-18   Nessus indicates the OS and service pack

Nessus works on even the most recent Windows versions. In Figure 6-19, Nessus identifies the remote host, a Windows Server 2003 system, as being vulnerable to an "Etherleak," which means the Ethernet driver is leaking bits of the contents of the OS's memory.

Figure 6-20 shows a firewall vulnerability that Nessus has detected on port 53 (DNS). Nessus suggests reviewing your firewall rules policy to help address this vulnerability. (Firewalls are covered in detail in Chapter 13.)

The Nessus tool does more than just enumerate Microsoft OSs, as you'll see in the following section. Nessus can also be used to enumerate NetWare systems.

6

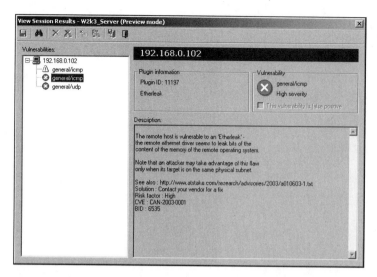

Figure 6-19   Nessus detects a vulnerability in a Windows Server 2003 system

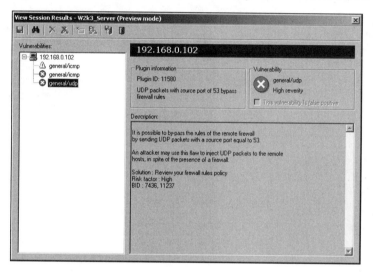

Figure 6-20   Nessus detects a firewall vulnerability

ENUMERATING THE NETWARE OPERATING SYSTEM

Many security professionals assume that knowledge of just one operating system is enough, but focusing on Microsoft and ignoring *NIX systems—or vice versa—can limit your career as a security professional. Similarly, some security professionals see Novell NetWare as a "dead horse" OS, but many corporations still rely on their faithful NetWare servers that keep plugging away. This section gives you a brief overview of NetWare and some of its vulnerabilities so that you can become a more versatile security tester.

Table 6-3 describes the NetWare OSs since version 4.11. Versions before 4.11 are rarely used now, but if you do encounter them, you can always do an Internet search to find information. Novell doesn't offer any technical support for versions before 4.11, so you might recommend that a business using a pre-4.11 version upgrade or consider moving to another platform.

 Security testers don't usually make recommendations for software. However, if you suspect that a hardware crash could cause irreparable damage to a company's data because of hardware or software malfunctions, offering suggestions on upgrading or switching platforms is useful.

Table 6-3 NetWare OS descriptions

NetWare Operating System	Description
NetWare 4.1	This version enhanced the database file system, called the Bindery, and introduced the NetWare Directory Services (NDS) directory structure. With the Bindery, data was maintained on each server. NDS, however, contained objects and login information from all NetWare servers on the network. This technology, based on the X.500 standard, allowed millions of objects to be stored in a hierarchical data structure.
Intranetware 4.11	This version added more intranet features.
NetWare 4.2	This version was easier to install than its predecessors and included services such as telephony, multimedia, and Web-browsing capabilities.
NetWare 5.0	This version emphasized the use of a windowed environment instead of command-line utilities. In addition, TCP/IP replaced IPX/SPX as the default protocol.
NetWare 5.1	This version emphasized the Internet as being an integral part of businesses. New features included IBM WebSphere Application Server; eDirectory (an enhancement to NDS); ConsoleOne, a graphical Java utility for centralized network administration; and the Novell Certificate Authority service, which enabled a server to issue digital certificates.
NetWare 6.0	This version offered more tools for accessing files and folders from remote Web browser clients and improvements to the eDirectory structure. It also added Apache Web Server, Tomcat Servlet Engine, and NetWare Enterprise Web Server as part of the OS.
NetWare 6.5	This version improved Web access and included Web development and software development tools, such as MySQL and the PHP scripting language, to create dynamic Web pages.
SUSE Linux Enterprise Server (NetWare 7.0)	The most recent NetWare OS; it uses SUSE Linux as its OS and eDirectory as its database.

Novell has worked over the years to improve its product, but the OS has vulnerabilities similar to the problem of NetBIOS null sessions in Microsoft. Although this book doesn't devote an entire chapter to a discussion of hacking NetWare, the following section includes several screen shots to familiarize you with the OS interface in case you need to conduct security testing on a network with a NetWare server.

NetWare Enumeration Tools

NetWare 5.1 is still used on many networks, so this section provides an example of enumerating a NetWare 5.1 system. For more recent NetWare versions, you might need to research vulnerabilities and exploits specific to that version, such as a Google search on "NetWare 6.5 vulnerabilities." New OS vulnerabilities are discovered daily, so you need to be vigilant in checking vendor sites and other Web sites that release information on security vulnerabilities. In Activity 6-3, you see how to research vulnerabilities in NetWare 5.1.

Activity 6-3: Discovering NetWare 5.1 Vulnerabilities

Time Required: 30 minutes

Objective: Learn to use search engines to discover NetWare 5.1 vulnerabilities.

Description: In this activity, you search the Internet for NetWare 5.1 vulnerabilities so that you can find a way to access the server's resources. Because you might not be familiar with NetWare, you also search the Internet for any sites that can assist you in using NetWare commands and conducting a security test.

1. From your Windows XP Professional system, open a Web browser, type **www.cve.mitre.org** in the Address text box, and press **Enter**.

2. Scroll down the Common Vulnerabilities and Exposures (CVE) home page, and click the **Search CVE** icon.

3. On the Search CVE page, type **NetWare 5.1** in the Keyword(s) text box, and click **Search**. How many CVE entries did you find?

4. CAN-2001-1233 pertains to enumerating user names, group names, and other information that could be obtained from a remote user. Click this entry and read the information. Should all NetWare users be concerned about this candidate?

5. Return to the page of entries, and click the **CVE-2002-1417** entry. What significance does it have, if any, for accessing user information?

6. If time permits, read other CVE or CAN entries. When you're done, close your Web browser, and shut down Windows XP.

To see how NetWare enumeration works, take a look at an example of using Nessus to scan a NetWare 5.1 server. Figure 6-21 shows a vulnerability detected in the NetWare server's Lightweight Directory Access Protocol (LDAP) configuration. LDAP (port 389) is the protocol used to access Novell's eDirectory tree and Microsoft Active Directory. Nessus also notes that LdapMiner could be used to exploit this vulnerability. (In Case Project 6-2, you research LdapMiner on the Internet.)

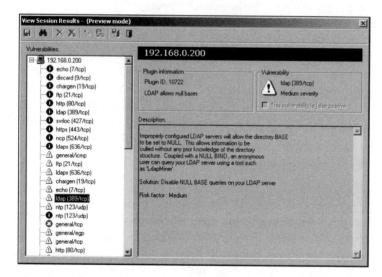

Figure 6-21   Nessus enumerates a NetWare server

In Figure 6-22, another vulnerability has been selected in the tree on the left. Nessus was able to determine eDirectory information, such as the Organization object's name (ZIONBANK) and the Common Name (CN) object of BankActsZionBank.com.

Figures 6-23 and 6-24 show the most dangerous vulnerabilities Nessus discovered: the user name and password for the FTP account (Figure 6-23) and the names of several user accounts (Figure 6-24). An attacker could use these login names and passwords to attempt access to the server.

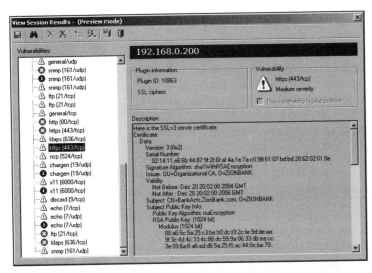

Figure 6-22   Enumerating eDirectory in Nessus

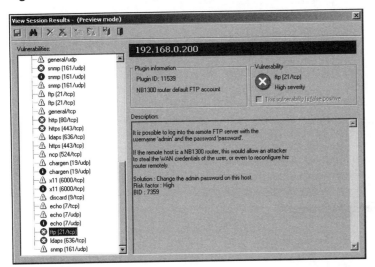

Figure 6-23   Nessus discovers the FTP account's user name and password

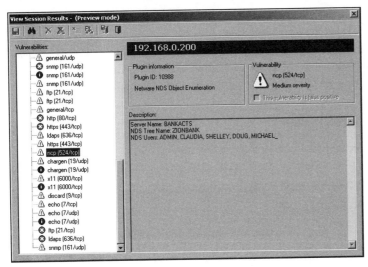

Figure 6-24   Nessus enumerates several user accounts

Like Microsoft, NetWare has its own tools for gathering information on shares and resources. If you know you might have to conduct security tests on a network with NetWare servers, consider installing Novell Client32, available via the Download link at *www.novell.com*. In this following example, the client for Windows 95/98 was downloaded, but clients for other OSs are available. After downloading the client software, you run the Setup program to install it. When you restart your computer, you're prompted with the Novell Login dialog box shown in Figure 6-25.

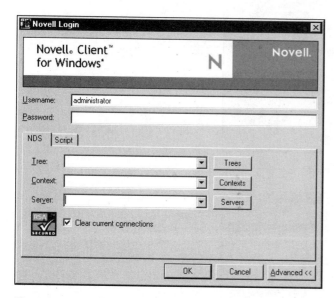

Figure 6-25   The Novell Login dialog box

If you click the Trees button, the Tree dialog box opens (see Figure 6-26). It's possible to access this dialog box without supplying a login name or password, a vulnerability of the NetWare OS.

Figure 6-26   The Tree dialog box

After you click OK, the Novell Login dialog box opens again. Clicking the Contexts button displays a list of available contexts (the location in the eDirectory tree). In Figure 6-27, the context name of New York is displayed, but no information on logging in to the server has been given yet.

Figure 6-27   Displaying available contexts in NetWare

If you click OK in the Contexts dialog box, you return to the Novell Login dialog box. Clicking the Server button displays a list of available servers to log in to (see Figure 6-28). The next step is selecting a server (BANKACTS is the only one available in this example) and clicking OK.

Figure 6-28   Displaying available servers in NetWare

The Novell Login dialog box now has data entered in all the login fields. The next step is trying to change the login name to "Admin" and the password to "password," the information Nessus gathered from the FTP account (see Figure 6-29).

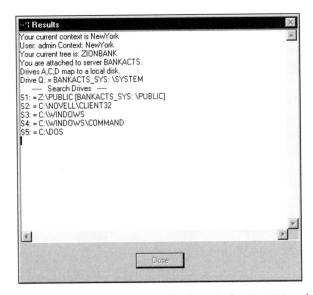

Figure 6-29   Logging in with credentials supplied by Nessus

After clicking OK, the window shown in Figure 6-30 is displayed, indicating that the correct login name and password were entered.

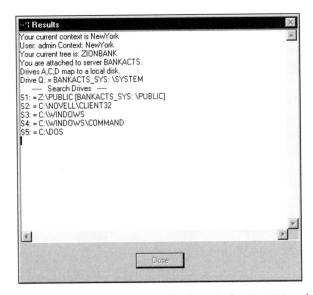

Figure 6-30   Information displayed after NetWare login is accepted

Now you have access to the NetWare server. If you open Windows Explorer, you can access the server through mappings the client software created (see Figure 6-31).

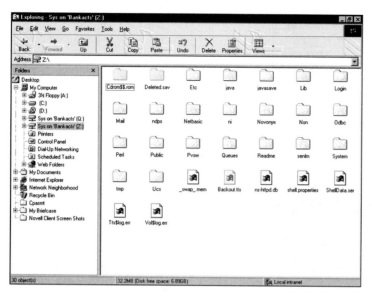

Figure 6-31   Accessing NetWare through mapped drives

ENUMERATING THE *NIX OPERATING SYSTEM

Of the OSs covered in this chapter, UNIX is the oldest. Most computer manufacturers have developed their own flavors of this popular OS, but because of copyright restrictions (only AT&T can use the name UNIX), they can't use "UNIX" in their product names. Other variations of UNIX include the following:

- Solaris (Sun Microsystems)
- SunOS (Sun Microsystems)
- Xenix (Microsoft)
- HP-UX (Hewlett-Packard)
- A/UX (Apple)
- Dynix (Sequent)
- Linux (developed by Linus Torvalds)
- Fedora Linux (developed by contributors and sponsored by Red Hat)
- Debian Linux (developed by world-wide contributors)
- SUSE Linux (Novell Corporation)
- Red Hat Linux (Red Hat Software)
- Ultrix (Digital Equipment)
- AIX (IBM)
- BSD UNIX (Univerity of California at Berkley)
- FreeBSD (BSD-based UNIX, developed by many contributors)
- OpenBSD (BSD-based UNIX, developed by contributors)
- NetBSD (BSD-based UNIX, developed by contributors)

As you can see, many companies have a version of the UNIX operating system. Linux, created by Linus Torvalds, is just that: a variation of UNIX. With all the UNIX variations available, it's no wonder that many computer professionals are trying out this operating system. Newer versions of Linux are easier to install and configure. They also include GUIs and Web browsers that make the software less complicated to use. With the use of Linux Loader (LILO, a bootloader for multiboot systems) or Grand Unified Bootloader (GRUB), having your home computer or laptop start in both Windows and Linux is possible. Even novice computer users can now install the latest version, Fedora Linux.

UNIX Enumeration

The most popular enumeration tool for security testers and hackers alike is the Finger utility, which enables you to find out who is logged in to a *NIX system with one simple command (see Figure 6-32).

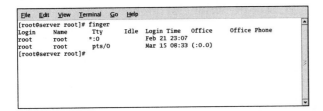

Figure 6-32   Using the Finger command

If you have any experience with UNIX, you might have used Finger to determine who was running a process that seemed to have taken over the OS, such as an endless loop or one that was causing other processes to freeze. Before stopping such a process, an administrator might want to find its owner and then contact that person to find out what's running and prevent the problem from happening again.

Nessus is also helpful in *NIX enumeration. Figure 6-33 shows what Nessus found when scanning a Red Hat Linux 3.0 Enterprise server and a Linux 7.2 system. As you can see, Nessus rates the vulnerability as "High Severity." Nessus claims that the vulnerability is related to buffer management functions that might give an attacker the ability to issue arbitrary commands on the host. In other words, a buffer overflow is a possibility on this system.

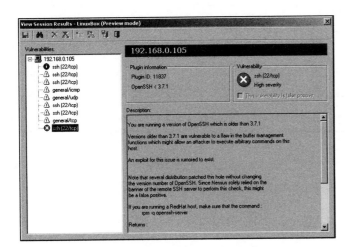

Figure 6-33   Nessus enumeration of a Linux system

Activity 6-4: Enumerating UNIX Systems with Finger

Time Required: 30 minutes

Objective: Learn to use the Finger command on local and remote *NIX systems.

Description: In this activity, you use the Finger command to enumerate your Linux computer and see how this powerful command can gather information from a remote system.

1. From your Windows XP Professional system, boot from the student Linux CD.

2. Open a shell, type **man finger**, and press **Enter**.

3. Read through the manual, using the spacebar to scroll through the document. Press Ctrl+Z to exit when you're finished.

4. From any shell, type **finger root**, and then press **Enter**. Note that the output displays the logon name, the directory in which the root account is currently located, the shell being used, and the date the root account logged on to the system.

5. To find out if there's a root account on a remote *NIX server, type the command **finger root@mit.edu** and press **Enter**. You can experiment with different remote addresses, but using root@mit.edu returned the information shown in Figure 6-34, as of the writing of this book.

```
[root@server /]# finger root@mit.edu
Student data loaded as of May 17, Staff data loaded as of May 17.

Notify Personnel or use WebSIS as appropriate to change your information.

Our on-line help system describes
  How to change data, how the directory works, where to get more info.
  For a listing of help topics, enter finger help@mit.edu. Try finger
  help_about@mit.edu to read about how the directory works.
  Directory bluepages may be found at http://mit.edu/communications/bp.

There were 2 matches to your request.

Complete information will be shown only when one individual matches
your query.  Resubmit your query with more information.
For example, use both firstname and lastname or use the alias field.

     name: Root, David
department: The Broad Institute
    title: Research Scientist II, RNAi Consortium Project Ldr
    alias: D-root

     name: Root, Philip J
    title: G
    alias: P-root
[root@server /]#
```

Figure 6-34   Using the Finger command on a remote system

6. Read the output that was returned, and note that two additional names were obtained: David and Philip. This account information could come in handy if you were attempting to enumerate this server.

7. To dig deeper, type the command **finger David@mit.edu** and press **Enter** to see whether you can gather more information on this person. Figure 6-35 shows the information returned.

```
[root@server /]# finger David@mit.edu
Student data loaded as of May 17, Staff data loaded as of May 17.

Notify Personnel or use WebSIS as appropriate to change your information.

Our on-line help system describes
  How to change data, how the directory works, where to get more info.
  For a listing of help topics, enter finger help@mit.edu. Try finger
  help_about@mit.edu to read about how the directory works.
  Directory bluepages may be found at http://mit.edu/communications/bp.

There were 5 matches to your request.

Complete information will be shown only when one individual matches
your query.  Resubmit your query with more information.
For example, use both firstname and lastname or use the alias field.

     name: Martin, David F
department: Media Laboratory
    title: Administrative Assistant II
    alias: D-martin1

     name: David, Edwin F
department: Lincoln Laboratory
    title: LL - Technical Staff
    alias: E-david

     name: David, James A.W.
department: Non-Institute  Harvard
     year: 4
    alias: J-david

     name: David, Lawrence Anthony
    title: G
    alias: L-david

     name: David, Robert
department: Mechanical Engineering
     year: G
    alias: R-david
[root@server /]#
```

Figure 6-35   Using the Finger command to gather information on a specific user

8. The plot is getting thicker! Next, choose one of the accounts that Finger identified. Type **finger -s E-david@mit.edu** and press **Enter**. Figure 6-36 shows the results of this command.

```
[root@server /]# finger -s E-david@mit.edu
Student data loaded as of May 17, Staff data loaded as of May 17.

Notify Personnel or use WebSIS as appropriate to change your information.

Our on-line help system describes
  How to change data, how the directory works, where to get more info.
  For a listing of help topics, enter finger help@mit.edu. Try finger
  help_about@mit.edu to read about how the directory works.
  Directory bluepages may be found at http://mit.edu/communications/bp.

There was 1 match to your request.

      name: David, Edwin F
     email: edavid@LL.MIT.EDU
     phone: (781) 981-4309
   address: LL-S3-357
department: Lincoln Laboratory
     title: LL - Technical Staff
     alias: E-david
[root@server /]#
```

Figure 6-36 Using Finger to gather additional information on a user

9. Take a few minutes to review the other accounts the Finger command revealed. Remember to use the Philip@mit.edu account, too.

10. Identifying the account logon names on a system can be damaging to the owner or administrator of that system. What other information did the Finger command supply that an attacker could use? Give specific examples.

11. Close any open windows, and shut down your system.

CHAPTER SUMMARY

❏ Enumeration is the process of extracting user names, passwords, and shared resources from a system.

❏ Enumerating Microsoft targets can be done with built-in Microsoft tools, such as the Nbtstat, Net view, and Net use commands, or with a variety of other utilities. Enumerating Microsoft systems relies heavily on the NetBIOS null session vulnerability.

❏ Many of the enumeration tools used on Microsoft targets can also be used on NetWare targets. In addition, the Novell Client software can be used for NetWare enumeration to view the eDirectory structure and shared resources.

❏ Enumeration of *NIX systems can be done with built-in UNIX utilities, such as the Finger command, and with tools used for enumerating other OSs, such as Nessus.

KEY TERMS

enumeration — The process of connecting to a system and obtaining information such as logon names, passwords, group memberships, and shared resources.

Network Basic Input Output System (NetBIOS) — A Microsoft programming interface that allows computers to communicate across a LAN.

null session — A null session is an unauthenticated connection to a Microsoft system.

Tar command — This command combines multiple files and folders into a file called a tape archive, but it does not compress files and folders.

REVIEW QUESTIONS

1. _____ is usually conducted after port scanning and is a more intrusive testing process.

   a. Port scanning

   b. Enumeration

   c. Null scanning

   d. Numeration

2. Security testers conduct enumeration for which of the following reasons? (Choose all that apply.)

   a. to gain access to shares and network resources

   b. to obtain user logon names and group memberships

   c. to discover services running on computers and servers

   d. to discover open ports on computers and servers

3. Which of the following tools can be used to enumerate Microsoft operating systems? (Choose all that apply.)

   a. Nessus

   b. DumpSec

   c. DumpIt

   d. Hyena

4. Enumeration can be more difficult to conduct if port _____ is filtered.

   a. 110/UDP

   b. 443/UDP

   c. 80/TCP

   d. 139/UDP

5. Which of the following commands can you use to uncompress the nbtscan-1.5.1.tar.gz file? (Choose two answers.)

   a. unzip nbtscan-1.5.1.tar.gz

   b. gzip nbtscan-1.5.1.tar.gz

   c. gzip –d nbtscan-1.5.1.tar.gz

   d. tar –zxvf nbtscan-1.5.1.tar.gz

6. Which of the following commands do you use to expand the nbtscan-1.5.1.tar file?

   a. tar –xvf nbtscan-1.5.1.tar

   b. tar –expand nbtscan-1.5.1.tar

   c. tar –xvf nbtscan-1.5.1.tar.gz

   d. tar –xvf nbtscan-1.5.1.gz

7. To identify the NetBIOS names of systems on the 193.145.85.0 network, which of the following commands do you use?

   a. nbtscan 193.145.85.0/24

   b. nbtscan 193.145.85.0-255

   c. nbtstat 193.145.85.0/24

   d. netstat 193.145.85.0/24

8. Which of the following is a Microsoft command-line utility for seeing NetBIOS shares on a Microsoft network?

   a. Net use

   b. Net user

   c. Net view

   d. Nbtuser

9. To view eDirectory information on a NetWare 5.1 server, which of the following tools should you use?

   a. Nmap

   b. Mmap

   c. Nbtstat

   d. Novell Client32

10. The Nbtstat command is used to enumerate *NIX systems. True or False?

11. A NetBIOS name can contain a maximum of _____ characters.

    a. 10

    b. 11

    c. 15

    d. 16

12. Which of the following commands connects a computer to another computer running the Server service?

    a. Net view

    b. Net use

    c. Netstat

    d. Nbtstat

13. Which port numbers are most vulnerable to NetBIOS attacks?

    a. ports 135 to 137

    b. ports 389 to 1023

    c. ports 135 to 139

    d. ports 110 and 115

14. Which of the following is a popular tool for enumerating Microsoft operating systems?

    a. DumpSec

    b. DumpIt

    c. Netcat

    d. Finger

15. Which of the following is the Nessus client that can be installed on a Windows operating system?

    a. Nessus

    b. NessusWX

    c. Nessus for Windows

    d. Nessus Client

16. Most NetBIOS enumeration tools connect to the target system by using which of the following?

    a. ICMP packets

    b. default logons and blank passwords

    c. null logons and null passwords

    d. Admin accounts

17. What is the best method of preventing NetBIOS type attacks?

    a. filter ports 135 to 139 at the firewall

    b. tell users to create difficult-to-guess passwords

    c. pause the Workstation service

    d. stop the Workstation service

18. Which of the following is a commonly used UNIX enumeration tool?

    a. Netcat

    b. Nbtstat

    c. Netstat

    d. Finger

19. Which of the following commands should you use to determine whether there are any shared resources on a Windows 98 computer with an IP address of 193.145.85.202?

    a. netstat –c 193.145.85.202

    b. nbtscan –a 193.145.85.202

    c. nbtstat –A 193.145.85.202

    d. nbtstat –A \\193.145.85.202

20. The Microsoft Net use command is a quick way to discover any shared resources on a computer or server. True or False?

CASE PROJECTS

Case 6-1: Enumerating Systems on the K. J. Williams Network

After conducting enumeration of the K. J. Williams network, you discover several Windows 98 computers with shared folders for the Help Desk Department. You're concerned when you access one of the shared folders containing information for help desk personnel and find an Excel spreadsheet listing e-mail addresses and passwords for all employees. The help desk staff use this shared folder to access the Excel spreadsheet if users call claiming that they have forgotten their passwords. Help desk staff need this information even when they're away from their office.

Based on the preceding information, write a one-page memo to the IT manager, Bob Jones, describing the steps you would take after this discovery. The memo should also mention any information you find in the OSSTMM that relates to your discovery and offer recommendations.

Case 6-2: Researching LdapMiner on the Internet

After using Nessus and other enumeration tools, you discover that K .J. Williams is running a NetWare 5.1 server to store billing information. Nessus has revealed five accounts on the NetWare server: TMulligan, CSmith, GPetrelli, PRichardson, and CRivera. Nessus also shows that a vulnerability in the NetWare server's LDAP service could be compromised with a program called LdapMiner, so you conduct an Internet search on this program.

Based on the information you found, write a one-page report to your supervisor describing how LdapMiner can be used to attack the NetWare server and discussing the exploits that could be launched by using the listed user accounts.

PROGRAMMING FOR SECURITY PROFESSIONALS

After reading this chapter and completing the exercises, you will be able to:

♦ Explain basic programming concepts

♦ Write a simple C program

♦ Explain how Web pages are created with HTML

♦ Describe and create basic Perl programs

♦ Explain basic object-oriented programming concepts

As a security professional, you need to know how both hackers and security testers use computer programming. This chapter describes the basic skills of programming. You won't be an expert programmer after this chapter, but you'll have a clearer idea of how computer programs are written. Removing the mystique eliminates the fear many networking professionals experience when hearing the word "programming." Having a basic understanding of programming can also help you in developing custom security tools or modifying existing tools when you're conducting security tests. In fact, most security tester positions require being able to create customized security tools. Just as a good carpenter knows how to modify a tool to fit a special job, security testers should know how to modify computer tools created for one purpose so that they can be used for other functions.

This chapter gives you a general overview of C, HTML, and Perl. Becoming a computer programmer takes a lot of time and practice, but this chapter gives you an opportunity to examine some computer programs and practice writing a couple of programs yourself.

INTRODUCTION TO COMPUTER PROGRAMMING

Just as book editors must understand the rules of the English language, computer programmers must understand the rules of programming languages. Instead of grammatical errors, programmers must deal with syntax errors. A command's syntax must be exact, right down to the placement of semicolons and parentheses. One minor mistake and the program won't run correctly or, even worse, it produces unpredictable results. Being a computer programmer takes a keen eye and patience; keep in mind that errors aren't unusual the first time you try to create a program.

Computer Programming Fundamentals

Manuals filled with a programming language's syntax and commands can take up a lot of space on your shelves, but there are some basics in any programming language that you can learn without consulting manuals. In fact, you can begin writing programs with just a little knowledge of some programming fundamentals, which you can remember with the acronym BLT (as in bacon, lettuce, and tomato): branching, looping, and testing.

Branching, Looping, and Testing (BLT)

Most programming languages have a way to branch, loop, and test. For example, a function in a C program can branch to another function in the program, perform a task there, and then return to its starting point. A **function** is a mini program within a main program that carries out a task. For example, you can write a function that adds two numbers and then returns the answer to the function that called it. **Branching** takes you from one area of a program (a function) to another area. **Looping** is the act of performing a task over and over. The loop usually completes after **testing** is conducted on a variable and returns a value of true or false. Although you don't need to worry about the syntax for now, examine the following program to see where it uses branching, looping, and testing:

```
main()
{
    int a = 1 /* Variable initialized as an integer, value 1 */
    if (a > 2) /* Testing if "a" is greater than 2 */
      printf("A is greater than 2");
    else
      GetOut(); /* Branching--calling a different function */
GetOut() /* Do something interesting here */
  {
      for(a=1; a<11; a++) /* Loop to print 10 times */
{
printf("I'm in the GetOut() function");
}
  }
}
```

There you have it: the BLT of computer programming. Of course, there's a lot more to learn in programming, but by knowing how to do these three actions, you can examine a computer program and understand its functionality.

A computer program contains different functions, or modules, that perform specific tasks. Say you're writing a program for making a BLT sandwich. The first step is to list the tasks in this process. In computer lingo, you're writing an **algorithm** (a recipe) to make a BLT sandwich. You keep an algorithm as simple as possible, but creating an algorithm is one of the most important programming skills to master.

Skipping a step in an algorithm can cause problems. For example, not rinsing the lettuce might result in a bug in your sandwich. Similarly, not reviewing your program's code carefully might result in having a **bug** in your program—an error that causes unpredictable results. Bugs are worse than syntax errors because a program can run successfully with a bug, but the output might be incorrect or inconsistent. Performing tasks in the incorrect order might also create havoc. For example, putting mayonnaise on the bread before toasting it can result in soggy toast. The following list is an example of an algorithm for making a BLT sandwich:

- Purchase the ingredients.
- Gather all the utensils needed for making the sandwich.
- Clean the tomatoes and lettuce.
- Slice the tomatoes and separate the lettuce leaves.
- Fry the bacon.
- Drain the bacon.
- Toast the bread.
- Put mayonnaise on the toast.
- Put the fried bacon, sliced tomato, and lettuce leaves on the toast.
- Join the two slices of toasted bread.

A programmer would then convert this algorithm into **pseudocode**. Pseudocode is not a programming language; it's an English-like language you can use to help create the structure of your program. The following example is the pseudocode that addresses purchasing all the ingredients needed for a BLT sandwich before you write the programming code:

```
PurchaseIngredients Function
    Call GetCar Function
    Call DriveToStore Function
    Purchase Bacon, Bread, Tomatoes, Lettuce, and Mayonnaise at store
End PurchaseIngredients Function
```

After writing pseudocode, you can then begin writing your program in the language of your choosing. Are writing an algorithm and pseudocode necessary for every computer program you write? No. If the program you're writing has very few lines of code, you can skip these steps, but for beginning programmers, these two steps are helpful.

Documentation

When writing any computer program, documenting your work is essential. To do this, you add comments to the code that explain what you're doing. Documentation not only makes your program easier for someone else to modify; it also helps you remember what you were thinking when you wrote the program. The phrase "No comment" might be appropriate for politicians or Wall Street investors with inside trading information, but not for computer programmers.

Although documentation is important, many programmers find it time consuming and tedious. Often they think their code is self-explanatory and easy enough for anyone to maintain and modify, so documenting their work isn't necessary. You'll soon discover, however, that without good documentation you won't understand the lines of code you wrote three weeks ago, let alone expect a stranger to figure out your train of thought. For example, the following comments can help the next programmer understand why a new function was added to an existing program:

```
// The following function was added to the program June 15, 2005
// per a request from the Marketing Department.
// It appears that reports generated by the sales() function were
// not giving the Marketing folks information about the sales in
// Asia. This new function now uses data from text files from the
// offices in Tokyo and Hong Kong. - Bob C. Twins
```

Software engineering firms don't retain computer programmers who do not document their work because they know that 80% of the cost of software projects is maintenance. They also know that an average of one bug for every 2000 lines of code is the industry standard. Windows 2000 contains almost 50 million lines of code. Microsoft software engineers, partly because of strict documentation rules, were able to limit bugs to fewer than 60,000 in this program. To a novice programmer, this number might seem extremely high, but Microsoft is way below the industry standard on the average number of bugs. With bugs being so prevalent in programs, it's easy to see how attackers can discover vulnerabilities in software. With thousands of lines of code, it's no wonder programmers can miss something that might create a security hole attackers can exploit.

Activity 7-1: Writing Your First Algorithm

Time Required: 10 minutes

Objective: Learn to write an algorithm.

Description: Computer programmers must be able to think logically and to approach problem solving in distinct steps or tasks. Missing a step can have disastrous affects, so you should train yourself to think in a structured and logical way. A good way to test whether you can follow a step-by-step approach is by doing exercises that encourage you to think in this manner. For this activity, list at least 10 steps for making scrambled eggs. When writing the steps, make sure you don't take anything for granted. That is, assume someone with no knowledge of cooking—or even of eggs—will try to follow your algorithm.

LEARNING THE C LANGUAGE

Many programming languages are available to security testers. You'll begin your journey with an introduction to one of the most popular programming languages: C, developed by Dennis Ritchie at Bell Laboratories in 1972. The C language is both powerful and concise. In fact, UNIX, which was first written in **assembly language**, was soon rewritten in C. Not many programmers would enjoy writing programs in binary (machine code) or machine language. Assembly language uses a combination of hexadecimal numbers and expressions, such as mov, add, and sub, making it easier for humans to write programs.

This chapter provides a simple overview of the C language. Many colleges devote an entire semester to learning this language; others skip C and teach C++, an enhancement of the C language. Many security professionals and hackers still use C because of its power and cross-platform usability.

A **compiler** is a program that converts a text-based program, called source code, into executable or binary code. Table 7-1 lists some of the available C compilers. Most C compilers can also create executable programs in C++. The Intel and Microsoft compilers must be purchased, but many other compilers are free and can be found with a simple Internet search.

Table 7-1   C language compilers

Compiler	Description
Intel Compilers for Microsoft Windows and Linux	Intel's C++ compiler for developing applications for Windows servers, desktops, and handheld PDAs. The Intel Linux C++ compiler claims to optimize the speed of accessing information from a MySQL database, an open-source database program used by many corporations and e-commerce companies.
Microsoft Visual C++ Compiler	This compiler is widely used by programmers developing C and C++ applications for Windows platforms.
GNU C and C++ compilers (GCC)	These free compilers can be downloaded for Windows and *NIX platforms. Most *NIX systems include the GNU GCC compiler.

The dangerous thing about C is that a beginner can make some big blunders. For example, a programmer can write to areas of memory that cause damage to the OS kernel. Keep in mind that the C language can do as much damage as assembly language, but is a lot easier to learn and use.

Anatomy of a C Program

Many veteran programmers can't think of the C language without remembering the "Hello, world!" program, the first computer program a C student learns:

```
/* The famous "Hello, world!" C program */

#include <stdio.h> /* Load the standard IO library. The library
contains functions your C program might need to call to perform
various tasks. */

main()
{
    printf("Hello, world!\n\n");
}
```

That's it. You can write these lines of code in almost any text editor, such as Notepad if you're using Windows or the vi editor if you're using Linux. The following sections examine each line of code in the "Hello, world!" program.

Many C programs use the /* and */ characters to comment large portions of text instead of using the // characters for one-line comments. For example, you can type the /* characters, add as many lines of comment text as needed, and then type the closing */ characters. Forgetting to add the */ at the end of comment text can cause errors when compiling the program, so be careful.

The #include statement is used to load libraries that hold the commands and functions used in your program. In the Hello, world! example, the #include <stdio.h> statement loads the stdio.h library, which contains many C functions.

The parentheses in C mean you're dealing with a function. C programs must contain a main() function, but you can also add your own functions to a C program. Note that after the main() function, an open brace (the { character) is on a line by itself. Braces show where a function begins and ends. In the Hello, world! program, the closing brace indicates the end of the program. Forgetting to add a closing brace is a common mistake.

Inside the main() function, the program calls another function: printf(). When a function calls another function, it uses parameters, also known as arguments. Parameters are placed between opening and closing parentheses. In this example, the parameters "Hello, world!\n\n" are passed to the printf() function. The printf() function then prints the words "Hello, world!" to the screen, and the \n\n characters print two line feeds after the "Hello, world!" statement. Table 7-2 lists some special characters that can be used with the printf() function.

Table 7-2 Special characters for use with the printf() function

Character	Description
\n	New line
\t	Tab
\0	Null (used to end or terminate a string of characters)

Declaring Variables

A variable, as you know, represents a numeric or string value. For example, you can solve x + y = z if you know two of the variable values. In programming, you can declare variables at the beginning of a program so that calculations can be carried out without user intervention. A variable might be defined as a character or characters, such as the letters of the alphabet, or it can be assigned a numeric value, as in the expression int x = 1. Table 7-3 shows some of the variable types used in C.

Table 7-3   Variable types in C

Variable Type	Description
int	Use this variable type for an integer (positive or negative number).
float	This variable type is for a real number that includes a decimal point, such as 1.299999.
double	Use this variable type for a double-precision floating point.
char	This variable type holds the value of a single letter.
string	This variable type holds the value of multiple characters or words.
const	A constant variable is one you create to hold a value that doesn't change for the duration of your program. For example, you can create a constant variable called TAX and give it a specific value: const TAX = .085. If this variable is used in areas of the program that calculate total costs after adding an 8.5% tax, it's easier to change the constant value to a different number if the tax rate changes, instead of changing every occurrence of 8.5% to 8.6%.

If the printf() function contains values other than a quoted sentence, such as numbers, you need to use **conversion specifiers**. Conversion specifiers for the printf() function are listed in Table 7-4. A conversion specifier tells the compiler how to convert the value in a function. For example, `printf("Your name is %s!", name)` prints the following if you have assigned the value Sue to the string variable called name:

```
Your name is Sue!
```

Table 7-4   Conversion specifiers in C

Specifier	Type
%c	Character
%d	Decimal number
%f	Floating decimal or double number
%s	Character string

In addition to conversion specifiers, programmers use operators to compare values, perform mathematical calculations, and the like. Most likely, programs you write will require calculating values based on mathematical operations, such as addition or subtraction. Table 7-5 describes the many mathematical operators used in C.

Table 7-5   Mathematical operators in C

Operator	Description
+ (unary)	Doesn't change the value of the number. Unary operators use a single argument; binary operators use two arguments. Example: +(2).
- (unary)	Returns the negative value of a single number.
++ (unary)	Increments the unary value by 1. For example, if a is equal to 5, the ++a command changes the value to 6.
-- (unary)	Decrements the unary value by 1. For example, if a is equal to 5, the --a command changes the value to 4.
+ (binary)	Addition. For example, a + b.
- (binary)	Subtraction. For example, a - b.
* (binary)	Multiplication. For example, a * b.
/ (binary)	Division. For example, a / b.
% (binary)	Modulus. For example, 10 % 3 is equal to 1 because 10 divided by 3 leaves a remainder of 1.

You might also need to test whether a condition is true or false when writing a C program. To do that, you need to understand how to use logical operators, described in Table 7-6.

Table 7-6   Logical operators in C

Operator	Description
==	Used to compare the equality of two variables. In a == b, for example, the condition is true if variable a is equal to variable b.
!=	Not equal. The exclamation mark negates the equal sign. For example, the statement if a != b is read as "if a is not equal to b."
>	Greater than.
<	Less than.
>=	Greater than or equal to.
<=	Less than or equal to.
&&	The AND operator; evaluated as true if both sides of the operator are equal. For example, if ((a > 5) && (b > 5)) printf ("Hello, world!"); prints only if both a and b are greater than 5.
||	The OR operator; evaluated as true if either side of the operator is equal.
!	The NOT operator; the statement a != 5, for example, means that variable a is not equal to the number 5.

Using operators, you can write rather cryptic-looking code in C. For example, TotalSalary += 5 is another way of writing TotalSalary = TotalSalary + 5. Similarly, TotalSalary -= 5 means the TotalSalary variable now contains the value of TotalSalary - 5.

TIP

Many beginning C programmers make the mistake of using a single equal sign (=) instead of the double equal sign (==) when attempting to test the value of a variable. A single equal sign is used to assign a value to a variable. For example, a = 5 assigns the value of 5 to the variable a. To test the value of variable a, you could use the command "if (a == 5)." If you mistakenly wrote the statement as "if (a = 5)," the value of 5 is assigned to the variable a, and then the statement is evaluated as true. This is because any value not equal to zero is evaluated as true, and a zero value is evaluated as false.

Although this chapter covers only the most basic elements of a computer program, with what you have learned so far, you can write a C program that prints something on the screen. Security testers should work to gain additional programming skills so that they can develop tools for performing specific tasks, as you'll see in "Understanding Perl" later in this chapter.

Branching, Looping, and Testing in C

Branching in C is as easy as placing a function in your program followed by a semicolon. The following C code does absolutely nothing, but it shows you how to begin writing a program that can be developed later:

```
main()
{
    prompt();      //Call function to prompt user with a question
    display();     //Call function to display graphics on screen
    calculate();   //Call function to do complicated math
    cleanup();     //Call function to make all variables equal to
                   //zero
```

```
prompt()
{
[code for prompt() function goes here]
}
display()
{
[code for display() function goes here]
}
[etc.]
}
```

When the program runs, it branches to the prompt() function and then continues branching to the functions listed subsequently. By creating a program in this fashion, you can develop each function or module one at a time. You can also delegate writing other functions to people with more experience in certain areas. For example, you can have a math wizard write the calculate() function if math is not your forte.

C has several methods for looping. The **while loop** is one way of having your program repeat an action a certain number of times. It checks whether a condition is true and then continues looping until the condition becomes false. Take a look at the following code and see whether you can understand what the program is doing:

```
main()
{
    int counter = 1;        //Initialize counter variable

    while (counter <= 10) //Do what's in the brackets until false
    {
        printf("Counter is equal to %d\n", counter);
        ++counter; //Increment counter by 1;
    }
}
```

Figure 7-1 shows the output of this program. In this example, when the counter variable is greater than 10, the while loop stops processing. This causes printf() to print 10 lines of output before stopping.

```
File   Edit   View   Terminal   Go   Help
[root@server /]# gcc -c while.c -o while.o
[root@server /]# gcc -o while.exe while.o
[root@server /]# ./while.exe
Counter is equal to 1
Counter is equal to 2
Counter is equal to 3
Counter is equal to 4
Counter is equal to 5
Counter is equal to 6
Counter is equal to 7
Counter is equal to 8
Counter is equal to 9
Counter is equal to 10
[root@server /]#
```

Figure 7-1   A while loop in action

The **do loop** performs an action first and then tests to see whether the action should continue to occur. In the following example, the do loop performs the print() function first and then checks whether a condition is true:

```
main()
{
    int counter = 1;           //Initialize counter variable
    do
        {
        printf("Counter is equal to %d\n", counter);
        ++counter;                //Increment counter by 1
```

```
    } while (counter <= 10); //Do what's in the brackets until
                             //false
}
```

NOTE Which is better to use: the while loop or the do loop? That's entirely up to the programmer.

The last loop type in C is the **for loop**, one of C's most interesting pieces of code. In the following for loop, the first part initializes the counter variable to 1, and then the second part tests a condition. It continues looping until the value of counter is equal to or less than 10. The last part of the for loop increments the counter variable by 1. Figure 7-2 shows an example of a for loop.

7

```
for (counter = 1;counter <= 10;counter++);
```

```
 File   Edit   View   Terminal   Go   Help
// The for loop program
//
main()
{
    int counter;

    for(counter = 1;counter <= 10;counter++)
    {
        printf("Counter is equal to %d\n",counter);
    }
}
```

Figure 7-2 A for loop

You might see some C programs with a for loop containing nothing but semicolons, as in this example:

```
for (;;)
        {
printf("Wow!");
        }
```

This code might look odd, but it's a powerful, yet dangerous, implementation of the for loop. The for(;;) tells the compiler to keep doing what's in the brackets over and over and over. You can create an endless loop with this statement if you don't have a way to exit the block of code that's running. Usually, a programmer has a statement inside the block that performs a test on a variable and then exits the block when a certain condition is met.

Activity 7-2: Learning to Use the GNU GCC Compiler

Time Required: 30 minutes

Objective: Understand how to use the GNU GCC compiler included with most *NIX operating systems.

Description: In the past, programmers had to read through their code line by line before submitting the job to the mainframe CPU. The job included all the commands the CPU would execute. If a program was full of errors, the mainframe operator notified the programmer, who had to go through the code again and fix the errors. With today's compilers, you can quickly write a program, compile it, and test it yourself. If the compiler finds errors, it usually indicates what they are so that you can correct the code and compile the program again. In this activity, you create a C program that contains errors and try to compile the program. After seeing the errors generated, you correct the program and then recompile it until you get it right.

1. Start your computer with the Linux CD. Open a shell, type **man gcc**, and press **Enter**.

2. Scroll through the manual by using the spacebar. As you can see, the manual contains more than enough information for learning how to use this compiler. Exit the man page when you're finished.

3. From the shell, type **vi syntax.c** and press **Enter** to use the vi editor.

4. Press **Esc** and type **i** to enter Insert mode.

5. Type the following code, pressing **Enter** after each line:

```
main()
{
        int age
        printf("Enter your age:    ");
        scanf("%d", &age);
        if (age > 0)
        {
            printf("You are %d years old\n", age);
        }
}
```

6. Exit and save the file by pressing **Esc** and then pressing **:** (the colon character). At the : prompt, type **wq** and press **Enter**.

7. To compile the program, enter the **gcc –c syntax.c –o syntax.o** command. The –c and –o switches tell the compiler to compile and create an output file called syntax.o. The compiler returns an error similar to the one shown in Figure 7-3. The error returned varies depending on the version of the compiler you use. In any event, you should be warned that there was a syntax error before printf because there should have been a semicolon after the "int age" statement.

```
[root@server root]# gcc -c syntax.c -o syntax.o
syntax.c: In function `main':
syntax.c:4: syntax error before "printf"
[root@server root]#
```

Figure 7-3   Example of a syntax error

If there are no errors in the source code you created, you get a shell prompt.

Sometimes you can correct an error easily by looking at the line number of the first error detected.

8. To correct the missing semicolon error, you can use the vi editor. Type **vi syntax.c** and press **Enter**. Press **Esc** and then type **a** to enter Append mode. Add a semicolon to the end of the line containing the variable declaration "int age."

9. Save and exit the program.

10. Compile the program again by typing **gcc –c syntax.c –o syntax.o** and pressing **Enter**. (You can also use the up arrow key to return to previous commands.)

11. At the shell prompt, type **gcc –o syntax.exe syntax.o** and press **Enter**.

12. If you entered everything correctly, you should be at the shell prompt. To run the program, type **./syntax.exe** and press **Enter**.

13. Remain in the Linux shell for the next activity.

Security Bytes

NOTE

There are two schools of thoughts on how to handle syntax errors. Many programmers believe the compiler should look for errors in their code and spend little time reading and stepping through the program looking for syntax or logic errors. They just compile it and see what errors pop up. Others refuse to compile the program until they have examined the code thoroughly and are confident it's accurate and syntactically correct. For beginning programmers, examining the code carefully before compiling helps make you a better programmer. You will increase your skills and develop the keen eye needed to spot a missing brace or semicolon.

7

Understanding HTML Basics

HTML is one of the many languages used to create Web pages on the Internet. Basically, HTML files are text files, so they don't contain the complex programming code you see in a C program. As a security professional, you should understand basic HTML syntax because it's still the foundation language used for Web development. No matter what language is used to create a Web page, HTML statements are still used in those pages, so basic HTML knowledge is the foundation for learning other Web-based languages.

Security professionals often need to examine Web pages and recognize when something looks suspicious. You should understand what HTML's limitations are, be able to read an HTML document, and have a basic understanding of what's happening. This section is not going to make you a Web developer, but it does introduce you to some HTML basics so that you have a foundation for exploring and learning other programming and scripting languages.

NOTE

Today, many Web sites use Extensible Markup Language (XML). Although this language isn't covered in this book, it's a good one to study if you want to specialize in Web security. Learning additional Web-development languages, such as DHTML, Perl, Java, and PHP, can also enhance your skill set as a security professional.

Creating a Web Page Using HTML

You can create an HTML Web page in Notepad and then view it in a Web browser, such as Internet Explorer. HTML doesn't use branching, looping, or testing. Basically, it's a static formatting language rather than a programming language. The following is a simple example of HTML code:

```
<!--This is how you add a comment to an HTML Web page-->
<HTML>
<HEAD>
<TITLE>Hello, world--again</TITLE>
</HEAD>
<BODY>
This is where you put page text, such as marketing copy for an
e-commerce business.
</BODY>
</HTML>
```

The < and > symbols denote HTML tags, which act on the data they enclose. Notice that each tag has a matching closing tag that's written with a forward slash (/) added. For example, the <HTML> tag has a closing tag of </HTML>, as do the <HEAD>, <TITLE>, and <BODY> tags. Most HTML Web pages contain these four tags. Table 7-7 describes some common formatting tags used in an HTML Web page.

Table 7-7 HTML formatting tags

Opening Tag	Closing Tag	Description
<H1>	</H1>	Formats text as a level 1 heading. (Level 1 is the largest font size, and level 6 is the smallest.)
<H2>, <H3>, <H4>, <H5>, and <H6>	</H2>, </H3>, </H4>, </H5>, and </H6>	Formats text as a level 2, 3, 4, 5, or 6 heading.
<P>	</P>	Used to mark the beginning and end of a paragraph.
 	</BR>	Used to insert a carriage return.
<B>	</B>	Formats enclosed text in bold.
<I>	</I>	Formats enclosed text in italics.

There are more tags for formatting tables and lists, but this table gives you a general overview of using HTML tags. You can find many books on this subject to learn more about creating HTML Web pages (refer to Appendix B). In Activity 7-3, you get a chance to practice creating a Web page with Notepad as the editor.

Activity 7-3: Creating an HTML Web Page

Time Required: 30 minutes

Objective: Create an HTML Web page.

Description: As a security tester, you might be required to view Web pages and possible Web security issues. A basic knowledge of HTML can help you with this task. In this activity, you create a simple HTML Web page and then view it in your Web browser.

1. Start your computer in Windows XP Professional. Click **Start**, **Run**, type **notepad MyWeb.html** in the Open text box, and press **Enter**. If you're prompted to create a new file, click **Yes**.

2. In the new Notepad document, type the following lines, pressing **Enter** after each line:

```
<!--This HTML Web page has many tags-->
<HTML>
<HEAD>
<TITLE> HTML for Security Testers </TITLE>
</HEAD>
```

3. Type the next two lines, pressing **Enter** *twice* after each line:

```
<BODY>
<H2> Security Tester Web Site </H2>
```

4. Type **<P><B> There are many good Web sites to visit for security testers. For vulnerabilities click </B>** and press **Enter**.

5. Type **<A HREF="HTTP://www.cve.mitre.org"><FONT COLOR="red">here!</FONT></A>** and press **Enter**.

6. Type **</P>** and press **Enter**.

7. Type **
<FONT SIZE="-1">Copyright 2005 Security Testers, Incorporated. </FONT></BR>** and press **Enter**.

8. Type **</BODY>** and press **Enter**. On the last line, type **</HTML>** to end your code.

9. Verify that you have typed everything correctly. Your file should look similar to Figure 7-4. When you're done, save the file.

```
<!-- This HTML web page has many tags -->
<HTML>
<HEAD>
        <TITLE> HTML For Security Testers </TITLE>
</HEAD>
<BODY>

<H2>Security Tester Web Site </H2>

<P><B>There are many good web sites to visit for security testers. For vulnerabilities click</B>
<A HREF="HTTP://www.cve.mitre.org"><FONT COLOR="red">here!</FONT></A>
</P>
<BR><FONT SIZE="-1">Copyright 2005 Security Testers, Incorporated. </FONT></BR>

</BODY>

</HTML>
```

Figure 7-4   HTML source code

10. To test whether you have created the Web page correctly, open Internet Explorer, and click **File**, **Open** from the menu. In the Open dialog box, click **Browse** and click the **MyWeb.html** file you created. Click **Open** and then click **OK**. Your Web page should look like the one in Figure 7-5 if you entered the information correctly.

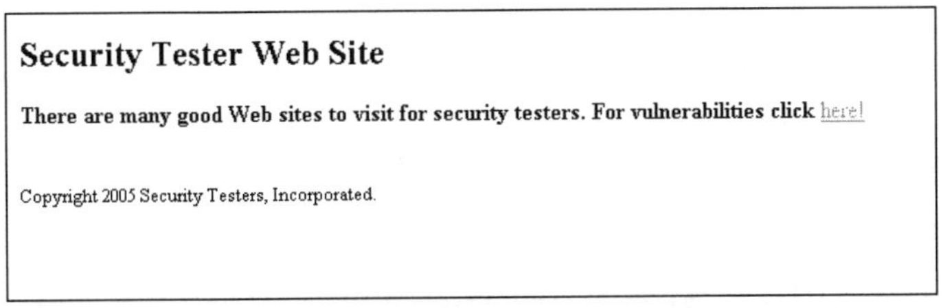

Security Tester Web Site

There are many good Web sites to visit for security testers. For vulnerabilities click here!

Copyright 2005 Security Testers, Incorporated.

Figure 7-5   An HTML Web page

11. Click the **here** hyperlink you created to check whether you're sent to the correct Web site. If not, make corrections to your HTML code.

12. When you're finished, close your Web browser, but leave Windows XP running for the next activity.

UNDERSTANDING PRACTICAL EXTRACTION AND REPORT LANGUAGE (PERL)

Many scripts and programs for security professionals are written in Practical Extraction and Report Language (Perl), a powerful scripting language. In fact, Perl is the next language of choice after C for both hackers and security professionals. In this section, you see why this language is so popular, examine the syntax of the language, and practice writing Perl scripts. You also create a utility for examining the configuration of a Windows XP computer.

Background on Perl

Perl, developed by Larry Wall in 1987, can run on almost any platform, and *NIX-based OSs already have Perl installed. The Perl syntax is similar to C, so C programmers have few difficulties learning Perl. Table 7-8 is a brief timeline of this language. For more details, visit *http://history.perl.org/PerlTimeline.html*.

Table 7-8   Perl timeline

Perl Version	Date	Description
Version 1.0000	December 1987	Wall describes his scripting language as being optimized for scanning text files and extracting information from those files.
Version 2.0000	June 1988	New features added, such as recursive subroutine calls, local variables allowed in blocks and subroutines, a sort operator, and much more.
Version 3.0000	October 1989	Perl now handles binary data, passes arguments to subroutines by reference (previously by value only), and offers debugger enhancements and new functions.

Table 7-8 Perl timeline (continued)

Perl Version	Date	Description
Version 4.0000	March 1991	Perl now includes an artistic license and GPL (GNU Public License). Wall receives the *Dr. Dobbs Journal* Excellence in Programming Award in his final 4.036 version released in 1993.
Version 5.0000	October 1994	Complete rewrite of Perl with more extensive documentation, additional functions, and the introduction of object-oriented programming for Perl. The most current version as of this writing is 5.8.6.
Version 6.000	Not released	Wall wants this version to be a rewrite of version 5.0, but wants the Perl community to participate in the rewriting. Perl 6 will also include Parrot (a language-independent interpreter) as part of its design.

Hackers use Perl to create viruses, worms, and Trojans, but security professionals use it to perform repetitive tasks and conduct security monitoring. Before examining the Perl syntax, in Activity 7-4 you download, install, and write your first Perl script. As with any programming language, the best way to learn Perl is by using it.

ACTIVITY

Activity 7-4: Downloading, Installing, and Running ActivePerl 5.8 for Windows

Time Required: 60 minutes

Objective: Download ActivePerl 5.8 from the Internet, install the program, and write your first Perl script.

Description: Security professionals and hackers alike use the Perl scripting language. Many hacking programs are written in Perl, so any skills you develop in this language will help you in your professional career. In this activity, you download a version of Perl for Windows, install the program on your Windows XP Professional computer, and write a basic Perl script. (*Note*: The version of Perl you download might be different from the one shown in this activity. Updates and enhancements are made to the software, and the dialog boxes might require you to perform different steps than what's indicated here. When in doubt, follow the software's installation instructions.)

1. Start your Web browser, type the URL **http://activestate.com/products/activeperl**, and press **Enter**. If you see a message about security, add the site to your trusted zones.

2. On the ActiveState home page, click the **DOWNLOAD** link.

3. If you're prompted to fill in contact information, skip this step by clicking **Next**.

4. On the ActivePerl page, click the **MSI** link under the Windows heading.

5. In the File Download - Security Warning dialog box, click **Save** and save the installation program to your desktop.

6. In the Download complete dialog box, click **Run** to install the program. (Installation might take 5 to 10 minutes.) If the download box closes automatically, simply double-click the file on the desktop.

7. If necessary, when the Internet Explorer - Security Warning dialog box prompts you about an unknown publisher, click **Run**.

8. In the ActivePerl Setup Wizard, click the **Next** button shown in Figure 7-6.

9. Read the license agreement, verify that the "I accept the terms in the License Agreement" option button is selected, and then click **Next**.

10. In the Custom Setup window, follow the instructions to install all components to your hard disk, as shown in Figure 7-7. If you want to see the total disk space required, click the **Disk Usage** button, and then click **OK**. Click **Next** to accept the features.

7

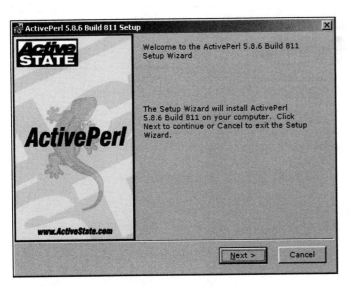

Figure 7-6   The ActivePerl Setup Wizard

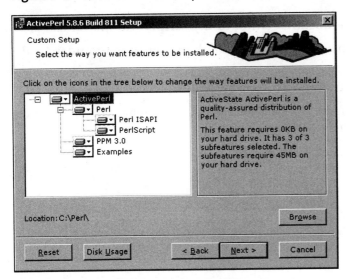

Figure 7-7   Installing ActivePerl features

11. If the New features in PPM window (see Figure 7-8) is displayed, click **Next**.

12. In the Choose optional setup actions window, click **Next** to accept the defaults, and then click **Install**. After several minutes, the program is installed.

13. In the last window, click **Finish**. Then read the release notes and table of contents before exiting the ActivePerl Setup Wizard.

14. To begin writing your Perl script, open a command prompt window and change to the **C:\Perl** directory.

15. Type **notepad first.pl** and press **Enter**. When prompted to create a new file, click **Yes**.

16. On the first line, type **# This is my first Perl script program** and press **Enter**.

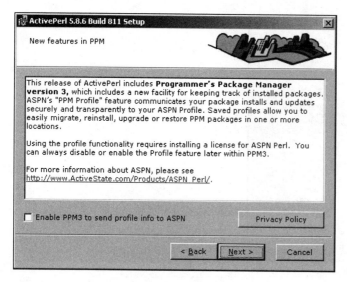

Figure 7-8 ActivePerl PPM features

17. Next, type **# I should always have documentation in my scripts--no matter** and press **Enter**.

18. Finish the previous comment by typing **# how easy I think the script is to understand!** and pressing **Enter** twice.

19. Next, type **print "Hello security testers!\n\n";** and press **Enter**.

20. Your script should look similar to Figure 7-9. Be careful not to miss a semicolon or quotation mark. Remember that programming requires a keen eye.

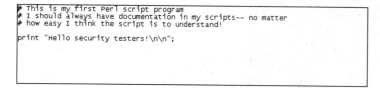

Figure 7-9 Creating the first.pl Perl script

21. Save the file and close Notepad.

22. At the command prompt, type **first.pl** and press **Enter**.

23. If you didn't make any errors, your screen should look like Figure 7-10. If you did receive errors, read through your code and compare it with the lines of code in this activity's steps. Correct any errors and save the file again.

Figure 7-10 Running your first.pl Perl script

24. Close the command prompt window, and leave Windows XP running for the next activity.

Understanding the Basics of Perl

Knowing how to get help quickly in any programming language is useful. The perl -h command gives you a list of parameters used with the perl command (see Figure 7-11).

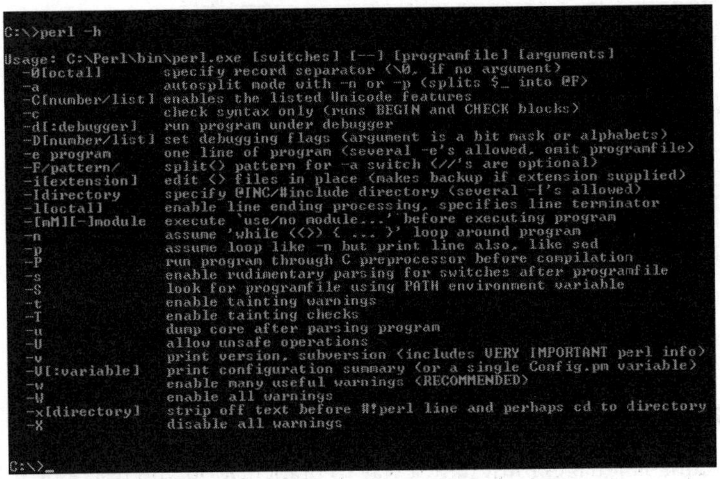

```
C:\>perl -h

Usage: C:\Perl\bin\perl.exe [switches] [--] [programfile] [arguments]
  -0[octal]         specify record separator (\0, if no argument)
  -a                autosplit mode with -n or -p (splits $_ into @F)
  -C[number/list]   enables the listed Unicode features
  -c                check syntax only (runs BEGIN and CHECK blocks)
  -d[:debugger]     run program under debugger
  -D[number/list]   set debugging flags (argument is a bit mask or alphabets)
  -e program        one line of program (several -e's allowed, omit programfile)
  -F/pattern/       split() pattern for -a switch (//'s are optional)
  -i[extension]     edit <> files in place (makes backup if extension supplied)
  -Idirectory       specify @INC/#include directory (several -I's allowed)
  -l[octal]         enable line ending processing, specifies line terminator
  -[mM][-]module    execute `use/no module...' before executing program
  -n                assume 'while (<>) { ... }' loop around program
  -p                assume loop like -n but print line also, like sed
  -P                run program through C preprocessor before compilation
  -s                enable rudimentary parsing for switches after programfile
  -S                look for programfile using PATH environment variable
  -t                enable tainting warnings
  -T                enable tainting checks
  -u                dump core after parsing program
  -U                allow unsafe operations
  -v                print version, subversion (includes VERY IMPORTANT perl info)
  -V[:variable]     print configuration summary (or a single Config.pm variable)
  -w                enable many useful warnings (RECOMMENDED)
  -W                enable all warnings
  -x[directory]     strip off text before #!perl line and perhaps cd to directory
  -X                disable all warnings

C:\>_
```

Figure 7-11 Using the perl -h command

If you want to know what the print command does, you can use perldoc -f print, which produces the output shown in Figure 7-12.

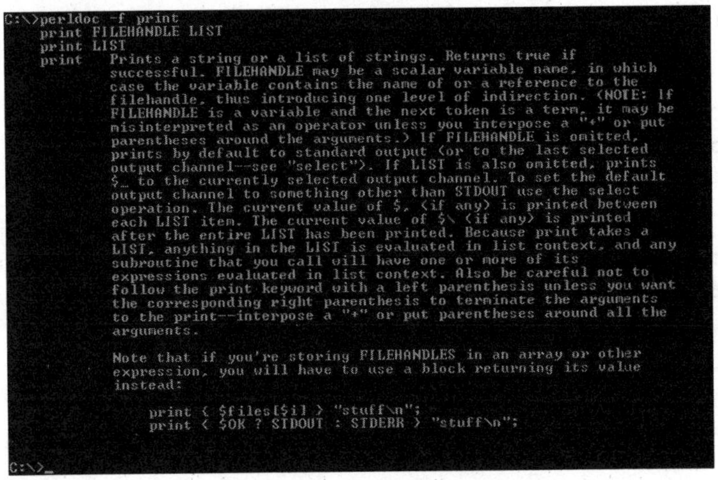

```
C:\>perldoc -f print
    print FILEHANDLE LIST
    print LIST
    print   Prints a string or a list of strings. Returns true if
            successful. FILEHANDLE may be a scalar variable name, in which
            case the variable contains the name of or a reference to the
            filehandle, thus introducing one level of indirection. (NOTE: If
            FILEHANDLE is a variable and the next token is a term, it may be
            misinterpreted as an operator unless you interpose a "+" or put
            parentheses around the arguments.) If FILEHANDLE is omitted,
            prints by default to standard output (or to the last selected
            output channel--see "select"). If LIST is also omitted, prints
            $_ to the currently selected output channel. To set the default
            output channel to something other than STDOUT use the select
            operation. The current value of $, (if any) is printed between
            each LIST item. The current value of $\ (if any) is printed
            after the entire LIST has been printed. Because print takes a
            LIST, anything in the LIST is evaluated in list context, and any
            subroutine that you call will have one or more of its
            expressions evaluated in list context. Also be careful not to
            follow the print keyword with a left parenthesis unless you want
            the corresponding right parenthesis to terminate the arguments
            to the print--interpose a "+" or put parentheses around all the
            arguments.

            Note that if you're storing FILEHANDLES in an array or other
            expression, you will have to use a block returning its value
            instead:

                print { $files[$i] } "stuff\n";
                print { $OK ? STDOUT : STDERR } "stuff\n";

C:\>_
```

Figure 7-12 Using the perldoc command

As you can see, this command gives you a detailed description of the print command. The print command for Perl is almost identical to the C print command. Perl also has the printf command for formatting complex variables. Table 7-9 shows how you can use the printf command to format specific data. Note the similarities to C.

Table 7-9 Using printf to format output

Formatting Character	Description	Input	Output
%c	Character	`printf '%c', "d"`	d
%s	String	`printf '%s', "This is fun!"`	This is fun!

Table 7-9 Using printf to format output (continued)

Formatting Character	Description	Input	Output
%d	Signed integer in decimal	`printf '%+d %d', 1, 1`	+1 1
%u	Unsigned integer in decimal	`printf '%u', 2`	2
%o	Unsigned integer in octal	`printf '%o', 8`	10
%x	Unsigned integer in hexadecimal	`printf '%x', 10`	a
%e	Floating point in scientific notation	`printf '%e', 10;`	1.000000e+001 (OS dependent)
%f	Floating point in fixed decimal notation	`printf '%f', 1;`	1.000000

Understanding the BLT of Perl

As you learned previously, all programming languages must have a way to branch, loop, and test. The following sections use examples of Perl code to show you how Perl handles these BLT functions. As you examine these examples, keep the following syntax rules in mind:

- The keyword "sub" is used in front of function names.
- Variables begin with the $ character.
- Comment lines begin with the # character.
- The & character indicates a function.

Except for these minor differences, Perl's syntax is much like the C syntax. This similarity is one of the reasons many security professionals with C programming experience choose Perl as a scripting language.

Branching in Perl

In a Perl program, to go from one function to another, you simply call the function by entering the function name in your code. In the following example, the &name_best_guitarist line branches the program to the sub name_best_guitarist function:

```
#  Perl program illustrating the branching function
#  Documentation is important
#  Initialize variables
$first_name = "Jimi";
$last_name = "Hendrix";
&name_best_guitarist;
sub name_best_guitarist
{
    printf "%s %s %s", $first_name, $last_name, "was the best guitarist!";
}
```

Looping in Perl

Suppose you want to send an important message to everyone in your class using the Net send command. Because you're sending the same message to multiple users, it's a repetitive task that requires looping. In Activity 7-5, you write a Perl script to do just that: send a message to everyone in the class. As you learned in C, you have several choices for performing a loop. In this section, you learn about two of Perl's looping mechanisms: the for loop and the while loop.

The Perl for loop is identical to the C for loop:

```
for (beginning variable assignment; test condition; increment variable)
{
    a task to do over and over
}
```

Substituting the variable a, you have the following code:

```
for ($a = 1; $a <= 10; $a++)
{
    print "Hello security testers!\n"
}
```

This loop prints the phrase 10 times. Next, try getting the same output by using the while loop, which has the following syntax:

```
while (test condition)
{
    a task to do over and over
}
```

The following code produces the same output as the for loop:

```
$a = 1;
while ($a <=10)
{
    print "Hello security testers!\n";
    $a++
}
```

Security Bytes

Chris Nandor, known for developing the Mac Classic version of Perl 5.8.0, became one of the first hackers to use a Perl script in an online election. Apparently, his Perl script added more than 40,000 votes to an online election for several Red Sox players in 1999. Similarly, in 1993, an online election involving the Denver Broncos traced more than 70,000 votes coming from one IP address. The power of the loop!

Testing Conditions in Perl

Most programs must be able to test the value of a variable or condition. The two looping examples shown previously use the less than and equal operators. Other operators used for testing in Perl are similar to C operators. Table 7-10 lists the operators you can use in Perl. Often you combine these operators with Perl conditionals, such as:

- *if*—Checks whether a condition is true. Example:

```
if ($age > 12) {
    print "You must be a know-it-all!";
}
```

- *else*—Used when there's only one option to carry out if the condition is not true. Example:

```
if ($age) > 12 {
    print "You must be a know-it-all!";
    }
else
    {
    print "Sorry, but I don't know why the sky is blue.";
    }
```

- *elsif*—Used when there are several conditionals to test. Example:

```
if (($age > 12) && ($age < 20))
{
     print "You must be a know-it-all!";
}
elsif ($age > 39)
{
     print "You must lie about your age!";
}
else
  {
     print "To be young...";
}
```

- *unless*—Executes unless the condition is true. Example:

```
unless ($age == 100)
{
     print "Still enough time to get a bachelor's degree.";
}
```

The message prints until the $age variable is equal to 100. With some practice and lots of patience, these examples provide enough information to create thousands of functional Perl scripts.

Table 7-10   Perl operators

Operator	Function	Example
+	Addition	$total=$sal + $commision
-	Subtraction	$profit = $gross_sales - $cost_of_goods
*	Multiplication	$total = $cost * $quantity
/	Division	$GPA = $total_points / $number_of_classes
%	Modulus	$a % 10 = 1
**	Exponent	$total = $a**10
Assignments		
=	Assignment	$Last_name = "Rivera"
+=	Add, then assignment	$a+=10; shorthand for $a=$a+10
-=	Subtract, then assignment	$a-=10; shorthand for $a=$a-10
*=	Multiply, then assignment	$a*=10; shorthand for $a=$a*10
/=	Divide, then assignment	$a/=10; shorthand for $a=$a/10
%=	Modulus, then assignment	$a%=10; shorthand for $a=$a%10
**=	Exponent and assignment	$a**=2; shorthand for $a=$a**2
++	Increment	$a++; increment $a by 1
--	Decrement	$a--; decrement $a by 1
Comparisons		
==	Equal to	$a==1; compare value of $a with 1
!=	Not equal to	$a!=1; $a is not equal to 1
>	Greater than	$a>10
<	Less than	$a<10
>=	Greater than or equal to	$a>=10
<=	Less than or equal to	$a<=10

ACTIVITY

Activity 7-5: Writing a Perl Script That Uses Net Send

Time Required: 30 minutes

Objective: Write a Perl script that uses branching, looping, and testing components.

Description: Security professionals often need to automate or create tools to help them conduct security tests. In this activity, you write a Perl script that uses the Windows XP Net send command and a for loop to select IP numbers from the classroom range your instructor has provided. In addition, you need to verify that the Messenger service is running on all Windows XP computers. Microsoft strongly recommends that all computers connecting to the Internet not run the Messenger service because of network vulnerabilities, so by default, Windows XP Service Pack 2 (SP2) disables it. For this activity, you need to enable the service so that a message can be sent to your computer.

1. Write down the IP address range used in the classroom.

2. To check whether the Messenger service is running on your computer, click **Start**, right-click **My Computer**, and click **Manage**.

3. Click to expand **Services and Applications**.

4. Click **Services** and then double-click **Messenger** in the details pane. If necessary, click the **General** tab. In the Startup type drop-down list, click **Automatic** and then click **Apply**.

5. In the Service status section, click the **Start** button and then click **OK**.

6. After the service starts, click **OK** to close the Messenger Properties dialog box.

7. Open a command prompt window, and switch to the **C:\Perl** directory. Type the command **notepad ping.pl** and press **Enter**. Click **Yes** when prompted to create a new file.

8. In the new Notepad document, type **# ping.pl** on the first line and press **Enter**.

9. Type **# Program to ping workstations in classroom** and press **Enter**.

10. Type **# If the ping is successful, a message is sent to my IP address using net send** and press **Enter**.

11. Type **# Program assumes a Class C address (w.x.y.z) where w.x.y is the network portion of the IP address** and press **Enter**.

12. Type **# The "y" octet will be incremented from 1 - 254 unless otherwise directed by the instructor** and press **Enter** twice.

13. The next lines initialize the variables you'll use. Type **$class_IP = '192.168.2'; # Network ID -- Change to reflect your topology** and press **Enter**. Type **$my_IP = '192.168.2.201'; # Use this address in Microsoft "net send" command** and press **Enter**.

14. The next lines of code are the for loop, which increments the last octet of your network IP address to all the available IP addresses in your classroom. Type **for ($y=1; $y<255; $y++) {** and press **Enter** three times to add some white space (blank lines) in your code, which improves readability.

15. Type the following lines, pressing **Enter** after each line:

```
$wkstation = "$class_IP.$y";
print "\nLooking for live systems to attack...\n";
@ping=("ping $wkstation");
unless (system(@ping)) {
    system("net send $my_IP $wkstation is ready to attack!");
}
```

16. Type **}** to end your program, which should look similar to Figure 7-13.

```
# ping.pl
# Program to ping workstations in classroom
# If the ping is successful, a message is sent to my IP address using net send
# Program assumes a Class C address (w.x.y.z) where w.x.y is the network portion of the IP address
# The "y" octet will be incremented from 1 - 254 unless otherwise directed by the instructor

$class_IP = '192.168.2';  # Network ID -- Change to reflect your topology
$my_IP = '192.168.2.201'; # Use this address in Microsoft "net send" command

for ($y=1; $y<255; $y++) {

    $wkstation = "$class_IP.$y";
    print "\nLooking for live systems to attack...\n";
    @ping=("ping $wkstation");
    unless (system(@ping)) {
        system("net send $my_IP $wkstation is ready to attack!");
    }
}
```

Figure 7-13   Creating the ping.pl Perl script

17. To improve this program's documentation, add comment lines to your code stating the author and date written and explaining any complex algorithms.

18. Be sure to go through each line of code and make sure the syntax is correct. Note that the variable "$class_IP" holds the network portion of your classroom network. Make sure your IP address is entered for the value of the "$my_IP" variable. After verifying the syntax and contents of the Perl script, save it and return to the command prompt.

19. Run your script by entering **ping.pl** from the C:\Perl directory and pressing **Enter**. If you have no errors, your program should begin pinging IP addresses, as shown in Figure 7-14.

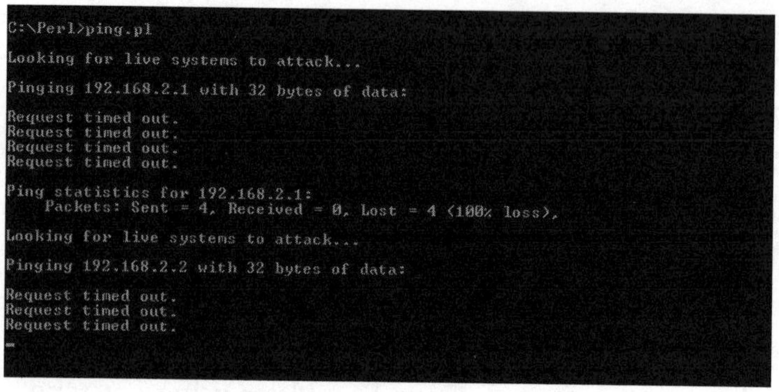

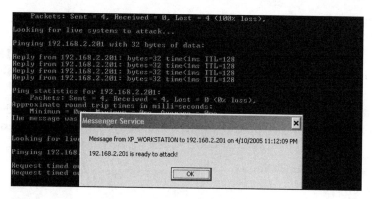

Figure 7-14   Running ping.pl on a live network

20. If a live IP address is found, a message similar to the one in Figure 7-15 is displayed.

Figure 7-15   Net send message displayed

21. To terminate the Perl script, press **Ctrl+C**. You can leave the command prompt window open for the next activity.

UNDERSTANDING OBJECT-ORIENTED PROGRAMMING CONCEPTS

Just when you think you're comfortable with a technology concept, something new comes along. Although the concept of object-oriented programming isn't new to experienced programmers, it might not be familiar to those just learning how to write their first Perl script, for example. Perl 5.0 uses object-oriented programming concepts, and Perl 6.0 will be based solely on this model, so this section covers some basic object-oriented concepts as a foundation for writing another Perl script. This is by no means a definitive study of a complex concept. Learning object-oriented programming takes time and practice, and this section merely introduces you to the fundamental concepts.

Components of Object-Oriented Programming

The version of Perl you installed has additional functions that make program calls to the Win32 Application Programming Interface (API). Programmers should know what functions are available in different OSs so that they can write programs that interact with those functions. For example, a C programmer knows that Win32 has the NodeName() function, which returns the NetBIOS computer name. To use this function, the programmer references it by using Win32::NodeName(). The :: is used to separate the name of the **class**, Win32, from the member function, NodeName(). In object-oriented programming, classes are the structures that hold pieces of data and functions. The following code example shows a class called Employee in the C++ language. Classes can be written in many object-oriented languages (Java, Object COBOL, or Perl). What's important here is recognizing what a class looks like:

```cpp
// This is a class called Employee created in C++
class Employee
{
    public:
        char firstname[25];
        char lastname[25];
        char PlaceOfBirth[30];
        [code continues]
};
void GetEmp()
{
    // Perform tasks to get employee info
    [program code goes here]
}
```

The structure created in this code can contain employee information as well as a function that performs a lookup. The function in a class is called a member function. As mentioned previously, to access a member function, you use the name of the class followed by two colons and the name of the member function:

```
Employee::GetEmp()
```

The Win32 class contains many functions you can call from your Perl script. Table 7-11 describes some of the most commonly used Win32 API functions.

Table 7-11   Win32 API functions

Function	Description
GetLastError()	Returns the last error that was generated when a call was made to the Win32 API.
OLELastError()	Returns the last error generated by the object linking and embedding (OLE) API.
BuildNumber()	Returns the Perl build number.
LoginName()	Returns the user name of the person running Perl.
NodeName()	Returns the NetBIOS computer name.
DomainName()	Returns the name of the domain of which the computer is currently a member.
FsType()	Returns the name of the file system, such as NTFS or FAT.
GetCwd()	Returns the current active drive.
SetCwd(newdir)	Enables you to change to the drive designated by the newdir variable.
GetOSVersion()	Returns the OS version.
FormatMessage(error)	Converts the error message number into a descriptive string.
Spawn(command, args, $pid)	Starts a new process using arguments supplied by the programmer and the process ID (pid).
LookupAccountSID(sys, sid, $acct, $domain, $type)	Returns the account name, domain name, and security ID (SID) type.

Table 7-11   Win32 API functions (continued)

Function	Description
InitiateSystemShutdown(machine, message, timeout, forceclose, reboot)	Shuts down a specified computer or server.
AbortSystemShutdown(machine)	Aborts the shutdown if it was done in error.
GetTickCount()	Returns the Win32 tick count (time elapsed since the system first started).
IsWinNT()	Returns true if the system is a Windows NT computer.
IsWin95()	Returns true if the system is a Windows 95 computer.
ExpandEnvironmentalStrings(envstring)	Returns the environmental variable strings specified in the envstring variable.
GetShortpathName(longpathname)	Returns the 8.3 version of the long pathname. In DOS and older Windows programs, file names could be only eight characters with a three-character extension.
GetNextAvailableDrive()	Return the next available drive letter.
RegisterServer(libraryname)	Loads the DLL specified by libraryname and calls the DLLRegisterServer function.
UnregisterServer(libraryname)	Loads the DLL specified by libraryname and calls the DLLUnregisterServer function.
Sleep(time)	Pauses the number of milliseconds specified by the time variable.

Attackers and security professionals can use these functions to discover information about a remote computer. Although these functions aren't difficult to understand, it takes time and discipline to become proficient at using them in a program. For security professionals who need to know what attackers can do, gaining this skill is worth the time and effort.

In Activity 7-6, you create a Perl script that uses some of the Win32 API functions listed in Table 7-11. This script gives you the following information about the Windows XP computer you have been using for this book's activities:

- Logon name of the user
- Computer name
- File system
- Current directory
- OS version

ACTIVITY

Activity 7-6: Creating a Perl Script That Uses the Win32 API

Time Required: 30 minutes

Objective: Learn how to access the Windows API from a Perl script.

Description: In this activity, you write a basic Perl script using the formatting functions you have already learned, and the Win32 API functions in Table 7-11. If possible, work in groups of three to four students.

1. If necessary, open a command prompt window and switch to the **C:\Perl** directory. Type the command **notepad Win32.pl** and press **Enter**. Click **Yes** when prompted to create a new file.

2. In the new Notepad document, type **# Win32.pl** on the first line and press **Enter**.

3. Use what you've learned previously in this chapter to write comments for documenting the program. Be sure to enter the author name, date, and a brief description of what the program does, such as the functions it accesses from the Win32 API.

4. After your lines of documentation, press **Enter** several times to create blank lines for separating your comments from the program code. Then type **use win32;** and press **Enter**. (*Note:* Don't forget the semicolon.)

5. You need five pieces of information (noted in the bulleted list before this activity) from the Win32 API. Attempt to write the code for getting this information, and then save the program. If you need assistance, use the following steps.

6. Type **$login = Win32::LoginName();** and press **Enter**. This line populates the $login variable with the information obtained from LoginName().

7. Next, type the following lines to populate the other variables needed to complete the task, pressing **Enter** after each line:

```
$NetBIOS = Win32::NodeName();
$filesystem = Win32::FsType();
$Directory = Win32::GetCwd();
$os_version = Win32::GetOSVersion();
```

8. The following variables need to be printed to the screen. Type the lines of code as shown, pressing **Enter** after each line. When you're done, your window should look similar to Figure 7-16.

```
print "$login\n";
print "$NetBIOS\n";
print "$filesystem\n";
print "$Directory\n";
print "$os_version\n";
```

```
# win32.pl
# Documentation here
#
#Author:
#Date Written:
#Comments:
#
#
#Modifications:
#
#

#Populate variables

use win32;
$login = Win32::LoginName();
$NetBIOS = Win32::NodeName();
$filesystem = Win32::FsType();
$Directory = Win32::GetCwd();
$os_version = Win32::GetOSVersion();

# Print output

print "$login\n";
print "$NetBIOS\n";
print "$filesystem\n";
print "$Directory\n";
print "$os_version\n";
```

Figure 7-16   Using the Win32 API from a Perl script

9. After typing all the code, save the program, run it, and debug any errors. Figure 7-17 shows the output. What's wrong with this report?

Figure 7-17   Running the win32.pl Perl script

10. Spend time improving the report's formatting so that anyone reading the output could understand its meaning.

11. Are there any improvements your group thinks should be made to the script? Explain. What other information might be beneficial for a security professional to get from such a report?

12. Select a spokesperson from your group to do a three- to five-minute presentation on the final product. All members must give feedback on what makes your program the most marketable. Choose a winner.

13. Close all open windows, and shut down your system.

CHAPTER SUMMARY

- ▢ Writing an algorithm and using pseudocode are good habits to adopt when writing computer programs.

- ▢ Clear documention of program code is essential.

- ▢ C is one of the most popular programming languages for security professionals and hackers alike.

- ▢ Learning the BLT of any programming language can help you quickly master the fundamentals of programming. Branching, looping, and testing are the most important aspects of programming.

- ▢ Many C compilers are available. GNU GCC is an open-source C compiler included with most Linux implementations.

- ▢ HTML is the primary language used to create Web pages. Security professionals need to recognize when something looks suspicious in a Web page, so they should be able to read an HTML document.

- ▢ Security professionals should have a basic knowledge of Perl and C because many security tools are written in these languages. Security professionals who understand these programming languages can modify or tweak security tools and or create their own customized tools.

- ▢ With object-oriented programming, programmers can create classes, which are structures containing both data and functions. Functions in these classes are computer programs that perform specific tasks.

- ▢ Win32 API is an interface to the Windows operating system that programmers can use to access information about a computer running Windows, such as the computer name, OS version, and so forth.

KEY TERMS

algorithm — A set of directions used to solve a problem.

assembly language — Uses a combination of hexadecimal numbers and expressions to program a more understandable set of directions.

branching — A method that takes you from one area of a program (a function) to another area.

bug — A programming error that causes unpredictable results in a program.

class — In object-oriented programming, the structure that holds pieces of data and functions.

compiler — A program that converts source code into executable or binary code.

conversion specifier — Tells the compiler how to convert the value indicated in a function.

do loop — A loop that performs an action and then tests to see whether the action should continue to occur.

for loop — A loop that initializes a variable, tests a condition, and then increments or decrements the variable.

function — A mini program within a main program that performs a particular task.

looping — The act of repeating a task.

pseudocode — An English-like language for creating the structure of a program.

testing — A process conducted on a variable that returns a value of true or false.

while loop — A loop that repeats an action a certain number of times while a condition is true or false.

REVIEW QUESTIONS

1. A C program must contain which of the following?

    a. the name of the computer programmer

    b. a main() function

    c. the #include <std.h> header file

    d. a description of the algorithm used

2. An algorithm is defined as which of the following?

    a. a list of possible solutions for solving a problem

    b. a method for automating a manual process

    c. a computer program written in a high-level language

    d. a set of instructions for solving a specific problem

3. A missing parenthesis or brace might cause a C compiler to return which of the following?

    a. system fault

    b. interpreter error

    c. syntax error

    d. machine language fault

4. List three logical operators used in C programming.

5. Most programming languages enable programmers to perform which of the following actions? (Choose all that apply.)

    a. branching

    b. testing

    c. faulting

    d. looping

6. Before writing a program in C or Perl, many programmers create a program by using which of the following?

    a. pseudocode

    b. machine code

    c. assembly code

    d. assembler code

7. Which of the following C statements has the highest risk of creating an infinite loop?

    a. while (a > 10)

    b. while (a < 10)

    c. for (a = 1; a < 100; ++a)

    d. for (;;)

8. To add comments to a Perl script, you use which of the following?

    a. //

    b. /*

    c. #

    d. <!--

9. Documentation of a computer program should include which of the following? (Choose all that apply.)

   a. author

   b. date written

   c. explanation of complex algorithms

   d. modifications to the code

10. Name two looping mechanisms used in Perl.

11. In C, which looping function performs an action first and then tests to see whether the action should continue to occur?

    a. for loop

    b. while loop

    c. do loop

    d. unless loop

12. What is the result of running the following C program?

```
main()
{
    int a = 2;
    if (a = 1)
       printf("I made a mistake!");
    else
       printf("I did it correctly!");
}
```

    a. "Syntax error: illegal use of ;" is displayed.

    b. "I made a mistake!" is displayed.

    c. "Syntax error: variable not declared" is displayed.

    d. "I did it correctly!" is displayed.

13. Using the following code, how many times will "This is easy..." be printed to the screen?

```
for ($count=1; $count <= 5; $count++)
{
    print "This is easy... ";
}
```

    a. 6

    b. 4

    c. none (syntax error)

    d. 5

14. HTML files must be compiled before users can see the resulting Web pages. True or False?

15. Which of the following HTML tags is used to create a hyperlink to a remote Web site?

    a. <A HREF=http://URL>

    b. <A HREF="http://URL">

    c. <A HREF="file:///c:/filename">

    d. <A HREF/>

16. In object-oriented programming, classes are defined as the structures that hold data and functions. True or False?

17. What are the three looping mechanisms in C? (Choose all that apply.)

    a. for loop

    b. while loop

    c. if-then-else loop

    d. do loop

18. Which of the following is the Win32 API function that can be used to verify the file system used on a Windows computer?

    a. Filesystem()

    b. FsType()

    c. System()

    d. IsNT()

19. Perl and C are the most widely used programming languages among security professionals. True or False?

20. Which of the following tags enables an HTML programmer to create a loop?

    a. <LOOP>

    b. <NEST>

    c. <WHILE>

    d. HTML does not have a looping function or tag.

7

Case Projects

CASE PROJECTS

Case 7-1: Determining Software Engineering Risks for K. J. Williams

After reviewing all the software programs K. J. Williams uses, you notice that many of them have been modified or changed during the past couple of months. Two of the company's financial applications are written in C and, according to Mark Thompson, the IT manager, monitor the company's accounts and financial data. Mr. Thompson notices that several modifications were made to one program, with no documentation indicating who made the changes or why.

Based on the preceding information, write a memo to Mr. Thompson informing him of your findings and any recommendations you might have for improving the security of the company's software engineering practices. Search the Internet for any information on securing company software. Does the OSSTMM address any of these issues? What improvements should you recommend to better protect this information?

CASE PROJECTS

Case 7-2: Developing a Security-Testing Tool

The security company where you are employed has asked you to develop a tool that can gather information from several hundred computers running Windows XP Professional at K. J. Williams. The tool needs to verify whether a computer is left running at certain hours in the evening. Management has requested that all computers be turned off no later than 6:00 p.m.

Write a memo to your supervisor describing the programming language you would use to develop this tool and the method for verifying the request from K. J. Williams.

8

MICROSOFT OPERATING SYSTEM VULNERABILITIES

After reading this chapter and completing the exercises, you will be able to:

♦ Describe the tools available to assess Microsoft system vulnerabilities

♦ Describe the vulnerabilities of Microsoft operating systems

♦ Describe the vulnerabilities of services running on Microsoft operating systems

♦ Explain techniques to harden Microsoft systems against common vulnerabilities

♦ Describe best practices for securing Microsoft systems

In Chapter 6, you learned how to enumerate Microsoft operating systems to discover open ports that can be used to access data and resources. In this chapter, you look at additional vulnerabilities that can be exploited to attack or compromise the Microsoft OS.

Microsoft OSs contain many security vulnerabilities and also support applications that can cause problems. Microsoft commonly integrates products, allowing code and common technologies to be used across the platform. This practice unfortunately introduces single points of failure and increases the impact a single vulnerability can pose. In this chapter, you learn about some powerful tools that security testers can use to examine Microsoft system vulnerabilities. You examine different services and components—such as NetBIOS, Internet Information Services (IIS), SQL Server, and remote access services—that contain serious security problems, which can be exploited to gain access to Microsoft systems. You also learn how Microsoft uses the Server Message Block (SMB) and Common Internet File System (CIFS) protocols to manipulate remote resources as though they were local, and how these protocols can expose a system to attack.

As a security tester, your job includes pinpointing potential security problems. You must also be familiar with methods of improving security on tested systems and correcting vulnerabilities you find. This chapter examines how a security tester of a Microsoft system analyzes the system for vulnerabilities and corrects them. Finally, techniques for hardening Microsoft systems and best security practices for Microsoft services are explored.

TOOLS TO IDENTIFY VULNERABILITIES ON MICROSOFT SYSTEMS

Many tools are available to discover vulnerabilities in Microsoft systems. Using more than one tool for analysis is advisable, so learning a variety of methods and tools is beneficial to your career. Familiarity with several tools also helps you pinpoint problems more accurately. Some tools might report deceptive results, and if these results aren't verified with another method, you might not have an accurate assessment to report.

Several tools are built into Microsoft products, and you learned about many of them in Chapter 6. In this chapter, you explore other tools used to assess Microsoft systems.

Built-in Microsoft Tools

This chapter focuses on the Microsoft Baseline Security Analyzer (MBSA), Winfingerprint, and HFNetChk tools for analyzing Microsoft systems.

Microsoft Baseline Security Analyzer (MBSA)

You already know that many security problems exist in computer systems, and Microsoft generally leads the pack in software vulnerabilities. That's not to say only Microsoft has problems; in fact, any software can have bugs that result in glitches and vulnerabilities. It could be argued that Microsoft has more of the market share, so it naturally follows that Microsoft systems would suffer more attacks. Although this is true, many attacks can be avoided with careful analysis and maintenance of systems, which can include anything from establishing an efficient and regular update scheme to reviewing log files for signs of unusual activity. Microsoft knows its software has problems and publishes patches, security updates, service packs, and hotfixes to address them as soon as possible after discovery.

Along this same line of reasoning, Microsoft has also addressed the problem of finding configuration errors, missing patches, and so on. The primary resource for doing this is the **Microsoft Baseline Security Analyzer (MBSA)**, shown in Figure 8-1. This effective tool is capable of checking for patches, security updates, configuration errors, blank or weak passwords, and much more.

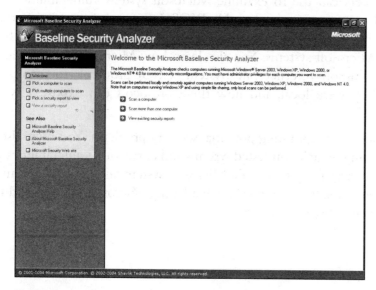

Figure 8-1   The MBSA Welcome window

Table 8-1 summarizes MBSA's scanning capabilities. Note that these scans aren't performed, even in full-scan mode, if the associated product isn't installed on the scanned machine. More information and complete instructions for MBSA are available from the MBSA Help interface or the Microsoft Security Web site (*www.microsoft.com/security/*).

Table 8-1 Checks performed by MBSA in full-scan mode

Security Checks	Checks For
Security update checks	Missing Windows, IIS, and SQL Server security updates Missing Exchange Server security updates Missing IE security updates Missing Windows Media Player and Office security updates Missing Microsoft Virtual Machine (VM) and Microsoft Data Access Components (MDAC) security updates Missing MSXML and Content Management Server security updates
Windows checks	Account password expiration and blank or simple local user account passwords File system type on hard drives Whether the Auto Logon feature is enabled Whether the Guest account is enabled and the number of local Administrator accounts RestrictAnonymous Registry key settings List shares on the computer and any unnecessary services running Windows version and whether Windows auditing is enabled Internet Connection Firewall and Automatic Updates status
IIS checks	Whether the IIS Lockdown tool (version 2.1) is running Whether IIS sample applications and the IIS Admin virtual folder are installed Whether IIS parent paths are enabled Whether MSADC and Scripts virtual directories are installed Whether IIS logging is enabled Whether IIS is running on a domain controller
SQL checks	Whether the Administrators group belongs in Sysadmin role and if CmdExec role is restricted to Sysadmin only Whether SQL Server is running on a domain controller Whether the SA account password is exposed and the Guest account has database access SQL Server installation folders access permissions Whether the Everyone group has access to SQL Server registry keys Whether SQL Server service accounts are members of the local Administrators group Whether SQL Server accounts have blank or simple passwords SQL Server authentication mode type and number of Sysadmin role members
Desktop Application Checks	Internet Explorer security zone settings for each local user Whether Internet Explorer Enhanced Security Configuration is enabled for Administrator accounts Whether Internet Explorer Enhanced Security Configuration is enabled for non-Administrators Office products security zone settings for each local user

8

Using MBSA

Any computer meeting the system requirements shown in Table 8-2 can scan another computer or be scanned locally or remotely by MBSA.

Table 8-2 Minimum system requirements for MBSA

Action	Requirements
To scan the local computer	Windows Server 2003, Windows 2000, or Windows XP Internet Explorer 5.01 or later XML parser (the most recent version of the MSXML parser is recommended) World Wide Web service to perform local IIS administrative vulnerability checks Workstation and Server services enabled
Requirements for a computer running the tool that's scanning remote machines	Windows Server 2003, Windows 2000, or Windows XP Internet Explorer 5.01 or later XML parser required for the tool to function correctly (the most recent version of the MSXML parser is recommended) IIS Common Files required on the computer on which the tool is installed if performing remote scans of IIS computers (*Note:* IIS 6.0 Common Files are required on the local machine when remotely scanning an IIS 6.0 server.) Workstation service and Client for Microsoft Networks enabled
Requirements for a computer to be scanned remotely	Windows NT 4.0 SP4 and above, Windows 2000, Windows XP (local scans only on Windows XP computers that use simple file sharing), or Windows Server 2003 Internet Explorer 5.01 or later (required for IE zone checks) IIS 4.0, 5.0, or 6.0 (required for IIS product and administrative vulnerability checks) SQL Server 7.0, 2000, or SQL Server Desktop Engine (MSDE) 1.0, 2000 (required for SQL product and administrative vulnerability checks) Office 2003, Office 2000, or Office XP (required for Office product and administrative vulnerability checks) Server and Remote Registry services and File and Print Sharing enabled

HFNetChk

The **HFNetChk** engine is part of MBSA but is available separately from Shavlik Technologies. You can find the advanced command-line version and the GUI version at *www.shavlik.com*.

After MBSA is installed, it can perform two types of scans from the command line:

- *MBSA-style scans*—Results stored in individual XML files for later viewing in the MBSA user interface. You can run the tool from the command line by using **Mbsacli.exe**. Table 8-3 summarizes the available parameters and switches.

- *HFNetChk-style scans*—The HFNetChk scan can be used with the /hf parameter to indicate an HFNetChk scan to the MBSA engine. The parameters for the HFNetChk-style scan are summarized in Table 8-3. Note that the MBSA-style scan parameters can't be combined with the /hf flag option. HFNetChk can be run from the command line by using mbsacli.exe /hf followed by any of the HFNetChk parameters shown in Table 8-3.

Table 8-3 MBSA and HFNetChk scan parameters

Scan Style	Parameter	Description
MBSA	No options	Scan the local computer.
MBSA	/c DomainName /c ComputerName	Scan the specified computer.
HFNetChk	-h HostName	Scan the specified NetBIOS computer name.
HFNetChk	-fh FileName	Scans the NetBIOS computer names listed in the specified text file.

Table 8-3   MBSA and HFNetChk scan parameters (continued)

Scan Style	Parameter	Description
MBSA	/l xxx.xxx.xxx.xxx −xxx.xxx.xxx.xxx	Scan a range of IP addresses.
HFNetChk	-l xxx.xxx.xxx.xxx	Scan an IP address; multiple IP addresses can be scanned by separating each entry with a comma.
HFNetChk	-r xxx.xxx.xxx.xxx − xxx.xxx.xxx.xxx	Scan specified IP address range.
HFNetChk	-fip *FileName*	Scan the IP addresses listed in the specified text file.
MBSA, HFNetChk	/d *DomainName*	Scan the specified domain.
HFNetChk	-n	Scan all computers on the local network.
MBSA	/n IIS	Skip IIS checks.
MBSA	/n OS	Skip Windows OS checks (also IE/Outlook zones and Office macro security checks).
MBSA	/n Password	Skip password checks.
MBSA	/n SQL	Skip SQL checks.
MBSA	/n Updates	Skip security update checks.
MBSA, HFNetChk	/sus *SUS Server* I *SUS FileName*	Check for security updates approved at the specified URL of the SUS server or the file path to the Approveditems.txt file.
MBSA, HFNetChk	/s 1	Suppress security update check notes.
MBSA, HFNetChk	/s 2	Suppress security update check notes and warnings.
MBSA, HFNetChk	/nosum, -nosum	Security update checks don't check file checksums.
HFNetChk	-sum	Force a checksum scan when scanning a non-English language system.
HFNetChk	-z	Do not perform Registry checks.
HFNetChk	-history	Display updates that have been explicitly, not explicitly, and successfully installed
MBSA, HFNetChk	/nvc	Don't check for new version of MBSA.
MBSA	/o *FileName*	Specify output file name template. The default format is d - c (t), with d=*domain*, c=*ComputerName*, and t=*date and time*. IP can also be used (IP is the IP address of the scanned machine). Note that Windows XP inserts a default name in the GUI scan. For the command-line scan, enter the desired file name in the format shown.
HFNetChk	-o (tab) -o (wrap)	Specify the output format; used with the (tab) or (wrap) options, it displays output in tab-delimited or word-wrapped formats.
HFNetChk	-f *FileName*	Specify the name of a file to store output.
HFNetChk	-unicode	Generate Unicode output.

8

Table 8-3   MBSA and HFNetChk scan parameters (continued)

Scan Style	Parameter	Description
MBSA	/e	List errors from latest scan.
MBSA	/l	List all reports available.
MBSA	/ls	List reports from latest scan.
MBSA	/lr *ReportName*	Display overview report.
MBSA	/ld *ReportName*	Display detailed report.
MBSA	/v	Display security update reason codes.
MBSA	/?	Display help.
MBSA	/qp	Don't display progress.
MBSA	/qe	Don't display error list.
MBSA	/qr	Don't display report list.
MBSA	/q	Don't display any of the above.
MBSA	/f	Redirect output to a file.
MBSA	/Unicode	Generate Unicode output.
HFNetChk	-t	Displays the number of threads used to run the scan.
HFNetChk	-u *UserName*	Specify the user name to use when scanning; must be used with the -p *Password* switch.
HFNetChk	-p *Password*	Specify the password to use when scanning; must be used with the -u *UserName* switch.
HFNetChk	-x	Specify the XML data source containing the available security update information.
HFNetChk	-?	Display a menu (help).

Running MBSA from the command line produces output as text in the command prompt window, as shown in Figure 8-2.

Of course, you can always run MBSA from the GUI window, as shown previously in Figure 8-1. Often, however, you need to scan for a particular report, and the command-line parameters give you more control over the scans. Note that you must be an administrator on the scanned machine to run the scan. If you don't have administrative privileges, you'll receive an error message. Figure 8-3 shows the results of scanning a remote machine with the IP address 192.168.1.18. Notice that the administrative user name and password are specified in the command. If you were entering this command to scan a remote machine (or a group of remote machines using a range of IP addresses), you would replace the words *administrator* and *password* with the actual administrative credentials for that machine or group. Later in this chapter, you work with MBSA using both the GUI and the command line.

Winfingerprint

Winfingerprint is an administrative tool that can be used to scan network resources. This tool can gather information without any logon credentials via the Windows null session and can detect NetBIOS shares, disk information and services, and null sessions. Although null sessions can be disabled easily by modifying the Registry (changing the HKEY_LOCAL_MACHINE\SYSTEM\CurrentControlSet\Control\LSA Add Value: RestrictAnonymous –REG_DWORD value to 1), many organizations fail to make these changes.

Winfingerprint's capabilities also include ICMP and DNS resolution, OS detection, service packs and hotfixes, and much more. Winfingerprint can be run in passive or interactive modes and can be run on a single machine or the entire Network Neighborhood. You can also specify IP addresses or ranges. If time permits, your instructor might want to conduct classroom activities using Winfingerprint, or you can explore this tool further on your own. You can download it free at *http://winfingerprint.sourceforge.net/*. Familiarity with many tools is important and an asset to your career as a security professional.

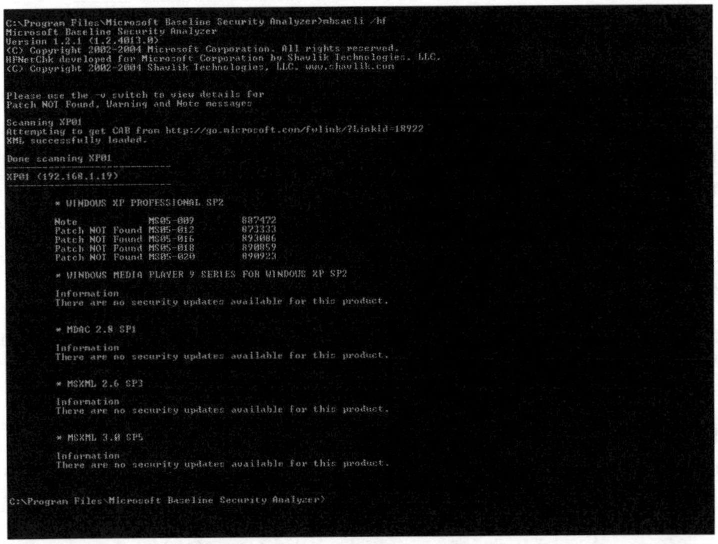

Figure 8-2   Output displayed when using the mbsacli.exe /hf command

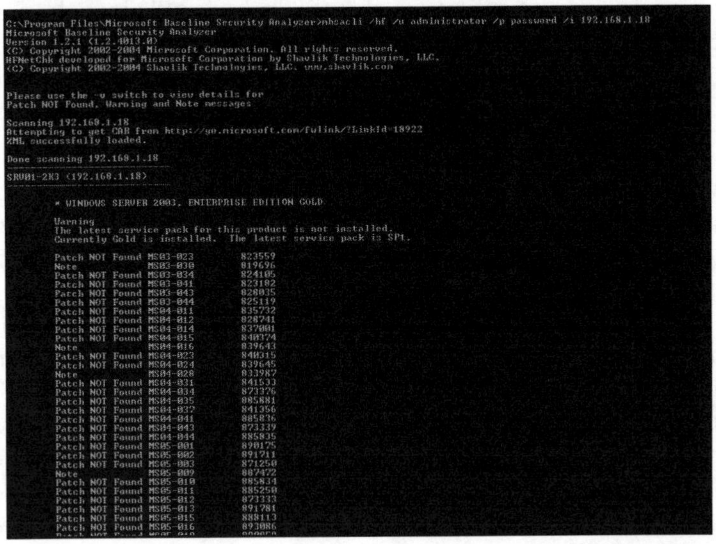

Figure 8-3   Mbsacli.exe output of the scan on the remote machine

8

MICROSOFT OS VULNERABILITIES

Computer networking had its humble beginnings at four universities in the late 1960s. Since then, computers have spread into nearly every aspect of our business and personal lives. Microsoft had a great deal of influence on this technology explosion. Although it didn't create networks, it did devise a way for the average person to use computers and networks. With the advent of Windows for Workgroups 3.11, small businesses could begin to leverage computers to increase productivity and share resources in a workgroup (peer-to-peer) setting. When Windows 95 hit the market with its GUI interface and straightforward workgroup networking, the spread of computers and the Internet into homes and businesses became a juggernaut.

Microsoft integrates many of its products into a single package, such as including the Internet Explorer Web browser as part of the OS installation. Although this recycling of common code and reuse of technologies is sound software engineering practice (why pay a developer to write the same code over and over if you can just reuse it?), unfortunately it introduces single points of failure into those products, and any single security vulnerability that exists is magnified. Many viruses, worms, Trojans, and other attack vectors have taken advantage of this fact.

Security testers should also search for any vulnerabilities associated with the OS they are testing or any applications running on the server (Exchange, SQL Server, and so forth). The port-scanning step reveals any open ports (services), which gives you a clue about applications that might be installed on the server. For example, port 53 indicates that the server is running DNS. Ports 25 and 110 indicate that the server processes e-mail. To determine vulnerabilities for this OS, you can check the Common Vulnerabilities and Exposures (CVE) Web site (*www.cve.mitre.org*). Table 8-4 briefly describes a few CVEs and CANs (candidates) found for Windows Server 2003 on the CVE site. (For a more detailed explanation, visit the Web site.)

Many of the explanations at the CVE Web site are complex and might be difficult to understand. What's important, however, is that you are able to research a vulnerability that's relevant to the security test you're conducting. For example, if the system you're testing uses the HyperTerminal system noted in CVE 2004-0568, you might need to do research on what HyperTerminal is and whether the version the company is running is vulnerable. You might also have to visit the Microsoft Web site to see whether any patches or security updates are available for this vulnerability. For example, performing a search on "hyperterminal vulnerability" at the Microsoft Web site reveals the following: "Microsoft Security Bulletin MS04-043: Vulnerability in HyperTerminal Could Allow Code Execution (873339). Customers should install the update at the earliest opportunity. Bulletin is rated Important. http://www.microsoft.com/technet/security/Bulletin/MS04-043.mspx."

NOTE   As a security tester, you must be able to go beyond the basics to perform your job effectively. A security tester is an investigator who doesn't stop at one piece of information. You are the Columbo of the IT world, always saying "Oh, and one more question . . ."

Table 8-4   Windows Server 2003 vulnerabilities from the CVE Web site

CVE/CAN	Description
2003-0825	The Windows Internet Naming Service (WINS) for Microsoft Windows Server 2003, and possibly Windows NT and Server 2000, does not properly validate the length of certain packets, which allows attackers to cause a denial of service and possibly execute arbitrary code.
2003-0352	Buffer overflow in a certain DCOM interface for RPC in Microsoft Windows NT 4.0, 2000, XP, and Server 2003 allows remote attackers to execute arbitrary code via a malformed message, as exploited by the Blaster/MSblast/LovSAN and Nachi/Welchia worms.

Table 8-4 Windows Server 2003 vulnerabilities from the CVE Web site (continued)

CVE/CAN	Description
2003-0533	Stack-based buffer overflow in certain Active Directory service functions in LSASRV.DLL of the Local Security Authority Subsystem Service (LSASS) in Microsoft Windows NT 4.0 SP6a, 2000 SP2 through SP4, XP SP1, Server 2003, NetMeeting, Windows 98, and Windows Me, allows remote attackers to execute arbitrary code via a packet that causes the DsRolerUpgradeDownlevelServer function to create long debug entries for the DCPROMO.LOG log file, as exploited by the Sasser worm.
2004-0119	The Negotiate Security Software Provider (SSP) interface in Windows 2000, Windows XP, and Windows Server 2003 allows remote attackers to cause a denial of service (crash from null dereference) or execute arbitrary code via a crafted SPNEGO NegTokenInit request during authentication protocol selection.

Security testers can use the information from the CVE site to test a Windows Server 2003 computer and make sure it's been patched with updates from Microsoft that address these known vulnerabilities. Hackers visit Web sites that offer exploit programs to run against these vulnerabilities, but launching exploits is not your job. In other words, you don't blow up a refinery to illustrate the company's safety violations; you inform the company when it isn't in compliance with safety regulations. Many known vulnerabilities use ports that port-scanning tools could easily detect as being open. For example, NNTP (port 119), SMTP (port 25), and RPC (port 135) might all be vulnerable to attack.

When you're conducting research on possible vulnerabilities, the CVE and CAN information should not be skimmed. Remember, attention to detail is what separates skillful security testers from the mediocre. As Pete Herzog states in the OSSTMM: "Do sweat the small stuff, because it's all small stuff." The steps you have performed in previous chapters can be carried out on any Microsoft OS as well as *NIX systems and other OSs.

Remote Procedure Call (RPC)

Remote Procedure Call (RPC) is an interprocess communication mechanism that allows a program running on one host to run code on a remote host. The MSBlast (LovSAN, Blaster) and Nachi worms took advantage of a vulnerability in Microsoft RPCs to run arbitrary code on susceptible hosts. Microsoft Security Bulletin MS03-026, posted July 16, 2003, advised users of this critical vulnerability that allowed attackers to run code of their choice, and provided a patch to correct the problem. Even though the vulnerability was published in advisories and a patch was available weeks before the Blaster worm hit in August 2003, millions of computers were affected.

To determine whether a system is vulnerable to an RPC-related issue, the best tool is MBSA. In Activity 8-1, you download and install this tool on your Windows XP computer.

Activity 8-1 Downloading and Installing MBSA

Time Required: 10 minutes

Objective: Download and install Microsoft Baseline Security Analyzer.

Description: MBSA is a vital tool for locating possible vulnerabilities in Microsoft systems. In this activity, you download MBSA from the Microsoft Web site, and then install the tool.

1. From Windows XP, start a Web browser, enter the URL **www.microsoft.com/technet/security/ tools/mbsahome.mspx**, and press **Enter**.

2. Scroll down the page, and click the download link for the English version of MBSA.

3. When a File Download dialog box opens asking what you want to do with this file, click **Save**.

4. Browse to the location where you want to save the files (or to the location your instructor designates), and click **Save**.

5. After the file download is finished, click **Open Folder** in the Download complete dialog box. Double-click the setup executable, or browse to the location of the saved file and double-click the setup executable to start setup. If you're prompted with a Security Warning dialog box, click **Run**. The MBSA Setup dialog box opens (see Figure 8-4).

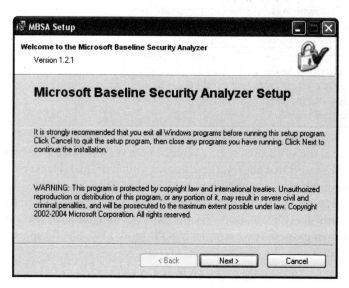

Figure 8-4 The MBSA Setup dialog box

6. After closing all running Windows applications, click **Next** in the MBSA Setup dialog box.

7. Click the **I accept the license agreement** option button, and then click **Next**.

8. Follow the prompts, accepting the defaults unless your instructor advises you otherwise.

9. When the installation is completed, start the application by clicking **Start**, **All Programs** and clicking **Microsoft Baseline Security Analyzer** in the list of programs, or double-click the shortcut on your desktop, if one has been placed there.

10. Take a few moments, if time permits, to explore the interface and familiarize yourself with the program. Close the MBSA window, but leave your system running for the next activity.

NetBIOS

Early Microsoft OSs communicated with each other by using NetBIOS. As you learned in Chapter 6, NetBIOS is software loaded into memory that enables a computer program to interact with a network resource or another device on a network. Network resources are identified with 16-byte NetBIOS names. The purpose of NetBIOS is to make disk space sharable over a LAN. NetBIOS is not a protocol; it's just the interface to a network protocol that enables an application to access a network resource. It usually works with **NetBIOS Extended User Interface (NetBEUI)**, a fast, efficient protocol that requires little configuration and allows NetBIOS packets to be transmitted over TCP/IP and various network topologies, such as token ring and Ethernet. NetBIOS over TCP/IP is called NBT in Windows 2000 Server; in Windows Server 2003, it's called NetBT.

The newer Microsoft OSs can share files and resources without using NetBIOS; however, NetBIOS is still used for backward compatibility, which is important when corporate budgets don't allow upgrading every computer on the network. In addition, customer expectations must be met. Customers expect, for example, that a document created in Word 97 can still be read in Word 2003. In fact, they demand it. Therefore, software developers face the challenge of improving an operating system's security yet must still ensure that the system is compatible with less secure predecessors. As long as newer Microsoft OSs have to work with older NetBIOS-based systems, security will always be a problem.

Server Message Block (SMB)

In Windows 95, 98, and NT, Microsoft used **Server Message Block (SMB)** to share files. SMB usually runs on top of NetBIOS, NetBEUI, or TCP/IP. Several hacking tools that target SMB can still cause damage to Windows networks. Two well-known SMB hacking tools are L0phtcrack's SMB Packet Capture utility and SMBRelay, which collects user names and password hashes from SMB traffic traversing a network.

Common Internet File System (CIFS)

The **Common Internet File System (CIFS)** protocol replaced SMB for Windows 2000, XP, and Windows Server 2003, but, to allow for backward compatibility, SMB is still used. In fact, CIFS relies on an enhanced version of SMB to function. CIFS is a remote file system protocol that enables computers to share network resources over the Internet. In other words, files, folders, printers, CD-ROM drives, and other items located on a computer can be made available to users throughout a network. For sharing to occur, there must be an infrastructure that allows these resources to be located on the network and a method to control access to resources. CIFS relies on other protocols to handle service announcements that notify users what resources are available on the network and to handle authentication and authorization for accessing these resources. CIFS is also available for AT&T Advanced Server for UNIX, Digital PATHWORKS, HP Advanced Server 9000, IBM Warp Connect, IBM LAN Server, and others.

Anyone who has used a Microsoft OS has heard of Network Neighborhood or My Network Places. These services announce the resources available on a network by using broadcast protocols. Essentially, a computer on the network shouts out over the network wire "Here I am! My NetBIOS name is Salesmgr, and I have lots of files and folders to share with anyone out there." To share those files or folders, CIFS relies on an updated version of SMB. However, CIFS offers many enhancements, including the following:

- Locking features that enable multiple users to access and update a file simultaneously without conflicts
- Caching and read-ahead/write-behind capability
- Support for fault tolerance
- Capability to run more efficiently over slow dial-up lines
- Support for anonymous and authenticated access to files for improved security

To prevent unauthorized access to these files, CIFS relies on the security model set forth in SMB. An administrator can select two methods for server security:

- *Share-level security*—A directory or folder on a disk is made available to users for sharing. A password can be configured for the share but is not required.
- *User-level security*—When user-level security is selected, the resource is again made available to users on the network; however, a user name and password are required to access the resource. The SMB server maintains an encrypted version of the user's password to enhance security.

Windows 2000 Server and Server 2003 use CIFS. However, these systems listen on most of the same ports as does Windows NT, which means that many of the old tricks might still work on newer systems. For example, recognizing which ports are open on a Windows 2000 Server system enables a security tester to locate vulnerabilities that make it possible to introduce a Trojan horse or other remote control program for capturing authorized users' passwords and logon names. Most attackers look for servers designated as **domain controllers** (servers that handle authentication). Windows 2000 domain controllers are used to authenticate user accounts, so they contain much of the information that attackers want to access. By default, a Windows 2000 domain controller using CIFS listens on the following ports:

- FTP (port 21)
- SMTP (port 25)
- DNS (port 53)
- HTTP (port 80)

- Kerberos (port 88)

- RPC (port 135)

- NetBIOS Name Service (port 137)

- NetBIOS Datagram Service (port 139)

- LDAP (port 389)

- HTTPS (port 443)

- Microsoft SMB/CIFS (port 445)

- LDAP over SSL (port 636)

- Active Directory global catalog (port 3268)

- Windows Terminal Server (port 3389)

In Windows 2000, a domain controller uses a global catalog (GC) server to locate resources in a domain containing thousands or even millions of objects. For example, if a user wants to locate a printer with the word "color" in its description, he or she can use a GC server, which contains attributes such as the resource's name and location and points the user to the network resource.

Activity 8-2: Understanding the Vulnerabilities of CIFS and SMB

Time Required: 30 minutes

Objective: Learn how CIFS and SMB are used to share network resources in a Microsoft environment and how they affect network security.

Description: In this activity, you learn about the vulnerabilities of the CIFS and SMB protocols.

1. From Windows XP or Linux, start a Web browser, enter the URL **www.microsoft.com**, and press **Enter**.

2. On the Microsoft home page, type **cifs/smb** in the Search Microsoft.com for text box and click **Search**.

3. Select two or three links and spend some time reading about this protocol. What new information about CIFS and SMB did you learn from your reading?

4. From your Web browser, type the URL **www.insecure.org** and press **Enter**.

5. On the Insecure.org home page, type **cifs** in the Search text box and click **Search**.

6. Click the **CIFS: Common Insecurities Fail Scrutiny** link, and read the paper. It gives you a good idea of the level of expertise you should aspire to reach and explains the weaknesses in CIFS. Don't be discouraged if some of the jargon is difficult to understand. After reading the paper, summarize the author's reason for writing it.

7. The "Groundwork: What's out there?" section identifies the methods for finding SMB servers on a network. List some methods attackers could use to locate these servers.

8. Close your Web browser.

Understanding Samba

Users expect to be able to share resources over a network, regardless of whether the systems are Microsoft, UNIX, NetWare, or Macintosh, and companies have discovered that customers no longer tolerate proprietary systems that can't co-exist in a network. To address the issue of interoperability, a group of programmers created **Samba** (*www.samba.org*) in 1992 as an open-source implementation of CIFS. With Samba, Linux and UNIX servers can share resources with Windows-based clients, and a Microsoft client can access a *NIX resource without realizing that the resource is located on a *NIX computer. Samba has been ported to non-*NIX systems, too, including VMS, NetWare, and AmigaOS. Security professionals should have a basic knowledge of SMB and Samba because many companies have a mixed environment of Microsoft and *NIX systems. In addition, Samba accessing Microsoft shares can make a network susceptible to attack, so you should understand how it works.

NOTE
Samba has continued to improve with each new version and is now used by millions of people all over the world. See *http://linuxdevices.com/news/NS8217660071.html* for an article about the use of Samba in making the blockbuster movie *Sin City*.

For a Microsoft computer to be able to access a Linux resource, CIFS must be enabled on both systems. On networks that require UNIX or Linux computers to access Microsoft resources, Samba is often used. It's not a hacking tool; this product was designed to enable *NIX computers to "trick" Microsoft services into believing that *NIX resources are Microsoft resources. A UNIX client can connect to a Microsoft shared printer and vice versa when Samba is configured on the UNIX computer. Most new versions of Linux come with Samba already installed, so you don't need to download, install, and compile it.

Activity 8-3: Visiting the Samba Web Site

ACTIVITY

Time Required: 20 minutes

Objective: Learn how Samba is used in mixed Windows and *NIX environments to allow both OSs to share files and printers.

Description: In this activity, you see how *NIX systems use Samba to enable Microsoft computers to access *NIX resources. The Samba Web site contains a wealth of information for security professionals. You aren't configuring Samba in this activity, but you see how it can be done. If you have two computers, one running Linux and the other running Windows XP, you should consider following the step-by-step directions in configuring Samba. You should also practice sharing a Linux folder so that the Windows XP computer can access its contents.

1. From Windows XP or Linux, start a Web browser, enter the URL **www.samba.org**, and press **Enter**.

2. Scroll through the home page and click the **Official HOWTO** link to access The Official Samba-3 HOWTO and Reference Guide. Scroll through the table of contents to get an idea of the topics covered in this document. It's an excellent resource if you have Windows systems that need to access *NIX resources, and vice versa.

3. Click the **What Is Samba?** link to read about the main goal of the Samba project.

4. As you discovered, the main goal of the Samba project is to make it possible for Microsoft products to interact with non-Microsoft OSs, such as Linux, UNIX, IBM, and VMS. Click the **Home** link at the bottom to return to the table of contents, and click **Configuring Samba (smb.conf)**. The Smb.conf file is the meat of Samba. A Linux or UNIX administrator can edit this file, which contains multiple configurable sections, or uncomment sections by removing the ; comment character. If you have worked with Microsoft Lmhosts and Hosts files, this file will seem familiar. The manual gives you a good look at a minimal configuration file. Figure 8-5 shows an excerpt from the Smb.conf file on a Linux Enterprise Server system named Server. This portion of the file identifies any shares on the Linux system.

5. Close your Web browser.

After configuring the Smb.conf file to include any files or printers a Windows XP client might need to access, a Linux administrator might want to run the Testparm program to identify any syntax errors in the file. Figure 8-6 shows the results of running the Testparm command on the Smb.conf file you saw in the previous activity.

To access the Linux server named Server from a Windows XP computer, users could enter the UNC \\192.168.0.105 in the Run dialog box. Figure 8-7 shows the result, which reveals several shared folders on the Linux server.

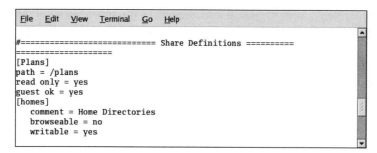

Figure 8-5   Share definitions in the Smb.conf file

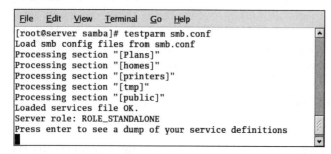

Figure 8-6   Running Testparm on the Smb.conf file

Figure 8-7   Windows XP showing shared resources on a Linux server

The Windows XP user is prompted for a user name and password after entering the UNC. For a Windows XP computer to be able to connect to the *NIX computer or server, the password on the Windows XP computer must match the password in the Linux Smbpasswd file. How does this file get this information? This account information is created on the Linux computer by using the Smbusers command. When this command is issued, the user is prompted to enter a name and password for the Samba user. This information is automatically entered into the Smbpasswd file.

Closing SMB Ports

The best way to protect a network from SMB attacks is to make sure routers filter out ports 137 to 139 and 445. Even Windows Server 2003 does not disable SMB on port 445 by default. In fact, if the computer is a domain controller, you probably need to provide access to SMB. The server's job is to make sure the person attempting to log on to the network is indeed authorized to access network resources. Because you usually want to share resources on a server, closing port 445 could create other problems, such as users not being able to access shared folders and printers.

Null Sessions

As you learned in Chapter 6, a null session is an anonymous connection established without credentials, such as a user name and password. Also called an anonymous logon, a null session can be used to display information about users, groups, shares, and password policies. Windows NT services running as the Local System account use null sessions to communicate with other services running on the network. Windows 2000 and later services running as the Local System account use the local computer account to communicate with other servers.

You can use the Nbtstat, Net view, Netstat, Ping, Pathping, and Telnet commands to enumerate NetBIOS vulnerabilities, as discussed in Chapter 6.

8

Default Installations of Microsoft OSs

Many Microsoft OSs install with serious vulnerabilities. Windows 2000 and earlier systems install with most services and features unsecured and open for access. To secure these systems, administrators must manually disable, reconfigure, uninstall, or otherwise secure these vulnerable services and features. Windows XP and Windows Server 2003 install with most services and features locked down. In these environments, the administrator must configure them to be available, or users can't access needed resources. This problem, as with most other Microsoft vulnerabilities, could have an entire chapter devoted to it, but for this book, you need only know that a default installation of a Microsoft system can contain serious vulnerabilities that can be exploited. MBSA can scan for and detect most of these vulnerabilities.

Passwords and Authentication

You already know that, in most systems, the most vulnerable point is the people legitimately using the system. Unfortunately, it's also the most difficult point to secure, because it relies on people who might not realize that their actions could expose their organization to a major security breach, resulting in damaged machines, stolen or destroyed information, malware infection, or other undesirable effects. There might also be legal issues to deal with after an attack, and a company can lose customer confidence as a result.

Companies can take steps to secure the people working for them. A comprehensive password policy is critical, because a user name and password are often all that stand between an attacker and access. A password policy should include rules such as the following:

- Change passwords regularly on system-level accounts (every 60 days at minimum).
- Require users to change their passwords regularly (at least quarterly).
- Require password length of at least six characters.
- Require complex passwords; in other words, passwords must include letters, numbers, symbols, punctuation characters, and preferably both uppercase and lowercase letters.
- Passwords may not be common words or words found in the dictionary.
- Passwords must not be personally identifiable to a particular user, such as birthdays, names, or company-related words.
- Passwords should not be a word in any language, slang, jargon, or dialect.
- Never write down a password or store it online or on the local system.
- Do not reveal a password to anyone over the phone, in e-mail, or in person, or hint at the password.
- Use caution when logging on to ensure that no one sees you enter your password.
- Limit reuse of old passwords.

In addition to these guidelines, administrators can configure domain controllers to enforce password age, length, and complexity. A Windows 2000 or Server 2003 domain controller can enforce some aspects of a password policy, such as:

- *Account lockout threshold*—Set the number of failed attempts before the account is temporarily disabled.

- *Account lockout duration*—Set the period of time the user account is locked out after a specified number of failed logon attempts.

Despite the best efforts to promote security through strong passwords and enforcement of a password policy, it's still entirely possible that a password can be cracked. With enough time and processing power, most passwords can be cracked.

Security Bytes

Never run a password-cracking program without explicit written permission from the owner of the system or a manager with enough authority to allow this activity. Even if you are the administrator of a system, get your employer's written permission first. Many well-intentioned administrators have been fired for running password scanners or crackers without permission to do so. It might also be wise to include details of the test, explaining what the program will do, how it will do it, and what it can reveal as well as the purpose for running the test. If you have a signed permission form with this information on it, and it is signed by someone with authority to do so, you're generally protected from termination or litigation.

Activity 8-4: Using MBSA to Scan the Local Computer

Time Required: 20 minutes

Objective: Use MBSA to scan the local computer to discover weak or missing passwords.

Description: In this activity, you scan your computer with the MBSA tool to determine vulnerabilities, including weak or missing passwords. At the end of the activity, submit a summary of your findings to your instructor, along with brief recommendations for correcting the problems you found.

1. From Windows XP, open MBSA, if it's not already open. Click **Scan a computer**.

2. The Pick a computer to scan window opens. Accept all defaults, and click **Start scan**.

3. When the scan is finished, the View security report window displays your results (see Figure 8-8). What problems did MBSA find? Did it find any unexpected results? Did it find any password vulnerabilities?

4. Write a brief summary of password-related problems the MBSA scanner found. If time permits, discuss your results with your classmates and instructor. Close the MBSA window, and leave Windows XP running for the next activity.

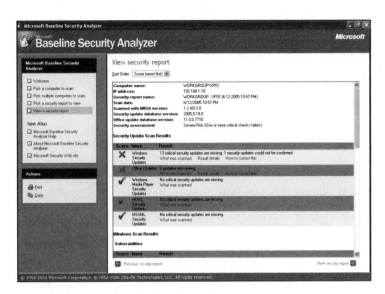

Figure 8-8   Results of a local machine scan

VULNERABILITIES IN MICROSOFT SERVICES

As if securing the operating system weren't challenging enough, you must remember that the purpose of a network is to share resources. In today's globalized world, the Internet is a critical resource that an overwhelming number of people and businesses use daily. To allow these services to be shared, installing additional software to support them is necessary. Unfortunately, any software added to the infrastructure increases the potential for security problems. In this section, you examine Internet Information Services (IIS) and SQL Server, two of the most common—and commonly attacked—applications running on Microsoft networks.

Web Services

Many Microsoft services expose the system to attack. The most critical are Microsoft Web services, IIS in particular. IIS installs with critical security vulnerabilities. Microsoft has developed the IIS Lockdown Wizard specifically for locking down IIS. You can download it from *www.microsoft.com/technet/security/tools/locktool.mspx*.

Although IIS 6.0 installs with a "secure by default" posture, previous versions left crucial holes that made it possible for attackers to sneak into a network. Regardless of the IIS version a system runs, keeping systems patched is important, and system administrators should still be familiar with their Web servers. Configuring only those services that are needed is a wise move. Also, IIS includes sample applications designed to demonstrate the server's functionality. These applications weren't designed to operate securely and should be removed before placing the server into production.

One of the biggest problems with IIS is that Windows 2000 ships with IIS installed by default, and many administrators have been unaware of its presence until a problem occurs. It pays to never assume that a Web server doesn't exist on your network just because you didn't specifically install one. Running MBSA can detect IIS running on your network, whether you know it's there or not.

SQL Server

The majority of Microsoft SQL vulnerability exploits can be classified in one of the following five areas:

- The SA account with a blank password
- SQL Server Agent
- Buffer overflow
- Extended stored procedures
- Default SQL port 1433

These vulnerabilities are all related to SQL Server 7.0 and SQL Server 2000 but are also present on some installations of Windows NT, 2000, and XP.

The SA Account

All versions of SQL Server, including SQL 2000, have a potential vulnerability that allows a remote user to obtain Administrator access to the system through the SA account on the server. During SQL Server 6.5 and 7 installations, the user is prompted, but not required, to set a password on this account. SQL Server 2000 defaults to using Windows Integrated authentication, but the user can also select mixed-mode authentication. If mixed mode is selected, an SA account is created by default, which can't be disabled and by default has a blank password. If an attacker finds such an account, he or she would have full access to the database.

SQL Server Agent

SQL Server Agent is a service mainly responsible for replication, running scheduled jobs, and restarting the SQL service. The problem comes from the Server Agent's willingness to comply with users' requests. An authorized but unprivileged user can create scheduled jobs that can be run by SQL Server Agent. For example, a user could schedule a job that might have weak permissions, and if a job step requires creating an output file, SQL Server Agent simply complies and uses its permissions to create it.

Buffer Overflow

As already discussed, with so many lines of code in programs, there are bound to be bugs, and SQL Server is no exception. The Database Consistency Checker in SQL Server 2000 contains commands that have identical buffer overflows. If exploited, they could allow an attacker to run arbitrary code with the privilege level of the SQL Server service account. These buffer overflows don't require an authenticated user and can be exploited remotely.

SQL Server 7 and 2000 have a number of functions that generate text messages in response to database queries. Because of flaws in the functions themselves, several functions don't properly verify that the text they generate fits in the buffer supplied to hold them. This can enable arbitrary code to run in the security context of the SQL Service. Another vulnerability is caused by the format string vulnerability in the C runtime functions. Because of the specific way in which this vulnerability occurs, the C runtime code would always be overrun with the same values, resulting in a denial of service.

Extended Stored Procedures

SQL Server 7 and 2000 provide for extended stored procedures that appear to users as normal stored procedures and are carried out in the same way. Several of the extended stored procedures have a flaw in which they fail to perform input validation correctly and are susceptible to buffer overruns. This could enable an attacker to cause the SQL Server service to fail or to cause code to run in the security context in which SQL Server is running.

Default SQL Port 1433

SQL Server is a Winsock application that communicates over TCP/IP using the sockets network library. The SQL server listens for incoming connections on port 1433 by default. The Spida worm scans for systems listening on TCP port 1433, and after it's connected, attempts to use the xp_cmdshell utility to enable and set a password for the Guest user account. Port 1433 is the official Internet Assigned Number Authority (IANA) socket number for SQL, but just changing to another port is not a simple matter. SQL Server calls stored procedures outside the database through port 1433, which means the port can't be disabled for many installations of SQL Server. In addition, if port 1433 is open to remote requests, and if SQL 7 receives a Tabular DataStream (TDS) packet with three or more null byes as data, it might crash the server. This attack wouldn't allow inappropriate access to data on the server, but it could indicate other possible risks, such as an attempt to install a Trojan program or rootkit. For a detailed analysis of the SQL.Spider-B worm, go to the SANS Web site at *www.sans.org/resources/idfaq/spider.php*.

BEST PRACTICES FOR HARDENING MICROSOFT SYSTEMS

As a penetration tester, your job is simply to find vulnerabilities and report them as defined in your contract. Your responsibility ends there. However, a security tester must not only find vulnerabilities; he or she must be familiar with methods of correcting them. Management staff typically want potential problems reported along with solutions for those problems, particularly for technologies they might not fully understand.

Although the only way to make a system truly secure is to unplug it and lock it away in a vault, this approach defies the purpose of a network. Because you can't lock network computers away to keep them secure, the best option is to be vigilant. A security breach is always one undiscovered vulnerability away, but with careful management, most systems can be adequately secured and still meet users' needs. Some general things you can do to make and keep a network secure are discussed in the following sections.

Patching Systems

The number-one way to keep your system secure, operating at peak performance, and using the newest features is to *keep the systems under your care up to date*. As noted, many attacks have taken advantage of a known vulnerability for which a patch is available. There are several methods for obtaining service packs hotfixes and patches. If you have only a few computers to maintain (10 or fewer), accessing Windows Update manually from each computer will probably work fine, but this method is still time consuming. Depending on the version of Windows you're working with, you can configure Automatic Updates on each machine. This is probably the better option because it helps ensure that machines are always up to date without the administrator or user's intervention. The downside is that some patches can cause problems. This is why testing the patch before applying it to a production system is preferable, particularly in large networks.

For a large network, applying updates manually isn't feasible. Configuring Automatic Updates is an option if you have physical access to all computers, but downloading patches to each machine can slow network performance. There are a couple of options for patch management. **Systems Management Server (SMS)** can manage security patches for all computers on your network. SMS is exactly what its name implies: a systems management server. It assesses all machines in a defined managed domain and can be configured to manage patch deployment. SMS has the capability to do much more, but that topic isn't within the scope of this book. For the purposes of this chapter, you simply need to know that SMS can be used for patch management.

The other option for patch management is **Software Update Services (SUS)**. SUS is a client-server technology designed specifically to manage patching and updating systems software from within the corporate network. Instead of downloading updates onto each computer, SUS downloads patches and publishes them internally to corporate servers and desktop systems. Unlike Automatic Updates where all updates are automatically downloaded and installed, with SUS, the administrator has control over which updates are deployed. This is a major advantage, considering that some updates can cause problems and should be tested for the environment before being deployed.

The downside to SUS is that it can work only with Windows 2000 Server/Professional, Windows XP, and Windows Server 2003. SUS consists of both server-side and client-side components. The server-side component must be installed and configured on a Windows 2000 Server (SP2 or later) computer with IIS enabled. The client-side component is included as part of the OS in Windows 2000 SP3 and later, Windows XP SP1 and later, and Windows Server 2003.

Whatever patch-management technique is the best fit, remember that keeping systems up to date is one of the most critical steps toward keeping systems secure. As a security tester, often you'll find that patches are not current on the system being tested. An effective patch-management scheme might seem like common sense, but administrators often get so busy with other complicated issues that they forget the simple solutions. You must recommend effective patch management and be able to explain why it's crucial to system security. In Activity 8-5, you use MBSA from the command line to scan your partner's computer for missing patches.

Activity 8-5: Using Mbsacli.exe to Scan a Remote Computer

Time Required: 20 minutes

Objective: Use the Mbsacli.exe command-line tool to scan a remote computer to discover weak or missing passwords.

Description: In this activity, you scan a remote computer (your partner's or another designated by your instructor) with the Mbsacli.exe command-line tool to detect vulnerabilities, including weak or missing passwords. At the end of the activity, submit a summary of your findings to your instructor, along with brief recommendations for correcting the problems you found.

1. From Windows XP, open a command prompt window.

2. Navigate to the **Microsoft Baseline Security Analyzer** directory on your computer. (*Hint:* If you aren't familiar with navigating via the command line, search for basic DOS navigation commands on the Web.)

3. At the C:\Program Files\Microsoft Baseline Security Analyzer> prompt (or the correct path to your MBSA directory), type **mbsacli /hf /u** *username* **/p** *password* **/i** *ipaddress* (replace *username* with the administrative user name, *password* with the administrative password, and *ipaddress* with the IP address of the remote computer you want to scan). Press **Enter** to start the scan.

4. When the scan is completed, you see the results in the command prompt window. What does your scan show? Discuss your results with your partner, and then submit a summary of your findings to your instructor. Close the command prompt window, but leave your system running for the next activity.

Antivirus Solutions

Whether you're working with an enterprise network consisting of hundreds of servers and thousands of clients, or a small business network of 15 systems and one server, an antivirus solution is essential. For small networks, desktop antivirus tools with automatic updating might be enough to protect the system. In a large network, a corporate-level solution is needed. Several excellent products are available, and selecting the right solution requires some research. What's important to remember about an antivirus solution is that it must be planned, installed, and configured correctly to offer the best protection. An antivirus tool is almost useless if it isn't updated regularly. Ideally, an antivirus solution should automatically obtain and install updates daily.

If your examination of a system reveals that no antivirus tool is running, you should recommend installing one immediately. You must also stress keeping it up to date to offer the best protection.

Enable Logging and Review Logs Regularly

Logging is an important step for monitoring many crucial areas, including performance, traffic patterns, and possible security breaches. It must be configured carefully to log only the statistics that are useful for a machine, because logging can have a negative impact on performance.

Review logs regularly for signs of intrusion or other problems on the network. Scanning through thousands of log entries is time consuming, and missing important entries is likely. A log-monitoring tool is best for this task. Several are available, depending on network needs and budget.

Disable Unused or Unneeded Services

It only makes sense to disable unneeded services and delete unnecessary applications or scripts. Unused services, applications, or scripts give an intruder a potential point of entry into a network. For example, if you have a Windows 2000 Server system acting as a file server, you certainly don't need DNS services running. Not only could this cause serious problems with any other DNS servers you have, but it leaves port 53 TCP/UDP open on this machine and vulnerable to attack. The idea is simple: Open *only* what needs to be open and close everything else. Some ports frequently subject to attack include the following:

- FTP (20 and 21 TCP)
- TFTP (69 UDP)
- Telnet (23 TCP)
- DNS (53 TCP/UDP)
- NNTP (119 TCP)
- NetBIOS (135 TCP/UDP, 137 and 138 UDP, 139 TCP)
- Windows 2000 NetBIOS (445 TCP/UDP)
- SNMP (161 and 162 TCP/UDP)
- Windows RPC programs (1025 to 1039 TCP/UDP)

An attacker can gain entry through many other ports. It isn't possible to close all avenues of attack and still offer necessary functionality for users, but with careful planning, an administrator can make sure there are fewer ways in. For a complete list of ports and services, consult IANA's Assigned Port Number page at *www.iana.org/assignments/port-numbers*.

Use caution when disabling services and blocking ports. Make sure that no required services depending on a port or other service are disabled.

Other Security Best Practices

In addition to keeping software up to date, running antivirus software, and disabling services, you can take the following steps to help minimize the risks to a Microsoft network:

- Use TCP/IP filtering in Windows 2000/XP or Windows Firewall in XP.
- Delete unused scripts and sample applications.
- Delete default hidden shares and unnecessary shares.
- Use a different unique naming scheme and passwords for public interfaces.
- Be careful of default permissions.
- Use appropriate packet-filtering technologies, such as a desktop software firewall or an enterprise-class hardware firewall, as suited to the environment.
- Use available tools to assess system security. Handy tools include MBSA, HFNetChk, IIS Lockdown Wizard, **SQL Critical Update Kit**, and the built-in tools on your Microsoft computer.
- Disable the Guest account.
- Rename the default Administrator account.
- Make sure there are no accounts with blank passwords. A good password policy is crucial.
- Develop a comprehensive security awareness program for users in compliance with your organization's security policy.
- Keep up with emerging threats. Check with Microsoft, SANS, US-CERT (*www.us-cert.gov*), and other security organizations for the newest developments.

TCP/IP filtering can filter only inbound traffic. This feature doesn't affect outbound traffic or response ports that are created to accept responses from outbound requests. Use IPSec Policies or packet filtering if you require more control over outbound access. Activity 8-6 walks you through the process of TCP/IP filtering.

Activity 8-6: Configuring TCP/IP Filtering Security

Time Required: 20 minutes

Objective: Configure TCP/IP inbound security.

Description: In this activity, you configure inbound TCP/IP filtering to secure your Microsoft system.

1. From Windows XP, click **Start**, **Control Panel**, and then double-click **Network Connections**. (*Note:* This step assumes you're in Classic view.)

2. Right-click the interface where you want to configure inbound access control, and then click **Properties**.

3. In the This connection uses the following items list box, click **Internet Protocol (TCP/IP)**, and then click **Properties**.

4. In the Internet Protocol (TCP/IP) Properties dialog box, click **Advanced**.

5. Click the **Options** tab.

6. Click **TCP/IP filtering**, if necessary, and then click the **Properties** button.

7. Click to enable the **Enable TCP/IP Filtering (All adapters)** check box. This option enables filtering for all adapters, but they are configured on a per-adapter basis, so the same filters don't apply to all adapters.

8. There are three columns labeled TCP ports, UDP ports, and IP protocols. In each column, you must select one of the following options:

   - **Permit All**: If you want to permit all TCP or UDP packets, leave this option activated.

   - **Permit Only**: If you want to allow only specified TCP or UDP traffic, click **Permit Only**, and then click **Add**. Type the appropriate port in the Add Filter text box. (*Hint:* If you want to block all UDP or TCP traffic, click **Permit Only**, but don't add any port numbers in the UDP or TCP port columns.)

9. Click **OK**, and close all windows. What did you learn from this activity? Did you find it more or less difficult than you expected? Discuss this activity with your classmates. When you're finished, shut down your system.

The security field is changing rapidly, and security professionals must keep up with new developments, threats, and tools. Securing Microsoft systems can be challenging, but a number of tools can be used to pinpoint problems.

CHAPTER SUMMARY

- ☐ Many tools are available to discover vulnerabilities in Microsoft systems. Using more than one tool for analysis is important, so learning a variety of methods and tools is beneficial to your career. Tools include Microsoft Baseline Security Analyzer (MBSA), Winfingerprint, and HFNetChk, in addition to built-in tools you learned about in Chapter 6.

- ☐ MBSA is an effective tool capable of checking for patches, security updates, configuration errors, blank or weak passwords, and much more. It can perform two types of scans from the command line: the MBSA-style scan and the HFNetChk-style scan. This tool is also the best one for determining whether a system is vulnerable to RPC-related issues.

❏ Winfingerprint is a free administrative tool that can be used to scan network resources. It can detect NetBIOS shares, disk information and services, and null sessions. It also can detect ICMP and DNS resolution, the operating system, service packs, hotfixes, and much more. Winfingerprint can be run in passive or interactive modes and can be run on a single machine or the entire Network Neighborhood.

❏ Microsoft's integration of several products into one package, as well as other factors associated with software development, increase the potential for problems and make a single vulnerability far more serious.

❏ Newer Microsoft OSs can share files and resources without using NetBIOS; however, NetBIOS is still used for backward compatibility.

❏ In Windows 95, 98, and NT, Microsoft used Server Message Block (SMB) to share files. SMB usually runs on top of NetBIOS, NetBEUI, or TCP/IP. Several hacking tools that target SMB can still cause damage to Windows networks. The best way to protect a network from SMB attacks is to make sure routers filter out ports 137 to 139 and 445.

❏ The Common Internet File System (CIFS) protocol replaced SMB for Windows 2000, XP, and Windows Server 2003, but to allow for backward compatibility, SMB is still used.

❏ To address the issue of interoperability, a group of programmers created Samba (*www.samba.org*) in 1992 as an open-source implementation of CIFS.

❏ Null sessions and default installations of systems can leave passwords blank and resources unprotected, causing major problems.

❏ A comprehensive password policy is critical, because a user name and password are often all that stand between an attacker and access.

❏ Many Microsoft services expose the system to attack. The most critical are Microsoft Web services—IIS in particular. Microsoft has developed the IIS Lockdown Wizard specifically for locking down this service.

❏ The majority of Microsoft SQL vulnerability exploits can be classified in one of these areas: SA account with a blank password, SQL Server Agent, buffer overflow, extended stored procedures, and default SQL port 1433.

❏ Some steps you can recommend to secure Microsoft systems include keeping systems updated with the most current patches and updates, running a good antivirus program, enabling logging and reviewing logs regularly, and disabling unused or unneeded services (ports).

KEY TERMS

Common Internet File System (CIFS) — A remote file system protocol that enables computers to share network resources over the Internet.

domain controller — A Windows server that stores user account information, authenticates domain logons, maintains the master database, and enforces security policies for a Windows domain.

HFNetChk — A Microsoft tool that enables administrators to check the patch status of all machines in a network from a central location.

Internet Information Services (IIS) — A Web server distributed with Windows. Originally supplied as part of the Option Pack for Windows NT and subsequently integrated with Windows 2000 and Windows Server 2003. The current version is IIS 6.0.

Mbsacli.exe — The command-line counterpart to MBSA used to check for security updates and patches. Being able to run from a command prompt enables administrators to schedule scans to run during slow periods of network use, such as at night or on weekends.

Microsoft Baseline Security Analyzer (MBSA) — A GUI tool that gives administrators a way to interactively scan local and remote servers and desktop computers for possible security vulnerabilities.

NetBIOS Extended User Interface (NetBEUI) — A fast, efficient protocol that allows NetBIOS packets to be transmitted over TCP/IP and various network topologies, such as token ring and Ethernet.

Remote Procedure Call (RPC) — An interprocess communication mechanism that allows a program running on one host to run code on a remote host.

Samba — An open-source implementation of CIFS that allows Linux and UNIX servers to share resources with a Windows client.

Server Message Block (SMB) — A protocol for sharing files and printers and providing a method for client applications to read, write to, and request services from server programs in a computer network. Windows operating systems have included SMB protocol support since Windows 95.

Software Update Services (SUS) — A free add-in component for Windows 2000 and Windows Server 2003. After it's installed, SUS simplifies the process of keeping Windows 2000, Windows XP, and Windows Server 2003 computers current with the latest critical updates, security updates, and service packs. SUS installs a Web-based application that runs on Windows 2000 Server or Windows Server 2003 computers.

SQL Critical Update Kit — To help protect editions of SQL Server 2000 and MSDE 2000 that are vulnerable to the Slammer worm, Microsoft has consolidated SQL Scan, SQL Check, and SQL Critical Update into a single download. The SQL Critical Update Kit also includes an SMS deployment tool and the Servpriv.exe utility.

Systems Management Server (SMS) — This service includes detailed hardware inventory, software inventory and metering, software distribution and installation, and remote troubleshooting tools. SMS is tightly integrated with SQL Server and the Windows Server OS, creating a complete solution for change and configuration management.

TCP/IP filtering — This feature enables users to specify which types of IP traffic are allowed to enter an interface. It's designed to isolate the traffic being processed by Internet and intranet clients. In the absence of other TCP/IP filtering, such as IPSec, Routing and Remote Access Service, or other TCP/IP applications or services, this feature can add security to a network by blocking unauthorized types of packets. TCP/IP filtering is disabled by default.

REVIEW QUESTIONS

1. The MBSA tool performs which of the following security checks?

   a. database checks

   b. IIS checks

   c. system time checks

   d. computer logon checks

2. One way to make sure IIS is secure is to do which of the following?

   a. Disable IIS logging.

   b. Install IIS on a domain controller.

   c. Run the IIS Lockup Wizard.

   d. Delete sample applications.

3. In Windows 2000, the administrator must manually enable IIS for it to run. True or False?

4. A computer must have which of the following to be scanned remotely?

   a. Server service, Remote Registry service, and DNS enabled

   b. Internet Explorer 5.01 or later

   c. Windows NT 4.0 SP3 or later

   d. none of the above

5. MBSA can run which of the following types of scans? (Choose all that apply.)

   a. Mbsacli.sys scans

   b. HFNetFix scans

   c. HFNetChk-style scans

   d. MBSA-style scans

6. To run an MBSA scan on a specified domain, you use which of the following commands? (Choose all that apply.)

   a. mbsacli.exe /d *DomainName*

   b. hfnetchk.exe /d *DomainName*

   c. mbsacli.exe /hf /d *DomainName*

   d. mbsacli.exe /hf -n

7. To prevent MBSA from checking for a new version of MBSA, you should enter which command?

   a. MBSA /n /chkver

   b. mbsacli.exe /nvc

   c. hfnetchk.exe −qr

   d. mbsacli.exe −n

8. Microsoft OSs were vulnerable to the MSBlast worm because of a(n) _____ vulnerability.

   a. arbitrary code

   b. SQL buffer overflow

   c. blank password

   d. Remote Procedure Call

9. Two well-known SMB hacking tools are _____ .

   a. NTPass and SMBRelay

   b. SMBsnag and Nessus Packet Sniffer

   c. CIFScrack and L0phtcrack's SMB Packet Capture Utility

   d. SMBRelay and L0phtcrack's SMB Packet Capture Utility

10. Which ports should be filtered to protect a network from SMB attacks?

    a. 134 to 138 and 445

    b. 135, 139, and 443

    c. 137 to 139 and 445

    d. 53 TCP/UDP and 445 UDP

11. A good password policy should include which of the following? (Choose all that apply.)

    a. specifies a minimum password length

    b. mandates password complexity

    c. states that passwords never expire

    d. recommends writing down passwords to avoid forgetting them

12. For a Microsoft computer to be able to access a Linux resource, CIFS must be enabled on at least one of the systems. True or False?

13. Microsoft SQL exploit areas are usually found in the SQL Server Agent, extended stored procedures, buffer overflows, _____ , and _____ .

    a. extensible storage procedures

    b. default SQL port 1433

    c. RPC vulnerabilities

    d. SA account with a blank password

8

14. SQL Server Agent is a service mainly responsible for which of the following?

    a. authenticating users to the SQL Server

    b. access control of resources

    c. replication

    d. password resets

15. The Database Consistency Checker in SQL 2000 contains commands that have identical
   _____ .

    a. remote access permissions

    b. buffer overflows

    c. C runtime code

    d. stored procedures

16. SQL uses port _____ by default.

    a. 1344

    b. 1443

    c. 1433

    d. all of the above

17. What can you do to secure Microsoft systems?

    a. Unplug them.

    b. Keep all software updated.

    c. Disable the Guest account.

    d. Do all of the above.

18. Windows RPC programs use which of the following ports?

    a. 119 TCP

    b. 161 and 162 TCP/UDP

    c. 53 TCP/UDP

    d. 1025 to 1039 TCP/UDP

19. Unused scripts and sample applications should be stored in your My Documents folder in case you
need to use them for diagnostic purposes. True or False?

20. Security testing requires running exploits against all computer systems the customer uses. True or False?

CASE PROJECTS

**CASE
PROJECTS**

Case 8-1: Protecting Computer Systems at K. J. Williams

After performing enumeration tests on the K. J. Williams network, you discover that the network consists of
110 Windows XP computers, 23 Windows 98 computers, three Windows NT servers, and four Windows
Server 2003 servers.

Based on the preceding information, write a one-page memo to Bob Lynch, the IT manager, outlining some
suggestions on possible weaknesses or vulnerabilities in these systems. The memo should reference specific
CVEs and CANs and include recommendations to reduce risks of network attacks.

Case 8-2: Validating Password Strength for K. J. Williams Corporation

After discovering that the majority of computers and servers at K. J Williams are running many different versions of the Windows OS, your supervisor has asked you to present a report on the issue of password vulnerabilities.

Based on the preceding information, write a one-page memo to your supervisor describing the password-cracking areas you will test. Your memo should be based on the information you find in Section 11, "Password Cracking," of the OSSTMM.

8

9

LINUX OPERATING SYSTEM VULNERABILITIES

After reading this chapter and completing the exercises, you will be able to:

♦ Describe the fundamentals of the Linux operating system

♦ Describe the vulnerabilities of the Linux operating system

♦ Describe Linux remote attacks

♦ Explain countermeasures for protecting the Linux operating system

As a security professional, you need to have a good understanding of operating systems and their vulnerabilities. This chapter reviews the Linux operating system and discusses methods for attacking the system remotely. You also learn about built-in features that help you protect the Linux OS and its system files.

Like any OS, Linux can be made more secure if users are aware of its vulnerabilities and keep current on new releases and fixes. For example, in this chapter, you see how Linux notifies users of available updates to the kernel.

REVIEW OF LINUX FUNDAMENTALS

When learning any operating system, starting with a good overview is important. Then you can gradually learn the many commands for using an OS effectively. This chapter reviews the basics of the Linux OS, but it's assumed that you have some experience working with a *NIX-based OS. Linux is a version of UNIX that's usually available free, although you can purchase a version that includes documentation and support, such as Red Hat. Whichever version you use, it's important to understand the basics of the Linux directory structure and file system, discussed in the following sections.

NOTE

Guide to Operating Systems, Third Edition (Course Technology, 2004, ISBN: 0-619-21347-7) is highly recommended for more information on Linux as well as the Microsoft, NetWare, and Macintosh OSs. A thorough understanding of OSs is essential for security testers.

Linux Directory Structure

To make it easy to find where specific information is stored on a Linux system, Linux creates default directories, listed in Table 9-1.

Table 9-1   Directories on a Linux system

Directory Name	Description
/	The root directory is the starting point of the *NIX directory structure and is a mandatory directory. It's the beginning of the file system and includes all directories beneath it. Every other file and directory on the system is under the root directory. Typically, the root directory contains only subdirectories. You don't normally store single files directly under root. Don't confuse the root (/) directory with the root user's home directory (/root).
/bin	This directory contains binaries (executable programs the system needs to operate, such as ls, grep, and mdir). For multiuser systems, binaries are usually stored in the /usr/bin directory. When you type a command such as ls or pwd, it's usually directed to one of these two directories where the program exists.
/dev	Devices that are available to a Linux system are stored in this directory. Linux devices are treated like files, and you can read and write to devices as though they were files. For example, /dev/hda is the first IDE hard drive, /dev/fd0 is your first floppy drive, and so forth. Devices in Linux are block or character devices. For example, a few character devices are your keyboard, mouse, and serial port. Block devices include the hard disk, floppy drive, and CD-ROM drive.
/etc	Pronounced "et-see," this directory holds configuration files for the system and is divided into several subdirectories. Most files located in this directory are text files and can be edited by hand, although caution is advised.
/home	This directory contains user account directories where users keep their personal files. Every user has his or her own directory under /home (such as /home/jane), and usually it's the only place where users are allowed to write files. Red Hat Linux creates a user's home directory by default; however, some versions of *NIX require the administrator to create the user's home directory separately.
/lib	This directory is used to hold shared library files needed to boot the system and contains files required by other programs, such as cp and ls. Shared libraries are similar to DLLs on Windows systems. Libraries that support users are usually stored in the /usr/lib directory.

Table 9-1   Directories on a Linux system (continued)

Directory Name	Description
/mnt	This directory is used for mounting temporary file systems. Physical storage devices, such as hard disk drives, floppy disks, or CD-ROMs must be attached to some directory in the file system tree before they can be accessed.
/proc	The currently running kernel creates and uses this special virtual directory. Within this directory is information about running processes, such as the amount of RAM available on the system or the CPU speed in megahertz. This directory is deleted when the system is shut down.
/root	This is the home directory for the super user (root) account and usually contains system administration files. The /root directory can't be viewed from regular user accounts.
/sbin	This directory contains most system administration and maintenance programs as well as executable programs needed to boot the system. In most cases, you must run these programs as the root user.
/tmp	This directory is used for temporary storage space. Programs can write their temporary files here; these files are often deleted on reboot or flushed out periodically by a regular job process.
/usr	This directory is used to hold user directories, programs, and applications. Used by all system users, /usr is typically the largest directory on a Linux system.
/var	This directory stores variable data that changes constantly, such as log files, mail, and process-specific files. Subdirectories (such as /var/log) are updated while the system runs and can give you helpful information about the condition of your system.

Linux File System

The purpose of any file system, regardless of the OS, is to store and manage information. The file system organizes information that users create as well as the OS files needed to boot the system, so the file system is the most vital part of any OS. It provides many functions, such as:

- Enables files to be organized through directories or folders

- Establishes a file-naming convention

- Includes utilities that enable users to compress or encrypt data files

- Provides for both file and data integrity

- Enables error recovery

- Stores information about directories and files, such as the creation date, last time modified, size, and information on the owner and permissions of directories and files

To store information about files, *NIX systems use information nodes (**inodes**) that contain the following information:

- An inode number

- Owner of the file

- Group the file belongs to

- Size of the file

- Date the file was created

- Date the file was last modified or read

On *NIX systems, any file created on the file system is associated with an inode. Note that a file system has a fixed number of inodes created when the file system is created. You can't change this amount, so the number of inodes needs to be large enough to allow for the number of files to be created on the file system. By default, most *NIX systems allocate one inode for each 4 KB of disk space.

To access a file system on a Microsoft OS, you use a letter of the alphabet. For example, the command Dir D:\Exploits accesses a folder called Exploits located on an NTFS partition, if that was the file system used on the D: partition. *NIX, however, mounts a file system as a subfile system of the root file system, which is identified as /. The mount command is used to mount a particular file system on a *NIX system. (In Activity 9-1, you practice using this command.) Figure 9-1 shows the command being entered without any parameters, which displays the mounted file systems on a computer running Red Hat Enterprise 3 Linux.

```
[root@server root]# mount
/dev/hda2 on / type ext3 (rw)
none on /proc type proc (rw)
none on /dev/pts type devpts (rw,gid=5,mode=620)
usbdevfs on /proc/bus/usb type usbdevfs (rw)
/dev/hda1 on /boot type ext3 (rw)
none on /dev/shm type tmpfs (rw)
[root@server root]#
```

Figure 9-1   Using the mount command to view mounted file systems

You can also use the df command to display the currently mounted file systems, as shown in Figure 9-2. When used with the correct switch, the df command gives more information in an easier-to-read output.

```
[root@server /]# df
Filesystem          1K-blocks       Used Available Use% Mounted on
/dev/hda2            37073224    6876240  28313768  20% /
/dev/hda1              101089      23754     72116  25% /boot
none                  319860          0    319860   0% /dev/shm
[root@server /]#
```

Figure 9-2   Using the df command

Linux uses several different file systems. Originally implemented as an extension to the Minix operating systems, Linux initially supported only the Minix file system. Because the Minix file system was too limiting (for example, a maximum file system size of 64 MB and a maximum file name length of 14 characters), developers started thinking about ways to implement new file systems into the Linux kernel. The **Extended File System (Ext)** removed the two major limitations of Minix. Its maximum file system size is 2 GB, and it supports file names up to 255 characters. The Ext file system is included in the standard Linux kernel and might be Ext, Second Extended File System (Ext2fs), or Third Extended File System (Ext3fs). Ext was an improvement over Minix, but it still had no support for separate access, inode modification, and data modification timestamps. It also used linked lists to keep track of free blocks and inodes; this approach gets messy as the file system is used. The lists became unsorted and the file system fragmented. It was inefficient.

Ext2fs was an improvement over Ext, allowing file system sizes up to 4 TB. In addition, Ext2fs supports standard UNIX file types, long file names, and variable-length directory entries and provides better performance and stability. Ext2fs also allows users to benefit from extensions and new features without having to reformat their file systems. In addition to other improvements, Ext2fs offers better scalability and flexibility than Ext.

Ext3fs, the newest major implementation in Linux file systems, offers even more improvements. Unlike Ext2fs, Ext3fs does not require a file system check, except after certain hardware failures, so a crashed system can be brought back online much faster. Ext2fs forces a check after an unclean shutdown, but Ext3fs removes this limitation because the data is written to disk in a way that's always consistent. Ext3fs also uses **journaling**, a method that keeps track of transactions written to disk. When a journaling system crashes, transactions will have been fully written or marked as not yet fully committed. If there are no inconsistencies, the system can be used immediately; if a problem is found, the file system driver can read the journal and fix it. This makes the recovery process much faster. Data integrity is improved, and Ext3fs optimizes hard drive head motion. Making the transition from Ext2fs to Ext3fs is straightforward and simple. Although Ext2fs is regarded as the de facto standard for Linux file systems, Ext3fs is now merged into the Linux kernel from Kernel 2.4.15 on.

Activity 9-1: Determining Which Linux File System Is Mounted

Time Required: 30 minutes

Objective: Use Linux commands to view the contents of default Linux directories and determine which file system is mounted.

Description: In this activity, you use the Linux mount command to discover what file system is mounted on your computer.

1. Start your system from your Linux CD. Open a shell and examine the contents of the bin directory by typing **cd /bin**, pressing **Enter**, typing **ls**, and pressing **Enter** again.

2. What are the contents of the directory?

3. List five programs that have been installed on your Linux version.

4. Use the **cd** command to change to each directory listed in Table 9-1. View the contents of each directory with the **ls** command.

5. Type **man mount** and press **Enter** to view information about the mount command. When you're finished, exit the man page by pressing **q**.

6. From your shell, type **mount** and press **Enter**.

7. Which file system is mounted on your Linux version?

8. From your shell, type **df** and press **Enter**. This is another way to display the currently mounted file systems.

9. Do not shut down your system.

Linux File System Commands

Getting around the Linux file system requires knowing commands for viewing, copying, and moving files from one area of the OS to another. Table 9-2 lists the most commonly used commands.

Table 9-2   Linux commands

Linux Command	Description
cat	Displays a file's contents, similar to the type command used in DOS. Used to list the contents of short files to the screen.
more	Used to view large files one screen at a time by pressing the spacebar.
less	Similar to the more command, but allows users to page up or down through the file by using the arrow keys.
cd	Used to change into different directories. For example, cd /mnt changes to the /mnt directory. The same command is used in DOS.
cp	Copies a file to another location; can be used just like the DOS copy command. For example, the command cp filename1 filename2 creates the filename2 file if it doesn't exist. If it does exist, normally the command overwrites the file without warning.
ifconfig	Displays the configuration of all active interfaces (see Figure 9-3); similar to the DOS ipconfig command. Also enables you to assign a static IP address to a particular interface when used with the command's many options.
fdisk	Brings up a utility for creating or deleting partitions on your hard drive.

Table 9-2 Linux commands (continued)

Linux Command	Description
format	Used to format hard disks and floppy disks.
ls	Lists files and directories within the current working directory; similar to the DOS dir command.
mkdir	Used to create a new directory. Similar to the DOS md command.
df	Used to show the amount of free disk space on file systems. Also displays the mounted file systems and the directory in which they're mounted.
mount	Allows a device or file system to be accessed; without parameters, displays the current mounted file system.
umount	Removes access to a file system; on most *NIX operating systems, you can't open the CD tray until you unmount the CD file system.
mv	Moves a file to a different directory or renames a file or directory; similar to the DOS ren command.
netstat	Lists information about the networking subsystem. The output is controlled by one or more arguments.
rm -R	Removes a directory. The r stands for recursive, meaning every file and subdirectory in the directory is removed. Similar to the DOS deltree command.
route	Displays the Linux internal routing table on the screen (see Figure 9-4). Similar to the DOS route print command.
touch	Updates the access and modification times and can be used to create an empty file. For example, the touch test command creates an empty file named test.

Many of the commands listed in Table 9-2 have multiple parameters and more functionality than what's described in the table. For example, to view more information on the touch command, type touch --help at the command prompt. Figure 9-5 shows that the touch command can be used to change an existing file's access time by using the -a parameter. When time permits, examine the commands in Table 9-2 by using the --help parameter.

```
[root@server root]# ifconfig
eth1      Link encap:Ethernet  HWaddr 00:C0:4F:09:09:8A
          inet addr:192.168.0.105  Bcast:192.168.0.255  Mask:255.255.255.0
          UP BROADCAST RUNNING MULTICAST  MTU:1500  Metric:1
          RX packets:37849 errors:0 dropped:0 overruns:0 frame:0
          TX packets:24132 errors:0 dropped:0 overruns:0 carrier:0
          collisions:0 txqueuelen:1000
          RX bytes:9282568 (8.8 Mb)  TX bytes:6006614 (5.7 Mb)
          Interrupt:11 Base address:0xd880

lo        Link encap:Local Loopback
          inet addr:127.0.0.1  Mask:255.0.0.0
          UP LOOPBACK RUNNING  MTU:16436  Metric:1
          RX packets:13634 errors:0 dropped:0 overruns:0 frame:0
          TX packets:13634 errors:0 dropped:0 overruns:0 carrier:0
          collisions:0 txqueuelen:0
          RX bytes:694841 (678.5 Kb)  TX bytes:694841 (678.5 Kb)

[root@server root]# █
```

Figure 9-3 Using the ifconfig command

```
[root@server root]# route
Kernel IP routing table
Destination     Gateway         Genmask         Flags Metric Ref    Use Iface
192.168.0.0     *               255.255.255.0   U     0      0        0 eth1
169.254.0.0     *               255.255.0.0     U     0      0        0 eth1
default         192.168.0.1     0.0.0.0         UG    0      0        0 eth1
[root@server root]# █
```

Figure 9-4 Using the route command

```
[root@server root]# touch --help
Usage: touch [OPTION]... FILE...
Update the access and modification times of each FILE to the current time.

Mandatory arguments to long options are mandatory for short options too.
  -a                         change only the access time
  -B SEC, --backward=SEC     date back SEC seconds
  -c, --no-create            do not create any files
  -d, --date=STRING          parse STRING and use it instead of current time
  -F SEC, --forward=SEC      date forward SEC seconds
  -f                         (ignored)
  -m                         change only the modification time
  -r, --reference=FILE       use this file's times instead of current time
  -t STAMP                   use [[CC]YY]MMDDhhmm[.ss] instead of current time
  --time=WORD                set time given by WORD: access atime use (same as -a)
                               modify mtime (same as -m)
      --help      display this help and exit
      --version   output version information and exit

Note that the -d and -t options accept different time-date formats.

Report bugs to <bug-coreutils@gnu.org>.
[root@server root]# 
```

Figure 9-5   Viewing available parameters for the touch command

Activity 9-2: Using Linux File System Commands

Time Required: 30 minutes

Objective: Learn to use Linux file system commands.

Description: Before you can hack or test a Linux computer, you should have a basic knowledge of the Linux file system and know how to use commands to get information.

1. If you're not already booted in Linux, start your system from your Linux CD. Open a shell, type **pwd**, and press **Enter**. The "print working directory" command should display the current directory you're in, which is /root.

2. Type **cd /** and press **Enter** to navigate to the root directory of Linux, and then type **ls –l** and press **Enter** to view the directory's contents. The –l parameter gives more details in the directory listing.

3. Type **cd ~** and press **Enter**. The tilde character can be used to return a user to his or her home directory from anywhere in the directory structure. (*Note*: Don't confuse /root with the root directory. The /root directory is a special directory used for the root user's home directory, separate from the /home directory used by regular system users.)

4. To create a directory called exploits, type the command **mkdir exploits** and press **Enter**. Type **ls** and press **Enter** to see whether the directory was created.

5. Next, you need to create three directories in the exploits directory called Microsoft, Linux, and NetWare. Type **mkdir Microsoft** and press **Enter**.

6. Type **ls** and press **Enter** to view the directory's contents. Note that the Microsoft directory was not created in the exploits directory but is in the root directory. To move the Microsoft directory, type **mv Microsoft exploits** and press **Enter**.

7. Type **cd exploits** and press **Enter**, and then use the ls command to view the contents of the exploits directory. The exploits directory now contains the Microsoft directory.

8. From the exploits directory, create the other two directories, Linux and NetWare, by typing **mkdir Linux NetWare** and pressing **Enter**. (The space between "Linux" and "NetWare" creates two directories called Linux and NetWare.) Use the **ls** command to verify that the exploits directory now contains three directories: Linux, Microsoft, and NetWare.

9. To create files in each of the directories you created, type **cd Linux** and press **Enter**. From the Linux directory, type **touch exploit1** and press **Enter**. Press the **up arrow** key to repeat the touch command while changing exploit1 to **exploit2** and then **exploit3** so that you have created three files in the Linux directory: exploit1, exploit2, and exploit3. Use the **ls** command to verify that you have created these files in the Linux directory.

10. To copy these three files to the Microsoft directory, type **cp exploit1 ../Microsoft** and press **Enter**. Press the **up arrow** key and change exploit1 to **exploit2** and then **exploit3**, and then check that the three files have been created in the Microsoft directory by using the commands you've learned. Repeat these steps to copy the files to the NetWare directory. Take advantage of using the up arrow key instead of typing the full commands. For example, after all three cp commands have been entered to copy the exploit files to the Microsoft directory, simply changing the word "Microsoft" to "Net-Ware" saves some keystrokes.

11. Verify that all three directories contain three files, and then change to the exploits directory. To navigate back one directory, type **cd ..** and press **Enter**. In Linux, you must place a space before the two periods, or you get an error. Microsoft OSs don't require this space.

12. From the exploits directory, type **rmdir Linux** and press **Enter**. Note that Linux returns the message "rmdir: 'Linux': Directory not empty." Before you can delete this directory, you must remove the files it contains. Type **rm –R Linux** and press **Enter**. This command does all the work for you, but prompts you before deleting each file and the directory. Type the letter **y** and press **Enter** to verify that you want to delete each file and the Linux directory.

13. Next, type **rm –R Microsoft –f** and press **Enter**.

14. Type **ls** and press **Enter**. Oops! The Microsoft directory and its files are gone. The -f parameter was used in Step 13 to tell Linux that you don't need to be prompted. This command is obviously a quick way of deleting directories that contain hundreds of files, but it can also be dangerous.

15. To delete the exploits directory and all its contents, type **cd /root** and press **Enter** to return to the /root directory.

16. Next, type **rm –R exploits –f** and press **Enter**. Verify that the exploits directory is deleted by using the **ls** command.

17. Close the shell, but leave Linux running for the next activity.

LINUX OS VULNERABILITIES

Because UNIX has been around for quite some time, and Linux is based on this OS, it's no wonder that attackers have had plenty of time to discover vulnerabilities in *NIX systems. Too many network administrators believe the Microsoft OS is easier to attack and view Linux or any UNIX-based OS as inherently more secure; therefore, they fail to understand that vulnerabilities exist for all OSs. Security professionals must understand that making these assumptions can be dangerous. Attackers didn't get their reputations from hacking Microsoft OSs; they got them from hacking UNIX systems. When conducting a security test on systems running Linux, you should follow the same rules that you would for any OS. Visiting the Common Vulnerabilities and Exposures Web site (*www.cve.mitre.org*) is your first step in discovering possible avenues attackers will take to break into a Linux system.

In Chapter 6, you learned how tools such as Nessus can be used to enumerate multiple OSs. A security tester using enumeration tools is able to do the following:

- Identify a computer on the network by using port scanning and zone transfers
- Identify the operating system the computer is using by conducting port scanning and enumeration
- Identify via enumeration any logon accounts and passwords configured on the computer
- Obtain the names of shared folders by using enumeration
- Identify services running on the computer

The following example shows Nessus enumerating a Linux computer that's running Knoppix, a bootable, open-source version of Linux included on your student CD that accompanies this book. Figure 9-6 shows the Windows NessusWX tool scanning a Linux computer with an IP address of 192.168.0.102. You don't have to use a Windows client to perform this test, as you see in Activity 9-3 later in this section.

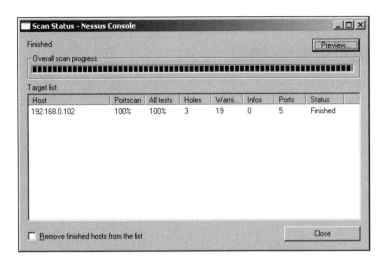

Figure 9-6   Using NessusWX to scan a Linux computer

Note in the figure that Nessus discovered three security holes and 19 vulnerabilities—not bad for less than one minute! After you click the Preview button, expand the IP address icon, and select one of the listed vulnerabilities, you see the screen shown in Figure 9-7.

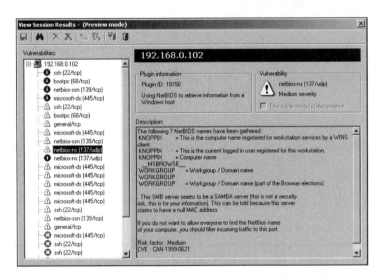

Figure 9-7   Viewing the details of a vulnerability

Nessus discovered that the Linux computer is an SMB server and was able to enumerate the server's NetBIOS names—so far, not exactly damaging information, but certainly information that attackers can use. You can see why understanding Samba, covered in Chapter 8, is important and how a security professional's knowledge can help prevent possible attacks. A beginning security tester would be surprised to see any references to NetBIOS on a Linux computer unless he or she understood the important role that Samba plays. Figure 9-8 shows how Nessus enumerated shares on this computer.

There is enough information in Figure 9-8 to devote an entire chapter to, but take a look at two more figures to see how you can use Nessus for security testing. Figure 9-9 shows more damaging information on Samba.

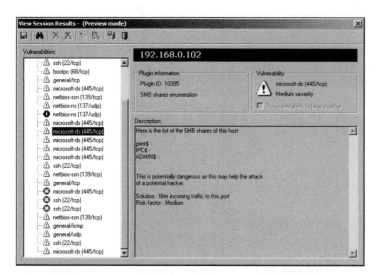

Figure 9-8   Viewing SMB shares that Nessus discovered

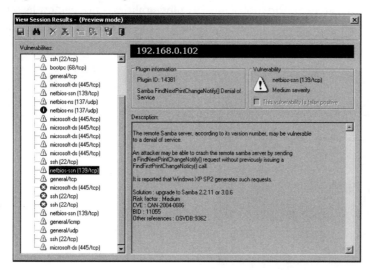

Figure 9-9   DoS attack possible through a Samba vulnerability

 NOTE   The Samba version running on the bootable CD included with this book is not the most recent version. A security tester would most likely recommend an upgrade before spending too much time looking for vulnerabilities. However, this is a good example of how to use a security-testing tool to perform your job.

Probably the most damaging information Nessus discovered is shown in Figure 9-10. After an attacker learns the root password of a *NIX system, all bets are off. The attacker can do anything he or she wants. Most likely, the attacker will create multiple accounts with root permissions that can be used later if the administrator discovers the attack and attempts to change the password as quickly as possible.

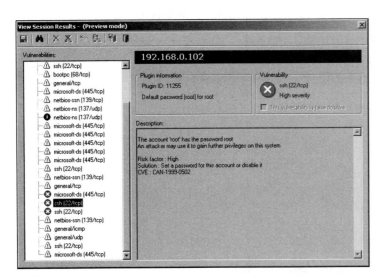

Figure 9-10   Nessus discovers the root password

Activity 9-3: Using Nessus to Discover Vulnerabilities on Your Partner's Linux Computer

Time Required: 30 minutes

Objective: Use Nessus to discover any vulnerabilities on your partner's Linux computer.

Description: Nessus is a great tool for enumerating an operating system. Not only does the tool warn the tester of any possible vulnerabilities, but it also makes recommendations to help correct any problems discovered. In this activity, you configure Nessus to scan your partner's Linux computer and discover any vulnerabilities or security holes an attacker might use to gain access.

1. Your system should already be running from your bootable Linux CD. Open a shell of your choice and determine your computer's IP address by typing **ifconfig** and pressing **Enter**.

2. Write down the IP address of your computer, and give it to your partner.

3. Type **nessusd –D** and press **Enter**. This command starts the Nessus daemon on the Linux server. You'll receive error messages on your system that can be ignored. However, the last line displayed on the screen should indicate that nessusd 2.0.10 started. This is an older version of Nessus, but it still produces helpful results in performing a security test on your partner's computer.

4. From the console, type **nessus** and press **Enter**. You see a screen similar to Figure 9-11.

5. Type **root** in the Password text box and click the **Log in** button. If you see a warning that certain plug-ins with the capability to crash remote services or hosts have been disabled, click **OK**.

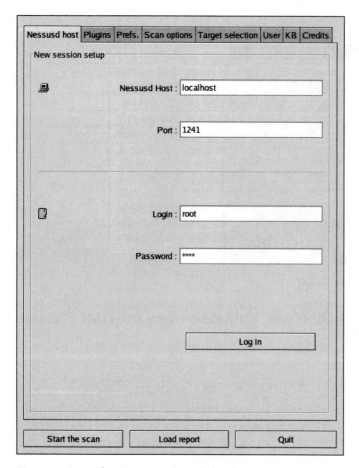

Figure 9-11   The Nessus Setup dialog box

6. Click the **Plugins** tab if necessary, and then click the **Enable all** button (see Figure 9-12). The grayed boxes in the Nessus Setup dialog box indicate that a selection is made. (*Note:* The newer version of Nessus in Figure 9-12 shows check boxes instead of grayed boxes.) If you click the Disable all button, the boxes turn white. Be sure to click the Enable all button so that all plug-ins are selected. You should be careful doing this on a production system because some plug-ins Nessus uses might crash the system.

7. Click the **Prefs.** tab and note the different types of scans Nessus can conduct and the many options available to testers.

8. Next, click the **Scan options** tab and review the available options. Do not make any selections.

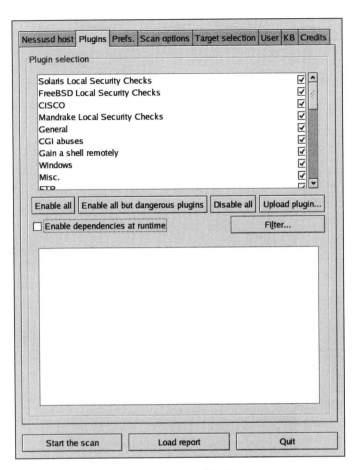

Figure 9-12 Nessus plug-ins enabled

9. Click the **Target selection** tab, and enter your partner's IP address number in the Target(s) text box (see Figure 9-13). Be sure you enter your partner's IP address, not the one shown in the figure, and then click the **Start the scan** button at the bottom.

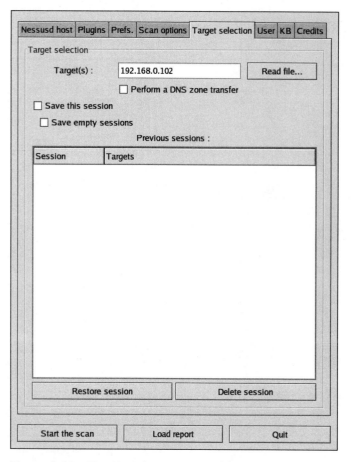

Figure 9-13   Entering the target IP address

10. After several minutes, you see a screen similar to Figure 9-14. Click the **Subnet** icon, and then click the **Host** icon to display the open ports Nessus discovered.

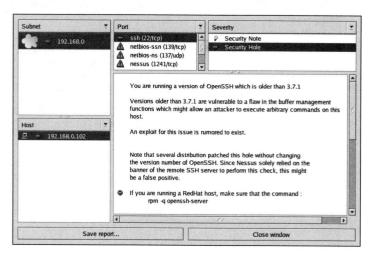

Figure 9-14   Nessus discovers security holes

11. Using the information Nessus discovered, write down what port SMB is running on and what port CIFS is running on. What recommendation does Nessus make to prevent users from finding out the NetBIOS name on your Linux computer?

12. To end Nessus, click the **Close window** button. When prompted to save the report, click **No**, and then click **Quit** in the Nessus Setup dialog box. Leave Linux running for the next activity.

Table 9-3 lists a small portion of the CVEs and CANs found when entering the word "Linux" in the CVE site's search box. To give you an idea of the multitude of Linux vulnerabilities, more than 500 entries were found. Many of these vulnerabilities are no longer possible on systems that have been upgraded.

Table 9-3   Linux vulnerabilities from the CVE Web site

CVE/CAN	Description
2002-1319	The Linux kernel 2.4.20 and earlier and 2.5.x, when running on x86 systems, allows local users to cause a denial of service (hang) via the emulation mode, which does not properly clear TF and NT EFLAGs.
2003-0018	Linux kernel 2.4.10 through 2.4.21-pre4 does not properly handle the O_DIRECT feature, which allows local attackers with write privileges to read portions of previously deleted files or cause file system corruption.
2004-1137	Multiple vulnerabilities in the IGMP functionality for Linux kernel 2.4.22 to 2.4.28 and 2.6.x to 2.6.9 allow local and remote attackers to cause a denial of service or execute arbitrary code via (1) the ip_mc_source function, which decrements a counter to -1, or (2) the igmp_marksources function, which does not properly validate IGMP message parameters and performs an out-of-bounds read.
2005-0086	Heap-based buffer overflow in Red Hat Enterprise Linux 3 allows attackers to cause a denial of service (application crash) or possibly execute arbitrary code via a crafted file, as demonstrated using the UTF-8 locale.

A security tester could use the information in Table 9-3 and test the Linux computer against these known vulnerabilities. Security testers should review the CVE and CAN information carefully to ensure that a customer's system is not still vulnerable to any entries listed on the CVE Web site and should make sure the system in question has been updated. Note that some vulnerabilities describe a local attacker and some a remote attacker. Attacking a system remotely is usually more difficult than conducting a local attack when sitting in front of the computer. You learn about some methods remote attackers use in the "Remote Access Attacks on Linux Systems" section later in this chapter.

After an attacker discovers a vulnerability, he or she can go to a Web site that offers exploits that take advantage of the vulnerability. In Activity 9-4, you visit another Web site with lots of information on exploits as well as many articles and tools for security testers.

ACTIVITY

Activity 9-4: Discovering Exploits for Linux Operating Systems

Time Required: 20 minutes

Objective: Using the Web to discover Linux OS exploits.

Description: In this activity, you visit a Web site listing exploits you can use to attack different OSs. As a security tester, you should be aware of the resources available to both security testers and attackers.

1. From Linux, start a Web browser, type the URL **www.governmentsecurity.org**, and press **Enter**. Figure 9-15 shows the *GovernmentSecurity.org* Web site.

2. On the *GovernmentSecurity.org* home page, click the **Exploit Archive** link on the left.

3. On the Exploits & Vulnerabilities Archive page, click the **Ethereal** link in the list (see Figure 9-16).

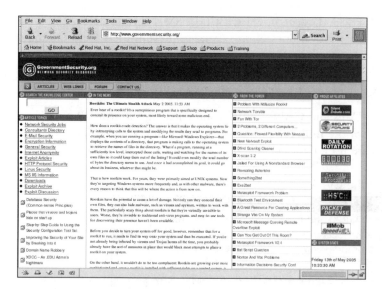

Figure 9-15   Using the *GovernmentSecurity.org* Web site to discover vulnerabilities

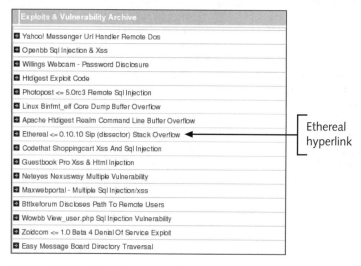

Figure 9-16   Selecting an exploit to investigate

4. Read the code displayed on your screen. The author did a nice job of documenting the program and describes how this exploit can be used. What version of Ethereal would this exploit work on?

5. To determine the version of Ethereal running on your computer, open a new shell, type **ethereal**, and press **Enter**.

6. In the Ethereal Network Analyzer window, click **Help**, **About Ethereal** from the menu. Your screen should look similar to Figure 9-17, but you're running an older version on your bootable CD. Figure 9-17 shows version 0.10.10 being used. What version of Ethereal is running on your system?

7. Would the exploit in question work on your system?

8. Would the exploit in question work on the system shown in Figure 9-17?

9. Close your Web browser, but leave Linux running for the next activity.

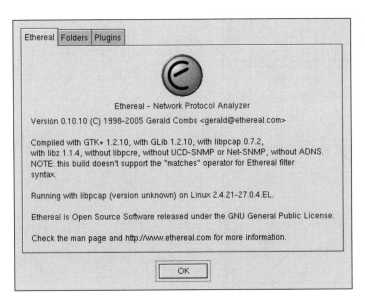

Figure 9-17   The About Ethereal dialog box

REMOTE ACCESS ATTACKS ON LINUX SYSTEMS

Attacking a network remotely requires knowing what system a remote user is operating and the attacked system's passwords and login accounts. You have examined some of these topics in previous chapters and should understand the steps for finding this information. The following sections focus on putting those steps together.

Footprinting an Attacked System

Before launching an attack on a computer system or network, attackers use footprinting techniques to find out as much as possible about the organization they plan to attack. First, attackers need to find out what OS version the attacked computer is running. Finding out what operating system a company is using can be done in many ways. Many attackers check newsgroups for any postings by technical personnel that not only give the version of Linux the company is running but also any patches or applications that might be causing problems.

A simple search at *http://groups.google.com* for the e-mail format the company uses can reveal a lot of information. For example, Figure 9-18 shows the results of searching for @linux at *http://groups.google.com*. The user who posted his question gave too much information to the forum. The IP addresses give attackers information they might not have been able to gather on their own. What other information has the administrator inadvertently let slip?

Of course, knowing a company's e-mail address can make the search even easier. Attackers who aren't targeting a specific company can simply go directly to support newsgroups and read postings from thousands of users. It's amazing how many people list their entire security infrastructure and pose questions that open them up to bigger problems than they started out with.

NOTE

Security Bytes

The amount of information you can find from visiting newsgroups is astounding. In one case, a security tester, armed with the e-mail address of only one employee at a government agency, found more than 15 messages posted to professional newsgroups. He was able to determine the OSs, software applications, and firewall hardware the agency used and discovered the names of seven employees working in different IT positions at the agency. It is important to train employees to use different e-mail addresses when they're posting questions on OSs or revealing application-specific information.

Figure 9-18   A newsgroup search

Attackers can use the following tools for further footprinting of a target system:

- Whois databases
- DNS zone transfers
- Nessus
- Port-scanning tools, such as Nmap and Netcat

Nmap is still one of the best tools for detecting the OS that's running and determining the services running on a system.

Activity 9-5: Determining the OS of Your Partner's Computer

Time Required: 30 minutes

Objective: Use Nmap to determine the OS your partner is running.

Description: Before you can hack a system, you need to determine what OS the computer is running. In this activity, you use Nmap to determine the OS your partner is running.

1. Your system should already be running from your bootable Linux CD. Open a shell of your choice and determine the IP number of your computer by typing **ifconfig** and pressing **Enter**.

2. Write down the IP address of your computer and give it to your partner.

3. Type **nmap –sS –O** *IPaddress*, substituting your partner's IP address number for *IPaddress*, and press **Enter**. Depending on the speed of your network, the command might take a few seconds or a few minutes. It should return information similar to what's shown in Figure 9-19.

```
Interesting ports on  (192.168.0.102):
(The 1597 ports scanned but not shown below are in state: closed)
Port       State       Service
22/tcp     open        ssh
68/tcp     open        dhcpclient
139/tcp    open        netbios-ssn
445/tcp    open        microsoft-ds
Remote operating system guess: Linux Kernel 2.4.0 - 2.5.20
Uptime 0.118 days (since Tue Feb 22 07:48:33 2005)

Nmap run completed -- 1 IP address (1 host up) scanned in 319 seconds
[root@server home]#
```

Figure 9-19   Nmap results

4. The –O parameter is used to determine the operating system of the attacked computer. In Step 3, what is the –sS parameter used for? (*Hint:* Type **man nmap** or **nmap** without any parameters if you need a reminder on Nmap commands.)

5. After the instructor has notified you that the classroom computer has been started in Windows XP Professional, type **nmap –sS –O *IPaddress*** (using the IP address number of your instructor's PC), and press **Enter**.

6. What are the results of running the Nmap command on the Windows XP computer?

7. Close the shell, but leave Linux running for the next activity.

Nmap might not always be able to determine the OS running on a computer, especially if the computer is using a firewall. You can still make an educated guess by looking at the ports or services running. Figure 9-20 shows Nmap attempting to determine the OS running on an XP computer with a software firewall installed. This version of Nmap was not able to give a firm answer on which OS was running, but the open ports it discovered, such as 139 (NetBIOS), at least let you know that the OS is Microsoft.

9

```
Interesting ports on  (192.168.0.101):
(The 1598 ports scanned but not shown below are in state: filtered)
Port      State      Service
135/tcp    open       loc-srv
139/tcp    open       netbios-ssn
445/tcp    open       microsoft-ds
No exact OS matches for host (test conditions non-ideal).
TCP/IP fingerprint:
SInfo(V=3.00%P=i386-redhat-linux-gnu%D=2/22%Time=421BA421%O=135%C=-1)
TSeq(Class=TR%IPID=I%TS=0)
T1(Resp=Y%DF=Y%W=FFFF%ACK=S++%Flags=AS%Ops=MNWNNT)
T2(Resp=N)
```

Figure 9-20   Nmap problem determining the OS

Using Social Engineering to Attack Remote Linux Systems

If attackers find that determining the OS with footprinting tools is too challenging, remember that they often resort to social engineering. Security testers can also use this technique to gather information. Instead of spending time running Nmap or searching through newsgroups, you can try using social engineering skills to get OS information from company employees. As you learned in Chapter 4, the following are some common techniques:

- Urgency
- Quid pro quo
- Status quo
- Kindness
- Position

Determining which OS a company is using is probably the easiest information to obtain. Most users see this information as being innocuous and freely report the OS they're running if they believe it might improve their work environment.

Don't underestimate the power of using social engineering skills to attack remote systems. As a security tester, you will probably gain the most information by using these techniques. In addition, a training program should be established to ensure that users are aware of this type of attack.

Installing Trojan Programs

Another method of attacking remote networks is installing Trojan programs that record keystrokes and other processes without users' knowledge. Trojan programs can be installed after a user clicks an attachment in an e-mail message, or worse, the user might download it over the Internet thinking it's a patch or a security fix for the OS they are currently running. This makes it easier for attackers because the Web server logs the

IP address of all visitors, so they now know the IP address of the person who downloaded the Trojan. When a Trojan is installed on a computer, it advertises information it obtains to a specific port, so the attacker needs to monitor or connect to that port to gather the information. Most Trojan programs perform one or more of the following functions:

- Allow for remote administration of the attacked system

- Create a file server (FTP) on the attacked computer so that files can be loaded and downloaded without the user's knowledge

- Steal passwords from the attacked system and e-mail them to the attacker

- Log all keystrokes a user enters, and e-mail the results to the attacker or store the results in a hidden file that the attacker can access remotely

Linux Trojan programs are sometimes disguised as legitimate programs, such as df or tar, but contain program code that can wipe out file systems on a Linux computer. Trojan programs are more difficult to detect today because programmers develop them to make legitimate calls on outbound ports that an IDS or a firewall wouldn't detect. Because the traffic generated is normal network traffic, it's difficult to detect. For example, a Trojan program called Sheepshank makes HTTP GET requests over port 80. There's certainly nothing strange about that occurring on a network. The Web server could then be configured to issue commands or keywords that are carried out on a Linux computer. The HTTP traffic would appear to be normal traffic traversing a network, but the keywords sent from the Web server could contain commands that request the attacked computer to download or copy sensitive files to a remote Web server.

Protecting Linux computers from Trojan attacks is difficult because these new types of Trojan programs are being developed. It's easier to protect Linux computers against Trojan programs that IT professionals have already identified. For example, the Trojan.Linux.JBellz program was identified as a vulnerablility on SUSE Linux 8.0 and Slackware Linux 8.0 systems. A security professional would know of this fact and take appropriate action. In this Trojan program, a user plays an MP3 file he or she received in an e-mail attachment, and the Trojan program deletes all files in the user's home directory. Another Linux Trojan program called Remote Shell also disseminates through e-mail messages by installing a backdoor that listens for incoming connections on UDP port 5503 or higher. Remote attackers then can take control of the system. This Remote Shell Trojan is similar to the Windows Back Orifice Trojan. Recently, another Linux Trojan program called Backdoor.Dextenea was released. The program creates the following files on the attacked system:

- /usr/secure

- /usr/doc/sys/qrt

- /usr/doc/run

- /usr/doc/sys/crond

- /usr/sbin/kfd

It then replaces the following legitimate files with copies of Trojan programs:

- /bin/ps or /usr/bin/ps

- /bin/netstat or /usr/bin/netstat

The Trojan creates multiple directories and installs a Telnet and modified SSH daemon as backdoors as well as a user account named r00t to access the attacked computer using SSH.

More dangerous Trojan programs are those contained in a rootkit. Rootkits contain Trojan binary programs ready to be installed by an intruder who has already gained root access to the system. The attacker can now hide the tools he uses to perform further attacks on the system and also have access to backdoor programs. A popular Linux rootkit is Linux Rootkit 5 (LRK5), released in 2000. Numerous rootkits are available for the Linux platform. When a rootkit is installed, legitimate commands are replaced with Trojan programs. For example, if the LRK5 rootkit is installed on a Linux computer, entering the Trojaned killall command allows the attacker's processes to continue running even though the Linux administrator thinks he killed all processes. The familiar ls command doesn't show the files the attacker uses, and the netstat command doesn't show suspicious network connections the attacker makes. So everything looks normal to the Linux administrator because he or she is using commands that have been Trojaned.

Activity 9-6: Finding Linux Rootkits on the Internet

Time Required: 15 minutes

Objective: Learn how Linux rootkits can be found and installed easily.

Description: Attackers can easily locate Linux rootkits for many Linux platforms. In this activity, you visit the *www.packetstormsecurity.org* Web site. This site has thousands of tools and exploits that attackers or security professionals can use.

1. Your system should already be running from your bootable Linux CD. Start a Web browser, type the URL **www.packetstormsecurity.org**, and press **Enter**.

2. On the Packet Storm home page, type **Linux rootkit** in the text box at the top, and click **search**. If you scroll to the bottom of the screen, you'll see that more than 3000 results were returned for this search.

3. Look through the list for Linux rootkit 5. The description shows some Linux commands that are Trojaned when using this rootkit. List five of these commands.

4. Leave your Web browser open and Linux running for the next activity.

As a security tester, you should periodically check Linux systems for installed rootkits. Activity 9-7 gives you a basic overview of a Trojan rootkit detector.

Activity 9-7: Checking for Linux Rootkit Trojans

Time Required: 60 minutes

Objective: Learn how to detect the presence of a rootkit installed on a Linux system by using two of the most popular rootkit detection programs: Rootkit Hunter and Chkrootkit.

Description: After gaining access to a Linux system, an attacker might install a rootkit containing Trojan programs and backdoors that can be used to further exploit the attacked system. In this activity, you download two tools to help you check for rookit installations.

1. Your system should already be running from your bootable Linux CD. Open a Web search engine, type **rootkit hunter**, and press **Enter**.

2. On the search engine page, click the **Rootkit Hunter** link.

3. On the Rootkit Web page shown in Figure 9-21, click the **Rootkit Hunter** link on the right under Projects.

4. Read the information about Rootkit Hunter and scroll through the document. Under the Project related documentation heading, click the **Rootkit Hunter FAQ (including installation)** link.

5. Use the browser back arrow to return to the previous page, and click the **1.2.7** link at the bottom of the page for the latest release.

6. If you're prompted to open the file, click **OK** to accept the default Save to Disk option. When prompted to enter the name of the file to save, accept the default file name rkhunter-1.2.7.tar.gz file name by clicking the **Save** button shown in Figure 9-22.

7. After the file is downloaded, open a shell and navigate to the directory where you downloaded the file.

8. Verify that the file is located in the directory by typing **ls** and pressing **Enter**.

9. Type the command **tar -zxvf rkhunter-1.2.7.tar.gz** and press **Enter**.

10. Change to the rkhunter directory that was created with the tar command by typing **cd rkhunter**.

11. From the shell, type the command **./installer.sh**.

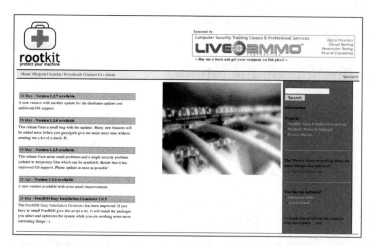

Figure 9-21   Selecting the Rootkit Hunter project

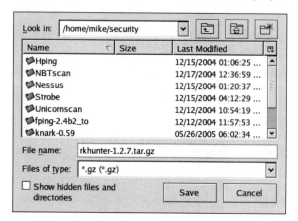

Figure 9-22   Saving the Rootkit Hunter program to your computer

NOTE

The installation might fail if you're using a read-only file system. Examine the errors that were returned. If the installer shell script is run on a computer that has a writable disk, a directory named files is created. The rkhunter program can be run in this directory. Entering the command without parameters displays the screen shown in Figure 9-23.

```
Rootkit Hunter 1.2.7, Copyright 2003-2005, Michael Boelen

Rootkit Hunter comes with ABSOLUTELY NO WARRANTY. This is free software,
and you are welcome to redistribute it under the terms of the GNU General
Public License. See LICENSE for details.

Valid parameters:
--checkall (-c)            : Check system
--createlogfile*           : Create logfile
--cronjob                  : Run as cronjob (removes colored layout)
--display-logfile          : Show logfile at end of the output
--help (-h)                : Show this help
--nocolors*                : Don't use colors for output
--report-mode*             : Don't show uninteresting information for reports
--report-warnings-only*    : Show only warnings (lesser output than --report-mode
                             more than --quiet)
--skip-application-check*  : Don't run application version checks
--skip-keypress*           : Don't wait after every test (non-interactive)
--quick*                   : Perform quick scan (instead of full scan)
--quiet*                   : Be quiet (only show warnings)
--update                   : Run update tool and check for database updates
--version                  : Show version and quit
--versioncheck             : Check for latest version

--bindir <bindir>*         : Use <bindir> instead of using default binaries
--configfile <file>*       : Use different configuration file
--dbdir <dir>*             : Use <dbdir> as database directory
--rootdir <rootdir>*       : Use <rootdir> instead of / (slash at end)
--tmpdir <tempdir>*        : Use <tempdir> as temporary directory

Explicit scan options:
--allow-ssh-root-user*     : Allow usage of SSH root user login
--disable-md5-check*       : Disable MD5 checks
--disable-passwd-check*    : Disable passwd/group checks
--scan-knownbad-files*     : Perform besides 'known good' check a 'known bad' che
ck

Multiple parameters are allowed
*) Parameter can only be used with other parameters

[root@localhost files]#
```

Figure 9-23   Running rkhunter without parameters

12. To perform a system check, enter the parameter **--checkall** at the shell and press **Enter**. Figure 9-24 shows the first screen displayed.

```
[root@localhost files]# rkhunter --checkall

Rootkit Hunter 1.2.7 is running

Determining OS... Ready

Checking binaries
* Selftests
    Strings (command)                       [ OK ]

* System tools
  Performing 'known good' check...
    /bin/ls                                 [ OK ]
    /bin/netstat                            [ OK ]
    /bin/ps                                 [ OK ]
    /usr/bin/strings                        [ OK ]
    /usr/bin/top                            [ OK ]
[Press <ENTER> to continue]
```

Figure 9-24   Running rkhunter with the --checkall parameter

If you continue pressing Enter, Rootkit Hunter checks the system for known rootkit vulnerabilities (see Figures 9-25 and 9-26). This tool does a good job of comparing known Trojans and backdoors to software installed on the computer.

13. Close the shell and return to your Web browser.

14. Type the URL **www.chkrootkit.org** and press **Enter**.

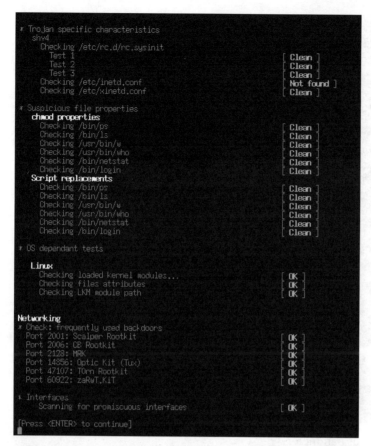

Figure 9-25   Scanning for Trojans

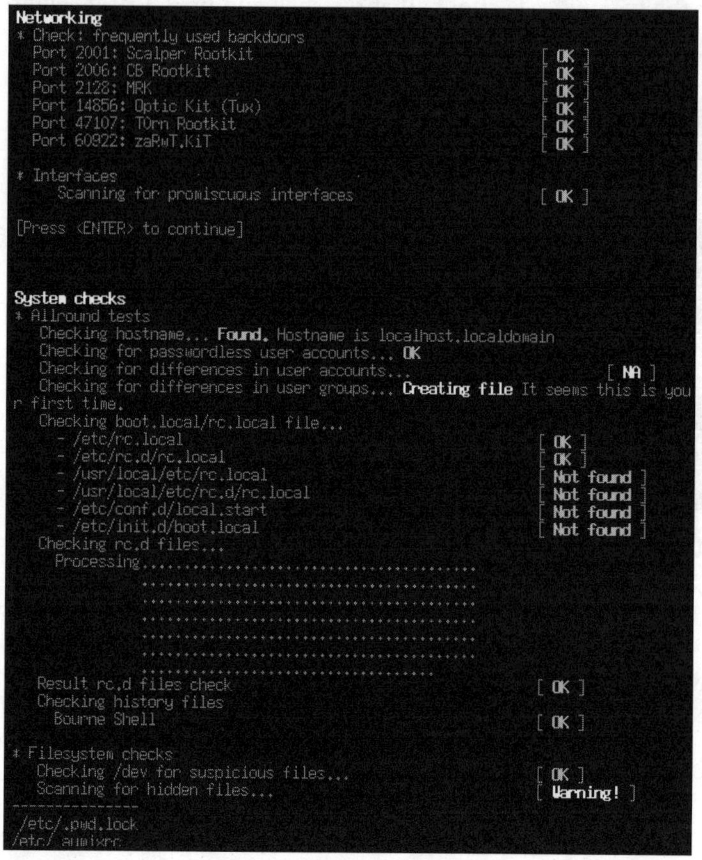

Figure 9-26   Rootkit Hunter continues to scan for Trojans

15. On the home page, click the **chkrootkit 0.45 is now available!** link, shown in Figure 9-27.

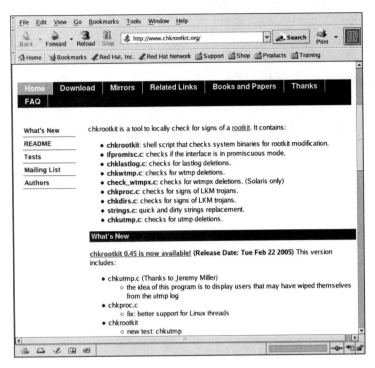

Figure 9-27   The Chkrootkit home page

16. On the next page, click the **Latest Source tarball** link at the bottom (see Figure 9-28) to begin downloading the tool.

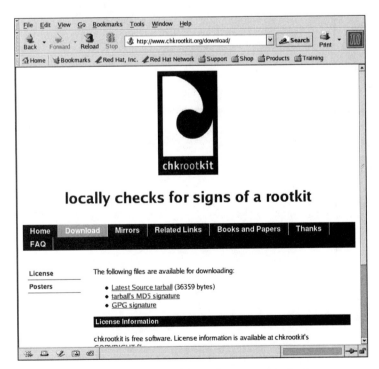

Figure 9-28   Selecting the Chkrootkit source tarball

17. If prompted to save the file, click **OK** and save the program in any directory you choose. Be sure to note this directory so that you can navigate there in the next step. When the file is saved, close your Web browser and open a new shell.

18. Change to the directory where you saved the program, type **ls**, and press **Enter** to view the directory's contents.

19. Type **tar –zxvf chkrootkit.tar.gz** and press **Enter**.

20. Change to the new directory created in Step 18 by typing **cd chkrootkit-0.45** and pressing **Enter**.

21. From the chkrootkit-0.45 directory, type **make** and press **Enter**.

22. To see a list of the commands that can be used with Chkrootkit, type **./chkrootkit –h** and press **Enter**. The available options are shown (see Figure 9-29).

```
[root@server chkrootkit-0.45]# ./chkrootkit -h
Usage: ./chkrootkit [options] [test ...]
Options:
        -h              show this help and exit
        -V              show version information and exit
        -l              show available tests and exit
        -d              debug
        -q              quiet mode
        -x              expert mode
        -r dir          use dir as the root directory
        -p dir1:dir2:dirN path for the external commands used by chkrootkit
        -n              skip NFS mounted dirs
[root@server chkrootkit-0.45]# 
```

Figure 9-29   Options for the Chkrootkit program

23. To run a test on your Linux computer, type **./chkrootkit** and press **Enter**. The test takes a minute or so; while it runs, watch the programs and files that are tested for possible infection. You might want to use the **|less** parameter so that you can view one screen at a time (see Figure 9-30).

```
ROOTDIR is `/'
Checking `amd'... not infected
Checking `basename'... not infected
Checking `biff'... not found
Checking `chfn'... not infected
Checking `chsh'... not infected
Checking `cron'... not infected
Checking `date'... not infected
Checking `du'... not infected
Checking `dirname'... not infected
Checking `echo'... not infected
Checking `egrep'... not infected
Checking `env'... not infected
Checking `find'... not infected
Checking `fingerd'... not found
Checking `gpm'... not infected
Checking `grep'... not infected
Checking `hdparm'... not infected
Checking `su'... not infected
Checking `ifconfig'... not infected
Checking `inetd'... not tested
Checking `inetdconf'... not found
Checking `identd'... not found
Checking `init'... not infected
Checking `killall'... not infected
Checking `ldsopreload'... not infected
Checking `login'... not infected
Checking `ls'... not infected
Checking `lsof'... not infected
Checking `mail'... not infected
Checking `mingetty'... not infected
Checking `netstat'... not infected
Checking `named'... not found
Checking `passwd'... not infected
Checking `pidof'... not infected
Checking `pop2'... not found
Checking `pop3'... not found
:
```

Figure 9-30   Running the Chkrootkit program

Figure 9-31 shows the last screen of the Chkrootkit program. This tool is helpful for checking whether any rootkit Trojan programs have been installed on your system. As you'll discover when visiting security Web sites, a new Trojan program is identified every day.

```
Searching for LPD Worm files and dirs... nothing found
Searching for Ramen Worm files and dirs... nothing found
Searching for Maniac files and dirs... nothing found
Searching for RK17 files and dirs... nothing found
Searching for Ducoci rootkit... nothing found
Searching for Adore Worm... nothing found
Searching for ShitC Worm... nothing found
Searching for Omega Worm... nothing found
Searching for Sadmind/IIS Worm... nothing found
Searching for MonKit... nothing found
Searching for Showtee... nothing found
Searching for OpticKit... nothing found
Searching for T.R.K... nothing found
Searching for Mithra... nothing found
Searching for LOC rootkit... nothing found
Searching for Romanian rootkit... nothing found
Searching for HKRK rootkit... nothing found
:/proc/28129/fd: No such file or directory
Searching for Suckit rootkit... nothing found
Searching for Volc rootkit... nothing found
Searching for Gold2 rootkit... nothing found
Searching for TC2 Worm default files and dirs... nothing found
Searching for Anonoying rootkit default files and dirs... nothing found
Searching for ZK rootkit default files and dirs... nothing found
Searching for ShKit rootkit default files and dirs... nothing found
Searching for AjaKit rootkit default files and dirs... nothing found
Searching for zaRwT rootkit default files and dirs... nothing found
Searching for Madalin rootkit default files... nothing found
Searching for Fu rootkit default files... nothing found
Searching for ESRK rootkit default files... nothing found
Searching for anomalies in shell history files... nothing found
Checking `asp'... not infected
Checking `bindshell'... not infected
Checking `lkm'... chkproc: nothing detected
Checking `rexedcs'... not found
Checking `sniffer'... eth1: PF_PACKET(/sbin/dhclient)
Checking `w55808'... not infected
Checking `wted'... chkwtmp: nothing deleted
Checking `scalper'... not infected
Checking `slapper'... not infected
Checking `z2'... chklastlog: nothing deleted
Checking `chkutmp'... chkutmp: nothing deleted
(END)
```

Figure 9-31 Chkrootkit continues search for Trojans

24. After viewing the output, close all shells and your Web browser, but leave Linux running for the next activity.

Countermeasures for Trojan attacks are the same as the standard set of rules a security tester should follow:

- Remove any unneeded services running on the system.

- Apply security updates in a timely fashion.

- Isolate infected computers as soon as possible to prevent further corruption of data or systems.

- Train employees not to open attachments or install programs on their systems without IT authorization.

- Train employees on methods attackers might use to gather information from them.

- Enforce a strong password policy so that if a system is compromised, it would be difficult for an attacker to crack passwords.

- If you suspect a rootkit has been installed, visit *www.chkrootkit.org* and download the Chkrootkit tool to check your system.

Creating Buffer Overflow Programs

Another method attackers use to compromise remote Linux systems is to create programs that cause a buffer overflow. As you learned in Chapter 3, buffer overflows write code to the operating system's memory that then runs some type of program. For example, the code might open a shell and issue commands that shut down the Linux OS or, even worse, elevate the attacker's permissions to the level of owner.

The steps for creating a buffer overflow program are beyond the scope of this book, but you can find hundreds of Web sites with step-by-step directions if you're interested in investigating this topic. Simply type "Creating buffer overflow" in any search engine. However, security testers should focus first on learning what a buffer overflow program looks like. The following C code shows how a program can cause a buffer overflow. Some of the code might look a little confusing because arrays were not covered in Chapter 7. (An **array**, in programming, is a structure that holds multiple values of the same type. After creation, an array is a fixed-length structure.) However, for this example, you should still be able to follow the code:

```
1. main()
2. {
3.     char fish_name[1]; //Assign a buffer area (array) of 1
                          //character
4.     char hawaii_fish_name[25] = "Humuhumukununukuapuaa"
5.     strcpy(fish_name, hawaii_fish_name); //Copy long name to
                                            //small area
6.             }
```

Line 3 defines an array (a buffer area) called fish_name that can hold one character. Line 4 allocates an array of 25 characters called hawaii_fish_name and stores the string Humuhumukununukuapuaa (the name of a Hawaiian fish; translates to "fish with a pig's nose"). Line 5 copies the contents of hawaii_fish_name into the one-character array, fish_name. The program compiles with no errors, but when it runs, the error shown in Figure 9-32 is returned.

```
[root@server /]# ./fish.exe
Segmentation fault
[root@server /]#
```

Figure 9-32   A segmentation fault error caused by a buffer overflow

A cleverly crafted buffer overflow replaces an area of memory, specifically the stack segment, with the shell code it wants to run. (The stack is a contiguous portion of memory that contains data.) When a function or program is called, it's pushed onto the stack. The following code fills that area in memory with **shell code**. The following C snippet of hexadecimal shell code shows you that a program is being run. You would probably want to know exactly what the program is doing if you suspect foul play. A security tester who has access to the source code needs to decode the data stored in the info[] buffer to determine whether it is indeed a buffer overflow program.

```
    include <string.h>
    char info[] = "\xeb\x2a\x08\x09\x00\x00\x89\x05\xed\xff"
        "\xeb\x2a\x03\x09\x00\x00\x89\x05\xed\xff"
        "\xeb\x2a\x02\x09\x00\x00\x89\x05\xed\xdf"
  "\xeb\x2a\x08\x01\x01\x02\x83\x04\xef\xcf"
        "\x6e\x2a\x08\x09\x00\x00\x89\x05\xed\xff"
        "\xeb\x2a\x08\x11\x00\x00\x89\x05\xed\xae"
  "\xca\x2a\x08\x09\x00\x00\x67\xcc\xed\xef"
        "\x22\x2a\x08\xaa\x00\x00\xff\x05\xed\xff"
        "\xdd\x2a\x08\x09\x00\x00\xcc\x05\xed\xcd"
  "\xfa\x2a\x08\x09\x00\x00\x00\x11\xed\xde"
        "\xeb\x2a\x08\x09\x00\x00\x89\x05\xed\xff"
main()
{   //Contains a function that copies the info[] array into a
    //buffer area.
        [Remaining code omitted]
}
```

To help prevent buffer overflow attacks, security professionals must understand the importance of writing code that minimizes the possibility of such an attack. Without any computer programming experience, this could be difficult, so you should make sure that someone on your security team has the necessary experience. The following list describes some guidelines to help reduce this type of attack on Linux systems:

- Write secure code that avoids the use of functions known to have buffer overflow vulnerabilities, such as strcpy(), strcat(), sprintf(), and gets().

- On Linux systems, it's possible to configure the OS to not allow code in the stack to run any other executable code in the stack. Remember, buffer overflow attacks usually place executable code in the stack so that a computer attack can be carried out.

- Use compilers, such as GCC, that warn programmers when a function such as the ones listed in the first item in this list are used. The compiler issues a warning message, such as "The gets() function is dangerous and should not be used."

Using Sniffers to Gain Access to Remote Linux Systems

Configuring a network adapter card in promiscuous mode can also be an entry point into a network for an intruder. When an intruder installs a packet analyzer or protocol analyzer, such as Tcpdump or Ethereal, on his computer, the intruder's NIC accepts all packets that traverse the network cable. This is called **promiscuous mode** because the NIC accepts all packets addressed to it. Sniffing network packets and viewing logon names and passwords are possible if the attacker is running a computer on the same network segment as the attacked computer. If the packet sniffer or protocol analyzer is capturing packets while the unsuspecting user is entering a password to a Telnet session, the information the user enters can easily be captured by the attacker and used to launch an attack later.

The best countermeasure for this type of attack is to prevent unauthorized personnel from having access to your network. Many hackers install a sniffer on the attacked computer after they gain root access to the system. You should also avoid using protocols that send data in clear text, such as FTP, Telnet, HTTP, and so on. These protocols send passwords and logon names in clear text that a sniffer could easily retrieve.

Activity 9-8: Using a Packet Sniffer

Time Required: 30 minutes

Objective: Learn to use the Ethereal packet sniffer to review network traffic from your partner's computer.

Description: Packet sniffers are good tools for obtaining information needed to hack into a Linux computer. In this activity, you use Ethereal to capture and analyze network packets as they leave your partner's Linux computer.

1. Your system should already be running from your bootable Linux CD. Right-click a blank area of the desktop to display the Local Area Security menu. Click **Apps, l.a.s.**, and click **ethereal** from the l.a.s menu. You should see a window similar to Figure 9-33.

2. Click **Capture, Start** from the menu. Accept the defaults in the Ethereal: Capture Options dialog box by clicking **OK**. The Ethereal: Capture dialog box shown in Figure 9-34 opens and displays captured packets.

3. To create additional network traffic, you need to perform some activity on your Linux computer. Open another shell and ping any IP address in your classroom. Next, open a Web browser and visit several Web sites. If you have access to an SMTP mail server, telnet the site by typing **telnet mail.*webmailserver*.com 25** and pressing **Enter**. (Substitute the name of your classroom mail server for *webmailserver*.) If a password is required for any accounts, be sure to enter an incorrect password because this information can be sniffed on the network wire. If you have access to an FTP server, type **FTP *server_name*** and press **Enter**. Don't enter any password information unless you want other classmates to see it.

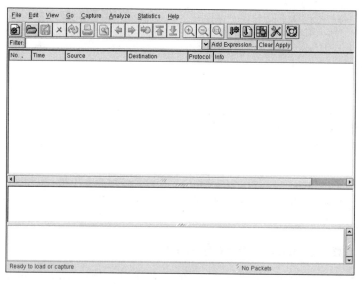

Figure 9-33   The main window of Ethereal

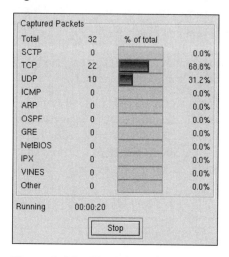

Figure 9-34   The Ethereal: Capture dialog box

4. When you think you have collected enough traffic, end the capture by clicking **Stop** in the Ethereal: Capture dialog box. You should see a results window similar to the one in Figure 9-35. Your output will vary depending on the network traffic you generated.

5. Click the **Protocol** header to sort the output file by protocol. In Figure 9-35, the top pane shows all the Address Resolution Protocol (ARP) requests generated during the capture period. (*Note*: For a complete user guide on Ethereal, visit *www.ethereal.com*.)

6. Scroll through the list and note the protocols. Click a record that identifies DNS as the protocol. What Web sites did your partner visit?

7. Spend time looking at the traffic captured. Does Ethereal display the contents of captured packets or just the protocol information?

8. Shut down your Linux system.

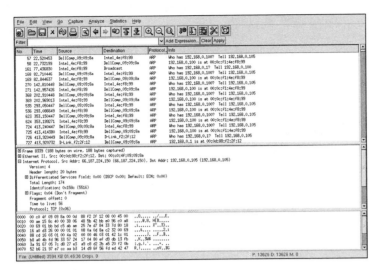

Figure 9-35   Ethereal capture results

COUNTERMEASURES AGAINST LINUX REMOTE ATTACKS

Protecting a Linux system from remote attacks is not much different from protecting any system from remote attacks. The most critical concerns are training users and keeping up on new kernel releases and security updates. Having a handle on these two tasks is an essential start to protecting any network.

User Awareness Training

Making it difficult for social engineers to obtain information from company employees is the place to start protecting your Linux system from outside attacks. Users must be told that no information should be given to outsiders, no matter how harmless it might seem. Inform employees that if attackers know what OS the company is running, they can use that information to conduct attacks on the company's network. Make your customers aware that many exploits can be downloaded from Web sites. Emphasize that knowing which OS is running makes it easier for attackers to select an exploit.

Teach users to be suspicious of people asking questions about the systems they are using and to verify that they are talking to someone claiming to be from the IT Department. Asking for a telephone number to call back is a good way to ensure that the person does work for the same company. A 30-minute training session on security procedures can alert staff to how easily outsiders can compromise a system and gain proprietary information.

Keeping Current

Software vendors are in a never-ending battle to address vulnerabilities that attackers discover. As soon as a bug or vulnerability is discovered and posted on the Internet, OS vendors usually notify customers of upgrades or patches. Installing these fixes promptly is essential to protecting your system.

Red Hat has improved its method for informing users when they're running outdated versions. Figure 9-36 shows the warning icon that's displayed when an administrator logs on to a Linux system that isn't current.

 — Warning icon

Figure 9-36   The Red Hat warning icon

If you click the red exclamation mark, you see the Red Hat Update Agent welcome window shown in Figure 9-37.

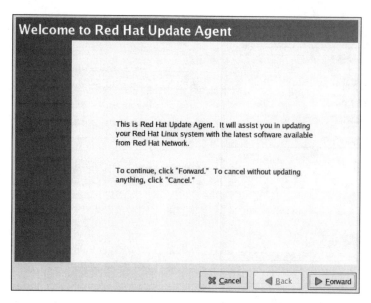

Figure 9-37 The Red Hat Update Agent welcome window

Click Forward to see the window shown in Figure 9–38. This window lists all available updates, and you can click the Launch up2date button to download and install the items you select.

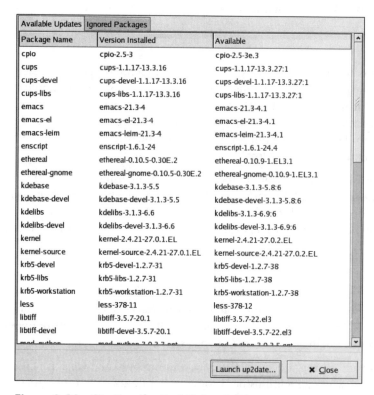

Figure 9-38 Starting the Red Hat up2date program

After you install the updates successfully, the icon on the status bar at the far right changes to a check mark (see Figure 9–39).

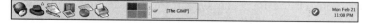

Figure 9-39 Red Hat icon showing that no updates are needed

CHAPTER SUMMARY

- File systems for all operating systems are important because they handle storing and managing user data and system data. File systems also enable users to compress, format, encrypt, and view information on the creation and owner of all files and directories.

- Linux uses default directories (called folders in some newer Linux versions) to store user data and system data. Examples of some default directories are bin, dev, etc, home, lib, and proc.

- The default Linux file system is the Extended File System (Ext), but *NIX systems allow users to mount many different file systems depending on their needs.

- Information about *NIX files, such as the file owner, file size, file creation date, last modification date, and so on, is stored in an information node (inode).

- Vulnerabilities of the Linux OS can be determined by the use of security tools, such as Nessus and Nmap, and from accessing the CVE Web site.

- Remote attacks on Linux systems can be accomplished by using footprinting, social engineering, Trojan programs, and buffer overflows.

- Social engineering can be the most effective way to gather information on the Linux OS because it doesn't require breaking into a system directly or running special programs or security utilities.

- Countermeasures to Trojan program attacks might include removal of any unneeded services running on the system, applying tested security updates in a timely fashion, isolating infected computers to prevent further corruption of data or systems, and implementing training programs.

- Countermeasures to buffer overflow attacks on a Linux system include writing secure code that avoids functions known to be susceptible to buffer overflows, configuration of the Linux OS to prevent code from being run in the stack, and using compilers that warn when a function is dangerous or risky.

- Protecting a Linux system begins with ensuring that the most recent OS or tested security updates are being used and that employees are trained on social engineering tactics.

- Keeping current on OS versions and security updates is critical in protecting a Linux system or network from remote attacks.

KEY TERMS

array — In programming, this structure holds multiple values of the same type. After creation, an array is a fixed-length structure.

Extended File System (Ext) — The Ext file system is included in the standard Linux kernel and might be Ext, Second Extended File System (Ext2fs), or Third Extended File System (Ext3fs).

inodes — Information nodes store information, such as file size and creation date, about files on a *NIX system.

journaling — A method of providing fault-resiliency to a file system by writing updates to a log before the original disk is updated. In the event of a system crash, the system can check logs to see whether all updates were written to disk and can correct inconsistencies quickly if any incomplete transactions are found.

promiscuous mode — Installing a sniffer program so that all packets passing through the NIC are captured instead of being dropped.

segmentation fault — An error that occurs when a program attempts to access a memory location it isn't allowed to access or in a way that's not permitted.

shell code — An assembly language program that executes a shell and can be used as an exploit payload.

REVIEW QUESTIONS

1. Which Linux folder holds configuration files?

   a. etc

   b. bin

   c. home

   d. usr

2. What Linux command displays the file system being used? (Choose all that apply.)

   a. display all

   b. ls -l

   c. df

   d. mount

3. What Linux command displays the configuration of all interfaces on a Linux computer?

   a. ipconfig

   b. ifconfig

   c. config

   d. iptables

4. Name three commands for listing the contents of a text file.

5. What methods can be used to install a Trojan program on a remote Linux computer? (Choose all that apply.)

   a. attaching the program to an e-mail

   b. disguising the program as a security patch or fix

   c. running a port-scanning tool

   d. using the -sS parameter in Nmap

6. Many buffer overflow attacks against Linux systems use _____ code to issue commands.

   a. pseudo

   b. machine

   c. shell

   d. assembly

7. Which of the following is a tool for analyzing network traffic and collecting logon account names and passwords?

   a. Nmap

   b. Ethereal

   c. Passwd

   d. Ethernet

8. Write the Nmap command to determine the OS running on a host computer with the IP address 193.145.85.10.

9. System binary files are located in which of the following default Linux directories?

   a. /sbin

   b. /bin

   c. /proc

   d. /etc

10. Which file system is considered the "de facto standard" on all versions of the Linux OS?

    a. Network File System (NFS)

    b. Third Extended File System (Ext3fs)

    c. Second Extended File System (Ext2fs)

    d. EFS (EFS)

11. NFS supports sharing and saving files to remote disks. True or False?

12. The following C snippet is most likely a _____ .

```
#include <stdio.h>
#include <string.h>
#define OFFSET 0
#define ALIGN 0
#define BUFFER 470
// Date written: 3/23/2005
#ifdef Linux

char shellcode[] = "\x31\xdb\x89\xd8\xb0\x16\xcd\x81" /*setuid(0)
*/
. . . . . .
"\xeb\x1f\x5e\x89\x76\x08\x31\xc0\x88\x46\x07\x89\x46\x0c"
. . . . . .
"\xb0\x0b\x89\xf3\x8d\x4e\x08\x8d\x56\x0c\xcd\x80\x31\xdb"
. . . . . .
"\x89\xd8\x40\xcd\x80\xe8\xdc\xff\xff\xff/bin/sh";
#endif
```

    a. virus

    b. Trojan program

    c. worm

    d. buffer overflow

13. IT professionals should never post technical questions through online sources, such as newsgroups. True or False?

14. Which of the following is the most efficient way to determine which operating system a company is using?

    a. Run Nmap or other port-scanning programs.

    b. Use the Whois database.

    c. Install a sniffer on the company's network segment.

    d. Call the company and ask.

15. Write the Linux command to create a file named security.

16. List three countermeasures for Trojan attacks on a Linux system.

17. To help prevent social-engineering attacks on Linux systems, security testers should recommend which of the following measures?

    a. implementing an employee awareness training program

    b. monitoring all incoming and outgoing e-mail

    c. reducing newsgroups

    d. implementing current updates of security programs

18. Employees should be able to install programs on their company computers as long as the programs are not copyrighted. True or False?

19. Which tool can be used to determine the OS and services running on a computer?

   a. Host

   b. Nmap

   c. Netstat

   d. Traceroute

20. List three techniques social engineers use to get information from company employees.

CASE PROJECTS

Case 9-1: Determining Vulnerabilities of the Linux OS

After conducting footprinting and using social-engineering techniques on the K. J. Williams network, you have determined that the company is running several applications on Linux computers. You discover that one of the systems is running Red Hat Linux, and you need to ensure that the most current version is being used.

Based on the preceding information, write a brief report stating the most current Red Hat version and describe any vulnerabilities in this version.

Case 9-2: Detecting Unauthorized Applications

In conducting a review of the operating systems running on the K. J. Williams network, you detect a computer program that appears to be unauthorized. No one in the department knows how the program got on the Linux computer. The manager thinks the program was installed on the computer before his start date three years ago. When you review the program's source code, you discover that it contains a buffer overflow exploit.

Based on the preceding information, write a report to the IT manager stating what course of action should be taken and listing recommendations for management.

10

HACKING WEB SERVERS

After reading this chapter and completing the exercises, you will be able to:

♦ Describe Web applications

♦ Explain Web application vulnerabilities

♦ Describe the tools used to attack Web servers

C ompanies recognize the power of the Web to improve sales. Many Web development platforms are available to users, such as Microsoft Active Server Pages (ASP), Sun's Java Server Pages (JSP), and ColdFusion. With all the available platforms and e-commerce Web sites, it's no wonder that security vulnerabilities abound.

This chapter gives you an overview of Web applications, explains the vulnerabilities of many Web components, and describes the tools used to hack Web servers.

UNDERSTANDING WEB APPLICATIONS

As you learned in Chapter 7, it is nearly impossible to write a program without bugs. The bigger the program, the more bugs are possible, and some bugs create security vulnerabilities. Web applications are no exception, and because they generally have a larger user base than standalone applications, bugs are even more of a problem. The more people who have access to a program, the bigger the risks of security vulnerabilities. The following sections describe the components of a Web application and discuss different platforms for developing Web applications.

Web Application Components

HTML is still the foundation of most Web applications and is commonly used for creating **static Web pages**. Static Web pages display the same information regardless of the time of day or the user who activates the page. **Dynamic Web pages** can vary the information that's displayed depending on variables such as the current time and date, user name, and purchasing history (information collected via cookies or Web bugs). For Web pages to be dynamic, their HTML code must consist of more than just the basic tags discussed in Chapter 7. These pages need special components for displaying information that changes depending on user input or information obtained from a back-end server. To do this, dynamic Web pages can use the <form> tag, Common Gateway Interface (CGI), Active Server Pages (ASP), PHP, ColdFusion, scripting languages, and database connector strings, such as Open Database Connector (ODBC). These components are covered in the following sections.

Web Forms

Web servers use the <form> element or tag in an HTML document to allow customers to submit information to the Web server. You have probably filled out a form when purchasing a product online or registering for an e-mail newsletter, for example. Some forms can be quite long and ask for a lot of information; some have only a couple of input fields, such as user name and password. A Web server processes information from a form by using a Web application. The following HTML code shows the syntax for a simple form:

```
<html>
<body>
<form>
Enter your username:
<input type="text" name="username">
<br>
Enter your password:
<input type="text" name="password">
</form></body></html>
```

Figure 10-1 shows the Web page created with this HTML code.

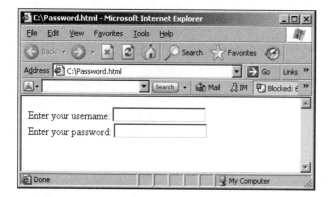

Figure 10-1   An HTML Web page with a form

Gaining skills in creating HTML forms can help you recognize vulnerabilities in Web applications. Forms are an easy way for attackers to intercept data that users enter and submit to a Web server, so security testers should be able to recognize when forms are being used.

Common Gateway Interface (CGI)

Another standard that handles moving data from a Web server to a Web browser is **Common Gateway Interface (CGI)**, which enables Web designers to create dynamic HTML Web applications. The majority of dynamic Web pages on the Internet are created with CGI and scripting languages. CGI is the interface that describes how a Web server passes data to a Web browser. It relies on Perl or another scripting language to create dynamic Web pages, which is quite different from Active Server Pages (covered in the next section). CGI's main role is passing data between a Web server and Web browser. In fact, the term "gateway" describes this movement of data between the Web server and the Web browser.

CGI programs can be written in many different programming and scripting languages, such as C/C++, Perl, UNIX shells, Visual Basic, and FORTRAN. Programming languages such as C or C++ require compiling the program before running it. If CGI is implemented through a scripting language, compilation isn't necessary. The following CGI program prints "Hello Security Testers!" to the user's browser. This Hello.pl program is written in Perl and would be placed in the cgi-bin directory on the Web server.

```
#!/usr/bin/perl
print "Content-type: text/html\n\n";
print "Hello Security Testers!";
```

To check whether the CGI program works, save the program to the cgi-bin directory of your Web server, and then enter the URL in your Web browser, such as *http://www.myweb.com/cgi-bin/hello.pl*.

Active Server Pages (ASP)

The main difference between HTML pages and **Active Server Pages (ASP)** is that with ASP, developers can display HTML documents to users on the fly. That is, when a user requests a Web page, one is created at that time. ASP is not a programming language. It uses scripting languages, such as JScript (Microsoft's implementation of JavaScript) or VBScript. ASP is a technology that enables developers to create dynamic, interactive Web pages.

Not all Web servers support ASP, so if you want to develop pages using ASP, the server you're using must support this technology. Of course, Internet Information Services (IIS) 4.0 and later supports ASP, and several projects provide ASP or ASP-like functionality for Apache, such as Apache::ASP, mod_mono, and Chilisoft_ ASP. (For more information, visit *http://httpd.apache.org*.) It's important to understand that the Web server, not the Web browser, must support ASP. In Activities 10-1 and 10-2, you work with IIS to get a better understanding of Web applications.

Activity 10-1: Installing Internet Information Services (IIS) 5.1

Time Required: 30 minutes

Objective: Install IIS 5.1 on your Windows XP Professional computer.

Description: To create a Web site, you need to install IIS on your Windows XP Professional computer. Microsoft includes IIS 5.1 with Windows XP Professional, but it isn't installed by default; IIS requires a separate installation from the OS installation. In this activity, you install IIS 5.1 and use your Web browser to test that it was installed correctly. You need your Windows XP Professional CD, or your instructor will share a folder on his or her computer that you can access during this activity.

1. From your Windows XP Professional computer, insert the Windows XP Professional CD in the CD-ROM drive, or, if you don't have the CD, write down the path of the instructor's shared folder.

2. Click **Start**, **Control Panel**, and then double-click **Add or Remove Programs**.

3. Click the **Add/Remove Windows Components** icon on the left. When the Windows Components Wizard starts, click to select the **Internet Information Services (IIS)** check box (see Figure 10-2). Do not clear any options already selected in this window. Click **Next**, and follow the on-screen instructions. If you're prompted for a CD, click **Browse** and enter the path from Step 1. Click **Finish** and close all windows.

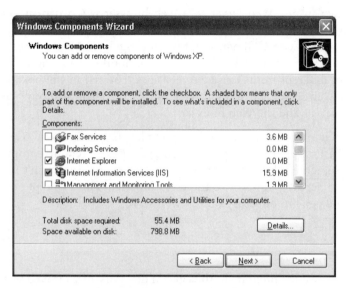

Figure 10-2   The Windows Components Wizard

4. After IIS is installed, test it by clicking **Start**, **All Programs**, pointing to **Administrative Tools**, and then clicking **Internet Information Services**. The Internet Information Services Microsoft Management Console (MMC) opens (see Figure 10-3). What version of IIS is installed on your computer?

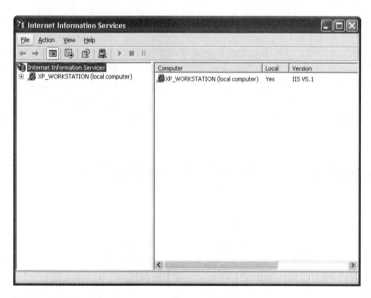

Figure 10-3   The Internet Information Services MMC

5. Start a Web browser, type the URL **http://localhost**, and press **Enter**. The window shown in Figure 10-4 is displayed. Read the Help information in this window. Note that a visitor to your Web site would get an "under construction" message because you haven't created a default HTML Web page yet. When you're finished, close the window.

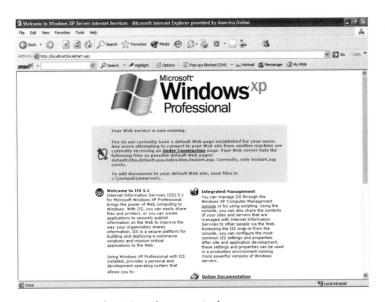

Figure 10-4   The IIS welcome window

6. Next, you need to create a folder on your Web server to hold any HTML pages you create. When IIS is installed, a new folder called Inetpub is created on your C: drive. Right-click **Start** and click **Explore** to open Windows Explorer. Under the C: drive (substitute the correct drive letter if your installation is different), click to expand the **Inetpub** folder and the **wwwroot** folder.

7. Click **File** on the Windows Explorer menu, point to **New**, and click **Folder**. For the folder name, type *YourFirstName* (substituting your own first name).

8. Close any open windows, and leave Windows XP running for the next activity.

To keep attackers from knowing the directory structure you create on an IIS Web server, creating a **virtual directory** is recommended so that the path a user sees on the Web browser is not the actual path on the Web server. A virtual directory is a pointer to the physical directory. For example, with virtual directories, a user might see *http://www.mycompany.com/jobs/default.asp* instead of *http://www.mycompany.com/security/positions/CEH_Cert/default.asp*.

The simpler structure a virtual directory offers is often easier for users to memorize and makes it simpler to navigate to a particular folder on the Web server. Using this design strategy also helps hide the actual directory structure from attackers.

Activity 10-2: Creating a Virtual Directory

Time Required: 15 minutes

Objective: Learn how to create a virtual directory on an IIS Web server.

Description: After IIS is installed and physical directories are created, a Web designer should create virtual directories that prevent customers from seeing how the physical directory structure is implemented. A virtual directory is a good security feature and makes it easier for users to navigate the folder structure. In this activity, you create a virtual directory using the directory you created in Activity 10-1.

1. From your Windows XP Professional computer, click **Start**, **All Programs**, point to **Administrative Tools**, and then click **Internet Information Services**. In the Internet Information Services MMC, click to expand **Web Sites** and **Default Web Site** (see Figure 10-5).

2. Right-click the *YourFirstName* folder you created in Activity 10-1, point to **New**, and then click **Virtual Directory**. The Virtual Directory Creation Wizard starts (see Figure 10-6).

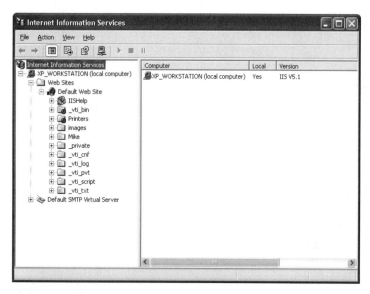

Figure 10-5   Viewing IIS Web sites

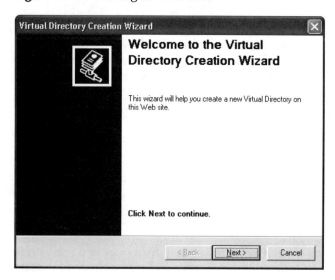

Figure 10-6   The Virtual Directory Creation Wizard

3. Click **Next**. When prompted to enter an alias, enter your first name, specify the directory path of the folder you created in Activity 10-1, and follow the on-screen instructions. In the final wizard window, click **Finish** to create a virtual directory that users can access over the Web.

4. Close all open windows, and leave Windows XP running for the next activity.

The Web server uses the ASP scripting language to generate HTML pages for the Web browser. How does the Web server know when ASP code is being used? You wrote an HTML Web page in Chapter 7; now look at a Web page containing ASP statements in Activity 10-3. The best way to learn ASP is to create a Web page with it. To do this, you need three components: a text editor (Notepad, for example), a Web server (such as IIS Web Server), and a Web browser (such as Internet Explorer).

Activity 10-3: Creating an ASP Web Page

Time Required: 30 minutes

Objective: Understand how Microsoft uses ASP to create dynamic Web pages and be able to recognize ASP Web pages.

Description: ASP Web pages are created on the Web server and enable a developer to create dynamic Web pages that can be displayed on a user's Web browser. In this activity, you create an ASP Web page and use a Web browser to view the page.

1. From your Windows XP Professional computer, start Notepad and type the following code:

```
<HTML>
<HEAD><TITLE> My First ASP Web Page </TITLE></HEAD>
<BODY>
     <H1>Hello, security professionals</H1>
     The time is <% = Time %>.
</BODY>
</HTML>
```

2. Save the file as **First.asp** in the C:\Inetpub\Wwwroot*YourFirstName* directory. Be sure the file is saved with the .asp extension, not the .txt extension. Close Notepad.

3. To test your First.asp Web page, start your Web browser, type the URL **http://localhost/** *YourFirstName***/First.asp**, and press **Enter**. Note that the Web page shows the current time of your location, meaning it's dynamic. That is, it changes each time your Web browser calls for the Web page. The <% and %> tags tell the Web server that ASP is being used as the script language.

4. Click **View**, **Source** from the Web browser menu. Does the source code show you the ASP commands you entered?

5. Close the Web browser, and leave Windows XP running for the next activity.

Microsoft does not want users to be able to view an ASP Web page's source code. If users can access ASP Web pages easily, problems could arise. For example, a Web page containing a connection string that reveals user name and password information to users could be used for an attack. Not being able to view the source code makes ASP more secure than basic HTML Web pages. Connection strings are covered later in the "Connecting to Databases" section.

Apache Web Server

As a security tester, you should also be aware of another Web server program: Tomcat Apache. Apache Web Server is said to host anywhere from 50% to 60% of all Web sites in the world. You can see why a little knowledge of this Web server can be helpful in the security-testing profession. Apache has several advantages over the competition: It works on just about any *NIX platform as well as Microsoft Windows, and it's free. Installing Apache is not as easy as installing Windows IIS. First you need to install Java 2 Standard Runtime Environment (J2SE, version 5.0). Activity 10-4 gives you a chance to look at the product and install it on a Windows XP Professional computer. You would most likely see this Web server on a UNIX or Linux system, but because you're using a bootable Linux CD that creates everything in RAM, installing it on a Windows XP computer gives you the opportunity to look over the software after reboots without having to reinstall.

Activity 10-4: Installing J2SE and Tomcat Apache Web Server

Time Required: 45 minutes

Objective: Install Apache Web server.

Description: Without a doubt, you'll run across an Apache Web server when conducting a security test. In this activity, you install J2SE and Tomcat 5.5 on your Windows XP computer.

Remember that version numbers as well as instructions for downloading and installing products are subject to change. If this occurs, just follow the onscreen instructions.

NOTE

1. From your Windows XP Professional computer, start Internet Explorer, type the URL **http://java.sun.com/j2se/1.5.0/install.html**, and press **Enter**.

2. On the installation page, shown in Figure 10-7, click the **JDK for Windows** link in the 32-bit Installation column.

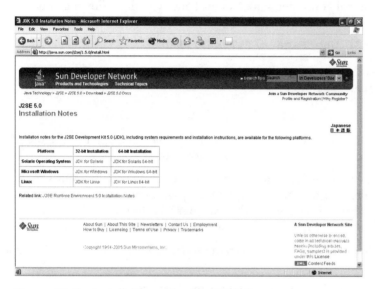

Figure 10-7 Installation notes for JDK 5.0

3. Read the information on the Installation Notes JDK 5.0 Microsoft Windows (32-bit) Web page, and then click your browser's **Back** button to return to the previous page.

4. On the Installation Notes page, click the **Download** link at the top. You see the page shown in Figure 10–8.

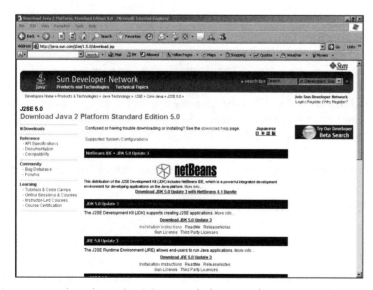

Figure 10-8 The J2SE download page

5. Click the **Download JDK 5.0 Update 3 with NetBeans 4.1 Bundle** link.

6. On the Download J2SE Web page, click the **Download** button at the right (see Figure 10-9).

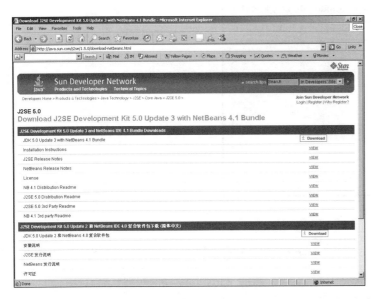

Figure 10-9   Downloading J2SE

7. When prompted to accept a license agreement, click the **accept** option button and then click the **continue** button at the bottom.

8. On the Download Web page, click the link to select the Windows Platform download. When prompted with the File Download - Security Warning dialog box, click **Save** (see Figure 10-10).

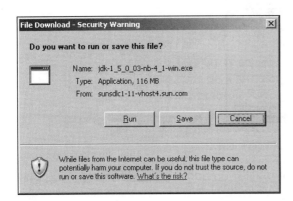

Figure 10-10   The File Download - Security Warning dialog box

9. Create a folder called **J2se** on the D: drive if your computer is configured with two or more partitions. If not, create the J2se folder on the C: drive. The file you're saving is rather large and might take 10 to 15 minutes to download depending on your Internet connection and classroom bandwidth.

10. When the download is finished, close the dialog box and navigate to the folder where you downloaded the J2SE file.

11. Double-click the icon in your J2se folder to begin the installation.

12. When prompted with the Open File - Security Warning dialog box, click **Run**.

13. In the welcome window of the Java installation wizard (see Figure 10-11), click **Next**.

14. Click the **I accept the terms in the license agreement** option button, and then click **Next**.

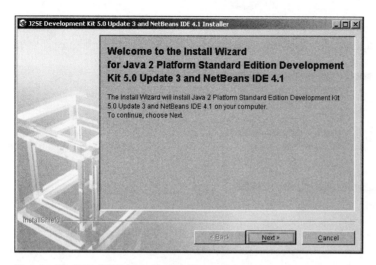

Figure 10-11   The Java installation wizard

15. When prompted for an installation directory, as shown in Figure 10-12, click **Next** to accept the default.

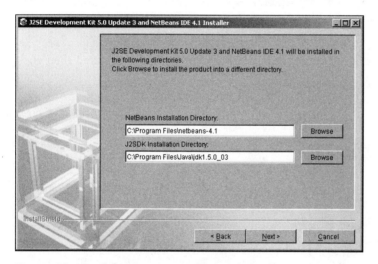

Figure 10-12   Selecting an installation directory

16. Click **Next** when prompted with a summary of installation information. After reviewing the information shown in Figure 10-13, click **Finish**.

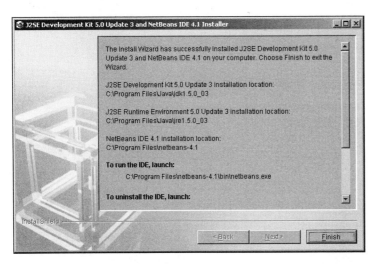

Figure 10-13   Summary of installation information

17. You can now create Web applications with an easy-to-use GUI, if you want to explore this tool later. Next, you install the Apache Web browser. Return to your Web browser, type the URL **http://jakarta.apache.org/site/binindex.cgi**, and press **Enter**.

18. On the Apache Jakarta Project home page (see Figure 10-14), click **Tomcat** in the Downloads list.

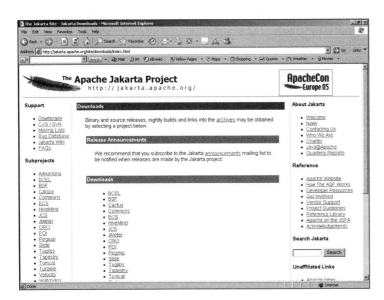

Figure 10-14   The Apache Jakarta Project home page

19. On the Tomcat Downloads page, click **Tomcat 5**.

20. Next, click the **5.5.9.exe** link. When prompted with the File Download - Security Warning dialog box, click **Save**.

21. Create a folder called **Tomcat** to save the downloaded file, and then click **Save**. When the download is finished, click **Close** and leave your browser open.

22. Navigate to the Tomcat folder and double-click the **Apache Tomcat Installer** icon. Click **Run** to begin the installation.

23. In the welcome window of the Apache Tomcat Setup Wizard (see Figure 10-15), click **Next**.

24. Click **I Agree** to accept the license agreement.

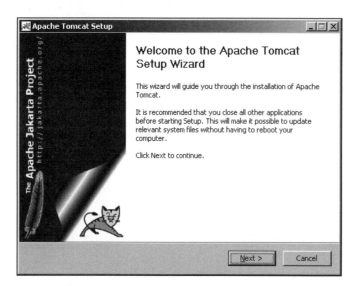

Figure 10-15   The Apache Tomcat Setup Wizard

25. In the Choose Components window, click to select all components (see Figure 10-16), and then click **Next**.

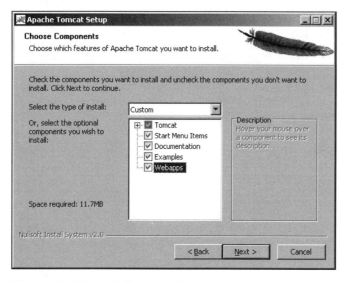

Figure 10-16   Installing Apache components

26. Click **Next** to accept the destination folder to install Apache.

27. When prompted to enter an administrator logon account and password, enter your logon account for the Windows XP Professional computer (see Figure 10-17), and click **Next**. If you didn't configure your computer to use a logon account and password, create an account and password now. Your account must have administrative rights.

28. When prompted for the path of J2SE 5.0 JRE, accept the default by clicking **Install**.

29. In the window stating that Apache has been successfully installed, click **Finish**.

30. To see whether your Apache Web server is installed, start your Web browser if it's not already open, type the URL **http://localhost:8080**, and press **Enter**. If all went well, you should see the Apache Jakarta Project welcome page (see Figure 10-18).

31. If time permits, click some links in the Administration, Documentation, and Examples sections, and read the material.

32. Close any open windows, and leave Windows XP running for the next activity.

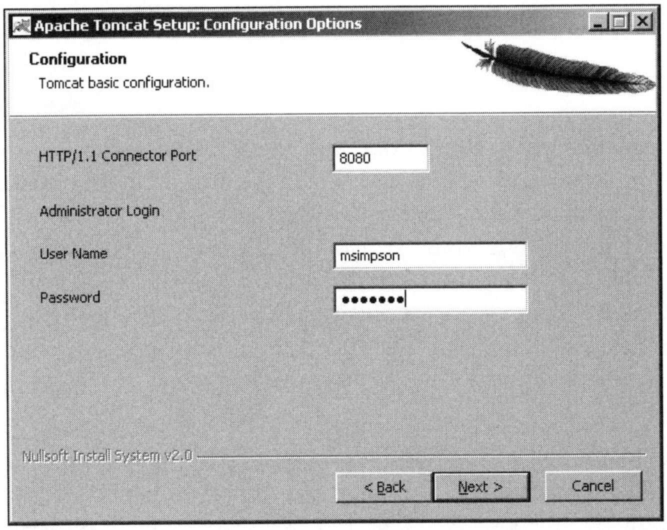

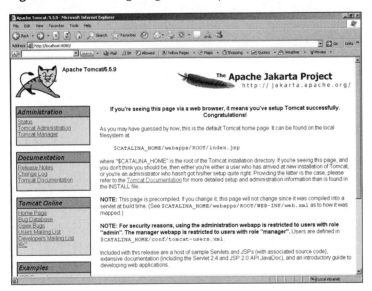

Figure 10-17   Configuring an HTTP port and administrator account

Figure 10-18   The Apache Tomcat welcome page

Using Scripting Languages

Web pages can be developed by using several different scripting languages, such as VBScript and JavaScript. You won't learn how to be a Web developer by reviewing the scripting languages covered in this chapter, but you should be able to recognize when one is being used. According to some estimates, nearly 70% of all new viruses, such as Nimda and Melissa, are based on some type of scripting language.

PHP: Hypertext Processor (PHP)

Similar to ASP, PHP also enables Web developers to create dynamic Web pages. PHP, an open-source server-side scripting language, is embedded in an HTML Web page by using the PHP tags <?php and ?>. Because PHP Web pages run on the server, users can't view the source code in their Web browsers. PHP is used primarily on UNIX systems but is also supported on Macintosh and Windows platforms. The following excerpt is an example of code for a basic PHP static Web page illustrating the use of PHP tags:

```
<html>
<head>
<title>My First PHP Program </title>
</head>
```

```
<body>
<?php echo '<h1>Hello, Security Testers!</h1>'; ?>
</body>
</html>
```

This page would need to be created on your Web server as you did with the ASP Web page you created in Activity 10-3. After you have identified the Web server as using PHP, you should use the methods you have learned in this book to investigate further for specific vulnerabilities. For example, several versions of PHP running on Linux platforms can be exploited because of a line of code in the Php.ini file. The line `file_uploads=on` permits file uploads; however, this setting might allow a remote attacker to run arbitrary code with elevated privileges. The best solution is to upgrade to PHP version 4.2.1, but if that's not possible, change the line of code to `file_uploads=off`. Many companies use PHP with MySQL databases, so security testers should investigate Web sites such as *www.php.net* and *www.mysql.com* for more information.

ColdFusion

ColdFusion is another server-side scripting language used to develop dynamic Web pages. Created by the Allaire Corporation, it integrates Web browser, Web server, and database technologies. It uses its own proprietary tags written in ColdFusion Markup Language (CFML), and Web applications written in CFML can also contain other client technologies, such as HTML and JavaScript. The following code is an example of HTML using a CFML tag that redirects the user to a ColdFusion home page. All CFML tags begin with the letters CF. For example, the column tag is CFCOL.

```
<html>
<head>
<title>Using CFML</title>
</head>
<body>
<CFLOCATION URL="www.isecom.org/cf/index.htm" ADDTOKEN="NO">
</body>
</html>
```

As with the PHP example, security testers should become well acquainted with any vulnerabilities associated with a Web server using ColdFusion. A quick search of the Macromedia security page (*www.macromedia.com/ devnet/security/security_zone/*) can narrow your research time, allowing you to focus on the vulnerabilities that affect your situation.

VBScript

Visual Basic Script (VBScript) is a scripting language developed by Microsoft. You can insert VBScript into your HTML Web pages to convert static Web pages into dynamic Web pages. The biggest advantage of using a scripting language is that the functionality of powerful programming languages is at your disposal. For those who have programming experience, there's no learning curve. You can start writing VBScript faster than a dual-processor 3 GHz PC. Take a look at a simple example to help you recognize when VBScript is being used. The following code is entered in an HTML document in Notepad, as you did earlier:

```
<html>
<body>
<script type="text/vbscript">
document.write("<h1>Hello Security Testers!</h1>")
document.write("Date Activated: " & date())
</script>
</body>
</html>
```

Figure 10-19 shows the Web page generated from the preceding VBScript code.

The Microsoft Security Bulletin Search page (*www.microsoft.com/technet/security/current.aspx*) is an excellent starting point when investigating VBScript vulnerabilities. A search on a specific Security Bulletin provides a wealth of information, including the severity rating and patch information.

Figure 10-19   A VBScript Web page

 For a quick example of a VBScript Security Bulletin, visit *www.microsoft.com/ technet/security/bulletin/MS02-009.mspx.*

NOTE

10

JavaScript

Another popular scripting language used to create dynamic HTML Web pages is JavaScript. JavaScript also has the power of a programming language. As with VBScript, you can branch, loop, test, and create functions and procedures within your HTML Web page. The following code is a simple HTML snippet with JavaScript code added:

```
<html>
<head>
<script type="text/javascript">
function chastise_user()
{
alert("So, you like breaking rules?")
document.getElementByld("cmdButton").focus()
}
</script>
</head>
<body>
<h3>"If you are a Security Tester, please do not click the command
button below!"</h3>
<form>
<input type="button" value="Don't Click!" name="cmdButton"
onClick="chastise_user()" />
</form>
</body>
</html>
```

This code is a little more complex than the previous samples, but it shows you how scripting languages can include functions and alerts. Notice that the third line specifies that JavaScript is the language being used. Next, a function is defined as chastise_user(); this function simply displays a pop-up message box. The getElementByld() function is a method (a computer program in itself) defined by the World Wide Web Consortium (W3C) Document Object Model (DOM). Basically, it returns an object—in this case, a command button you click. The remaining code is fairly self-explanatory. To see how this code works, take a look at the output screen shown in Figure 10-20.

If the user clicks the command button, the alert box shown in Figure 10-21 is displayed.

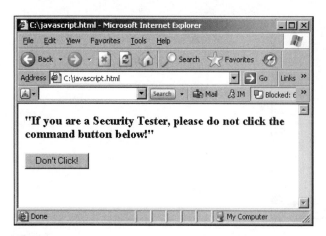

Figure 10-20   A JavaScript command button

Figure 10-21   A JavaScript alert box

JavaScript is widely used, and a variety of vulnerabilities have been exploited in older Web browsers. It's in the best interest of security testers and the client to inspect every computer for unpatched or outdated browser versions. The Cert Advisory CA-1997-20 (*www.cert.org/advisories/CA-1997-20.html*) outlines one such vulnerability.

Connecting to Databases

Most Web pages that display company information to users are stored on a database server. Web pages that prompt a user for information, such as name, telephone number, address, and so on, store information entered by users in a database. The technology used to connect a Web application to a database server might vary depending on the OS used, but the theory is the same. The following sections discuss some of the technologies used to connect to a database or an external file system from a Web application.

Open Database Connectivity (ODBC)

Open Database Connectivity (ODBC) is a standard database access method developed by the SQL Access Group. The ODBC interface allows an application to access data stored in a database management system (DBMS), such as Microsoft SQL, Oracle, or any system that understands and can issue ODBC commands. Interoperability among back-end database management systems is a key feature of the ODBC interface, allowing application developers to focus on the application without worrying about any specific DBMS. The ODBC interface accomplishes this by defining the following:

- A standardized representation for data types
- A library of ODBC function calls that permit an application to connect to a DBMS, run SQL statements, and then retrieve the results
- A standard method of connecting to and logging on to a DBMS

Object Linking and Embedding Database (OLE DB)

Object Linking and Embedding Database (OLE DB) is a set of interfaces that enable applications to access data stored in a database management system. It was developed by Microsoft and was designed to be faster, more efficient, and more stable than its predecessor, ODBC. OLE DB relies on connection strings that enable the application to access the data stored on an external device. Depending on to what data source you are connecting, you could use a different provider. For example, connecting to an SQL database requires using SQLOLEDB as the provider instead of Microsoft.Jet. Table 10-1 shows some of the OLE DB providers available for developers. When conducting a security test on a Web server, you should verify how the Web server is connecting to a database and, of course, what type of database or resource data is being collected. The following code line is a sample of a connection string used to access data in a Microsoft Access database named Personnel:

```
Provider=Microsoft.Jet.OLEDB.4.0;Data Source=C:\Personnel.mdb;User
ID=; Password=;
```

Table 10-1   OLE DB providers

OLE DB Provider	Description in Connection String
Microsoft Active Directory Service	"Provider=ADSDSOOBJECT"
Advantage	"Provider=Advantage OLE DB Provider"
AS/400(from IBM)	"Provider=IBMDA400"
AS/400 and VSAM (from Microsoft)	"Provider=SNAOLEDB"
MS Commerce Server	"Provider=Commerce.DSO.1"
DB2	"Provider=DB2OLEDB"
MS Exchange	"Provider=EXOLEDB.DataSource"
MySQL	"Provider=MySQLProv"
Oracle (from Microsoft)	"Provider=msdaora"
Oracle (from Oracle)	"Provider=OraOLEDB.Oracle"
MS SQL Server	"Provider=SQLOLEDB"

ActiveX Data Objects (ADO)

ActiveX Data Objects (ADO) is another technology for connecting a Web application to data in a database. ActiveX defines a set of technologies that allow applications, such as Word or Excel, to interact with the Web. For example, you could place an Excel spreadsheet in a Web page. ADO is a programming interface that enables a Web application to access data in a database. To access a database from within an ASP Web page, you would do the following:

1. Create an ADO connection to the database you want to access.

2. Open the database connection you created in Step 1.

3. Create an ADO recordset, which contains rows from the table you will access.

4. Open the recordset.

5. Select the data you need from the recordset based on particular criteria.

6. Close the recordset.

7. Close the database connection.

Next, take a look at how these steps are performed and what the result looks like in an ASP Web page. The following ASP code creates and opens the ADO connection:

```
<%
set conn=Server.CreateObject("ADODB.Connection")
conn.Provider="Microsoft.Jet.OLEDB.4.0"
conn.Open "c:\MyDatabase\employee.mdb"
%>
```

Now you need to create a recordset to contain records from a table in your employee database (employee.mdb):

```
<%
set rs=Server.CreateObject("ADODB.recordset")
rs.Open "Select * FROM Employee", conn
```

```
.....
rs.close
conn.close
%>
```

You would most likely use a loop to print all the records to the HTML Web page, but that's not important here. You want to understand the technology so that you can recognize vulnerabilities when they exist. Now that you have a good foundation on the components of a Web application, the following section discusses some of these vulnerabilities.

UNDERSTANDING WEB APPLICATION VULNERABILITIES

Many platforms and programming languages can be used to design a Web site. Each platform has its advantages and disadvantages. Some are free and require only basic skills in creating Web applications; others cost quite a bit and require an in-depth knowledge of programming. Regardless of the system in place, security professionals need to assess the system and examine potential methods for attacking that system.

There's no doubt that network security is important to protect data and company resources from attack. The problem is that many security professionals don't see the importance of application security. One reason is that many security professionals have experience in networking but little or no experience in programming. In fact, most network security books have little programming coverage because the topic frightens many students. No matter how efficient a company's firewalls or intrusion detection systems are, most systems ignore the content of HTTP traffic. Therefore, an attacker can bypass these security boundaries as well as any operating system hardening that security professionals have implemented. Simply stated, network layer protection does not prevent application layer attacks from occurring. All an attacker needs is an understanding of some basic programming concepts or scripting languages. To add to the mayhem, attackers usually don't need special tools, and there's little chance of being detected. After an attacker gains control of a Web server, he or she could do the following:

- Deface the Web site.

- Destroy the company's database or offer to sell its contents.

- Gain control of user accounts.

- Perform secondary attacks from the Web site.

- Gain root access to other application servers that are part of network infrastructure.

Application Vulnerabilities and Countermeasures

Luckily, there's an organization that helps security professionals understand the vulnerabilities in Web applications. Much like ISECOM, **Open Web Application Security Project (OWASP)** is an open, not-for-profit foundation dedicated to finding and fighting the causes of software vulnerabilities. OWASP (*www.owasp.org*) publishes the Ten Most Critical Web Application Security Vulnerabilities paper that has been built into the Payment Card Industry (PCI) Data Security Standard. The PCI Data Security Standard will soon be a requirement for all businesses that sell products online. You visit the OWASP Web site in Activity 10-5, but first, take a look at what OWASP has deemed the top-10 Web application vulnerabilities:

- *Unvalidated parameters*—Attackers can make HTTP requests from a browser that's not validated by the Web server. Form fields, hidden fields, cookies, headers, and so on can be inserted into the HTTP request. To prevent this type of attack, all HTTP requests sent to the Web server must be verified, and any requests not specifically allowed should be rejected. All validation should be done on the server side, not the client side, because an attacker can delete any validation occurring on his or her Web browser (client) and then perform the attack. Checking for min/max values entered into a form and the type of character set being used is vital to protecting the Web server. Although not foolproof, one method of preventing users from entering potentially dangerous long strings of text is to use the text box's MaxLength property.

- *Broken access control*—In this flaw, developers implement access controls but fail to test them properly. Even though authentication is present, an authenticated user might have access to another user's information. The attacker can exploit this flaw to access sensitive information in user accounts. To reduce this risk, a company should develop a good access control policy that can be centrally administered. The policy should be written down and should not be so complex as to create holes or any ambivalence.

- *Broken account and session management*—Flaws in this area enable attackers to compromise passwords or session cookies to gain access to accounts. To reduce this risk, it's critical that you use strong authentication methods, and credentials must be kept secret at all times. You can also incorporate back-end servers to authenticate credentials instead of just relying on the Web server.

- *Cross-site scripting (XSS) flaws*—In this flaw, a Web browser might carry out code sent from a Web site. An attacker can use a Web application to run a script on the Web browser of the system he or she is attacking. XSS is one of the easiest types of attacks to perform; the attacker simply saves the form to his or her local computer and changes the form field values. Luckily, this type of attack is also one of the easiest to protect against by making sure that any "post" action is coming from your Web site.

- *Buffer overflows*—Because Web applications can read all types of input from users, such as libraries, DLLs, and so on, it's possible for an attacker to use C or C++ code that includes a buffer overflow. You should be cautious about reading data into buffers and you might not want to use C or C++ because they are susceptible to buffer overflows. There's no single method to prevent these types of attacks; however, care in coding practices can reduce the risk. If developers do use C or C++, they should avoid using any vulnerable functions, such as strcpy(), sprintf(), and strcat(), which do not perform bounds checking.

- *Command injection flaws*—Many Web applications pass parameters when accessing an external system. For example, a Web application that accesses a database server needs to pass logon information to the database server. An attacker can embed malicious code and run a program on the database server. Malicious code can also be sent in an HTTP request.

- *Error-handling problems*—If an error occurs during normal operations and is not handled correctly, information sent to the user might reveal information that an attacker can use. For example, attackers can use error screens that reveal what was executed on the stack or that give a message showing what Web software is being used.

- *Insecure use of cryptography*—Storing keys, certificates, and passwords on a Web server can be dangerous. If an attacker can gain access to these mechanisms, the server is vulnerable to attack. To decrease the chances of a compromise, do not store customer credit card numbers on your Web server. Instead, require that confidential data such as credit card numbers be entered each time the user visits the Web site.

- *Remote administration flaws*—Many Web applications allow the administrator to manage the Web site remotely. If the site isn't protected, an attacker can also gain access to the Web server through the same interface. You might want to eliminate the possibility of administration over the Internet or at least limit the scope of what can be done remotely.

- *Web and application server misconfiguration*—Any Web server software out of the box is usually vulnerable to attack. Most have default accounts and passwords, overly informative error messages, and administrative services that aren't used. A Web server must be configured carefully, and administrators should keep up with all patches and security updates. You should also require a log of all patches and updates and include who the responsible party is, the time and date of the update, and the reason for the update. Of course, it's always a good idea to perform updates on a test network, if one is available.

The OWASP paper on the top-10 vulnerabilities might cover some areas beyond the skill set of a beginning security tester, so OWASP offers a product called **WebGoat** that helps beginning Web application security testers gain a better understanding of the areas covered in this list. In Activity 10-5, you visit the OWASP Web site and see what else is available to help protect Web applications.

10

Activity 10-5: Visiting the OWASP Web Site

Time Required: 30 minutes

Objective: Learn more about the OWASP foundation.

Description: OWASP is more than just a Web site that lists the top-10 Web application vulnerabilities. At this site, you can find many tools that help you protect Web applications. In this activity, you examine the top-10 list in detail and gain a better understanding of the steps you can take to protect an organization from an application attack.

1. From your Windows XP Professional computer, start Internet Explorer, type the URL **http://www.owasp.org**, and press **Enter**.

2. On the OWASP home page, click the **Top Ten** link in the Quick Links section.

3. On the Welcome page, scroll down to the table that summarizes the Top Ten vulnerabilities and click the **A1** link in the table.

4. The Unvalidated Input page gives you more detailed information about this type of flaw in a Web application. Read through the document and then return to the previous page by clicking your browser's **Back** button.

5. Spend the next 10 to 15 minutes reviewing the other nine vulnerabilities accessible through the links in the table (A2 to A10), and return to the home page when you're finished.

6. On the home page, click the **WebGoat** link and read about this exciting project. You don't install WebGoat in this activity, but following this activity, you get a chance to see how WebGoat can be used to learn about some basic Web application attacks.

7. Leave your Web browser open for the next activity.

OWASP developed the WebGoat project to help security testers learn how to perform vulnerability testing on Web applications. Solutions to the problems posed aren't given. Instead, you're given hints for solving the puzzles. The OWASP developers want to encourage security students to think and figure out how to perform an attack. For this reason, not all solutions for the exercises shown in this section are given. Before running WebGoat, you must install the J2SE Development Kit and Apache Server on your computer. Because this was already done on your XP computer in Activity 10-4, the next step is downloading WebGoat from the OWASP Web site. If you already have Java installed, you can download the WebGoat standalone version, as shown in Figure 10-22. Check with your instructor before downloading and running WebGoat.

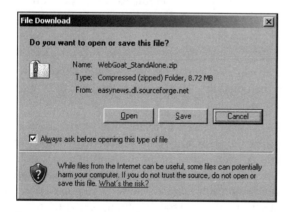

Figure 10-22 Downloading the WebGoat standalone version

After making some minor configuration changes, you can enter the URL *http://localhost:8080/WebGoat/attack* to run WebGoat (see Figure 10-23). This URL takes you to the first exercise, which reviews HTTP basics. After you enter a name, the server accepts the HTTP request and reverses the input. For example, entering the name "student" returns the value "tneduts." You can click the buttons shown in Figure 10-23 to reveal HTML or Java code and any cookies or parameters used.

Figure 10-23   Displaying HTML, parameters, and cookies

The exercises get more complex than this example, so you probably won't be able to do all of them quickly. For example, the exercise "How to Discover Clues in the HTML" adds more complexity for beginners. In this exercise, you're expected to hack a logon name and password. Figure 10-24 shows the user being prompted for a user name and password that are unknown.

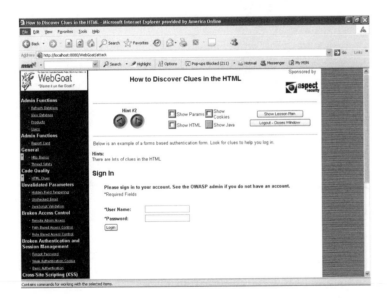

Figure 10-24   Discovering clues in HTML code

Clicking the Hint button points you in the right direction, but you're still required to find the answer somewhere in the 173 lines of HTML code. After entering the logon and password you discovered, you're prompted with the page shown in Figure 10-25.

End your overview of WebGoat by looking at one last attack. This attack allows you to traverse a file system on a Windows XP computer running Apache (see Figure 10-26).

10

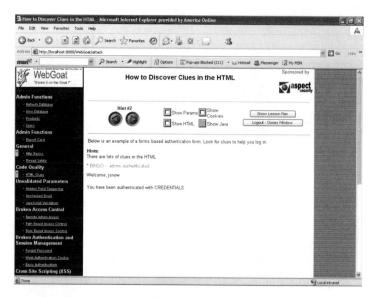

Figure 10-25   A successful logon

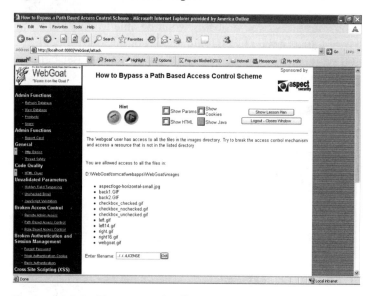

Figure 10-26   Traversing the file system

Note in Figure 10-26 that the user should have access only to the D:\WebGoat\tomcat\webapps\WebGoat\ images directory. You are tasked with attempting to break the access control mechanism and access a resource that's not listed. The attack was possible by using the solution shown in Figure 10-27.

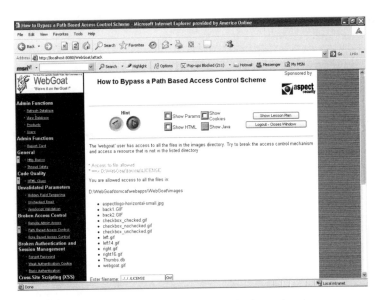

Figure 10-27   Breaking the access control mechanism

Traversing the file structure was possible by using the ../../../LICENSE command in the URL. Figure 10-28 shows the URL entered in the browser, which takes the user to the License file (shown in Figure 10-29) to which he or she wasn't supposed to have access. Anyone with the time and inclination can learn much more from using WebGoat. The last exercise, called the Challenge (see Figure 10-30), takes beginning students to a higher level.

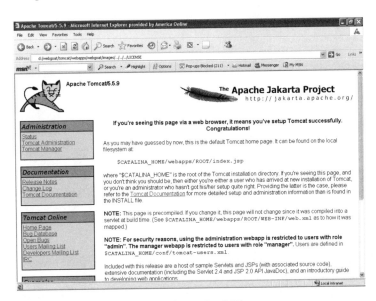

Figure 10-28   Using Unicode in the URL

In this exercise, you're challenged with breaking an authentication scheme, stealing credit cards from a database, and then defacing a Web site. Remember, there are no solutions for this exercise; you do all the work. However, knowing how to use the Web can give you even more hints. Many people from all over the world use WebGoat and offer their input.

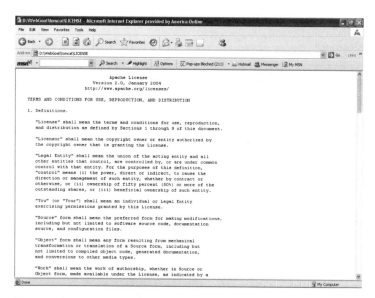

Figure 10-29   Accessing the License file

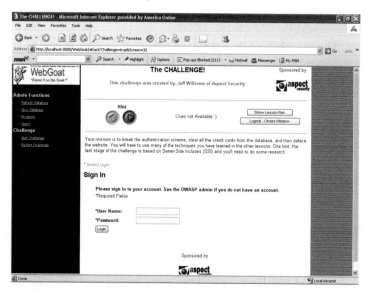

Figure 10-30   WebGoat's big challenge

Assessing Web Applications

When looking for possible vulnerabilities in a Web application, security testers look for answers to some important questions. Depending on the tester's experience level and amount of training in securing Web infrastructures, these questions might be difficult to answer. Remember, most of the time, teams are used when performing a security test. If you have only a little experience with Web applications, you might want to consider including a team member who has expertise in this subject. Each area covered in the following sections might require specialized knowledge.

Does the Web Application Use Dynamic Web Pages?

If static Web pages are used, there is less likelihood of an attacker inserting program code into forms or fields displayed in the Web browser. However, static Web pages by no means create a secure environment. A form of attack that has been used for at least a decade and is still used at the time of this writing involves submitting a specially formatted URL to the attacked Web server. This attack was carried out on IIS servers until Microsoft issued a security patch. That's not to say everyone applied that security patch or that no companies run IIS without it. Therefore, you should be sure to verify that the vulnerability is not possible on the Web server you have been asked to test.

The vulnerability is that IIS didn't correctly parse the URL information a user entered, which allowed attackers to launch a Unicode exploit. For example, if a user entered the /../.. sequence of characters into a URL, IIS would indicate an error. Recall from DOS that the two dots traverse the user up or down the directory tree. This is also true for Web applications. To bypass this check by IIS, attackers substituted the Unicode equivalent of ../ with ..%255c. ASCII uses 8 bits to store characters. Unicode is a more sophisticated character standard that uses 16 bits to store characters. This number of bits makes it possible for computers to handle Chinese and Japanese characters as well as Middle Eastern language sets. Understanding how Unicode works isn't essential; all you need to know is that every character you enter at a keyboard can be represented in Unicode. The following URL would traverse a Windows IIS server, run the Cmd.exe program, and pass the dir c:\ parameter to it, which gives the attacker the contents of the C: drive:

```
http://www.nopatchiss.com/scripts/..%255c..%255cwinnt/system32
/cmd.exe?/c+dir+c
```

Installing a Trojan horse program on a Web server is even possible if the URL is formed correctly. For example, the URL can use Trivial File Transfer Protocol (TFTP) to connect to a server and install the Trojan program. A second URL can then run the Trojan program. Unicode exploits are still possible today and should be part of your security test.

If the application is using dynamic Web pages, your next questions should be: "How is it done? Is CGI being used as the mechanism for moving information from the Web server to the Web browser, or is Active Server Pages (ASP) or another methodology in place?" This leads you to the next question.

Does the Web Application Connect to a Backend Database Server?

Web applications that prompt users for information or display available inventory to users usually have a database backend server storing all this information. The inventory database has tables containing the information to display to the customer, and a customer database usually stores data about users that might include credit card information. If this is the case, database security is of paramount importance. Who has access to the tables? What database software and version is being used—for example, Oracle 9*i*, Microsoft SQL Server 2000, or MySQL? Is there a possibility of SQL injection being used to attack the system? **SQL injection** involves the attacker supplying SQL commands when prompted to fill in a Web application field.

A basic SQL statement to select records (rows) in a table named "books" would look like the following:

```
SELECT * FROM books WHERE lname = "Leno";
```

In an SQL injection, attackers "inject" their own SQL statements inside this statement. Remember the logon form created with HTML in the "Web Application Components" section. An ASP Web page that prompts the customer for a user name and password would look almost identical.

```
<form name="Validate" action="validate.asp" method="post">
   Username: <input type="text" name="username">
   Password: <input type="text" name="password">
    <input type="submit">
</form>
```

The contents of the "username" and "password" parameters are passed to the ASP page called Validate.asp. To validate that the user name and password are correct, many Web applications have a secured database of valid user names and passwords. The Validate.asp page could look something like the following:

```
<%

1.  Dim username, password, sql_statement
2.  Dim conn, rs
3.  username = Request.Form("username")
4.  password =  Request.Form("password")
```

10

```
5.   set conn = server.createObject("ADODB.Connection")
6.   set rs = server.createObject("ADODB.Recordset")
7.   sql_statement = "SELECT * FROM customer
WHERE tblusername='" & username & "' AND tblpassword='" & password
& "'"
8.   conn.Open "Provider=SQLOLEDB; Data Source=(local);
Initial Catalog=CustomerDB; User Id=sa; Password="
9.   rs.activeConnection = conn
10.  rs.open sql_statement
11.   if not rs.eof then
12.  response.write "Welcome!"
13.  else
14.  response.write "Please reenter your username and password"
15.  end if

%>
```

 The line numbers would not be in an actual ASP Web application. They are here as a reference point only.

NOTE

Lines 1 and 2 declare the variables used in the rest of the code: username, password, sql_statement, conn (for the connection), and rs (for the recordset). Dim stands for dimension, which was used in the days of BASIC programming to declare variables.

Lines 3 and 4 define the username and password variables. In Lines 5 and 6, the set conn and set rs commands create the connection string object and recordset objects that will be used. In Line 7, the sql_statement variable holds the SQL statement used to query the database.

Lines 8 and 9 show that SQLOLEDB, the OLE DB provider for SQL Server, is used to connect to the database server. In this case, a database named CustomerDB is accessed, as shown in the Catalog statement.

Line 10 shows that by storing the SQL statement in a variable, you can run it later with the rs.open sql_statement. Line 11 checks for the end-of-file (EOF) marker. If no records are found that match what the customer entered (lastname, password), the Web browser displays the message to reenter the user name and password information. If a match is found, the SELECT statement lists all the records in the Customer table. So what's the problem, you ask?

Take a look at the customer table that was created and the command for inserting four records into it:

```
CREATE TABLE customer (
tblCustomerID CHAR(10);
tblusername VARCHAR(25);
tblpassword  VARCHAR(25);
/
INSERT INTO customer (tblusername, tblpassword)
VALUES ("bob", "password");
INSERT INTO customer (tblusername, tblpassword)
VALUES ("ted", "pa$$w0rd");
INSERT INTO customer (tblusername, tblpassword)
VALUES ("alice", "G0uLd");
INSERT INTO customer (tblusername, tblpassword)
VALUES ("carol", "n@tw00d");
```

If Bob logged on with his credentials, the SELECT statement would be as follows:

```
SELECT * FROM customer
WHERE tblusername = 'bob' AND tblpassword = 'password'
```

But suppose Bob entered the following when prompted for his user name:

```
' OR 1=1 --
```

The SQL statement would then be the following:

```
SELECT * FROM customer
WHERE tblusername = ' ' OR 1=1 -- ' AND tblpassword = ' '
```

Because 1=1 will always be true, the query is carried out successfully. Double hyphens (--) are used in SQL to represent a comment. Are there more tricks to hacking into a database? Take a look at a couple of other things an attacker could have entered when prompted for a user name and password.

```
Please enter username: ' OR "="
Please enter password: ' OR "="
```

The SQL statement would then be the following:

```
SELECT * FROM customer
WHERE tblusername = ' OR "=" AND tblpassword = ' OR "="
```

Instead of the SQL statement comparing the values the user entered with the values in the Customer table, it compares a quotation mark to another quotation mark, which of course returns a true condition. Hence, all rows are returned. It is surprising that this vulnerability exists on many systems connected to the Internet. You should not test for this vulnerability by attempting SQL injections on Web sites because this attack is considered intrusive and is subject to criminal prosecution. However, you should test any Web applications when you're performing a security test and are authorized in writing to do so. Some basic testing should look for the following:

- Whether you can enter text containing punctuation marks of any kind

- Whether you can enter a single quotation mark followed by any SQL keywords, such as WHERE, SELECT, INSERT, UNION, and so on

- Whether you get any sort of database error when attempting to inject SQL (meaning SQL injection is possible)

By determining that the Web application is using a backend database server, you have discovered an additional way to conduct a penetration test of the system.

Security Bytes

When students apply for graduate school, waiting for an acceptance letter can be painful. A computer hacker offered those impatient students a way of getting an answer quickly. The hacker, who has yet to be identified as of this writing, gained access to internal admissions records for Harvard, Stanford, MIT, and other top business schools by exploiting vulnerabilities discovered in a Web application called ApplyYourself. The hacker then posted hacking hints on *Business Week*'s online forum. (To see the instructions, visit *http://poweryogi. blogspot.com/2005/03/hbsapplyyourself-admit-status-snafu.html*.) Many applicants without any hacking background could find out whether they had been accepted into the college for which they applied. Harvard Business School identified 119 applicants who hacked the system and stated that it would reject their admissions because of an ethics violation. Some people thought the problem was the lack of security on the ApplyYourself Web server, which allowed an attacker to simply modify the Web server's displayed URL. The applicants who were caught used their logon names and changed only the URL when connected to the Web server. They didn't attempt to hide their tracks or guess passwords. Was it unethical to do what they did? This might be a difficult question to answer, but Harvard had no problem doing just that.

10

Activity 10-6: Identifying SQL Injection Vulnerabilities

Time Required: 30 minutes

Objective: Recognize the vast number of platforms that have SQL injection vulnerabilities.

Description: After identifying that a Web application is using a backend database server to store data, a security tester should attempt to test the Web application for SQL injection vulnerabilities. In this activity, you visit the Common Vulnerabilities and Exposures (CVE) Web site to identify some known vulnerabilities.

1. From your Windows XP Professional computer, start Internet Explorer, type the URL **www.cve.mitre.org**, and press **Enter** to visit the CVE Web site.

2. On the CVE home page, scroll to the bottom and click the **search CVE** button.

3. On the CVE page, type **SQL injection** in the Keyword(s) text box and click **Search**. How many CVE entries or candidates are found?

4. Scroll through the list of vulnerabilities and candidates, and read the descriptions for each entry. When you get to end of the list, enter a new query in the Search again text box. Type **SQL injection login.asp** and click **Search**. How many entries are found?

5. What versions of Brooky eStore software are vulnerable to an SQL injection attack?

6. When an attacker discovers a vulnerability as you did in this activity, the next step is trying to find out which businesses are using the software. To find this information, you could do a quick search using Google or another search engine. Many Web sites using the eStore software add a footnote to their home pages stating "Powered by eStore." Use a search engine of your choice and type "Powered by eStore" for your search criteria. How many Web sites did your search engine return? Do you think the majority of sites corrected the vulnerability you discovered?

7. Spend some time visiting Web sites your search engine found that use the eStore software. Did many of the sites indicate the version of the software they were running? What are the security ramifications of listing the version of software you're running on a system?

8. Close the Web browser, and shut down your system.

As you saw in this activity, thousands of Web sites use eStore software. After attackers discover a vulnerability, they look for as many targets as possible to attack. This is why it's crucial that you notify your client when you discover a vulnerability—and the faster, the better!

Does the Web Application Require Authentication of the User?

Many Web applications require that a server other than the Web server authenticate users. For example, a Web application might require using a Windows Server 2003 server running Active Directory Services for authentication. If this is the case, you should examine how authentication information is passed between the two servers. Is an encrypted channel used, or is data passed in clear text that can be easily retrieved? Are logon and password information stored in a secured location, or is it possible for an intruder to access and retrieve the information? If attackers recognize that an additional authentication server must validate customer credentials, they have another target to go after. The Web server might not be an attacker's only point of entry.

On What Platform Was the Web Application Developed?

With so many platforms available for Web developers, it's no wonder that so many vulnerabilities exist. Knowing whether a Web application was developed on an IIS server with ASP and SQL Server or on a Linux Apache Web server using PHP and MySQL, for example, gives attackers and security testers the ammunition needed to do their job. Remember, the reason you conduct footprinting is to discover what operating and database systems the attacked system is using. The more you know about the system, the easier it is to gather information about its vulnerabilities. For example, knowing that ASP is the mechanism used to move information from the Web server to the Web browser is critical information for security testers. If CGI is used instead, the attack or security test will be quite different.

Tools of Web Attackers and Security Testers

After vulnerabilities of a Web application or OS platform are discovered, security testers or attackers then look for the tools that enable them to attack or test the system. For example, if you learn of a vulnerability indicated for CGI, the next step is discovering whether any systems are using CGI. As you saw in the previous section, all platforms and Web application components have vulnerabilities. No matter on which platform the Web application was developed, there is unfortunately a hole in it and a tool to use to break in.

Web Tools

You have already seen that the majority of tools for performing a security test or attacking a network can be obtained over the Internet and are usually free. The following sections cover some popular tools for hacking Web applications. One of the best Web sites to find such tools is *http://packetstormsecurity.org*. As a security tester, you should visit this site weekly to keep track of any new tools and to browse through the multitude of available exploits.

10

Cgiscan.c: CGI Scanning Tool

Cgi Scanner v1.4 (Cgiscan.c), written in 1999 by Bronc Buster, is a tool for searching Web sites for CGI scripts that can be exploited. Cgiscan.c, a C program that must be compiled, is by far one of the best tools for scanning the Web for systems with CGI vulnerabilities. Security testers can also run this tool against company Web servers. Many of these programs are available on the Internet, but Packetstormsecurity.org recommends this one in particular. The programmer has written helpful directions for users, even though the following documentation has many spelling and grammatical errors:

```
/* Cgi Scanner v1.4

I got tired of looking at a ton of cgi hole scanners and none of
them had everything included, so I made one for all the kode
kiddies out there. I ripped some of this code from 9x's shell
script they echo'ed to netcat to update this, and some other code
for storage from someone elses broken version that looked for a
few of these already.

This will basicly ask a web server (Unix or NT) if they have
these programs open to the general public, and if they do, it
tells you. I could of made this exploit the holes as well, but I
have to leave something for you to do (well in the LoU released
version it did exploit them). Sometimes it will tell you that the
files DO EXIST, but you may not have access to them. By using
another hole you may be able to access them though. So if the
scan returns that it found something, don't instantly think you
can exploit it. If they have changed their '404' page it will
also sometimes return a false reading.

To complie:
luser$ gcc cgiscan.c -o cgiscan
To use:
luser$ ./cgiscan somedomain.com    (i.e. ./cgiscan antionline.com)

coded by Bronc Buster of LoU - Nov 1998
updated Jan 1999

[gh] uses this to preform all their eLe3t h4cKs, shouldn't you?

*/

#include <sys/types.h>
#include <netinet/in.h>
```

```c
#include <string.h>
#include <netdb.h>
#include <ctype.h>
#include <arpa/nameser.h>
#include <strings.h>
#include <stdio.h>
#include <stdlib.h>
#include <unistd.h>
#include <sys/socket.h>
#define MAX_SIZE 21  /* make this the size of temp[] if you change
it */

int main(int argc, char *argv[])
{
int s;
struct in_addr addr;
struct sockaddr_in victem;
struct hostent *bad;
char foundmsg[] = "200";
char *cgistr;
char buffer[1024];
char cgibuff[1024];
int num,i=0;
char *temp[22];
char *name[22];

temp[1] = "GET /cgi-bin/phf HTTP/1.0\n\n";
temp[2] = "GET /cgi-bin/Count.cgi HTTP/1.0\n\n";
temp[3] = "GET /cgi-bin/test-cgi HTTP/1.0\n\n";
temp[4] = "GET /cgi-bin/php.cgi HTTP/1.0\n\n";
temp[5] = "GET /cgi-bin/handler HTTP/1.0\n\n";
temp[6] = "GET /cgi-bin/webgais HTTP/1.0\n\n";
temp[7] = "GET /cgi-bin/websendmail HTTP/1.0\n\n";
temp[8] = "GET /cgi-bin/webdist.cgi HTTP/1.0\n\n";
temp[9] = "GET /cgi-bin/faxsurvey HTTP/1.0\n\n";
temp[10] = "GET /cgi-bin/htmlscript HTTP/1.0\n\n";
temp[11] = "GET /cgi-bin/pfdispaly.cgi HTTP/1.0\n\n";
temp[12] = "GET /cgi-bin/perl.exe HTTP/1.0\n\n";
temp[13] = "GET /cgi-bin/wwwboard.pl HTTP/1.0\n\n";
temp[14] = "GET /cgi-bin/www-sql HTTP/1.0\n\n";
temp[15] = "GET /_vti_pvt/service.pwd HTTP/1.0\n\n";
temp[16] = "GET /_vti_pvt/users.pwd HTTP/1.0\n\n";
temp[17] = "GET /cgi-bin/aglimpse HTTP/1.0\n\n";
temp[18] = "GET /cgi-bin/man.sh HTTP/1.0\n\n";
temp[19] = "GET /cgi-bin/view-source HTTP/1.0\n\n";
temp[20] = "GET /cgi-bin/campas HTTP/1.0\n\n";
temp[21] = "GET /cgi-bin/nph-test-cgi HTTP/1.0\n\n";

name[1] = "phf";
name[2] = "Count.cgi";
name[3] = "test-cgi";
name[4] = "php.cgi";
name[5] = "handler";
name[6] = "webgais";
name[7] = "websendmail";
name[8] = "webdist.cgi";
name[9] = "faxsurvey";
name[10] = "htmlscript";
name[11] = "pfdisplay";
name[12] = "perl.exe";
name[13] = "wwwboard.pl";
name[14] = "www-sql";
```

```
name[15] = "service.pwd";
name[16] = "users.pwd";
name[17] = "aglimpse";
name[18] = "man.sh";
name[19] = "view-source";
name[20] = "campas";
name[21] = "nph-test-cgi";

if (argc!=2)
    {
    exit(printf("\nUsage : %s domain.com\n",argv[0]));
    }
if ((bad=gethostbyname(argv[1])) == NULL)
    {
    exit(printf("Error getting hostname\n"));
    }

printf("New web server hole and info scanner for elite kode
kiddies\n");
printf("coded by Bronc Buster of LoU - Nov 1998\n");
printf("updated Jan 1999\n");

system("sleep 2");

s=socket(AF_INET, SOCK_STREAM, 0);
if(s<0) exit(printf("Socket error"));
bcopy(bad->h_addr, (char *)&victem.sin_addr, bad->h_length);
victem.sin_family=AF_INET;
victem.sin_port=htons(80);

if (connect(s, (struct sockaddr*)&victem, sizeof(victem))<0)
    {
    exit(printf("Connect error\n"));
    }
printf("\nGetting HTTP version\n\n");
send(s, "HEAD / HTTP/1.0\n\n",17,0);
recv(s, buffer, sizeof(buffer),0);
printf("Version:\n%s",buffer);
close(s);
system("sleep 2");

while(i++ < MAX_SIZE)
    {
    s=socket(AF_INET, SOCK_STREAM, 0);
    bcopy(bad->h_addr, (char *)&victem.sin_addr, bad->h_length);
    victem.sin_family=AF_INET;
    victem.sin_port=htons(80);
    if (connect(s, (struct sockaddr*)&victem, sizeof(victem))<0)
        {
        exit(printf("Connect error\n"));
        }
    printf("Searching for %s : ",name[i]);
    for(num=0; num<1024; num++)
        {
        cgibuff[num] = '\0';
        }

    send(s, temp[i],strlen(temp[i]),0);
    recv(s, cgibuff, sizeof(cgibuff),0);
    cgistr = strstr(cgibuff,foundmsg);
    if(cgistr != NULL)
```

10

```
        printf(" * * Found * * \n");
    else
        printf(". . Not Found . .\n");

    close(s);
    }
printf("\n[gH] - aka gLoBaL hElL - are lame kode kiddies\n");
return 0;
    }
/* EOF */
```

Figure 10-31 shows the program being compiled and run on a Linux computer. A security tester could use the information this program retrieved to dig further into possible attacks that could be made on the organization's Web server. For example, several CGI programs are running on the server that could be exploited. The Perl.exe program, a known vulnerability, is also listed.

```
[root@server mike]# gcc cgiscan.c -o cgiscan
[root@server mike]# ./cgiscan isecom.org
New web server hole and info scanner for elite kode kiddies
coded by Bronc Buster of LoU - Nov 1998
updated Jan 1999


Getting HTTP version

Version:
HTTP/1.1 200 OK
Date: Wed, 02 Mar 2005 18:55:42 GMT
Server: Apache/1.3.29
Identity: The Institute for Security and Open Methodologies
P3P: Not supported at this time
Connection: close
Content-Type: text/html

7⊢Searching for phf :   * * Found * *
Searching for Count.cgi :   * * Found * *
Searching for test-cgi :   * * Found * *
Searching for php.cgi :   * * Found * *
Searching for handler :   * * Found * *
Searching for webgais :   * * Found * *
Searching for websendmail :   * * Found * *
Searching for webdist.cgi :   * * Found * *
Searching for faxsurvey :   * * Found * *
Searching for htmlscript :   * * Found * *
Searching for pfdisplay :   * * Found * *
Searching for perl.exe :   * * Found * *
Searching for wwwboard.pl :   * * Found * *
Searching for www-sql :   * * Found * *
Searching for service.pwd :   * * Found * *
Searching for users.pwd :   * * Found * *
Searching for aglimpse :   * * Found * *
Searching for man.sh :   * * Found * *
Searching for view-source :   * * Found * *
Searching for campas :   * * Found * *
Searching for nph-test-cgi :   * * Found * *

[gH] - aka gLoBaL hElL - are lame kode kiddies
[root@server mike]#
```

Figure 10-31   Compiling and running Cgiscan

Phfscan.c

Phfscan.c was written to scan Web sites looking for hosts that could be exploited by the PHF bug, which is an exploit that enables an attacker to download the victim's /etc/passwd file. After this information is obtained, an attacker has access to the victim's server using the list of passwords in that file. The exploit also allows attackers to run programs on the victim's Web server by using a particular URL. This bug is an old one, and any *NIX administrator should know to stop this PHF script from running. Attackers still look for administrators who don't keep up on security issues and refuse to patch their systems, and Phfscan.c is one tool for doing so.

Wfetch

If you're tired of all these text mode programs, Wfetch is a GUI tool that can be downloaded free from Microsoft and is included in the IIS Resource Kit. The 1.3 version is supported on Windows XP and Windows Server 2003 platforms. Microsoft warns users that the utility has advanced features that might expose a server to potential security risks, so be careful. Despite this caution, this helpful tool makes it possible for security testers to query the status of a Web server and attempt authentication using any of the methods listed in the fourth bullet item. The current version of Wfetch offers the following features:

- Multiple HTTP methods, such as GET, HEAD, TRACE, POST, and OPTIONS
- Configuration of host name and TCP port
- HTTP 1.0 and HTTP 1.1 support
- Anonymous, Basic, NTLM, Kerberos, Digest, and Negotiate authentication types
- Multiple connection types, such as HTTP, HTTPS, PCT 1.0, SSL 2.0, SSL 3.0, and TLS 3.1
- Proxy support
- Client-certificate support
- Capability to enter requests manually or have them read from a file
- On-screen and file-based logging

Figure 10-32 shows the information obtained from an IIS 5.1 server. Note that an attacker would know the version of IIS the user is running as well as the type of authentication (Basic) the Web server is using.

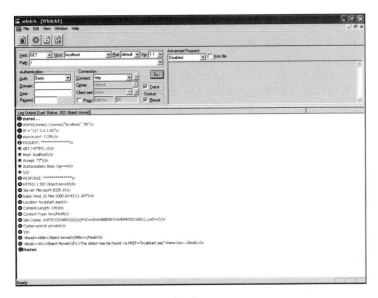

Figure 10-32   Using the Wfetch program

CHAPTER SUMMARY

- Web applications can be developed on many different platforms. HTML Web pages can contain forms, ASP, CGI, and scripting languages, such as VBScript and Javascript. Note, however, that scripting languages account for over half of Web server attacks.

- Static Web pages have been replaced by dynamic Web pages, which are created on the fly or when a user calls the page. Dynamic Web pages can be created through Common Gateway Interface (CGI), Active Server Pages (ASP), and Java Server Pages (JSP).

- Web forms allow developers to create Web pages that visitors can interact with. Care should be taken, however, to ensure that form fields are not manipulated by attackers.

- Web applications use a variety of technologies to connect to databases, such as ODBC, OLE DB, and ADO. These technologies create a front-end interface, allowing a Web application to connect to the back-end database.

❑ Windows XP Professional can be used to test your Web pages by installing IIS. Although the concurrent user logon limit is 10, this should be sufficient for most testing purposes.

❑ Web application vulnerabilities can have damaging consequences to a company. An attacker might be able to deface the company Web site, destroy a critical database, gain access to user accounts, or even gain access to the admin account or root access to other application servers on the network.

❑ When conducting a security test on a Web application, testers should ask questions about whether the Web application connects to a database source and if the user is authenticated though a different server.

❑ Many tools are available to security testers for testing Web application vulnerabilities, such as Cgiscan and Wfetch. In addition, OWASP offers open-source software.

❑ Web applications that interact with databases might be vulnerable to SQL injection exploits. Unicode exploits are possible on older versions of IIS.

❑ Many free tools for attacking Web servers can be downloaded from the Internet. There are also organizations such as the Open Web Application Security Project to help security professionals understand Web application vulnerabilities.

KEY TERMS

Active Server Pages (ASP) — A scripting language used to create dynamic Web pages.

ActiveX Data Objects (ADO) — A programming interface used to connect a Web application to a database.

ColdFusion — Created by Allaire, ColdFusion is a server-side scripting language used to create dynamic Web pages and supports a wide variety of databases. ColdFusion uses a proprietary markup language known as CFML.

Common Gateway Interface (CGI) — An interface that passes data between a Web server and a Web browser.

dynamic Web pages — A Web page that can change on the fly depending on variables, such as the date or time of day.

Object Linking and Embedding Data Base (OLE DB) — A set of interfaces enabling Web applications to access diverse database management systems.

Open Database Connectivity (ODBC) — A standard database access method that allows a Web application to interact with a variety of database management systems.

Open Web Application Security Project (OWASP) — A not-for-profit foundation dedicated to fighting and finding Web application vulnerabilities.

PHP Hypertext Processor (PHP) — An open-source server-side scripting language.

SQL injection — A type of exploit that takes advantage of improperly written applications. An attacker is able to issue SQL statements using a Web browser to retrieve data, change server settings, or possibly gain control of the server.

static Web pages — A Web page that displays the same information whenever it's accessed.

virtual directory — A pointer to a physical directory on a Web server.

WebGoat — A J2EE Web-based application designed to teach security professionals about Web application vulnerabilities.

REVIEW QUESTIONS

1. The following code snippet is an example of what language?

```
<Body>
<%
Dim strLastname, strFirstname
strLastname = Request.Form("Last")
strFirstname = Request.Form("First")
%>
```

   a. PHP

   b. HTML

   c. ASP

   d. JScript

2. Which of the following can be used to create dynamic Web pages? (Choose all that apply.)

   a. ColdFusion

   b. PHP

   c. ASP

   d. MySQL

3. Which of the following might be used to connect a Web server to a backend database server? (Choose all that apply.)

   a. ODBC

   b. OLE DB

   c. ADO

   d. HTML

4. What tag is used in an HTML document to represent the ASP scripting language?

5. What is the default Web server that comes with Windows XP Professional?

   a. PWS (Personal Web Server)

   b. IIS 6.0

   c. IIS 5.0

   d. IIS 5.1

6. Entering the URL http://www.abc.com/%55/%55/%55/%55/%55 in a Web browser is an example of what exploit?

   a. buffer overflow

   b. Unicode exploit

   c. worm injection

   d. SQL injection

7. Entering the value ' OR 1=1 in a Web browser application that has an "Enter Your PIN" field is most likely an example of a(n) _____ attack.

   a. SQL injection

   b. code injection

   c. buffer overflow

   d. Ethernet

8. HTML Web pages that contain connection strings are more vulnerable to attack. True or False?

9. Which of the following is a good tool for searching the Web for sites containing vulnerable CGI scripts?

    a. 10phtcrack

    b. Paros

    c. Cgiscan.c

    d. Nmap

10. Which of the following is an open-source technology that can be used to create dynamic HTML Web pages?

    a. ASP

    b. PHP

    c. Java

    d. Oracle

11. Microsoft uses CGI in its ASP pages. True or False?

12. Name three Web application vulnerabilities from OWASP's top 10 list.

13. If a Web server isn't protected, an attacker can gain access through remote administration interfaces. True or False?

14. _____ is a technology used to connect an ASP Web page to an Oracle database. (Choose all that apply.)

    a. ADO

    b. HTML

    c. CGA

    d. OLE DB

15. What organization is dedicated to fighting and finding the causes of software vulnerabilities?

16. What tags identify ColdFusion as the scripting language?

    a. <# #>

    b. <% %>

    c. the letters CF

    d. <! /!>

17. What HTML tags identify PHP as the scripting language?

    a. <# #>

    b. <% %>

    c. <? ?>

    d. <! /!>

18. An HTML Web page containing ASP scripting language must be compiled before running. True or False?

19. Which tool can be used to download a user's /etc/passwd file after connecting to his or her Web server?

    a. Cgiscan

    b. Nmap

    c. Phfscan

    d. Wfetch

20. IIS Web servers account for more than 50% of all Web sites. True or False?

CASE PROJECTS

Case 10-1: Determining Vulnerabilities of Web Servers

After conducting preliminary security testing on the K. J. Williams network, you have identified that the company has seven Web servers. One is a Windows NT 4.0 server running IIS 4.0. Curt Cavanaugh, the Web master and network administrator, says the Web server is used only by sales personnel as a front-end to update inventory data on an Oracle database server. He says this procedure needs to be done remotely and that it is convenient for sales personnel to use a Web browser when out of the office.

Based on the preceding information, write a one-page report on any vulnerabilities that might exist for the current configuration of the company's Web server. Use the tools you have learned to date to search for possible vulnerabilities of IIS 4.0. Your report should include any recommendations that might increase Web security.

Case 10-2: Discovering Web Attack Tools

After discovering that K. J. Williams has multiple Web servers running on different platforms, you wonder whether your security tools can do a proper job of assessing Web application vulnerabilities. You currently have only two tools for conducting the Web security portion of a security test: Cgiscan and Wfetch.

Based on the preceding information, write a two-page report on the tools available for security testers conducting Web application vulnerability testing. Use the skills you have gained to search the Internet for tools for Microsoft and *NIX platforms. The report should state the name of the tool, describe the method of downloading and installing, and include a brief description of what the tool does.

10

11

HACKING WIRELESS NETWORKS

After reading this chapter and completing the exercises, you will be able to:

♦ Explain wireless technology

♦ Describe wireless networking standards

♦ Describe the process of authentication

♦ Describe wardriving

♦ Describe wireless hacking and tools used by hackers and security professionals

As defined at the online encyclopedia Wikipedia (*http://en.wikipedia.org/wiki/Wireless_technology*), wireless technology is ". . . generally used for mobile IT equipment [and] encompasses cellular telephones, personal digital assistants (PDAs), and wireless networking." Although wireless technology also includes "nonmobile" technology, such as garage door openers and satellite television, this chapter's focus is on wireless networking as it relates to security. There's no doubt that wireless technology is here to stay. However, securing a wireless network from attackers is a primary concern.

This chapter gives you an overview of wireless networking technology and standards, explains the process of authentication, describes wardriving, and covers some tools wireless attackers use.

UNDERSTANDING WIRELESS TECHNOLOGY

For a wireless network to function, you must have the right hardware and software. There must also be a technology in place that allows those electrons to travel in space. At one time, when seeing the comic strip character Dick Tracy talk to his wristwatch, people wondered whether that would ever be possible. For those of another generation, the idea that a phone could work without a wire connected to it astounded them, even though the walkie-talkie was invented by Alfred J. Gross in 1938. In fact, the creator of the "Dick Tracy" comic asked Gross's permission before using the wireless wristwatch in his comics. (To read more about Al Gross, visit *www.retrocom.com*.) In 1973, 35 years after the walkie-talkie, Martin Cooper invented the first cell phone, which weighed in at close to two pounds.

Wireless technology is part of our lives. Here are some of the wireless devices many people use daily:

- Baby monitors
- Cell phones
- Cordless phones
- Pagers
- Global positioning systems (GPSs) in cars
- Remote controls
- Garage door openers
- Two-way radios
- Wireless PDAs

Components of a Wireless Network

Any network has certain components that make it work: protocols, network cards, and a medium (a wire) or a method for transmitting data. As complex as a wireless network might seem, it has only three basic components:

- Access point (AP)
- Wireless network interface card (WNIC)
- Ethernet cable

The following sections explain how an AP and a wireless NIC function in a wireless LAN.

Access Points

An **access point (AP)** is a transceiver that connects to an Ethernet cable. It bridges the wireless network with the wired network. It's possible to have a wireless network that doesn't connect to a wired network, but this topology isn't covered in this book. Most companies where you conduct security tests will use a **wireless LAN (WLAN)** that connects to the company's wired network topology.

The AP is where channels are configured. Figure 11-1 shows the channels detected by NetStumbler (an AP-scanning program covered in "Understanding Wardriving" later in this chapter). APs are what hackers look for when they drive around with an antenna and a laptop computer scanning for access.

An AP enables users to connect to a LAN using wireless technology. The AP can listen to or receive traffic from only a defined area or square footage, depending on the technology. If you are 20 miles away from an AP, you most likely are out of range.

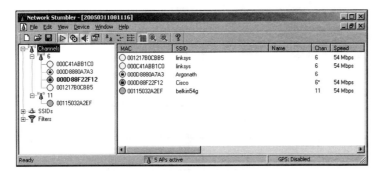

Figure 11-1 AP channels detected

Service Set Identifiers (SSIDs)

A **service set identifier (SSID)** is the name used to identify the **wireless local area network (WLAN)**, much the same way a workgroup is used on a Windows network. The SSID is configured on the AP with a unique, 1- to 32-character alphanumeric name and is case sensitive. For wireless computers to access the WLAN, they must also be configured with the same SSID as the AP. The SSID name, or "code," is attached to each packet to identify it as belonging to that wireless network. The AP usually broadcasts the SSID several times a second so that users who have wireless NICs (WNICs) in their computers can see a display of all WLANs within range of the AP's signal. Figure 11-2 shows the SSIDs advertised by the APs in the wireless computer.

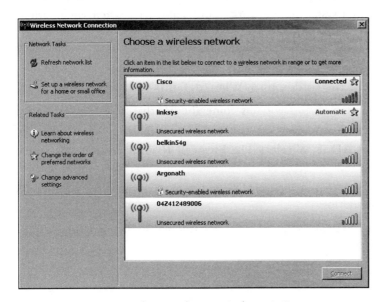

Figure 11-2 SSIDs advertised to a wireless station

Many vendors have SSIDs set to a default value that companies never change. For example, Cisco APs use the default SSID of Tsunami. Table 11-1 shows some of the default SSIDs used as of this writing. This list changes often, sometimes daily. As a security professional, you must constantly research and gather information to keep abreast of the many changes in this industry. If an AP is configured not to provide its SSID until after authentication, many wireless hackers can attempt to guess the SSID by using the information in Table 11-1. Be sure the client or customer for whom you're conducting a security test is not using a default SSID.

Table 11-1   Default SSIDs

Vendor	Default SSIDs
3Com	3Com
Apple	Airport Network
Belkin (54G)	Belkin54g
Cisco	Tsunami
Compaq	Compaq
D-Link	WLAN, default
Dell	Wireless
Intel	Intel, 101, xlan, 195
Linksys	linksys, Wireless, linksys-g
Microsoft	MSNHOME
Netgear	Wireless, NETGEAR
SMC	WLAN, BRIDGE, SMC
Symantec	101
US Robotics	WLAN, USR9106, USR808054

ACTIVITY

Activity 11-1: Finding Vulnerabilities in SSIDs

Time Required: 30 minutes

Objective: Learn how recognizing a default SSID can open the door to discovering vulnerabilities.

Description: As you learned in Chapter 6, recognizing which OS a customer or client is using is essential before you can detect vulnerabilities in a system or network. This is also true when you're attempting to discover vulnerabilities in an AP. When conducting a security test on a WLAN, you start by looking for SSIDs advertised over the air to determine the type of AP the company is using.

1. If necessary, start your computer in Windows XP Professional and open a Web browser. Next, type the URL **http://new.remote-exploit.org/index.php/Wlan_defaults** and press **Enter**.

2. Read the information in the document. It lists wireless vulnerabilities that have been compiled from various sources and can be quite helpful when conducting a security test on a wireless network.

3. Click the **3Com OfficeConnect ADSL Wireless 11g Firewall Router Authentication Bypass Vulnerability** link.

4. Read the information on the page shown in Figure 11-3, and then click the **discussion** tab. What vulnerability does this document address?

5. What solution would you offer to a client using the router mentioned in Step 3 with version 1.23 firmware? (*Hint*: Click the **solution** tab.)

6. Leave your Web browser open and XP running for the next activity.

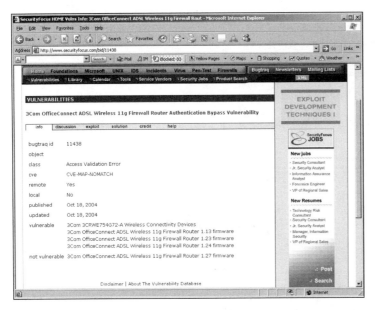

Figure 11-3   Vulnerabilities listed on the SecurityFocus site

Configuring an Access Point

Configuring an AP varies depending on the hardware. Most devices allow users to access the software interface through any Web browser. The following example shows some options for configuring an AP and how an AP administrator can determine the SSID and channel and configure security (covered later in this chapter in the "Understanding Authentication" section). This example outlines the steps a security professional takes to access and reconfigure a D-Link wireless router with an IP address of 192.168.0.1:

1. After entering the IP address into a Web browser, the user is prompted for a logon name and password (see Figure 11-4). If this is the user's first time accessing the router, no password is needed. The default logon name for this D-Link wireless router is "admin." Changing the default name is strongly recommended for security purposes.

Figure 11-4   Logging on to a D-Link wireless router

2. After a successful logon, you see the window displayed in Figure 11-5.

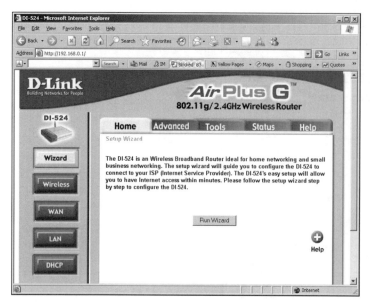

Figure 11-5   The D-Link main window

3. After clicking the Wireless button on the left, the window in Figure 11-6 is displayed. Note that the user entered "Cisco" for the SSID but could have entered any name. (Remember: The default SSID for Cisco wireless routers is Tsunami, not Cisco.) The user changed the default name to "Cisco" to try to fool potential attackers into believing the wireless router is a Cisco product. Channel 6, the default channel for D-Link wireless routers, has been selected. In this configuration, the user has created a Wired Equivalent Privacy (WEP) key that must be supplied by the wireless computer. The 10 characters in the key are hexadecimal, not alphanumeric. For example, a Windows XP Professional computer that wants to connect to the AP with the SSID "Cisco" must enter the WEP key in the Properties dialog box shown in Figure 11-7. The software supplied with the WNIC enables the user to access available APs in the area.

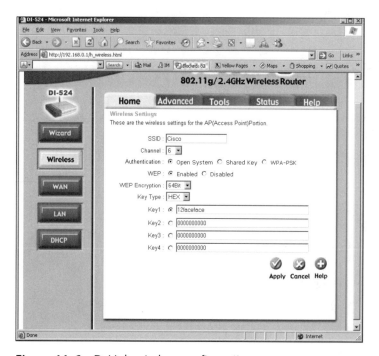

Figure 11-6   D-Link wireless configuration

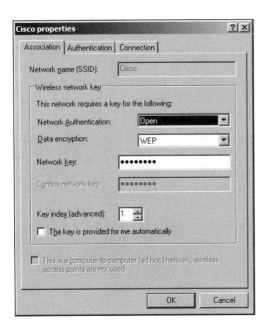

Figure 11-7 Entering a WEP key

4. The next thing an administrator should do to better protect the wireless LAN from attack is to turn off SSID broadcasts. You have already seen how attackers can discover vulnerabilities for devices by using the Internet. Broadcasting who you are and whether you're using any form of encryption just makes their attacks easier. For D-Link, disabling SSID broadcasts is easy to do, so it's puzzling why it is not emphasized in the documentation. Figure 11-8 shows disabling SSID broadcasts in the Advanced tab.

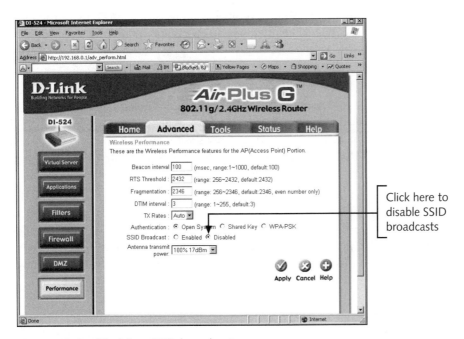

Figure 11-8 Disabling SSID broadcasts

If a company does not change its default SSID but decides to disable SSID broadcasts, an intruder can play a guessing game and attempt to connect to the wireless LAN by trying different default names from a wireless client. If the user did not assign a password to the AP, you can see how easy it is for an attacker to access the WLAN. As a security tester, you must verify that these vulnerabilities don't exist on a WLAN; if they do, you should close the holes as quickly as possible.

Wireless NICs

For a computer to be able to send information over any medium, it must be able to understand the medium it's traversing; the correct software and drivers for the network card must be installed. For example, data that travels over a copper wire must follow rules for how electrons are placed on that wire. For wireless technology to work, each node or computer must have a wireless NIC. The NIC's main function is converting the radio waves it receives into digital signals the computer understands.

There are many wireless NICs on the market, but be careful deciding which ones to purchase if you're considering using specific tools for detecting APs, decrypting WEP keys, or using antennas that can cover a large distance. For example, AirSnort, a program for cracking WEP encryption used on a WLAN, requires using a specific chipset on a NIC, so only certain brands of NICs can be used.

UNDERSTANDING WIRELESS NETWORK STANDARDS

A standard is a set of rules formulated by an organization. All industries have standards, and a WLAN is no exception. Just as the **Institute of Electrical and Electronics Engineers (IEEE)** has standards that specify how long a cable can be in an Ethernet network, there are rules to follow for wireless networks.

Institute of Electrical and Electronics Engineers (IEEE) Standards

A group of people from the electrical and electronics industry meet to create a standard. This group is called a working group (WG). Proposals of new standards, or drafts, are voted on, and if a consensus is achieved in favor of the proposed standard, it must then be approved by another group of people who are members of the Sponsor Executive Committee (SEC). Finally, after being recommended by the Standards Review Committee (RevCom) and approved by the IEEE Standards Board, you have a new standard.

IEEE Project 802 was developed to create LAN and WAN standards. The first meeting was held in February 1980, so the project was given the number 802. When a project is approved in a WG, a letter is added to the group name, such as 802.11a or 802.11b. In this chapter, you learn about the 802 standards that pertain to wireless networks.

The 802.11 Standard

The first wireless technology standard, 802.11, defined the specifications for wireless connectivity at 1 Mbps and 2 Mbps within a LAN. The standard applied to layers 1 and 2 of the OSI model: the physical layer, which deals with the wireless connectivity issues of fixed, portable, and moving stations within a local area, and the data link layer, specifically the Media Access Control (MAC) layer. Because wireless networks can't detect a collision, carrier sense multiple access/collision avoidance (CSMA/CA) is used instead of CSMA/CD (collision detection).

Many definitions of terms are discussed in the more than 500 pages of the 802.11 standard. One important distinction is that wireless LANs do not have an address associated with a physical location, as does a wired LAN. In 802.11, an addressable unit is called a **station (STA)**. This station is defined as a message destination and might not be a fixed location. Another distinction is made between mobile stations and portable stations. A mobile station is defined as a station that accesses the LAN while moving; a portable station is one that can move from location to location, but is used only while in a fixed location.

The Basic Architecture of 802.11

802.11 uses a **basic service set (BSS)** as its building block. As long as a station is within its BSS, or coverage area, it can communicate with other stations in the BSS. You have probably experienced losing connectivity on your cell phone when you're out of range of your service area. Similarly, you can lose network connectivity if you aren't in the wireless LAN's coverage area. To connect two BSSs, 802.11 requires a distribution system (DS) as an intermediate layer. Basically, BSS1 connects to the DS, which in turn connects to BSS2. But how does a station called STA1 in BSS1 connect to STA2 located in BSS2? 802.11 defines one more component, called an access point (AP), which is a station that provides access to the DS. Data moves between a BSS and the DS through the AP. This sounds complicated, but Figure 11-9 should clear up any confusion.

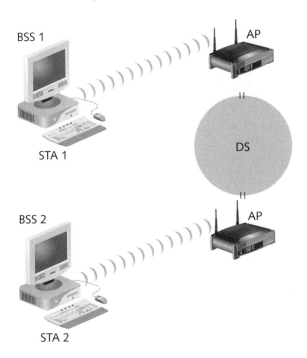

Figure 11-9   Connecting two wireless remote stations

IEEE 802.11 also defines the operating frequency range of 802.11. In the United States, it's 2.400 to 2.4835 GHz. Think of the frequency as a superhighway in the sky where data travels, and this superhighway encompasses many highways (frequency bands). Each frequency band contains **channels**. A channel is a frequency range. For example, channel 1 of a frequency band that ranges from 2.4 GHz to 2.4835 GHz might use the 2.401 GHz frequency. Channel 2 of that frequency band might use 2.402 GHz. The 802.11 standard defines 79 channels in the 2.400 to 2.4835 GHz range. If channels overlap, interference could occur.

Sound travels through the air just as waves move in the ocean. Just as a wave in the ocean has a wavelength measure from the peak of one wave to the next, sound waves also have a wavelength. The length and **frequency** of a sound wave are what make it have a distinct sound and volume. Surfers know that they must wait for the next set of waves to occur and get quite accurate in determining the frequency, or the time it takes for a set of waves to repeat. The completion of this repeating pattern of sound waves is called a cycle. For surfers, a cycle can sometimes be minutes. Sound waves, however, repeat at a much faster rate, or frequency. For example, a tuning fork vibrates at 440 hertz (Hz), or cycles per second. That's 440 waves per second—too fast for a surfer. Different frequencies, referred to as bands, are used by various technologies to transmit sound. Table 11-2 lists frequency bands. For example, the medium frequency (MF) band is used by commercial AM radio stations. Very high frequency (VHF) is used by FM radio listeners and by the Search and Rescue band. The distance sound waves need to travel also determines which frequency band to use.

Table 11-2   Frequency bands

Frequency	Range	Wavelength
Extremely low frequency (ELF)	30–300 Hz	10,000–1000 km
Voice frequency (VF) or ultra low frequency (ULF)	300 Hz–3 KHz	1000–100 km
Very low frequency (VLF)	3–30 KHz	100–10 km
Low frequency (LF)	30–300 KHz	10–1 km
Medium frequency (MF)	300 KHz–3 MHz	1 km–100 m

Table 11-2 Frequency bands (continued)

Frequency	Range	Wavelength
High frequency (HF)	3–30 MHz	100–10 m
Very high frequency (VHF)	30–300 MHz	100 km
Ultra high frequency (UHF)	300 MHz–3 GHz	100 km
Super high frequency (SHF)	3–30 GHz	10–1 cm
Extremely high frequency (EHF)	30–300 GHz	1 cm–1 mm

When you purchase a wireless router, you might be asked whether you have a wireless telephone in your home or office because many wireless telephones operate at the same frequency as wireless routers. This can cause interference if the telephone is close to the wireless router or AP.

An Overview of Wireless Technologies

Now that you understand the different frequencies on which sound waves can travel, take a look at the three technologies in which wireless LANs operate:

- *Infrared (IR)*—Infrared light can't be seen by the human eye. **Infrared (IR)** technology is restricted to a single room or line of sight because IR light can't penetrate walls, ceilings, or floors. This technology is used for most remote controls and PDAs.

- *Narrowband*—**Narrowband** technology uses microwave radio band frequencies to transmit data. The most popular uses of this technology are cordless phones and garage door openers.

- *Spread spectrum*—For data to be moved over radio waves, it must be modulated on the carrier signal or channel discussed earlier. **Modulation** defines how data is placed on a carrier signal. **Spread spectrum** means that data is spread across a large-frequency bandwidth instead of traveling across just one frequency band. In other words, a group of radio frequencies are selected, and the data is "spread" across them. Spread spectrum, the most popular type of WLAN technology, uses the following methods:

  - *Frequency-hopping spread spectrum (FHSS)*—Data hops to other frequencies to avoid any interference that might occur over a frequency band. This hopping from one frequency to another occurs at split-second intervals and makes it difficult for an intruder or attacker to jam the communication channel.

  - *Direct sequence spread spectrum (DSSS)*—Sub-bits are added to a packet as it travels across the frequency band and are used for recovery, in much the same way that RAID uses parity bits to rebuild a hard disk that crashes in a RAID-5 configuration. Sub-bits are called "chips," and every bit of the original message is represented by multiple bits, called the **chipping code**.

  - *Orthogonal frequency division multiplexing (OFDM)*—The bandwidth is divided into a series of frequencies called tones and allows a higher throughput than do FHSS and DSSS.

IEEE Additional 802.11 Projects

The IEEE WG had some additional projects in 802.11, covered in the following paragraphs.

The 802.11a specification, created in 1999, had two major changes since 802.11: The operating frequency range changed from 2.4 GHz to 5 GHz, and throughput increased from 11 Mbps to 54 Mbps. In fact, three distinct bands or frequencies are used in 802.11a:

- Lower band—5.15 to 5.25 GHz

- Middle band—5.25 to 5.35 GHz

- Upper band—5.75 to 5.85 GHz

The 802.11b standard also operates in the 2.4 GHz range, but increased throughput from 1 or 2 Mbps to 11 Mbps. 802.11b is also referred to as Wi-Fi (wireless fidelity). The standard allows for a total of 11 separate channels to prevent overlapping signals. However, because of each channel's bandwidth requirements, effectively only three channels (1, 6, and 11) can be used in combination without overlapping and creating interference. This standard introduced Wired Equivalent Privacy (WEP), which gave many users a false sense of security that data traversing the WLAN was protected. WEP is covered later in this chapter in "Understanding Authentication."

The 802.11e standard had improvements to address the problem of interference. When interference is detected, the signal can jump to another frequency more quickly, improving quality of service over 802.11b.

The 802.11g standard operates in the 2.4 GHz range, but because this standard uses a different modulation, it uses OFDM, which increased the top speed of 11 Mbps in 802.11b to 54 Mbps.

The 802.11i standard introduced **Wi-Fi Protected Access (WPA)**, which is covered in "Understanding Authentication." For now, just know that 802.11i corrected many of the security vulnerabilities of 802.11b. For security professionals, the 802.11i standard is probably the most important.

The 802.15 standard addresses networking devices within one person's workspace, which is called the **wireless personal area network (WPAN)**. The distance covered is usually no more than 10 meters. For example, a user can connect her PDA to her PC and print a document without any wires connecting these devices. One implementation of this technology is Bluetooth, covered later in this section.

The 802.16 standard addresses the issue of wireless metropolitan area networks (MANs). This standard defines the WirelessMAN Air Interface for wireless MANs and addresses the limited distance available for 802.11b WLANs. This new technology will have a range of up to 30 miles and throughput of up to 120 Mbps.

The 802.20 standard addresses wireless MANs for mobile users who are sitting in trains, subways, or cars traveling at speeds up to 150 miles per hour.

Bluetooth is a telecommunications specification that defines a method for interconnecting portable devices, such as PDAs, cell phones, and computers, without wires. The maximum distance allowed between each device is 10 meters. Bluetooth uses the 2.45 GHz frequency band and can exchange data up to a speed of 12 Mbps. It's not compatible with the 802.11 standards. Bluetooth is more secure than a WLAN but is still vulnerable to attack.

HiperLAN2 is a European WLAN standard that's not compatible with 802.11 standards, so compatibility with devices you already own is an important factor in deciding whether to purchase a HiperLAN2 device.

Table 11-3 is a summary of the wireless standards in use today.

Table 11-3   Summary of wireless standards

Standard	Frequency	Rate	Modulation
802.11	2.4 GHz	1 or 2 Mbps	FHSS/DSSS
802.11a	5 GHz	54 Mbps	OFDM
802.11b	2.4 GHz	11 Mbps	DSSS
802.11g	2.4 GHz	54 Mbps	OFDM
802.11e	2–6 GHz	22 Mbps	DSSS
802.11i	2.4 GHz	11 Mbps	DSSS
802.15	2.4 GHz	2 Mbps	FHSS
802.16	10–66 GHz	120 Mbps	OFDM
802.20 (Mobile Wireless Access Working Group)	Below 3.5 GHz	1 Mbps	OFDM proposed (might change)
Bluetooth	2.4 GHz	12 Mbps	Gaussian frequency shift keying (GMSK)
HiperLAN2	5 GHz	54 Mbps	OFDM

Activity 11-2: Visiting the IEEE 802.11 Web Site

Time Required: 30 minutes

Objective: Learn more about IEEE wireless standards.

Description: You can find a wealth of information at the IEEE Web site, and the standards are currently available for download. In this activity, you visit the IEEE Web site and research some standards covered in this section.

1. If necessary, start your computer in Windows XP Professional and open a Web browser. Type the URL **http://grouper.ieee.org/groups/802/** and press **Enter**.

2. In the IEEE 802 GENERAL INFORMATION section of the IEEE 802 LAN/MAN Standards Committee page, click **Tutorial Materials**.

3. On the IEEE Plenary Tutorials page, scroll down the document to the "March 15-19, 2004, Walt Disney World, FL" section. Click Tutorial #1, **Wireless Performance Prediction**, and then click **Open**.

4. Review the PowerPoint presentation to get an idea of how standards are formulated. Note the slide on Microsoft's current WLAN network. How many authentications occur each day?

5. Leave your Web browser open and Windows XP running for the next activity.

UNDERSTANDING AUTHENTICATION

The problem of unauthorized users accessing resources on a network is a big concern for security professionals. An organization that introduces wireless technology to the mix increases the potential for security problems. For example, if an employee installs an AP that's not configured correctly, unauthorized users could log on to her AP after obtaining her logon name and password. The 802.1X standard, discussed in the following section, addresses the issue of authentication.

The 802.1X Standard

The **802.1X standard** defines the process of authenticating and authorizing users on a WLAN. There must be a methodology to ensure that not everyone with a wireless NIC can access resources on your wireless network. 802.1X addresses the concern of authentication. To understand how authentication can take place on a wireless network, review some basic concepts in the following sections.

Point-to-Point Protocol (PPP)

Many ISPs use PPP to connect dial-up or DSL users. PPP handles authentication by requiring a user to enter a valid user name and password. PPP verifies that users attempting to use the link are indeed who they say they are.

Extensible Authentication Protocol (EAP)

Extensible Authentication Protocol (EAP) is an enhancement to PPP. The EAP framework was designed to allow a company to select its authentication method. For example, a company can use certificates or Kerberos authentication to authenticate a user connecting to an AP. A **certificate** is a record that authenticates network entities, such as a server or client. It contains X.509 information that identifies the owner, the certificate authority (CA), and the owner's public key.

If you have never seen a certificate, you can use the following steps to view a certificate from Amazon.com. Otherwise, skip to the list describing EAP methods.

1. In any Web browser, type the URL **www.amazon.com** and press **Enter**.

2. On the Amazon.com home page, click the **Books** link at the left.

3. On the Books page, click any book title, and then click the **Add to cart** button at the right.

4. On the next page displayed, click the **Proceed to Checkout** button.

5. When prompted to enter your e-mail address, type **test.com** and click the **Sign in using our secure server** button.

6. Ignore the error message stating that there's a slight problem with your order, and note the small lock icon at the bottom of the Web page. Double-click the **lock** icon. You should see the Certificate dialog box, similar to what's shown Figure 11-10.

Figure 11-10   Viewing information about an X.509 certificate

7. Click the **Details** tab to view the information in the certificate. To view the public key, click it.

8. Click the **Certification Path** tab to identify the CA.

9. Click **OK** and close your Web browser.

The following EAP methods can be used to improve security on a wireless network:

- *Extensible Authentication Protocol-Transport Layer Security (EAP-TLS)*—This method requires that both the client and server be assigned a digital signature signed by a CA they both trust. This CA can be a commercial company that charges a fee, or a network administrator can configure a server, such as a Windows Server 2003 machine, to issue certificates. In this way, both the server and the client mutually authenticate. In addition to servers requiring that clients prove they are who they say, clients also want servers to verify their identity.

- *Protected EAP (PEAP)*—**Protected EAP (PEAP)** uses TLS to authenticate the server to the client but not the client to the server. With PEAP, only the server is required to have a public certificate. See RFC2246 for more information on TLS.

- *Microsoft PEAP*—In Microsoft's implementation of PEAP, a secure channel is created by using TLS to protect from eavesdropping.

802.1X uses the following components to function:

- *Supplicant*—A **supplicant** is the wireless user attempting access to a WLAN.

- *Authenticator*—The AP functions as the authenticator.

■ *Authentication server*—This server, which might be a Remote Access Dial-In User Service (RADIUS) server, is used as a centralized component that authenticates the user and performs accounting functions. For example, an ISP using RADIUS can verify who logged on to the ISP service and how long the user was connected. Most RADIUS servers are *NIX based, but the Microsoft implementation of RADIUS is called Internet Authentication Service (IAS).

Figure 11-11 shows the process of 802.1X.

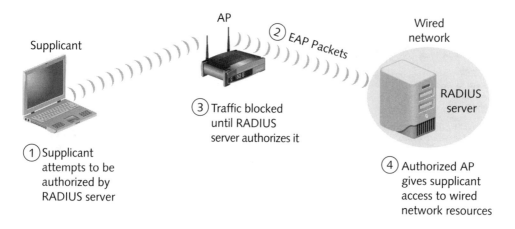

Figure 11-11   A supplicant connecting to an AP and a RADIUS server

In Figure 11-11, the following steps take place:

1. An unauthenticated client (supplicant) attempts to connect with an authenticator (RADIUS) server.

2. The access point (AP) responds by enabling a port that passes only EAP packets from the supplicant to the RADIUS server located on the wired network.

3. The AP blocks all other traffic until the RADIUS server authenticates the supplicant.

4. After being authenticated by RADIUS, the AP gives the supplicant access to network resources.

Until EAP and 802.1x were implemented on wireless LANs, a device, not a user, was authenticated on the WLAN. That is, if a computer was stolen from a company, the thief would be able to connect to the resources on the WLAN. The following sections describe the security features introduced in 802.11b.

Wired Equivalent Privacy (WEP)

Wired Equivalent Privacy (WEP) is part of the 802.11b standard. It was implemented specifically to encrypt data that traversed a wireless network. For some time, it gave many security professionals a false sense of security that wireless technology could be just as safe as wired network security. Unfortunately, WEP has been torn to shreds by security professionals, professors from major universities, and hackers who have no problem posting ways to crack WEP encryption. Some argue that WEP is still better than no security at all, and that when combined with the security of a virtual private network (VPN), WEP works well for home users or small businesses. Still, many saw a need for a more secure way to protect WLANs.

Wi-Fi Protected Access (WPA)

Wi-Fi Protected Access (WPA) is specified in the 802.11i standard and is the replacement for WEP (802.11b), known to have cryptographic weakness problems. WPA improves encryption by using Temporal Key Integrity Protocol (TKIP). TKIP is composed of four enhancements that address the encryption vulnerabilities in WEP:

■ *Message Integrity Check (MIC)*—MIC, called Michael, is a cryptographic message integrity code. Its main purpose is to prevent forgeries, which are packets that attackers create to look like legitimate packets. For example, a MIC uses a secret authentication key, which only the sender and receiver know, and creates a tag generated from the key and message that is sent to the receiver. A tag is also referred to as a message integrity code. The sender sends the message and tag to the receiver, who must enter the key, tag, and message into a program that verifies whether the tag created with the three input fields is equal to the tag the program should have created. You don't need to memorize how this process takes place, but understanding that MIC corrects a known vulnerability in WEP is important.

- *Extended Initialization Vector (IV) with sequencing rules*—This enhancement was implemented to prevent replays. In a replay, an attacker records or captures a packet, saves it, and retransmits the message later. To prevent this from occurring, a sequence number is applied to the WEP IV field. If a packet is received with an IV equal to or less than the sequence number received earlier, the packet is discarded.

- *Per-packet key mixing*—This enhancement helps defeat weak key attacks that occurred in WEP. MAC addresses are used in creating an intermediate key, which prevents the same key from being used by all links.

- *Rekeying mechanism*—This enhancement provides fresh keys that help prevent attacks that relied on reusing old keys. That is, if the same key was used repeatedly, someone running a program to decipher the key could likely do so after collecting a large number of packets. The same key being used repeatedly was a big problem with WEP.

WPA also added an authentication mechanism implementing 802.1X and EAP, which wasn't available in WEP.

UNDERSTANDING WARDRIVING

It's probably no secret that hackers use **wardriving**—driving around with inexpensive hardware and software that enables them to detect access points that haven't been secured. It is surprising, but most APs have no passwords or security implemented, so wardriving can be quite rewarding for hackers. As of the writing of this book, wardriving isn't illegal; using the resources of these networks is, of course, a different story. Wardriving has now been expanded to include warflying, which is accomplished by using an airplane wired with an antenna and the same software used in wardriving. In one test conducted by warflyers, more than 3000 APs were discovered, and two-thirds of them used no encryption. The testers used Kismet, covered later in this section, which identifies APs that attempt to "cloak" or hide their SSIDs.

How It Works

To conduct wardriving, an attacker or a security tester simply drives around with a laptop computer containing a wireless NIC, an antenna, and software that scans the area for SSIDs. Not all wireless NICs are compatible with scanning software, so you might want to look at the software requirements first before purchasing the hardware. Antenna prices vary depending on their quality and the range they can cover. Some are as small as the antenna on a cell phone and some as large as a small bazooka, which you might have seen in old war films. The larger ones can sometimes return results on networks miles away from the attacker. The smaller ones might require being in close proximity to the AP.

Most scanning software packages indicate the company's SSID, the type of security enabled (WEP), and the signal strength, indicating how close the AP is to the attacker. The following section introduces a tool that most wireless hackers and security professionals use when conducting a security test on a WLAN.

Security Bytes

An ethical hacker in Houston, previously employed by the county's Technology Department, was accused of breaking into a Texas court's wireless network. He noticed this vulnerability while he was scanning wireless networks in Houston and was concerned. He demonstrated to a county official and a local reporter how easily he could gain access to the court's wireless network using just a laptop computer and a wireless NIC. He was later charged with two counts of unauthorized access of a protected computer system and unauthorized access of a computer system used in justice administration. After a three-day trial and 15 minutes of jury deliberation, he was acquitted. If he had been found guilty of all charges, he would have faced 10 years in prison and a $500,000 fine.

NetStumbler

NetStumbler (*www.netstumbler.com*) is a shareware tool written for Windows that enables you to detect WLANs using 802.11a, 802.11b, and 802.11g. It's easy to install, but not all wireless hardware works with the software, so you must follow the directions carefully and verify that the hardware you have is compatible. NetStumbler was primarily designed to assist security testers in the following:

- Verifying your WLAN configuration
- Detecting other wireless networks that might be interfering with your WLAN
- Detecting unauthorized APs that might have been placed on your WLAN

NetStumbler is also used in wardriving, but remember that in most parts of the world, using someone's network without permission is illegal. This also includes using someone's Internet connection without his or her knowledge or permission.

Another feature of NetStumbler is its capability to interface with a GPS, enabling a security tester or hacker to map out locations of all the WLANs the software detects (see Figure 11-12).

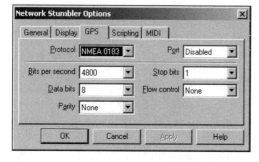

Figure 11-12   Configuring GPS settings in the Network Stumbler Options dialog box

When the program identifies an AP's signal, it logs the SSID, MAC address of the AP, manufacturer of the AP, channel on which it was heard, strength of the signal, and encryption (WEP), if any. Attackers can detect any APs within a 350-foot radius, but with a good antenna, they can locate APs a couple of miles away. For those with mechanical ability, numerous Web sites have directions on building your own antenna. Instructions range from using empty bean cans to a potato chip can. You can also purchase a decent antenna for about $50.

For directions on building an antenna from a potato chip can, visit *www.oreillynet.com/cs/weblog/view/wlg/448*.

Activity 11-3: Installing NetStumbler

Time Required: 15 minutes

Objective: Install NetStumbler on your Windows XP Professional computer.

Description: When testing a network for vulnerabilities, don't neglect to check for vulnerabilities in the corporate network's WLAN. NetStumbler enables you to verify available SSIDs and APs and to see whether nearby WLANs might be interfering with your company's wireless network. In this activity, you download NetStumbler and install it on your Windows XP Professional computer. It's unlikely that your classroom will have wireless NICs or an AP, but you can do the activity later where equipment is available, such as your home or office.

1. If necessary, start your computer in Windows XP Professional and open a Web browser. Type the URL **http://www.netstumbler.com/downloads** and press **Enter**.

2. On the NetStumbler download page, click **Release Notes (PDF)**. Read the document, paying close attention to the author's comments on OS requirements, configuration, and legal issues of using the product.

3. After reading the document, click the **Back** button to return to the NetStumbler.com home page. On the home page, click the **NetStumbler 0.4.0 Installer** link to begin downloading the program. (*Note:* The version might have changed since the writing of this book.)

4. After being prompted to run or save the application, click **Save** and create a new folder on your C: drive called **NetStumbler**. Change to that folder, click **Save** to save the default file name to the folder, and then click **Run** twice to install the program.

5. After downloading the product, you're prompted with the license agreement. Click the **I Agree** button, and then click **Next** in the Choose Components window shown in Figure 11-13.

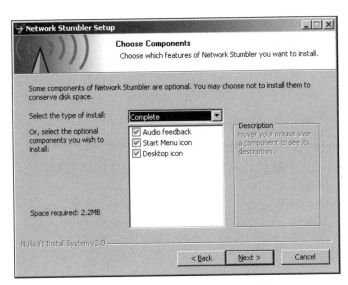

Figure 11-13   Selecting NetStumbler components

6. When prompted to choose the install location, click **Install** to accept the default location and install Network Stumbler.

7. Click **Close** when the Network Stumbler Setup Installation Complete window opens.

8. To run the program, click **Start**, point to **All Programs**, and click **Network Stumbler**. If you have a wireless adapter card that's compatible with the software, you see a window similar to Figure 11-14.

9. If you can view any SSIDs, click to expand **Channels**, **SSIDs**, and **Filters**. Figure 11-15 shows how Network Stumbler separates SSIDs by channel.

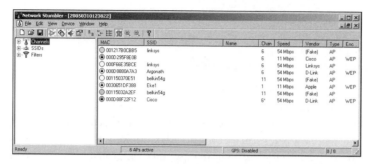

Figure 11-14 The Network Stumbler main window

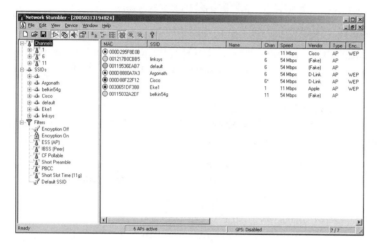

Figure 11-15 Viewing SSIDs, channels, and filters in Network Stumbler

10. Click **File**, **Exit** from the menu, and click **No** when prompted to save changes.

11. Close any open windows, and shut down your system.

Kismet

Another common product for conducting wardriving attacks is Kismet (*www.kismetwireless.net*), written by Mike Kershaw. This product is free and runs on Linux, BSD, Mac OS X, and even Linux PDAs. The software is advertised as being more than just a wireless network detector. Kismet's documentation states that Kismet is also a sniffer and an intrusion detection system (IDS, covered in detail in Chapter 13). Kismet can sniff 802.11b, 802.11a, and 802.11g traffic and offers the following features:

- Ethereal- and Tcpdump-compatible data logging
- AirSnort compatible (covered later in the "Tools of the Trade" section)
- Network IP range detection
- Hidden network SSID detection
- Graphical mapping of networks
- Client-server architecture (similar to Nessus) that allows multiple clients to view a single Kismet server at the same time
- Manufacturer and model identification of APs and clients
- Detection of known default access point configurations
- XML output
- Supports 20 card types

Kismet can be used to conduct wardriving, but can also be used to detect rogue APs placed on a company's network. If you require global positioning system (GPS) support, you need to download additional software from Web sites that furnish the GPS daemon (GPSD). When Kismet is configured to use the GPSD, the output displays coordinates that pinpoint the location of the AP being scanned.

UNDERSTANDING WIRELESS HACKING

Hacking a wireless network is not much different from hacking a wired LAN. Many of the port-scanning and enumeration tools you've learned about can be applied to wireless networks. The following sections describe some additional tools that attackers use and that you can use in conducting a security test.

Tools of the Trade

A wireless hacker usually has a laptop computer, a wireless NIC, an antenna, sniffers (Tcpdump, Ethereal), tools such as NetStumbler or Kismet, and lots of patience. After using NetStumbler or Kismet to determine the network name, SSID, MAC address of the AP, channel used, signal strength, and whether WEP is enabled, a security tester is ready to continue his or her test. Wireless routers that perform DHCP functions can pose a big security risk. If a wireless computer is automatically issued an IP address number, subnet mask, and DNS information, a hacker can use all the skills learned in hacking wired networks on the wireless network. If DHCP is not used, the hacker simply relies on Ethereal to sniff packets passing through the wireless network to gather this IP configuration information. (As a security professional, you should recommend that DHCP be disabled and that IP addresses are statically assigned to wireless stations.) He or she can then configure the wireless NIC with the correct IP information. But what does a hacker or security tester do if WEP is enabled on the AP being tested? Several tools address this issue. AirSnort and WEPCrack, covered in the following sections, are what prompted organizations to replace WEP with the more secure WPA as their authentication method. However, many companies are still using 802.11b with WEP enabled, and many more are using 802.11b with WEP disabled.

AirSnort

As a security professional, your job is to protect a network so that it's difficult for attackers to break in. AirSnort (created by Jeremy Bruestle and Blake Hegerle and available at *http://sourceforge.net/projects/airsnort/*) is the tool most hackers wanting to access WEP-enabled WLANs use. Bruestle and Hegerle set out to prove that WEP encryption was faulty and easy to crack, and AirSnort woke up nonbelievers who thought WEP was enough protection for a WLAN.

AirSnort has some limitations. For example, you can't run it on a Microsoft OS; AirSnort runs only on Linux and requires specific drivers. In addition, only the following NICs function with AirSnort as of this writing:

- Addtron AWP-100
- Bromax Freeport
- Compaq WL100
- D-Link DWL-650
- GemTex (Taiwan) WL-211
- Linksys WPC11
- Samsung SWL2000-N
- SMC 2632W
- Z-Com x1300
- Zoom Telephonics ZoomAir 4100
- LeArtery Solutions SyncbyAir LN101

- Cisco Aironet 340

- Cisco Aironet 350

- Lucent Orinoco Silver

- USR 2410

WEPCrack

WEPCrack, released about a week before AirSnort, is another open-source tool used to crack WEP encryption. It also works on *NIX systems and can be downloaded free at *http://wepcrack.sourceforge.net/*. WEPCrack uses Perl scripts to carry out attacks on wireless systems. Future versions are expected to include features for attackers to conduct brute-force attacks. (See Chapter 12 for more on brute force attacks.)

Countermeasures for Wireless Attacks

Protecting a wireless LAN is a challenge for security professionals because of the inherent design flaws of wireless technology and because, to some extent, engineers are attempting to place a band-aid over a hemorrhaging system. Some of the countermeasure techniques discussed in this section, such as using certificates on all wireless devices, are time consuming and costly. If you approach securing a wireless LAN as you would a wired LAN, you'll have a better chance of protecting corporate data and network resources. Would you allow users to have access to network resources simply because they plugged their NICs into the company's switch or hub? Of course not. Then why would you allow users to have access to a wireless LAN simply because they have wireless NICs and know the company's SSID?

If a company must use wireless technology, your job is to make it as secure as possible. Be sure wireless users are authenticated before being able to access any network resources. Here are some additional guidelines to help secure a wireless LAN:

- Consider using anti-wardriving software to make it more difficult for attackers to discover your wireless LAN. In Chapter 13, you learn about honeypots, which are hosts or networks available to the public for the purpose of enticing hackers to attack them instead of a company's real network. IT personnel can study how an attack is made on the honeypot, which can be useful in securing the company's actual network. To make it more difficult for wardrivers to discover your WLAN, you can use Fakeap, software that creates fake APs. This keeps wardrivers so busy trying to connect to nonexistent wireless networks that they won't have time to discover your legitimate AP. Another software package that does this is Black Alchemy Fake AP. It creates thousands of fake APs so that wardrivers have difficulty finding the company's actual AP. The product has been fully tested on Linux 7.3 and can be downloaded free from *www.blackalchemy.to/project/fakeap/*.

- There are measures for preventing radio waves from leaving or entering a building so that wireless technology can be used only by people located in the facility. One is using a certain type of paint on the walls, but this method isn't foolproof because some radio waves can leak out if the paint isn't applied properly.

- Allow only predetermined MAC addresses and IP addresses to have access to the wireless LAN. Unfortunately, some exploits enable attackers to spoof these addresses, but this measure makes exploits more difficult for typical attackers.

- Consider using an authentication server instead of relying on a wireless device to authenticate users. A RADIUS server that can refer all users to a server running Windows Server 2003 with Active Directory can be used to authenticate wireless users attempting to access network resources. This method can also prevent an intruder from sending or receiving HTTP, DHCP, SMTP, or any network packets over the network before being authenticated.

- Consider using EAP, which allows different protocols to be used that enhance security. For example, EAP enables using certificates for authentication, or wireless vendors can implement a password-based authentication using the EAP standard. EAP offers more options for increasing security.

- Consider placing the AP in the demilitarized zone (DMZ), covered in Chapter 13, and using a firewall in front of the company's internal network that filters out all traffic from unauthorized IP addresses.

- If you use WEP, consider using 104-bit encryption rather than 40-bit encryption. If possible, replace WEP with WPA for better security. Remember, WEP encryption has been cracked.

- Assign static IP addresses to wireless clients instead of using DHCP.

- Change the default SSID and disable SSID broadcasting, if possible. If you cannot disable broadcasting of the SSID, rename the default SSID to make it more difficult for intruders to determine the router's manufacturer. For example, leaving the default SSID of Netgear makes it easy for an attacker to determine what router is being used. Changing its SSID to "Cisco" might dupe an attacker into believing you are using a Cisco product.

These methods aren't foolproof. In fact, by the time you read this book, there will undoubtedly be ways to crack WPA or any other security method for protecting a wireless LAN. That's what makes the security field dynamic. There are no easy fixes. And if there were, those fixes wouldn't last long, unfortunately.

To determine whether you have the skills necessary to secure a wireless LAN, see if you can pass this test:

1. Fill a pitcher with water.

2. Pour all the water into a colander or sieve.

3. Attempt to prevent the water from leaking out of the small holes.

If you were able to stop the water from passing through all the holes, you would be able to secure a wireless LAN—or any network, for that matter. Think of the water as an attacker finding a vulnerability or hole in your system security. Plugging up every hole is impossible, but that doesn't mean you don't keep trying to make it as difficult as possible for attackers to discover those holes.

CHAPTER SUMMARY

- IEEE's main purpose is to create standards for LANs and WANs. IEEE consists of engineers, scientists, and students from all over the world. IEEE, the largest technical society, is most well known for its work in developing the IEEE 802 standards for local and wide area networking.

- 802.11 is the IEEE standard for wireless networking. It incorporates many additional standards that address security and authentication.

- Wireless technology defines how and at what frequency data travels over carrier sound waves.

- The three basic components of a wireless network are access points (APs), which are receivers that connect to an Ethernet cable; wireless network interface cards (WNICs), which convert radio waves into digital signals that computers can understand; and Ethernet cables, the media used to connect components to the network.

- A service set identifier (SSID) is assigned to an AP and represents the wireless segment of a network for which the AP is responsible.

- Data must be modulated over carrier signals. DSSS, FHSS, and OFDM are the most common modulations for wireless networks.

- Wardriving and warflying involve driving in a car or flying in a plane with a laptop computer, a wireless NIC, an antenna, and software that scans for any available access points.

- WLANs can be attacked with many of the same tools used for hacking wired LANS. For example, a sniffer such as Ethereal can also be used to scan WLANs for logon and password information.

- Some of the methods used to protect a wireless network are disabling SSID broadcasts, renaming default SSIDs, using an authentication server, placing the AP in the DMZ, and using a router to filter any unauthorized MAC and IP addresses from network access.

KEY TERMS

access point (AP) — A transceiver that connects to an Ethernet cable. It bridges the wireless network with the wired network.

basic service set (BSS) — The coverage area of a wireless LAN (WLAN).

certificate — A record that authenticates network entities, such as a server or client.

channel — A frequency range in which data is transmitted.

chipping code — Multiple bits that can be used for recovery of a corrupted packet that travels across a frequency band. Sub-bits are called "chips," and every bit of the original message is represented by multiple bits, called the chipping code.

Extensible Authentication Protocol (EAP) — A framework designed to allow an organization to select an authentication method.

Institute of Electrical and Electronics Engineers (IEEE) — An organization that creates standards for the IT industry.

frequency — The number of sound waves that vibrate in a specified time.

infrared (IR) — An area in the electromagnetic spectrum with a frequency above microwaves; an infrared signal is restricted to a single room or line of sight. IR light can't penetrate walls, ceilings, or floors. This technology is used for most remote controls and PDAs.

modulation — A process that defines how data is placed on a carrier signal.

narrowband — A technology that uses microwave radio band frequencies to transmit data. The most popular uses of this technology are cordless phones and garage door openers.

Protected EAP (PEAP) — An authentication protocol that uses Transport Layer Security (TLS) to authenticate the server to the client, but not the client to the server.

service set identifier (SSID) — The name of a wireless LAN that can be broadcast by an AP.

spread spectrum — In this technology, data is spread across a large-frequency bandwidth instead of traveling across one frequency band.

station (STA) — An addressable unit in a wireless network. A station is defined as a message destination and might not be a fixed location.

supplicant — The client or wireless computer that connects to an AP.

wardriving — The act of driving around an area with a laptop computer that has a WNIC, scanning software, and possibly an antenna to obtain a list of available SSIDs in that area.

Wi-Fi Protected Access (WPA) — A standard that addressed WEP security vulnerabilities in 802.11b with the new 802.11i standard. *See also* Wired Equivalent Privacy (WEP).

Wired Equivalent Privacy (WEP) — An 802.11b standard implemented to encrypt data traversing a wireless network.

wireless LAN (WLAN) — A network that relies on wireless technology (radio waves) to operate.

wireless personal area network (WPAN) — A wireless network for one user only; usually refers to Bluetooth technology.

REVIEW QUESTIONS

1. Which IEEE standard defines authentication and authorization in wireless networks?
   a. 802.11
   b. 802.11a
   c. 802.11b
   d. 802.1X

2. Which EAP method requires that public certificates be installed on both the server and the client?
   a. EAP-TLS
   b. PEAP
   c. EAP-SSL
   d. EAP-CA

3. Which of the following tools can be used to hack a wireless network? (Choose all that apply.)

    a. AirSnort

    b. NetStumbler

    c. Kismet

    d. WEPCrack

4. Name a tool that can help reduce the risk of a wardriver attacking your WLAN.

5. What protocol was added to 802.11i to address WEP's encryption vulnerability?

    a. MIC

    b. TKIP

    c. TTL

    d. EAP-TLS

6. What IEEE standard defines wireless technology?

    a. 802.3

    b. 802.5

    c. 802.11

    d. all 802 standards

7. What information can be obtained by wardriving? (Choose all that apply.)

    a. SSIDs of wireless networks

    b. whether WEP is enabled

    c. whether SSL is enabled

    d. signal strength

8. Disabling SSID broadcasts must be configured on the computer and the AP. True or False?

9. What TKIP enhancement addressed the WEP vulnerability of forging packets?

    a. Extended Initialization Vector (IV) with sequencing rules

    b. per-packet key mixing

    c. rekeying mechanism

    d. Message Integrity Check (MIC)

10. Wi-Fi Protected Access (WPA) was introduced in which IEEE 802 standard?

    a. 802.11a

    b. 802.11b

    c. 802.11i

    d. 802.11

11. Wardriving requires expensive hardware and software. True or False?

12. What is a known weakness of wireless network SSIDs?

    a. broadcast in clear text

    b. difficult to configure

    c. use large amounts of bandwidth

    d. consume excessive amount of computer memory

13. Bluetooth technology is more vulnerable to network attacks than WLANs. True or False?

11

14. Which of the following channels is available in 802.11b when attempting to avoid overlapping? (Choose all that apply.)

    a. 1

    b. 5

    c. 6

    d. 11

15. List three technologies in which wireless LANs can operate.

16. An access point (AP) provides _____ .

    a. access to the BSS

    b. access to the DS

    c. access to a remote station

    d. access to a secure node

17. The IEEE 802.11 standard pertains to the _____ and _____ layers of the OSI model.

18. The operating frequency range of 802.11a is 2.4 GHz. True or False?

19. The supplicant must be authenticated by the _____ before being granted access to a WLAN.

    a. access point (AP)

    b. authenticator

    c. certificate authority (CA)

    d. public key issuer

20. List three tools for conducting wireless security testing.

CASE PROJECTS

CASE PROJECTS

Case 11-1: Determining Vulnerabilities of Wireless Networks

After conducting a security test on the K. J. Williams network, you discover that the company has a wireless router configured to issue IP addresses to connecting stations. NetStumbler indicates that channel 6 is active, the SSID is Linksys, and WEP is not enabled.

Based on the preceding information, write a one-page report listing possible vulnerabilities for the WLAN's current configuration. Your report should include recommendations for increasing wireless security.

CASE PROJECTS

Case 11-2: Maintaining Security on Wireless Systems

Bob Smith from the IT procurement office of K. J. Williams has just purchased a laptop computer. The company has asked you to ensure that privacy and security are maintained on this wireless system.

Based on the preceding information, write a one-page report using the information in the OSSTMM, Section E, Wireless Security (pp. 70 to 84). Your report should list the steps for ensuring the laptop's security.

# CHAPTER 12

CRYPTOGRAPHY

After reading this chapter and completing the exercises, you will be able to:

♦ Describe the history of cryptography

♦ Describe symmetric and asymmetric cryptography algorithms

♦ Explain public key infrastructure (PKI)

♦ Describe possible attacks on cryptosystems

Protecting data as it traverses a network or while it's stored on a computer is one of the most important jobs of a network security professional. Companies as well as private individuals don't want others to be able to view confidential documents and files.

In this chapter, you examine the various cryptography technologies that security professionals use to protect a company's data. You see how information can be converted into an unreadable format and how only those with the correct key or "decoder" can read the message. You also look at various cryptography attacks and some of the tools used to conduct these attacks.

UNDERSTANDING CRYPTOGRAPHY BASICS

Cryptography is the process of converting **plaintext**, which is readable text, into **ciphertext**, which is unreadable or encrypted text. Cryptography can be used on data that people or organizations want to keep private or accessible to only certain users. In other words, cryptography is used to hide information from unauthorized users. Decryption is the process of converting ciphertext back to plaintext (also called cleartext). As a kid, you might have had a decoder ring from a box of cereal that you could use to write a letter to a friend in secret code. If your friend had the same decoder ring, he or she could decode your letter and read it.

History of Cryptography

Cryptography has been around for thousands of years. Some Egyptian hieroglyphics found on ancient monuments were encrypted. The Book of Jeremiah was written using a **cipher**, or key, known as atbash. Basically, the key mapped each letter of the alphabet to a different letter, so only the person who knew the mapping could decipher or decrypt the message. This type of cryptography is called a **substitution cipher**. Julius Caesar developed a similar method of encrypting messages by shifting each letter of the alphabet three positions. For example, A would be encoded as the letter D. Every culture seems to have used some form of hiding or disguising plaintext. *The Kama Sutra*, written by the religious scholar Vatasayna more than 2000 years ago, recommends that men and women learn and practice the art of cryptography, which it defines as "the art of understanding writing in cipher, and the writing of works in a peculiar way."

You can find an excellent timeline of cryptography in *The Codebreakers*, written by David Kahn (Macmillan, 1967, ISBN: 0684831309).

NOTE

As long as people attempt to create encryption algorithms to protect data, others will endeavor to break those encryption algorithms. This study is called **cryptanalysis**. It's taught in universities and by government organizations, but hackers also find the challenge of breaking an encryption algorithm intriguing and continue to push the envelope for developers of encryption algorithms. When a new encryption algorithm is developed, cryptanalysis is performed on it to ensure that breaking the code is impossible or would take so much time and so many resources to break that it would be impractical for hackers to attempt. That is, if breaking the secrecy of an encryption algorithm requires the processing power of a super mainframe computer and 200 years of processing time, the algorithm could be considered successful.

The War Machines

The most famous encryption device was the Enigma machine developed by Arthur Scherbius and used by the Germans during World War II. Every book on the subject of cryptography has a chapter devoted to this encryption device. How did it work? The operator typed a letter that he or she wanted encrypted, and the machine would display the substitution character for the letter entered. For example, if the operator entered the letter "A," the Enigma machine substituted the letter "N." The operator then wrote down this substitution letter and turned a rotor or switch. He or she then entered the next letter in the machine, again writing down the substitution letter Enigma provided. When the message was completely encrypted, it was transmitted over the airwaves. Of course, the message could be decrypted only by the Enigma machine at the other end, which knew in what positions to shift the rotors. The code was broken first by a group of Polish cryptographers, and then by the British and Americans. The machine for breaking the code was called the "Bombe." For a picture of both machines, see the Smithsonian photograph taken by Laurie Minor-Penland at *http://photo2.si.edu/infoage/infoage.html*.

Another notable war machine, called the Purple Machine, was developed and used by the Japanese during World War II. This machine used techniques discovered by Herbert O. Yardley. The code was broken by William Frederick Friedman, a cryptanalyst for the U.S. government and known as the "Father of U.S. Cryptanalysis." The FBI employed both Mr. Friedman and his wife to assist in decrypting messages sent by bootleggers during the 1930s. These encryption codes proved to be more difficult and complex than those used during wartime. Today, drug cartels have some of the most skilled cryptologists working to create unbreakable encryption codes for their operations, making it difficult for law enforcement agencies to decipher these coded messages.

The main purpose of cryptography is to hide something from unauthorized personnel. Today, there are other methods of hiding data without using encryption. One method is called **steganography**, which is a form of hiding data in plain view in pictures, graphics, or text. For example, a picture of a man standing in front of the White House might have a hidden message embedded that gives a spy information about troop movements. In 1623, Sir Francis Bacon used a similar form of steganography by hiding bits of information in variations of the typeface used in books.

Activity 12-1: Creating a Cipher Key

Time Required: 30 minutes

Objective: Learn how to create a cipher key and encrypt a message.

Description: To better understand cryptography, break into groups of four students. Each group should create a short message no longer than five words in plaintext. Your group encrypts the message using a substitution cipher, and then the other groups (the decrypters) try to decode the message. Each group should create one encrypted message and decrypt each message created by the other groups.

1. The encrypting group writes a five-word message on a blank sheet of paper.

2. Create a substitution cipher to encrypt the message. For example, each character can be shifted four characters over so that, for example, the letter A becomes the letter D.

3. Write down the ciphertext message you created with your group's cipher key.

4. When instructed to do so, hand your ciphertext messages to the other groups to decrypt.

5. When a group decrypts the message, the group leader should shout "Finished!" so that the instructor can see which group completed the task the fastest.

6. After all groups have had a chance to try decrypting messages, discuss the cipher keys each group created.

Security Bytes

Did you know that Thomas Jefferson invented a wheel cipher in the 18th century that the Navy redeveloped and used during World War II and named Strip Cipher, M-138-A? The more things change, the more they remain the same.

UNDERSTANDING SYMMETRIC AND ASYMMETRIC ALGORITHMS

Modern cryptography uses algorithms to encrypt data, banking transactions, online Web transactions, wireless communications (WEP and WPA), and so on. An **algorithm** is a mathematical function or program that works with a key, similar to the decoder ring discussed earlier. The strength of the algorithm and the secrecy of the key determine how secure the encrypted data is. In most cases, the algorithm is not a secret but is known to the public. What *is* secret is the key. A **key** is a sequence of random bits generated from a range of allowable values called a **keyspace**, which is contained in the algorithm. The larger the keyspace, the more random sequenced keys that can be created. The more random keys that can be created, the more difficult it is for hackers to guess the key being used to encrypt the data. Of course, using only eight random keys (as shown in Figure 12-1) would be too easy to crack and is used as an example only.

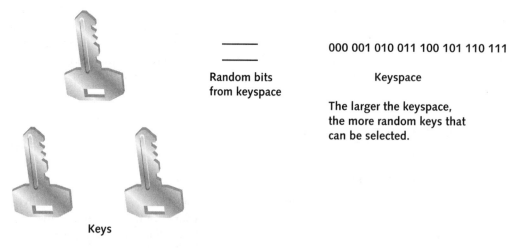

Key length of 3 bits would allow for 2^3 or 8 different random keys to be used.

Random bits from keyspace

000 001 010 011 100 101 110 111

Keyspace

The larger the keyspace, the more random keys that can be selected.

Keys

Figure 12-1   Selecting random keys from a keyspace

Most attempts to break a cryptosystem are related to guessing the key. No matter how strong the algorithm is or how large the keyspace is, if the key is not protected, an attacker can decrypt the message. That is, if a user shares his key with someone, all bets are off!

Table 12-1 gives you a quick look at the three types of algorithms.

Table 12-1   Symmetric, asymmetric, and hashing algorithms

Type of Algorithm	Description
Symmetric	Uses a single key to encrypt and decrypt data. Both the sender and receiver must agree on the key before data is transmitted. Symmetric algorithms support confidentiality, but not authentication and nonrepudiation (covered later in "Asymmetric Cryptography Algorithms"). However, they are faster than asymmetric algorithms.
Asymmetric	Uses two keys, one to encrypt and one to decrypt data. Asymmetric algorithms support authentication and nonrepudiation but are slower than symmetric algorithms. Asymmetric algorithms are also known as public key cryptography.
Hashing	A modern algorithm used for verification. Hashing takes a variable-length input and converts it to a fixed-length output string called a hash value.

Having the skills of a cryptologist isn't necessary for security testers, but understanding basic cryptology terms is helpful. For example, if you read the description "Blowfish is a block cipher having a key size of up to 448 bits," you want to know enough to understand what that means. The following sections examine these algorithm types in more detail and explain some basic terms.

Symmetric Cryptography Algorithms

Cryptosystems using **symmetric algorithms** have one key that encrypts and decrypts data. If a user wants to send a message to a colleague, he or she encrypts the message with the secret key and the colleague, who must have a copy of that same key, decrypts the message. If that same user wants to encrypt a different message and send it to a different colleague, a different secret key must be maintained. If hundreds of colleagues are placed in the equation, keeping track of which secret key to use becomes a big problem. To calculate the number of keys needed to support a symmetric system, you use the formula n(n-1)/2. For example, if five users need to use secret keys to transmit data, you need 5(5-1)/2 keys, or 10 keys.

Another problem associated with the secret keys is how to send the secret key to the colleague you want to decrypt your message. E-mailing it can be dangerous because the e-mail message can be intercepted. You can try putting the secret key on a floppy disk or CD-R, but either medium can be misplaced or stolen.

Because two users share the same key in symmetric algorithms, there's no way to know which user sent the message. In other words, symmetric algorithms don't support authenticity and nonrepudiation (covered in more detail in the "Asymmetric Cryptography Algorithms" section).

As you can see, there are some problems associated with symmetric algorithms, but as Table 12-1 states, symmetric algorithms are fast. They are perfect mechanisms for encrypting large blocks of data quickly and are difficult to break if a large key size is used. The advantages and disadvantages of symmetric algorithms are as follows:

Advantages:

- Much faster than asymmetric algorithms

- Difficult to break if a large key size is used

- Only one key needed to encrypt and decrypt data

Disadvantages:

- Requires each pair of users to have a unique secret key, making key management a challenge

- Difficult to deliver keys without risk of theft

- Does not provide authenticity or nonrepudiation for users

Two types of symmetric algorithms are used currently: stream ciphers and block ciphers. **Stream ciphers** operate on plaintext one bit at a time. Messages are treated as a stream of bits, and the stream cipher performs mathematical functions on each bit, which makes stream ciphers great candidates for hardware or chip-level encryption devices. **Block ciphers** operate on blocks of plaintext. The blocks of bits are used as input to mathematical functions that perform substitution and transposition of the bits, making it difficult for someone to reverse-engineer or attempt to figure out what mathematical functions were applied to the blocks of bits.

In the following sections, you take a look at some of the symmetric systems that have become standards in the industry: Data Encryption Standard (DES) and Advanced Encryption Standard (AES). Regardless of the standard, however, symmetric algorithms rely on one and the same key to encrypt and decrypt data.

ACTIVITY

Activity 12-2: Hacking the Encryption Method Used to Encrypt DVDs

Time Required: 20 minutes

Objective: Learn how to use the Internet to obtain information on encryption and decryption methodologies.

Description: In this activity, you use the Internet to research the encryption method used for DVDs.

1. From your Windows XP computer, start a Web browser, open a search engine of your choice, and type **DeCSS** for the search keyword. How does DeCSS relate to DVD encryption?

2. On the search page, type **Why the DVD Hack was a Cinch** as the search phrase. It should take you to an article at *www.wired.com* by Andy Patrizio. Read the two-page article. What does CSS stand for?

3. Open several other links related to CSS encryption. Were any lawsuits brought against the DeCSS program? If yes, briefly describe them.

4. Leave your system running for the next activity.

Data Encryption Standard (DES)

A discussion of symmetric algorithms could not take place without a mention of the **Data Encryption Standard (DES)**. The National Institute of Standards and Technology (NIST) wanted a means of protecting sensitive but unclassified data, so in the early 1970s, it invited vendors to submit data encryption algorithms. The best algorithm would become the standard encryption method for government and private-sector companies. IBM had already created a 128-bit algorithm called Lucifer. NIST accepted it as the standard encryption algorithm; however, the National Security Agency (NSA) wanted to make some modifications to it before allowing it to be used. The NSA decided to reduce the key size from 128 bits to 64 bits and named it **Data Encryption Algorithm (DEA)**. Not the most creative name, but the NSA probably thought the name Lucifer didn't have an official government ring to it. The reason that the NSA reduced the algorithm's keyspace is not known. What is known is that 128-bit encryption is far more difficult to crack than 64-bit encryption.

 Even though DES uses 64-bit encryption, only 56 bits are effectively being used. Eight of the 64 bits are used for parity.

NOTE

Like most things, time took its toll on DES. In 1988, NSA thought the standard, because of its longevity, was at risk of being broken. Any system, no matter how secure, is vulnerable when hackers have years to look for holes. NSA proved to be correct in its assumption. The increasing processor power of computers soon made it possible for the encryption to be broken. In fact, in 1998 a computer system was designed that was able to break the encryption key in only three days. There are also examples of hackers combining the CPU power of tens of thousands of computer systems (without the system owners' knowledge) over the Internet to crack complex encryption algorithms. Many cryptologists are too quick to make statements that the encryption algorithm they use would take several Cray mainframe computers 200 years to figure out a secret key, when only a couple of years of improvements in processor speed technology proves it can be done with a powerful laptop and access to the Internet.

Triple DES (3DES)

A new standard needed to be put into place because DES was no longer the solution. **Triple Data Encryption Standard (3DES)** served as a quick fix to the vulnerabilities of DES. To make it more difficult for attackers to crack the encryption code, it performed a complex computation on the data that made it 2^{56} times stronger than DES. This improvement did have a price on performance. 3DES takes longer to encrypt and decrypt data than its predecessor, but that's a small price to pay for better security.

Advanced Encryption Standard (AES)

After DES was in service for many years, NIST decided that a new standard was in order: **Advanced Encryption Standard (AES)**. In 1997, NIST again put out a request to the public for a new encryption standard. The request required all submittals for a symmetric block cipher be capable of supporting 128-, 192-, and 256-bit keys. There were five finalists, but the winning standard was Rijndael, developed by Joan Daemon and Vincent Rijmen. To quote NIST, "When considered together, Rijndael's combination of security, performance, efficiency, implementability, and flexibility make it an appropriate selection for AES." The other four finalists were MARS, RC6, Serpent, and Twofish. Visit *http://csrc.nist.gov* for more details.

International Data Encryption Algorithm (IDEA)

International Data Encryption Algorithm (IDEA) is a block cipher that operates on 64-bit blocks of plaintext. It uses a 128-bit key and is used in PGP encryption software (covered in the "Asymmetric Cryptography Algorithms" section). IDEA was developed by Xuejia Lai and James Massey to work more efficiently in computers used at home and in businesses. IDEA is free for noncommercial use, but a license agreement must be purchased for commercial use. It was developed in Zurich, Switzerland and is patented in the United States and most European countries.

Blowfish

Blowfish is a block cipher that also operates on 64-bit blocks of plaintext. However, the key length for this algorithm can be as large as 448 bits. Blowfish was developed by Bruce Schneier, a leading cryptologist. He is the author of the book *Applied Cryptography, Second Edition* (John Wiley & Sons, 1996, ISBN: 0471117099), which is highly recommended for those wanting to learn more about the algorithm and to view its C language source code.

RC5

RC5 is another block cipher that can operate on different block sizes: 32, 64, and 128. The 32-bit key size is used only for experimentation and evaluation purposes. The key size can reach 2048 bits. The algorithm was created by Ronald L. Rivest in 1994 for RSA Data Security (*www.rsasecurity.com*).

Asymmetric Cryptography Algorithms

Recall that in symmetric algorithms, a single key is used for both encrypting and decrypting data. **Asymmetric algorithms** use two keys that are mathematically related, so data encrypted with one key can be decrypted only with the other key. Another name for asymmetric key cryptography is **public key cryptography**, and these terms are often used interchangeably. A **public key** is the key that can be known by the public; in many cases, public keys can be downloaded from Web sites for the public to use. The **private key** is the secret key known only by the key owner and should never be shared. Even if people can discover the public key used to encrypt a message, they won't be able to figure out the key owner's private key. So with asymmetric cryptosystems, a public key being intercepted in transmission isn't a concern.

Before looking at some of the more popular asymmetric algorithms, take a look at a simple example of public key cryptography. There are different ways to encrypt a message with asymmetric algorithms, depending on whether the goal is to ensure that the message is indeed from the person claiming to have sent it (authenticity) and to provide nonrepudiation of the sent message. **Authenticity** refers to validating the sender of a message, assuring the receiver that the message was indeed sent by the sender identified in the message header. **Nonrepudiation** means that a user can't deny he or she sent a message to a recipient, and the receiver of a message can't deny ever receiving the message. These two functions aren't supported in symmetric algorithms.

If User A encrypts a message with her private key and sends the message to User B, User B can decrypt the message with User A's public key. So User A is able to encrypt a message with her private key and another person can use User A's public key to decrypt the message. Remember, a user's private and public keys are mathematically joined. That is, a public key can only decrypt a message that has been encrypted with the corresponding private key.

If confidentiality is a major concern for User A, the one sending a message, she encrypts the message using the public key of the person to whom she's sending the message. That way, only the receiver of the message can decrypt the message with his private key. If User A wants to assure User B that she is indeed the person sending the message (authentication), she can encrypt the message with her private key. After all, she is the only person who possesses her private key.

Asymmetric algorithms are more scalable than symmetric systems. However, they are slower than symmetric algorithms.

RSA

RSA was developed by three MIT professors: Ronald L. Rivest, Adi Shamir, and Leonard M. Adleman. It's one of the most popular asymmetric algorithms used today, even though it was developed in 1977. The authors offered their findings to anyone who sent them a self-addressed envelope. The NSA took a jaundiced view to this approach and suggested the professors cease and desist. But when the NSA was questioned about the legality of its request, it did not respond and the algorithm was published in 1978.

12

Many Web browsers that use the Secure Sockets Layer (SSL) protocol use the RSA algorithm. Without having to get into too much math, the algorithm is based on the difficulty of factoring large numbers. It is important to understand that RSA uses something called a one-way function to generate a key. A one-way function is a mathematical formula that is easy to compute in one direction but difficult or nearly impossible to compute in the opposite direction. For example, it is easier to multiply two large prime numbers and get the product of the two numbers, but it is more difficult to determine what numbers were used initially in the calculation when supplied with only the product. A simple analogy would be making a smoothie. It is fairly simple to blend a banana, strawberries, and ice cubes in a blender, but if after blending them you had to reconstruct the banana, strawberries, and ice cubes into their original state, you might find the task impossible.

Diffie-Hellman

This algorithm, developed by Whitfield Diffie and Martin Hellman, originators of the public and private key concept, does not provide encryption but is used for key exchange. Key management is an important component of securing data. If a key is transmitted and intercepted, the network is vulnerable to attack. The Diffie-Hellman algorithm is used for secure key distribution. With this methodology, users can send secret keys electronically without the fear of interception.

Elliptic Curve Cryptosystems (ECC)

ECC is used for encryption as well as digital signatures and key distribution. It is an efficient algorithm requiring few resources (memory, disk space, bandwidth, and so on), so it's a perfect candidate for wireless devices and cellular telephones.

Elgamal

Elgamal is another public key algorithm that can be used to encrypt data as well as create a digital signature and exchange secret keys. Written by Taher Elgamal in 1985, the algorithm uses discrete logarithm problems that are mathematically complex to solve. Solving a discrete logarithm problem can take many years and require CPU-intensive operations.

Digital Signatures

Asymmetric algorithms have a useful feature that enables a public key to decrypt a message that was encrypted using a private key, or vice versa. The only way a public key can decrypt a message that has been encrypted with a private key is when that message was encrypted by the corresponding private key's holder. Figure 12-2 shows how a message and hash value encrypted with a private key ensures that the sender cannot deny sending the message (nonrepudiation) and the receiver is also assured that the message did indeed come from the sender. This type of encryption is called a **digital signature**.

Digital Signature Standard (DSS)

In 1991, NIST established a standard called Digital Signature Standard (DSS) to ensure that digital signatures rather than written signatures could be verified. The federal government required that RSA and Digital Signature Algorithm (DSA) be used for all digital signatures, and that a hashing algorithm be used to ensure the integrity of the message. NIST required that the **Secure Hash Algorithm (SHA)** be used, which is covered in "Understanding Hash Algorithms" later in this chapter. Basically, a digital signature can be created using only a user's private key, and the user's signature could be verified by anyone using that same user's public key.

Pretty Good Privacy (PGP)

Pretty Good Privacy (PGP) was developed by Phil Zimmerman as a free e-mail encryption program that allowed average users to encrypt e-mail messages. Sounds harmless, but Zimmerman was almost arrested for his innovation. The Justice Department initiated an investigation of Mr. Zimmerman that could have made it a crime for the PGP program to be made available to the public. Back in the mid-1990s, any kind of "unbreakable" encryption was seen as a weapon and compared to selling arms to the enemy.

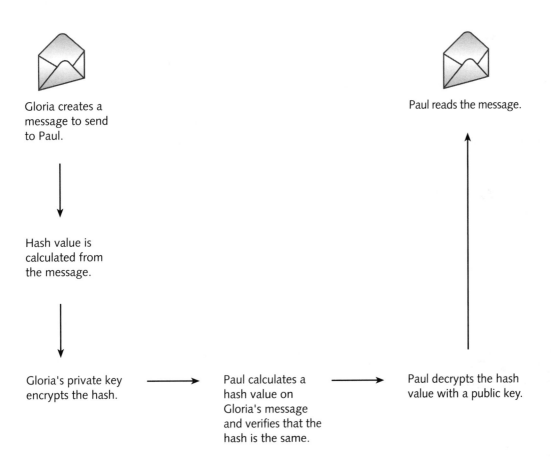

Figure 12-2 Using a digital signature

PGP is a free public key encryption program. It uses certificates similar to those in public key infrastructure (PKI), but because a centralized certification authority (CA) is not used (remember, it's free), verification of a CA is not as efficient as PKI. PGP uses the IDEA, RSA, DSA, Message Digest 5 (MD5), and SHA-1 algorithms for providing encryption, authentication, message integrity, and key management. PGP is a great way to learn how a public key encryption algorithm might be used without having to spend a lot of money. You can also purchase a commercial copy of the software if you need technical support.

Activity 12-3: Using Hotmail and PGP (Optional)

Time Required: 60 minutes

Objective: Learn how to use PGP with a Hotmail account.

Description: Sending e-mail messages that contain private information can be a big risk. In fact, a good rule to follow is to pretend that any e-mail message you send will be read live on CNN the following morning. That should keep you from revealing your innermost thoughts in an e-mail message. A "pretty good" way of preventing someone from sniffing an e-mail message you sent is to encrypt the message with PGP. In this activity, you install Hotmail and PGP and configure PGP to sign and encrypt all your e-mail messages.

1. Start your Web browser, type the URL **www.hotmail.com**, and press **Enter**. Click the **Sign Up** link, and then click the **Get It FREE** button.

2. Enter the registration information, and click the **I Agree** button to accept the license agreement. Click **Continue** when prompted that registration is complete.

3. If you're shown a list of newsletters, scroll to the bottom and click the **Continue** button.

4. On the MSN Hotmail home page, click the **Sign Out .net** button.

5. Start Outlook Express. Click **Tools**, **Accounts** from the menu.

6. Click the **Mail** tab. Click the **Add** button, and then click **Mail**.

7. Enter your name, and click **Next**. Enter your new e-mail address, and click **Next**.

8. Click **HTTP server**, click to select **Hotmail** as your HTTP mail service provider, and then click **Next**.

9. Verify that your Hotmail account name is listed correctly, and then enter your password. Also, verify that the Log on using Secure Password Authentication (SPA) check box is selected. Your screen should be similar to Figure 12-3. Click **Next**.

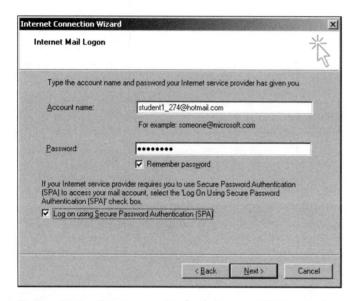

Figure 12-3   Creating an Outlook Express HTTP e-mail account

10. In the Congratulations window, click **Finish**.

Because free e-mail accounts might be discontinued or configuration requirements can change at any time, downloading a product different from the one covered in this activity might be necessary. Another free e-mail program you can try is Google Mail (Gmail), which at the time of this writing was offered as a preview release. To configure Gmail with Outlook Express, for example, you simply use a wizard that does all the work for you. Figure 12-4 shows selecting the Enable POP for all e-mail option. Then you would click the Configuration instructions link.

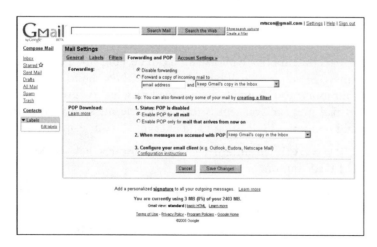

Figure 12-4   Using Gmail as a POP client

Next, the window shown in Figure 12-5 is displayed, where you could select Outlook Express from the Mail Clients list.

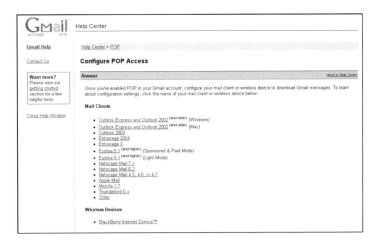

Figure 12-5 Selecting Outlook Express for Gmail access

In the next window that's displayed (see Figure 12-6), you can click the Run the auto-configuration tool link and have Outlook Express configured to use Gmail automatically.

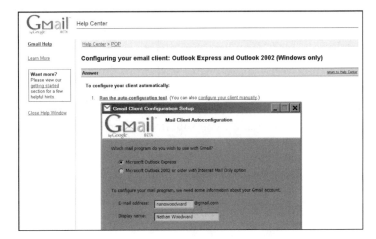

Figure 12-6 Running Gmail's auto-configuration tool

To find out more about this product, visit *http://mail.google.com*. If Gmail is not available, visit *www.hotpop.com*, which claims that HotPOP won't be discontinued. If it is, however, you should be able to do some detective work and find a free POP e-mail provider easily. Remember that the objective of this activity is to see how PGP can be used to secure your e-mail, not to learn how to install free e-mail software.

To download and install PGP, follow these steps:

1. From your Web browser, type the URL **www.pgpi.org/download**, press **Enter**, and download the version of PGP for Windows XP. You might have to click the **pgp @** link first, and then the **Microsoft Windows XP** link.

2. On the Freeware versions for Windows XP Web page, click the **PGP 8.0.2** link. You're then prompted to download a German or English version of PGP. Choose the English version (unless you're reading this book in German). (*Note:* The version number and installation instructions for downloading any program might change. Be sure to follow the vendor's instructions because these steps might be outdated by the time this book is published.)

3. If you're prompted to download a beta version, scroll down the screen and click the link that takes you to the PGP freeware page.

4. Accept the license agreement, and then click the **PGP Desktop 9 for Windows** button.

5. Fill out the contact information in the PGP Desktop Trial Download window, and then click the **Email My Trial License Key** button at the bottom. If you're prompted with a Security Alert, click **Yes**.

6. A Download window displays a message that an e-mail will be sent to you describing the next steps to follow. You need to check the e-mail account you listed in the previous steps.

7. Check your e-mail account and click the hyperlink in the e-mail to download the program. A PDF file is also included in the e-mail containing license numbers needed to install the product.

8. On the PGP Customer Information page, click the **Download** link, and click **Save** when prompted to save or open the file. (You can save the file to the desktop or anywhere you choose. The file might take several minutes to download.)

9. Click **Close** when prompted by the Download Complete dialog box.

10. When instructed to do so, locate the downloaded compressed folder, double-click the icon, and click **Folder Tasks**, **Extract all files**. Accept the default location for extracting the files, and then click **Finish**.

11. Double-click the **PGPDesktop902_Inner.exe** icon to begin installation. If prompted with an Open File - Security Warning dialog box, click **Run**.

12. In the PGP Desktop dialog box, select your language.

13. After reading the license agreement, click **I accept the license agreement**, and then click **Next**.

14. Read the Readme Information to learn about the new features of PGP, and then click **Next** to begin the installation process. After the installation, click **Yes** when prompted to restart your system.

15. After your system starts, you're asked whether you want to enable PGP from this account. If directed to do so by your instructor, click **Next**.

16. In the PGP Setup Assistant dialog box, enter your name, organization, and e-mail address, and then click **Next**. This information must match the information you supplied earlier.

17. When prompted to enter your license number, enter the number from the e-mail sent to you earlier, click **Next**, and follow the instructions to finish the installation.

To create PGP keys, follow these steps:

1. Start Outlook Express. Click **Tools**, **PGP**, **Launch PGPkeys** from the menu.

2. Click **Keys**, **New Key** from the menu.

3. Click **Next** to start the PGP Key Generation Wizard.

4. Enter your full name and e-mail address, and then click **Next**.

5. Enter a passphrase (the longer, the better), and then click **Next** to generate the key.

6. Click **Next**, and then click **Finish**.

To configure PGP, use the following steps:

1. Start Outlook Express. Click **Tools**, **PGP**, **Options** from the menu.

2. Click the **E-mail** tab.

3. Click to select the **Encrypt new messages by default** and **Sign new messages by default** check boxes, and then click **OK**.

4. Send a message by clicking the **Send Mail** button. Note that the Encrypt Message (PGP) and Sign Message (PGP) check boxes are selected by default.

5. Enter your partner's e-mail address in the Address text box.

6. Enter **Test** for the subject and enter **PGP** in the body of the message.

7. Click the **Send Message** button. When you're prompted for your passphrase, enter it and note that the Hide Typing check box is selected to prevent anyone from reading the text you enter. Click **OK** to send the message.

8. Close all windows, but leave Windows XP running for the next activity.

As you can see, PGP is a great way of sending e-mail with a layer of security added. PGP is not the only technology used to send secure e-mail. The following sections briefly cover two more secure e-mail standards: S/MIME and PEM.

Secure Multipurpose Internet Mail Extension (S/MIME)

S/MIME is another public key encryption standard used to encrypt and digitally sign e-mail. S/MIME can also encrypt e-mail messages containing attachments and use PKI certificates for authentication. See RFC 2311 for details on S/MIME version 2 and RFC 2633 for information on S/MIME version 3.

Privacy-Enhanced Mail (PEM)

PEM is an Internet standard that is compatible with both symmetric and asymmetric methods of encryption. PEM can use the X.509 certificate standards and encrypt messages with DES (a symmetric encryption algorithm). It is not used as much today, but newer implementations of the standard might resurface under a different name: MIME Object Security Services (MOSS). See RFC 1848 for more details. Many of the PEM features are included with MOSS.

12

Hashing Algorithms

Several hashing algorithms are in use today. Table 12-2 summarizes some of the most common. A **hashing algorithm** is a function that takes a variable-length string or message and produces a fixed-length value called a **message digest**. If a message stating "How are you?" is sent to a user, for example, a specific hash value is calculated for this message. In a sense, a hash value is equivalent to a fingerprint of the message in that it's unique. If the message is changed later to "Who are you?" the hash value changes, too, so that the recipient knows the original message changed during transmission. If two different messages produce the same hash value, it results in a collision. Therefore, a good hashing algorithm is one that's collision free.

One of the most popular hashing algorithms used to be SHA-1. As of the writing of this book, SHA-1 has been broken. A team of researchers from Shandong University in eastern China circulated a draft of a paper showing that a key hash function used in state-of-the-art encryption could be less resistant to an attack by hackers than had been thought. In fact, as of March 15, 2005, the NIST recommends not using SHA applications. Federal agencies have been instructed to remove SHA-1 from all existing applications. That SHA-1 is no longer safe emphasizes that security professionals must be vigilant in keeping aware of changes. An article at *Money.cnn.com* warned of Internet security problems with SHA-1. Panic over this popular encryption method being cracked struck many in the security profession. Banks, e-commerce Web sites, credit card companies, and the like had used this form of encryption for many years.

Table 12-2   Hashing algorithms

Algorithm	Description
MD2	Developed by Ronald L. Rivest in 1989, this algorithm was optimized for 8-bit machines.
MD4	Developed by Rivest in 1990. Using a PC, collisions can now be found in this version in less than one minute.
MD5	Developed by Rivest in 1991. It was estimated in 1994 that it would cost $10 million to create a computer that could find collisions using brute force.
SHA	SHA-1 was a federal standard used by the government and private sector for handling sensitive information and was the most widely used hashing function.
HAVAL	A variation of the MD5 hashing algorithm that processes blocks twice the size of MD5.

Activity 12-4: Breaking a Hashing Algorithm

Time Required: 30 minutes

Objective: Learn more about the SHA-1 hashing algorithm fiasco.

Description: As a security professional, you can't rely on information in a textbook being up to date. The field of data security changes so rapidly that technical writers can't keep up with those changes. By the time this book is published, there will be numerous changes in encryption algorithms and other areas of security. The SHA-1 algorithm was widely accepted as being one of the best and most unlikely to be cracked, yet it was cracked. In this activity, you read an article by Charles Forelle, a staff reporter for *The Wall Street Journal*, and answer the questions. This activity can be done as a group project.

1. Start your Web browser, type the URL **www.mail-archive.com/ cryptography@metzdowd.com/msg03700.html**, and press **Enter**.

2. Read the article. What does the author think is the most immediate threat of the exploit the three cryptologists discovered?

3. Even though some believe the cracking of SHA-1 poses no immediate danger, what are some indicators that a major problem exists?

4. The article mentions the concerns of Bruce Schneier, a cryptologist. What, if any, credence should be given to his statement that the flaw is "real"?

5. What is the term for two different chunks of data that yield the same hash value?

6. What does the article say about collisions that might affect the common Internet user?

7. The article mentions problems with the MD4 and MD5 hashing algorithms. How much time did it take a cryptographer to find collisions for the MD5 hashing algorithm?

8. Choose someone in your group to give a five-minute presentation on the group's position as to whether a company should stop using SHA-1 or whether the article is overreacting to the claims of university cryptologists.

9. Close your Web browser, but leave Windows XP running for the next activity.

UNDERSTANDING PUBLIC KEY INFRASTRUCTURE (PKI)

A discussion of public key encryption cannot take place without mentioning **public key infrastructure (PKI)**. PKI is not an algorithm; rather, it's a structure or base that consists of programs, protocols, and security policies. PKI uses public key cryptography as its method of protecting data that traverses the Internet. The topic of PKI can take up an entire book, so this section just gives you an overview of its major components and how PKI is used in creating certificates.

Components of PKI

Another way authentication can take place over a communication channel is through the use of **certificates**. A certificate is a digital document that verifies that the two parties exchanging data over the Internet are really who they claim to be. Each certificate contains a unique serial number and must follow the X.509 standard that describes the makings of a certificate. SSL, a major component of security over the Internet, also requires PKI.

Public keys are issued by a **certification authority (CA)**. The CA vouches for the company to which you might send your credit card number when ordering that Harley-Davidson motorcycle online. You would probably want to know that the company from which you were ordering the bike was a viable company, not someone who started up a bogus Web site to collect credit card numbers from unsuspecting victims. Think of a CA as a passport agency. When a U.S. citizen shows her passport at Customs in a foreign country, the person viewing the passport doesn't necessarily trust the American woman. The custom agent does, however, trust the passport agency that issued the passport, so the woman is allowed to enter the country.

A certificate that the CA issues to a company binds a public key to the recipient's private key. In this way, if you encrypted an e-mail message using the public key of your friend Sue, you know only she would be able to decrypt the message with her private key that was mathematically related to her public key. You also know that the public key you used was indeed Sue's public key because you trust the CA that issued it.

Expiration, Revocation, and Suspension of Certificates

Just because a certificate is issued by a CA today, it doesn't necessarily mean it's good for a lifetime. A period of validity is assigned to each certificate, and after that date, the certificate expires. If the keys are still valid and remain uncompromised, the certificate can be renewed with a new expiration date assigned.

At times, a certificate might need to be suspended or revoked before its expiration date, such as in the following circumstances:

- A user leaves the company.
- A hardware crash causes a key to be lost.
- A private key is compromised.

The CA compiles a Certificate Revocation List (CRL) that contains all revoked and suspended certificates. Suspension of a certificate might be done when one or more parties fail to honor agreements set forth at the issuance of the certificate. Instead of revoking the certificate, suspension makes it easier to restore if the parties come to an agreement at a later date.

12

Backing Up Keys

Just as backing up data is important for a network administrator, backing up keys is just as critical. If keys are destroyed and not backed up properly, encrypted business-critical information might be irretrievable. The CA is usually responsible for backing up keys, and a key recovery policy is also part of the CA's responsibility. There are too many CAs to list in this book, but in Activity 12-5, you can research companies that offer CA services and see the types of certificates they issue.

Activity 12-5: Identifying Root CAs

Time Required: 20 minutes

Objective: Gain a better understanding of certificates and the CAs that issue them.

Description: A CA issues certificates that can be used to transmit e-mail or conduct business on the Internet. In this activity, you search the Web to look at the many companies that offer CA services and spend some time learning what a certificate looks like.

1. Start Internet Explorer. Click **Tools**, **Internet Options** from the menu. In the Internet Options dialog box, click the **Content** tab.

2. Click the **Certificates** button to open the Certificates dialog box, and then click the **Trusted Root Certification Authorities** tab (see Figure 12-7).

3. Scroll down the list and click the **VeriSign Trust Network** entry. Then click the **View** button at the bottom right of the Certificates dialog box to view the certificate shown in Figure 12-8.

4. List at least five purposes of the certificate.

5. To see more information about this certificate, click the **Details** tab. Figure 12-9 shows the output when selecting the Public key option in the Field column. What algorithm is being used to generate the public key?

6. Click **OK**, and then click **Close**. Finally, click **OK** in the Internet Options dialog box.

7. Close your Web browser, and shut down your system.

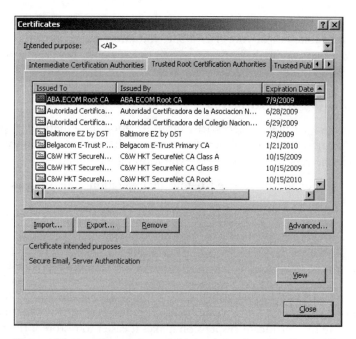

Figure 12-7   Using Internet Explorer to view the Root CA

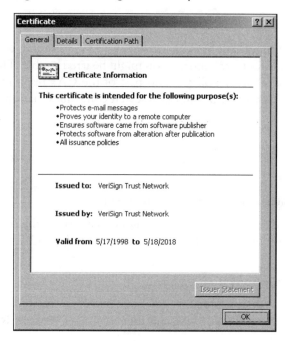

Figure 12-8   Viewing a certificate from the VeriSign Trust Network CA

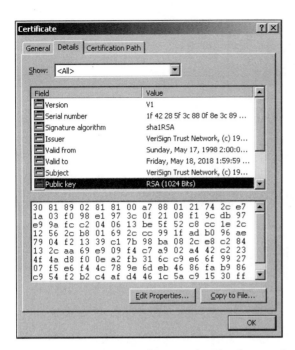

Figure 12-9   Viewing the Details tab of a certificate

Microsoft Root CA

You have seen that many third-party CAs can be used to issue certificates. In Windows Server 2003 and Windows 2000 Server, administrators can configure a server as a CA. For example, from the Windows Component Wizard, an administrator selects Certificate Services, as shown in Figure 12-10.

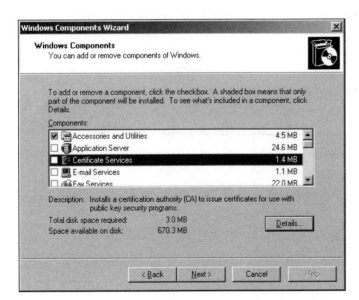

Figure 12-10   Selecting Certificate Services in the Windows Components Wizard

Selecting this option immediately displays a warning to the administrator (see Figure 12-11) because after a Windows domain controller takes on the role of a CA, there is no turning back. That is, the name of the domain or computer cannot change.

After accepting that the name of this server can't be changed, the administrator can view the details of what will be installed on the server. Figure 12-12 shows two components that will be installed. Note that the description in the figure shows a CA will be installed that can issue and manage digital certificates.

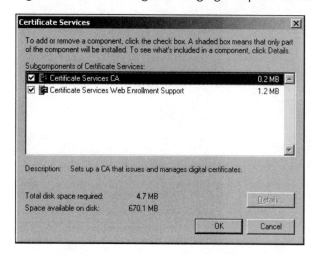

Figure 12-11   Warning on changing computer or domain names

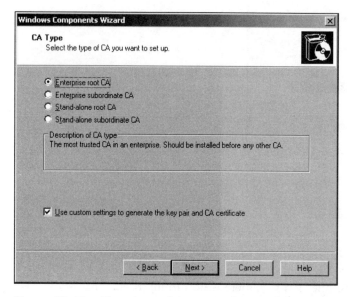

Figure 12-12   The Certificate Services dialog box

When configuring a Windows server as a CA, the administrator has four options, as shown in Figure 12-13:

- Enterprise root CA
- Enterprise subordinate CA
- Stand-alone root CA
- Stand-alone subordinate CA

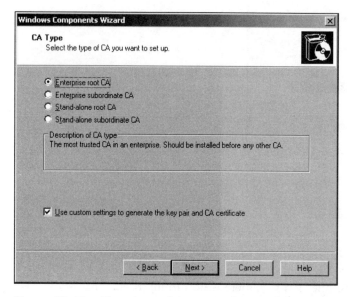

Figure 12-13   Choosing a CA type in the Windows Components Wizard

You don't need to memorize these options. What's important is understanding that a company can configure its own server to be a CA, just as the commercial CAs you saw earlier, and that the administrator can choose from several parameters shown in Figure 12-14. If the administrator selects the Enterprise root CA option and the option "Use custom settings to generate the key pair and CA certificate," the screen shown in Figure 12-14 is displayed.

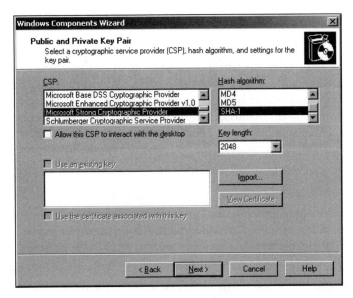

Figure 12-14   Selecting Enterprise root CA and custom settings

Figure 12-14 shows the three parameters an administrator can select for generating certificates. Note that the default Cryptographic Service Provider (CSP) is Microsoft Strong Cryptographic Provider and that SHA-1 is the hashing algorithm used. Also, note that by default the key length is 2048. Of the seven CSP options available, four are Microsoft based. These are the other available options:

- *Gemplus GemSAFE Card CSP v1.0*—Gemplus specializes in smart card solutions. In this form of security, digital certificates, encryption keys, and other information are placed in a PIN-protected token carried by the end user. This is a more secure method than storing the information on a computer system.

- *Infineon SICRYPT Base Smart Card CSP*—Developed by Infineon Technologies, this smart-card technology is supported by Windows Server 2003 and Windows XP.

- *Schlumberger Cryptographic Service Provider*—Also uses a smart-card technology to store digital certificates and encryption keys.

No matter which CA a company chooses, you should be aware of the type of algorithm used so that you know whether the company is vulnerable to an attack if information about the algorithm is later compromised. Certificates at risk of being compromised can create a major security flaw for a company and shouldn't be overlooked when conducting a security test.

UNDERSTANDING CRYPTOGRAPHY ATTACKS

As you have learned from reading and performing the activities in this book, a hacker can perform many attacks on a network. Using tools to eavesdrop (Tcpdump, Ethereal) or perform port scanning (Nmap, Unicornscan, Hping, and so on) are considered passive attacks because the attacker is not affecting the algorithm (key), message, or any parts of the encryption system.

Active attacks attempt to determine the secret key being used to encrypt plaintext. Remember, the algorithm is usually known by the culprit and the general public because the companies that develop encryption algorithms realize that the general population might discover vulnerabilities in their algorithms that the company's programmers missed. This is the philosophy of software engineers who develop open-source code products. By releasing their source code to the world, suggestions are made and users are given the freedom to modify or add to the programming code. Ostensibly, this can create a better product. Of course, agencies such as NSA and the CIA do not release information on the encryption algorithms they are using. The following sections describe some common active attacks.

Birthday Attack

You have probably heard the old adage that if 23 people are in a room, two will share the same birthday. **Birthday attacks** are used to find the same hash value for two different inputs. A birthday attack is used to reveal any mathematical weaknesses in the hashing algorithm. For example, if an attacker has one hash value and wants to find another message that creates the same hash value, he or she could possibly do so in a couple of hours. SHA-1, a hashing function once used by thousands of businesses and government agencies, uses a 160-bit key. Theoretically, it would require 2^{80} computations to break; however, as you learned earlier, SHA-1 has indeed been broken.

Mathematical Attacks

In a **mathematical attack**, properties of the algorithm are attacked by using mathematical computations. The attacker performs this type of attack in different ways, depending on the information to which he or she has access. Basically, there are four categories for this attack:

- *Ciphertext-only attack*—The attacker has the ciphertext of several messages that were encrypted with the same encryption algorithm but has no access to the plaintext, so he or she must try to figure out the key used to encrypt the data. Getting a copy of ciphertext is relatively easy. Using a sniffer such as Tcpdump or Ethereal can give you all the ciphertext you probably need, but this type of attack is by far the most difficult to perform because little or no information is known about the encryption method the company uses.

- *Known plaintext attack*—The attacker has messages in both encrypted form and decrypted forms. This attack is easier to perform than the ciphertext-only attack because now patterns can be looked at from the plaintext showing how a letter from the company was formulated. For example, if a bank letter to any of its customers always begins with a particular salutation and ends with the familiar "Thanks for your business," the attacker can use reverse-engineering techniques to determine the key used to encrypt the data.

- *Chosen-plaintext attack*—The attacker has access to plaintext and ciphertext and the ability to choose which messages to encrypt. This obviously makes it easier to determine the key that was used because the whole plaintext message and the whole ciphertext message are available. The attacker can obtain this information by sending an e-mail message to someone stating that the contents are not to be divulged to anyone except, say, Bob Smith. The attacker would most likely spoof the e-mail message so that the recipient believes the message is from someone known and trusted. When the recipient forwards the message as ciphertext, the attacker sniffs the contents and then has both the cleartext he or she wrote and the ciphertext document the user sent.

- *Chosen-ciphertext attack*—The attacker has access to the ciphertext to be decrypted and to the resulting plaintext. He or she also needs access to the cryptosystem to perform this type of attack.

Regardless of which type of attack is used, the attacker builds on the information gained and then conducts another type of attack. Patience and curiosity are usually part of cryptologists' personalities, whether they're working for good or bad purposes.

Brute Force Attack

Despite its name, this type of attack doesn't require a hammer or martial art skills; it just requires lots of time and patience. In a **brute force attack**, an attacker uses a password-cracking program, such as John the Ripper, to guess passwords by attempting every possible combination of letters.

Man-in-the-Middle Attack

In a **man-in-the-middle attack**, attackers place themselves between the victim computer and another host computer. They then intercept messages sent from the victim to the host and pretend to be the host computer. This type of attack follows this process:

1. Gloria sends her public key to Bruce, and you, the attacker, intercept the key and send Bruce your public key. Bruce thinks he just received Gloria's public key, but he received your public key.

2. Bruce sends Gloria his public key. You intercept this key also and send Gloria your public key.

3. Gloria sends a message to Bruce, encrypted in what she thinks is Bruce's public key, but because she is using your public key, you can decrypt the message with your private key!

4. You then can reencrypt the message using Bruce's public key and send it to Bruce.

5. Bruce answers Gloria by encrypting his message with Gloria's public key. You intercept the message, decrypt it with your private key, and then encrypt it with Gloria's real public key and send it to Gloria.

You might have to read these steps several times to get a good understanding of how this type of attack works. Using index cards with the names of participants written on them might help you get a clearer picture of what is taking place. Activity 12-6 will help you better understand a man-in-the-middle attack.

ACTIVITY

Activity 12-6: Conducting a Man-in-the-Middle Attack

Time Required: 20 minutes

Objective: Gain a better understanding of how a man-in-the-middle attack works.

Description: Using index cards and breaking into teams of three students, you perform a manual man-in-the-middle attack.

1. Two students should create two index cards. Label one card as *FirstName* PublicKey and the second card as *FirstName* PrivateKey. (Substitute your own first name for *FirstName*.)

2. The attacker performing the man-in-the-middle attack should name his or her cards Attacker PublicKey and Attacker PrivateKey.

3. As the first student hands his or her *FirstName* PublicKey to the second student, the attacker should intercept the transfer and substitute his or her Attacker PublicKey.

4. The student receiving this attacker card would be under the impression that he or she has received the real public key and would then encrypt a message using this public key and send it back to the sender.

5. The attacker should intercept this card and use his or her private key card to simulate decrypting the message.

Dictionary Attack

In a **dictionary attack**, after an attacker has access to a password file, he or she can run a password-cracking program that uses a dictionary of known words or passwords as an input file. Most of these input files are available on the Internet and can be downloaded free. Remember that using such programs is illegal in most parts of the world. In fact, a conviction for using a password-cracking program in the United States results in about five years' prison time for each occurrence.

Replay Attack

In a **replay attack**, the attacker captures data and attempts to resubmit the captured data so that the device, which can be a computer or router, thinks a legitimate connection is in effect. If the captured data was logon information, the attacker could gain access to a system and be authenticated. Many systems have countermeasures to prevent such attacks from occurring, such as packets using sequence numbers that detect when a packet is out of order or not in a correct sequence.

12

Understanding Password Cracking

As a security professional, you might come across files that are encrypted or password protected. In most cases, passwords can be easily guessed (pet names, relatives, spouses, and anniversary and birth dates). A study conducted by NSA almost 30 years ago indicated that 70% of all passwords are written in an area within four feet of a user's computer. Also, to paraphrase a social engineer when asked about cracking passwords, "Why spend time trying to decrypt a password when you can just ask for it?"

It's important to understand that in most countries, including the United States, cracking someone else's passwords is illegal. (You're allowed to crack your own password if you forgot it.) It might also be illegal in many countries to just try to figure out the encryption method being used. For example, DVD movies use encryption to prevent people from making bootleg copies. It is illegal for anyone to research how that encryption is used.

Many Web sites sell automated password crackers that decrypt PDF, Microsoft Word, or Microsoft Excel documents. Some of these password crackers are illegal, so you must be careful when using them to perform a security test. Many of these "underground" Web sites might contain offensive materials that are unsuited for the faint of heart, as do many hacking Web sites. It might also be wise to disable JavaScript and ActiveX on your Web browser before browsing because viruses can be carried out through these programs. Examples of some Web sites that offer password cracking tools are *www.cracks.am*, *www.cracks.ru*, and *http://astalavista.box.sk*.

If you're going to conduct password cracking, you must first obtain the password file from the system that stores user names and passwords. This varies based on the OS you're testing. For *NIX systems, the file is stored in the /Etc/Passwd or /Etc/Shadow directory. For older Microsoft NT systems, the file is stored in the \WINNT\repair\SAM._ directory or other variations of this directory that are more difficult to find. Most vendors don't freely advertise where password files are stored, for obvious reasons. This is why visiting those "underground" Web sites can be quite educational. After the file is located, a dictionary attack can be performed on the file by using the following programs. The Web sites for downloading these programs come and go as quickly as viruses are created, so you get better results by using a search engine to find them.

- *John the Ripper*—One of the best programs available today for cracking password files
- *Hydra (THC)*—Good program for testing over the Internet
- *EXPECT*—A scripting language for Windows and Linux that performs repetitive tasks, such as password cracking
- *L0phtcrack*—The original password-cracking program now used by many government agencies to test for password strength
- *Pwdump3v2*—An enhancement of the Pwdump3 program used to extract hash values of user accounts on a Windows computer (versions of the program can be downloaded from *www.openwall. com/passwords/nt.shtml*)

A security tester can use the following steps to obtain passwords on a Windows XP computer. It should be noted that performing these steps on a computer other than your own can be illegal in most parts of the world. In fact, using password cracking software on a computer other than yours can be dangerous. In this example, Pwdump2 and John the Ripper are used to obtain passwords from a Windows XP Home Edition computer:

1. The security tester first runs the Pwdump2 program to get hash values of user accounts on the Windows XP computer (see Figure 12-15).
2. If the program returns hash values, the security tester runs Pwdump2 again, but this time uses a redirector to send the output to a file named Pass.txt: pwdump2 > pass.txt.
3. Using John the Ripper with the Pass.txt file as the input file, the security tester can perform a brute force attack on the hash values discovered with Pwdump2. Figure 12-16 shows the attempts made to crack the passwords of accounts on the Windows XP computer.

```
C:\PWDump2>pwdump2
Administrator:500:aad3b435b51404eeaad3b435b51404ee:31d6cfe0d16ae931b73c59d7e0c08
9c0:::
Guest:501:aad3b435b51404eeaad3b435b51404ee:31d6cfe0d16ae931b73c59d7e0c089c0:::
HelpAssistant:1005:4de3894c7163da748da3c95a4bd00e59:a65517d8e29a67065a831d78f780
feb6:::
Michael Simpson:1006:aad3b435b51404eeaad3b435b51404ee:31d6cfe0d16ae931b73c59d7e0
c089c0:::
SUPPORT_388945a0:1002:aad3b435b51404eeaad3b435b51404ee:8f2483172e8152f8b59ac5020
c3c3894:::

C:\PWDump2>
```

Figure 12-15 Running Pwdump2

```
C:\john-16>john pass.txt
Loaded 10 passwords with no different salts (NT LM DES [24/32 4K])
                (Administrator:1)
                (Administrator:2)
                (Guest:1)
                (Guest:2)
                (Michael:1)
                (Michael:2)
                (SUPPORT:1)
                (SUPPORT:2)
guesses: 8  time: 0:00:02:40 (3)  c/s: 1963773  trying: YEJLD - YN1EE
guesses: 8  time: 0:00:02:41 (3)  c/s: 1964601  trying: CLUHVD2 - HMMSCLA
guesses: 8  time: 0:00:02:47 (3)  c/s: 1969358  trying: OGCCHA - ONFFAB
guesses: 8  time: 0:00:02:51 (3)  c/s: 1972345  trying: RM5EF12 - DDGNNDO
guesses: 8  time: 0:00:02:52 (3)  c/s: 1973069  trying: TYKSS P - PEOSK10
guesses: 8  time: 0:00:02:54 (3)  c/s: 1974494  trying: SHJUDHN - GLCEDRT
guesses: 8  time: 0:00:03:08 (3)  c/s: 1972465  trying: N5J4SA - OLDWKO
guesses: 8  time: 0:00:03:09 (3)  c/s: 1973124  trying: J1NUZ2 - 163D2T
guesses: 8  time: 0:00:03:10 (3)  c/s: 1973776  trying: SNUC0S - ATCOYR
guesses: 8  time: 0:00:03:11 (3)  c/s: 1974421  trying: UVYP? - URDGT
guesses: 8  time: 0:00:03:12 (3)  c/s: 1975060  trying: NJCPUCT - NOPKSPO
guesses: 8  time: 0:00:03:13 (3)  c/s: 1975692  trying: NGNRYS1 - NJTBUZA
guesses: 8  time: 0:00:03:14 (3)  c/s: 1976317  trying: NTRRSDS - NGPUGLL
guesses: 8  time: 0:00:03:15 (3)  c/s: 1976936  trying: NULCBUN - NTSSP94
guesses: 8  time: 0:00:03:16 (3)  c/s: 1977549  trying: NOMSA79 - NUMBLJN
guesses: 8  time: 0:00:03:17 (3)  c/s: 1978156  trying: NJSKVAM - NORKFOL
guesses: 8  time: 0:00:03:18 (3)  c/s: 1978756  trying: NGMAM68 - NJMMBNN
guesses: 8  time: 0:00:03:19 (3)  c/s: 1979350  trying: NTMKTNY - NGRALMY
guesses: 8  time: 0:00:03:20 (3)  c/s: 1979939  trying: NUSURDL - NTGOLLL
guesses: 8  time: 0:00:03:21 (3)  c/s: 1980521  trying: NOTLBLM - NUCEEGG
guesses: 8  time: 0:00:03:22 (3)  c/s: 1981098  trying: SATKWOR - DURLKER
guesses: 8  time: 0:00:03:23 (3)  c/s: 1981669  trying: JL7TAKA - BKEBAIL
guesses: 8  time: 0:00:03:24 (3)  c/s: 1982234  trying: TRB1CCS - LMRGGGA
```

Figure 12-16 Running John the Ripper with the Pass.txt input file

The command "john pass.txt" performs a brute force attack on the passwords. To see the commands that can be used with John the Ripper, you can type the command "john" without any other parameters. Figure 12-17 shows you the commands available in John the Ripper.

```
C:\john-16>john

John the Ripper  Version 1.6  Copyright (c) 1996-98 by Solar Designer

Usage: john [OPTIONS] [PASSWORD-FILES]
-single                    "single crack" mode
-wordfile:FILE -stdin      wordlist mode, read words from FILE or stdin
-rules                     enable rules for wordlist mode
-incremental[:MODE]        incremental mode [using section MODE]
-external:MODE             external mode or word filter
-stdout[:LENGTH]           no cracking, just write words to stdout
-restore[:FILE]            restore an interrupted session [from FILE]
-session:FILE              set session file name to FILE
-status[:FILE]             print status of a session [from FILE]
-makechars:FILE            make a charset, FILE will be overwritten
-show                      show cracked passwords
-test                      perform a benchmark
-users:[-]LOGIN|UID[,..]   load this (these) user(s) only
-groups:[-]GID[,..]        load users of this (these) group(s) only
-shells:[-]SHELL[,..]      load users with this (these) shell(s) only
-salts:[-]COUNT            load salts with at least COUNT passwords only
-format:NAME               force ciphertext format NAME (DES/BSDI/MD5/BF/AFS/LM)
-savemem:LEVEL             enable memory saving, at LEVEL 1..3

C:\john-16>
```

Figure 12-17 Using John the Ripper parameters

This method is not the fastest one for breaking a password, but it's effective. Many hackers leave a program like this running for days on a computer devoted to breaking passwords. What's important to note is that these programs were run on a Windows XP Home Edition computer using SP2. Many of the old tools used to crack passwords on Microsoft NT products are still effective today.

CHAPTER SUMMARY

❑ Cryptography has been in existence since the dawn of civilization, from Egyptian hieroglyphics to the Enigma machine and on to the 21st century.

❑ Ciphertext is data that has been encrypted, whereas cleartext, also called plaintext, is used to define data that can be intercepted and read by anyone.

❑ Symmetric cryptography uses one key to encrypt and decrypt data. Both sender and receiver must agree on the key before data is transmitted. DES, DEA, 3DES, and AES are symmetric algorithm standards.

❑ Asymmetric cryptography uses two keys: one key to encrypt and another to decrypt data. Asymmetric cryptography is also referred to as public key cryptography. In public key cryptography, a public key can be downloaded from a Web site and is mathematically related to a private key known only to the user. A private key is never shared or revealed to anyone. Blowfish, IDEA, and RC5 are block ciphers used in symmetric algorithms.

❑ RSA uses only a one-way function to generate a key. Diffie-Hellman, ECC, and Elgamal use encryption, key distribution, and digital signatures to secure data.

❑ Digital Signature Standard (DSS) ensures that digital signatures rather than written signatures can be verified. To create a digital signature, the hash value must be encrypted with the sender's private key.

❑ PGP is a free public key encryption program developed by Phil Zimmerman to encrypt e-mail messages. Two other programs used to encrypt email are S/MIME and PEM.

❑ Hashing algorithms are used to verify data integrity. One of the most popular hashing algorithms is SHA-1. However, because of recent exploits, the algorithm has been cracked and is no longer recommended by NIST.

❑ Public key infrastructure (PKI) is a structure or base made up of many different components used to encrypt data. PKI includes protocols, programs, and security policies and uses public key cryptography as its method of protecting data that traverses the Internet.

❑ A digital certificate is a digital file issued by a certification authority (CA). It binds a public key to information about its owner. A CA is a trusted third party that accepts certificate applications from entities, authenticates applications, issues certificates, and maintains all information about the certificates.

❑ An active attack on a cryptosystem attempts to determine the secret key being used to encrypt plaintext. Examples of active attacks are birthday attacks, brute force attacks, man-in-the-middle attacks, replay attacks, and dictionary attacks.

❑ A passive attack on a cryptosystem uses tools such as Ethereal, Tcpdump, Nmap, Unicornscan, and others that don't affect the algorithm (key), message, or any parts of the encryption system.

KEY TERMS

Advanced Encryption Standard (AES) — A new symmetric block cipher standard from NIST that replaced DES.

asymmetric algorithm — Encryption methodology that uses two keys that are mathematically related. Also referred to as public key cryptography.

authenticity — The process of validating the sender of a message.

birthday attacks — An attack used to find the same hash value for two different inputs. Based on the theory that if 23 people are in a room, two will share the same birthday.

block cipher — An algorithm that encrypts data a block at a time. The blocks of bits are used as input to mathematical functions that perform substitution and transposition of the bits, making it difficult for someone to reverse-engineer the mathematical functions that were applied to the blocks of bits.

Blowfish — A block cipher developed by Bruce Schneier, author of *Applied Cryptography*, that can use a key length as large as 448 bits.

brute force attack — An attack when the attacker uses software that attempts every possible combination of letters to guess passwords.

certificates — Digital documents that verify whether two parties exchanging data over the Internet are really who they claim to be. Each certificate contains a unique serial number and must follow the X.509 standard.

certification authority (CA) — A third-party company, such as VeriSign, that vouches for another company's financial stability and issues a certificate that binds a public key to a recipient's private key .

cipher — A key that maps each letter or number to a different letter or number. The book of Jeremiah was written using a cipher known as atbash that mapped each letter of the alphabet to a different letter.

ciphertext — Plaintext (readable text) that has been encrypted.

cryptanalysis — A field of study devoted to breaking encryption algorithms.

Data Encryption Algorithm (DEA) — The NIST standard encryption algorithm that was originally named Lucifer and later renamed DEA by the NSA.

Data Encryption Standard (DES) — The NIST standard for protecting sensitive but unclassified data. DES is a symmetric algorithm that uses 56 bits for encryption.

dictionary attack — An attack where the attacker runs a password-cracking program that uses a dictionary of known words or passwords as an input file against the password file of the attacked system.

digital signature — Asymmetric encryption that ensures the sender cannot deny sending the message and the receiver of the message is assured that the message did indeed come from the sender.

hashing algorithm — A function that takes a variable-length string or message and produces a fixed-length value called a message digest.

International Data Encryption Algorithm (IDEA) — A block cipher that operates on 64-bit blocks of plaintext and uses a 128-bit key.

key — The bits of information used in an encryption algorithm to transform plaintext into ciphertext or vice versa.

keyspace — A sequence of random bits generated from a range of allowable values.

man-in-the-middle attack — An attack where the attackers place themselves between the victim computer and another host computer. They then intercept messages sent from the victim to the host and pretend to be the host computer.

mathematical attack — An attack where properties of the encryption algorithm are attacked using mathematical computations. Examples include ciphertext-only attack, known plaintext attack, chosen-plaintext attack, and chosen-ciphertext attack.

message digest — The fixed-length string value created from using a hashing algorithm.

nonrepudiation — A user cannot deny that they sent a message to a recipient and the receiver of a message cannot deny receiving the message.

plaintext — Readable text that has not been encrypted.

Pretty Good Privacy (PGP) — A free public key encryption program developed by Phil Zimmerman that allowed the common person to encrypt e-mail messages.

private key — The secret key used in an asymmetric algorithm that is known only by the key owner and is never shared. Even if the public key that encrypted a message is known, the owner's private key cannot be determined.

public key — The key that can be known by the public and in many cases is downloaded from Web sites for public use. It works with a private key in asymmetric key cryptography, which is also known as public key cryptography.

public key cryptography — Also known as asymmetric key cryptography, public key cryptography is an asymmetric algorithm which uses two keys that are mathematically related.

public key infrastructure (PKI) — A structure or base that consists of programs, protocols, and security policies. PKI uses public key cryptography as its method of protecting data that traverses the Internet.

RC5 — A block cipher created by Ronald L. Rivest that can operate on different block sizes: 32, 64, and 128 bits.

replay attack — An attack where the attacker captures data and attempts to resubmit the data captured so that a device, such as a workstation or router, thinks a legitimate connection is in effect.

Secure Hash Algorithm (SHA) — NIST standard hashing algorithm that has recently been cracked. NIST recommends not using SHA applications.

steganography — The process of hiding data in plain view in pictures, graphics, or text.

stream cipher — An algorithm that operates on plaintext one bit at a time.

symmetric algorithm — An encryption algorithm that uses only one key to both encrypt and decrypt data. A user who is sent a message encrypted by a key must have a copy of the same key to decrypt the message.

substitution cipher — An algorithm that maps each letter of the alphabet to a different letter of the alphabet. The book of Jeremiah was written using a substitution cipher called Atbash.

Triple Data Encryption Standard (3DES) — A quick fix to the vulnerabilities of DES that improved on security but takes longer to encrypt and decrypt data.

REVIEW QUESTIONS

1. Digital signatures are used to do which of the following?
   a. ensure that the receiver of a message can't deny receiving it
   b. ensure that repudiation is provided
   c. ensure that the sender's identity is provided and to prevent repudiation
   d. encrypt sensitive messages

2. What is the standard used for PKI certificates?
   a. X.500
   b. X.400
   c. X.509
   d. MySQL.409

3. List the three MIT professors who developed the RSA algorithm.

4. A hash value is a fixed-length value used as a message fingerprint. True or False?

5. Pretty Good Privacy (PGP) is focused on protecting which of the following?
   a. Web content
   b. e-mail messages
   c. database systems
   d. IPSec traffic

6. An intruder can perform which kind of attack if she has possession of the company's password file?
   a. dictionary
   b. scan
   c. ciphertext
   d. buffer overflow

7. Intercepting messages destined for another computer and sending back messages while pretending to be the other node is an example of what type of attack?
   a. man-in-the-middle
   b. smurf
   c. buffer overflow
   d. Ethereal

8. A certification authority (CA) issues private keys to recipients. True or False?

9. Write the equation to calculate how many keys are needed to have 20 people communicate with symmetric keys.

10. Why did the NSA decide to drop support for DES?

    a. high cost of use

    b. encryption algorithm was too slow

    c. claims it had been popular for too long

    d. claims it was too difficult for government agencies to implement

11. DES is a symmetric algorithm. True or False?

12. Which of the following describes a chosen-plaintext attack?

    a. The attacker has ciphertext and algorithm.

    b. The attacker has plaintext and algorithm.

    c. The attacker has plaintext, can choose what part of the text gets encrypted, and has access to the ciphertext.

    d. The attacker has plaintext, ciphertext, and the password file.

13. Two different messages producing the same hash values result in which of the following?

    a. duplicate key

    b. corrupt key

    c. collision

    d. message digest

14. Which of the following is a program that can be used to output the hash values of Microsoft accounts?

    a. Nmap

    b. Pwdump2

    c. John the Ripper

    d. l0phtcrack

15. The Advanced Encryption Standard (AES) replaced DES with which algorithm?

    a. Rijndael

    b. Blowfish

    c. IDEA

    d. Twofish

16. What encryption devices were used during World War II? (Choose all that apply.)

    a. Enigma machine

    b. Black Box

    c. Purple Machine

    d. Bombe

17. Asymmetric cryptography systems are which of the following?

    a. faster than symmetric cryptography systems

    b. slower than symmetric cryptography systems

    c. the same speed as symmetric cryptography systems

    d. practical only on systems with multiple processors

18. The Diffie-Hellman algorithm is used to encrypt e-mail messages. True or False?

12

19. Hiding data within a photograph is an example of which of the following?

   a. steganography

   b. stenography

   c. ciphertext

   d. cryptology

20. Which of the following is an asymmetric algorithm?

   a. DES

   b. AES

   c. RSA

   d. Blowfish

CASE PROJECTS

Case 12-1: Determining Possible Vulnerabilities of Microsoft CA Root Server

In conducting security testing on the K. J. Williams network, you have identified that the company configured one of its Windows Server 2003 computers as an Enterprise root CA server. You have also determined that Ronnie Jones, the administrator of the CA server, selected SHA-1 as the default hashing algorithm for creating digital signatures.

Based on the preceding information, write a one-page report explaining possible vulnerabilities on the CA root server caused by the SHA-1 exploit. The report should cite any articles written about the SHA-1 vulnerability and include any recommendations from Microsoft about its use of the SHA-1 algorithm in its software applications.

Case 12-2: Exploring Moral Versus Legal Issues

After conducting the research for Case 12-1, you have gathered a lot of background on the release of information as it pertains to encryption algorithms. Articles on vulnerabilities of SHA-1, MD4, and MD5 abound. The proliferation of computer programs that break DVD encryption codes and the recent imprisonment of an attacker who broke Japan's encryption method for blocking certain images from pornographic movies have raised many questions on what is moral or legal in releasing information that exposes the algorithms used to encrypt data.

Based on the preceding information, write a two-page report that addresses the moral and legal issues for the release of software or programmable code that breaks encryption algorithms. Your paper should also answer these questions:

1. If a person is able to break the encryption of a particular algorithm, should he or she be allowed to post the findings on the Internet?

2. Do you think the reporters of the DVD (DeCSS) crack were exercising their First Amendment rights when including the source code that breaks the DVD encryption key in an article? What about the source code being displayed on a T-shirt?

3. As a security professional, do you think you have to abide by a higher standard when it comes to sharing or disseminating source code that breaks encryption algorithms? Explain.

13

PROTECTING NETWORKS WITH SECURITY DEVICES

After reading this chapter and completing the exercises, you will be able to:

♦ Describe network security devices

♦ Describe firewall technology

♦ Describe intrusion detection systems

♦ Describe honeypots

Hackers have many tools at their disposal to attack a network. You have seen how port scanning and enumeration make it possible for attackers to determine the services running on computers and to gain access to network resources. In this chapter, you look at security devices that can be used to reduce the risks of many of these attacks.

Routers, hardware and software firewalls, intrusion detection systems (IDSs), and honeypots are covered in this chapter. Because Cisco routers and the Cisco PIX firewall products are popular, you learn about these products as well as Microsoft Internet Security and Acceleration (ISA) Server.

UNDERSTANDING NETWORK SECURITY DEVICES

To protect a network from attack, security professionals must know how to use routers, firewalls, intrusion detection systems, and honeypots. You start by seeing how routers can be used to reduce network attacks.

Understanding Routers

Routers, which operate at the network layer of the OSI model, are hardware devices used on a network to send packets to different network segments. Their main purpose is to reduce broadcast traffic that passes over a network and to choose the best path for moving those packets. For example, if Router A in Spain wants to send a packet to Router B in Iowa, the packet could most likely take several paths. Routers use routing protocols in this best-path decision-making process that function in the following ways:

- **Link-state routing protocol**—If a router is using a link-state routing protocol, it uses link-state advertisements sent to other routers that identify the network topology and any changes or paths that have recently been discovered on the network. For example, if a new router or path becomes available for a packet to travel, that information is sent to all other routers participating in the network. This method is efficient because only new information is sent over the wires. An example of a link-state routing protocol is Open Shortest Path First (OSPF).

- **Distance-vector routing protocol**—If a router is using a distance-vector routing protocol, it passes its routing table (containing all possible paths it has discovered) to all routers participating on the network. If the router learns one new path, it sends the entire routing table, which is not as efficient as a link-state routing protocol. An example of a distance-vector routing protocol is Routing Internet Protocol (RIP).

For more information about routing protocols, see *CCNA Guide to Cisco Routing, Second Edition* (Course Technology, 2002, ISBN: 0-619-03477-7).

As a security professional, your main concern is configuring a router to filter certain traffic, not designing a router infrastructure and determining the routing protocol an organization uses. The following section explains how a Cisco router is configured to filter traffic.

Understanding Basic Hardware Routers

In this section, Cisco routers are used as an example because they are widely used in the networking community. More than one million Cisco 2500 series routers are currently being used by companies around the world. The information in this section can assist you in performing security tests on companies that use Cisco routers in their networks. In Activity 13-1, you visit the Cisco Web site and browse through some Cisco products. If you've never seen a router or worked with the interfaces discussed in this section, the product photographs on this site can help give you an idea of what you'll be working with as a security professional.

Activity 13-1: Visiting the Cisco Web Site

Time Required: 30 minutes

Objective: Learn more about Cisco routing products.

Description: The Cisco family of routing products will undoubtedly become an important part of your job as a security professional because of the many companies using its products. In this activity, you visit the company's Web site and look at some of the vulnerability information Cisco releases to its customers. This information can be helpful if you're performing a security test on a company that uses Cisco routers to protect its network.

1. Start a Web browser, type the URL **www.cisco.com**, and press **Enter**. On the Cisco home page, type **2500** in the Search text box at the right, and click **GO**. Even though the 2500 series might not be supported by Cisco as of the writing of this book, it's still one of the most popular series.

2. Click the first link listed, **Cisco 2500 Series Routers – Technical Support & Documentation**.

3. On the Cisco 2500 Series Routers page, scroll down and click the **Security Advisories and Notices (84)** link under the Troubleshoot and Alerts heading.

4. On the Security Advisories and Notices page, click the **Cisco Security Advisory: TCP Vulnerabilities in Multiple IOS-Based Cisco Products 13/Apr/2005** link under the Cisco 2525 Router heading.

5. On the Cisco Security Advisory page, click the **Summary** link in the Table of Contents and read the information on this vulnerability. Scroll through the document and look for any details that interest you.

6. Click the browser **Back** button to return to the Security Advisories and Notices page.

7. Browse through the Security Advisories and Notices page and pay close attention to the types of vulnerabilities associated with Cisco routers. Click two or three links of your choosing and read the summary information.

8. Close your Web browser, but leave your system running for the next activity.

As you can see from your reading, vulnerabilities exist in Cisco as they do in any operating system, so security professionals must consider the type of router being used when conducting a security test.

Security Bytes

NOTE

At a recent Black Hat computer-security conference, a 24-year-old researcher named Michael Lynn was instructed by Cisco Systems, Inc. not to give a presentation on vulnerabilities he found in Cisco's Internet routers. Mr. Lynn claimed the vulnerabilities would allow hackers to take over corporate and government networks. Cisco argued that releasing his findings to the general public was illegal and that Mr. Lynn was able to find the vulnerabilities by reverse-engineering Cisco's product, also illegal in this country. Most technology companies don't want vulnerabilities in their products to be released to the public until they have the chance to correct the problem themselves or they can control what information is given to the public. The issue of disclosure will be here for quite some time and will most certainly affect security testers.

Cisco Router Components

To help you understand how routers are used as security devices, this section describes the components of a Cisco router. A Cisco router uses the Cisco Internetwork Operating System (IOS) to function. Just as a system administrator must understand commands for configuring a server, Cisco router administrators must know commands for configuring a Cisco router. Many components of a Cisco router are similar to those of a computer, so the following components should seem familiar:

- *Random access memory (RAM)*—This component holds the router's running configuration, routing tables, and buffers. If you turn off the router, the contents stored in RAM are wiped out. Any changes you make to a router's configuration, such as changing the prompt displayed, are stored in RAM and aren't permanent unless you explicitly save the configuration.

- *Nonvolatile RAM (NVRAM)*—This component holds the router's configuration file, but the information is not lost if the router is turned off.

- *Flash memory*—This component holds the IOS the router is using. It's rewritable memory, so you can upgrade the IOS if Cisco releases a newer version or the current IOS version becomes corrupted.

- *Read-only memory (ROM)*—This component contains a minimal version of the IOS used to boot the router if flash memory gets corrupted. You can boot the router and then correct any problems with the IOS, possibly installing a new, uncorrupted version.

■ *Interfaces*—These components are the hardware connectivity points to the router and are the component you're most concerned with. An Ethernet port, for example, is an interface that connects to a local area network (LAN) and can be configured to restrict any traffic from a specific IP address, subnet, or network.

As a security professional, you should know some basic Cisco commands to view information in these components. For example, to see what information is stored in RAM, a Cisco administrator would type this command (with the bolded text indicating the actual command that's typed):

RouterB# **show running-config**

The output of this command is similar to Figure 13-1.

```
RouterB#show running-config
Building configuration...

Current configuration:
!
version 11.1
service udp-small-servers
service tcp-small-servers
!
hostname RouterB
!
enable secret 5 $1$RHhg$ngXce3OBeC7GprpPjtqsP1
!
ipx routing 0060.474f.6506
!
interface Ethernet0
 ip address 172.22.2.1 255.255.255.0
 ipx access-group 800 out
 ipx network 300
!
interface Serial0
 no ip address
!
interface Serial1
 ip address 172.22.3.2 255.255.255.0
!
router rip
 network 172.22.0.0
!
no ip classless
access-list 800 deny 300 500
access-list 800 permit FFFFFFFF FFFFFFFF
!
!
!
!
line con 0
line vty 0 4
 password password
 login
!
end

RouterB#
```

Figure 13-1 Output from the show running-config command

Cisco Router Configuration

Two modes are available on a Cisco router: user mode and privileged mode. In **user mode**, an administrator can perform basic troubleshooting tests and list information stored on the router. In **privileged mode**, an administrator can perform full router configuration tasks. You can see which mode you are in by looking at the prompt. The router name followed by a greater-than sign (>), such as Router>, indicates that you're in user mode. A router name followed by a # sign, such as Router#, indicates that you're in privileged mode, also called enable mode. When first logging on to a Cisco router, you're in user mode by default. To change to privileged mode, you simply type the word "enable," which can be abbreviated as "en." Usually, you have to enter a password to do this, unless the administrator of the Cisco router has little experience and hasn't specified a password.

After you're in privileged mode, you need to enter another command for one of the following modes to configure the router:

- *Global configuration mode*—In this mode, you can configure router settings that affect overall router operation, such as changing the router's displayed banner when a user telnets in from a remote host. The banner might indicate that the router is secured or should not be accessed by unauthorized personnel. To use this mode, you enter the command config t (which means "configure terminal") at the Router# prompt. The prompt then changes to Router (config)#, which tells the user she's in global configuration mode. When using a Cisco router or switch, being aware of the prompts is critical.

- *Interface configuration mode*—In this mode, you're configuring an interface on the router, such as a serial port or an Ethernet port. To use this mode, first you enter global configuration mode (with the command config t). Next, you enter the command for interface configuration mode and the interface name you want to configure, such as "interface ethernet 0." The prompt then changes to Router(config-if)# to indicate you're in interface configuration mode.

Now that you understand the basic modes in which a Cisco router can operate, take a look at some commands for viewing the components of a Cisco router. Table 13-1 lists some commonly used commands. If you want to know all the commands available in global configuration mode, after the Router(config)# prompt, simply type a question mark.

13

Table 13-1   Cisco commands

Mode	Command	Description
Privileged	show running-config	Displays the currently running router configuration file
Privileged	show startup-config	Displays the contents of NVRAM
Privileged or user	show version	Displays the router's version information, including the IOS version number
Privileged or user	show ip route	Displays the router's routing table
Privileged or user	show interfaces	Lists configuration information and statistics for all interfaces on the router
Privileged or user	show flash	Shows the contents of flash memory and the amount of memory used and available
Privileged	copy running-config startup-config	Copies the running configuration to NVRAM so that changes made are carried out the next time the router is started
Privileged	copy startup-config running-config	Copies the startup configuration from NVRAM to memory (RAM)
Global configuration	interface serial [#]	Allows you to configure the serial interface you identify, such as serial 0
Global configuration	interface ethernet [#]	Allows you to configure the Ethernet interface you specify

A Cisco administrator needs to know many additional commands that aren't covered in this book. The most critical configuration that security professionals perform is on a router's interfaces. Packets can be filtered or evaluated on a router's Ethernet and serial interfaces before passing to the next router or a company's internal network. To control the flow of traffic through a router, access lists are used, as explained in the following section.

Understanding Access Control Lists

There are several types of access control lists, but this section focuses on IP access lists. **IP access lists** are lists of IP addresses, subnets, or networks that are allowed or denied access through a router's interface. On a Cisco router, an administrator can create two different types of access lists:

- Standard IP access lists

- Extended IP access lists

NOTE   IPX access lists aren't covered in this book. However, you might want to research this type if you're working with a network that includes Novell NetWare servers because IPX is sometimes still used as the protocol in NetWare networks.

NOTE   Cisco refers to IP access lists as "access control lists," but refers to the specific file containing the list of commands as an "access list."

Standard IP Access Lists

Standard IP access lists can restrict IP traffic entering or leaving a router's interface based on only one criterion: source IP address. Figure 13-2 illustrates a network composed of two routers. Network 1 (10.0.0.0/8) is connected to an Ethernet interface on Router A. Router A's serial interface (s1) is connected to Router B's serial interface (s0). Network 2 (192.168.10.0/24) is connected to Router B's Ethernet interface (e0), and Network 3 (173.110.0.0/16) is connected to Router B's Ethernet interface (e1).

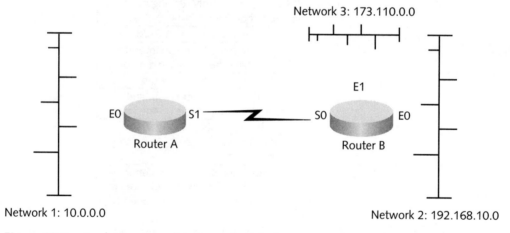

Figure 13-2   Applying access lists to router interfaces

If a Cisco administrator wants to restrict all traffic from Network 3 from entering Network 1, he or she can create a standard IP access list that looks like the following:

```
access-list 1 deny 173.110.0.0 0.0.255.255
access-list permit any
```

Don't worry about understanding the syntax now. What's important is to see how simple an access list can be. With just two lines of code, a whole network can be prevented from accessing another network. For example, the two-line access list command shown previously can be applied to one of these interfaces:

- Serial interface s0 on Router B

- Serial interface s1 on Router A

A network administrator can decide to which interface to apply the access list based on variables beyond the scope of this book. Access lists are nothing more than lists; they don't become effective until they are applied to interfaces. The syntax of a standard access list is as follows:

```
access-list [list #] [permit|deny] [source address]
[source wildcard mask]
```

The following list describes the parameters that can be used:

- [list #]—A standard access list must be assigned a number in the range of 1 to 99.
- [permit|deny]—The access list must have one of these keywords to permit or deny traffic flowing through a router interface.
- [source address]—This parameter specifies the IP address of the source host, subnet, or network.
- [source wildcard mask]—Also referred to as an inverse mask, the wildcard mask signifies which bits of the source address are significant.

A wildcard mask is similar to a subnet mask, which determines which part of an IP address number is the network portion and which is the host portion. For example, an IP address of 10.10.1.112 with a subnet mask of 255.255.255.0 signifies that 10.10.1.0 is the subnet on which host 112 resides. In a subnet mask, 1s are used to show the significant bits. In an inverse mask, 0s perform this duty. Take a look at some examples to make this important point clearer:

```
access-list 1 deny 10.10.1.112 0.0.0.0
```

The 0s used after the IP address signify that every octet in the IP address must match the IP address being filtered. That is, the first octet must be 10, the second octet must contain a 10, the third octet must contain a 1, and the last octet must contain the number 112. For a standard IP access list, 0.0.0.0 is the default wildcard mask, so it's not necessary to add it.

In the following command, the deny keyword applies to any IP address with the first two octets containing 10.10. The 255.255 signifies that the last two octets can contain any number.

```
access-list 1 deny 10.10.1.112 0.0.255.255
```

So to deny access to all users from subnet 192.168.10.0, the access list is as follows:

```
access-list 1 deny 192.168.10.0 0.0.0.255
access-list 1 permit any
```

Any IP address from the subnet 192.168.10 is denied access because the 0.0.0 matches these first three octets. The 255 signifies that the last octet of the IP address attempting access doesn't matter, so it can be any number from 0 to 255. Luckily, Cisco allows a shortcut so that you don't have to type 0.0.0.0 when permitting or denying access to a specific host IP address. The shortcut is "host," as shown in this example:

```
access-list 1 deny host 192.168.10.112
```

The preceding command is equivalent to this one:

```
access-list 1 deny 192.168.10.112 0.0.0.0
```

When creating any access list on a Cisco router, you need to know one critical piece of information. Access lists always end with an implicit deny, even when you don't add it. For example, the following access list denies everyone access to the interface on which this access list is assigned:

```
access-list 1 deny 192.168.10.112
```

The administrator thought she was denying only this one user from accessing the corporate LAN, but Cisco automatically places an implicit deny at the end of the access list for any IP address not included. Think of it as a security enhancement. By default, after you create an access list and apply it to an interface, Cisco denies every access to the interface unless you explicitly give permission (permit) access to that interface. This means that after you deny 192.168.10.112 access, you must add the "permit any" statement, as shown here:

```
access-list 1 deny host 192.168.10.112
access-list 1 permit any
```

This is also true when using a permit statement, as shown here:

```
access-list 1 permit 192.168.0.0
```

Applying this command to an interface on a router denies everyone else on a different subnet from accessing the interface. To correct this problem, you need to add lines to permit other subnets to access the interface. To apply the access list to an interface, you perform the following steps:

1. Enter global configuration mode (with the config t command).

2. Create the access list by entering the commands shown previously.

3. Enter interface configuration mode.

4. Use the ip access-group command to apply the access list to the interface.

Here's an example of applying a basic access list to Ethernet interface e0 on a 2500 series Cisco router. The bold text is what the user configuring the router enters. Note that the prompts change as commands are entered:

```
Router> en
Password ******
Router# config t
Router(config)# access-list 1 deny 172.16.5.0 0.0.0.255
Router(config)# access-list 1 permit any
Router(config)# int e0
Router(config-if)# ip access-group 1 out
Router(config-if) Ctrl+z [to save and exit global configuration mode]
Router#
```

The ip access-group 1 command applies the access list 1 you created. The "out" keyword indicates that the filter acts on packets leaving the interface, not entering it.

Security Bytes

NOTE

Recently, a military base network was shut down for several hours when a probationary security professional inadvertently denied access to multiple routers. When creating an access list, he didn't take the implicit deny command into account. In other words, he did not place a "permit any" entry in his access list. He thought he was tightening security by restricting access to the router's interfaces using ranges of IP addresses his superior gave him. In the military, a list of IP addresses called a "black list," which contains IP addresses of known threats, is given to security personnel. These IP addresses are then entered into access lists. The security professional was terminated for this blunder.

Extended IP Access Lists

A standard IP access list is restricted to source IP addresses. So if you want to restrict a user from sending a packet to a specific IP address (destination IP address), you could not use a standard IP access list. Extended IP access lists can restrict IP traffic entering or leaving a router's interface based on the following criteria:

- Source IP address

- Destination IP address

- Protocol type

- Application port number

Configuring an extended IP access list is much the same as configuring a standard IP access list. The syntax, however, is a little more complex:

```
access-list [list #] [permit|deny] [protocol] [source IP address]
[source wildcard mask] [destination IP address] [destination
wildcard mask] [operator] [port] [log]
```

The following list explains the parameters you can use in this syntax:

- [*list #*]—Extended IP lists are represented by numbers in the range of 100 to 199. Newer versions of the Cisco IOS can also use names instead of numbers, as you'll see in the "Configuration of the PIX Firewall" section of this chapter.
- [permit | deny]—As with standard IP access lists, you can permit or deny access.
- [*protocol*]—Protocols to be filtered can be IP (which includes all protocols in the TCP/IP suite), TCP, UDP, ICMP, and so on.
- [*source IP address*]—The IP address of the source.
- [*source wildcard mask*]—A wildcard mask to determine significant bits of source IP address.
- [*destination IP address*]—The IP address of the destination.
- [*destination wildcard mask*]—A wildcard mask to determine the significant bits of the destination address
- [*operator*]—The operator can be lt (less than), gt (greater than), eq (equal to), or neq (not equal to). If the extended access list is filtering by port numbers, one of these operators can be used.
- [*port*]—Port number of the protocol to be filtered.
- [*log*]—Logs all activity of the access list for the administrator.

Next, take a look at an example of an extended IP access list to see how to use the syntax:

```
access-list 100 deny tcp host 172.16.1.112 host 172.30.1.100 eq
www
```

The access list number is 100, signifying an extended IP access list. The tcp entry is the protocol on which you're filtering. Unlike standard IP access lists, there is no default 0.0.0.0, so you must enter the 0.0.0.0 wildcard mask following the source IP address or use the keyword "host." Note that the first IP address in an extended IP access list is the source, and the second IP address is always the destination. This information is especially important for those seeking CCNA certification.

In this final example, you examine the commands entered at the Cisco router. The 172.30.1.100 in this example is a Web server. The access list is denying the user's computer with an IP address of 172.16.1.112 from accessing Web services. Note that the filtering is done on an Ethernet port as the packets enter the router. This is indicated by the "in" keyword used with the access-group command:

```
Router> en
Password ******
Router# config t
Router(config)# access-list 100 deny tcp host 172.16.1.112 host
172.30.1.100
Router(config)# access-list 100 permit any
Router(config)# int e0
Router(config-if)# ip access-group 100 in
Router(config-if) Ctrl+z
Router#
```

Activity 13-2: Creating Standard and Extended IP Access Lists

Time Required: 30 minutes

Objective: Learn how to create standard and extended IP access lists.

Description: Many routers and firewalls use a command-line interface to allow administrators to accept or deny access to the device's interfaces. Having a good background in creating access lists will help you better protect a company's internal network from the outside world. In this activity, you create standard and extended access lists.

1. Start Windows XP Professional, and open Notepad. Many Cisco and PIX firewall professionals create access lists with a basic text editor, such as Notepad, and then copy and paste the information in the device interface to which they have connected by Telnet.

2. Type the first line of a standard access list that prevents packets sent from the 193.145.85.0 network from entering the router's Ethernet interface named e0.

3. What command do you enter to assign the access list you created in Step 2 to the Ethernet e0 interface? Type the next line of the access list you created in Step 2 that must be present, or no packets from any other network can enter the router's Ethernet interface e0.

4. Save the access list you created as **Access-1**, and then open a new Notepad document by clicking **File**, **New** from the menu.

5. Create an extended access list that prevents a computer with an IP address of 193.145.85.200 from being able to telnet to an FTP server with an IP address of 172.16.1.10.

6. What command do you enter to apply the access list created in Step 5 to serial interface s1?

7. On a Cisco router, what mode must you be in to assign an access list to the router's serial interface?

8. Close Notepad and click **No** when prompted to save changes. Leave your system running for the next activity.

Understanding Firewalls

Firewalls are hardware devices or software installed on a system. They serve two purposes: controlling access to all traffic that enters an internal network, and controlling all traffic that leaves an internal network. In other words, firewalls are specifically installed on a network to protect a company's internal network from dangers that exist on the Internet. In this section, you look at the Cisco PIX hardware firewall and Microsoft Internet Security and Acceleration (ISA) Server, which is software that runs on Microsoft server OSs.

There are advantages and disadvantages to hardware and software firewalls; however, this book doesn't attempt to make recommendations, but to educate security professionals on how firewalls fit into a security strategy. Briefly, the disadvantage of hardware firewalls is that you are locked into the firewall's hardware, such as the number of interfaces it includes. With a software firewall, you can easily add NICs to the server running the firewall software. A disadvantage of a software firewall is that you might have to worry about configuration problems, such as memory requirements, hard disk space requirements, number of CPUs supported, and so on. Software firewalls rely on the OS on which they're running, such as Windows 2000 Server or Windows Server 2003, which are needed to implement versions of ISA. Hardware firewalls are usually faster and can handle a larger throughput than software firewalls.

As you have seen, a router can also be used to filter traffic entering or leaving a router's interface. Filtering can be implemented through access lists that can restrict traffic based on the source IP address, destination IP address, and protocol. However, a firewall is specifically designed as a security device and has more security features than a router.

Understanding Firewall Technology

You have seen numerous methods an attacker can use to scan a network and launch exploits. Firewalls can help reduce these attacks by using several technologies:

- Network address translation (NAT)
- Access control lists
- Packet filtering
- Stateful packet inspection (SPI)

Network Address Translation (NAT)

The most basic security feature of a firewall is **Network Address Translation (NAT)**. One job of a security professional is to hide the corporate internal network from outsiders. With NAT, internal private IP addresses are mapped to public external IP addresses, hiding the internal infrastructure from unauthorized personnel. For example, a user with a private IP address of 10.1.1.15 has her address mapped to an external IP address of 193.145.85.200. The outside world sees only this number and doesn't know the internal IP addresses the company uses.

After hackers know a computer or server's IP address, they scan that system for open or vulnerable ports. Hiding IP address numbers from hackers can help prevent this from happening. To accommodate the many addresses that need to be mapped, many organizations use Port Address Translation (PAT), which is derived from NAT. This allows thousands of internal IP addresses to be mapped to one external IP address.

Access Control Lists

As you'll recall from the router section, access lists are used to filter traffic based on source IP address, destination IP address, and ports or services. Firewalls also use this technology, as you see in the Cisco PIX firewall output section later in this chapter. After you understand how to create an access list on a router, creating one on a firewall is a similar process. Visit *www.cisco.com/warp/public/105/acl_wp.html* for more information on Cisco's access control lists.

Packet Filtering

Another basic security function a firewall performs is packet filtering. Packet filters screen packets based on information contained in the packet header, such as:

- Protocol type
- IP address
- TCP/UDP port

Stateful Packet Inspection (SPI)

Firewalls usually take the basic filtering done by a router a step further by performing stateful packet inspection. **Stateful packet filters** record session-specific information about a network connection, including the ports a client uses, in a file called a **state table**. Table 13-2 is an example of a state table.

Table 13-2 State table example

Source IP	Source Port	Destination IP	Destination Port	Connection State
10.1.1.100	1022	193.145.85.201	80	Established
10.1.1.102	1040	193.145.85.1	80	Established
10.1.1.110	1035	193.145.85.117	23	Established
192.145.85.20	1080	10.1.1.210	25	Established

In this state table, several internal hosts using private IP addresses have established connections to various external IP addresses. One host has established a Telnet session (port 23), two hosts have established HTTP connections (port 80), and one host has established a connection to an e-mail server (port 25). This can help reduce port scans that rely on spoofing or sending packets after a three-way handshake. If a hacker attempted to send a SYN/ACK packet from an IP address not in the state table, the packet would be dropped. As you learned in Chapter 5, a SYN/ACK packet is sent only after a SYN packet has been received.

Stateful packet filters recognize types of anomalies that most routers ignore, such as hundreds or thousands of SYN/ACK packets being sent to a computer or server, even though the computer or server hasn't sent out any SYN packets. **Stateless packet filters** handle each packet on an individual basis, so spoofing or DoS attacks are more prevalent.

13

Implementing a Firewall

Placing a firewall between a company's internal network and the Internet is dangerous because it leaves the company open to attack if a hacker compromises the firewall and then has complete access to the internal network. To reduce this risk, most firewall topologies use a demilitarized zone to add a layer of defense.

Demilitarized Zone (DMZ)

A **demilitarized zone (DMZ)** is a small network containing resources that a company wants to make available to Internet users; this setup helps maintain security on the company's internal network. A DMZ sits between the Internet and the internal network and is sometimes referred to as a "perimeter network." Figure 13-3 shows how outside users can access the e-mail and Web servers located in the DMZ, but the internal network is protected from these outside Internet users.

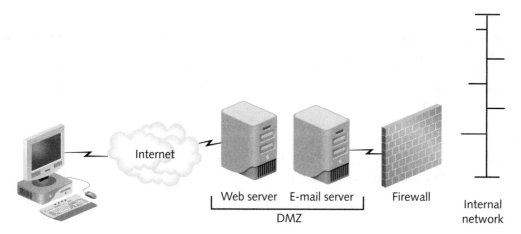

Figure 13-3   A DMZ protecting an internal network.

Note that Internet users can access the DMZ without going through the firewall. A better security strategy is to place an additional firewall in the design, as shown in Figure 13-4.

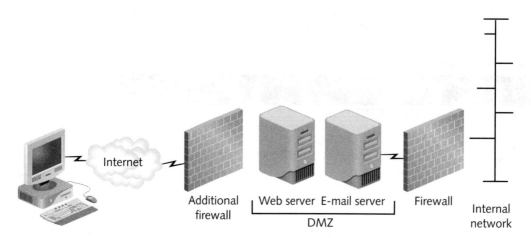

Figure 13-4   An additional firewall used to protect the DMZ

For users to access the internal network from the Internet, they need to pass through two firewalls. This is probably the most popular design for a firewall topology.

Understanding the Private Internet Exchange (PIX) Firewall

A good way to learn how a firewall operates is to look at the configuration of one of the most popular firewalls on the market: the Cisco PIX firewall. In the following sections, you view the configuration file of a PIX firewall that was used to protect a large multimillion-dollar business to get an idea of what security professionals need to know.

 Cisco has classes and books on configuring this firewall product, so the information in this section is just the tip of the iceberg.

NOTE

Configuration of the PIX Firewall

After telneting into a PIX firewall, you can see the similarity of connecting to a Cisco router. A login prompt appears that's similar to the Cisco prompt you saw earlier in this chapter:

```
If you are not authorized to be in this XYZ Hawaii network device,
log out immediately!
User Access Verification
Password:
```

The administrator of this company created a banner warning anyone attempting to connect that he or she should be authorized before continuing. This banner might seem like a waste of time, but it serves a legal purpose. If the banner had said "Welcome, please log on," an intruder might not be prosecuted if he or she hacked into your network. The U.S. legal system has already dropped charges against hackers who entered sites with the word "Welcome" used in banners.

After you log on with the correct password, the firewall displays the following information:

```
Type help or '?' for a list of available commands.
xyz>
```

Note that the prompt is the same one you saw when logging on to a Cisco router. You are now in user mode. After entering the ? character at the prompt, you see the following information:

```
xyz> ?

At end of show <command>, use the pipe character '|' followed by:
begin|include|exclude|grep [-v] <regular_exp>, to filter show
output.

enable    Turn on privileged commands
help      Help list
login     Log in as a particular user
logout    Exit from current user profile, and to unprivileged mode
pager     Control page length for pagination
quit      Quit from the current mode, end configuration or logout
xyz>
```

To enter privileged mode, the user types the enable command (as you saw previously for a Cisco router) and then is prompted to enter a password as shown:

```
Password: ********
xyz#
```

13

After entering the correct password, the user is placed in privileged mode, indicated by the # prompt. Entering the ? character reveals several more commands available to the privileged mode user. The following excerpt shows some of the information you see on-screen :

```
xyz# ?

At end of show <command>, use the pipe character '|' followed by:
begin|include|exclude|grep [-v] <regular_exp>, to filter show
output.

arp          Change or view arp table
capture      Capture inbound and outbound
configure    Configure from terminal
copy         Copy image or PDM file from TFTP server into flash
debug        Debug packets or ICMP tracings
disable      Exit from privileged mode
eeprom       Show or reprogram the 525 onboard i82559 devices
flashfs      Show, destroy, or preserve filesystem information
help         Help list
kill         Terminate a telnet session
logout       Exit from current user profile
logging      Clear syslog entries from the internal buffer
memory       System memory utilization
pager        Control page length for pagination
passwd       Change Telnet console access password
ping         Test connectivity from specified interface to <ip>
quit         Quit from the current mode
reload       Halt and reload system
shun         Manages the filtering of packets from undesired hosts
who          Show active administration sessions on PIX
xyz#
```

To enter configuration mode in PIX, you use the same command as on a Cisco router. To see the commands available in global configuration mode, you would enter the following commands:

```
xyz# configure terminal
xyz(config)# ?
```

You then see a long list of available commands that illustrate the complexity of configuring a firewall. Learning how to configure a PIX firewall would take more than one chapter in a security book, but you can learn quite a bit by examining this configuration file. Some names and several IP addresses were changed, but most of the information was left unmodified. The following code block shows the beginning of the running configuration file:

```
: Written by enable_15 at 12:24:53.789 HST Mon Mar 14 2005
PIX Version 6.3(4)
interface ethernet0 auto
interface ethernet1 auto
interface ethernet2 auto
interface ethernet3 auto shutdown
interface ethernet4 auto shutdown
interface ethernet5 auto shutdown
nameif ethernet0 outside security0
nameif ethernet1 inside security100
nameif ethernet2 dmz security50
nameif ethernet3 intf3 security6
nameif ethernet4 intf4 security8
nameif ethernet5 intf5 security10
enable password VKFoztttwQo/asdU encrypted
passwd dcccrcF.Fuyyy0sF encrypted
hostname xyz
domain-name ciscopix.com
```

You can see that the PIX firewall has several Ethernet interfaces. Interfaces ethernet3 through ethernet5 are currently shut down. Nameif is a PIX command to name an interface, and you see this command used with entries such as security0 and security100. PIX allows the administrator to assign values to an interface that designate its security level. Zero means low security, and 100 signifies the highest security. Note that the outside interface, perhaps going to the Internet, has the lowest security, whereas the inside network has the highest. The administrator also assigned an encrypted password to this firewall.

So far, this is not too difficult to understand. Next, look at how the firewall uses access lists to filter traffic. Instead of numbers to identify the type of access list, PIX enables an administrator to use descriptive names for the access list. In this configuration, the administrator has created an access control list (ACL) with the name acl_to_outside.

```
access-list acl_to_outside remark     Allow Bob Jones/Exchange to
smtp access-list acl_to_outside remark
**************************************************
access-list acl_to_outside permit tcp host 172.16.100.41 any eq
smtp access-list acl_to_outside permit tcp host 172.16.1.109 any
eq smtp
**** permits user's laptop to use smtp
```

The administrator has documented this section of the configuration file well, so a beginner can read through this section and understand what's happening. To allow Bob Jones to send mail, his specific computer IP addresses are permitted to connect to the outside. Next, the administrator decided to block gaming ports, as shown in the following lines:

```
access-list acl_to_outside remark     Block the gaming ports
access-list acl_to_outside remark
**************************************************
access-list acl_to_outside deny tcp any any range 9992 9998
access-list acl_to_outside deny udp any any range 9992 9998
access-list acl_to_outside deny tcp any any eq 26000
access-list acl_to_outside deny udp any any eq 26000
access-list acl_to_outside deny tcp any any range 28800 29000
access-list acl_to_outside deny udp any any range 28800 29000
access-list acl_to_outside deny tcp any any eq 666
access-list acl_to_outside deny udp any any eq 666
access-list acl_to_outside deny tcp any any eq 36794

access-list acl_to_outside remark     Allow everything else
access-list acl_to_outside remark
**************************************************
access-list acl_to_outside permit ip any any
access-list acl_from_outside remark
```

This administrator remembered the rule of an implicit deny being the last line of an access list. By denying the gaming ports, he needed to add the "permit any" statement, or he might have forgotten to place the command at the end of this file. This error could have inadvertently denied everyone from accessing any outside addresses. Next, look at a few more lines in the PIX firewall access list:

```
access-list acl_from_outside remark     Allow Dave into SSH (PMS
servers) access-list acl_from_outside remark
**************************************************
access-list acl_from_outside permit tcp host 123.61.64.54 host
60.12.241.182 eq ssh
```

Note that the administrator is allowing Dave (123.61.64.54) to use SSH from his host IP address to the destination IP address of 60.12.241.182. For the acl_from_outside and acl_to_outside access lists to be implemented, the following lines are the most important:

```
access-group acl_from_outside in interface outside
access-group acl_to_outside in interface inside
```

In these code lines, the access lists are assigned to both the outside and inside interfaces as an "in" filter.

Finally, take a look at a large section of the PIX configuration to give you a better perspective of what a firewall access list looks like. This section of code shows that the administrator configured a computer located in the DMZ (192.168.1.14) to connect to a domain controller running Windows Server 2003 and Microsoft Exchange located behind the firewall on the customer's network. If a hacker tried to access any ports shown in the following list, the packet would be dropped because the filter on those ports is denied. Only the 192.168.1.14 host can access ports 389, 88, 1120, and so on that are open on the 172.16.100.31 server:

```
access-list acl_from_dmz remark    Allow Webmail access to
DC/Exchange (exb1) access-list acl_from_dmz remark
*************************************************
access-list acl_from_dmz permit tcp host 192.168.1.14 host
172.16.100.41 eq https
access-list acl_from_dmz permit tcp host 192.168.1.14 host
172.16.100.41 eq www
access-list acl_from_dmz permit tcp host 192.168.1.14 host
172.16.100.41 eq imap4
access-list acl_from_dmz permit tcp host 192.168.1.14 host
172.16.100.31 eq 691
access-list acl_from_dmz permit tcp host 192.168.1.14 host
172.16.100.31 eq ldap
access-list acl_from_dmz permit udp host 192.168.1.14 host
172.16.100.31 eq 389
access-list acl_from_dmz permit tcp host 192.168.1.14 host
172.16.100.31 eq 3268
access-list acl_from_dmz permit tcp host 192.168.1.14 host
172.16.100.31 eq 88
access-list acl_from_dmz permit udp host 192.168.1.14 host
172.16.100.31 eq 88
access-list acl_from_dmz permit tcp host 192.168.1.14 host
172.16.100.31 eq 135
access-list acl_from_dmz permit tcp host 192.168.1.14 host
172.16.100.31 eq 1120
access-list acl_from_dmz permit tcp host 192.168.1.14 host
172.16.100.32 eq 691
access-list acl_from_dmz permit tcp host 192.168.1.14 host
172.16.100.32 eq ldap
access-list acl_from_dmz permit udp host 192.168.1.14 host
172.16.100.32 eq 389
access-list acl_from_dmz permit tcp host 192.168.1.14 host
172.16.100.32 eq 3268
access-list acl_from_dmz permit tcp host 192.168.1.14 host
172.16.100.32 eq 88
access-list acl_from_dmz permit udp host 192.168.1.14 host
172.16.100.32 eq 88
access-list acl_from_dmz permit tcp host 192.168.1.14 host
172.16.100.32 eq 135
access-list acl_from_dmz permit tcp host 192.168.1.14 host
172.16.100.32 eq 1120
access-list acl_from_dmz permit tcp host 192.168.1.14 host
172.16.100.31 eq 445
access-list acl_from_dmz permit tcp host 192.168.1.14 host
172.16.100.32 eq 445
```

ACTIVITY

Activity 13-3: Understanding the PIX Firewall

Time Required: 30 minutes

Objective: Learn more about configuring a PIX firewall.

Description: The Cisco PIX firewall is one of the most popular firewalls on the market. As a network security professional, you will most likely need to configure a PIX firewall or, at minimum, review its configuration. In this activity, you use the Internet to get a better understanding of this important firewall.

1. Start a Web browser, type the URL **www.google.com**, and press **Enter**. On the Google search page, type **Cisco PIX firewall VPN guide Version 6.2** and click **Google Search**.

2. On the results page, click the **Cisco PIX Firewall and VPN Configuration Guide Version 6.2** link.

3. On the Cisco PIX Firewall and VPN Configuration Guide, Version 6.2 page, click the **Getting Started** link in the table of contents.

4. On the Cisco Systems Getting Started page, click the **How the PIX Firewall Works** link.

5. Read the "How the PIX Firewall Works" section, which discusses the security levels a PIX firewall uses. What is the security level of an outside interface? What is the security level of an inside interface?

6. Scroll through the document and read the "Protecting Your Network from Attack" section, which discusses Unicast RPF. What is it used for? Why is the Flood Defender feature of a PIX firewall used?

7. Spend the next 5 to 10 minutes browsing the document. Cisco does an excellent job of preparing users to optimize hardware they purchase. You might want to download this manual to your laptop for quick access when performing security tests.

8. Leave your Web browser open for the next activity.

Understanding Microsoft ISA

Many vendors have seen the need for protecting networks through the use of firewalls. Some companies, such as Microsoft, have approached the problem via software instead of manufacturing hardware devices. Microsoft **Internet Security and Acceleration (ISA) Server** functions as a software router, firewall, and IDS. This section covers the firewall and IDS functionality of ISA.

ISA has the same functionality as any hardware router, except that it uses the Windows OS to perform these functions. ISA provides the following security features:

- Packet filtering to control incoming traffic

- Application filtering through the examination of protocols

- Intrusion detection filters

- Access policies to control outgoing traffic

IP Packet Filters

ISA enables administrators to filter IP traffic based on the following:

- Source and destination IP address

- Network protocol, such as HTTP

- Source port or destination port

This filtering isn't different from how most firewalls operate. However, with ISA Server, you can use a GUI for these configurations (see Figure 13-5) instead of the text-mode creation of access lists.

A network segment can be denied or allowed HTTP access in the Remote Computer tab of the HTTP Port 80 Properties dialog box shown in Figure 13-6.

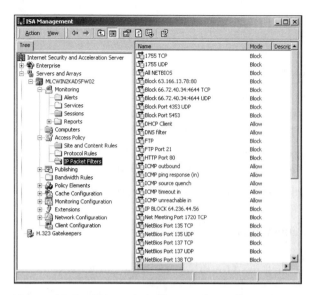

Figure 13-5 ISA packet filtering through an access policy

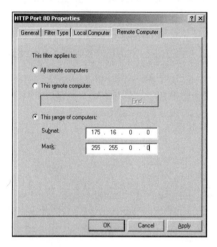

Figure 13-6 Denying access to Port 80 for the specified subnet

Application Filters

ISA application filters can accept or deny data from specific applications or data containing specific content. For example, an SMTP filter can restrict e-mail with specific attachments, e-mail from a specific user or domain, e-mail containing specific keywords, and SMTP commands a user enters from a command prompt. As shown in Figure 13-7, the administrator selects the Application Filters option and then selects the protocol he or she wants to configure.

In the SMTP Filter Properties dialog box, the administrator can filter a specific e-mail attachment based on a rule he or she configures. In this example, any e-mail containing an attachment named loveNote is deleted (see Figure 13-8).

The Attachments tab shows the rule that was configured. In this tab, an administrator can also easily remove, add, or edit rules (see Figure 13-9).

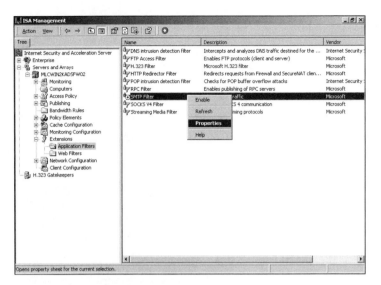

Figure 13-7 SMTP filter configuration

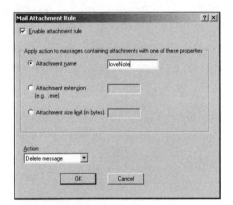

Figure 13-8 Creating an attachment rule

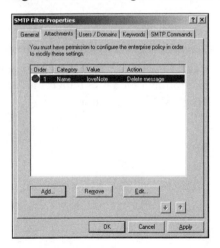

Figure 13-9 Viewing a rule in the Attachments tab

By selecting the Users/Domains tab in the SMTP Filter Properties dialog box, an administrator can filter e-mail messages sent from a user or from specific domains. You can perform this task by using access list commands on a PIX firewall, but with ISA Server, you simply add the user or domain name in this tab (see Figure 13-10).

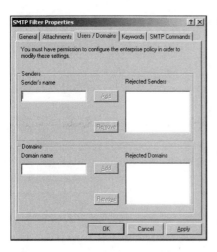

Figure 13-10   The Users/Domains tab of the SMTP Filter Properties dialog box

As a security professional, you might be asked to restrict e-mails containing certain keywords to reduce spam or prevent introducing spyware and adware to a network. In Figure 13-11, the administrator is configuring a keyword rule to delete all emails with the word "Mortgage" in the header or message body.

Figure 13-11   Configuring a keyword rule

The last tab in the SMTP Filter Properties dialog box is SMTP Commands (see Figure 13-12). If you recall from Chapter 2, SMTP commands can be entered at the command prompt after a user telnets into an SMTP server. In this tab, the administrator can prevent a user from running SMTP commands.

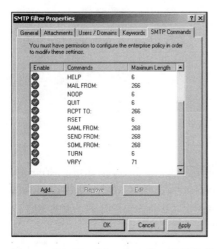

Figure 13-12   Viewing the SMTP Commands tab

As you can see, ISA Server can be a helpful tool for protecting the network you are testing. ISA simplifies many tasks for security professionals.

Intrusion Detection Filters

ISA Server includes intrusion detection filters that analyze all traffic for possible known intrusions:

- *DNS intrusion detection filter*—This filter analyzes DNS traffic destined to an internal network and checks for any known DNS attacks.

- *POP intrusion detection filter*—This filter looks for any known attacks made on POP servers and drops the packet before it reaches the POP server. Figure 13-13 shows a filter checking for a known POP buffer overflow.

- *FTP Access filter*—This filter analyzes FTP traffic so that an ISA server can support FTP.

- *H.323 filter*—This filter analyzes traffic generated by multimedia programs, such as telephony and conferencing, that use the H.323 protocol, such as Microsoft Exchange.

- *HTTP Redirector filter*—This filter redirects Web clients to a proxy server (the Web site the user requested) or blocks the user from connecting to the requested Web site.

- *RPC filter*—This filter enables servers to use the Remote Procedure Call (RPC) protocol, such as Microsoft Exchange Server (e-mail).

- *SMTP filter*—This filter blocks unwanted e-mail messages based on properties of the message or the sender of the message. This filter is described in detail in the "Application Filters" section of this chapter.

- *SOCKS V4 filter*—This filter allows clients to use the Internet protocol called SOCKS, which is an abbreviation of the word "sockets."

- *Streaming Media filter*—This filter allows clients to use streaming video services on the network, such as the Microsoft Media Server (MMS) protocol.

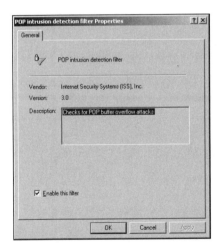

Figure 13-13 A POP intrusion detection filter that checks for buffer overflows

ISA also includes intrusion detection functionality that enables an administrator to filter out known attacks. Figure 13-14 shows the known attacks that ISA's IDS recognizes.

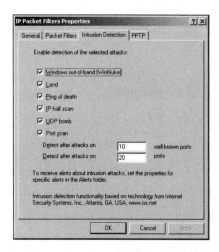

Figure 13-14   An IDS detecting known attacks

Access Policies

ISA allows an administrator to control outgoing traffic through the use of access policies and rules. An **access policy** consists of the following rules:

- Policy rules
- Site and content rules
- IP filter rules

A discussion of Microsoft's use of policies for server administration is beyond the scope of this book, but you can see how a policy or a rule can restrict access to a protocol or even to a destination network. As shown in Figure 13-15, an administrator selects IP Packet Filters under Access Policy, and then selects the protocol he or she wants to configure.

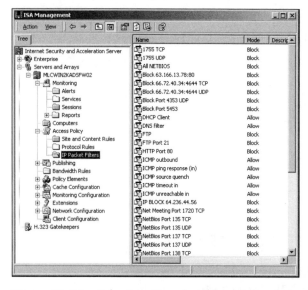

Figure 13-15   Selecting IP packet filters through an access policy

UNDERSTANDING INTRUSION DETECTION SYSTEMS (IDSs)

Intrusion detection systems (IDSs) monitor network devices so that security administrators can identify attacks in progress and stop them. For example, for users to be able to access a Web server, a firewall must allow Port 80 to be open. Unfortunately, opening this port also allows a hacker to attack the Web server. An IDS looks at the traffic traversing the wire that connects to Port 80 and compares it with known exploits, similar to virus software using a signature file to identify viruses. The following section describes two types of intrusion detection systems: network-based and host-based.

Network-Based and Host-Based IDSs

Network-based IDSs monitor activity on network segments. Essentially, they sniff traffic as it flows over the network and alert a security administrator when something suspicious occurs. **Host-based IDSs** are used to protect a critical network server or database server. The software is installed on the server you're attempting to protect, just like antivirus software you install on your PC.

IDSs are categorized by how they react when they detect suspicious behavior. Systems that don't take any action to stop or prevent an activity are called **passive systems**. They do, of course, send out an alert and log the activity, much like an underpaid security guard at a shopping mall witnessing an armed robbery. **Active systems** also log events and send out alerts, but they can also interoperate with routers and firewalls. For example, an active IDS can send an access list to a router that closes an interface to prevent attackers from damaging the network.

Table 13-3 lists some of the many IDSs on the market. You might recognize Snort on the list, which is covered in the Security+ course. Airsnort, covered briefly in Chapter 11, is the wireless equivalent of Snort. Spend some time visiting the Web sites listed in the table to learn more about these products. IDSs are probably the best defense against network attacks. When combined with routers and firewall technology, they can help you protect the network you have been asked to secure.

13

Table 13-3   Intrusion detection systems

Company	Description
Aladdin Knowledge Systems (www.aladdin.com)	Provides security against known and unknown security threats
Entercept Security Technologies (www.mcafeesecurity.com/us/products/mcafee/host_ips/desktop_server_agents.htm)	Host-based IDS that focuses on protecting OSs and applications
Cisco Systems, Inc. (www.cisco.com)	Network-based IDS formerly known as NetRanger
Computer Associates International, Inc. (www.ca.com)	Part of the eTrust suite of security products
CyberSafe Corp. (www.cybersafe.com)	Combines host-based and network-based IDSs
Internet Security Systems, Inc. (www.iss.net)	Provides integrated host- and network-based IDSs
Raytheon Co. (www3.ca.com/products/)	Designed to detect threats in an organization
Snort (www.snort.org)	Open-source IDS
Sourcefire, Inc. (www.sourcefire.com)	Open-source network intrusion detection software
Symantec Corp. (www.symantec.com)	Host-based and network-based IDSs

UNDERSTANDING HONEYPOTS

A **honeypot** is a computer placed on the perimeter of a network that contains information or data intended to lure and then trap hackers. A security professional configures the computer to have vulnerabilities so that hackers spend time trying to exploit those vulnerabilities. One goal of a honeypot is to have hackers connect to the "phony" computer long enough to be traced, just as in movies when the FBI wants a criminal to stay on the telephone long enough to trace his or her location.

For more information on honeypots, visit *www.honeynet.org*. This Web site offers exercises and challenges that encourage user participation, contains white papers on the subject of honeypots, and includes workshop presentations that describe the Honey Pot Project. If you decide to participate in any of the exercises, you might want to use a computer lab isolated from any production servers or network. A test computer should be used because of the possibility of virus infection or data corruption.

How They Work

If attackers can get to your internal network, they can create havoc. A honeypot appears to have important data or sensitive information stored on it. For example, it could store fake financial data that tempts hackers into attempting to browse through the data. The government and private industry have used the concept of creating honeypots to lure attackers into network areas away from the real data for many years. Basically, the belief is that if hackers discover a vulnerability in a system, they will spend time exploiting that vulnerability and stop looking for other areas to exploit and access a company's resources.

Honeypots also enable security professionals to collect data on attackers. In this way, the hunter becomes the hunted. Honeypots are available commercially and through open-source avenues. Tables 13-4 and 13-5 show some of the many products available for security professionals.

Table 13-4 Commercial honeypots

Name	Description
Decoy Server (*www.symantec.com/*)	Defined by Symantec as a deception-based IDS. Threats are logged in real time as a hacker is placed in an isolated area called a "cage."
KFSensor (*www.keyfocus. net/kfsensor/*)	A Windows honeypot that detects the nature of attacks on file shares and Windows services.
NetBait (*www2.netbaitinc. com:5080*)	Makes it possible to create thousands of fake services while taking an intruder away from the real network. NetBait also enables administrators to track and analyze an intruder's activity.
Specter (*www.specter.com* or *www.spectorcne.com*)	Lists configuration settings and statistics for all interfaces on a router.

Table 13-5 Open-source honeypots

Name	Description
Jackpot (*http://jackpot.uk.net/*)	An SMTP-relay honeypot that catches spammers. The program runs on Linux and enables you to watch in real time as spammers use HELO commands.
Back Officer Friendly (BOF) (*www.nfr.com/resource/ backOfficer.php*)	Detects attempted connections to services such as Telnet, FTP, SMTP, POP3, and IMAP4 and gives a fake reply, thus keeping hackers busy. Runs on the Windows platform.
LaBrea Tarpit (*http://labrea. sourceforge.net/labrea-info.html*)	Honeypot that answers connection requests in such a way that the attacking machine gets "stuck." Works on FreeBSD, Linux, Solaris, and Windows platforms.
Honeyd (*www.honeyd.org/*)	Written in C for *NIX platforms, it can monitor millions of unused IP addresses, simulate hundreds of OSs, and monitor TCP and UDP ports.
Tiny Honeypot (*www.alpinista. org/thp/*)	A honeypot that creates thousands of bogus services that make it difficult for hackers to sift through information. No matter what attack a hacker attempts, it will be successful.

The good news is that creating a honeypot without dedicating a powerful server to the task is possible now. Virtual honeypots are created by using a programming language rather than configuring a physical device. You can download free open-source code and install it on a GNU Linux or BSD UNIX computer. In Activity 13-4, you examine one such product: Honeyd, created and maintained by Niels Provos.

Activity 13-4: Examining an Open-Source Honeypot

Time Required: 30 minutes

Objective: Learn about the virtual honeypot program called Honeyd.

Description: As a security professional, you might need to set up a honeypot to reduce the possibility of a network attack. Many products are available that can help reduce attacks by tricking hackers into accessing fake information; while they're busy breaking into the honeypot, you can log their activities. In this activity, you look at an open-source product called Honeyd.

1. Start a Web browser if necessary, type the URL **www.honeyd.org**, and press **Enter**.

2. On the Developments of the Honeyd Virtual Honeypot Web page, read the information, and then click the **Frequently Asked Questions** link in the Honeyd Resources section.

3. From the Honeyd Resources menu, click the **Sample Configurations** link. Read the information on configurations to get an idea of how a honeypot works.

4. Close your Web browser, and shut down your system.

If time permits, you might want to download the Honeyd program from *www.honeyd.org* and install it on a Linux system. You might also want to set up a lab and get some practice using the program, which does an excellent job of tracking hackers who are attempting to access resources on a company's network. It can even trick Nmap into believing it has detected the OS running on a system. For example, you can create templates that emulate whatever OS you want the attacker to believe is running on a particular IP address.

Honeyd monitors all unused IP addresses on a network. It assumes that anyone monitoring one of these addresses is a malicious user. After all, why would anyone monitor an IP address that's not being used? Honeyd generates an alert and indicates what the attacker is attempting to do. For more information on using this program, visit *www.securityfocus.com/infocus/1659*.

CHAPTER SUMMARY

- Security professionals can use a variety of security devices to protect a network, such as routers, firewalls, and intrusion detection systems.

- Routers use access lists to accept or deny traffic through their interfaces. On Cisco routers, access lists can be used to filter IP, IPX, and other traffic coming into a network and leaving a network. The access lists are applied to various interfaces on the router.

- Firewalls can be hardware devices or software installed on computer systems. Firewalls are used to control access to (and data from) an internal network. The Cisco PIX firewall is one of the most popular firewalls.

- Firewalls use NAT, IP filtering, and access control lists to filter incoming and outgoing network traffic. The basic function performed by a firewall is packet filtering, in which packets are filtered or screened based on information in the packet header.

- Stateful packet filters record session-specific information about network connections, whereas stateless packet filters handle each packet individually.

- The DMZ is used to add a layer of defense between the Internet and a company's internal network. The DMZ sits between the Internet and a company's internal network and is sometimes referred to as a perimeter network.

- Many hardware firewalls are on the market. A popular one is Cisco's PIX firewall. PIX uses a syntax similar to that of Cisco routers, so administrators can easily learn how to configure a PIX firewall.

❑ Software firewalls are installed on a computer. One of the most popular is Microsoft ISA, which functions as a software router, firewall, and IDS. ISA provides security through IP packet filters, application filters, and intrusion detection filters.

❑ Intrusion detection systems monitor network devices so that administrators can identify any anomalies that might occur on a network. For example, a computer that receives thousands of SYN packets over a short period might indicate that an intruder is scanning the network.

❑ Network-based intrusion systems monitor activity on network segments, whereas host-based intrusion detection systems are used to protect a critical network server or database server.

❑ Passive IDSs do not take any action or prevent an activity from continuing to occur. Rather, they simply alert and log the activity for the administrator. Active IDSs log and send alerts but also interoperate with the routers and firewalls and can close a port or interface on a router that's possibly being compromised.

❑ Honeypots are computer systems that contain bogus information and vulnerabilities specifically designed to lure hackers away from legitimate network resources. Instead of attacking your production network, they are distracted by the honeypot and spend their time exploring the emulated software and data it contains.

KEY TERMS

access policy — A set of rules and policies that an administrator can use to control outgoing traffic.

active systems — An IDS that logs events, sends out alerts, and can interoperate with routers and firewalls.

demilitarized zone (DMZ) — A small network containing resources that sits between the Internet and the internal network, sometimes referred to as a "perimeter network." It's used when a company wants to make resources available to Internet users yet keep the company's internal network secure.

distance-vector routing protocol — A routing protocol that passes its routing table (which contains all possible paths it has discovered) to all routers participating on the network. If the router learns one new path, it sends the entire routing table, which is not as efficient as a link-state routing protocol.

firewalls — Hardware devices or software installed on a system that serve two purposes: controlling access to all traffic that enters an internal network and controlling all traffic that leaves an internal network. Firewalls are specifically installed on a network to protect a company's internal network from dangers on the Internet.

honeypot — A computer placed on the perimeter of a network that contains information or data intended to lure and then trap hackers.

host-based IDS — Software used to protect a critical network server or database server. The software is installed on the server you're attempting to protect, just like antivirus software you install on your PC.

Internet Security and Acceleration (ISA) Server — Microsoft software that functions as a router, a firewall, and an IDS.

intrusion detection systems (IDSs) — Hardware or software devices that monitor network devices so that security administrators can identify attacks in progress and stop them.

IP access lists — A list of IP addresses, subnets, or networks that are allowed or denied access through a router's interface.

link-state routing protocol — A routing protocol that uses link-state advertisements to send any changes in topology or new paths learned to other routers participating on the network. This method is efficient because only new information is sent over the wire.

Network Address Translation (NAT) — A basic security feature of a firewall used to hide the corporate internal network from outsiders. With NAT, internal private IP addresses are mapped to public external IP addresses, hiding the internal infrastructure from unauthorized personnel.

network-based IDS — A device that monitors activity on network segments. Essentially, a network-based IDS sniffs traffic as it flows over the network and alerts a security administrator when something suspicious occurs.

passive systems — An IDS that does not take any action to stop or prevent an activity.

privileged mode — A method used on Cisco routers that allows an administrator to perform full router configuration tasks. Privileged mode is also called enabled mode.

stateful packet filters — A filter on a router that records session-specific information into a file about a network connection, including the ports a client uses.

stateless packet filters — A filter that handles each packet on an individual basis, so spoofing or DoS attacks are more prevalent.

state table — A file created by a stateful packet filter that contains information on network connections.

user mode — The default method used on a Cisco router in which an administrator can perform basic troubleshooting tests and list information stored on the router. In this mode, administrators can't make any changes to the router's configuration.

REVIEW QUESTIONS

1. Which routing protocol broadcasts the entire routing table to all routers when a new path is discovered?

   a. RIP

   b. IP

   c. TCP

   d. OSPF

2. A distance-vector routing protocol uses OSPF to determine the best path. True or False?

3. Which of the following Cisco components stores the router's running configuration, routing tables, and buffers?

   a. NVRAM

   b. RAM

   c. ROM

   d. Flash

4. If the Flash memory of a Cisco router becomes corrupted, the router can boot from which of the following components?

   a. ROM

   b. NVRAM

   c. RAM

   d. CD-ROM

5. Which prompt is displayed if a user logs into a Cisco router in privileged mode?

   a. Router>

   b. Router+

   c. Router#

   d. Router\>

6. To change from user mode to privileged mode, the administrator of a Cisco router enters which command?

   a. priv

   b. chmod

   c. config

   d. en

13

7. What prompt is displayed if a Cisco administrator is in global configuration mode?

   a. Router(config)#

   b. Router(config)>

   c. Router(config-if)#

   d. Router(config-if)>

8. A standard IP access list can't filter IP packets based on the destination address of an IP packet. True or False?

9. There are three networks that connect to a Cisco router's interfaces: 12.0.0.0, 172.16.15.0, and 192.168.10.0. The following access list is created by an administrator:

   ```
   access-list 1 deny 12.0.0.0
   ip access-group 1 in
   ```

   If this access list is assigned to Ethernet interface e0, which of the following networks can't access that interface?

   a. 12.0.0.0

   b. 172.16.15.0

   c. 192.168.10.0

   d. all of the above

10. Write the four steps an administrator performs to apply an access list to an interface.

11. An extended IP access list can be used to filter IP traffic based on source IP address, destination IP address, and protocol. True or False?

12. What is the main purpose of a firewall? (Choose all that apply.)

    a. control access to all traffic that enters an internal network

    b. control all traffic that leaves an external network

    c. control all traffic that leaves an internal network

    d. control all traffic that enters an external network

13. Firewalls are installed on a network to protect a company's internal network from dangers on the Internet. True or False?

14. _____ is a technology used by firewalls to hide the internal network topology from outside users.

    a. packet filtering

    b. SPI

    c. ACL

    d. NAT

15. Which packet filter type handles each packet on an individual basis?

    a. stateful

    b. state table

    c. protocol type

    d. stateless

16. A DMZ is also referred to as a _____ .

    a. perimeter network

    b. stateful network

    c. stateless network

    d. honeypot

17. Microsoft Internet Security and Acceleration Server can function as which of the following? (Choose all that apply.)

    a. an intrusion detection system

    b. a router

    c. a firewall

    d. a honeypot

18. Host-based IDS can protect smaller subnets that contain fewer than 255 hosts. True or False?

19. Which type of IDS can send an access list to a router or firewall when an intrusion is detected on a network?

    a. active system

    b. passive system

    c. firewall system

    d. host-based

20. What is the main rationale for deploying a honeypot in an organization? (Choose all that apply.)

    a. lure hackers

    b. entrap hackers

    c. distract hackers from attacking legitimate network resources

    d. protect the DMZ from internal attacks

13

CASE PROJECTS

Case 13-1: Determining Possible Firewall Vulnerabilities of a Company's Network

CASE PROJECTS

The security test you have conducted for K. J. Williams Corporation has revealed the potential for ICMP type exploits to occur on the network. You were able to perform multiple scans and ping sweeps from outside the company's internal network and are concerned that hackers could do the same and attempt to shut down the network by using a DoS attack. Paul Edwards, a system administrator, informs you that he needs to be able to ping computers from his office when testing connectivity problems. His computer connects to the company's internal network through a switch on the main building's second floor.

Based on the preceding information, write a brief report on your recommendations for configuring the company's firewall or routers. The report should give an example of what an access list might contain to prevent outside users from pinging computers on the internal network.

Case 13-2: Attracting Hackers to K. J. Williams Corporation

CASE PROJECTS

After conducting a thorough security test on the K. J. Williams network, you have identified several intrusion attempts from various sources over the Internet. The hackers have not gained access to the internal network, but you are concerned that it's only a matter of time before the attempts become successful.

Based on the preceding information, write a one-page report describing what can be done to attract intruders and keep them connected to the network long enough so that the hackers can be traced. The report should discuss the pros and cons of using this strategy and should mention any legal issues the company might face.

Table A-1 Comparing computer crime laws in Vermont and New York

Law	Description
Vermont statutes, Title 13, Chapter 87: Computer Crimes	
§ 4101. Definitions	(1) "Access" means to instruct, communicate with, store data in, enter data in, retrieve data from, or otherwise make use of any resources of a computer, computer system, or computer network.
	(2) "Computer" means an electronic device which performs logical, arithmetic, and memory functions by the manipulations of electronic, photonic or magnetic impulses, and includes all input, output, processing, storage, software, or communications facilities which are connected or related to such a device in a system or network, including devices available to the public for limited or designated use or other devices used to access or connect to such a system or network.
	(3) "Computer network" means the interconnection of remote user terminals with a computer through communications lines, or a complex consisting of two or more interconnected computers.
	(4) "Computer program" means a series of instructions or statements or related data that, in actual or modified form, is capable of causing a computer or a computer system to perform specified functions in a form acceptable to a computer, which permits the functioning of a computer system in a manner designed to provide appropriate products from such computer system.
	(5) "Computer software" means a set of computer programs, procedures, and associated documentation concerned with the operation of a computer system.
	(6) "Computer system" means a set of connected computer equipment, devices and software.
	(7) "Data" means any representation of information, knowledge, facts, concepts, or instructions which are being prepared or have been prepared and are intended to be entered, processed, or stored, are being entered, processed, or stored, or have been entered, processed, or stored in a computer, computer system, or computer network.
	(8) "Property" includes electronically-produced data, and computer software and programs in either machine or human readable form, and any other tangible or intangible item of value.
	(9) "Services" includes computer time, data processing, and storage functions. (Added 1999, No. 35, § 1.)
§ 4102. Unauthorized access	A person who knowingly and intentionally and without lawful authority, accesses any computer, computer system, computer network, computer software, computer program, or data contained in such computer, computer system, computer program, or computer network shall be imprisoned not more than six months or fined not more than $500.00, or both. (Added 1999, No. 35, § 1.)
§ 4103. Access to computer for fraudulent purposes	(a) A person shall not intentionally and without lawful authority access or cause to be accessed any computer, computer system, or computer network for any of the following purposes:
	(1) executing any scheme or artifice to defraud;
	(2) obtaining money, property, or services by means of false or fraudulent pretenses, representations, or promises; or
	(3) in connection with any scheme or artifice to defraud, damaging, destroying, altering, deleting, copying, retrieving, interfering with or denial of access to, or removing any program or data contained therein.
	(b) Penalties. A person convicted of the crime of access to computer for fraudulent purposes shall be,
	(1) if the value of the matter involved does not exceed $500.00, imprisoned not more than one year or fined not more than $500.00, or both;
	(2) if the value of the matter involved does not exceed $500.00, for a second or subsequent offense, imprisoned not more than two years or fined not more than $1,000.00, or both; or
	(3) if the value of the matter involved exceeds $500.00, imprisoned not more than ten years or fined not more than $10,000.00, or both. (Added 1999, No. 35, § 1.)

Table A-1 Comparing computer crime laws in Vermont and New York (continued)

Law	Description
§ 4104. Alteration, damage, or interference	(a) A person shall not intentionally and without lawful authority, alter, damage, or interfere with the operation of any computer, computer system, computer network, computer software, computer program, or data contained in such computer, computer system, computer program, or computer network. (b) Penalties. A person convicted of violating this section shall be, (1) if the damage or loss does not exceed $500.00 for a first offense, imprisoned not more than one year or fined not more than $500.00, or both; (2) if the damage or loss does not exceed $500.00 for a second or subsequent offense, imprisoned not more than two years or fined not more than $1,000.00, or both; or (3) if the damage or loss exceeds $500.00, imprisoned not more than ten years or fined not more than $10,000.00, or both. (Added 1999, No. 35, § 1.)
§ 4105. Theft or destruction	(a) A person shall not intentionally and without claim of right deprive the owner of possession, take, transfer, copy, conceal, or retain possession of, or intentionally and without lawful authority, destroy any computer system, computer network, computer software, computer program, or data contained in such computer, computer system, computer program, or computer network.Copying a commercially available computer program or computer software is not a crime under this section, provided that the computer program and computer software has a retail value of $500.00 or less and is not copied for resale. (b) Penalties. A person convicted of violating this section shall be, (1) if the damage or loss does not exceed $500.00 for a first offense, imprisoned not more than one year or fined not more than $500.00, or both; (2) if the damage or loss does not exceed $500.00 for a second or subsequent offense, imprisoned not more than two years or fined not more than $1,000.00 or both; or (3) if the damage or loss exceeds $500.00, imprisoned not more than ten years or fined not more than $10,000.00, or both. (Added 1999, No. 35, § 1.)
§ 4106. Civil liability	A person damaged as a result of a violation of this chapter may bring a civil action against the violator for damages and such other relief as the court deems appropriate. (Added 1999, No. 35, § 1.)
§ 4107. Venue	For the purposes of venue under this chapter, any violation of this chapter shall be considered to have been committed in the state of Vermont if the state of Vermont is the state from which or to which any use of a computer or computer network was made, whether by wires, electromagnetic waves, microwaves, or any other means of communication. (Added 1999, No. 35, § 1.)
New York Penal Law	
N.Y. Penal Law § 155.00	Larceny; definitions of terms
N.Y. Penal Law § 156.00	Offenses involving computers; definition of terms
N.Y. Penal Law § 156.05	Unauthorized use of a computer
N.Y. Penal Law § 156.10	Computer trespass
N.Y. Penal Law § 156.20	Computer tampering in the fourth degree
N.Y. Penal Law § 156.25	Computer tampering in the third degree
N.Y. Penal Law § 156.26	Computer tampering in the second degree
N.Y. Penal Law § 156.27	Computer tampering in the first degree
N.Y. Penal Law § 156.30	Unlawful duplication of computer related material
N.Y. Penal Law § 156.35	Criminal possession of computer related material
N.Y. Penal Law § 156.50	Offenses involving computers; defenses

Table A-2 Computer crime statutes by state

State	Statute
Alabama	Alabama Code § 13A-8-100 to § 13A-8-103
Alaska	Alaska Statute Title 11, Chapters 46 and 81. §§ 11.46.200(a)(3), 11.46.484.740, 11.46.985, 11.46.990, 11.81.900(a)(46) & (52)
Arizona	Arizona Revised Statutes, Title 13, §§ 13-2301(E), 13-2316

Table A-2 Computer crime statutes by state (continued)

State	Statute
Arkansas	Arkansas Code §§ 5-41-101 to 107
California	California Penal Code §§ 484j, 499c, 502, 502.1, 502.7(h), 503, 1203.047, 2702, 484–502.8, 503–514, 1191–1209, 2700–2716
Colorado	Colorado Revised Statutes. §§ 18.5.5-101 to 18.5.5-102
Connecticut	Connecticut General Statutes. §§ 53a-250 to 53a-261
Delaware	Delaware Code Annotated, Title 11. §§ 931–939
Florida	Florida Statutes, Chapter 775, 815, and 934.
Georgia	Georgia Code Annotated. §§ 16-7-22, 16-9-90 to 16-9-94
Hawaii	Computer Crime, Hawaii Revised Statutes. §§ 708-890 to 708-895
Idaho	Idaho Code. §§ 18-2201 to 2202, 48-801
Illinois	Computer Crime Prevention Law, Illinois Revised Statutes, Chapter 38. §§ 16D-1 to 7
Indiana	Indiana Code. §§ 35-43-1-4, 35-43-2-3, 35-43-4-1, 35-43-4-2, 35-43-4-3, 35-43-5-1, 35-43-7-3
Iowa	Iowa Code. §§ 716A.1 to 716A.16
Kansas	Kansas Statutes Annotated. §§ 21-3775
Kentucky	Kentucky Revised Statutes Annotated. §§ 434-840 to 434.860
Louisiana	Louisiana Revised Statutes Annotated. §§ 14:73.1 to 14:73.5
Maine	Maine Revised Statutes Annotated, Title 17-A, Chapter 18. §§ 431–433
Maryland	Maryland Code Annotated, Criminal Law. §§ 27-45A, 27-145, 27-146, 27-340
Massachusetts	Massachusetts General Laws, Chapter 266. §§ 30, 60A
Michigan	Michigan Computer Laws. §§ 752.791 to 752.797
Minnesota	Crimes Against Commerce, Minnesota Statutes, Chapter 609. §§ 609.52, 609.87, 609.88, 609.89, 609.891, 609.8911, 609.892, 609.893
Mississippi	Computer Crimes, Mississippi Code Annotated, Chapter 45
Missouri	Missouri Revised Statutes, Chapter 569. §§ 569.093, 569.094, 569.095, 569.097, 569.099
Montana	Montana Code Ann. §§ 45-1-205(4), 45-2-101, 45-6-310, 45-6-311
Nebraska	Computer Crimes Act, Nebraska Revised Statutes. §§ 28-1341 to 28-1348, 28-1332 to 28-1341, 28-1342 to 28-1402
Nevada	Crimes Against Property; Unlawful Acts Regarding Computers, Nevada Revised Statutes. §§ 205.473 – 205.477, 205.481, 205.485, 205.491. Infringements of Trade Secrets, Nevada Revised Statutes. §§ 603.050
New Hampshire	New Hampshire Revised Statutes Annotated. §§ 638:16 to 638:19
New Jersey	New Jersey Statutes Annotated. §§ 2A:38A-1 to 2A:38A-6, 2C:20-1, 2C:20-23 to 2C:20-34
New Mexico	Computer Crimes Act, New Mexico Statutes Annotated. §§ 30-45-1 to 30-45-7
New York	N.Y Penal Law. §§ 156.00, 156.05, 156.10, 156.20, 156.25, 156.26, 156.27, 156.30, 156.35, 156.50
North Dakota	North Dakota Century Code. §§ 12.1-06.1-01, 12.1-06.1-08
Ohio	Ohio Revised Code Annotated. §§ 2901.01(J), (M); 2901.1(I); 2901.12; 2912.01(F), (L)-(R), (T); 2913.04 (B), (D); 2913.42; 2913.81; 2933.41 (A)(7)
Oklahoma	Oklahoma Statutes Annotated, Title 21. §§ 1951–1958
Oregon	Oregon Revised Statutes. § 164.377
Pennsylvania	Pennsylvania Consolidated Statutes. § 3933
Rhode Island	Road Island General Laws. § 11-52 -1 to 11-52-8
South Carolina	Computer Crime Act, South Carolina Code Annotated. §§ 16-16-10 to 16-16-40
South Dakota	South Dakota Codified Laws Annotated. §§ 43-43B-1 to 43-43B-8
Tennessee	Tennessee Computer Crimes Act: Tennessee Code Annotated. §§ 39-14-601 to 39-14-603
Texas	Texas Penal Code Annotated. §§ 33.01 to 33.05
Utah	Utah Code Annotated. §§ 76-6-701 to 76-6-705
Vermont	Vermont's revised statutes, Chapter 87: Computer Crimes. §§ 4101 to 4107
Virginia	Virginia Computer Crimes Act: Virginia Code. §§ 18.2-152.1 to 18.2-152.14
Washington	Washington Revised Code. §§ 9A.52.110, 9A.52.120, 9A.52.130
West Virginia	West Virginia Code. §§ 61-3C-1 to 61-3C-21
Wisconsin	Wisconsin Statutes. § 943.70
Wyoming	Wyoming Statute. § 6-3-401

NATIONAL COMPUTER FRAUD AND ABUSE ACT OF 1986

A

Sec. 1030. Fraud and related activity in connection with computers

- (a) Whoever –

  - (1) having knowingly accessed a computer without authorization or exceeding authorized access, and by means of such conduct having obtained information that has been determined by the United States Government pursuant to an Executive order or statute to require protection against unauthorized disclosure for reasons of national defense or foreign relations, or any restricted data, as defined in paragraph y. of section 11 of the Atomic Energy Act of 1954, with reason to believe that such information so obtained could be used to the injury of the United States, or to the advantage of any foreign nation willfully communicates, delivers, transmits, or causes to be communicated, delivered, or transmitted, or attempts to communicate, deliver, transmit or cause to be communicated, delivered, or transmitted the same to any person not entitled to receive it, or willfully retains the same and fails to deliver it to the officer or employee of the United States entitled to receive it;

  - (2) intentionally accesses a computer without authorization or exceeds authorized access, and thereby obtains –

    - (A) information contained in a financial record of a financial institution, or of a card issuer as defined in section 1602(n) of title 15, or contained in a file of a consumer reporting agency on a consumer, as such terms are defined in the Fair Credit Reporting Act (15 U.S.C. 1681 et seq.);

    - (B) information from any department or agency of the United States; or

    - (C) information from any protected computer if the conduct involved an interstate or foreign communication;

  - (3) intentionally, without authorization to access any nonpublic computer of a department or agency of the United States, accesses such a computer of that department or agency that is exclusively for the use of the Government of the United States or, in the case of a computer not exclusively for such use, is used by or for the Government of the United States and such conduct affects that use by or for the Government of the United States;

  - (4) knowingly and with intent to defraud, accesses a protected computer without authorization, or exceeds authorized access, and by means of such conduct furthers the intended fraud and obtains anything of value, unless the object of the fraud and the thing obtained consists only of the use of the computer and the value of such use is not more than $5,000 in any 1-year period;

  - (5)

    - (A) knowingly causes the transmission of a program, information, code, or command, and as a result of such conduct, intentionally causes damage without authorization, to a protected computer;

    - (B) intentionally accesses a protected computer without authorization, and as a result of such conduct, recklessly causes damage; or

    - (C) intentionally accesses a protected computer without authorization, and as a result of such conduct, causes damage;

  - (6) knowingly and with intent to defraud traffics (as defined in section 1029) in any password or similar information through which a computer may be accessed without authorization, if –

    - (A) such trafficking affects interstate or foreign commerce; or

    - (B) such computer is used by or for the Government of the United States;

- (7) with intent to extort from any person, firm, association, educational institution, financial institution, government entity, or other legal entity, any money or other thing of value, transmits in interstate or foreign commerce any communication containing any threat to cause damage to a protected computer; shall be punished as provided in subsection (c) of this section.

- (b) Whoever attempts to commit an offense under subsection (a) of this section shall be punished as provided in subsection (c) of this section.

- (c) The punishment for an offense under subsection (a) or (b) of this section is –

- (1)

  - (A) a fine under this title or imprisonment for not more than ten years, or both, in the case of an offense under subsection (a)(1) of this section which does not occur after a conviction for another offense under this section, or an attempt to commit an offense punishable under this subparagraph; and (B) a fine under this title or imprisonment for not more than twenty years, or both, in the case of an offense under subsection (a)(1) of this section which occurs after a conviction for another offense under this section, or an attempt to commit an offense punishable under this subparagraph;

- (2)

  - (A) a fine under this title or imprisonment for not more than one year, or both, in the case of an offense under subsection (a)(2), (a)(3), (a)(5)(C), or (a)(6) of this section which does not occur after a conviction for another offense under this section, or an attempt to commit an offense punishable under this subparagraph; and

  - (B) a fine under this title or imprisonment for not more than 5 years, or both, in the case of an offense under subsection (a)(2), if –

    - (i) the offense was committed for purposes of commercial advantage or private financial gain;

    - (ii) the offense was committed in furtherance of any criminal or tortuous act in violation of the Constitution or laws of the United States or of any State; or

    - (iii) the value of the information obtained exceeds $5,000;

  - (C) a fine under this title or imprisonment for not more than ten years, or both, in the case of an offense under subsection (a)(2), (a)(3) or (a)(6) of this section which occurs after a conviction for another offense under this section, or an attempt to commit an offense punishable under this subparagraph; and (3)(A) a fine under this title or imprisonment for not more than five years, or both, in the case of an offense under subsection (a)(4), (a)(5)(A), (a)(5)(B), or (a)(7) of this section which does not occur after a conviction for another offense under this section, or an attempt to commit an offense punishable under this subparagraph; and (B) a fine under this title or imprisonment for not more than ten years, or both, in the case of an offense under subsection (a)(4), (a)(5)(A), (a)(5)(B), (a)(5)(C), or (a)(7) of this section which occurs after a conviction for another offense under this section, or an attempt to commit an offense punishable under this subparagraph; and

- (d) The United States Secret Service shall, in addition to any other agency having such authority, have the authority to investigate offenses under subsections (a)(2)(A), (a)(2)(B),

  - () The United States Secret Service shall, in addition to any of the United States Secret Service shall be exercised in accordance with an agreement which shall be entered into by the Secretary of the Treasury and the Attorney General.

  - (e) As used in this section –

    - (1) the term "computer" means an electronic, magnetic, optical, electrochemical, or other high speed data processing device performing logical, arithmetic, or storage functions, and includes any data storage facility or communications facility directly related to or operating in conjunction with such device, but such term does not include an automated typewriter or typesetter, a portable hand held calculator, or other similar device;

- (2) the term "protected computer" means a computer –

  - (A) exclusively for the use of a financial institution or the United States Government, or, in the case of a computer not exclusively for such use, used by or for a financial institution or the United States Government and the conduct constituting the offense affects that use by or for the financial institution or the Government; or (B) which is used in interstate or foreign commerce or communication;

- (3) the term "State" includes the District of Columbia, the Commonwealth of Puerto Rico, and any other commonwealth, possession or territory of the United States;

- (4) the term "financial institution" means –

  - (A) an institution, with deposits insured by the Federal Deposit Insurance Corporation;

  - (B) the Federal Reserve or a member of the Federal Reserve including any Federal Reserve Bank;

  - (C) a credit union with accounts insured by the National Credit Union Administration;

  - (D) a member of the Federal home loan bank system and any home loan bank;

  - (E) any institution of the Farm Credit System under the Farm Credit Act of 1971;

  - (F) a broker-dealer registered with the Securities and Exchange Commission pursuant to section 15 of the Securities Exchange Act of 1934;

  - (G) the Securities Investor Protection Corporation;

  - (H) a branch or agency of a foreign bank (as such terms are defined in paragraphs (1) and (3) of section 1(b) of the International Banking Act of 1978); and (I) an organization operating under section 25 or section 25(a) of the Federal Reserve Act.

- (5) the term "financial record" means information derived from any record held by a financial institution pertaining to a customer's relationship with the financial institution;

- (6) the term "exceeds authorized access" means to access a computer with authorization and to use such access to obtain or alter information in the computer that the accesser is not entitled so to obtain or alter;

- (7) the term "department of the United States" means the legislative or judicial branch of the Government or one of the executive departments enumerated in section 101 of title 5; and

- (8) the term "damage" means any impairment to the integrity or availability of data, a program, a system, or information, that –

  - (A) causes loss aggregating at least $5,000 in value during any 1-year period to one or more individuals;

  - (B) modifies or impairs, or potentially modifies or impairs, the medical examination, diagnosis, treatment, or care of one or more individuals;

  - (C) causes physical injury to any person; or

  - (D) threatens public health or safety; and (9) the term "government entity" includes the Government of the United States, any State or political subdivision of the United States, any foreign country, and any state, province, municipality, or other political subdivision of a foreign country.

- (f) This section does not prohibit any lawfully authorized investigative, protective, or intelligence activity of a law enforcement agency of the United States, a State, or a political subdivision of a State, or of an intelligence agency of the United States.

- (g) Any person who suffers damage or loss by reason of a violation of this section may maintain a civil action against the violator to obtain compensatory damages and injunctive relief or other equitable relief. Damages for violations involving damage as defined in subsection (e)(8)(A) are limited to economic damages. No action may be brought under this subsection unless such action is begun within 2 years of the date of the act complained of or the date of the discovery of the damage.

- (h) The Attorney General and the Secretary of the Treasury shall report to the Congress annually, during the first 3 years following the date of the enactment of this subsection, concerning investigations and prosecutions under subsection (a)(5).

INDEPENDENT COMPUTER CONSULTANTS ASSOCIATION
STANDARD FORM CONSULTING CONTRACT

THIS AGREEMENT is made as of _____, 20___

between

_____

_____ ("Client")

and

_____

_____("Consultant").

WITNESSETH, THAT:

WHEREAS, Client desires to retain the services of Consultant, and Consultant desires to provide such services; and

WHEREAS, the parties desire to enter into a Consulting Contract setting forth the terms and conditions of their agreement and their understandings.

NOW, THEREFORE, in consideration of the premises and the mutual covenants, promises, and agreements herein contained and for other good and valuable considerations, the receipt and sufficiency of which are hereby acknowledged, the parties, intending to be legally bound hereby, agree as follows:

1. Services. Consultant agrees to perform for Client the services listed in the Scope of Services as set forth on Exhibit A attached hereto and incorporated herein by reference (the "Services"). Consultant shall have access to Client's staff and resources as deemed necessary by Consultant, in Consultant's sole and absolute discretion, to perform the Services provided for by this Agreement.

2. Rate of Payment for Services. Client agrees to pay Consultant for Services in accordance with the schedule contained in Exhibit B attached hereto and incorporated herein by reference and executed by both Client and Consultant.

3. Invoicing. Consultant shall invoice Client, at Client's address as set forth in Section 15 hereof, for the Services rendered, and Client shall pay the amount set forth on such invoices to Consultant, at Consultant's address as set forth in Section 15 hereof, within ten (10) days of receipt thereof.

4. Confidential Information. (a) In the course of performing the Services referenced herein, Consultant and Client may come into possession of the other parties' financial and/or other business information pertaining to such other parties' business which is not published or readily available to the public, including, but not limited to, trade secrets, research, development, marketing concepts and plans, training, pricing information, sales techniques, lists of customers and vendors and other information pertaining to the business conducted by either Consultant or Client which is received from the agents or employees of either party ("Confidential Information"). Confidential Information shall not include information which is generally known or easily ascertainable by third parties of ordinary skill and competence in computer system design and programming, nor shall it include information already known to the receiving party or disclosed to the receiving party by a third party without violation of a duty of confidentiality to the disclosing party.

(b) Consultant and Client each acknowledge and agree that Confidential Information is important to, and greatly affects the success of, both parties in a competitive marketplace. Consultant and Client agree that during the course of their relationship and at all times thereafter, Consultant and Client shall hold in the strictest confidence, and shall not use for either parties' personal benefit, or disclose, duplicate or communicate to or use for the direct or indirect benefit of any other person, firm, corporation or entity, any Confidential Information without the prior written consent of the other party, or unless Consultant is required to do so in order to perform the Services, or pursuant to a court order or by operation of law.

Figure B-1   A sample contract from the Independent Computer Consultants Association (ICCA)

5. Staff. Consultant is an independent contractor and neither Consultant nor Consultant's staff is or shall be deemed to be employed by Client. Client is hereby contracting with Consultant for the Services described on Exhibit A and Consultant reserves the right to determine the method, manner and mean by which the Services will be performed. Consultant is not required to perform the Services during a fixed hourly or daily time and if the Services are performed at the Client's premises, then Consultants time spent at the premises is to be at the discretion of the Consultant; subject to the Client's normal business hours and security requirements. Consultant hereby confirms to Client that Client will not be required to furnish or provide any training to Consultant to enable Consultant to perform Services required hereunder. The Services shall be performed by Consultant or Consultant's staff, and Client shall not be required to hire, supervise or pay any assistants to help Consultant perform the Services under this Agreement. Consultant shall not be required to devote Consultant's full time nor the full time of Consultant's staff to the performance of the services required hereunder, and it is acknowledged that Consultant has other clients and Consultant offers services to the general public. The order or sequence in which the work is to be performed shall be under the control of Consultant. Except to the extent that the Consultant's work must be performed on or with Client's computers or Client's existing software, all materials used in providing the Services shall be provided by Consultant. Consultant's Services hereunder cannot be terminated or cancelled short of completion of the Services agreed upon except for Consultant's failure to perform the Agreement's specification as required hereunder and conversely, subject to Client's obligation to make full and timely payment(s) for Consultant's Services as set forth in Exhibit B, Consultant shall be obligated to complete the Services agreed upon and shall be liable for nonperformance of the Services to the extent and as provided in Paragraph 10 hereof. Client shall not provide any insurance coverage of any kind for Consultant or Consultant's staff, and Client will not withhold any amount that would normally be withheld from an employee's pay. Consultant shall take appropriate measures to insure that Consultant's staff is competent and that they do not breach Section 4 hereof.

Each of the parties hereto agrees that while Consultant is performing Services under this Agreement and for a period six (6) months following the performance of such Services or the termination of this Agreement, whichever is later, neither party will, except with the other party's written approval, solicit or offer employment as an employee, consultant, independent contractor, or in any other capacity to the other party's employees or staff engaged in any efforts under this Agreement.

6. Use of Work Product. Except as specifically set forth in writing and signed by both Client and Consultant, Consultant shall have all copyright and patent rights with respect to all materials developed in the course of performing the Services under this Agreement, and Client is hereby granted a non-exclusive license to use and employ such materials within the Client's business.

7. Client Representative. The following individual_____ shall represent the Client during the performance of this Agreement with respect to the Services and deliverables as defined herein and has authority to execute written modifications or additions to this Agreement as defined in Section 14.

8. Disputes. Any disputes that arise between the parties with respect to the performance of this contract shall be submitted to binding arbitration by the American Arbitration Association, to be determined and resolved by said Association under its rules and procedures in effect at the time of submission and the parties hereby agree to share equally in the costs of said arbitration.

The final arbitration decision shall be enforceable through the courts of the state of Consultant's address [15(ii)] or any other state in which the Client resides or may be located. In the event that this arbitration provision is held unenforceable by any court of competent jurisdiction, then this contract shall be as binding and enforceable as if this section 8 were not a part hereof.

9. Taxes. Any and all taxes, except income taxes, imposed or assessed by reason of this Agreement or its performance, including but not limited to sales or use taxes, shall be paid by the Client.

LIMITED WARRANTY

10. LIABILITY. CONSULTANT WARRANTS TO CLIENT THAT THE MATERIAL, ANALYSIS, DATA PROGRAMS AND SERVICES TO BE DELIVERED OR RENDERED HEREUNDER, WILL BE OF THE KIND AND QUALITY DESIGNATED AND WILL BE PERFORMED BY QUALIFIED PERSONNEL. SPECIAL REQUIREMENTS FOR FORMAT OR STANDARDS TO BE FOLLOWED SHALL BE ATTACHED AS AN ADDITIONAL EXHIBIT AND EXECUTED BY BOTH CLIENT AND CONSULTANT. CONSULTANT MAKES NO OTHER WARRANTIES, WHETHER WRITTEN, ORAL OR IMPLIED, INCLUDING WITHOUT

Figure B-1 A sample contract from the Independent Computer Consultants Association (ICCA) (continued)

LIMITATION, WARRANTY OF FITNESS FOR A PARTICULAR PURPOSE OR MERCHANTABILITY. IN NO EVENT SHALL CONSULTANT BE LIABLE FOR SPECIAL OR CONSEQUENTIAL DAMAGES, INCLUDING, BUT NOT LIMITED TO, LOSS OF PROFITS, REVENUE, DATA, OR USE BY CLIENT OR ANY THIRD PARTY, REGARDLESS OF WHETHER A CLAIM OR ACTION IS ASSERTED IN CONTRACT OR TORT, WHETHER OR NOT THE POSSIBILITY OF SUCH DAMAGES HAS BEEN DISCLOSED TO CONSULTANT IN ADVANCE OR COULD HAVE BEEN REASONABLY FORESEEN BY CONSULTANT, AND IN THE EVENT THIS LIMITATION OF DAMAGES IS HELD UNENFORCEABLE THEN THE PARTIES AGREE THAT BY REASON OF THE DIFFICULTY IN FORESEEING POSSIBLE DAMAGES ALL LIABILITY TO CLIENT SHALL BE LIMITED TO ONE HUNDRED DOLLARS ($100.00) AS LIQUIDATED DAMAGES AND NOT AS A PENALTY.

11. Complete Agreement. This agreement contains the entire Agreement between the parties hereto with respect to the matters covered herein. No other agreements, representations, warranties or other matters, oral or written, purportedly agreed to or represented by or on behalf of Consultant by any of its employees or agents, or contained in any sales materials or brochures, shall be deemed to bind the parties hereto with respect to the subject matter hereof. Client acknowledges that it is entering into this Agreement solely on the basis of the representations contained herein. In the event of a conflict in the provisions of any attachments hereto and the provisions set forth in this Agreement, the provisions of such attachments shall govern.

12. Applicable Law. Consultant shall comply with all applicable laws in performing Services but shall be held harmless for violation of any governmental procurement regulation to which it may be subject but to which reference is not made in Exhibit A. This Agreement shall be construed in accordance with the laws of the State indicated by the Consultant's address [15(ii)].

13. Scope of Agreement. If the scope of any of the provisions of the Agreement is too broad in any respect whatsoever to permit enforcement to its full extent, then such provisions shall be enforced to the maximum extent permitted by law, and the parties hereto consent and agree that such scope may be judicially modified accordingly and that the whole of such provisions of this Agreement shall not thereby fail, but that the scope of such provisions shall be curtailed only to the extent necessary to conform to law.

14. Additional Work. After receipt of an order which adds to the Services initially provided for as set forth in Exhibit A of this Agreement, Consultant may, at its discretion, take reasonable action and expend reasonable amounts of time and money based on such order. In the event Consultant provides such additional services requested by Client, Client agrees to pay Consultant for such action and expenditure as set forth in Exhibit B of this Agreement for payments related to Services.

15. Notices. All notices, requests, demands and other communications hereunder shall be in writing and shall be deemed to have been duly given when personally delivered or two (2) business days after deposited with the United States Postal Service, certified or registered mail, postage prepaid, return receipt requested, addressed as follows (or to such other address as either party may designate by notice given in accordance with the provisions of this Section):
(i) Notices to Client should be sent to:

(ii) Notices to Consultant should be sent to:

16. Assignment. This Agreement may not be assigned by either party without the prior written consent of the other party. Except for the prohibition on assignment contained in the preceding sentence, this Agreement shall be binding upon and inure to the benefits of the heirs, successors and assigns of the parties hereto.

IN WITNESS WHEREOF, the parties hereto have signed this Agreement as of the date first above written. **THIS CONTRACT CONTAINS A BINDING ARBITRATION PROVISION WHICH MAY BE ENFORCED BY THE PARTIES.**

Client

Type Name and Title

Figure B-1   A sample contract from the Independent Computer Consultants Association (ICCA) (continued)

Consultant

(This is a Standard Form Contract which may or may not require revision by the individual consultant's legal counsel. It is recommended that each consultant review the legal requirements pertaining to the consultant's State of operation with counsel licensed to practice in that State. Various States have laws that require that disclaimers of liability or arbitration provisions must be printed in enlarged print or that specific language be used, which may or may not be contained in this form. This should be reviewed with the counsel in the State in which each Consultant operates.)

For use by ICCA Members only. Copyright© 1996, Independent Computer Consultants Association.
Independent Computer Consultants Association 11131 South Towne Sq., Suite F, St. Louis, MO 63123, Phone 314-892-1675
(Revised 1/97)

Figure B-1   A sample contract from the Independent Computer Consultants Association (ICCA) (continued)

Resource Books

Chapter 1

Computer Consultants Guide (Janet Ruhl, 1997, ISBN: 0471176494)

Getting Started in Computer Security (Peter Meyer, 1999, ISBN: 0471348139)

Chapter 9

Guide to Operating Systems, Third Edition (Course Technology, 2004, ISBN: 0619213477)

Chapter 12

The Code Breakers (David Kahn, Macmillan, 1967, ISBN: 0684831309)

Applied Crytopgraphy (Bruce Schneier, Wiley and Sons, 1996, ISBN: 0471117090)

Chapter 13

CCNA Guide to Cisco Routing, Second Edition (Course Technology, 2002, ISBN: 0619034777)

Resource Web Sites

Chapter 1
Professional Certifications and Security Jobs

www.comptia.org

www.eccouncil.org

www.giac.org

www.isc2.org

www.isecom.org

www.monster.com

www.isecom.org/osstmm/

www.sans.org

Chapter 2
Protocols

www.iana.org

www.ietf.org

Chapter 3
Identifying Malware

www.cert.org/advisories

www.spywareguide.com

Search for Known Vulnerabilities and Exposures

http://archives.neohapsis.com

www.cve.mitre.org

www.google.com

www.kb.cert.org/vuls

www.microsoft.com/security/bulletins/default.mspx

www.neworder.box.sk

www.osvdb.org

www.packetstormsecurity.com

www.securityfocus.com/swsearch

www.symantec.com

Chapter 4

Footprinting Web Tools

www.arin.net

www.bugnosis.org/download.html

http://groups.google.com

www.namedroppers.com

www.samspade.org

www.severus.org/sacha/metis

www.whitepages.com

www.whois.net

Commands

http://atstake.com/research/tools

http://directory.fsf.org/All_Packages_in_Directory/Greenwich.html

http://gnu.org/software/wget/wget.html

www.parosproxy.org

http://pigtail.net/LRP/dig

www.sysinternals.com/Utilities/Hostname.html

Chapter 5

Port-Scanning Tools

www.atelierweb.com

www.fping.com/download

www.hping.org/download

www.nessus.org

www.netscantools.com

Chapter 6:

Enumeration Tools

www.atstake.com/products/lc/

www.inetcat.org/software/nbtscan.html

www.systemtools.com

Chapter 7

Programming

http://activestate.com/products/activeperl

http://history.perl.org/PerlTimeline.html

Chapter 8

Microsoft Tools

www.microsoft.com/technet/security/tools/mbsahome.mspx

http://winfingerprint.sourceforge.net/

Vulnerabilities

www.insecure.org

www.samba.org

www.us-cert.gov

Chapter 9

Linux Tools

www.chkrootkit.org

www.ethereal.com

Chapter 10

Web Security Sites

http://httpd.apache.org

http://jakarta.apache.org/site/downloads/index.html

http://java.sun.com/j2se/1.5.0/install.html

www.macromedia.com/devnet/security/security_zone/

www.mysql.com

www.owasp.org

www.php.net

Chapter 11

Wireless-Related Web Sites

www.blackalchemy.to/project/fakeap/

http://grouper.ieee.org/groups/802/

www.kismetwireless.net

www.netstumbler.com

www.oreillynet.com/cs/weblog/view/wlg/448

http://new.remote-exploit.org/index.php/Wlan_defaults

www.retrocom.com

http://sourceforge.net/projects/airsnort/

http://wepcrack.sourceforge.net

B

Chapter 12

Cryptography

http://astalavista.box.sk

http://csrc.nist.gov

www.infosec.sdu.edu.cn/WSJ_com.htm

www.openwall.com/passwords/nt.shtml

www.pgpi.org/download

http://photo2.si.edu/infoage/infoage.html

www.rsasecurity.com

www.wired.com

Free e-mail Programs

www.hotmail.com

www.hotpop.com

http://mail.google.com

Chapter 13

Security Devices

www.alpinista.org/thp/

www.symantec.com

www.cai.com

www.cisco.com

www.mcafeesecurity.com/us/products/mcafee/host_ips/desktop_server_agents.htm

www.cybersafe.ltd.uk/

www.aladdin.com

www.honeyd.org

www.honeynet.org

www.iss.net

http://jackpot.uk.net/

www.keyfocus.net/kfsensor/

http://labrea.sourceforge.net/labrea-info.html

http://www2.netbaitinc.com:5080/

www.nfr.com/resource/backOfficer.php

www.securityfocus.com/infocus/1659

http://www3.ca.com/products/

www.snort.org

www.sourcefire.com

www.specter.com or *www.spectorcne.com*

DOCUMENTATION FORMS FOR PENETRATION TESTS

The reports in this appendix will give you a good idea of what security testers do and how they should present findings to managers and IT personnel. The sample reports show how methodical a security tester must be and emphasize that nothing should be overlooked or assumed to be unimportant. Security testers must consider all factors that might affect the security of a business.

The two reports in this appendix are sample documents shared by ISECOM. Few organizations give examples of documentation for a security test, so these reports will be extremely helpful. Some material in the reports might be beyond the scope of information covered in this book, but remember that you can delve into any areas in which you aren't well versed.

The first sample report is an executive summary usually given to management staff, who typically aren't interested in all the details of a security test. Instead, they want a summary of important areas that they can read over quickly to get the bottom line. For these people, you need to emphasize what problems were found and how they can be fixed. The second sample is the technical report that would most likely be given to IT personnel. This type of report includes details of vulnerabilities and exploits as well as possible solutions for the identified problems.

Clients who hire security professionals to assess their organizations want a report that details what was found and offers recommendations to help protect their resources. Documentation—the task most IT professionals hate—is probably the most important part of a security professional's job. When a team is used to conduct a security test, the person most skilled in report writing should handle creating these reports to management and IT staff.

Testing
Executive Summary

Client Company

Prepared for
John Smith

May 2003

Testing Company. 12456 Main Street Southside, MO 00000
Phone (888) 888-8888 Fax (888) 888-8889
http://www.testingco.com

Table of Contents

Testing Company Logo

Limitations on Disclosure and Use

This document contains sensitive and confidential information concerning vulnerabilities within Client's 193.145.85.0/24 DMZ Network, as well as methods for exploiting these vulnerabilities. Testing Company recommends that special precautions be taken to protect the confidentiality of the information contained in this report. Testing Company has securely retained a copy of the report for future Client reference. All subsequent copies of this report will be delivered by Testing Company to the appropriate Client representative.

While Testing Company is confident that the major security vulnerabilities of the target systems have been identified, there can be no assurance that an assessment of this nature will identify all possible security exposures. Additionally, the findings and recommendations presented in this document are based on the technologies and known threats as of the date of this report. As technologies and risks change over time, the vulnerabilities and the recommendations associated with the Client 193.145.85.0/24 DMZ Network, may also change.

C

Executive Summary

Testing Overview

In an effort to assess the security of Client's presence on the Internet, Client requested that Testing Company perform Testing service against those systems supporting the Client 193.145.85.0/24 DMZ Network. The purpose of the Testing service was to identify network-level security weaknesses that may be exploited from the Internet.

The Testing service was performed via the Internet from Testing Company's security labs located in Southside, MO between 10-9-2003 and 11-11-2003. All vulnerabilities identified, as well as any security concerns encountered, were communicated to Client contact John Smith throughout the Testing service process.

Testing was limited to the target networks and IP addresses specifically, and did not include any third-party networks or systems that were out of the immediate scope of the project. Furthermore, Testing Company did not perform any Denial of Service (DoS) based attacks against the target systems.

Processes and Techniques

Testing Company's consultants rely on vetted testing practices to determine how susceptible a Client's network is to security exposure. These testing practices have been continuously developed over a period of years and are constantly refined to better represent the threats facing a business's Internet presence.

Testing Company uses various scanning products that have been recognized as industry standards, including Retina by eEye, CANVAS by ImmunitySec, and Nessus by the Security Community. A variety of scanners are used so that the Testing service is not bias to one product and the results are not restricted to the findings of one individual vendor. Testing Company also incorporates what are considered industry standard testing tools into its testing process, such as scanrand, nikto, netcat, and other tools made by security testers for security testers. In addition to using tools that are publicly available, Testing Company's consultants have a variety of testing tools, scripts and processes that have been developed in-house or in conjunction with the Institute for Security and Open Methodologies (ISECOM).

Testing Company implements a multi-phased testing process that is designed to test for all known vulnerabilities, as well as the discovery of unknown vulnerabilities within custom configurations. This multi-phased testing process allows Testing Company to be "self-checking", ensuring that its consultants have thoroughly identified all apparent vulnerabilities.

Testing Company implements separate testing processes for each type of Testing service it offers, including external network testing, internal network testing and web application testing. Each process is specifically designed to target the type of service being performed and implements the best testing practices available.

While performing the Testing service, Testing Company consultants assume the role of an attacker by portraying a "think outside of the box" mindset. This approach allows Testing Company to provide a more accurate representation of the threats an environment is susceptible to. Testing Company uses ISECOM's Open Source Security Testing Methodology Manual (OSSTMM) as the base methodology for all Testing engagements.

Risks

During the security assessment, Testing Company discovered various vulnerabilities and security concerns relating to the 193.145.85.0/24 DMZ Network. It is important to note that the vulnerabilities documented in this report reflect the conditions of the 193.145.85.0/24 DMZ Network at the time of the Testing service and do not necessarily reflect current conditions.

Below is a table highlighting the risks identified during this assessment. Each risk is associated with a Risk Assessment Value that classifies its degree of exposure. For additional details concerning these risks and their associated recommendations, please refer to the appropriate pages of the technical reports.

System	Service	RAV	TR Page
193.145.85.22	Email	Vulnerability – Identified – 1.6	11
193.145.85.43	File Transfer	Weakness – Verified – 1.6	21
	Remote Control	Weakness – Verified – 1.6	21
	Website	Weakness – Verified – 1.6	22
193.145.85.44	Website	Vulnerability – Identified – 1.6	23
193.145.85.58	DNS	Weakness – Verified – 1.6	23
193.145.85.59	DNS	Weakness – Verified – 1.6	24
	DNS	Vulnerability – Identified – 1.6	24
193.145.85.72	Website	Vulnerability – Identified – 1.6	28
	Remote Control	Weakness – Verified – 1.6	28
193.145.85.79	Website	Vulnerability – Identified – 1.6	31

Testing Company Logo

System	Service	RAV	TR Page
193.145.85.90	DNS	Vulnerability – Identified – 1.6	33
	DNS	Weakness – Verified – 1.6	33
193.145.85.91	DNS	Weakness – Verified – 1.6	34
193.145.85.100	File Transfer	Vulnerability – Identified – 1.6	35
193.145.85.150	File Transfer	Vulnerability – Identified – 1.6	36

About Testing Company

Testing Company markets Information Security Protection and Security Education services to large and medium-sized businesses worldwide.

Questions or comments regarding this Testing service, the contents of this report, or Testing Company should be directed to Mike Jones (mike.jones@testingco.com) at (888) 888-8888. Additionally, please visit our website at http://www.testingco.com.

Section
1 Introduction

At the request of Client, Testing Company performed a Testing service of Client's 193.145.85.0/24 DMZ Network. The objective of this Testing service was to determine the overall security of the 193.145.85.0/24 DMZ Network. The security assessment performed was focused on the target systems identified in the Section 1.1. These results are not intended to be an overall assessment of all Client hosts, but only of those systems that fell within the scope of this project.

The Testing service was performed via the Internet from Testing Company's security labs located in Southside, MO between October 9th 2003 and November 11th 2003. All vulnerabilities identified, as well as any security concerns encountered, were communicated to Client employee John Smith throughout the Testing service process.

This testing did not attempt any active Denial of Service (DoS) attacks. In some cases, however, it may be possible to determine if a host is susceptible to a DoS attack without performing the attack itself.

1.1   Target Systems

The following table displays the target systems and networks identified for this network test. Each of the identified systems were tested with all three stages of Testing Company's standard network-level Testing service process (see Section 1.2).

IP Address/Netmask	Host/Network Name	Host/Network Description
193.145.85.0/24	Client DMZ	This is the main DMZ network for Client.
193.145.85.22	mail2.school.mo.us.	Linux 2.4/2.6 (NAT)
193.145.85.23	listserv.school.mo.us.	Windows 2000 SP4, XP SP1
193.145.85.25	Relay.school.mo.us.	NAVGW on NT
193.145.85.28	Sped.school.mo.us.	Mac OS9
193.145.85.29	is.school.mo.us.	Windows NT
193.145.85.33	Clientschools.org.	Mac OS9
193.145.85.36	techctr-backup.school.mo.us.	Microsoft Windows Server 2003 Enterprise Edition, Microsoft Windows 2000 SP3
193.145.85.37	web.school.mo.us.	Windows 2000
193.145.85.38	uxy38.school.mo.us.	Windows 2000

C

193.145.85.39	193.145.85.39	Mac? (No up ports, only down, Web and Timbuktu)
193.145.85.43	uxy43.school.mo.us.	Polycom Viewstation 512 – Software 7.0.3
193.145.85.44	classrooms.school.mo.us.	Windows
193.145.85.48	uxy48.school.mo.us.	Mac? (No up ports, only down, ftp, web, Frame Maker, Timbuktu)
193.145.85.58	ns1.school.mo.us.	Windows? (no response on any TCP port)
193.145.85.59	ns2.school.mo.us.	Windows? (no response on any TCP port)
193.145.85.68	support.school.mo.us., dap.school.mo.us.	Windows 2000
193.145.85.72	register.school.mo.us.	Windows 2000 (why TS & VNC on same box?)
193.145.85.79	ysystems.com.	Windows 2000
193.145.85.80	uxy80.school.mo.us.	Ridgeway IP Freedom?
193.145.85.90	dns1.Clientschools.org.	Windows? (No response on any TCP port)
193.145.85.91	dns2.Clientschools.org.	Windows? (No response on any TCP port)
193.145.85.100	uxy100.school.mo.us.	Windows 2000
193.145.85.150	web.school.mo.us.	Windows 2000
193.145.85.248	uxy248.school.mo.us.	Mac? (Weird DNS server, not Bind)
193.145.85.251	mail.school.mo.us.	Windows NT 4.0
193.145.84.206	MO.cust-rtr.bigcablemodem.net.	Cisco 801/1720 router running IOS 12.2.8, Cisco router running IOS 12.2(8)T

1.2 Tools & Techniques

For each network-level penetration test, Testing Company follows a robust, peer-reviewed methodology to ensure a complete and accurate security assessment. This documented process includes three individual stages of testing. Each stage utilizes commercial scanners, freely available tools, public resources, and proprietary tools and procedures. Below is a description of each of the stages performed by Testing Company during a network test.

Stage I - Discovery

The first stage of a network-level Testing service is devoted to information gathering and discovery. In this stage, Testing Company will attempt to gather all publicly available information concerning the target environment. This includes:

examining DNS records (both authoritative and non-authoritative), querying various whois servers, utilizing standard network utilities such as ping and traceroute, and analyzing the BGP tables of various backbone Internet routers.

After researching and recording the public information concerning the target environment, Testing Company attempts to map the network architecture of the target systems. This includes attempting to identify any filtering devices, i.e. firewalls or routers, which protect the environment, as well as, recording the various routes to the individual targets. To accomplish this mapping of the target environment, Testing Company used TCP, UDP, and ICMP echo request sweeps, lft, sing, dig, and several other tools designed to perform various queries that flush out live hosts.

Stage II - Enumeration

In the second stage of a network-level Testing service, Testing Company utilizes the information and hosts discovered in Stage I to enumerate specific host configurations and settings. This includes identifying any open TCP and UDP services, detecting, if possible, the software version of the open services and operating systems, and the purpose of the host, i.e. firewall, mail server, DNS server, web server etc. In addition, Testing Company will attempt to ascertain, through experience and research, if the software versions of the services or operating systems are vulnerable to remote exploitation.

To determine the open TCP and UDP ports, Testing Company performs a sweep of all 65,535 TCP ports and attempts protocol specific requests against the most commonly used and exploited UDP ports. Please refer to Appendix A for the complete list of open TCP and UDP services for each target system. Testing Company utilizes several different techniques to identify the software version of the services and operating systems of each target host. These include: OS detection through examination of network packets, system configuration and feedback profiling, and banner grabbing.

During this stage of a network-level Testing service, Testing Company uses various commercial, publicly available, and in-house developed proprietary tools. These include, but are not limited to:

❖ Retina by eEye

- ❖ CANVAS by Immunitysec
- ❖ Nessus by Renaud Deraison
- ❖ Sing by Alfredo Andres
- ❖ Nmap by Fyodor
- ❖ Scanrand by Dan Kaminsky

Stage III - Exploitation

The third and final stage of a network-level Testing service is the exploitation phase. In this stage Testing Company will attempt to exploit any vulnerabilities or weaknesses discovered during Stage II. The goal of this stage is to obtain user-level or privileged-level access on the target systems. Typical methods of gaining system-level access include successful brute force attacks or the execution of buffer overflow exploits. If access is obtained, Testing Company will attempt to further penetrate all systems and networks connected to the compromised host. The purpose of this continued penetration is to test the security controls in place to protect confidential assets from compromised systems. Additionally, this test demonstrates the depth of exposure of the target network after one of the hosts has been compromised. Testing Company will immediately alert the appropriate representative if any host is compromised during the Testing service.

Denial-of-Service (DoS)

DoS attacks are special tests designed to determine the susceptibility of a target system or network to unauthorized malicious downtime. Testing Company has accumulated a large database of various DoS programs and methods. These programs range from ICMP DoS attacks, such as smurf, to network flooding DoS attacks, such as SYN Floods. Testing Company does not perform a DoS attack unless specifically requested. In the event that a DoS attack is requested, a time-window will be agreed upon and the DoS attack will only occur during this time period.

1.3 Risk Classification

In Section 2.0 of this document, Testing Company presents all of the vulnerabilities that were discovered during this security assessment. Each of these vulnerabilities has been organized into four different severity classifications: Severe-Risk, Moderate-

Risk, Minimal-Risk, and Security Concerns.   Below is a brief definition of each of the four severity categories.

Vulnerability

A flaw inherent in the security mechanism itself or which can be reached through security safeguards that allows for privileged access to the location, people, business processes, and people or remote access to business processes, people, infrastructure, and/or corruption or deletion of data.

A vulnerability may be a metal in a gate which becomes brittle below 0° C, a thumbprint reader which will grant access with rubber fingers, an infrared device that has no authentication mechanism to make configuration changes, or a translation error in a web server which allows for the identification of a bank account holder through an account number.

Weakness

A flaw inherent in the platform or environment of which a security mechanism resides in – a misconfiguration, survivability fault, usability fault, or failure to meet the requirements of the Security Posture. A weakness may be a process which does not save transaction data for the legal time limit as established by regional laws, a door alarm which does not sound if the door is left open for a given amount of time, a firewall which returns ICMP host unreachable messages for internal network systems, a database server that allows unfiltered queries, or an unlocked, unmonitored entrance into a otherwise secured building.

Information Leak

A flaw inherent in the security mechanism itself or which can be reached through security safeguards which allow for privileged access to privileged or sensitive information concerning data, business processes, people, or infrastructure.

An information leak may be a lock with the combination available through audible signs of change within the lock's mechanisms, a router providing SNMP information about the target network, a spreadsheet of executive salaries for a private company, the private mobile telephone number of the marketing staff, or a website with the next review date of an organization's elevators.

Concern

C

A security issue which may result from not following best practices however does not yet currently exist as a danger.

A concern may be FINGERD running on a server for an organization that has no business need for the FINGER service, a guarded doorway which requires the watchman to leave the door to apprehend a trespasser with no new guard to replace the one who left and maintain a presence at the door, or employees who sit with their monitors and whiteboards viewable from outside the perimeter security.

Unknowns

An unidentifiable or unknown element in the security mechanism itself or which can be reached through security safeguards that currently has no known impact on security as it tends to make no sense or serve any purpose with the limited information the tester has.

An unknown may be an unexpected response possibly from a router in a network that is repeatable and may indicate network problems, an unnatural radio frequency emanating from an area within the secure perimeter however offers no identification or information, or a spreadsheet which contains private data about a competing company.

1.4 Risk Assessment Values

In addition to the risk classifications described above in Section 1.3, Testing Company has associated a Risk Assessment Value for every risk discovered during this security assessment.

	Verified	Identified
Vulnerability	.032	.016
Weakness	.016	0.008
Concern	0.008	0.004
Information Leak	0.004	0.002
Unknown	0.002	0.001

1.5 Use of this Report

The remainder of this document has been organized into the following sections.

Section 2 – Risks & Recommendations

In this section, Testing Company describes the findings and recommendations associated with the 193.145.85.0/24 DMZ Network that was tested during this Testing service. The findings and recommendations have been divided into two different categories: **Vulnerability & Weakness.** Risks classified as **Concern, Information Leak** or **Unknown** will be mentioned only in the companion technical document. Please refer to Section 1.3 on page 10 for detailed explanations of these categories.

Section 3 - Concluding Remarks

In this final section, Testing Company presents the concluding remarks concerning the 193.145.85.0/24 DMZ Network. This includes a brief recap of the risks and recommendations, comments on the security of the environment, and a summary of the Testing service.

Appendix A – Open TCP Ports

In Appendix A, Testing Company has supplied Client with the raw output from the port scans performed during the security assessment. The output will highlight the TCP ports currently and historically open on all of the network devices tested during this assessment. Please refer to Section 1.1 for additional details of the target systems for this Testing service.

Testing Company Logo

Section

2 Risks & Recommendations

The Risks & Resolutions section of this document highlights all of the risks and security concerns identified during the assessment of the Client 193.145.85.0/24 DMZ Network. Each risk will have a Risk Assessment Value (see Section 1.4), a list of the vulnerable systems, a discussion, and a recommendation. The discussion is a brief description of how Testing Company was able to identify this particular risk and what affect it has on the security of the system and the rest of the environment, inserting text and screen captures where appropriate. Finally, the recommendation section will contain Testing Company's recommendations for eliminating the respective vulnerability. These recommendations are based on years of information security experience and extensive research.

2.1 Vulnerability

In this section, Testing Company has documented the **Severe-Risk** vulnerabilities associated with the Client 193.145.85.0/24 DMZ Network. **Severe-Risk** vulnerabilities are the most critical findings and may pose a serious, immediate threat to your information assets. All **Severe-Risk** vulnerabilities should be remedied as soon as possible.

2.1.1   Sendmail Buffer Overflows

Relevancy: Identified

Vulnerable Systems: 193.145.85.22

Impact

According to the Fingerprint and the banners shown, this version of Sendmail is vulnerable to many different buffer overflows. There are also a few minor local information leaks with this version. Either way, please consider updating to a newer non-vulnerable version.

CVE : CAN-2002-1337, CVE-2001-1349

Recommendation

Upgrade to Sendmail 8.12.10. (http://www.sendmail.org/)

2.1.2   shtml.dll–Frontpage Extensions 2000 & 2002

Relevancy: Identified

Vulnerable Systems: 193.145.85.44, 193.145.85.72

Impact

Did not validate this, but it seems that this machine is vulnerable to a flaw in the shtml.dll file that can allow a remote attacker the ability to run arbitrary code. This affects both Frontpage Server Extensions 2000 and 2002.

Recommendation

Install the appropriate Microsoft hotfix.

http://www.microsoft.com/technet/treeview/default.asp?url=/technet/security/bulletin/MS02-053.asp

http://support.microsoft.com/default.aspx?scid=kb;en-us;Q329085

See page 28 of the Technical Report for more information.

2.1.3   Bind 9.2.2rc1 Buffer Overflow

Relevancy: Identified

Vulnerable Systems: 193.145.85.59

Impact

This version of bind (based solely on the reported revision number) is known to be vulnerable to a buffer overflow which may allow an attacker to gain a shell on this host or disrupt access to this server (DoS).

Recommendation

If this indeed is a problem, then upgrade to bind 9.2.3 (http://www.isc.org/products/BIND/) or downgrade to the 8.x series. This may not be a problem for you if you're running bind on a windows platform as this specific vulnerability is tied to the GNU DNS resolver library as part of glibc.

2.1.4   Bind 9.2.2rc1 Buffer Overflow

Relevancy: Identified

Vulnerable Systems: 193.145.85.59

Impact

This version of bind (based solely on the reported revision number) is known to be vulnerable to a buffer overflow which may allow an attacker to gain a shell on this host or disrupt access to this server (DoS).

Recommendation

If this indeed is a problem, then upgrade to bind 9.2.3 (http://www.isc.org/products/BIND/) or downgrade to the 8.x series. This may not be a problem for you if you're running bind on a windows platform as this specific vulnerability is tied to the GNU DNS resolver library as part of glibc.

2.1.5   Allaire ColdFusion DoS

Relevancy: Identified

Vulnerable Systems: 193.145.85.79

Impact

Due to a faulty mechanism in the password parsing implementation in authentication requests, it is possible to launch a denial of service attack against Allaire ColdFusion 4.5.1 or previous by inputting a string of over 40 000 characters to the password field in the Administrator login page. CPU utilization could reach up to 100%, bringing the program to halt. The default form for the login page would prevent such an attack. However, a malicious user could download the form locally to their hard drive, modify HTML tag fields, and be able to submit the 40 000 character string to the ColdFusion Server.

Recommendation

Workaround:

Back up all existing data and implement the steps outlined in the following knowledge base article:

http://www.macromedia.com/support/coldfusion/ts/documents/tn17254.htm

http://www.macromedia.com/v1/cfdocs/allaire_support/admin
security.htm

2.1.6   Bind 8.2.5-REL Buffer Overflow

Relevancy: Identified

Vulnerable Systems: 193.145.85.90

Impact

Remote shells and DoS.
http://www.securityfocus.com/bid/6160/discussion/
http://xforce.iss.net/xforce/xfdb/10333

When a DNS lookup is requested on a non-existent sub-domain of a valid
domain and an OPT resource record with a large UDP payload is attached,
the server may fail.

Recommendation

Upgrade to 8.4.1 or 9.2.3

http://www.isc.org/products/BIND/bind8.html

http://www.isc.org/products/BIND/

2.1.7   MS FTP DoS

Relevancy: Identified

Vulnerable Systems: 193.145.85.100

Impact

Based on the version in the banner, it may be possible to crash the ftp server
(DoS). This would only be possible after logging in, which would require a
valid username/password.

Recommendation

Apply relevant hotfix:

http://www.microsoft.com/technet/security/bulletin/ms02-
018.asp

Microsoft Patch Q319733 IIS 5.0

http://download.microsoft.com/download/iis50/Patch/Q319733/
NT5/EN-US/Q319733_W2K_SP3_X86_EN.exe

2.1.8   Rumpus FTP DoS

Relevancy: Identified

Vulnerable Systems: 193.145.85.150

Impact

The remote system may be vulnerable to one or more remote buffer overflow attacks.

Recommendation

Contact Rumpus http://www.maxum.com/Rumpus/ for more information.

2.2   Weakness

In this section, Testing Company has documented the **Weakness** risks associated with the Client 193.145.85.0/24 DMZ Network.

2.2.1   FTP Default Password

Relevancy: Verified

Vulnerable Systems: 193.145.85.43

Impact

The FTP server allows logging in as user admin or administrator with any password combination.

Once logged in as an admin level account, you can read files, write files, reboot the device, and update the firmware on the device.

Recommendation

Restrict access to this port at the firewall. Change the admin and administrator passwords.

2.2.2   Telnet Default Password

Relevancy: Verified

Vulnerable Systems: 193.145.85.43

Impact

You can obtain and modify configurations on port 23 and port 24 without being prompted for authentication

Recommendation

Restrict access to these ports at the firewall.

2.2.3   WWW Default Password

Relevancy: Verified

Vulnerable Systems: 193.145.85.43

Impact

Through the admin and administrator accounts on the website you can view and modify the configuration. You can make long distance calls. You can also wipe the logs.

Recommendation

Restrict access to this port at the firewall.

2.2.4   Recursive DNS

Relevancy: Verified

Vulnerable Systems: 193.145.85.58, 193.145.85.59, 193.145.85.90, 193.145.85.91, 193.145.85.248

Impact

This DNS server is allowing recursive queries from the outside. This would allow an attacker to poison the DNS servers local cache. The next victim to request that information may be unknowingly directed to the attackers site.

Recommendation

Disable recursive queries for those outside of the Client IP space.

C

2.2.5 VNC Enabled

Relevancy: Verified

Vulnerable Systems: 193.145.85.72

Impact

There is a VNC server running on this host. VNC (Virtual Network Computing) allows remote users to control the host machine as though they were physically at the terminal.

VNC is not encrypted in its default form, and authentication is not a part of the Windows standard authentication. There is no username, only a password which can be brute forced.

It's very odd to see VNC and TS running on the same machine, as it's twice the administrative load to properly secure.

Recommendation

Disable VNC.

If you must run VNC, limit access to it with firewall ACL's.

Section

3 Concluding Remarks

This analysis is based on known threats as of the date of this report. Testing Company recommends that the actions suggested for identified risks be applied as quickly as possible.

All in all we found that the current security posture for the systems within the scope was in decent shape from an external point of view. Although, as with most networks we've tested, there is room for improvement. After Client has implemented the changes suggested in this document and the companion technical report, we recommend that Client contact Testing Company for a follow on retest to verify that the suggested changes were made.

Testing Company has appreciated this opportunity to perform the Testing service for Client. We hope that the information contained in these documents is of benefit to your organization. As Client security related needs arise again in the future, it would be our pleasure to serve you again. For more information about our services, please contact our Sales Staff at (888) 888-8888, or visit our website (http://www.testingco.com).

Appendix A: Open TCP Ports

In this appendix, Testing Company has inserted the raw results of the port scans performed against the target systems listed in Section 1.1. For each target host, the list of open TCP ports has been attached. All open ports should be closely examined for their business purpose. Unnecessary open ports should be disabled to avoid any additional vulnerability exposures.

<removed for anonymity>

C

Testing
Technical Report

Client Company

Prepared for
John Smith

November 12, 2003

Domains	Subdomain.Domain.Root
xxx.mo.us Clientschools.org ysystems.com Clientonline.com	School.mo.us

Principal Services	Protocol, Port, Service
File transfer, Remote administration, Email, Web pages, Database, Video Conferencing, Routing, Unknown, VoIP	FTP, 21, File Transfer Telnet, 23, Remote Administration Telnet, 24, Remote Administration SMTP, 25, Email DNS, 53, Domain Name Service HTTP, 80, Web Timbuktu, 407, Timbuktu HTTP, 591, Filemaker Database

Number of Domains	
5	

IP Addresses	IP (types of system)
193.145.85.1-254, 2193.145.84.206	T1, 1 class C, one boarder GW router.

Gateway Routers	IP (physical location)
2193.145.84.206	Client Organization 200 Broad Street Richland, MO 00000-0000 US (UNITED STATES)

Number of Visible Systems	
	20

Primary Operating Systems	OS Name
	Linux, Windows, Mac OS 9,Windows NT, Windows 2000 (XP?)

Firewall	IP, OS, type
Could not determine	Inline? Could not determine

IDS	IP, OS, type
Could not determine	Could not determine

Web Technologies	IP Technology
	193.145.85.100Microsoft-IIS/5.0 WebLogic Server 8.x 193.145.85.150 Down 11/6/2003 193.145.85.23 Tcl-Webserver/3.4.2 193.145.85.28 WebSTAR/3.0 193.145.85.33 WebSTAR/4.4(SSL) 193.145.85.37 Microsoft-IIS/5.0 193.145.85.44 Says Microsoft-IIS/5.0, might be Microsoft-IIS/4.0 193.145.85.68 Microsoft-IIS/5.0 193.145.85.72 Microsoft-IIS/5.0 ASP.NET 193.145.85.79 Microsoft-IIS/5.0 193.145.85.43 Polycom Viewstation 512 Administrative Web GUI

ISP One primary	**Name, Address, website** MO Internet Services 111 Street St. #5000 City, Mo, 12345 http://www.mointernetservice.net
Test Conditions	**Hops** 10,11,15 **Speed** 120kB/s downloading from websites **Restrictions** Many networking changes throughout testing cycle

Notes

Overall, not bad. There is definitely room for improvement, but we've seen far worse☺. Keep your eye out for anything .8 and higher. The 0.0-0.4 is nit picky, but if you have time, fix those too.

We look forward to working with you again soon. If anything is unclear, please don't hesitate to drop us a line via email or phone.

Testing Team

Document Grinding Assessment

Persons Discovered

person	telephone	e-mail
John xxx		john@School.mo.us
		board @School.mo.us
Lucy xxx	(888) 888-1234	lucy@School.mo.us, lucy_2@School.mo.us
		joe@School.mo.us
Kris xxx		kris @School.mo.us
Susan xxx	(888) 888-2345, (456) 888-XXXX	susan@School.mo.us, susan_2@access.xxx.mo.us
Suey xxx		suey_2@School.mo.us
		pam@School.mo.us
		beth@XXX.us
Scott xxx	(888) 888-3456	scott_2@School.mo.us
John xxx	Ext 4567	john_2@School.mo.us, john @School.mo.us
John xxx	Ext 5678	John_xxx@School.mo.us
Winnona xxx	(888) 888-7890	winnona_xxx@School.mo.us
Joseph xxx	(888) 888-8901	Jo.xxx@School.mo.us
Ariel xxx		ariel_xxx@access.xxx.mo.us
Carl xxx		carl_xxx@access.xxx.mo.us
Kassandra xxx		kassandra.xxx@School.mo.us
Greg xxx		greg_xxx@School.mo.us
Luis xxx	Ext 123	
Fiona xxx	Ext 234	
Charles xxx	Ext 345	
Jessica xxx	Ext 456	
Helpdesks	Ext 222, 333, 444, 555, 666	

External Postings

Link	description
http://www.School.mo.us/directory.html	Who should we call first?
http://groups.google.com/groups?q= 1	Old networking problem
http://www.another.net/cs/pt/view/eg_e/1332	National Board Certification General Meeting
http://www.another.net/cs/pt/view/eg_e/1319	National Board Certification Support Network
http://www.sssss.edu/ed174/resources/information_forms/ informational_handouts/ Info_Bhasha.doc	SUBJECT EXAMINATIONS
http://www.xxxxxxx.com/sgro	Hobby
http://wwwstatic.xxx.org/gems/Mtg.Minutes.htm	BUSINESS AND ADMINISTRATION STEERING COMMITTEE (BASC

http://wwwstatic.xxx.org/gems/Minutes.htm	BUSINESS AND ADMINISTRATION STEERING COMMITTEE (BASC)
www.xxx.org/docs/	Great Technology To Enhance Language Arts
http://www.xxx.org/xxx/lists/rre/Networks	Ancient Post for John

Systems and Technologies

Technology name	description or link to information
Linux	http://www.linux.org – Free operating system
Windows	http://www.microsoft.com – Commercial Operating System
Mac	http://www.apple.com – Commercial Operation System
Polycom Viewstation 512	http://www.polycom.com/products_services/0,1816,pw-4353-4430,00.html – Video Conferencing
WebLogic	http://www.bea.com/framework.jsp?CNT=index.htm&FP=/content/products/server
Tcl-Webserver – Lyris List Manager	http://www.lyris.com/products/listmanager/lm_flyer.pdf
WebStar	http://www.4d.com/products/webstar.html
IIS	http://www.microsoft.com/WindowsServer2003/iis/default.mspx
Elluminate	http://www.elluminate.com/ – Virtual Classroom
WebQuota	http://www.flicks.com/msystems/webquota/ – Advanced Authentication controls
Coldfusion	http://www.macromedia.com/software/coldfusion/
Rumpus	http://www.maxum.com/Rumpus/ – FTPD for the Mac
MacHTTP	http://www.machttp.org/ – the original Web server for Macintosh

E-mail Header

Header Information

Return-Path: <>
Received: from mail.School.mo.us ([193.145.85.251] verified)
  by xxx.xxx.net (PicoOS Mailserv SMTP 5.5.5)
  with ESMTP id 670434 for lsl@xxx.com; Fri, 07 Nov 2003 01:20:18 -0800
X-MIMETrack: Itemize by SMTP Server on mail/xxx/CLIENT(Release 5.0.10 | March 22, 2002)
at
 11/07/2003 01:11:54 AM,
        Serialize by Router on mail/xxx/CLIENT(Release 5.0.10 | March 22, 2002) at
 11/07/2003 01:11:54 AM,
        Serialize complete at 11/07/2003 01:11:54 AM
From: Postmaster@School.mo.us
Date: Fri, 7 Nov 2003 01:11:54 -0800
Message-ID: <OFB3D1E476.86C1FD7A-ON88256DD7.0032872A@School.mo.us>
MIME-Version: 1.0
Subject: DELIVERY FAILURE: User xxx (xxx@School.mo.us) not listed in
 public Name & Address Book
To: lsl@xxx.com
Content-Type: multipart/report; report-type=delivery-status;
boundary="==IFJRGLKFGIR419UHRUHIHD"

=-=-=-=-=-=-=-=-=
Return-Path: <lyris-noreply@listserv.School.mo.us>
Received: from listserv.School.mo.us ([193.145.85.23] verified)
  by xxx.xxx.net (PicoOS Mailserv SMTP 5.5.5)
  with SMTP id 670426 for root@xxx.com; Fri, 07 Nov 2003 00:46:21 -0800
Message-Id: <LYRIS0-1068194735--1540-lyris-noreply@listserv.School.mo.us>
X-lyris-type: command-notify
From: "Lyris ListManager" <lyris-noreply@listserv.School.mo.us>
Reply-To: "Lyris ListManager" <lyris-noreply@listserv.School.mo.us>
To: root@xxx.com
Subject: Re: your help request
Date: Fri, 07 Nov 2003 00:45:35 -0800

Network Profile

IP ranges to be tested and details of these ranges
193.145.85.1-254 – CLIENT Class C
193.145.84.206 – Border GW Router

Domain information and configurations

user64x248.School.mo.us.   193.145.85.248
Resolved xxx.in-addr.arpa and xxx.in-addr.arpa into Clientonline.com.
This is a very curious name server. It only responds for two IP addresses in this range.
It returns non-authoritive for all lookups (recursive queries allowed) except for other reverse lookups in this IP space.

=-=-=-=-=-=

DNS1.CLIENTSCHOOLS.ORG 193.145.85.90
Bind: 8.2.5-REL

=-=-=-=-=-=

DNS2.CLIENTSCHOOLS.ORG 193.145.85.91
Bind: 9.2.2

=-=-=-=-=-=

NS1.SCHOOL.MO.US   193.145.85.58
Bind: 8.4.1-REL

=-=-=-=-=-=

NS2.SCHOOL.MO.US   193.145.85.59
Bind: 9.2.2rc1

Zone Transfer Highlights

193.145.85.248
None allowed

=-=-=-=-=-=

DNS1.CLIENTSCHOOLS.ORG 193.145.85.90
None allowed

=-=-=-=-=-=

DNS2.CLIENTSCHOOLS.ORG 193.145.85.91
None allowed

=-=-=-=-=-=

NS1.SCHOOL.MO.US   193.145.85.58
None allowed

=-=-=-=-=-=

NS2.SCHOOL.MO.US   193.145.85.59
None allowed

Server List

IP Address/Netmask	Host/Network Name	Host/Network Description
193.145.85.0/24	Client DMZ	This is the main DMZ network for Client.
193.145.85.22	mail2.school.mo.us.	Linux 2.4/2.6 (NAT)
193.145.85.23	listserv.school.mo.us.	Windows 2000 SP4, XP SP1

193.145.85.25	Relay.school.mo.us.	NAVGW on NT
193.145.85.28	Sped.school.mo.us.	Mac OS9
193.145.85.29	is.school.mo.us.	Windows NT
193.145.85.33	Clientschools.org.	Mac OS9
193.145.85.36	techctr-backup.school.mo.us.	Microsoft Windows Server 2003 Enterprise Edition, Microsoft Windows 2000 SP3
193.145.85.37	web.school.mo.us.	Windows 2000
193.145.85.38	user64x38.school.mo.us.	Windows 2000
193.145.85.39	193.145.85.39	Mac? (No up ports, only down, Web and Timbuktu)
193.145.85.43	user64x43.school.mo.us.	Polycom Viewstation 512 – Software 7.0.3
193.145.85.44	classrooms.school.mo.us.	Windows
193.145.85.48	user64x48.school.mo.us.	Mac? (No up ports, only down, ftp, web, Frame Maker, Timbuktu)
193.145.85.58	ns1.school.mo.us.	Windows? (no response on any TCP port)
193.145.85.59	ns2.school.mo.us.	Windows? (no response on any TCP port)
193.145.85.68	support.school.mo.us., dap.school.mo.us.	Windows 2000
193.145.85.72	register.school.mo.us.	Windows 2000 (why TS & VNC on same box?)
193.145.85.79	ysystems.com.	Windows 2000
193.145.85.80	user64x80.school.mo.us.	Ridgeway IP Freedom?
193.145.85.90	dns1.Clientschools.org.	Windows? (No response on any TCP port)
193.145.85.91	dns2.Clientschools.org.	Windows? (No response on any TCP port)
193.145.85.100	user64x100.school.mo.us.	Windows 2000
193.145.85.150	web.school.mo.us.	Windows 2000
193.145.85.248	user64x248.school.mo.us.	Mac? (Weird DNS server, not Bind)
193.145.85.251	mail.school.mo.us.	Windows NT 4.0
193.145.84.206	MO.cust-rtr.bigcablemodem.net.	Cisco 801/1720 router running IOS 12.2.8, Cisco router running IOS 12.2(8)T

Document Grinding

Primary Contacts	John Smith	
Method of Contact	**Phone** (888) 888-8888	**Email** John_Smith@School.mo.us

Organizational Information	
Business Name	Client Company
Business Address	200 Broad Street Richland, MO 00000-0000 US (UNITED STATES)
Business Telephone	(888) 888-8888
Business Fax	(888) 888-8889
Line of Business	Customer services

IP Information	
Domain Names	School.mo.us xxx.mo.us Clientschools.org ysystems.com Clientonline.com

Network Blocks	209.76.0.0/14
Network Block Owner	MO Cable Internet Services
Records Created	1997-04-29
Records Last Updated	2001-09-26

Email Information	
Email Server Addresses	5 relay.School.mo.us. 10 mail.School.mo.us. 20 infoserv.School.mo.us. 20 listserv.School.mo.us. 25 mail2.School.mo.us. 25 newsletter.School.mo.us.
Email Server Types	relay.School.mo.us. Norton Antivirus GW? mail.School.mo.us. Lotus Domino Release 5.0.10-6.0.1CF1 infoserv.School.mo.us. <Dead>? listserv.School.mo.us. MailShield (Lyris Email) mail2.School.mo.us. Sendmail 8.11.6/8.11.6 - 8.12.2-8.12.5? newsletter.School.mo.us. <Dead>?
Email Clients	Notes
Email System	Lotus Domino/Notes
Email Address Standard	Firstname.lastname@domain Firstname_lastname@domain FirstinitialLastname@domain
E-mail Footer	None
Encryption / Standard	None
Bounced mails	The linux email server doesn't bounce email, nor does it forward them. The main mail server (relay) sends all email after processing it to the main lotus notes server (mail). That machine will bounce email back. The listserv also bounces email back.

Web Information	
Website Address	193.145.85.23 listserv.School.mo.us. 193.145.85.28 sped.School.mo.us. 193.145.85.33 www.Clientschools.org. 193.145.85.37 tegrityweb.School.mo.us. 193.145.85.43 user64x43.School.mo.us. 193.145.85.44 classrooms.School.mo.us. 193.145.85.68 ctap.School.mo.us. 193.145.85.72 register.School.mo.us. 193.145.85.79 www.ysystems.com.

Web Server Type	193.145.85.23 Tcl-Webserver/3.4.2
	193.145.85.28 WebSTAR/3.0
	193.145.85.33 WebSTAR/4.4(SSL)
	193.145.85.37 Microsoft-IIS/5.0
	193.145.85.44 Says Microsoft-IIS/5.0, might be Microsoft-IIS/4.0
	193.145.85.68 Microsoft-IIS/5.0
	193.145.85.72 Microsoft-IIS/5.0 ASP.NET
	193.145.85.79 Microsoft-IIS/5.0
	193.145.85.100 Microsoft-IIS/5.0 WebLogic Server 8.x
	193.145.85.150 Down 11/6/2003
	193.145.85.43 Polycom Viewstation 512 Administrative Web GUI
Server Locations	Client Company
	200 Broad Street
	Richland, MO 00000-0000
	US (UNITED STATES)
Technologies Used	Asp, Coldfusion, Frontpage, Weblogic
Encryption standards	None in use
Web-Enabled Languages	Java

Name Services	
Primary (Authoritative) Name Server	ns1.School.mo.us.
Secondary	ns2.School.mo.us.
Additional Name Servers	193.145.85.248
	DNS1.CLIENTSCHOOLS.ORG
	DNS2.CLIENTSCHOOLS.ORG

Firewall Information	
Firewall Address	Unknown
Firewall Type	Inline Pix FW?
IDS system	Unknown

Routing Information	
Router Addresses	2193.145.84.206
Router Types	Cisco
Router Capabilities	

Server Information

IP Address	domain name
193.145.85.22	mail2.School.mo.us.

Hop	Port	Protocol	Service	Service Details
11	25	SMTP	Sendmail 8.12.2-8.12.5	25 on priority (tied for last)

Banner(s):

Port	Protocol	Banner
11	SMTP	220 mail2.School.mo.us ESMTP Sendmail 8.11.6/8.11.6; Fri, 7 Nov 2003 07:18:34 -0800

TCP Sequencing:

TCP Sequence Prediction
Class=truly random
TCP ISN Seq. Numbers
AF224E1E D58A928A EEF2CEF3 D2CC66FE ED5DAF25 EEFB4754
IPID Sequence Generation
Incremental
Uptime
337 hours (or just over 14 days)

Concern or Vulnerability
Vulnerability – Identified – 1.6
According to the Fingerprint and the banners shown, this version of Sendmail is vulnerable to many different buffer overflows. There are also a few minor local information leaks with this version. Either way, please consider updating to a newer non-vulnerable version.
CVE : CAN-2002-1337, CVE-2001-1349
Example
For example, if you had working exploit code (see http://packetstormsecurity.nl/), you could in theory obtain remote root access to the box.
Solution
Upgrade to Sendmail 8.12.10. (http://www.sendmail.org/)

Concern or Vulnerability
Information Leak – Verified – .4
Based on the current configuration it is possible to enumerate local system accounts.
Example
Telnet to 193.145.85.22 on port 25
220 mail2.School.mo.us ESMTP Sendmail 8.11.6/8.11.6; Fri, 7 Nov 2003 07:32:17 -0800
helo foo
250 mail2.School.mo.us Hello xxx.xxx.net [193.145.84.43], pleased to meet you
mail from: test@test.com
250 2.1.0 test@test.com... Sender ok
rcpt to: rooot@mail2.School.mo.us
550 5.1.1 rooot@mail2.School.mo.us... User unknown
rcpt to: root@mail2.School.mo.us
250 2.1.5 root@mail2.School.mo.us... Recipient ok
Solution

C

Create a "Catch all" virtual user table. See http://www.sendmail.org/virtual-hosting.html for more information.

Concern or Vulnerability

Information Leak – Verified – .4

When you connect to 193.145.85.22 on TCP port 25, 193.145.85.22 send a tcp syn packet to your host on tcp port 113. This allows for "passive" OS fingerprinting.

Example

telnet 193.145.85.22 25

=-=-=-=-=-=

193.145.85.22:2632 - Linux 2.4/2.6 (NAT!) (up: 338 hrs) -> 193.145.84.43:113 (distance 11, link: GPRS or FreeS/WAN)

Solution

Disable the IdentD check in sendmail. See the online sendmail documentation at http://www.sendmail.org

---

Concern or Vulnerability

Information Leak – Verified – .4

This system allows for Information Leakage. We are able to obtain system information remotely, such as uptime, etc.

Example

nmap –P0 -O 193.145.85.22 -p25
(see
http://groups.google.com/groups?q=ICMP+linux+uptime+netcraft&hl=en&lr=&ie=UTF-8&oe=UTF-8&selm=4yUY5.4218%24TU6.379536%40ptah.visi.com&rnum=1

and http://www.insecure.org/nmap/ for more information)

Solution

Because this test relies on the characteristics of the packets rather than any data inside the packet, it's subject to failure if there is a firewall or filtering router in between the server and the outside world.

IP Address	domain name
193.145.85.23	listserv.School.mo.us.

Hop	Port	Protocol	Service	Service Details
11	25	SMTP	Lyris ListManager	MailShield SMTP server for ListManager software http://www.lyris.com/products/listmanager/
11	80	HTTP	Lyris Webserver	Web interface to Lyris ListManager software

Banner(s):

Port	Protocol	Banner
25	SMTP	220 listserv.School.mo.us ESMTP Lyris ListManager service ready
80	HTTP	Tcl-Webserver/3.4.2 September 3, 2002

TCP Sequencing:

TCP Sequence Prediction
Class=truly random
TCP ISN Seq. Numbers
649CCE60 5A901405 85077E1A 73995316 3C77D84D 36CFECAF
IPID Sequence Generation
Incremental
Uptime
Not available

Concerns and Vulnerabilities:

Concern or Vulnerability
Weakness – Identified – .8
Allows for brute force login attempts
Example
http://listserv.School.mo.us/
Solution
Consult with 4D and implement attempt lockouts thresholds.

Concern or Vulnerability
Information Leak – Verified – .4
Remote users are able to get the statistics for the web interface. This will help them know which URL's are most commonly accessed.
Example
http://193.145.85.23/status/
Solution
Reconfigure Lyris ListServ to disallow access to that directory

Concern or Vulnerability
Information Leak – Verified – .4
Bounced messages make the server connect to attackers machine. The "passive" fingerprinting methods used in tools such as p0f (http://www.stearns.org/p0f/) are far more accurate than in "active" fingerprinting tools such as nmap, xprobe2, etc.   If you can get the mail server to bounce email to an IP of your choice, you can use "passive" fingerprinting to map the OS.
Example

```
xxx.xxx:~/jobs/Client/Phase 2/Nameserver# nc 193.145.85.23 25
220 listserv.School.mo.us ESMTP Lyris ListManager service ready
helo foo
250 listserv.School.mo.us Hello foo [193.145.84.43], pleased to meet you
mail from: test@193.145.84.43
250 < test@193.145.84.43>... Sender ok
rcpt to: lyris@listserv.School.mo.us
250 < lyris@listserv.School.mo.us>... Recipient ok
data
354 Enter mail, end with "." on a line by itself
Subject: help me
1
2
3
.
2
50 518 Message accepted for delivery.

=-=-=-=-=-=
193.145.85.23:14362 - Windows 2000 SP4, XP SP1 -> 193.145.84.43:25 (distance 11, link:
GPRS or FreeS/WAN)
```

Solution
This is a nit-picky vulnerability. The business justifications to allow a bounce message might outweigh the need to block bounces

IP Address	domain name
193.145.85.25	relay.School.mo.us.

Hop	Port	Protocol	Service	Service Details
11	25	SMTP	Norton Antivirus Gateway	This service scrubs email before passing it to the Lotus Notes server

Banner(s):

Port	Protocol	Banner
25	SMTP	220 relay.School.mo.us SMTP; Fri, 07 Nov 2003 07:15:58 -0800

TCP Sequencing:

TCP Sequence Prediction
Class=truly random
TCP ISN Seq. Numbers
DAC37A60 A3293DCC B9510BBC FAE67E91 B54288AE B1F479CA
IPID Sequence Generation
Broken little-endian incremental
Uptime
Not available

Concerns and Vulnerabilities:

Concern or Vulnerability
No concerns currently
Example
n/a
Solution

IP Address	domain name
193.145.85.28	sped.School.mo.us.

Ho p	Port	Protocol	Service	Service Details
11	80	HTTP	WebSTAR Webserver	Simple webserver

Banner(s):

Port	Protocol	Banner
80	HTTP	WebSTAR/3.0 ID/59734

TCP Sequencing:

TCP Sequence Prediction
Class=truly random
TCP ISN Seq. Numbers
98574FDC AE31A86A 52B32D3A 4C50D1AB 9B547615 48E0F13F
IPID Sequence Generation
Broken little-endian incremental
Uptime
Not available

Concerns and Vulnerabilities:

Concern or Vulnerability
Weakness – Identified – .8
The admin and log protected areas are protected with basic authentication with no apparent lock out feature. This means that given enough time, these accounts will be brute forced.
Example
Get a copy of http://www.hoobie.net/brutus/ and throw it at this server. http://193.145.85.28/pi_admin.admin http://sped.School.mo.us/webstar.log http://sped.School.mo.us/logs/webstar.log Go take a walk ☺.
Solution
Contact 4D for a solution.

IP Address	domain name
193.145.85.29	is.School.mo.us

Ho p	Port	Protocol	Service	Service Details
11	80	HTTP	IIS Webserver	IS "Internal" Server?

Banner(s):

Port	Protocol	Banner
80	HTTP	Microsoft-IIS/4.0

TCP Sequencing:

TCP Sequence Prediction
Class=truly random
TCP ISN Seq. Numbers
5C66B382 935A476A 7B3DD619 76365366 8E0EC76E 55C8DF4B
IPID Sequence Generation
Incremental
Uptime
Not available

Concerns and Vulnerabilities:

Concern or Vulnerability
Weakness – Identified – .8
This allows an attacker to be able to bruteforce login and password attempts to the Front Page Extension Authoring interface. With enough time an attacker could potentially access the authoring portion of Front Page and deface your website.
Example
http://is.School.mo.us/_vti_bin/_vti_aut/author.dll
Solution
Consider disallowing public access to this url.

IP Address	domain name
193.145.85.33	www.Clientschools.org. School.mo.us. Clientschools.org. www.School.mo.us.

Hop	Port	Protocol	Service	Service Details
11	21	FTP	File transfer	Mac ftp
11	80	HTTP	Website	Mac webserver
11	591	HTTP	FileMaker Pro	File Maker Pro webserver
11	1417	Timbuktu	Remote Administration	Closed
11	1418	Timbuktu	Remote Administration	Closed
11	1419	Timbuktu	Remote Administration	Closed
11	1420	Timbuktu	Remote Administration	Closed
11	8080	HTTP	Web Cache Proxy	Closed

Banner(s):

Port	Protocol	Banner
21	FTP	220-Welcome to the CLIENT Web server 220 Service ready for new user
80	HTTP	WebSTAR/4.4(SSL) ID/73202
591	HTTP	FileMakerPro/4.0

TCP Sequencing:

TCP Sequence Prediction
Class=truly random
TCP ISN Seq. Numbers
F7F9CA69 715FCCF E00C6489 17DFCACC B8DB4507 C260272D
IPID Sequence Generation
Busy server or unknown class
Uptime
Up since Tue Nov 4 03:36:05 2003

Concerns and Vulnerabilities:

Concern or Vulnerability
Weakness – Identified – .8
The admin and log protected areas are protected with basic authentication with no apparent lock out feature. This means that given enough time, these accounts will be brute forced.
Example

Get a copy of http://www.hoobie.net/brutus/ and throw it at this server.
http://193.145.85.33/pi_admin.admin
Go take a walk ☺.

Solution
Contact 4D for a solution.

Concern or Vulnerability
Concern – Verified – .8
This url gives up information about the internal IP scheme (10.94.1.75)
Example
http://www.School.mo.us/docushare/
Solution
Fix this link on the server.

Concern or Vulnerability
Concern – Verified – .8
There are "closed" ports. Because everything else is filtered (firewalled), to see a closed port means that the firewall allows those connections through even though the OS isn't listening for any connections
Example
Send a syn packet to 193.145.85.33 on port 1417. You'll get a tcp rst back showing that the port is closed. If it were open you would get a syn ack. If it were filtered (firewalled) you would get nothing back.
Solution
Update your firewall to filter those ports.

Concern or Vulnerability
Concern – Verified – .8
You are allowing FTP sessions. The username, password, and all data sent over FTP are not encrypted by the protocol.
Example
Open up a packet analyzer (Like Ethereal http://www.ethereal.com/) and collect the data as you transfer files to 193.145.85.33 over ftp.
Solution
Migrate to sftp or scp (part of the SSH suite).

Concern or Vulnerability
Information Leak – Verified – .4
The FileMakerPro access is currently showing demo databases. These don't seem to have any business justifiable reason to be on there.
Example
http://193.145.85.33:591/
Solution
Remove the demo content, or restrict access to this port all together.

IP Address	domain name
193.145.85.36	Techctr-backup.School.mo.us.

Ho p	Port	Protocol	Service	Service Details
11	3389	RDP	Remote admin.	Microsoft Remote Desktop Protocol for Terminal Server

Banner(s):

Port	Protocol	Banner
3389	RDP	

TCP Sequencing:

TCP Sequence Prediction
Class=truly random
TCP ISN Seq. Numbers
DAD4274A 55703E9 A9E993C2 1B6BAB5A 9FFA4E40 103C1B4A
IPID Sequence Generation
Incremental
Uptime
Not Available

Concerns and Vulnerabilities:

Concern or Vulnerability
Concern – Verified – .8
There is a Terminal Services remote desktop server running on this host. TS/RDP allows remote users to control the host machine as though they were physically at the terminal.
The username and password can be brute forced.
Example
http://www.microsoft.com/windowsxp/pro/downloads/rdClientdl.asp
http://www.hammerofgod.com/download/tsgrinder-2.03.zip
Solution
Disable Terminal Services if you don't need it.
If you must run Terminal Services, limit access to it with firewall ACL's.

IP Address	domain name
193.145.85.37	tegrityweb.School.mo.us .

Hop	Port	Protocol	Service	Service Details
11	80	http	Website	No site comes up.
11	1417	Timbuktu	Remote Admin	Should be filtered
11	1418	Timbuktu	Remote Admin	Closed
11	1419	Timbuktu	Remote Admin	Closed
11	1420	Timbuktu	Remote Admin	Closed

Banner(s):

Port	Protocol	Banner
80	HTTP	Microsoft-IIS/5.0
1417	Timbuktu	

TCP Sequencing:

TCP Sequence Prediction
Class=truly random
TCP ISN Seq. Numbers
7567D129 CD0DBB5F 74F788B8 902ED12B 8A28CD62 B7D562CD
IPID Sequence Generation
Incremental

Uptime
Not available

Concerns and Vulnerabilities:

Concern or Vulnerability
Concern – Verified – .8
There are "closed" ports. Because everything else is filtered (firewalled), to see a closed port means that the firewall allows those connections through even though the OS isn't listening for any connections
Example
Send a syn packet to 193.145.85.37 on port 1418. You'll get a tcp rst back showing that the port is closed. If it were open you would get a syn ack. If it were filtered (firewalled) you would get nothing back.
Solution
Update your firewall to filter those ports.

Concern or Vulnerability
Concern – Identified – .4
If you make a Timbuktu remote administrative shell open to the world it can be brute forced.
Example
Play with http://www.macanalysis.com/download.php3
Solution
All remote administrator shells should be limited either via Firewall rule-sets or via VPN's.

Concern or Vulnerability
Concern – Identified – .4
Another brute force opportunity.
Example
http://tegrityweb.School.mo.us./printers
Solution
Consider restricting access to this URL

Concern or Vulnerability
Unknown – Verified – .2
If there is not supposed to be a website on this server why have that port open?
Example
http://193.145.85.37/ comes up with error 403 Forbidden
Solution
Put up a website, or filter this port at the firewall.

IP Address	domain name
193.145.85.38	user64x38.School.mo.us.

Hop	Port	Protocol	Service	Service Details
11	21	FTP	File transfer	Non-encrypted, non-anonymous

Banner(s):

Port	Protocol	Banner
21	FTP	220 TEGRITYWEB Microsoft FTP Service (Version 5.0).

TCP Sequencing:

TCP Sequence Prediction
Class=truly random
TCP ISN Seq. Numbers
5C0B4F6B 9E02BC10 D86853DB 85FA0380 7ABBF049 B3E281EE

IPID Sequence Generation
Busy server or unknown class
Uptime
Not available

Concerns and Vulnerabilities:

Concern or Vulnerability
Concern – Verified – .8
You are allowing FTP sessions. The username, password, and all data sent over FTP are not encrypted by the protocol.
Example
Open up a packet analyzer (Like Ethereal http://www.ethereal.com/) and collect the data as you transfer files to 193.145.85.38 over ftp.
Solution
Migrate to sftp or scp (part of the SSH suite).

IP Address	domain name
193.145.85.43	user64x43.School.mo.us.

Hop	Port	Protocol	Service	Service Details
15	21	FTP	File Transfer	Non-anonymous, non-encrypted
15	23	TELNET	Remote Administration	Non-encrypted, non-authenticated
15	24	TELNET	Remote Administration	Non-encrypted, non-authenticated
15	80	HTTP	Remote Administration Website	Non-encrypted, null password for admin and administrator
15	1720	NetMeeting	Chat, collaboration	Not-filtered
15	5001	UNKNOWN	Video Conferencing	UNKNOWN
15	5003	UNKNOWN	Video Conferencing	UNKNOWN
15	5004	UNKNOWN	Video Conferencing	UNKNOWN
15	All others	n/a	n/a	Closed

Banner(s):

Port	Protocol	Banner
21	FTP	220 FTP Server, type 'quote help' for help

C

23	TELNET	Hi, my name is : Client company
		Here is what I know about myself: Serial Number: 001573 Brand: Polycom Software Version: Release 7.0.3 - 21 Aug 2001 Model: VS Network Interface: ISDN_QUAD_BRI MP Enabled: No H323 Enabled: Yes IP Address: 193.145.85.43 Time In Last Call: 0:01:44 Total Time In Calls: 190:48:52 Total Calls: 924 Switch Type: NI-1 Country Code: 1 Area Code: 714 Client company Client company ISDN 1 a is: 4444063 SPID 1 a is: 71444440630101 ISDN 1 b is: 4441327 SPID 1 b is: 71444413270101 ISDN 2 a is: 4444960 SPID 2 a is: 71444449600101 ISDN 2 b is: 4441463 SPID 2 b is: 71444414630101 ISDN 3 a is: 4444066 SPID 3 a is: 71444440660101 ISDN 3 b is: 4441721 SPID 3 b is: 71444417210101
24	TELNET	Hi, my name is : Client company
		Here is what I know about myself: Serial Number: 001573 Brand: Polycom Software Version: Release 7.0.3 - 21 Aug 2001 Model: VS Network Interface: ISDN_QUAD_BRI MP Enabled: No H323 Enabled: Yes IP Address: 193.145.85.43 Time In Last Call: 0:01:44 Total Time In Calls: 190:48:52 Total Calls: 924 Switch Type: NI-1 Country Code: 1 Area Code: 714 ISDN 1 a is: 4444063 SPID 1 a is: 71444440630101 ISDN 1 b is: 4441327 SPID 1 b is: 71444413270101 ISDN 2 a is: 4444960 SPID 2 a is: 71444449600101 ISDN 2 b is: 4441463 SPID 2 b is: 71444414630101 ISDN 3 a is: 4444066 SPID 3 a is: 71444440660101 ISDN 3 b is: 4441721 SPID 3 b is: 71444417210101

80	HTTP	Viavideo-Web
1720	NetMeeting	
5001	UNKNOWN	
5003	UNKNOWN	
5004	UNKNOWN	

Concerns and Vulnerabilities:

Concern or Vulnerability
Weakness – Verified – 1.6
The FTP server allows logging in as user admin or administrator with any password combination. Once logged in as an admin level account, you can read files, write files, reboot the device, and update the firmware on the device.
Example
Connected to 193.145.85.43. 220 FTP Server, type 'quote help' for help Name (193.145.85.43:root): admin 331 User name okay, need password. Password: 230 User logged in, proceed. Remote system type is UNIX. ftp> quote help 214- Usage from FTP 　ls　　　- directory listing 　bin　　 - set image mode for put 　get filename - read file from ffs 　put filename - write file to ffs 　del filename - delete file in ffs 　quote swup   - set software update mode 　quote boot   - reboot 214 end of help
Solution
Restrict access to this port at the firewall. Change the admin and administrator passwords.

Concern or Vulnerability
Weakness – Verified – 1.6
You can obtain and modify configurations on port 23 and port 24 without being prompted for authentication
Example
telnet 193.145.85.43 23 Or telnet 193.145.85.43 24
Solution
Restrict access to these ports at the firewall.

Concern or Vulnerability
Weakness – Verified – 1.6
Through the admin and administrator accounts on the website you can view and modify the configuration. You can make long distance calls. You can also wipe the logs.
Example
Visit http://193.145.85.43/a_adminindex.htm Login: admin Password:
Solution

Restrict access to this port at the firewall.	
Change the admin and administrator account passwords.	

Concern or Vulnerability
Concern – Verified – .8
Anyone can establish a netmeeting connection to 193.145.85.43:1720
Example
Open Netmeeting. Connect to 193.145.85.43
Solution
Restrict access to this port.

Concern or Vulnerability
Concern – Verified – .8
You are allowing FTP sessions. The username, password, and all data sent over FTP are not encrypted by the protocol.
Example
Open up a packet analyzer (Like Ethereal http://www.ethereal.com/) and collect the data as you transfer files to 193.145.85.43 over ftp.
Solution
Migrate to sftp or scp (part of the SSH suite).

Concern or Vulnerability
Unknown – Identified – .1
Not sure what ports 5001, 5003, and 5004 are used for. Find out and determine if they need to be world accessible.
Example
Visit http://www.polycom.com/products_services/0,1816,pw-4353-4430,00.html
Grab the documentation files.
Solution
Restrict access to this port.

IP Address	domain name
193.145.85.44	Classrooms.School.mo.us.

Hop	Port	Protocol	Service	Service Details
11	80	http	Website	Allows students to navigate to the virtual classrooms
11	2187	JINX	Virtual Classroom	Java based
11	2188	JINX	Virtual Classroom	Java based

Banner(s):

Port	Protocol	Banner
80	HTTP	Microsoft-IIS/5.0
2187	JINX	400 Goodbye
2188	JINX	400 Goodbye

TCP Sequencing:

TCP Sequence Prediction
Class=truly random

TCP ISN Seq. Numbers
F379BDC7 E52C7DD1 381FEC4C 21BBD424 2AF4241D DD83F25C
IPID Sequence Generation
Incremental
Uptime
Not available

Concerns and Vulnerabilities:

Concern or Vulnerability
Vulnerability – Identified – 1.6
Did not validate this, but it seems that this machine is vulnerable to a flaw in the shtml.dll file that can allow a remote attacker the ability to run arbitrary code. This affects both Frontpage Server Extensions 2000 and 2002.
Example
Solution
Install the appropriate Microsoft hotfix. http://www.microsoft.com/technet/treeview/default.asp?url=/technet/security/bulletin/MS02-053.asp http://support.microsoft.com/default.aspx?scid=kb;en-us;Q329085

Concern or Vulnerability
Concern – Identified – .4
The authentication over port 2187-2188 are not encrypted.
Example
Open up a packet analyzer (Like Ethereal http://www.ethereal.com/) and collect the data as you authenticate to 193.145.85.44 over the Java interface.
Solution
Contact Elluminate – http://www.elluminate.com/

IP Address	domain name
193.145.85.58	ns1.School.mo.us.

Hop	Port	Protocol	Service	Service Details
11	53(UDP)	DNS	Domain Name Service	Primary nameserver for School.mo.us domain.

Banner(s):

Port	Protocol	Banner
53	DNS	8.4.1-REL

Concerns and Vulnerabilities:

Concern or Vulnerability
Weakness – Verified – 1.6
This DNS server is allowing recursive queries from the outside. This would allow an attacker to poison the DNS servers local cache. The next victim to request that information may be unknowingly directed to the attackers site.
Example
http://www.giac.org/practical/gsec/Doug_Sax_GSEC.pdf http://www.cert.org/advisories/CA-1997-22.html
Solution
Disable recursive queries for those outside of the CLIENT IP space.

IP Address	Domain name

193.145.85.59	ns2.School.mo.us.

Hop	Port	Protocol	Service	Service Details
11	53(UDP)	DNS	Domain Name Service	Secondary nameserver for School.mo.us domain.

Banner(s):

Port	Protocol	Banner
53	DNS	9.2.2rc1

Concerns and Vulnerabilities:

Concern or Vulnerability
Weakness – Verified – 1.6
This DNS server is allowing recursive queries from the outside. This would allow an attacker to poison the DNS servers local cache. The next victim to request that information may be unknowingly directed to the attackers site.
Example
http://www.giac.org/practical/gsec/Doug_Sax_GSEC.pdf http://www.cert.org/advisories/CA-1997-22.html
Solution
Disable recursive queries for those outside of the CLIENT IP space.

Concern or Vulnerability
Vulnerability – Identified – 1.6
This version of bind (based solely on the reported revision number) is known to be vulnerable to a buffer overflow which may allow an attacker to gain a shell on this host or disrupt access to this server (DoS).
Example
http://www.cert.org/advisories/CA-2002-19.html http://cert.uni-stuttgart.de/archive/bugtraq/2003/03/msg00075.html http://www.cve.mitre.org/cgi-bin/cvename.cgi?name=CAN-2002-0684
Solution
If this indeed is a problem, then upgrade to bind 9.2.3 (http://www.isc.org/products/BIND/) or downgrade to the 8.x series. This may not be a problem for you if you're running bind on a windows platform as this specific vulnerability is tied to the GNU DNS resolver library as part of glibc.

IP Address	domain name
193.145.85.68	ctap.School.mo.us. support.School.mo.us.

Hop	Port	Protocol	Service	Service Details
11	21	FTP	File Transfer	Non-anonymous
11	21	HTTP	Website	Getting Results
11	1417	Timbuktu	Remote Admin	Closed
11	1418	Timbuktu	Remote Admin	Closed
11	1419	Timbuktu	Remote Admin	Closed
11	1420	Timbuktu	Remote Admin	Closed

Banner(s):

Port	Protocol	Banner
21	FTP	220 vtserver Microsoft FTP Service (Version 5.0).
80	HTTP	Server: Microsoft-IIS/5.0 Content-Location: http://193.145.85.68/index.htm WebQuota Version 5.0f2: 8864247000 WebQuota Version 5.0f2: 8864247000 Date: Tue, 11 Nov 2003 05:28:48 GMT Content-Type: text/html Accept-Ranges: bytes Last-Modified: Thu, 21 Aug 2003 01:03:05 GMT ETag: "448d6efa7f67c31:89c" Content-Length: 5765

TCP Sequencing:

TCP Sequence Prediction
Class=truly random
TCP ISN Seq. Numbers
46ADBCA0 A9F8B4C 326D4CBD 1D10968B E636BC3B D1E76F71
IPID Sequence Generation
Incremental
Uptime
Not available

Concerns and Vulnerabilities:

Concern or Vulnerability
Concern – Verified – .8
You are allowing FTP sessions. The username, password, and all data sent over FTP are not encrypted by the protocol.
Example
Open up a packet analyzer (Like Ethereal http://www.ethereal.com/) and collect the data as you transfer files to 193.145.85.68 over ftp.
Solution
Migrate to sftp or scp (part of the SSH suite).

Concern or Vulnerability
Weakness – Identified – .8
Internet Printing (IPP) is enabled, and there are other signs that show that ISAPI extensions are enabled. The system appears to be patched, but you could save yourself the headache of people trying to exploit things by disabling those features all together.
Example
http://193.145.85.68/NULL.printer
Solution
http://www.microsoft.com/technet/treeview/default.asp?url=/technet/security/bulletin/ms01-023.asp http://www.securityfocus.com/bid/2674

Concern or Vulnerability
Concern – Identified – .4
This webserver is configured to support the TRACE method. Attackers may abuse HTTP TRACE functionality to gain access to information in HTTP headers such as cookies and authentication data. In the presence of other cross-domain vulnerabilities in web browsers, sensitive header information could be read from any domains that support the HTTP TRACE method
Example
http://www.kb.cert.org/vuls/id/867593 http://www.cgisecurity.com/whitehat-mirror/WhitePaper_screen.pdf

Solution

Use the URLScan tool to deny HTTP TRACE requests or to permit only the methods needed to meet site requirements and policy. The default configurations of Urlscan 2.5 (both baseline and SRP) only permit GET and HEAD methods.

Concern or Vulnerability
Information Leak – Verified – .4
It's possible to get the Coldfusion debug information from this server by calling for any cfm file (whether or not it exists) and appending ?mode=debug
Example
http://193.145.85.68/xxxxxx.cfm?mode=debug
Solution

As taken from
http://www.macromedia.com/support/coldfusion/ts/documents/tn17642.htm

1. Go into Debugging IPs in the ColdFusion Administrator.
2. Go to the box that states: Restrict debug output to selected IP addresses.
3. Enter only one IP Address - 127.0.0.1.
4. Click Add.
5. Click Apply.
6. Restart ColdFusion.

Concern or Vulnerability
Information Leak – Verified – .4
Certain DOS reserved filenames, such as NUL or PRN, can cause Coldfusion to display the path to the web root directory in an error message.
Example
http://193.145.85.68/nul..cfm
Solution

Two solutions are available to prevent IIS from passing DOS reserved filenames to ColdFusion for processing.

1. Install and configure the Microsoft URLScan Security Tool
2. Change IIS properties to check that files exist

See http://www.macromedia.com/v1/handlers/index.cfm?ID=22906 for more details.

Concern or Vulnerability
Information Leak – Verified – .4
Coldfusion 4.0-5.0 reveal file system paths of .cfm or .dbm files when the request contains invalid DOS devices.
Example
http://193.145.85.68/nul.dbm http://193.145.85.68/nul.cfm
Solution

Two solutions are available to prevent IIS from passing DOS reserved filenames to ColdFusion for processing.

1. Install and configure the Microsoft URLScan Security Tool
2. Change IIS properties to check that files exist

See http://www.macromedia.com/v1/handlers/index.cfm?ID=22906 for more details.

Concern or Vulnerability
Information Leak – Verified – .4
Coldfusion 4.0-5.0 reveal file system paths of .cfm or .dbm files when the request contains invalid DOS devices.
Example

http://193.145.85.68/nul.dbm
http://193.145.85.68/nul.cfm

Solution

Two solutions are available to prevent IIS from passing DOS reserved filenames to ColdFusion for processing.
 	
  1. Install and configure the Microsoft URLScan Security Tool
  2. Change IIS properties to check that files exist
 	
See http://www.macromedia.com/v1/handlers/index.cfm?ID=22906 for more details.

Concern or Vulnerability
Concern – Identified – .4
It appears this system has WebDAV enabled. If this feature isn't being used, consider disabling it.
Example
OPTIONS * HTTP/1.0 HTTP/1.1 200 OK Server: Microsoft-IIS/5.0 Date: Tue, 11 Nov 2003 17:05:26 GMT Content-Length: 0 Accept-Ranges: bytes DASL: <DAV:sql> DAV: 1, 2 Public: OPTIONS, TRACE, GET, HEAD, DELETE, PUT, POST, COPY, MOVE, MKCOL, PROPFIND, PROPPATCH, LOCK, UNLOCK, SEARCH Allow: OPTIONS, TRACE, GET, HEAD, DELETE, PUT, POST, COPY, MOVE, MKCOL, PROPFIND, PROPPATCH, LOCK, UNLOCK, SEARCH Cache-Control: private
Solution
To disable WebDAV on IIS 5.0: Create a DWORD registry value called "DisableWebDAV" in the HKEY_LOCAL_MACHINE\SYSTEM\CurrentControlSet\Services\W3SVC\Parameters key, and set it to 1.

IP Address	domain name
193.145.85.72	register.School.mo.us

Hop	Port	Protocol	Service	Service Details
11	21	FTP	File Transfer	Allows anonymous ftp
11	80	HTTP	Website	"Under construction"
11	3389	RDP	Remote admin.	Microsoft Remote Desktop Protocol for Terminal Server http://www.microsoft.com/windowsxp/pro/downloads/rdClientdl.asp
11	5632	Status for PC Anywhere	http://www.symantec.com	Closed
11	5800	VNC	Remote admin.	http://www.uk.research.att.com/vnc - why RDP and VNC? Version RFB 003.003
11	5900	VNC	Remote admin.	http://www.uk.research.att.com/vnc why RDP and VNC? Version RFB 003.003

Banner(s):

Port	Protocol	Banner
21	FTP	220 register Microsoft FTP Service (Version 5.0)
80	HTTP	Microsoft-IIS/5.0
3389	RDP	Windows 2000 Server
5800	VNC	<APPLET CODE=vncviewer.class ARCHIVE=vncviewer.jar WIDTH=800 HEIGHT=632>

TCP Sequencing:

TCP Sequence Prediction
Class=truly random
TCP ISN Seq. Numbers
A95DAFD6 801268D2 91FD17E8 A1B56489 69E3E14C B3A64BA4
IPID Sequence Generation
Busy server or unknown class
Uptime
Not available

Concerns and Vulnerabilities:

Concern or Vulnerability
Vulnerability – Identified – 1.6
A flaw in the shtml.dll file can allow a remote attacker the ability to run arbitrary code. This affects both Frontpage Server Extensions 2000 and 2002. The IIS server appears to have the .SHTML ISAPI filter mapped. At least one remote vulnerability has been discovered for the .SHTML filter. This is detailed in Microsoft Advisory MS02-018 and results in a denial of service access to the web server. It is recommended that even if you have patched this vulnerability that;you unmap the .SHTML extension, and any other unused ISAPI extensions if they are not required for the operation of your site. An attacker may use this flaw to prevent the remote service from working properly (DoS).
Example
Could not find working exploit code. This system may or may not be vulnerable to the issue.
Solution
Install patch: http://download.microsoft.com/download/FrontPage2002/fpse1002/1/W98NT42KMeXP/EN-US/fpse1002.exe Also see: http://cve.mitre.org/cgi-bin/cvename.cgi?name=CAN-2002-0692 http://www.microsoft.com/technet/treeview/default.asp?url=/technet/security/bulletin/MS02-053.asp http://www.microsoft.com/technet/security/bulletin/ms02-018.asp http://support.microsoft.com/default.aspx?scid=kb;en-us;Q329085 Also consider unmapping the shtml/shtm isapi filters. To unmap the .shtml extension: 1.Open Internet Services Manager. 2.Right-click the Web server choose Properties from the context menu. 3.Master Properties 4.Select WWW Service -> Edit -> HomeDirectory -> Configuration ;and remove the reference to .shtml/shtm and sht from the list.

Concern or Vulnerability

Weakness – Verified – 1.6

There is a VNC server running on this host. VNC (Virtual Network Computing) allows remote users to control the host machine as though they were physically at the terminal.

VNC is not encrypted in its default form, and authentication is not a part of the Windows standard authentication. There is no username, only a password which can be brute forced.

It's very odd to see VNC and TS running on the same machine, as it's twice the administrative load to properly secure.

Example

http://193.145.85.72:5800/

or download VNC Client from
http://www.realvnc.com/
http://www.phenoelit.de/vncrack/

Solution

Disable VNC.

If you must run VNC, limit access to it with firewall ACL's.

Concern or Vulnerability

Concern – Verified – .8

More brute force opportunities. Also worth noting I was able to create a student account and register for classes.

Example

http://register.School.mo.us/dev_supervisors.asp
http://register.School.mo.us/dev_instructors.asp?action=login&caller=&routine=

Solution

Consider restricting public access to these URLs.

Concern or Vulnerability

Concern – Verified – .8

There is a Terminal Services remote desktop server running on this host. TS/RDP allows remote users to control the host machine as though they were physically at the terminal.

The username and password can be brute forced.

It's very odd to see VNC and TS running on the same machine.

Example

http://www.microsoft.com/windowsxp/pro/downloads/rdClientdl.asp
http://www.hammerofgod.com/download/tsgrinder-2.03.zip

Solution

Disable Terminal Services if you don't need it.

If you must run Terminal Services, limit access to it with firewall ACL's.

Concern or Vulnerability

Concern – Verified – .8

You are allowing FTP sessions. The username, password, and all data sent over FTP are not encrypted by the protocol. This system also allows for anonymous FTP access, although no write/mkdir permissions were enabled, and there were no files available to download.

Example

Open up a packet analyzer (Like Ethereal http://www.ethereal.com/) and collect the data as you transfer files to 193.145.85.72 over ftp.

Solution

Migrate to sftp or scp (part of the SSH suite).

Concern or Vulnerability

Weakness – Identified – .8

/xxxxx.htw - Server may be vulnerable to a Webhits.dll arbitrary file retrieval.

Example

Could not verify, and this is an old vulnerability.

http://www.microsoft.com/technet/treeview/default.asp?url=/technet/security/bulleti n/MS00-006.asp

Solution

Ensure Q252463i, Q252463a or Q251170 are installed installed. See http://www.microsoft.com/technet/treeview/default.asp?url=/technet/security/bulleti n/MS00-006.asp for more information.

Concern or Vulnerability

Concern – Identified – .4

It appears this system has WebDAV enabled. If this feature isn't being used, consider disabling it.

Example

OPTIONS * HTTP/1.0

HTTP/1.1 200 OK
Server: Microsoft-IIS/5.0
Date: Tue, 11 Nov 2003 20:15:47 GMT
Content-Length: 0
Accept-Ranges: bytes
DASL: <DAV:sql>
DAV: 1, 2
Public: OPTIONS, TRACE, GET, HEAD, DELETE, PUT, POST, COPY, MOVE, MKCOL,
PROPFIND, PROPPATCH, LOCK, UNLOCK, SEARCH
Allow: OPTIONS, TRACE, GET, HEAD, DELETE, PUT, POST, COPY, MOVE, MKCOL,
PROPFIND, PROPPATCH, LOCK, UNLOCK, SEARCH
Cache-Control: private

Solution

To disable WebDAV on IIS 5.0:
Create a DWORD registry value called "DisableWebDAV" in the
HKEY_LOCAL_MACHINE\SYSTEM\CurrentControlSet\Services\W3SVC\Parameters key, and set it to 1.

Concern or Vulnerability

Concern – Identified – .4

This webserver is configured to support the TRACE method.
Attackers may abuse HTTP TRACE functionality to gain access to information in HTTP headers such as cookies and authentication data. In the presence of other cross-domain vulnerabilities in web browsers, sensitive header information could be read from any domains that support the HTTP TRACE method

Example

http://www.kb.cert.org/vuls/id/867593
http://www.cgisecurity.com/whitehat-mirror/WhitePaper_screen.pdf

Solution

Use the URLScan tool to deny HTTP TRACE requests or to permit only the methods needed to meet site requirements and policy. The default configurations of Urlscan 2.5 (both baseline and SRP) only permit GET and HEAD methods.

Concern or Vulnerability
Information Leak – Identified – .2
SQL injection is a technique for exploiting web applications that use Client-supplied data in SQL queries without stripping illegal characters first. This vulnerability can allow people to extract sensitive information from the server's database, and possibly even execute arbitrary commands.
Example
http://register.School.mo.us/events/DayView.asp?daterequest=10/6/2003&day=char%4039%41%2b%40SELECT
Solution
Contact Mediablend (www.Mediablend.com) for assistance in fixing the script.

Concern or Vulnerability
Information Leak – Identified – .2
SQL injection is a technique for exploiting web applications that use Client-supplied data in SQL queries without stripping illegal characters first. This vulnerability can allow people to extract sensitive information from the server's database, and possibly even execute arbitrary commands.
Example
http://register.School.mo.us/events/DayView.asp?daterequest=10/6/2003&day='http://register.School.mo.us/events/DayView.asp?daterequest=10/6/2003&day='
Solution
Contact Mediablend (www.Mediablend.com) for assistance in fixing the script.

IP Address	domain name
193.145.85.79	ysystems.com.

Hop	Port	Protocol	Service	Service Details
11	21	FTP	File Transfer	
11	80	HTTP	Website	Virtual Training
11	407	Timbuktu	Control port	Closed
11	1417	Timbuktu	Remote admin.	Timbuktu
11	1418	Timbuktu	Remote admin.	Closed
11	1419	Timbuktu	Remote admin.	Closed
11	1420	Timbuktu	Remote admin.	Closed

Banner(s):

Port	Protocol	Banner
21	FTP	
80	HTTP	Microsoft-IIS/5.0
3389	RDP	Windows 2000 Server
5800	VNC	<APPLET CODE=vncviewer.class ARCHIVE=vncviewer.jar WIDTH=800 HEIGHT=632>

TCP Sequencing:

TCP Sequence Prediction
Class=truly random
TCP ISN Seq. Numbers
A95DAFD6 801268D2 91FD17E8 A1B56489 69E3E14C B3A64BA4
IPID Sequence Generation
Busy server or unknown class
Uptime
Not available

Concerns and Vulnerabilities:

Concern or Vulnerability

Vulnerability – Identified – 1.6
Due to a faulty mechanism in the password parsing implementation in authentication requests, it is possible to launch a denial of service attack against Allaire ColdFusion 4.5.1 or previous by inputting a string of over 40 000 characters to the password field in the Administrator login page. CPU utilization could reach up to 100%, bringing the program to halt. The default form for the login page would prevent such an attack. However, a malicious user could download the form locally to their hard drive, modify HTML tag fields, and be able to submit the 40 000 character string to the ColdFusion Server.

Restarting the application would be required in order to regain normal functionality.

You appear to be running Coldfusion 4.5.

This administrative login screen can also be brute forced.

Example
The Administrator login page can be typically accessed via: http://193.145.85.79/cfide/administrator/index.cfm Modify the field size and POST action in the HTML tags to allow for the input of a character string consisting of over 40 000 characters. Also play with Brutus (http://www.hoobie.net/brutus/)
Solution
Workaround: Back up all existing data and implement the steps outlined in the following knowledge base article: http://www.macromedia.com/support/coldfusion/ts/documents/tn17254.htm http://www.macromedia.com/v1/cfdocs/allaire_support/adminsecurity.htm

Concern or Vulnerability
Information Leak – Verified – .4
Several Coldfusion default directories are available. This can in some cases divulge exact versions of installed code.
Example
http://193.145.85.79/cfide/administrator/include/ http://193.145.85.79/CFIDE/administrator/docs/ http://193.145.85.79/CFIDE/administrator/images/
Solution
Ensure Q252463i, Q252463a or Q251170 are installed installed. See http://www.microsoft.com/technet/treeview/default.asp?url=/technet/security/bulletin/MS00-006.asp for more information.

Concern or Vulnerability
Concern – Identified – .4
Another brute force availability.
Example
http://www.ysystems.com/youthsystems/admin/
Solution
Consider disallowing public access to this url.

Concern or Vulnerability
Concern – Identified – .4
It appears this system has WebDAV enabled. If this feature isn't being used, consider disabling it.
Example

OPTIONS * HTTP/1.0

HTTP/1.1 200 OK
Server: Microsoft-IIS/5.0
Date: Wed, 12 Nov 2003 02:41:30 GMT
IISExport: This web site was exported using IIS Export v3.0
Content-Length: 0
Accept-Ranges: bytes
DASL: <DAV:sql>
DAV: 1, 2
Public: OPTIONS, TRACE, GET, HEAD, DELETE, PUT, POST, COPY, MOVE, MKCOL,
PROPFIND, PROPPATCH, LOCK, UNLOCK, SEARCH
Allow: OPTIONS, TRACE, GET, HEAD, DELETE, PUT, POST, COPY, MOVE, MKCOL,
PROPFIND, PROPPATCH, LOCK, UNLOCK, SEARCH
Cache-Control: private

Solution

To disable WebDAV on IIS 5.0:
Create a DWORD registry value called "DisableWebDAV" in the
HKEY_LOCAL_MACHINE\SYSTEM\CurrentControlSet\Services\W3SVC\Parameters key,
and set it to 1.

Concern or Vulnerability

Concern – Identified – .4

This webserver is configured to support the TRACE method.
Attackers may abuse HTTP TRACE functionality to gain access to information in HTTP
headers such as cookies and authentication data. In the presence of other cross-
domain vulnerabilities in web browsers, sensitive header information could be read
from any domains that support the HTTP TRACE method

Example

http://www.kb.cert.org/vuls/id/867593
http://www.cgisecurity.com/whitehat-mirror/WhitePaper_screen.pdf

Solution

Use the URLScan tool to deny HTTP TRACE requests or to permit only the methods
needed to meet site requirements and policy. The default configurations of Urlscan 2.5
(both baseline and SRP) only permit GET and HEAD methods.

IP Address	Domain name
193.145.85.90	dns1.Clientschools.org

Hop	Port	Protocol	Service	Service Details
11	53(UDP)	DNS	Domain Name Service	Primary nameserver for Clientschools.org Bind on Windows

Banner(s):

Port	Protocol	Banner
53(UDP)	DNS	8.2.5-REL

Concerns and Vulnerabilities:

Concern or Vulnerability
Vulnerability – Identified – 1.6
There are several major vulnerabilities based on this version information.
Example

Remote shells and DoS.

http://www.securityfocus.com/bid/6160/discussion/
http://xforce.iss.net/xforce/xfdb/10333

When a DNS lookup is requested on a non-existent sub-domain of a valid domain and an OPT resource record with a large UDP payload is attached, the server may fail.

Solution
Upgrade to 8.4.1 or 9.2.3 http://www.isc.org/products/BIND/bind8.html http://www.isc.org/products/BIND/

Concern or Vulnerability
Weakness – Verified – 1.6 This DNS server is allowing recursive queries from the outside. This would allow an attacker to poison the DNS servers local cache. The next victim to request that information may be unknowingly directed to the attackers site.
Example
http://www.giac.org/practical/gsec/Doug_Sax_GSEC.pdf http://www.cert.org/advisories/CA-1997-22.html
Solution
Disable recursive queries for those outside of the CLIENT IP space.

IP Address	domain name
193.145.85.91	Dns2.Clientschools.org.

Hop	Port	Protocol	Service	Service Details
11	53(UDP)	DNS	Domain name service	Secondary nameserver for Clientschools.org Bind on windows

Banner(s):

Port	Protocol	Banner
11	DNS	9.2.2

Concerns and Vulnerabilities:

Concern or Vulnerability
Weakness – Verified – 1.6 This DNS server is allowing recursive queries from the outside. This would allow an attacker to poison the DNS servers local cache. The next victim to request that information may be unknowingly directed to the attackers site.
Example
http://www.giac.org/practical/gsec/Doug_Sax_GSEC.pdf http://www.cert.org/advisories/CA-1997-22.html
Solution
Disable recursive queries for those outside of the CLIENT IP space.

Concern or Vulnerability
Information: There is a newer 9.2.x tree available
Example
n/a
Solution
Upgrade to 9.2.3 http://www.isc.org/products/BIND/

IP Address	domain name
193.145.85.100	user64x100.School.mo.us. www.Clientschools.org

Ho p	Port	Protocol	Service	Service Details
11	21	FTP	File Transfer	www.Clientschools.org ftp site
11	80	HTTP	Website	www.Clientschools.org

Banner(s):

Port	Protocol	Banner
21	FTP	220 webserver Microsoft FTP Service (Version 5.0).
80	HTTP	Microsoft-IIS/5.0

TCP Sequencing:

TCP Sequence Prediction
Class=truly random
TCP ISN Seq. Numbers
D0546289 B64E6218 E1BE3211 CE884108 C369C71F DB1C99BB
IPID Sequence Generation
Incremental
Uptime
Not available

Concerns and Vulnerabilities:

Concern or Vulnerability
Vulnerability – Identified – 1.6
Based on the version in the banner, it may be possible to crash the ftp server (DoS). This would only be possible after logging in, which would require a valid username/password.
Example
An example request that can cause the crash: STAT ?*<240 x X>   More information can be found here: http://www.securiteam.com/windowsntfocus/5XP0H206VM.html
Solution
Apply relevant hotfix: http://www.microsoft.com/technet/security/bulletin/ms02-018.asp   Microsoft Patch Q319733 IIS 5.0 http://download.microsoft.com/download/iis50/Patch/Q319733/NT5/EN-US/Q319733_W2K_SP3_X86_EN.exe

Concern or Vulnerability
Weakness – Identified – .8
This allows an attacker to be able to bruteforce login and password attempts to the Front Page Extension Authoring interface. With enough time an attacker could potentially access the authoring portion of Front Page and deface your website.
Example
http://www.Clientschools.org/_vti_bin/_vti_aut/author.dll/admin.dll/
Solution
Consider disallowing public access to this url.

Concern or Vulnerability

Concern – Verified – .8
You are allowing FTP sessions. The username, password, and all data sent over FTP are not encrypted by the protocol.
Example
Open up a packet analyzer (Like Ethereal http://www.ethereal.com/) and collect the data as you transfer files to 193.145.85.100 over ftp.
Solution
Migrate to sftp or scp (part of the SSH suite).

IP Address	domain name
193.145.85.150	web.School.mo.us

Ho p	Port	Protocol	Service	Service Details
11	21	FTP	File Transfer	
11	80	HTTP	Website	

Banner(s):

Port	Protocol	Banner
21	FTP	220-Welcome to Rumpus! 220 Service ready for new user
80	HTTP	MACHTTP/2.5

TCP Sequencing:

TCP Sequence Prediction
Class=truly random
TCP ISN Seq. Numbers
A9CF4368 A3F03E63 B550E91E 994FFD63 AE3BC539 DE745F1B
IPID Sequence Generation
Broken little-endian incremental
Uptime
Not available

Concerns and Vulnerabilities:

Concern or Vulnerability
Vulnerability – Identified – 1.6
The remote system may be vulnerable to one or more remote buffer overflow attacks.
Example
Using automated FTP vulnerability "fuzzers" you can look for patterns of past weaknesses. This ftpd exhibited potential weaknesses for exploitation.
Solution
Contact Rumpus http://www.maxum.com/Rumpus/ for more information.

Concern or Vulnerability
Concern – Verified – .8
You are allowing FTP sessions. The username, password, and all data sent over FTP are not encrypted by the protocol.
Example
Open up a packet analyzer (Like Ethereal http://www.ethereal.com/) and collect the data as you transfer files to 193.145.85.150 over ftp.
Solution
Migrate to sftp or scp (part of the SSH suite).

IP Address	Domain name
193.145.85.248	user64x248.School.mo.us.

Ho p	Port	Protocol	Service	Service Details
11	53(UDP)	DNS	Domain Name Service	Not sure what function this one is serving.

Concerns and Vulnerabilities:

Concern or Vulnerability
Weakness – Verified – 1.6
This DNS server is allowing recursive queries from the outside. This would allow an attacker to poison the DNS servers local cache. The next victim to request that information may be unknowingly directed to the attackers site.
Example
http://www.giac.org/practical/gsec/Doug_Sax_GSEC.pdf http://www.cert.org/advisories/CA-1997-22.html
Solution
Turn off DNS services on this machine or disable recursive queries for those outside of the CLIENT IP space.

IP Address	Domain name
193.145.85.251	mail.School.mo.us

Ho p	Port	Protocol	Service	Service Details
11	25	SMTP	Email	This is the secondary email server for the CLIENT domains.
11	1352	NRPC	Notes Configurati on	

Banner(s):

Port	Protocol	Banner
25	SMTP	220 MAIL.SCHOOL.MO.US ESMTP SERVICE (LOTUS DOMINO RELEASE 5.0.10) READY AT THU, 6 NOV 2003 21:25:13 -0800
1352	NRPC	(CN=mail/OU=KalmusC/O=CLIENT)

TCP Sequencing:

TCP Sequence Prediction
Class=truly random
TCP ISN Seq. Numbers
27AABDDC 96B10C65 6442E324 7E05B2F0 54C9418F 56CA30F7
IPID Sequence Generation
Incremental
Uptime
Not available

Concerns and Vulnerabilities:

Concern or Vulnerability
Information Leak – Verified – .4
There is no need for port 1352 to be open to the world. This simply gives up more information about the site than needed.
Example
n/a
Solution
Update the FW rulesets to disallow access to port 1352.

Glossary

access point (AP) — A transceiver that connects to an Ethernet cable. It bridges the wireless network with the wired network.

access policy — A set of rules and policies that an administrator can use to control outgoing traffic.

ACK — A TCP flag that acknowledges a TCP packet with SYN-ACK flags set.

Active Server Pages (ASP) — A scripting language used to create dynamic Web pages.

active systems — IDSs that log events, send out alerts, and can interoperate with routers and firewalls.

ActiveX Data Objects (ADO) — A programming interface used to connect a Web application to a database.

Advanced Encryption Standard (AES) — A new symmetric block cipher standard from NIST that replaced DES.

adware — Software that can be installed without user knowledge; its main purpose is to determine users' purchasing habits.

algorithm — A set of directions used to solve a problem.

array — In programming, this structure holds multiple values of the same type. After creation, an array is a fixed-length structure.

assembly language — Uses a combination of hexadecimal numbers and expressions to program a more understandable set of directions.

asymmetric algorithm — Encryption methodology that uses two keys that are mathematically related. Also referred to as public key cryptography.

attack — Any attempt of an unauthorized person to access or use resources of a network or computer system.

authenticity — The process of validating the sender of a message.

backdoor — A program that can be used to gain access to a computer system at a later date.

basic service set (BSS) — The coverage area of a wireless LAN (WLAN).

birthday attacks — An attack used to find the same hash value for two different inputs. Based on the theory that if 23 people are in a room, two will share the same birthday.

black box model — Management does not divulge to IT security personnel that penetration testing will be conducted, nor does it give the testing team a description of the network topology. In other words, penetration testers are on their own.

block cipher — An algorithm that encrypts data a block at a time. The blocks of bits are used as input to mathematical functions that perform substitution and transposition of the bits, making it difficult for someone to reverse-engineer the mathematical functions that were applied to the blocks of bits.

Blowfish — A block cipher developed by Bruce Schneier, author of *Applied Cryptography*, that can use a key length as large as 448 bits.

branching — A method that takes you from one area of a program (a function) to another area.

brute force attack — An attack when the attacker uses software that attempts every possible combination of letters to guess passwords.

buffer overflow attack — An exploit written by a programmer that finds a vulnerability in poorly written code that doesn't check for a predefined amount of space usage and writes executable code in this overflow area.

bug — A programming error that causes unpredictable results in a program.

certificates — Digital documents that verify whether two parties exchanging data over the Internet are really who they claim to be. Each certificate contains a unique serial number and must follow the X.509 standard.

certification authority (CA) — A third-party company, such as VeriSign, that vouches for another company's financial stability and issues a certificate that binds a public key to a recipient's private key .

Certified Ethical Hacker (CEH) — A certification for security testers designated by the EC-Council.

Certified Information Systems Security Professional (CISSP) — Non-vendor-specific certification issued by the International Information Systems Security Certifications Consortium, Inc. (ISC^2). Visit *www.isc2.org* for more information.

channel — A frequency range in which data is transmitted.

chipping code — Multiple bits that can be used for recovery of a corrupted packet that travels across a frequency band. Sub-bits are called "chips," and every bit of the original message is represented by multiple bits, called the chipping code.

cipher — A key that maps each letter or number to a different letter or number. The book of Jeremiah was written using a cipher known as atbash that mapped each letter of the alphabet to a different letter.

ciphertext — Plaintext (readable text) that has been encrypted.

class — In object-oriented programming, the structure that holds pieces of data and functions.

closed ports — Ports are designated as closed when they're not listening or responding to a packet.

ColdFusion — Created by Allaire, ColdFusion is a server-side scripting language used to create dynamic Web pages and supports a wide variety of databases. ColdFusion uses a proprietary markup language known as CFML.

Common Gateway Interface (CGI) — An interface that passes data between a Web server and a Web browser.

Common Internet File System (CIFS) — A remote file system protocol that enables computers to share network resources over the Internet.

competitive intelligence — A means of gathering information about a business or an industry by using observation, accessing public computer information, speaking with employees, and so on.

compiler — A program that converts source code into executable or binary code.

computer security — The security of standalone computers that are not part of a network infrastructure.

connectionless — With a connectionless protocol, no session connection is required before data is transmitted. UDP and IP are examples of connectionless protocols.

connection-oriented — A method of transferring data over a network that requires a session connection before data is sent. With TCP/IP, this step is accomplished by sending a SYN packet.

conversion specifier — Tells the compiler how to convert the value indicated in a function.

cookie — A text file containing a message sent from a Web server to a user's Web browser to be used later when the user revisits the Web site.

crackers — Hackers who break into systems with the intent of doing harm or destroying data.

cryptanalysis — A field of study devoted to breaking encryption algorithms.

Data Encryption Algorithm (DEA) — The NIST standard encryption algorithm that was originally named Lucifer and later renamed DEA by the NSA.

Data Encryption Standard (DES) — The NIST standard for protecting sensitive but unclassified data. DES is a symmetric algorithm that uses 56 bits for encryption.

demilitarized zone (DMZ) — A small network containing resources that sits between the Internet and the internal network, sometimes referred to as a "perimeter network." It's used when a company wants to make resources available to Internet users yet keep the company's internal network secure.

denial-of-service (DoS) attack — An attack made to deny legitimate users from accessing network resources.

dictionary attack — An attack where the attacker runs a password-cracking program that uses a dictionary of known words or passwords as an input file against the password file of the attacked system.

digital signature — Asymmetric encryption that ensures the sender cannot deny sending the message and the receiver of the message is assured that the message did indeed come from the sender.

distance-vector routing protocol — A routing protocol that passes its routing table (which contains all possible paths it has discovered) to all routers participating on the network. If the router learns one new path, it sends the entire routing table, which is not as efficient as a link-state routing protocol.

distributed denial-of-service (DDoS) attack — An attack made on a host from multiple servers or workstations to deny legitimate users from accessing network resources.

do loop — A loop that performs an action and then tests to see whether the action should continue to occur.

domain controller — A Windows server that stores user account information, authenticates domain logons, maintains the master database, and enforces security policies for a Windows domain.

dumpster diving — Gathering information by examining the physical trash that people thoughtlessly discard.

dynamic Web pages — A Web page that can change on the fly depending on variables, such as the date or time of day.

enumeration — The process of connecting to a system and obtaining information such as logon names, passwords, group memberships, and shared resources.

ethical hackers — Users who access a computer system or network with the owner's permission.

Extended File System (Ext) — The Ext file system is included in the standard Linux kernel and might be Ext, Second Extended File System (Ext2fs), or Third Extended File System (Ext3fs).

Extensible Authentication Protocol (EAP) — A framework designed to allow an organization to select an authentication method.

filtered ports — Ports designated as not open or closed, but possibly filtered by a network-filtering device, such as a firewall.

firewalls — Hardware devices or software installed on a system that serve two purposes: controlling access to all traffic that enters an internal network and controlling all traffic that leaves an internal network. Firewalls are specifically installed on a network to protect a company's internal network from dangers on the Internet.

footprinting — Gathering information about a company before performing a security test or an attack.

for loop — A loop that initializes a variable, tests a condition, and then increments or decrements the variable.

Fping — An enhanced Ping utility for pinging multiple targets simultaneously.

frequency — The number of sound waves that vibrate in a specified time.

function — A mini program within a main program that performs a particular task.

Global Information Assurance Certification (GIAC) — An organization founded by the SANS Institute in 1999 to validate the skills of security professionals. GIAC certifications encompass many areas of expertise in the security field. Visit *www.giac.org* for more information.

gray box model — A hybrid of the black box model and the white box model. For example, the company might give a tester some information about which OSs are running, but not provide any network topology information (diagrams of routers, switches, intrusion-detection systems, firewalls, and so forth).

hacker — A user who accesses a computer system or network without authorization from the owner.

hashing algorithm — A function that takes a variable-length string or message and produces a fixed-length value called a message digest.

HFNetChk — A Microsoft tool that enables administrators to check the patch status of all machines in a network from a central location.

honeypot —A computer placed on the perimeter of a network that contains information or data intended to lure and then trap hackers.

host-based IDS — Software used to protect a critical network server or database server. The software is installed on the server you're attempting to protect, just like antivirus software you install on your PC.

Hping — An enhanced Ping utility for creating TCP and UDP packets to be used in port-scanning activities.

infrared (IR) — An area in the electromagnetic spectrum with a frequency above microwaves; an infrared signal is restricted to a single room or line of sight. IR light can't penetrate walls, ceilings, or floors. This technology is used for most remote controls and PDAs.

initial sequence number (ISN) — A number that keeps track of what packets a node has received.

inodes — Information nodes store information, such as file size and creation date, about files on a *NIX system.

Institute for Security and Open Methodologies (ISECOM) — ISECOM is a nonprofit organization that provides security training and certification programs for security professionals. Visit *www.isecom.org* for more information.

Institute of Electrical and Electronics Engineers (IEEE) — An organization that creates standards for the IT industry.

International Data Encryption Algorithm (IDEA) — A block cipher that operates on 64-bit blocks of plaintext and uses a 128-bit key.

Internet Assigned Numbers Authority (IANA) — The organization responsible for assigning IP addresses.

Internet Control Message Protocol (ICMP) — The protocol used to send informational messages and test network connectivity.

Internet Information Services (IIS) — A Web server distributed with Windows. Originally supplied as part of the Option Pack for Windows NT and subsequently integrated with Windows 2000 and Windows Server 2003. The current version is IIS 6.0.

Internet Security and Acceleration (ISA) Server — Microsoft software that functions as a router, a firewall, and an IDS.

intrusion detection systems (IDSs) — Hardware or software devices that monitor network devices so that security administrators can identify attacks in progress and stop them.

IP access lists — A list of IP addresses, subnets, or networks that are allowed or denied access through a router's interface.

journaling — A method of providing fault-resiliency to a file system by writing updates to a log before the original disk is updated. In the event of a system crash, the system can check logs to see whether all updates were written to disk and can correct inconsistencies quickly if any incomplete transactions are found.

key — The bits of information used in an encryption algorithm to transform plaintext into ciphertext or vice versa.

keyloggers — Hardware devices or software (spyware) that record keystrokes made on a computer and store the information for later retrieval.

keyspace — A sequence of random bits generated from a range of allowable values.

link-state routing protocol — A routing protocol that uses link-state advertisements to send any changes in topology or new paths learned to other routers participating on the network. This method is efficient because only new information is sent over the wire.

looping — The act of repeating a task.

macro virus — A computer program written in a macro programming language, such as Visual Basic Application.

malware — Malicious software, such as a virus, worm, or Trojan program, that is used to shut down a network and prevent a business from operating.

man-in-the-middle attack — An attack where the attackers place themselves between the victim computer and another host computer. They then intercept messages sent from the victim to the host and pretend to be the host computer.

mathematical attack — An attack where properties of the encryption algorithm are attacked using mathematical computations. Examples include ciphertext-only attack, known plaintext attack, chosen-plaintext attack, and chosen-ciphertext attack.

Mbsacli.exe — The command-line counterpart to MBSA used to check for security updates and patches. Being able to run from a command prompt enables administrators to schedule scans to run during slow periods of network use, such as at night or on weekends.

message digest — The fixed-length string value created from using a hashing algorithm.

Microsoft Baseline Security Analyzer (MBSA) — A GUI tool that gives administrators a way to interactively scan local and remote servers and desktop computers for possible security vulnerabilities.

modulation — A process that defines how data is placed on a carrier signal.

narrowband — A technology that uses microwave radio band frequencies to transmit data. The most popular uses of this technology are cordless phones and garage door openers.

Nessus — A security tool installed on a *NIX server that conducts port scanning, OS identification, and vulnerability assessments. A client computer (*NIX or Microsoft OS) must connect to the server to perform the tests.

NetBIOS Extended User Interface (NetBEUI) — A fast, efficient protocol that allows NetBIOS packets to be transmitted over TCP/IP and various network topologies, such as token ring and Ethernet.

Network Address Translation (NAT) — A basic security feature of a firewall used to hide the corporate internal network from outsiders. With NAT, internal private IP addresses are mapped to public external IP addresses, hiding the internal infrastructure from unauthorized personnel.

network-based IDS — A device that monitors activity on network segments. Essentially, a network-based IDS sniffs traffic as it flows over the network and alerts a security administrator when something suspicious occurs.

Network Basic Input Output System (NetBIOS) — A Microsoft programming interface that allows computers to communicate across a LAN.

network security — The security of computers or devices that are part of a network infrastructure.

Nmap — A security tool used to identify open ports and detect services and OSs running on network systems.

nonrepudiation — A user cannot deny that they sent a message to a recipient and the receiver of a message cannot deny receiving the message.

null session — A null session is an unauthenticated connection to a Microsoft system.

Object Linking and Embedding Data Base (OLE DB) — A set of interfaces enabling Web applications to access diverse database management systems.

Open Database Connectivity (ODBC) — A standard database access method that allows a Web application to interact with a variety of database management systems.

open ports — Ports are designated as open when they respond to packets.

Open Source Security Testing Methodology Manual (OSSTMM) — This security manual developed by Peter Herzog has become one of the most widely used security testing methodologies to date. Visit *www.osstmm.org* for more information.

Open Web Application Security Project (OWASP) — A not-for-profit foundation dedicated to fighting and finding Web application vulnerabilities.

OSSTMM Professional Security Tester (OPST) — An ISECOM-designated certification for penetration testers.

packet monkeys — A derogatory term for unskilled crackers or hackers who steal program code to hack into network systems instead of creating the programs themselves.

passive systems — IDSs that do not take any action to stop or prevent an activity.

penetration test — In this test, a security professional performs an attack on a computer network with permission from the network's owner.

PHP Hypertext Processor (PHP) — An open-source server-side scripting language.

piggybacking — A method attackers use to gain access to restricted areas in a company. The attacker closely follows an employee and enters the area with that employee.

Ping of Death attack — A crafted ICMP packet larger than the maximum 65,535 bytes. It causes the recipient system to crash or freeze.

ping sweep — Pinging a range of IP addresses to identify live systems on a network.

plaintext — Readable text that has not been encrypted.

port — The logical component of a connection that identifies the service running on a network device. For example, port 110 is the POP3 mail service.

port scanning — A method of finding out which services a host computer offers.

Pretty Good Privacy (PGP) — A free public key encryption program developed by Phil Zimmerman that allowed the common person to encrypt e-mail messages.

private key — The secret key used in an asymmetric algorithm that is known only by the key owner and is never shared. Even if the public key that encrypted a message is known, the owner's private key cannot be determined.

privileged mode — A method used on Cisco routers that allows an administrator to perform full router configuration tasks. Privileged mode is also called enabled mode.

promiscuous mode — Installing a sniffer program so that all packets passing through the NIC are captured instead of being dropped.

Protected EAP (PEAP) — An authentication protocol that uses Transport Layer Security (TLS) to authenticate the server to the client, but not the client to the server.

protocol — A language used to transmit data across a network infrastructure.

pseudocode — An English-like language for creating the structure of a program.

public key — The key that can be known by the public and in many cases is downloaded from Web sites for public use. It works with a private key in asymmetric key cryptography, which is also known as public key cryptography.

public key cryptography — Also known as asymmetric key cryptography, public key cryptography is an asymmetric algorithm which uses two keys that are mathematically related.

public key infrastructure (PKI) — A structure or base that consists of programs, protocols, and security policies. PKI uses public key cryptography as its method of protecting data that traverses the Internet.

RC5 — A block cipher created by Ronald L. Rivest that can operate on different block sizes: 32, 64, and 128 bits.

red team — A group of penetration testers who work together to attack a network.

Remote Procedure Call (RPC) — An interprocess communication mechanism that allows a program running on one host to run code on a remote host.

replay attack — An attack where the attacker captures data and attempts to resubmit the data captured so that a device, such as a workstation or router, thinks a legitimate connection is in effect.

rootkit — A set of tools created after an attack for later use by the attacker.

Samba — An open-source implementation of CIFS that allows Linux and UNIX servers to share resources with a Windows client.

script — Lines of code that run in sequence to perform tasks on a computer. Many experienced penetration testers write or modify scripts using the Perl or C programming language.

script kiddies — Similar to packet monkeys, a term for unskilled hackers or crackers who use scripts or computer programs written by others to penetrate networks.

Secure Hash Algorithm (SHA) — NIST standard hashing algorithm that has recently been cracked. NIST recommends not using SHA applications.

security test — In this test, a security professional performs an attack on a network; in addition, the tester analyzes the organization's security policy and procedures and reports any vulnerabilities to management.

segmentation fault — An error that occurs when a program attempts to access a memory location it isn't allowed to access or in a way that's not permitted.

Server Message Block (SMB) — A protocol for sharing files and printers and providing a method for client applications to read, write to, and request services from server programs in a computer network. Windows operating systems have included SMB protocol support since Windows 95.

service set identifier (SSID) — The name of a wireless LAN that can be broadcast by an AP.

session hijacking — An attack on a network that requires guessing ISNs. *See also* initial sequence number (ISN).

shell — An interface to an operating system that enables system commands to be executed.

shell code — An assembly language program that executes a shell and can be used as an exploit payload.

shoulder surfing — The ability of an attacker to observe the keys a user types when entering a password by simply looking over the unaware user's shoulder.

social engineering —Using an understanding of human nature to obtain information from people.

Software Update Services (SUS) — A free add-in component for Windows 2000 and Windows Server 2003. After it's installed, SUS simplifies the process of keeping Windows 2000, Windows XP, and Windows Server 2003 computers current with the latest critical updates, security updates, and service packs. SUS installs a Web-based application that runs on Windows 2000 Server or Windows Server 2003 computers.

spread spectrum — In this technology, data is spread across a large-frequency bandwidth instead of traveling across one frequency band.

spyware — Software installed on users' computers without their knowledge that records personal information from the source computer and sends it to a destination computer.

SQL Critical Update Kit — To help protect editions of SQL Server 2000 and MSDE 2000 that are vulnerable to the Slammer worm, Microsoft has consolidated SQL Scan, SQL Check, and SQL Critical Update into a single download. The SQL Critical Update Kit also includes an SMS deployment tool and the Servpriv.exe utility.

SQL injection — A type of exploit that takes advantage of improperly written applications. An attacker is able to issue SQL statements using a Web browser to retrieve data, change server settings, or possibly gain control of the server.

state table — A file created by a stateful packet filter that contains information on network connections.

stateful packet filters — A filter on a router that records session-specific information into a file about a network connection, including the ports a client uses.

stateless packet filters — A filter that handles each packet on an individual basis, so spoofing or DoS attacks are more prevalent.

static Web pages — A Web page that displays the same information whenever it's accessed.

station (STA) — An addressable unit in a wireless network. A station is defined as a message destination and might not be a fixed location.

steganography — The process of hiding data in plain view in pictures, graphics, or text.

stream cipher — An algorithm that operates on plaintext one bit at a time.

substitution cipher — An algorithm that maps each letter of the alphabet to a different letter of the alphabet. The book of Jeremiah was written using a substitution cipher called Atbash.

supplicant — The client or wireless computer that connects to an AP.

symmetric algorithm — An encryption algorithm that uses only one key to both encrypt and decrypt data. A user who is sent a message encrypted by a key must have a copy of the same key to decrypt the message.

SYN — A TCP flag that signifies the beginning of a session.

SYN-ACK — A reply to a SYN packet sent by a host.

SysAdmin, Audit, Network, Security (SANS) Institute — Founded in 1989, this organization conducts training worldwide and offers multiple certifications through GIAC in many aspects of computer security and forensics.

Systems Management Server (SMS) — This service includes detailed hardware inventory, software inventory and metering, software distribution and installation, and remote troubleshooting tools. SMS is tightly integrated with SQL Server and the Windows Server OS, creating a complete solution for change and configuration management.

Tar command — This command combines multiple files and folders into a file called a tape archive, but it does not compress files and folders.

TCP flag — The six flags in a TCP header are switches that can be set to on or off to indicate the status of a port or service.

TCP/IP filtering — This feature enables users to specify which types of IP traffic are allowed to enter an interface. It's designed to isolate the traffic being processed by Internet and intranet clients. In the absence of other TCP/IP filtering, such as IPSec,

Routing and Remote Access Service, or other TCP/IP applications or services, this feature can add security to a network by blocking unauthorized types of packets. TCP/IP filtering is disabled by default.

testing — A process conducted on a variable that returns a value of true or false.

three-way handshake — The method the transport layer uses to create a connection-oriented session.

Transmission Control Protocol/Internet Protocol (TCP/IP) — The main protocol used to connect computers over the Internet.

Triple Data Encryption Standard (3DES) — A quick fix to the vulnerabilities of DES that improved on security but takes longer to encrypt and decrypt data.

Trojan program — A computer program that disguises itself as a legitimate program or application but has a hidden payload that might send information from the attacked computer to the creator or to a recipient located anywhere in the world.

User Datagram Protocol (UDP) — A fast, unreliable transport layer protocol that is connectionless.

user mode — The default method used on a Cisco router in which an administrator can perform basic troubleshooting tests and list information stored on the router. In this mode, administrators can't make any changes to the router's configuration.

virtual directory — A pointer to a physical directory on a Web server.

virus — A computer program that attaches itself to an application or a program.

virus signature files — Antivirus software compares these files against the programming code of known viruses to determine whether a program you're installing is infected.

wardriving — The act of driving around an area with a laptop computer that has a WNIC, scanning software, and possibly an antenna to obtain a list of available SSIDs in that area.

Web bug — A small graphic image referenced in an <IMG> tag. This image is created by a third-party company specializing in data collection.

WebGoat — A J2EE Web-based application designed to teach security professionals about Web application vulnerabilities.

while loop — A loop that repeats an action a certain number of times while a condition is true or false.

white box model — In this model, testers can speak with company staff and are given a full description of the network topology and technology.

Wi-Fi Protected Access (WPA) — A standard that addressed WEP security vulnerabilities in 802.11b with the new 802.11i standard. *See also* Wired Equivalent Privacy (WEP).

Wired Equivalent Privacy (WEP) — An 802.11b standard implemented to encrypt data traversing a wireless network.

wireless LAN (WLAN) — A network that relies on wireless technology (radio waves) to operate.

wireless personal area network (WPAN) — A wireless network for one user only; usually refers to Bluetooth technology.

worm — A computer program that replicates and propagates without needing a host or program.

zone transfer — A method of transferring records from a DNS server to use in analysis of a network.

Index